A Handbook to

COUNTY BIBLIOGRAPHY

Being a Bibliography of Bibliographies relating to the County Towns of Great Britain and Ireland

by

Arthur L. Humphreys

DAWSONS OF PALL MALL

ISBN : 0 7129 0628 2
First printed for A.L. Humphreys 1917
Reprinted by Wm. Dawson & Sons Ltd. 1974

Printed in Belgium by Jos Adam
for Wm. Dawson & Sons Ltd.,
Cannon House, Folkestone, Kent, England

A Handbook to
COUNTY
BIBLIOGRAPHY.

A Handbook to COUNTY BIBLIOGRAPHY,

BEING A

Bibliography of Bibliographies *relating to* the *Counties* and *Towns* of

GREAT BRITAIN

AND IRELAND.

By Arthur L. Humphreys.

London,
187 PICCADILLY.

PREFACE.

THE purpose of this book is to provide a guide to the large amount of Bibliographical work which has been done to assist the study of the Topography of Great Britain and Ireland. I wish to make very clear at the outset that this book is not a Bibliography of each individual Town and Parish history, nor does it cover the same ground as any existing work, but attempts to go further than any book has hitherto done in providing clues to the discovery of the known as well as the obscure publications relating to every district in the Kingdom. I have cast my net widely, and what I have put together in the following pages is the result of many years' vigilance in taking notes, followed by four years of active work in amplifying, and preparing for the press.

All systematic bibliographies are included, and I have in addition called attention to source books, indexes, &c., of local, historical, or topographical material, because such books so often serve the purpose of bibliographies, and supplement them. The various local manuscript and printed collections are brought into the scheme of the book, especially those numerous and valuable collections which are lodged in the British Museum, and are easily accessible to students. I have searched the Transactions of County Antiquarian Societies, and unearthed a large amount of valuable bibliographical work buried therein. Until our public libraries catalogue, as they should do, each of the various items in these collections, they must remain almost an unexplored field. Bibliographical books and pamphlets relating to Ballads, Broadsides, Chap-books, Newspapers, Maps, and Portraits are included, and also any valuable local 'Garlands,' which often contain rare Street Ballads, giving accounts of local incidents, murders, &c.

Descriptive or bibliographical accounts of parochial documents are included, but Parish Registers themselves, unless accompanied by bibliographical notes, do not come within the scheme. Calendars of local documents are included, but not Calendars of Wills, because I hope later to issue a separate volume which will give a bibliography of books on Wills, arranged under counties.

The auxiliary lists at the end, printed as appendices, contain chiefly such references as I have thought might get overlooked. These appendices designedly omit many well-known books, and they are purposely limited to the less-known bibliographies, indexes, &c.

In surveying what has already been done for various counties bibliographically, one is obliged to regard what still remains to be accomplished. Certain counties have had the good fortune to find their bibliographers, while other counties, possessed of a wealth of topographical material, have not succeeded in securing one. As far back as 1837 the bibliography of the county of Kent was undertaken by that fine old pioneer, John Russell Smith. His book, *Bibliotheca Cantiana*, one of the first and one of the best, is excellent up to the time when it was issued.

London has yet to find its bibliographers. The duty of compiling a bibliography of London rightly belongs to the Corporation, which, with all its wealth, has never issued a satisfactory catalogue of its possessions in the Guildhall Library, nor has it even issued a periodical bulletin of bibliographical information, as is being done by all good libraries in America and by many here. The counties of Bedfordshire, Berkshire, Derbyshire, Hertfordshire, Leicestershire, and Shropshire are a few instances only of counties which have great claims bibliographically, but so far no one has been forthcoming to undertake the work required. Welsh and Irish counties are almost all untouched. In Scotland a band of zealous and capable bibliographers is producing good work.

Two fine models exist which may well be followed by any one who has the enterprise to embark upon a bibliography of his own county. These models are Boase and Courtney's *Bibliotheca*

Cornubiensis, and Hyett and Bazeley's *Manual of Gloucestershire Literature*. A third may be cited. John Taylor, a printer and newspaper proprietor of Northampton, gave up many years of his life, and with zeal collected a great body of valuable bibliographical information respecting Northamptonshire. In the end, he printed six copies only of his *magnum opus*. I had to journey to Northampton in order to see one of the six copies, which is fortunately in the Free Library in that town.

Perhaps too few writers and compilers of books of reference openly acknowledge their indebtedness to the resources of the Library of the British Museum. As a youth I began to study in that magnificent Library, and I have used the Reading Room almost daily ever since. I wish to pay a tribute to its admirable organization. I believe that there could be no better advice to a student beginning the study of Topography than to tell him to first make himself acquainted, as far as he can, with the books of reference, specially chosen and placed in the Reading Room of the British Museum, in the sections devoted to Topography, Genealogy, and History.

I have compiled this book as a labour of love and as a hobby in my spare hours. Mr. Walter Brown has been of the greatest assistance in arranging my manuscript and doing most valuable work in preparing it for the press. Furthermore, no praise could be too high for his patience in the construction of the Index.

During the progress of the book through the press, I have received many kindnesses from Mr. George Clinch, who ably fills the enviable post of Librarian to the Society of Antiquaries.

A. L. H.

February, 1917.

CONTENTS.

A HANDBOOK TO THE BIBLIOGRAPHY *of the* COUNTIES OF GREAT BRITAIN & IRELAND

ABERDEENSHIRE.

JOHNSTONE (James Fowler Kellas). **BIBLIOGRAPHY OF THE SHIRES OF ABERDEEN, BANFF, AND KINCARDINE.** New Spalding Club.

—— **A Concise Biblio. of the Hist. of the City of Aberdeen and its Institutions.** (*Aberdeen Univ. Lib. Bull.*, vol. i. pp. 699–738, 1913, and *Historical Assoc. of Scotland*, Pamphlet No. 3. 1913.)

—— **A Concise Biblio. of the Hist., Topo., and Institutions of the Shires of Aberdeen, Banff, and Kincardine.** (*Aberdeen Univ. Lib. Bull.*, vol. ii. pp. 73–120. 1913.) To be continued.

Anderson (**Peter John**). **Collections towards a Biblio. of the Universities of Aberdeen.** Edinburgh Biblio. Soc., vol. viii. 1907.

—— **Studies in the Hist. and Development of the Univ. of Aberdeen.** Collections towards a Biblio. of the Universities of Aberdeen, pp. 385–525. (*Aberdeen Univ. Studies. No.* 19. 1906.)

—— **Aberdeen Universities Bibliography.** Biblio. Note. ('*Aberdeen Journal*' *Notes & Queries*, vol. iii. pp. 197, 198. 1910.)

—— **Record of the Celebration of the Quatercentenary of the Univ. of Aberdeen, 1906.** Biblio. of Centenary Publications, pp. 590–598. (*Aberdeen Univ. Studies. No.* 29. 1907.)

—— **Biblio. Note on Aberdeen 'Theses.'** ('*Aberdeen Journal*' *Notes & Queries*, vol. i. pp. 3, 4. 1908.)

—— **Biblio. of the Writings of Professor Alexander Bain,** b. at Aberdeen, 1818; d. 1903. In '*Autobiography.*' 1904.

—— **A Biblio. of Duncan Liddel, M.A., M.D.,** b. at Aberdeen, 1561; d. 1613. Professor in the Univ. of Helmstedt, 1591-1607. 1910.

—— **Note on Academic Theses: with a Biblio. of Duncan Liddel.** App. a, Theses of Aberdeen Universities, pp. 17-23; App. c, Liddel's Career and Writings, pp. 27-44. (*Edinburgh Biblio. Soc.*, vol. x. 1913.)

—— **Hist. Notes on the Libraries of the Universities of Aberdeen.** 1893.

—— **Catal. of Books added to the Lib. in Marischal College, 1874-96.** 1897.

—— **The University Library: Past and Present.** (*Aberdeen Univ. Rev.*, vol. i. pp. 123–136. 1914.)

—— **Biblio. Note on Aberdeen Almanacs.** ('*Aberdeen Journal*' *Notes & Queries*, vol. ii. pp. 369-370. 1909.)

—— **Inventories of Records illustrating the Hist. of Aberdeen.** 1890.

—— **Charters and other Writs illustrating the Hist. of the Royal Burgh of Aberdeen, 1171-1804.** New Spalding Club. 1890.

—— **Inventories of Ecclesiastical Records of North-Eastern Scotland.** Aberdeen, pp. 165–172. New Spalding Club, vol. vi. *Miscellany*, vol. i. 1890.

ABERDEENSHIRE (*continued*).

Robertson (Alexander W.). Hand-List of Biblio. of the Shires of Aberdeen, Banff, and Kincardine. New Spalding Club. 1893.

Local Bibliography. (*Scottish Notes & Queries*, vols. viii.–xi. 1895–98.)

Watt (William). A Hist. of Aberdeen and Banff. The County Histories of Scotland. 1900. List of Books and Maps relating to Aberdeen and Banff, pp. 389–425.)

Bulloch (John Malcolm). Biblio. of Aberdeen Periodical Literature. (*Scottish Notes & Queries*, vols. i.–x.; Ser. 2, vols. ii.–viii. 1887–1907.)

—— **Chron. List of Aberdeen Newspapers, Magazines, &c.** Privately printed. 1889.

—— **Files of the Local Aberdeen Press,** past and present. (*Scottish Notes & Queries*, vol. ix. p. 170. 1896.)

Anderson (Robert). Biblio. of Aberdeen Publications. 1890–1899. (*Scottish Notes & Queries*, vols. iv.–ix., xi., xii. ; Ser. 2, vols. iii., v. 1891–1903.)

Thomson (James B.). Biblio. of Aberdeen and North-Eastern Publications, issued during 1909, 1910, 1911. ('*Aberdeen Journal' Notes & Queries*, vol. iii. pp. 168–170 ; vol. iv. pp. 67–71 ; vol. v. pp. 77–80. 1910–12.) Also issued separately.

Aberdeen Bibliographies. ('*Aberdeen Journal' Notes & Queries*, vol. iii. pp. 191, 192. 1910.)

Aberdeenshire References in Acts of Parliament of Scotland. ('*Aberdeen Journal' Notes & Queries*, vol. i. pp. 164, 171, 184, 185, 192 ; vol. ii. pp. 5, 12, 20, 27, 35, 48, 53, 58, 64, 71. 1908–09.)

A Bibliography of Local Poetry to 1860. Aberdeen 1887.

Walker (George). Aberdeen: Its Literature, Bookmaking, and Circulating. (*The Library*, vol. vi. pp. 238, 266. 1894.)

Aberdeen Books and those of Local Interest. (*Aberdeen Book Lover*, vol. i. No. 1., etc. 1913, etc.)

Aberdeen Booksellers of Bygone Days. (*Aberdeen Book Lover*, vol. i. No. 1, etc. 1913, etc.)

Terry (Chas. Sanford). The Aberdeen Historians, *vide* Anderson (P. J.) '*Studies in the Hist. and Development of the Univ. of Aberdeen.*' 1906.

Bulloch (John Malcolm). The House of Gordon. Biblio. of Gordon Genealogy, in vols. i. and ii. New Spalding Club, vols. xxvi., xxxiii. 1903, 1907.

Johnston (William). Biblio. and Portraits of Arthur Johnston, b. at Caskieben, now Keith Hall, co. Aberdeen, *circa* 1587 ; d. 1641. Physician to James I., '*Scottish Notes & Queries*,' vol. ix. pp. 49, 65, 82. 1895 ; also in '*Musa Latina Aberdonensis*,' vol. ii. pp. xli.–lvi. New Spalding Club, vol. xv. 1896. Also issued separately.

Aberdeen University. References in Acts of Parliament of Scotland. ('*Aberdeen Journal' Notes & Queries*, vol. ii., pp. 96, 103, 109. 1909.)

Robertson (Alexander W.). The Public Libraries of Aberdeen. (*The Library*, vol. vi. pp. 1–12. 1894.

—— **Catal. of Anderson Lib. at Woodside** (includes a large collection of local books).

Proposals for a Publick Library at Aberdeen. 1764. [Reprinted 1893.]

Scottish Univ. Libraries. Lists of Printed Catalogues. Aberdeen. (*Aberdeen Univ. Lib. Bull.*, vol. i. pp. 397–401. 1912.)

The Aberdeen Univ. Library has a special collection of North of Scotland Literature.

Murray (David). 'Museums.' Glasgow. 1904. Biblio. Note on Aberdeen Museums, vol. ii. pp. 71, 72.

ABERDEENSHIRE (continued).

Anderson (Joseph). Report on Local Museums in Scotland. Aberdeen Museums. By Geo. F. Black. (*Soc. of Antiq. Scot. Proc.*, vol. xxii. pp. 356-364. 1888.)

Dickson (Robert). Introduction of Printing into Scotland. Aberdeen. 1885. (Contains valuable information about Aberdeen Printing.)

Edmond (John Philip). Aberdeen Printers from Edward Raban to James Nicol, 1620-1736: being biblio. notices of their work and lives. Facsimiles and Index. 4 pts. Aberdeen. 1884-86.

—— **Handlist of Books printed at Aberdeen, or by Aberdeen Printers, 1620-1736.** Aberdeen. 1884.

—— **Last Notes on the Aberdeen Printers.** Privately printed. Aberdeen. 1888.

Axon (William E. A.). On an unrecorded issue of the Aberdeen Press of Edward Raban in 1627. With a handlist of the production of his presses at Edinburgh, St. Andrews, and Aberdeen. (*Soc. of Antiq. Scot. Proc.*, vol. xliii. pp. 24-53. 1909.)

Fraser (G. M.) An Aberdeenshire Rural Press. [John Cumming, of Hatton of Fintray], with List of Ballads issued at the Fintray Press. (*The Lone Shieling*, pp. 169-179. 1908.)

Livingstone (Matthew). Guide to the Public Records of Scotland. 1905. Aberdeenshire, pp. 111, 112, 173.

Turnbull (William B.). Scottish Parochial Registers. 1849. List of Aberdeenshire Registers, pp. 1-12, 159.

Hist. MSS. Comm. Reports. Aberdeenshire Collections.

Aberdeen, Burgh of	1st Rep. p. xii. and App. pp. 121-123.
—— University	2nd Rep. p. xix. and App. pp. 199-201.
—— Earl of, at Haddo House ...	5th Rep. p. xix. and App. pp. 608-610.
Blairs, Roman Catholic College ...	2nd Rep. p. xx. and App. pp. 201-203.
Buchan, Mr. James, at Auchmacoy	4th Rep. p. xxiii. and App. p. 528.
Crawford and Balcarres, Earl of, at Dunecht	2nd Rep. p. xvii. and App. 181-182.
Farquharson, Col. James, at Invercauld	4th Rep. p. xxii. and App. pp. 533-535.
Forbes, Lord, at Castle Forbes ...	2nd Rep. p. xix. and App. 193-196.
—— Sir William, at Fintray House	5th Rep. p. xx. and App. pp. 626-629.
Gordon, Mr. Hugh Mackay, at Abergeldie...	6th Rep. p. xix. and App. p. 712.
—— Mr. W. Cosmo, at Fyvie Castle	5th Rep. pp. xx. and App. pp. 644-646.
Grant, Sir Archibald, at Monymusk	9th Rep. p. xix. and App. II. pp. 238-241.
Huntly, Marquess of, at Aboyne Castle	2nd Rep. p. xvii. and App. p. 180.
Irvine, Mr. Alex. Forbes, at Drum Castle	2nd Rep. p. xix. and App. p. 198.
King, Lt.-Col. W. Ross, at Kinellar	3rd Rep. p. xvii. and App. p. 416.
Leith, Mr. James Forbes, at Whitehaugh	2nd Rep. p. xix. and App. p. 198.
Webster, Mr. John, Advocate in Aberdeen	3rd Rep. p. xxv. and App. pp. 420, 421.

Burgh Records, 1189, etc., with MS. and printed Indexes, at Town House, Aberdeen. (*Local Records Comm. Rep.*, 1902, App. III. p. 88.)

County Council Records, at Aberdeen. (*Local Records Comm. Rep.*, 1902, App. III. p. 82.)

Aberdeen Records, at various depositories. (*Local Records Comm. Rep.*, 1902, App. III. p. 132.)

Aberdeen. Franciscan Convent. List of Books and MSS. at the time of the Reformation. (*Arch. Scotia*, vol. ii. pp. 129-133. 1822.)

ABERDEENSHIRE (continued).

Aberdeen Friars and Hospital. References in Acts of Parliament of Scotland. ('*Aberdeen Journal' Notes & Queries*, vol. ii. pp. 90–91, 357. 1909.)

Aberdeen. Dean and Chapter. References in Acts of Parliament of Scotland. ('*Aberdeen Journal' Notes & Queries*, vol. ii. p. 76. 1909.)

Trimen (Henry). Botanical Biblio. of the British Counties. Aberdeenshire. (*Journ. of Botany*, vol. xii. p. 236. 1874.)

Christy (Miller). Biblio. Note on Aberdeenshire Birds. (*Catal. of Local Lists of British Birds.* London, 1891, p. 29.) **Mammals.** (*The Zoologist*, Ser. 3, vol. xvii. p. 209. 1893.) **Reptiles.** (*Ibid.* p. 249. 1893.) **Fishes.** (*Ibid.* p. 260. 1893.)

Anderson (John P.). Book of Brit. Topo., 1881. Aberdeenshire, pp. 276–278.

Gatfield (George). Guide to Heraldry. 1892. Aberdeenshire, p. 215.

Gough (Richard). Brit. Topo., 1780. Aberdeenshire, vol. ii. pp. 642–651.

PETERHEAD.

Taylor (William L.). Biblio. of Peterhead Periodicals. (*Scottish Notes & Queries*, vol. ii. p. 147; vol. iii. pp. 29, 42. 1889.)

Cameron (James). A Biblio. of Peter Buchan's Publications. (*Edinb. Biblio. Soc. Pubns.*, vol. iv. pp. 105–116. 1900.)

Fairley (John A.). Peter Buchan, Printer and Ballad-Collector. (*Buchan Field Club Trans.*, vol. vii. 1902–3.)

Burgh Records, at Peterhead. (*Local Records Comm. Rep.*, 1902, App. III. p. 98.)

Buchan Field Club. List of Papers from 1887 to 1908 in Transactions, vol. i.–ix. (*Twenty-one Years' Research in Buchan*, pp. 111–116. 1909.)

Anderson (Joseph). Reports on Local Museums in Scotland. Arbuthnot Museum, Peterhead. By Geo. F. Black. (*Soc. of Antiq. Scot. Proc*, vol. xxii. pp. 364–368. 1888.)

ANGLESEY.

Hist. MSS. Comm. Report. Anglesey Collection.
Miss Conway Griffith, at Carreglwyd. 5th Rep. p. xi. and App. pp. 405–423.

Miss Conway Griffith's Carreglwyd MSS. (*Archæol. Camb.*, Ser. 4, vol. ix. pp. 225–233, 302–311; vol. x. pp. 304–317. 1878–79.)

County Records. 17th Cent., etc., at Beaumaris and Holyhead. (*Local Records Comm. Rep.*, 1902, App. III. p. 28.)

Trimen (Henry). Botanical Biblio. of the British Counties. Anglesey. (*Journ. of Botany*, vol. xii. p. 158. 1874.)

Anderson (John P.). Book of Brit. Topo., 1881. Anglesey, p. 342.

Gatfield (George). Guide to Heraldry. 1892. Anglesey, p. 222.

Gough (Richard). Brit. Topo., 1780. Anglesey, vol. ii. p. 535.

Bandinel (Bulkeley). Catal. of Books bequeathed to Bodleian Library by Richard Gough 1814. Anglesey, p. 337.

ANTRIM.

ANDERSON (John). CATAL. OF EARLY BELFAST PRINTED BOOKS, 1694 to 1830. With Lists of Early Belfast Printers, 1700–1830, p. v. Booksellers, p. ix. Newspapers, &c., 1700–1830, p. x. New and Enlarged Edition. 1890.

——— **Supplements.** 1894 and 1902.

——— **Hist. of The Belfast Library and Soc. for Promoting Knowledge,** commonly known as The Linen Hall Library. With Chronological List of Catalogues, 1793–1887. Appendix, pp. 102–104. Belfast, 1888.

ANTRIM (*continued*).

Linen Hall Library. General Catalogue. Compiled by George Smith. 1896. (Contains a large number of works on the Linen Industry.)

—— **Supplementary Catalogue of Books added, 1903 and 1904.** Compiled by George Maxwell. 1904, 1905.

Descriptive Catal. of the Collection of Antiquities, etc., illustrative of Irish Hist., exhibited in the Museum, Belfast, at the 22nd meeting of the British Association, 1852. Belfast, 1852.

Murray (David). 'Museums.' Glasgow. 1904. Biblio. Note on Belfast Museums, vol. ii. p. 107.

Dix (Ernest Reginald McClintock). Irish Provincial Printing prior to 1701. Biblio. Note on Belfast Printing. (*The Library.* New Ser. vol. II. p. 347. 1901.)

Benn (George). Early Printing in Belfast. (*Hist. of the Town of Belfast*, 1877, pp. 424–445.)

Young (Robert M.). Some Notes on the Early Belfast Press and its Productions. (*Belfast Naturalists' Field Club. Ann. Report & Proc.*, Ser. 2, vol. iii. pp. 55–58. 1888.)

—— **An Account of some Notable Books Printed in Belfast.** (*The Library*, vol. vii. pp. 135–144. 1895.)

Hist. MSS. Comm. Report. Antrim Collection.
Lord Macartney, at Belfast. 9th Rep. p. xx. and App. II. pp. 330–340.

Inventory of the Pinkerton MS. Collection, and Lists of Belfast Books. See Young (R. M.) *Hist. Notices of Old Belfast.* 1896. Appendix, pp. 249–251. (The Collection was in the possession of Mr. R. M. Young in 1902.)

Garstin (J. R.). Descriptive Catal. of a Collection of MSS. formerly belonging to, and mainly the handiwork of William Reeves, Bishop of Down, now deposited in the Diocesan Library, Belfast. 1899. Not published. (Contains many Antrim entries.)

Christy (Miller). Biblio. Note on Antrim Birds. (*The Zoologist*, Ser. 3, vol. xiv. p. 266, 1890; and reprinted in pamph., 1891, p. 40.) **Mammals.** (*The Zoologist*, Ser. 3, vol. xvii, p. 215. 1893). **Reptiles.** (*Ibid.* p. 251. 1893.) **Fishes.** (*Ibid.* p. 263. 1893.)

Anderson (John P.). Book of Brit. Topo., 1881. Antrim, pp. 427, 428.
Gough (Richard). Brit. Topo., 1780. Antrim, p. 780.
Bandinel (Bulkeley). Catal. of Books bequeathed to Bodleian Lib. by Richard Gough, 1814. Antrim, p. 376.

CARRICKFERGUS.

Young (Robert M.). Notes on the Ancient Records of Carrickfergus. (*Soc. Antiq. Irel. Journ.*, Ser. 5, vol. iii. pp. 64–68. 1893.)

ARGYLLSHIRE.

Hist. MSS. Comm. Report. Argyllshire Collections.
Duke of Argyll, at Inveraray Castle (14th to 18th Cent.) 4th Rep. p. xix. and App. pp. 470–492; 6th Rep. p. xvi. and App. pp. 606–634.

County Council Records. 1688, etc., at Argyll. (*Local Records Comm. Rep.*, 1902. App. III. p. 82.)

Livingstone (Matthew). Guide to the Public Records of Scotland. 1905. Argyllshire, p. 173.

Turnbull (William B.). Scottish Parochial Registers. 1849. List of **Argyllshire** Registers, pp. 12–19.

ARGYLLSHIRE (continued).

Couper (W. J.). Biblio. of the Campbeltown Declaration of 1685. (*Glasgow Biblio. Soc. Records*, vol. i. pp. 118–124. 1914.)

Trimen (Henry). Botanical Biblio. of the British Counties. Argyllshire. (*Journ. of Botany*, vol. xii. p. 237. 1874.)

Christy (Miller). Biblio. Note on Argyllshire Birds. (*The Zoologist*, Ser. 3, vol. xiv. p. 262, 1890; and reprinted in pamph., 1891, p. 30.) **Mammals,** (*The Zoologist*, Ser. 3, vol. xvii. p. 209. 1893.) **Reptiles.** (*Ibid.* p. 249. 1893.) **Fishes.** (*Ibid.* p. 260. 1893.)

Anderson (John P.). Book of Brit. Topo., 1881. Argyllshire, p. 378.

Gatfield (George). Guide to Heraldry. 1892. Argyllshire, p. 215.

Gough (Richard). Brit. Topo., 1780. Argyllshire, pp. 653–655.

Bandinel (Bulkeley). Catal. of Books bequeathed to Bodleian Lib. by Richard Gough, 1814. Argyllshire, p. 356.

INVERARAY.

Burgh Records, 1655, etc., at Court House, Inveraray. (*Local Records Comm. Rep.*, 1902. App. III. p. 94.)

ARMAGH.

Dix (Ernest Reginald McClintock). List of Books and Pamphlets printed at Armagh in the 18th Century. Dublin. 1901. Second Edit. Cuala Press. Dundrum. 1910.

Gross (Charles). Biblio. of Brit. Municipal Hist. (*Harvard Hist. Studies*, vol. v. 1897.) Armagh, p. 158.

Catal. of MSS. in the Public Lib. at Armagh. Founded 1771; established by the Irish Parliament, 1774. (Printed.)

Reeves (William). Bishop of Down. Memoir of the Public Library at Armagh.

Garstin (J. R.). Descriptive Catal. of a Collection of MSS. formerly belonging to, and mainly the handiwork of Bishop Reeves, now deposited in the Diocesan Library, Belfast. 1899. Not published.

Anderson (John P.). Book of Brit. Topo., 1881. Armagh, p. 428.

Gough (Richard). Brit. Topo., 1780. Armagh, pp. 781-783.

Bandinel (Bulkeley). Catal. of Books bequeathed to Bodleian Lib. by Richard Gough, 1814. Armagh, p. 376.

AYRSHIRE.

Hist. MSS. Comm. Reports. Ayrshire Collections.

Ailsa, Marquess of, at Culzean Castle	5th Rep. p. xix. and App. pp. 613–617.
Eglinton and Winton, Earl of, at Eglinton Castle (14th to 17th cent.)	10th Rep. pp. 30, 31, and App. pp. 1–58.
Glasgow, Earl of, at Kelburne... ...	3rd Rep. pp. xxiii. and App. p. 405; 8th Rep. p. xvii. and App. pp. 304–308.

County Council Records, at County Buildings, Ayr. (*Local Records Comm. Rep.*, 1902, App. III. p. 82.)

Livingstone (Matthew). Guide to the Public Records of Scotland. 1905. Ayrshire, p. 174.

Turnbull (William B.). Scottish Parochial Registers. 1849. List of Ayrshire Registers, pp. 20–28, 160.

Gross (Charles). Biblio. of Brit. Municipal Hist. (*Harvard Hist. Studies*, vol. v. 1897.) Ayrshire, p. 160.

AYRSHIRE (continued).

Black (Geo. F.). Descriptive Catal. of Antiquities found in Ayrshire and Wigtonshire. (*Ayrshire & Galloway Archæol. Assoc. Collections*, vol vii. pp. 1-47. 1894.)

Mason (Thomas). Biblio. Notes on Zachary Boyd in his '*The Public and Private Libraries of Glasgow.*' 1885.

Trimen (Henry). Botanical Biblio. of the British Counties. Ayrshire. *Journ. of Botany*, vol. xii. p. 234. 1874.)

Christy (Miller). Biblio. Note on Ayrshire Birds. (*The Zoologist*, Ser. 3, vol. xiv. p. 262, 1890; and reprinted in pamph., 1891, p. 30.)

Anderson (John P.). Book of Brit. Topo., 1881. Ayrshire, pp. 379, 380.

AYR.

Burgh Records, 1202, etc., at Town Buildings, Ayr. (*Local Records Comm. Rep.*, 1902, App. III. p. 88.)

The Carnegie Public Library, Ayr, has special collections of Ayrshire and Burns literature.

ALLOWAY.

Ewing (J. C.). A Biblio. of Robert Burns, 1759-1796. (*Edinb. Biblio. Soc. Proc.*, vol. ix. pp. 57-72. 1909.)

Courtney (William Prideaux). A Register of National Bibliography. 3 vols. 1905-12. List of Burns Bibliographies, vol. i. p. 92; and vol. iii. p. 48.

Murray (David). 'Museums.' Glasgow, 1904. Biblio. Note on Burns Museum, vol. ii. p. 150.

Gibson Collection of Burns and Burnsiana in Linen Hall Library, Belfast.

KILMARNOCK.

Anderson (Joseph). Reports on Local Museums in Scotland. Kilmarnock Museum. (*Soc. of Antiq. Scot. Proc.*, vol. xxii. p. 411. 1888.)

AUCHINLECK.

Dibdin (Rev. T. F.). Account of Auchinleck Press. (*Biblio. Decameron*, 1817, vol. iii. p. 453.)

Martin (John). Auchinleck Press, with illustration. (*Biblio. Catal. of Books Privately Printed*, 1834, vol. i. pp. 347-358.)

Eyton (J. Walter K.). Sir AlexanderBoswell's Private Press at Auchinleck. (*Sale Catal. of his Library of Privately Printed Books, Sotheby's*, 1848, p. 10.)

Lowndes (W. T.). List of Books printed at Auchinleck Press. (*Bibliographer's Manual*, 1871, App. pp. 197-199.)

BANFFSHIRE.

JOHNSON (James Fowler Kellas). BIBLIOGRAPHY OF THE SHIRES OF ABERDEEN, BANFF, AND KINCARDINE. New Spalding Club.

——— **A Concise Biblio. of the Hist., Topo., and Institutions of the Shires of Aberdeen, Banff, and Kincardine.** (*Aberdeen Univ. Lib. Bull.*, vol. ii. pp. 73-120, 1913.) To be continued.

Robertson (Alexander W.) Hand-List of Biblio. of the Shires of Aberdeen, Banff, and Kincardine. New Spalding Club. 1893.

Local Bibliography. (*Scottish Notes & Queries*, vols. viii.-xi. 1895-98.)

BANFFSHIRE (continued).

Watt (William). A Hist. of Aberdeen and Banff. The County Histories of Scotland. 1900. List of Books and Maps relating to Aberdeen and Banff, pp. 389–425.

Livingstone (Matthew). Guide to the Public Records of Scotland. 1905. Banffshire, p. 174.

Inventories of Northern Records. I. The Sheriff Court of Banffshire. By G. M. Hossack. (*Scottish Notes & Queries*, vol. xi. pp. 138, 139. 1898.)

Anderson (Joseph). Report on Local Museums in Scotland. Museum of the Banff Institute. (*Soc. of Antiq. Scot. Proc.*, vol. xxii p. 368. 1888.)

Turnbull (William B.). Scottish Parochial Registers. 1849. List of Banffshire Registers, pp. 28–33.

Gross (Charles). Biblio. of Brit. Municipal Hist. (*Harvard Hist. Studies*, vol. v. 1897.) Banffshire, p. 161.

Hist. MSS. Comm. Reports. Banffshire Collections.

Fife, Duke of, at Duff House	4th Rep. p. xxiii. and App. pp. 515, 516.
Richmond, Duke of, at Gordon Castle	1st Rep. p. xiii. and App. p. 114.
Seafield, Earl of, at Cullen House ...	3rd Rep. p. xxii. and App. pp. 403, 404.
——— Dow. Countess of, at Cullen House	14th Rep. pp. 50, 51, and App. III. pp. 191–238.
Buckie, Catholic MSS. at	1st Rep. App. p. 120.

Banff. Burgh Records, 1372, etc., at Banff. (*Local Records Comm. Rep.*, 1902, App. III. p. 88.)

Cramond (William). Inventory of the Charters, Burgh Court Books, Books of Sasines, etc., belonging to the Burgh of Banff. 1887.

Anderson (Peter John). Inventories of Ecclesiastical Records of North-Eastern Scotland. Banffshire, pp. 238, etc. New Spalding Club, vol. vi. *Miscellany*, vol. i. 1890.

Trimen (Henry). Botanical Biblio. of the British Counties. Banffshire. (*Journ. of Botany*, vol. xii. p. 236. 1874.)

Christy (Miller). Biblio. Note on Banffshire Birds. (*The Zoologist*, Ser. 3, vol. xiv. p. 262, 1890, and reprinted in pamph., 1891, p. 30) **Mammals.** (*The Zoologist*, Ser. 3, vol. xvii. p. 209. 1893.) **Fishes.** (*Ibid.* p. 260. 1893.)

Anderson (John P.). Book of Brit. Topo., 1881. Banffshire, p. 380.

Gough (Richard). Brit. Topo., 1780, Banffshire, vol. ii. p. 656.

CULLEN.

Burgh Records, 1455, etc., at Cullen, with a Printed Index. (*Local Records Comm. Rep.*, 1902, App. III., p. 90.)

Cramond (William). Inventory of the Charters, Burgh Court Books, Books of Sasines, etc., belonging to the Burgh of Cullen, together with copy and translation of the Charter of the Burgh. 1887.

BEDFORDSHIRE.

Indexes to the Reports and Papers of the Associated Architectural Societies, etc. Vols. i.–viii. (1850–66); vols. ix.–xiv. (1867–78); vols. xv.–xix. (1879–88); and vols. xx.–xxv. (1889–1900). Lincoln. 1867–1905.

Index of References to Articles in the 'Gentleman's Magazine' relating to Bedfordshire. (*Beds. Notes & Queries*, vol. i. pp. 128–142. 1886.)

Index to the Victoria History of the County of Bedford. London: Constable & Co. 1914.

BEDFORDSHIRE (*continued*).

Genealogical Notes extracted from the 'Gentleman's Magazine.' 1731–1756. (*Beds. Notes & Queries*, vol. ii. pp. 141–156. 1889.)

List of Topographical Works relating to Bedfordshire. (*Book-Lore*, vol. iv. pp. 21–24. 1886.)

Bedfordshire Books. (*Notes & Queries*, Ser. 7, vol. xii. pp. 132, 233–234, 332. 1891.)

Bedford Literary and Scientific Institute and General Library. Catal. of the Circulating and Reference Libraries, and of the Old Library founded in 1700. [By T. G. Elger.] Bedford, 1892.

Gross (Charles). Biblio. of Brit. Municipal Hist. (*Harvard Hist. Studies*, vol. v. 1897.) Bedfordshire, pp. 165–166.

Davenport (Frances G.). List of Printed Materials for Manorial Hist. 1894. Biblio. Note on Beds. Manorial Hist., p. 38.

Dove (Patrick Edward). Domesday Studies. 1891. Domesday Biblio. Beds. vol. ii. pp. 669–670.

Lyell (Arthur H.). Biblio. List of Romano-British Remains. 1912. Bedfordshire, p. 1.

Macklin (Herbert Walter). Monumental Brasses. London: Geo. Allen & Co., 1913. Biblio. Note on Beds. Brasses, p. 139, with a List, pp. 144–145.

Matthews (A. Weight). MS. Biblio. of Works relating to Bedfordshire containing copies of Monumental Inscriptions. (In Library of Soc. of Genealogists, London.)

Hist. MSS. Comm. Reports. Bedfordshire Collections.

Bedford, Duke of, at Woburn	2nd Rep. p. ix. and App. pp. 1–4.
Cowper, Countess, at Wrest Park ...	2nd Rep. p. ix. and App. pp. 4–9.
Harvey, Mr. J. J., of Ickwell Bury, Herts.	1st Rep. p. x. and App. pp. 62–63; 2nd Rep. App. pp. 89–91.
Orlebar, Mr. R., of Hinwick House ...	3rd Rep. p. xix. and App. pp. 274–276.
Osborn, Sir George, at Chicksands ...	2nd Rep. p. xi. and App. p. 65.

Pomfret and Warburton's MS. Collections for Bedfordshire in British Museum.

Bedfordshire County Records. Vol. I. Notes and Extracts from the County Records in the Quarter Sessions Rolls, 1714–1832. Vol. II. Notes & Extracts from the County Records, being a Calendar of Vol. I. of the Sessions Minute Books, 1651–1660. Compiled by Messrs. Hardy and Page. 1907.

County Records, 1711, etc., at the Shire Hall, Bedford. (*Local Records Comm. Rep.*, 1902, App. III. p. 14.

Corporation of Bedford. A Schedule of the Records and other Documents. Printed by order of the Corporation. 1883.

Borough of Bedford. A Schedule of the Ancient Charters and Muniments. (Preface by F. A. Blaydes). 1895.

Borough Records, Hen. II., etc., at Town Hall, Bedford, with printed Index. (*Local Records Comm. Rep.*, 1902, App. III. p. 48.)

Fowler (G. Herbert). Early Charters of the Priory of Chicksands. Beds. Hist. Record Soc., vol. i. pp. 101–128. 1913.

For Biblio. of Elstow and John Bunyan see Dr. John Brown's '*Life of Bunyan*,' 3rd ed., 1887, pp. 453–489.

Luton Public Library. Spec. Colln. of Local Prints, Books, etc.

Trimen (Henry). Botanical Biblio. of the British Counties. Bedfordshire. (*Journ. of Botany*, vol. xii. p. 111. 1874.)

BEDFORDSHIRE (*continued*).

Christy (Miller). Biblio. Note on Bedfordshire Birds. (*The Zoologist*, Ser. 3, vol. xiv. p. 429, 1890; and reprinted in pamph., 1891, p. 8.) **Mammals.** (*The Zoologist*, Ser. 3, vol. xvii. p. 176. 1893.) **Reptiles.** (*Ibid.* p. 241. 1893.) **Fishes.** (*Ibid.* p. 252. 1893.)

Anderson (John P.). Book of Brit. Topo., 1881. Bedfordshire, pp. 48, 49.

Gatfield (George). Guide to Heraldry. 1892. Bedfordshire, pp. 117, 118.

Sims (Richard). Manual for the Genealogist. 1861. Bedfordshire, pp. 161, 198, 199, 229.

Upcott (William). English Topo., 1818. Bedfordshire, vol. i. pp. 1–8, 581, 582.

Smith (Alfred Russell). Catal. of Topo. Tracts, etc. 1878. Bedfordshire, pp. 1–5, 457.

Gough (Richard). Brit. Topo., 1780. Bedfordshire, vol. i. pp. 157–160.

Bandinel (Bulkeley). Catal. of Books bequeathed to Bodleian Library by Richard Gough. 1814. Bedfordshire, pp. 43, 44.

BERKSHIRE.

Reading Public Library. Catal. of the Reference Section. 1893. Appendix: List of Books, Prints, etc., arranged under Parishes, pp. 99–121.

Sherwood (George F. Tudor). County Collections for Berks. (*Berks., Bucks. & Oxon. Archæol. Journ.*, vol. vii. pp. 90–93; vol. viii. pp. 13–16. 1901–02.)

Berkshire Records and their Places of Deposit: I. The British Museum. (*Berks. Notes & Queries*, vol. i. pp. 7–15, 53–57. 1890.)

List of Books relating to the History of Berkshire. (*Berks. Archæol. Soc. Quart. Journ.*, vol. i. pp. 106, 107, 138. 1890.)

List of Topographical Works relating to Berkshire. (*Book-Lore*, vol. iv. pp. 33–38. 1886.)

Berkshire Books. (*Notes & Queries*, Ser. 4, vol. vi. pp. 14, 15. 1870.)

List of the Papers relating to Berkshire published in the '*Archæologia*' of the Soc. of Antiquaries, London, 1770–1885, vols. 1–50. (*Berks. Notes & Queries*, vol. i. pp. 100–102. 1890.)

Index to Berkshire Marriage Registers. By Mrs. J. H. Cope and L. Treacher. (*Berks., Bucks. & Oxon Archæol. Journ.*, vol. vi. p. 91; vol. vii. pp. 26, 51; vol. viii. pp. 88, 120; vol. ix. pp. 58, 83; vol. x. pp. 16–18. 1900–04.)

Sherwood (George F. Tudor). Berkshire Non-Parochial Registers in the Custody of the Registrar-General, from the Return of 1859. (*Berks. Notes & Queries*, vol. i. pp. 21–23, 51, 52. 1890.)

Gross (Charles). Biblio. of Brit. Municipal Hist. (*Harvard Hist. Studies*, vol. v. 1897.) Abingdon, p. 156. Reading, pp. 376, 377. Windsor, pp. 419, 420.

Davenport (Frances G.). List of Printed Materials for Manorial Hist. 1894. Biblio. Note on Berks. Manorial Hist., p. 38.

Dove (Patrick Edward). Domesday Studies. 1891. Domesday Biblio. Berks., vol. ii. p. 670.

Lyell (Arthur H.). Biblio. List of Romano-British Remains. 1912. Berkshire, pp. 1–3.

Macklin (Herbert Walter). Monumental Brasses. London: Geo. Allen & Co., 1913. Biblio. Note on Berks. Brasses, with a List, p. 145.

Hist. MSS. Comm. Reports. Berkshire Collections.

Bouverie-Pusey, Mr. S. E. E., at Faringdon	7th Rep. App. p. 681.
Eyston, Mr. C. J., at East Hendred, Wantage	3rd Rep. p. xxi. and App. pp. 260, 261.
Loder-Symonds, Capt. F. C., at Hinton Waldrist Manor, Berks	13th Rep. pp. 47, 48 and App. IV. pp. 378–404.

BERKSHIRE (continued).

Hist. MSS. Comm. Reports.

Throckmorton, Sir N. W., at Coughton Court, Warwickshire	3rd Rep. p. xxi. and App. pp. 256–258; 10th Rep. p. xxv. and App. IV. pp. 168–176.
Stuart MSS. at Windsor Castle ...	16th Rep. pp. 12–14; vol. i. (1902); vol. ii. (1904); 17th Rep. pp. 13–19; vol. iii. (1907).
Willes, Mrs., at Goodrest, Berks. ...	2nd Rep. p. xxi. and App. p. 103; 3rd Rep. p. xxvi. and App. p. 435.
Abingdon Corporation	1st Rep. App. p. 98; 2nd Rep. p. xv. and App. pp. 149, 150.
——— Hospital of Christ	1st Rep. App. p. 98.
Reading Corporation	11th Rep. pp. 26–29 and App. VII. pp. 167–227.
Wallingford Corporation	6th Rep. App. pp. 572–595.

Suckling's Collections for Berkshire, 1821–1839, in the British Museum. (Add. MSS. 18489; 18490. Index, Add. MS. 18491.)

Ashmolean MSS. Descriptive, Analytical, and Critical Catal. of the MSS. bequeathed unto the Univ. of Oxford by Elias Ashmole. By W. H. Black. Oxford, 1845.

——— **Index to the Catal. of the MSS. of Elias Ashmole,** formerly preserved in the Ashmolean Museum, and now in the Bodl. Lib., Oxford. By W. D. Macray and H. Gough. Oxford, 1866. (Parts 10 and 11 of the *Catalogus Codicum MSS. Bibl. Bodl.*)

Gough (Richard). Topographical Collections in Bod. Lib. The Berkshire MSS. increased by the William Nelson Clarke Collection (consisting of a Parochial Hist. of the County, transcripts of Herald's Visitations, early records, etc.). See Macray, '*Annals of the Bodleian*,' p. 287, note.

Berkshire Court Rolls. By N. J. Hone. (*Berks. Archæol. Soc. Quart. Journ.*, vol. iii. pp. 153, 173. 1894; *Berks. Bucks. & Oxon. Archæol. Journ.*, vol. xv. p. 81; vol. xvi. p. 22; vol. xvii. p. 85. 1909–11.)

List of Berkshire Deeds and other Documents on sale by F. Marcham, 9 Tottenham Terrace, White Hart Lane, London, N. A valuable and well-arranged list.

Trimen (Henry). Botanical Biblio. of the British Counties. Berkshire. (*Journ. of Botany*, vol. xii. p. 109. 1874.)

Christy (Miller). Biblio. Note on Berks. Birds. (*The Zoologist*, Ser. 3, vol. xiv. p. 249, 1890; and reprinted in pamph., 1891, p. 8.)

Anderson (John P.). Book of Brit. Topo., 1881. Berkshire, pp. 50–54.

Gatfield (George). Guide to Heraldry. 1892. Berkshire, pp. 118, 119.

Sims (Richard). Manual for the Genealogist. 1861. Berkshire, pp. 161, 199, 229.

Upcott (William). English Topo., 1818. Berkshire, vol. i. pp. 9–25, 583–585.

Smith (Alfred Russell). Catal. of Topo. Tracts, etc., 1878. Berkshire, pp. 5–12, 457.

Gough (Richard). Brit. Topo., 1780. Berkshire, vol. i. pp. 161–184.

Bandinel (Bulkeley). Catal. of Books bequeathed to Bodleian Library by Richard Gough, 1814. Berkshire, pp. 45–49.

READING.

Macray (W. Dunn). The MSS. of the Corporation of Reading. (*Hist. MSS. Comm. 11th Rep.*, 1887, App. VII. pp. 167–227.)

Guilding (Rev. J. M.). Reading Records. Schedule of MSS. belonging to the Corporation of Reading. Vol. i. pp. xi.–xiv. 1892.

Borough Records. Henry III., etc., at Town Hall, Reading. (*Local Records Comm. Rep.*, 1902, App. III. p. 38.)

BERKSHIRE (continued).

Report of the Municipal Commissioners appointed to enquire into the state of Corporations in England and Wales. Corporation of Reading, Oct. 24, 1833.

List of Reading Municipal Records Printed. (*Notes & Queries*, Ser. 11, vol. vi. p. 91. 1912.)

Harrison (W. H.). Reading and Some of its Literary Associations. (*Book-Auction Records*, vol. 8, pp. liii.-lviii. 1911.)

Ditchfield (P. H.). The Books and Bookmen of Reading. (*Walford's Antiq. Mag.*, vol. xi. pp. 233-238. 1887.)

Murray (David). 'Museums.' Glasgow, 1904. Biblio. Note on Reading Museum, vol. iii. p. 122.

ABINGDON.

Richardson (William H.). A Short Biblio. of Abingdon. London, 1902.

Challenor (Bromley). Selections from the Municipal Chronicles of the Borough of Abingdon, from 1555 to 1897. Abingdon. 1898.

Borough Records, 1556, etc., and Christ's Hospital Deeds, 12th Cent., etc. (*Local Records Comm. Rep.*, 1902, App. III. p. 46.)

Allnutt (W. H.). English Provincial Presses—Early Printing at Abingdon. (*Bibliographica*, vol. ii. pp. 30, 31. 1896.)

WINDSOR AND FROGMORE.

Records of Dean and Canons, 1154, etc., at Windsor, with MS. Index. (*Local Records Comm. Rep.* 1902, App. III. p. 116.)

Eyton (J. Walter K.). Publications of the Private Press at Frogmore Lodge. (*Sale Catal. of his Library of Privately Printed Books*, Sotheby's, 1848, p. 80.)

Lowndes (Wm. Thomas). List of Publications of the Frogmore Lodge Press. (*Bibliographer's Manual*, 1871, App. p. 216.)

Plomer (Henry R.). Frogmore Lodge Private Press. (*Some Private Presses of the Nineteenth Century*, in '*The Library*.' New Ser., vol. i. pp. 408, 409. 1900.)

MAIDENHEAD.

Borough Records, 1392, etc., at Town Hall, Maidenhead, with MS. Index. (*Local Records Comm. Rep.*, 1902, App. III. p. 64.)

Walker (J. W.). A Cal. of the Ancient Charters and Documents of the Corporation of Maidenhead. 1908.

NEWBURY.

Money (Walter). Notes on the Parish Registers of Newbury. (*Brit. Archæol. Assoc. Journ.* New Series, vol. ii. pp. 157–183. 1896.)

SYDMONTON.

Kingsmill (Andrew). The MSS. of Andrew Kingsmill, at Sydmonton Court, being ancient deeds relating to Hampshire and Berkshire. (*Hist. MSS. Comm. 15th Rep.*, App. X. pp. 173, 174. 1899.)

GRAZELEY.

Macray (Rev. W. D.). Early Berkshire Deeds relating to Grazeley, Berks. (*Berks., Bucks. and Oxon. Archæol. Journ.*, vol. ii. pp. 13–15. 1896.)

WOKINGHAM.

Borough Records, with MS. list, at Town Hall, Wokingham. (*Local Records Comm. Rep.*, 1902, App. III. p. 74.)

BERWICKSHIRE.

Hist. MSS. Comm. Reports. Berwickshire Collections.

Campbell, Sir Hugh Hume, at Marchmont House	14th Rep. pp. 47–49, and App. III. pp. 56–173.
Home, Earl of, at the Hirsel, Coldstream	12th Rep. p. 51, and App. VIII.
——— Col. David Milne, at Wedderburn Castle	16th Rep. p. 122, and vol. 1902.
Lauderdale, Earl of, at Thirlestaine Castle	5th Rep. p. xix. and App. pp. 610–613.
Stirling, Miss M. Eleanor, at Renton...	5th Rep. p. xxi. and App. pp. 646–650.
Hay, Mr. Robert Mordaunt, of Duns Castle	Rep. on MSS. in various Collections, vol. v. pp. 1–71. 1909.

County Council Records, at Greenlaw and Duns. (*Local Records Comm. Rep.*, 1902, App. III. p. 82.)

Livingstone (Matthew). Guide to the Public Records of Scotland, 1905. Berwickshire, p. 174.

Turnbull (William B.). Scottish Parochial Registers. 1849. List of Berwickshire Registers, pp. 33–38.

Black (George F.). Descriptive Catal. of Loan Collections of Prehistoric and other Antiquities from the Shires of Berwick, Roxburgh, and Selkirk. (*Soc. of Antiq. Scot. Proc.*, vol. xxviii. pp. 321–342. 1894.)

Biblio. of Historical Monuments in the Co. of Berwick, in Inventory of Monuments, etc., in the County of Berwick. (*Hist. Monuments (Scot.) Comm.*, 1*st Rep.* pp. xiv., xv. 1909.)

Anderson (Joseph). Report on Local Museums in Scotland. Berwick Museum. (*Soc. of Antiq. Scot. Proc.*, vol. xxii. p. 418. 1888.)

——— **Report on Local Museums in Scotland.** Duns Museum. (*Soc. of Antiq. Scot. Proc.*, vol. xxii. p. 383. 1888.)

Trimen (Henry). Botanical Biblio. of the British Counties. Berwickshire. (*Journ. of Botany*, vol. xii. p. 234. 1874.)

Christy (Miller). Biblio. Note on Berwickshire Birds. (*The Zoologist*, Ser. 3, vol. xiv. p. 262, 1890; and reprinted in pamph., 1891, p. 30.) **Mammals.** (*The Zoologist*, Ser. 3, vol. xvii. p. 209. 1893.) **Fishes.** (*Ibid.* p. 260. 1893.)

Anderson (John P.). Book of Brit. Topo., 1881. Berwickshire, pp. 380-382.

Gough (Richard). Brit. Topo., 1780. Berwickshire, vol. ii. pp. 657, 658.

Bandinel (Bulkeley). Catal. of Books bequeathed to Bodleian Lib. by Richard Gough, 1814, p. 356.

LAUDER.

Burgh Records, 1653, etc., at Lauder. (*Local Records Comm. Rep.*, 1902, App. III. p. 96.)

BRECKNOCKSHIRE.

Ballinger (John). The Trevecca Press. (*The Library*, New Ser. vol. vi. pp. 225-250. 1905.)

Anderson (John P.). Book of Brit. Topo., 1881. Brecknockshire, p. 343.

Gough (Richard). Brit. Topo., 1780. Brecknockshire, vol. ii. p. 509.

Bandinel (Bulkeley). Catal. of Books bequeathed to Bodleian Lib. by Richard Gough, 1814. Brecknockshire, p. 334.

Lyell (Arthur H.). Biblio. List of Romano-British Remains. 1912. Brecknockshire, p. 142.

BRECKNOCKSHIRE (*continued*).

Trimen (Henry). Botanical Biblio. of the British Counties. Brecknockshire. (*Journ. of Botany*, vol. xii. p. 157. 1874.)

Christy (Miller). Biblio. Note on Breconshire Birds. (*The Zoologist*, Ser. 3, vol. xiv. p. 261, 1890; and reprinted in pamph., 1891, p. 8.)

BUCKINGHAMSHIRE.

GOUGH (HENRY). BIBLIOTHECA BUCKINGHAMIENSIS: A LIST OF BOOKS RELATING TO THE COUNTY OF BUCKINGHAM. Aylesbury. 1890.

(Originally issued by Archit. & Archæol. Soc. for the County of Buckinghamshire in '*Records of Buckinghamshire*,' vol. v., vi. 1885–90.)

Gross (Charles). Biblio. of Brit. Municipal Hist. (*Harvard Hist. Studies*, vol. v. 1897.) Buckinghamshire, p. 90. Buckingham, pp. 181, 182. Wycombe, pp. 423, 424.

Davenport (Frances G.). List of Printed Materials for Manorial Hist. 1894. Biblio. Note on Bucks. Manorial Hist., p. 38.

Dove (Patrick Edward). Domesday Studies. 1891. Domesday Biblio. Bucks., vol. ii. p. 670.

Lyell (Arthur H.). Biblio. List of Romano-British Remains. 1912. Bucks., p. 4.

Macklin (Herbert Walter). Monumental Brasses. London: Geo. Allen & Co. 1913. Biblio. Note on Bucks. Brasses, with a List, pp. 147–149.

Martin (John). Private Printing Press at Hartwell. (*Biblio. Catal. of Books Privately Printed*, 1854, p. xvii.)

An Inventory of the Historical Monuments in Buckinghamshire. 2 vols. 1913. (*Royal Comm. on Hist. Monuments—England.*) Combined Index of Inventories of South and North Bucks., vol. ii. pp. 362–457.

Hist. MSS. Comm. Reports. Buckinghamshire Collections.

Buckinghamshire, Earl of	14th Rep. pp. 23–25 and App. IX. pp. 1–154.
Clayton, Sir William, at Harleyford, Marlow...	17th Rep. p. 130; various Collections, vol. iv. pp. 326–341.
Fortescue, Hon. G. M., at Dropmore	2nd Rep. p. xiii. and App. pp. 49–63.
Fortescue, Mr. J. B., at Dropmore ...	Vol. i. (13th Rep. pp. 36–47 and App. III.). Vol. ii. (14th Rep. pp. 36–37 and App. V. 16th Rep. pp. 68–79). Vol. iii. 1889 (17th Rep. pp. 77–97). Vol. iv. 1905. Vol. v. 1906. Vol. vi. 1908. Vol. vii. 1910. Vol. viii. 1912.
Frankland - Russell - Astley, Mrs., at Chequers Court, Bucks.	16th Rep. pp. 86–91 and vol. 1900.
Somerset, Duke of, at Maiden Bradley, Wilts.	15th Rep. App. VII. pp. 127–133.
Verney, Sir H., at Claydon House. co. Bucks.	7th Rep. p. xiv. and App. pp. 433–509.
Eton College	9th Rep. p. x. and App. I. pp. 349–358.
High Wycombe Corporation	5th Rep. p. xvii. and App. pp. 554–565.

Hare's MSS. in College of Arms contain an extensive Collection of Bucks material.

Browne Willis's MSS. in Bodleian Library contain large Collections for Bucks.

BUCKINGHAMSHIRE (*continued*).

Cole (**William**). 1714–82. **MS. Collections in British Museum**, relating to Bucks. and other Counties. See Index to the Contents of the Cole Manuscripts, by George J. Gray. 1912.

County Records, 1678, etc., with MS. Indexes, at the County Hall, Aylesbury. (*Local Records Comm. Rep.*, 1902. App. III. p. 14.)

Bucks. and Oxon. Marriage Bonds. By G. F. Tudor Sherwood. (*Berks., Bucks. & Oxon. Archæol. Journal*, vol. ii. pp. 52, 77, 117. 1896–97.)

Trimen (**Henry**). **Botanical Biblio. of the British Counties.** Buckinghamhamshire. (*Journ. of Botany*, vol. xii. p. 110. 1874.)

Christy (**Miller**). **Biblio. Note on Bucks. Birds.** (*The Zoologist*, Ser. 3, vol. xiv. p. 249, 1890; and reprinted in pamph., 1891, p. 8.)

Anderson (John P.). Book of Brit. Topo., 1881. Buckinghamshire, pp. 54–57.
Gatfield (George). Guide to Heraldry. 1892. Buckinghamshire, pp. 119–121.
Sims (Richard). Manual for the Genealogist. 1861. Buckinghamshire, pp. 162, 199, 200, 230.
Upcott (William). English Topo., 1818. Buckinghamshire, vol. i. pp. 26–31, 586, 587.
Smith (Alfred Russell). Catal. of Topo. Tracts, etc. 1878. Buckinghamshire, pp. 13–18, 458.
Gough (Richard). Brit. Topo., 1780. Buckinghamshire, vol. i. pp. 183–190.
Bandinel (Bulkeley). Catal. of Books bequeathed to Bodleian Lib. by Richard Gough, 1814. Buckinghamshire, pp. 50–52.

ETON.

Harcourt (**Lewis Vernon**). **An Eton Bibliography.** 1898. New ed. enlarged, 1902.

The Eton Collection of Books, etc., by the Rt. Hon. L. V. Harcourt is perhaps the largest in existence.

Loan Collection of Portraits, Views, and Other Objects connected with the Hist. of Eton, on occasion of the 450th anniversary of the foundation. Eton College, 1891. Privately Printed. Second Edition, revised and enlarged. Eton, 1891.

Cust (**Sir Lionel**). **Eton College Portraits.** (Spottiswoode & Co.)

Harvey (**Francis**). **A Catal. of Rare Mezzotint Portraits of Celebrated Etonians.** London: 4 St. James's Street, n.d.

Thackeray (**Rev. F. St. John**). **Eton College Library.** Reprinted from '*Notes & Queries.*' Eton, 1881.

James (**Montague R.**). **A Descriptive Catal. of the MSS. in the Library of Eton College.** 1895.

Allnutt (**W. H.**). **English Provincial Presses**—Sir H. Savile's Eton Press, 1610–13. (*Bibliographica*, vol. ii. pp. 276–278. 1896.)

Proctor (**Robert**). **The French Royal Greek Types and the Eton Chrysostom.** (*Biblio. Soc. Trans.*, vol. vii. pp. 49–74. 1904.)

Peddie (**R. A.**). **The Greek Type of the Eton Chrysostom.** (*Bibliographical Register*, vol. i. no. 3. 1906.)

BEACONSFIELD.

Summers (**W. H.**). **Some Documents in the State Papers relating to Beaconsfield.** (*Bucks. Archit. & Archæol. Soc.—Records of Bucks.*, vol. vii. pp. 97–114. 1893.)

HIGH WYCOMBE.

Summers (**W. H.**). **Some Documents in the State Papers relating to High Wycombe.** (*Bucks. Archit. & Archæol. Soc.—Records of Bucks.*, vol. vii. pp. 304–313. 1895.)

Chipping Wycombe. Charters relating to the Borough. 1817.

BUTESHIRE.

Hist. MSS. Comm. Reports. Buteshire Collection.

Bute, Marquess of, at Mountstuart ... 3rd Rep. pp. xiii., xxii. and App. pp. 202–209, 402, 403; 5th Rep. p. xix. and App. pp. 617–620.

County Council Records, 1650, etc., at County Buildings, Bute. (*Local Records Comm. Rep.*, 1902, App. III. p. 82.)

Burgh Records, 1400, etc., at Rothesay. (*Local Records Comm. Rep.*, 1902, App. III. p. 98.)

Livingstone (Matthew). Guide to the Public Records of Scotland. 1905. Buteshire, p. 173.

Turnbull (William B.). Scottish Parochial Registers. 1849. List of Buteshire Registers, pp. 38, 39.

Gross (Charles). Biblio. of Brit. Municipal Hist. (*Harvard Hist. Studies*, vol. v. 1897.) Buteshire, p. 131.

Trimen (Henry). Botanical Biblio. of the British Counties. Buteshire. (*Journ. of Botany*, vol. xii. p. 237. 1874.)

Christy (Miller). Biblio. Note on Buteshire Birds. (*The Zoologist*, Ser. 3, vol. xiv. p. 262, 1890; and reprinted in pamph., 1891, p. 31.) **Mammals.** (*The Zoologist*, Ser. 3, vol. xvii. p. 210, 1893.) **Fishes.** (*Ibid.* p. 261, 1893.)

Anderson (John P.). Book of Brit. Topo., 1881. Buteshire, p. 382.

CAITHNESS.

MOWAT (John). A BIBLIOGRAPHY OF CAITHNESS: WITH NOTES. Wick and Glasgow. 1909.

——— **A List of Books and Pamphlets** relating to the North of Scotland, with special reference to Caithness and Sutherland. (*Old-Lore Miscellany—Viking Club*, vol. ii. pp. 238–242; vol. iii. pp. 49–54, 170–176, 224, 225; vol. iv. pp. 45–47, 99–101, 151, 152, 201–205; vol. v. pp. 38–43, 82–89, 134–136. 1909–12.) Reprinted as 'Biblio. of Caithness and Sutherland.' London: Viking Club. 1910.

Caithness and Sutherland Records. Extracts from Documents, etc., with translations. Viking Club, London. 1909, etc. In progress.

Livingstone (Matthew). Guide to the Public Records of Scotland. 1905. Caithness, pp. 114, 174, 177.

Turnbull (William B.). Scottish Parochial Registers. 1849. List of Caithness Registers, pp. 39–40.

Gross (Charles). Biblio. of Brit. Municipal Hist. (*Harvard Hist. Studies*, vol. v. 1897.) Caithness, p. 131.

Biblio. of Historical Monuments, etc., in the Co. of Caithness, in Inventory of Monuments, etc., in the County of Caithness. (*Hist. Monuments* (*Scot.*) *Comm.*, *3rd Rep.*, pp. xvi.–xviii. 1911.)

Catal. of Heraldic, Geneal. and Antiq. Books and MSS. which belonged to Alex. Sinclair, son of Sir John Sinclair, of Ulbster. 1877. Privately Printed by the Earl of Glasgow.

Mackay (Angus). Sutherland and Caithness in Ancient Geography and Maps. (*Soc. of Antiq. Scot. Proc.*, vol xlii. pp. 79–94. 1908.)

Historicus. Some References to Witchcraft and Charming from Caithness and Sutherland Church Records. (*Old-Lore Miscellany— Viking Club*, vol. ii. pp. 110–115, 171, 172, 193; vol. iii. pp. 47, 48. 1909–10.)

CAITHNESS (*continued*).

Trimen (Henry). Botanical Biblio. of the British Counties. Caithness. (*Journ. of Botany*, vol. xii. p. 237. 1874.)

Christy (Miller). Note on Caithness Birds. (*The Zoologist*, Ser. 3, vol. xiv. p. 263, 1890, and reprinted in pamph., 1891, p. 31.) **Mammals.** (*The Zoologist*, Ser. 3, vol. xvii. p. 210. 1893.) **Reptiles.** (*Ibid.* p. 249. 1893.) **Fishes.** (*Ibid.* p. 261. 1893.)

Anderson (John P.). Book of Brit. Topo., 1881. Caithness, p. 383.
Gough (Richard). Brit. Topo., 1780. Caithness, vol. ii. p. 659.

CAMBRIDGESHIRE.

BOWES (Robert). **A CATALOGUE OF BOOKS PRINTED AT, OR RELATING TO, THE UNIVERSITY, TOWN, AND COUNTY OF CAMBRIDGE FROM 1521 TO 1893,** with Biblio. and Biog. Notes. (Index by Ernest Worman). 2 vols. Cambridge. 1894. Appendix III. List of Maps, Views, Caricatures, &c., pp. 497–504.

Bartholomew (Augustus Theodore). Cambridge University Library. Catal. of the Books and Papers, for the most part relating to the University, Town, and County of Cambridge, bequeathed to the University by John Willis Clark, M.A. Cambridge. 1912.

The principal sources of the collection were these: (1) An important 'Catalogue of tracts, etc., relating to Cambridgeshire' was issued by A. R. Smith, of Soho Square, in 1878, and from this Mr. Clark bought extensively. (2) The Rev. Stephen Parkinson, Fellow of St. John's College (B.A. 1815, M.A. 1818), was in the habit of preserving all Cambridge papers which came into his hands; his collection was acquired by Mr. Clark and filled numerous gaps in the long series of fly-sheets, programmes, proposals, &c., which is a particularly valuable feature of the Clark Collection (see the Catalogue, s.v. 'Cambridge Papers' and 'Fly Sheets'). (3) Mr. Henry Bradshaw, University Librarian, added many tracts to the collection; and at the sale which followed his death in 1886, Mr. Clark acquired many more Cambridge items. (4) Dr. H. R. Luard, Registrary, who died in 1891, left Mr. Clark his University pamphlets and Bentleiana. (5) In 1894 Mr. Robert Bowes published his remarkable 'Catalogue of Cambridge Books,' and a large number of the pieces there described made their way into the Cambridge collection at Scroope House. In addition to these main sources, Mr. Clark rarely missed an opportunity of securing any books which came within the scope of his collection wherever and whenever he happened to see them.

Mr. Clark's main idea in forming the collection was to illustrate the history and development of Cambridge by means of its literature; he collected from an historical and biographical rather than from a bibliographical point of view. Most of the books of typographical interest which were originally included in his Cambridge Collection he gave to the Library in 1902, in order that they might appear in Mr. Sayle's 'Early English Printed Books' in the University Library, Cambridge.

In addition to the books and papers here described, Mr. Clark left to the University a collection of prints and drawings of the University, Town, and County of Cambridge. Besides topographical engravings and plans the collection includes a series of original pencil sketches by George Nicholson (1816); architectural drawings by Professor Willis; and photographs of University ceremonies.

It is hoped that these may be fully described in a projected comprehensive Catalogue of Cambridge Prints and Plans.

Cambridge University Library, Clark Collection, p. 282.

A Short Bibliography of J. W. Clark, by A. T. B. and C. G., appears in the J. W. Clark Memorial Volume, '*Fasciculus Joanni Willis Clark dicatus.*' 1909.

Documents relating to the University and Colleges of Cambridge. Published by the Commissioners on the Univ. and Colleges. 3 vols. London, 1852.

Sandars (Samuel). An Annotated List of Books printed on vellum, to be found in the University and College Libraries at Cambridge. With an Appendix containing a List of Works referring to the Bibliography and Palæography of Cambridge Libraries. Camb. Antiq. Soc. Octavo Publication. No. xv. 1878.

Luard (H. R.). List of Documents in the University Registry, 1266–1544. (*Camb. Antiq. Soc. Communications*, vol. iii. pp. 385–403. 1876.)

CAMBRIDGESHIRE (*continued*).

Pink (**John**). **Catal. of Cambridge Books, Maps, and Prints.** 1874, and New Edn. 1889.

An Index to the Reports and Abstracts of Proceedings, including Subjects and Authors of Communications and Publications, from 1840 to 1897, **of the Cambridge Antiquarian Society.** (Octavo Publication. No. xxx. 1898.)

Bowes (**Robert**). **The First Printing in Cambridge.** Prospectus of a reprint of Linacre's edition of Galen, 1521, and other early Cambridge Books. 1879.

——— **The First Printing in Cambridge.** Prospectus of a reprint of Bullock's Oratio, 1521, and other early Cambridge Books. 1886.

——— **Facsimiles of title-pages and colophons of Early Cambridge Books.** (A series of photographs and lithographs.) 1879.

——— **Biog. Notes on the University Printers,** from the Commencement of Printing in Cambridge to the present time. (*Camb. Antiq. Soc. Communications*, vol. v. pp. 283–362. 1886.)

——— **Note on the Cambridge University Press,** 1701–07. (*Camb. Antiq. Soc. Communications*, vol. vi. pp. 362–367. 1887.)

——— **Cambridge Bookshops and Booksellers,** 1846–1858. (*Publishers' Circular*, vol. xcvii. pp. 7, 127. 1912.)

——— **On the First and Other Early Cambridge Newspapers.** (*Camb. Antiq. Soc. Proc.*, vol. viii. pp. 347–358. 1894.)

Bowes (**Robert**) and **Gray** (**George J.**). **John Siberch: Biblio. Notes,** 1886–1905. Cambridge, 1906.

Gross (**Charles**). **Biblio. of Brit. Municipal Hist.** (*Harvard Hist. Studies*, vol. v. 1897.) Cambridgeshire, pp. 90, 91. Cambridge, pp. 184, 185. Ely, p. 439. Wisbech, pp. 420, 421.

Davenport (**Frances G.**). **List of Printed Materials for Manorial Hist.** 1894. Biblio. Note on Cambs. Manorial Hist., pp. 38, 39.

Dove (**Patrick Edward**). **Domesday Studies.** 1891. Domesday Biblio. Cambs. vol. ii. p. 671.

Lyell (**Arthur H.**). **Biblio. List of Romano-British Remains.** 1912. Cambridgeshire, p. 5.

Macklin (**Herbert Walter**). **Monumental Brasses.** London: Geo. Allen & Co., 1913. Biblio. Note on Cambs. Brasses, with a List, pp. 139 and 149, 150.

Murray (**David**). **'Museums,' Glasgow.** 1904. Biblio. Note on Cambridge Museums, vol. ii. pp. 156–160.

Cambridge Antiquarian Society. Catal. of the First Exhibition of Portraits in the Camb. Antiq. Society's Collection, and Cambridge Caricatures to 1840, held May and June, 1908. Cambridge. 1908.

Porter (**Charles P.**). **Cambridge Libraries.** (*Book-Auction Records*, vol. iv. pt. 3, pp. xxv.–xxx. 1907.)

Allnutt (**W. H.**). **English Provincial Presses**—Earliest Printing at Cambridge. (*Bibliographica*, vol. ii. pp. 28, 29, 165–168. 1896.)

Bradshaw (**Henry**). **Books printed by J. Siberch at Cambridge,** 1521–2.

——— **Biblio. Introduction to facsimile of Henrici Bulloci Oratio, &c.** 1521. Cambridge, 1886.

Vide also **Jenkinson** (**F. J. H.**). **On a Letter from P. Kaetz to J. Siberch.** (*Camb. Antiq. Soc. Proc.*, vol. vii. pp. 186–189) and 'On a Copy of Linacre's *Galen de Temperamentis*, 1521,' printed by J. Siberch, at Trinity Coll., Dublin. (*Ibid.*, vol. ix. pp. 1–3.)

CAMBRIDGESHIRE (continued).

Prothero (G. W.). A Memoir of Henry Bradshaw. 1888. App. III. List of the Published Work of Henry Bradshaw, pp. 432–437.

Foster (J. E.). On Two Books printed by John Siberch, in All Souls' Coll., Oxford. (*Camb. Antiq. Soc. Proc.*, vol. viii. p. 31. 1891.)

Jenkinson (F. J. H.). On a unique fragment of a book printed at Cambridge by John Siberch, early in the sixteenth century. (*Camb. Antiq. Soc. Proc.*, vol. vii. pp. 104, 105. 1890.)

—— **List of Books printed at Cambridge, 1521–1650.** See **Bowes (Robert). Catal. of Books** printed at, or relating to, Cambridge, 1894. App. iv. pp. 505–516.

Roberts (T. C.). The University Press. (*The Camb. Mag.*, vol. ii. pp. 299–303. 1913.)

Gray (George J.). The Earlier Cambridge Stationers and Bookbinders, and the First Cambridge Printer. (*Biblio. Soc. Monographs*, No. 13. 1904.)

—— **The Early Stationers, Bookbinders, and the First Printer of Cambridge.** (*Biblio. Soc. Trans.*, vol. vi. pp. 145–148. 1903.)

Gray (J. P.) and Sons. A Note upon the Early Camb. Binders of the sixteenth century. 1900.

Cambridge Booksellers and Printers. A List. (*Notes & Queries*, ser. 10, vol. vii. pp. 26, 75. 1907.)

Fordham (Sir Herbert G.). Cambridgeshire Maps: a descriptive Catal. of the Maps of the County, and of the Great Level of the Fens, 1579–1900. Camb. 1904–1908. (Also issued in *Camb. Antiq. Soc. Proc.*, vol. xi. pp. 101–172; vol. xii. pp. 152–231. 1905–08.)

Smith (G. C. Moore). Cambridge Plans before 1585. (J. W. Clark Memorial Volume, '*Fasciculus Joanni Willis Clark dicatus*,' 1909.)

Clark (John Willis). John Hamond's Plan of Cambridge, 1592. (*Camb. Antiq. Soc. Proc.*, vol. vii. pp. 13, 14. 1888.)

Willis (Robert) and **Clark (John Willis). List of Authorities,** MS. Collections of Baker and Cole, Plans and Views of Cambridge. (*Architectural Hist. of the Univ. of Camb.*, 1886, vol. 1, pp. xcii.–cxxxiv.)

Hist. MSS. Comm. Reports. Cambridgeshire Collections.

Cambridge Corporation	1st Rep. App. p. 99.
—— Christ's College	1st Rep. App. p. 63.
—— Clare College	2nd Rep. p. xiii. and App. pp. 110–116.
—— Corpus Christi College	1st Rep. App. pp. 64–67.
—— Downing College	The Bowtell Coll. 3rd Rep. p. xx. and App. pp. 320–27.
—— Emmanuel College	4th Rep. p. xviii. and App. pp. 417–421.
—— Gonville and Caius College	2nd Rep. p. xiv. and App. pp. 116–118.
—— Jesus College	2nd Rep. p. xiv. and App. pp. 118–121.
—— King's College...	1st Rep. App. pp. 67–69.
—— Magdalene College	5th Rep. p. xv. and App. pp. 481–484.
—— Pembroke College	1st Rep. App. pp. 69–72; 5th Rep. p. xvi. and App. pp. 484–88.
—— Queen's College	1st Rep. App. pp. 72–73.
—— St. Catherine's College	4th Rep. p. xvii. and App. pp. 421–428.
—— St. John's College	1st Rep. App. pp. 74–77.

CAMBRIDGESHIRE (*continued*).

Hist. MSS. Comm. Reports.

Cambridge, St. Peter's College	1st Rep. App. pp. 77–82.
—— Sidney Sussex College	3rd Rep. p. xx. and App. pp. 327–329.
—— Trinity College	1st Rep. App. pp. 82–86.
—— Trinity Hall	2nd Rep. p. xiv. and App. pp. 121–123.
—— Registry of the University	1st Rep. App. p. 73.
Ely, Bishop of	12th Rep. p. 44 and App. IX. pp. 375–388.
—— Dean and Chapter of...	12th Rep. p. 43 and App. IX. pp. 389–396.
Wisbech Corporation	9th Rep. p. xiv. and App. I. pp. 293–299.

Cole (Rev. W.). Collections of MSS. chiefly relating to the County of Cambridge in the Brit. Museum, in 92 vols. numbered. Add. MSS. 5798–5887. Gen. Index to the first forty-six vols. Add. MS. 5801. Other Indexes are at Add. MSS. 5799 and 5800.

Gray (George J.). Index to the Contents of the Cole MSS. in the British Museum. Bowes & Bowes. Cambridge. 1912.

Suckling's Collections for Cambridgeshire (1821–1839) in Brit. Museum, numbered Add. MSS. 18,476, 18,478, 18,481, 18,482.—Index. Add. MS. 18,491.

Baker's Collections for the University of Cambridge, in 42 vols., at St. John's College, Cambridge, and at the British Museum.

Index to the Baker MSS. By four members (*i.e.* J. J. Smith, C. C. Babington, C. W. Goodwin, and J. Power) of the Camb. Antiq. Society. Cambridge, 1848.

MS. Collections relating to Cambridgeshire are in Trinity Coll. Library, Cambridge.

Lamb (John), Dean of Bristol. Collection of Letters, Statutes, & other Documents from the MSS. Library of Corpus Christi Coll., illustrative of the Hist. of the Univ. of Camb. from MD. to MDLXII. London, 1838.

Bannister (Rev. H. M.) A Short Notice of some MSS. of the Cambridge Friars, now in the Vatican Library. (Brit. Soc. of Franciscan Studies. '*Collectanea Franciscana.*' vol. i. pp. 114–123, 154, 155. 1914.)

Coleman's Cambridgeshire Deeds. By C. Parsons and W. M. Palmer. (*East Anglian*, Ser. 3, vol. xiii. pp. 230, 267, 280, 291, 323, 354, 373. 1909–10.)

Lists of Depositories of Records in Cambridgeshire. (*Local Records Comm. Rep.*, 1902, pp. 242–243.)

Whitaker (W.). Geology of the Neighbourhood of Cambridge. With a Biblio. Appendix. 1881.

Trimen (Henry). Botanical Biblio. of the British Counties. Cambridgeshire. (*Journ. of Botany*, vol. xii. p. 111. 1874.)

Miller (Christy). Biblio. Note on Cambs. Birds. (*The Zoologist*, Ser. 3, vol. xiv. p. 249, 1890; and reprinted in pamph., 1891, p. 8.) **Mammals.** (*The Zoologist*, Ser. 3, vol, xvii. p. 176, 1893.) **Reptiles.** (*Ibid.* p. 241, 1893.) **Fishes.** (*Ibid.* p. 252, 1893.)

Anderson (John P.). Book of Brit. Topo., 1881. Cambridgeshire, pp. 54–63.

Gatfield (George). Guide to Heraldry. 1892. Cambridgeshire, pp. 121–125.

Sims (Richard). Manual for the Genealogist. 1861. Cambridgeshire, pp. 162, 200, 230.

Upcott (William). English Topo., 1818. Cambridgeshire, vol. i. pp. 32–60, 588–599.

Smith (Alfred Russell). Catal. of Topo. Tracts, etc., 1878. Cambridgeshire, pp. 19–34, 458–459.

Gough (Richard). Brit. Topo., 1780. Cambridgeshire, vol. i. pp. 191–246.

Bandinel (Bulkeley). Catal. of Books bequeathed to Bodleian Lib. by Richard Gough, 1814. Cambridgeshire, pp. 55–84.

CAMBRIDGESHIRE (*continued*).

ELY.

Ely Cathedral Records. William I., etc., with MS. Index, at Ely Cathedral. (*Local Records Comm. Rep.*, 1902. App. III. p. 110.)

Ely Diocesan Records, Court Rolls, etc., from 1337, with Printed Index, at the Palace, Ely. (*Local Records Comm. Rep.*, 1902. App. III. p. 104.)

Gibbons (Alfred). Ely Episcopal Records, Calendar and Concise View of Episcopal Records, preserved in the Muniment Room at Ely. Privately printed. 1891.

Chapman (F. R.). Sacrist Rolls of Ely. Vol. I.—Notes on Transcripts. Vol. II.—Transcripts. For Private Circulation. Camb., 1908.

Ecclesiastical Records, see *ante* Hist. MSS. Comm. Reports.

WISBECH.

Murray (David). 'Museums.' Glasgow, 1904. Biblio. Note on Wisbech Museum, vol. III. p. 275.

Corporation Records, see *ante* Hist. MSS. Comm. Reports.

Miller (S. H.). The Camp of Refuge: a Tale of the Isle of Ely. Wisbech. 1887. Biblio. of the Fenland, pp. 487–490.

CARDIGANSHIRE.

Evans (George Eyre). Aberystwyth Printed Books and Pamphlets, 1809–1902. (Supplement to '*Aberystwyth and its Court Leet*,' 1902.) Also issued separately.

—— **Cardiganshire: A personal Survey of some of its Antiquities, Chapels, Churches, Fonts, Plate and Registers.** Aberystwyth, 1903.

Hist. MSS. Comm. Report. Cardiganshire Collection.
Stewart, Capt. James, of Alltyrodyn,
Llandyssil ... ... 10th Rep. p. 5 and App. IV. pp. 59–146.

Notes on Records relating to Lampeter and Cardiganshire. By R. W. B. (*Archæol. Camb.* Ser. 4, vol. ix. pp. 292-302. 1878.)

Archdeaconry of Cardigan. Court Leet Records, 1690 - 1785, at Aberystwyth. (*Local Records Comm. Rep.*, 1902, App. III. p. 126.)

Index to a Volume of Pedigrees of Caermarthenshire, Cardiganshire, and Pembrokeshire, *circa* 1700, belonging to J. L. Philipps, of Dale, co. Pembroke, 1857. Privately Printed at Middle Hill Press.

An Index of Pedigrees of Caermarthenshire, Cardiganshire, and Pembrokeshire, in continuation of Lewis Dwnn, to about the years 1700–10. Privately printed at Middle Hill Press. 1859.

Catal. of Local Museum exhibited in St. David's Coll., Lampeter, 1878, includes Books, MSS., &c. (*Archæol. Camb.*, Ser. 4, vol. x. pp. 65–68. 1879.)

Lyell (Arthur H.). Biblio. List of Romano-British Remains, 1912. Cardiganshire, p. 143.

Plomer (Henry R.). Thomas Johnes Private Press at Hafod. (Some Private Presses of the Nineteenth Century, in *The Library*, New Ser., vol. i. pp. 407, 408. 1900.)

Trimen (Henry). Botanical Biblio. of the British Counties. Cardiganshire. (*Journ. of Botany*, vol. xii. p. 157. 1874.)

Christy (Miller). Biblio. Note on Cardiganshire Birds. (*Catal. of Local Lists of Brit. Birds*, 1891, p. 9.)

Anderson (John P.). Book of Brit. Topo., 1881. Cardiganshire, pp. 343, 344.

Gough (Richard). Brit. Topo., 1780. Cardiganshire, vol. ii. p. 506.

CARLOW.

Dix (**Ernest Reginald McClintock**). **Early Printing in the South-East of Ireland.** Part I. **Carlow.** Part II. **Clonmel.** Reprint, n.d.

——— **Irish Provincial Printing prior to 1701.** (*The Library*, New Ser. vol. ii. pp. 342–348. 1901.)

Anderson (**John P.**). **Book of Brit. Topo.**, 1881. Carlow, p. 428.

Gross (**Charles**). **Biblio. of Brit. Municipal Hist.** (*Harvard Hist. Studies*, vol. v. 1897.) Carlow, p. 118.

CARMARTHENSHIRE.

Bibliography of Carmarthen. (*Carmarthenshire Antiq. Soc. Trans.*, vol. i. pp. 61, 67, 72; vol. ii. p. 142; vol. v. pp. 5, 61, 77; vol. vi. pp. 35, 76; vol vii. pp. 60, 68, 69, 75, 76, 82, 88; vol. viii. pp. 8, 12, 22; vol. ix. pp. 8, 40, 44. 1905–14.) In progress.

Books printed at Carmarthen. (*Carm. Antiq. Soc. Trans.*, vol. i. pp. 60, 61, 63, 65, 67; vol. iv. p. 75. 1905–9.)

List of Carmarthen Books not recorded in Rowland's 'Llyfryddiaeth y Cymru.' (*Carm. Antiq. Soc. Trans.*, vol. i. p. 71. 1905.)

Biblio. of References to Carmarthenshire from the Archæol. Cambrensis, 1846–1900. By M. H. Jones. (*Carm. Antiq. Soc. Trans.*, vol. i. pp. 4, 30. 1905.)

Daniel-Tyssen (**J.R.**). **Royal Charters and Historical Documents** relating to the Town and County of Carmarthen, and the Abbeys of Talley and Tygwyn-ar-Daf. Edited and Annotated by A. C. Evans. 1878.

The Genealogical and Topographical MSS. relating to the Town and County of Carmarthen formerly belonging to the late Alcwyn C. Evans are now in private ownership in Carmarthen.

Lewis (**E. A.**). **A Collection of Hist. Documents** relating to Carmarthen Castle from the earliest times to the close of the reign of Henry VIII. ('*West Wales Hist. Records' in Hist. Soc. of West Wales. Trans.*, vol. iii. pp. 1–72. 1913.) In progress.

Gross (**Charles**). **Biblio. of Brit. Municipal Hist.** (*Harvard Hist. Studies*, vol. v. 1897.) Carmarthenshire, pp. 28, 190.

Carmarthen. Borough Records, 1580, etc., at Town Clerk's Office, Carmarthen. (*Local Records Comm. Rep.*, 1902. App. III., p. 48.)

Hist. MSS. Comm. Reports. Carmarthenshire Collection.

Williams, Sir John, at Plas Llan-Stephan	Reports on MSS. in Welsh language, Vol. ii. Part II. pp. 419–782.

Kidwelly Charters, 1357–1619. (*Archæol. Camb.*, Ser. 3, vol. ii. pp. 273–281; vol. iii. pp. 1–22. 1856–57.)

Carmarthenshire Antiquarian Society. Classification of Contents of Transactions, by M. H. Jones. ('*Gift Booke*,' by A. Stepney-Gulston, pp. 54–59. 1907.) Privately published.

Index to a Volume of Pedigrees of Caermarthenshire, Cardiganshire, and Pembrokeshire, *circa* 1700, belonging to J. L. Philipps, of Dale, co. Pembroke. 1857. Privately Printed at Middle Hill Press.

An Index of Pedigrees of Caermarthenshire, Cardiganshire, and Pembrokeshire, in continuation of Lewis Dwnn, to about the years 1700–10. Privately Printed at Middle Hill Press, 1859.

Summary of Ancient Records preserved in the Diocesan Registry at Carmarthen. (*Carm. Antiq. Soc. Trans.*, vol. i. p. 82. 1905.)

Dawson (**Mrs. M. L.**). **References to the Churches of Carmarthenshire** in the Papal Registers for 13th and 14th Centuries. (*Carm. Antiq. Soc. Trans.*, vol. i. p. 87. 1905.)

CARMARTHENSHIRE (continued).

Carmarthen Non-Parochial Registers in 1827. (*Carm. Antiq. Soc. Trans.*, vol. i. p. 59. 1905.)

Carmarthenshire Worthies in the Dictionary of National Biography. By G. Eyre Evans. (*Carm. Antiq. Soc. Trans.*, vol. i. p. 77. 1905.)

Lyell (Arthur H.). Biblio. List of Romano-British Remains. 1912. Carmarthenshire, p. 143.

Speed's Map of Carmarthenshire in 1610. (*Carm. Antiq. Soc. Trans.*, vol. i. pp. 5–11. 1905.)

Buckley (J.). Early Carmarthen Printers. 1770–1835. (*Carm. Antiq. Soc. Trans.*, vol. ii. p. 212; vol. vii. pp. 58, 88; vol. viii. p. 14. 1907–12.)

Waters (W.). John Ross, Printer. (*Carm. Antiq. Soc. Trans.*, vol. i. pp. 61, 65, 71, 75, 101; vol. ii. p. 222; vol. iii. pp. 74, 82; vol. viii. p. 53. 1905–13.)

Phillips (D. Rhys). Isaac Carter, the Pioneer of Welsh Printing. —Printing Presses at Newcastle Emlyn and Trefhedyn. (*Welsh Biblio. Soc. Journ.*, vol. i. pp. 129–132. 1912.)

J. Daniel, Bookseller. (*Carm. Antiq. Soc. Trans.*, vol. i. p. 109; vol. v. p. 57. 1905, 10.)

Carmarthen Booksellers. (*Carm. Antiq. Soc. Trans.*, vol. viii. pp. 2, 9, 12. 1912.)

Llanelly Bibliography. (*Carm. Antiq. Soc. Trans.*, vol. vi. p. 76; vol. viii. p. 84. 1911–13.)

Trimen (Henry). Botanical Biblio. of the British Counties. Carmarthenshire. (*Journ. of Botany*, vol. xii. p. 157. 1874.)

Anderson (John P.). Book of Brit. Topo., 1881. Carmarthenshire, p. 344.

Gough (Richard). Brit. Topo., 1780. Carmarthenshire, vol. ii. p. 510.

CARNARVONSHIRE.

Bangor, Archdeaconry of. Ecclesiastical Records, 1550, etc., at Rectory House, Trefdraeht. (*Local Records Comm. Rep.*, 1902, App. III. p. 118.)

Carnarvon. Borough Records, 1684, etc., at Town Clerk's Office, Carnarvon. (*Local Records Comm. Rep.*, 1902, App. III. p. 50.)

Conway Municipal Records. By Edward Owen. (*Archæol. Camb.*, Ser. 5, vol. vii. pp. 226–233. 1890.)

Jones (Rev. C. W. F.). A Catal. of the Books in the Bangor Cathedral Library. 1872.

Lyell (Arthur H.). Biblio. List of Romano-British Remains, 1912. Carnarvonshire, p. 143.

Trimen (Henry). Botanical Biblio. of the Brit. Counties. Carnarvonshire. (*Journ. of Botany*, vol. xii. p. 157. 1874.)

Christy (Miller). Biblio. Note on Carnarvonshire Birds. (*Catal. of Local Lists of Brit. Birds*, 1891, p. 9.) **Reptiles.** (*The Zoologist*, Ser. 3, vol. xvii. p. 241. 1893.)

Anderson (John P.). Book of Brit. Topo., 1881. Carnarvonshire, pp. 345–347.

Gough (Richard). Brit. Topo., 1780. Carnarvonshire, vol. ii. p. 521.

CAVAN.

Anderson (John P.). Book of Brit. Topo., 1881. Cavan, p. 428.

Gough (Richard). Brit. Topo., 1780. Cavan, p. 784.

Macalister (R. A. Stewart). Studies in Irish Epigraphy. Part II. Biblio. of Cavan Epigraphy. 1902.

CHANNEL ISLANDS.

JERSEY.

Duprey (Eugène). Essai de Bibliographie Jersiaise. Catal. d'auteurs qui ont écrit sur Jersey. (*Soc. Jersiaise Bull.*, vol. iv. pp. 157–192. 1899.) Liste des Cartes, pp. 179–185, 1er Supplément, 1902. (*Ibid.* vol. v. pp. 57–72. 1902.)

Liste des Livres, Manuscripts, et Objets qui appartiennent à la Soc. Jersiaise. (See *Bulletin*, vol. i. pp. 60–67, 131, 173, 229, 344–350. 1876–82.)

Documents relatifs aux Iles de la Manche tirés des Rôles des Lettres Closes conservés au 'Public Record Office' à Londres, 1205-1327. Édités par F. H. Barreau, H. M. Godfray, and W. Nicolle. (*Société Jersiaise. Publication IX., Partie* 1, 2. 1891-93.)

Documents relatifs aux Iles conservés à la Bibl. de Caen. Archives du Calvados. (*Soc. Jersiaise. Bull.*, vol. v. pp. 180–188. 1905.)

Mills (Col. D. A.). Cartographie Jersiaise. (*Soc. Jersiaise. Bull.*, vol. vi. pp. 319–381. 1908.) Bibliographie, p. 378.

Actes des États de l'Île de Guernesey, 1605 à 1651. Table alphabétique des Matières. Guernsey, 1851, etc.

Isle of Guernsey. Encyclopædic Catal. of the Lending Department of the Guille-Allès Library and Museum, compiled by A. Cotgreave and H. Boland. 1891. (Contains numerous entries relating to the Channel Isles.)

Christy (Miller). Biblio. Note on Channel Islands Birds. (*The Zoologist*, Ser. 3, vol. xiv. p. 250, 1890, and reprinted in pamph. 1891, p. 42.)

Anderson (John P.). Book of Brit. Topo., 1881. Channel Islands, pp. 25–28.

Smith (Alfred Russell). Catal. of Topo. Tracts, etc., 1878. Channel Islands, pp. 35, 36.

CHESHIRE.

[As many bibliographical works relating to this county include Lancashire as well, reference should be made under both 'Cheshire' and 'Lancashire.']

COOKE (JOHN HENRY). BIBLIOTHECA CESTRIENSIS, OR A BIBLIOGRAPHICAL ACCOUNT OF BOOKS, MAPS, PLATES, and other Printed Matter relating to, printed or published in, or written by Authors resident in the County of Cheshire. 1904.

List of Maps, Plates, &c., pp. 26, 51–52, 132–185. List of Newspapers, p. 143.

Fenwick (George Lee). Hist. of Chester. 1896. Bibliography, pp. 445–460.

Biblio. of Lancs. and Cheshire Publications during 1876. (*Manchester Lit. Club. Papers*, vol. iii. pp. 261–302. 1877.)

Biblio. of Lancs. and Cheshire Antiquities. 1889. By Ernest Axon. (*Lancs. & Cheshire Antiq. Soc. Trans.*, vol. vii. pp. 327–332. 1890.)

Biblio. of Lancs. and Cheshire Antiquities. 1890. By Ernest Axon. (*Ibid.* vol. viii. pp.195–204. 1891.)

Biblio. of Lancs. and Cheshire Antiquities, 1891, and **Subject-Index to Biblio. of Local Antiquities,** 1889–91. By Ernest Axon. (*Ibid.* vol. ix. pp. 217–221. 1892.)

Biblio. of Lancs. and Cheshire Antiquities, 1892, and **Subject-Index.** By Ernest Axon. (*Ibid.* vol. x. pp. 230–236. 1893.)

Biblio. of Lancs. and Cheshire Antiquities and Biography, with Subject-Indexes, 1893–99. By John Hibbert Swann. (*Ibid.* vol. xii. p. 148; vol. xiii. p. 201; vol. xiv. p. 212; vol. xv. p. 229; vol. xvi. p. 188; vol. xvii. p. 271. 1895–1900.)

CHESHIRE (continued).

Biblio. of Lancs. and Cheshire Antiquities, and Biographical Publications, 1900–03, and Subject-Indexes. By Norman Hollins. (*Ibid.* vol. xviii. pp. 165–176; vol. xix. pp. 276–287; vol. xx. pp. 265–275; vol. xxi. pp. 224–233. 1901–03.)

Barlow (Thomas Worthington). A List of Books and Tracts wholly or in part relating to Cheshire History. (*The Cheshire & Lancs. Hist. Collector*, vols. i. and ii. 1853–55.)

——— **MS. List of Cheshire Books** (in the possession of T. Cann Hughes).

Cheshire Authors. By 'A Cheshire Bookworm.' (*Advertiser Notes & Queries.* Stockport, vol. v. pp. 29, 43, 51. 1885.)

Cheshire Bibliography, arranged under Authors. Second Series. (*Advertiser Notes & Queries.* Stockport, vol. v. pp. 64, 74, 88, 113, 152, 170. 1885.) This is in continuation of the preceding entry.

Cheshire Bibliography. Arranged under Authors ending at Drinkwater. (*Cheshire Notes & Queries*, vol. vii. pp. 1, 30, 113, 175, 244; vol. viii. pp. 4, 60, 144, 229, 249. 1887–88.)

Sutton (Albert). Bibliotheca Cestriensis. An Appendix of Cheshire Books to the Bibliotheca Lancastriensis. 1893 and 1898.

Winstanley (R.). Sale Catal. of Works relating to Lancs. and Cheshire. (Collected by Thomas Heywood.) Manchester, 1835.

Forshaw (Charles F.). Bibliography of Cheshire. (*Cheshire Notes & Queries.* New Ser. vol. v. pp. 230, 231. 1900.) A few items, principally of Chester Books.

Hughes (Thomas). On Chester Literature, Its Authors and Publishers during the Sixteenth and Seventeenth Centuries. (*Chester Archit. Archæol. & Hist. Soc. Journ.*, vol. ii. pp. 21–30. 1856.)

Robson (John). The Materials for the Hist. of the Two Counties (Lancs. and Cheshire) and the Mode of Using Them. (*Lancs. & Cheshire Hist. Soc. Proc.*, vol. v. pp. 199–217; *Trans.*, vol. vii. pp. 99–114; vol. x. pp. 47–58. 1853–58.)

Nodal (John H.). Special Collections of Books in Lancs. and Cheshire. (*Lib. Assoc. of the U.K. Trans.*, 1879, pp. 54–60 and App. III., and *Manchester Literary Club. Papers*, vol. vi. pp. 31–57. 1880.)

Madeley (C.). Limits of Local Collections in the Town Libraries of Lancs. and Cheshire. (*Manchester Literary Club Papers*, vol. vi. 1880.)

Warrington Municipal Museum. Catal. of the Reference Library. By C. Madeley. (Cheshire Records, Books, Maps, etc., and includes the Hundred of Bucklow.) 1898–1908.

[**Gower (F.)**]. **Materials for a Hist. of Cheshire.** 1771. (Contains a list of curious old Cheshire MSS. in possession of Author.)

Gower's Sketch of Materials for a New Hist. of Cheshire, with a New Preface, and an Account of further materials for his History. 3rd Edn. 1800.

——— **A List of MSS. in the possession of Thos. Gower in 1771,** when he was collecting materials for a Hist. of Cheshire. See Cooke (John H.), '*Bibl. Cestriensis,*' pp. 130, 131.)

Foote Gower MS. Collections for Cheshire, at the British Museum. Add. MSS. 11335–11338.

General Index to the Remains, Historical and Literary, published by the Chetham Soc., vols. i.–xxx. and vols. xxxi.–cxiv. Manchester, 1863 and 1893.

CHESHIRE (continued).

Index to the Transactions of the Hist. Soc. of Lancs. and Cheshire, vol. i.–li., 1849–1909, in vol. liv., 1902. Compiled by F. C. Beazley, and Rough Index to Papers and Communications, vol. lii.–lxi. in vol. lxi. 1909.

Smith (H. Ecroyd). Catal. of the Library of the Hist. Soc. of Lancs. and Cheshire. 1876.

Indexes to the Transactions of the Lancs. and Cheshire Antiq. Soc., vols. i.–x. in vol. x., 1892; vols. xi.–xx. in vol. xx., 1902; and vols. xxi.–xxx. in vol. xxx., 1912.

Subject-Indexes to vols. i.–iii., 1849–85, and New Ser. vols. i.–xviii., 1887–1911, of the **Journal of the Chester and North Wales Archæol. and Hist. Soc.** Chester, 1912.

Chester and North Wales Archæol. and Hist. Soc. Records from fourteenth century at the Grosvenor Museum, Chester. (*Local Records Comm. Rep.*, 1902; App. III. p. 132.)

The Chester and North Wales Arch. Soc. has a large Topog. Library, but no Catal. has been published.

Indexes to the Reports and Papers of the Associated Architectural Societies, etc., vols. i.–viii. (1850–66); vols. ix.–xiv. (1867–78); vols. xv.–xix. (1879–88); and vols. xx.–xxv. (1889–1900). Lincoln, 1867–1905.

Sutton (C. W.). Lancs. and Cheshire Archæology: a List of some Contributions in some Archæological Journals, reprinted from 'The Palatine Note Book.' Manchester, 1881.

Hawkins (Edward). MS. Catal. of Cheshire Printed Books (in the possession of T. Cann Hughes).

Axon (W. E. A.) A Paper on Provincial Biblio. having special reference to Lancs. and Cheshire. (*Manchester Literary Club. Papers*, vol. iii. pp. 183–186. 1877.) Also issued separately.

——— **The Libraries of Lancs. and Cheshire.** (*Lib. Assoc. of the U.K. Trans.* 1879, pp. 47–53, and *Manchester Literary Club. Papers*, vol. vi. pp. 21–30. 1880.)

——— **Sir John Chesshyre's Library at Halton in Cheshire.** (*The Library Journ.*, New York. Vol. iv. pp. 35–38. 1879.)

A reprint of the Rules and Orders made by Sir John Chesshyre, Knt., for the Library, together with his Catal. of Books [dated 1733]. Preface by G. D. Wray. [1898].

Formby (Thomas) and Axon (Ernest.) List of the Writings of W. Thompson Watkin. (*Lancs. & Cheshire Antiq. Soc. Trans.*, vol. vi. pp. 173–178. 1888.)

Evans (George Eyre). Record of the Provincial Assembly of Lancs. and Cheshire (with lists of Non-Parochial Registers, and Biblio. Notes to Biographies and Places). Manchester, 1896.

Harrison (William). Early Maps of Cheshire. (*Lancs. & Cheshire Antiq. Soc. Trans.*, vol. xxvi. pp. 1–26. 1909.) See also Cooke (John H.), *Bibl. Cestriensis*, pp. 26, 51–52, 132–135.

List of Private Acts relating to the County of Chester. London: Stevens & Sons, *circa* 1912.

Gross (Charles). Biblio. of Brit. Municipal Hist. (*Harvard Hist. Studies*, vol. v. 1897.) Cheshire, pp. 91–92. Chester, pp. 191–194.

Davenport (Frances G.). List of Printed Materials for Manorial History. 1894. Biblio. Note on Cheshire Manorial History, p. 39.

CHESHIRE (continued).

Dove (Patrick Edward). Domesday Studies. 1891. Domesday Biblio. Cheshire, vol. ii. p. 672.

A Catal. of the Museum of Antiquities exhibited at the King's School, Chester, at the Sixth Annual Meeting of the Brit. Archæol. Assoc. Chester. 1849.

Lyell (Arthur H.). Biblio. List of Romano-British Remains. 1912. Cheshire, pp. 5–8.

Macklin (Herbert Walter). Monumental Brasses. London: George Allen & Co., 1913. Biblio. Note on Cheshire Brasses, with a List, p. 150.

Murray (David). 'Museums.' Glasgow, 1904. Biblio. Note on Chester Museum, vol. ii. p. 175.

Allnutt (W. H.). English Provincial Presses. Earliest Printing at Chester. (*Bibliographica*, vol. ii. pp. 293, 294. 1896.)

Special Collections of Cheshire Books, &c., at Birkenhead Public Library, Northwich Public Library, Hyde Public Library, and at Grosvenor Museum, Chester, and a Local Collection at Stockport.

Hist. MSS. Comm. Reports. Cheshire Collections.

Antrobus, Mr. J. C., at Eaton Hall, Congleton	2nd Rep. p. xi. and App. p. 69.
Bromley-Davenport, Mr. W., at Baginton Hall, co. Warwick ...	2nd Rep. p. xi. and App. pp. 78–81; 10th Rep. p. 20 and App. VI. pp. 98–103.
Grey-Egerton, Sir Philip de M., at Oulton Hall, co. Chester	3rd Rep. p. xviii. and App. pp. 244–246.
Legh, Mr. J. W., at Lyme Hall, co. Chester	3rd Rep. p. xvii. and App. pp. 268–271.
Mainwaring, Sir P. T., at Peover Hall, co. Chester	10th Rep. p. 4 and App. IV. pp. 199–210.
de Tabley, Lord, at Tabley House, co. Chester	1st Rep. p. ix. and App. pp. 46–50.
Egerton-Warburton, Mr. R. E., at Arley Hall, co. Chester	3rd Rep. p. xvii. and App. pp. 290–292.
Westminster, Duke of, at Eaton Hall	3rd Rep. p. xv. and App. pp. 210–216.
Wilbraham, Mr. G. F., at Delamere House, co. Chester	3rd Rep. p. xvii. and App. pp. 292–293; 4th Rep. p. xv. and App. p. 416.
Chester Corporation	8th Rep. p. xv. and App. pp. 355–403.

Randle Holmes' MS. Collections for Cheshire, in about 270 vols. at the Brit. Museum. (Harl. MSS. 1920–2187, 7568, 7569.

Helsby (T.) The MS. Collections of the Four Randle Holmes of Chester. (*The Cheshire Sheaf*, Ser. 3, vol. ii. pp. 106–108. 1898.)

Earwaker (J. P.). The Four Randle Holmes, of Chester, Antiquaries, Heralds, and Genealogists. *c.* **1571 to 1707.** Manchester. 1892. Reprinted from *Chester Archæol. & Hist. Soc. Journ.*, New Ser. vol. iv. pp. 113–170. 1892.

Harl. MS. 473, Brit. Mus. The Index to this Collection is in Harl. MS. 471. A Cheshire Collection apparently by Sampson Erdeswicke in 1574.

Other Collections relating to Cheshire in the Brit. Museum are:—Harl. MS. 139. Collections of Rob. Bostocke; Lansd. MS. 644. Collections formerly in possession of Warburton, Somerset Herald, purchased in 1759; Add. MSS. 5836 (f. 191) and 6031. Collections for the Hist. of the Townships of Cheshire by Dr. Williamson; Add. MS. 6032. Collections by John Woodnoth.

Rondeau (J. B.). Manuscript Collections towards a Biblio. of Lancs. and Cheshire. In Wigan Free Library.

CHESHIRE (continued).

Ormerod (George). A Memoir on the Cheshire Domesday Roll, formerly preserved in the Exchequer of that Palatinate, to which is appended a Calendar of fragments of this lost record, etc. Not published. 1851.

Lumby (J. H.). Chester, Birkenhead and Liverpool in the Patent and Close Rolls of the Three Edwards, with an Index of References. (*Hist. Soc. of Lancs. & Cheshire. Trans.*, vol. liv. pp. 45–72. 1902.)

—— **Chester and Liverpool in the Patent Rolls** of Richard II. and the Lancastrian and Yorkist Kings. (*Hist. Soc. of Lancs. and Cheshire. Trans.*, vol. lv. pp. 163–187. 1903.)

A Calendar of Lancs. and Cheshire Exchequer Depositions by Commission, 1558-1702. Edited by C. Fishwick. (*Record Soc. for Lancs. and Cheshire. Publications*, vol. xi. 1885.)

Moore Collection. A Calendar of that part of the Collection of Deeds and Papers of the Moore Family, of Bankhall, co. Lancs., now in the Liverpool Public Library. By J. Brownbill. With an Appendix containing a Calendar of a further portion of the same collection, now in the Univ. of Liverpool School of Local Hist. and Records. By Kathleen Walker. (*Record Soc. of Lancs. & Cheshire*, vol. lxvii. 1913.)

See also *Hist. MSS. Comm., 10th Rep.*, Pt. iv. pp. 59–146. Capt. Stewart's MSS., in which are described many of the Moore documents.

Morton (T. N.) The Family of Moore of Liverpool. Rough List of their Paper Records. (*Hist. Soc. of Lancs. & Cheshire. Trans.*, vol. xxxviii. pp. 149–158. 1886.) MS. Lists are also at the Liverpool Public Library.

Taylor (Henry.) Ten Early Chester Deeds, 1270-1490. (*Chester Archit. Archæol. & Hist. Soc. Journ.*, New. Ser. vol. x. pp. 101–116. 1904.)

Burke (H. Farnham). Some Cheshire Deeds. (*The Ancestor*, No. 6. pp. 19–45. 1903.)

County Records, 1559, etc. at Chester Castle, with MS. Index. (*Local Records Comm. Rep.*, 1902. App. III. p. 16.)

Selby (Walford D.). Lancs. and Cheshire Records in the Public Record Office, London. 2 vols. (*Record Soc. for Lancs. and Cheshire*, vols. vii., viii. 1882–3.)

List of Records of the Palatinates of Chester, Durham, and Lancaster, etc. preserved in the Public Record Office. (*Public Record Office Lists and Indexes.* No. XL. 1914.)

Black (W. H.) On the Records of the County Palatine of Chester. (*Brit. Archæol. Assoc. Journ.*, vol. v. pp. 187–195. 1850.)

MS. Calendars and Indexes of the Records of the County Palatine of Chester, formerly kept in the Exchequer Office, Chester, now in the Warrington Museum. See Madeley (C.) Warrington Municipal Museum. Catal. of the Reference Library, 1898, p. 204.

Cheshire Records, transcribed from Originals in the Public Record Office. (*Chester Archit. Archæol. & Hist. Soc. Journ.*, New Ser. vol. vi. pp. 283–345. 1895.)

Hughes (T. Cann). Cheshire MSS. in the Bodleian Lib. (*The Cheshire Sheaf*, vol. iii. pp. 140–141. 1884.)

Cheshire in the Calendars. (*The Cheshire Sheaf*, Ser. 3. vol. v. pp. 77, etc. 1903.)

Chester Diocesan Records, 1541, etc., with MS. Indexes, at the Episcopal Registry, Chester. (*Local Records Comm. Rep.*, 1902, App. III. p. 104.)

Chester Cathedral Records, at Chester, with MS. Index. (*Local Records Comm. Rep.*, App. III. p. 110.)

Hall (James). Report on the Earwaker MS. Collection in the Grosvenor Museum Library, Chester. (*Chester Archit. Archæol. and Hist. Soc. Journ.*, New Ser. vol. xvii. pp. 97–106. 1910.)

CHESHIRE (continued).

Earwaker (J. P.). Notes on the Collection of Deeds preserved at the East Hall, High Legh, Cheshire, with Special Reference to those relating to Manchester and Neighbourhood. (*Lancs. & Cheshire Antiq. Soc. Trans.*, vol. v. pp. 259–271. 1887.)

Beamont (William). A Calendar of Family Charters at Arley Hall, Newton. 1866. See also *ante* Hist. MSS. Comm. Reports. Mr. R. E. Egerton-Warburton.

—— **A Calendar of Ancient Charters with Modern Transcripts, at Eaton Hall,** Warrington. 1862. Not printed for publication. See also *ante* Hist. MSS. Comm. Reports.

Whitaker (William). List of Books on the Geology, Mineralogy, and Palæontology of Cheshire. Liverpool, 1876.

Trimen (Henry). Botanical Biblio. of the British Counties. Cheshire. (*Journ. of Botany*, vol. xii. p. 179. 1874.)

Christy (Miller). Biblio. Note on Cheshire Birds. (*The Zoologist*, Ser. 3, vol. xiv. p. 250, 1890; and reprinted in pamph., 1891, p. 9.) **Mammals.** (*The Zoologist*, Ser. 3, vol. xvii. p. 177. 1893.) **Reptiles.** (*Ibid.* p. 242. 1893.) **Fishes.** *Ibid.* p. 252. 1893.)

Anderson (John P.). Book of Brit. Topo., 1881. Cheshire, pp. 63–68.
Gatfield (George). Guide to Heraldry. 1892. Cheshire, pp. 125–128.
Sims (Richard). Manual for the Genealogist. 1861. Cheshire, pp. 163, 201, 230, 231.
Upcott (William). English Topo., 1818. Cheshire, vol. i. pp. 61–75, 597, 598.
Smith (Alfred Russell). Catal. of Topo. Tracts, etc. 1878. Cheshire, pp. 38–41, 459.
Gough (Richard). Brit. Topo., 1780. Cheshire, vol. i. pp. 246–247.
Bandinel (Bulkeley). Catal. of Books bequeathed to Bodleian Library by Richard Gough. 1814. Cheshire, pp. 85–89.

CONGLETON.

Borough Records, Edw. I. etc., with MS. List, at Town Clerk's Office, Congleton. (*Local Records Comm. Rep.*, 1902, App. III. p. 52.)

MACCLESFIELD.

Borough Records, 1261, etc., with MS. Index, at Town Hall, Macclesfield. (*Local Records Comm. Rep.*, 1902, App. III. p. 64.)

CLACKMANNANSHIRE.

Hist. MSS. Comm. Reports. Clackmannanshire Collections.
Erskine-Murray, Hon. Mrs. Isabella, at Aberdona ... ... 4th Rep. p. xxi. and App. pp. 521–528.
Mar and Kellie, Earl of, at Alloa House 17th Rep. pp. 130–138, and a vol. 1904.

Livingstone (Matthew). Guide to the Public Records of Scotland. 1905. Clackmannanshire, p. 180.

Turnbull (William B.). Scottish Parochial Registers. 1849. List of Clackmannanshire Registers, pp. 41, 42.

Anderson (Joseph) and Black (Geo. F.). Reports on Local Museums in Scotland. Alloa Museum. (*Soc. of Antiq. Scot. Proc.*, vol. xxii. p. 355. 1888.)

Christy (Miller). Biblio. Note on Clackmannanshire Mammals. (*The Zoologist*, Ser. 3, vol. xvii. p. 210. 1893.)

Anderson (John P.). Book of Brit. Topo., 1881. Clackmannanshire, p. 383.
Gough (Richard). Brit. Topo., 1780. Clackmannanshire, vol. ii. p. 660.

CLARE.

Dix (Ernest Reginald McClintock). List of Books, Newspapers, and Pamphlets printed at Ennis, co. Clare, in the 18th Century. Cuala Press, Dundrum, 1912. (Irish Bibliography, no. viii.)

Coleman (James). Limerick and Clare Bibliography. List of the Topog. and Hist. Works relating to the Counties Limerick and Clare. (*Limerick Field Club Journ.*, vol. iii. pp. 139–142. 1907.)

Dix (Ernest Reginald McClintock). Early Printing in a Munster Town. —Ennis. (*Cork Hist. and Archæol. Soc. Journ.*, Ser. 2, vol. x. pp. 122-125. 1904.)

Gross (Charles). Biblio. of Brit. Municipal Hist. (*Harvard Hist. Studies*, vol. v. 1897.) Clare, p. 197.

Westropp (Thomas J.). The Cahers of Co. Clare: Their Names, Features, and Bibliography. (*Royal Irish Academy. Proc.*, Ser. 3, vol. vi. pp. 415–449. 1901.)

Anderson (John P.). Book of Brit. Topo., 1881. Clare, p. 429.
Gough (Richard). Brit. Topo., 1780. Clare, p. 784.

CONNAUGHT.

Coleman (James). Bibliographia Conaciensis: a list of Books relating to Connaught. (*Galway Archæol. and Hist. Soc. Journ.*, vol. v. pp. 28–34, 239. 1908.)

CORK.

Dix (Ernest Reginald McClintock). List of Books, Pamphlets, Journals, etc., printed in Cork in the 17th and 18th Centuries. 14 parts. Cork, 1904–12.

(Reprinted from the '*Journ. of the Cork Hist. and Archæol. Soc.*', Ser. 2, vol. vi. pp. 168–174, 233–240; vol. vii. pp. 104–110, 233–238; vol. viii. pp. 106–112, 249–253; vol. ix. pp. 27–32, 97–105, 264–268; vol. xi. pp. 24–26; vol. xiii. pp. 85, 86; vol. xv. pp. 111–114; vol. xvi. pp. 64–66; vol. xviii. p. 25. 1900–12.)

——— **List of all Pamphlets, Books, etc., printed in Cork during the 17th Century.** (*Royal Irish Academy, Proc.*, vol. xxx.. sect. C., pp. 71–82. 1912.)

——— **Irish Provincial Printing prior to 1701. Biblio. Note on Cork Printing.** (*The Library.* New Ser. vol. ii. p. 345. 1901.)

Local Bibliography. (Works dealing with the Literature of the District of Cork.) By C. G. Doran. (*Cork Hist. and Archæol. Soc. Journ.*, vol. i. pp. 60, 83, 84, 107, 108, 151, 152, 171, 172. 1892.)

Dr. Caulfield's Contributions to the 'Gentleman's Magazine.' (*Cork Hist. and Archæol. Soc. Journ.*, Ser. 2, vol. ix. pp. 189–198, 268–274; vol. x. pp. 48–56. 1903–04.)

Dix (Ernest Reginald McClintock). Two Rare 17th Century Cork Ballads. (*Cork Hist. and Archæol. Soc. Journ.*, Ser. 2, vol. xvi. pp. 44–48. 1910.)

Gross (Charles). Biblio. of Brit. Municipal Hist. (*Harvard Hist. Studies.* vol. v. 1897.) Cork, pp. 118, 201.

The Writers and Printers of Youghal. (*Cork Hist. and Archæol. Soc. Journ.*, Ser. 2, vol. v. pp. 133–146. 1899.)

Macalister (A. A. Stewart). Studies in Irish Epigraphy. Part III. Biblio. of Cork Epigraphy. 1907.

Sheehan (Rt. Rev. R. A.). Notes on the Literary History of Cork. (*Cork Hist. and Archæol. Soc. Journ.*, vol. i. pp. 4–10. 1892.)

CORK (*continued*).

Coleman (James). The Cork Library in 1801 and 1820. (*Cork Hist. and Archæol. Soc. Journ.*, vol. xi. pp. 82–93. 1905.)

Hist. MSS. Comm. Reports. Cork Collections.
Caulfield, Mr. Richard, at Cork ... ... 1st Rep. p. xii. and App. p. 129.
Hewitt, Mr. Thomas, at Cork ... ... 1st Rep. p. xii. and App. p. 129.
Cork, Corporation of ... ... 1st Rep. App. p. 128.

Historical MSS. relating to the County Cork. By J. Coleman. (*Cork Hist. and Archæol. Soc. Journ.*, vol. i. pp. 169, 170. 1892.) By W. A. Copinger. (*Ibid.* pp. 207–209. 1892.)

Brady (W. Maziere). Clerical and Parochial Records of Cork, Cloyne, and Ross, taken from Diocesan and Parish Registers, MSS. in principal Libraries of Oxford, Dublin, London, etc. 3 vols. London, 1864.

Christy (Miller). Biblio. Note on County Cork Birds. (*The Zoologist*, Ser. 3, vol. xiv. p. 267, 1890; and reprinted in pamph., 1891, p. 41.) **Mammals.** (*The Zoologist*, Ser. 3, vol. xvii. p. 215, 1893.) **Reptiles.** (*Ibid.* p. 251, 1893.) **Fishes.** (*Ibid.* p. 263, 1893.)

Anderson (John P.). Book of Brit. Topo., 1881. Cork, pp. 429–30.
Gough (Richard). Brit. Topo., 1780. Cork, pp. 785–787.
Bandinel (Bulkeley). Catal. of Books bequeathed to Bodleian Lib. by Richard Gough, 1814. Cork, pp. 376, 377.

CORNWALL.

BOASE (GEORGE CLEMENT) and COURTNEY (WILLIAM PRIDEAUX). BIBLIOTHECA CORNUBIENSIS. A CATALOGUE OF THE WRITINGS, BOTH MANUSCRIPT AND PRINTED, OF CORNISHMEN, AND OF WORKS RELATING TO THE COUNTY OF CORNWALL, with biographical memoranda and copious literary references. 3 vols. London. 1874–82. Vol. iii. is supplementary to the other vols., and has an Index to vols. i.–iii.

BOASE (GEORGE CLEMENT). COLLECTANEA CORNUBIENSIA: A COLLECTION OF BIOG. AND TOPO. NOTES RELATING TO THE CO. OF CORNWALL. Truro. 1890. This is in many respects a Supplement to the *Bibliotheca*.

Couch (Thomas Quiller) and Chorley (Charles). Bibliotheca Cornubiensis. Preparatory Lists with Maps, pp. 59–60, List of Cornish Portraits, pp. 70, etc. Royal Inst. of Cornwall. 1865.

Gen. Index to the Journals and Reports of the Royal Institution of Cornwall. 1818–1906. By Charles R. Hewitt. 1907.

The Library of the Royal Inst. of Cornwall has a large Collection of Books and MSS. relating to Cornwall. Among the George Freeth, of Duporth, bequest are MS. Copies of Deeds, Grants, Records, &c., also Materials for a New Survey of the Hist. and Antiq. of Cornwall.

Bellamy (John Cremer). An Alphabetical List of all Works relating to the Counties of Devon and Cornwall. (*A Thousand Facts in the History of Devon and Cornwall.* 1850, pp. 51–59.)

Stokes (H. Sewell). County and Parochial Histories and Books relating to Cornwall. (*Brit. Archæol. Assoc. Journ.*, vol. xxxiii. pp. 35–45. 1877.)

Maclean (Sir John). Address on Materials for History of Cornwall. (*Royal Inst. of Cornwall. Journ.*, vol. xi. pp. 220–234. 1893.)

Recent Cornish Writings. (Vols. and Articles.) (*Royal Inst. of Cornwall. Journ.*, vol. xvii. pp. 294, 295. 1908.)

CORNWALL (continued).

New Books relating to Cornwall. (*Royal Inst. of Cornwall. Journ.*, vol. xvii. pp. 405–416 ; vol. xviii. pp. 249–259. 1909–10.)

Lewis (G. R.). The Stanneries. A Study of the English Tin Miner. (*Harvard Economic Studies*, vol. iii., 1908.) *Biblio.*, pp. 281–288.

Simcoe (Rev. Henry Addington). Private Printing Press at Penheale. For Note and List of Books Printed, see Boase and Courtney, *Bibl. Cornubiensis*, pp. 650, 1457, *passim.*

Brushfield (T. N.). The Broadside Ballads of Devonshire and Cornwall. (*The Western Antiquary*, vol. vi., pp. v.–xiii., 1886.)

Worth (R. N.). Notes on the Ancient Topography of Cornwall, with a Map. (*Royal Inst. of Cornwall. Journ.*, vol. viii. pp. 343–353. 1885.)

Catal. of a Loan Exhibition of Portraits of Worthies connected with Devon and Cornwall. Exeter, 1873.

Index-Catal. to the Library of the Plymouth Institution. (Contains many Cornish entries.) (*Plymouth Inst. Ann. Rep. and Trans.*, vol. xi. pp. 315–384, 1894.)

Cornish Collections are to be found in Public Libraries at Penzance, Falmouth, Truro, and Plymouth.

Gross (Charles). Biblio. of Brit. Municipal Hist. (*Harvard Hist. Studies*, vol. v. 1897.) Cornwall, p. 92. Penzance, p. 362. St. Ives, p. 383. Launceston, p. 271. Bodmin, p. 171.

Davenport (Frances G.). List of Printed Materials for Manorial Hist. 1894. Biblio. Note on Cornish Manorial Hist., pp. 39, 40.)

Dove (Patrick Edward). Domesday Studies. 1891. Domesday Biblio. Cornwall, vol. ii. p. 672.)

Lyell (Arthur H.). Biblio. List of Romano-British Remains. 1912. Cornwall, p. 8.

Macklin (Herbert Walter). Monumental Brasses. London : Geo. Allen & Co. 1913. Biblio. Note on Cornish Brasses, p. 139, with a List, pp. 150–151.

Blight (J. T.) List of Antiquities in the Hundreds of Kirrier and Penwith, West Cornwall, with References to the Works in which they are described. Royal Inst. of Cornwall. 1862.

Hist. MSS. Comm. Reports. Cornwall Collections.

Mount-Edgcumbe, Earl of, at Mount Edgcumbe	2nd Rep. p. x. and App. pp. 20–24.
Rogers, Mr. J. J., at Penrose	2nd Rep. p. xii. and App. pp. 98, 99 ; 4th Rep. p. xv. and App. pp. 405, 406.
St. Germans, Earl of, at Port Eliot ...	1st Rep. p. x. and App. pp. 41–44.
Somerset, Duke of, at Maiden Bradley, Wilts	15th Rep. App. VII. pp. 133–146.
Trelawny, Sir John S., at Trelawne ...	1st Rep. p. x. and App. pp. 50–53.
Launceston Corporation	6th Rep. App. 524–526.
Lostwithiel Corporation	16th Rep. p. 101 ; Various Collections, vol. i. pp. 327–337.

Chanter (J. R.). Report on the Harding Collection of Manuscripts, Records, and Hist., Eccles., Heraldic, and Antiq. Documents relating to Devon and Cornwall. (*Devon Assoc. Trans.*, vol. xx. pp. 49–68. 1888.)

Worth (R. N.). Manuscript Materials for Cornish Hist. (*Royal Inst. of Cornwall. Journ.*, vol. viii. pp. 144–147. 1884.)

MSS. connected with published Histories of Cornwall. Biblio. Note. (*Royal Inst. of Cornwall. Journ.*, vol. iv. No. 15, pp. xxv.–xxviii. 1874.)

CORNWALL (continued).

Cornish MSS. Society. A Prospectus compiled by Wm. C. Borlase, of Laregan, and Henry Jenner, of the Brit. Museum, for a proposed Society, dated Oct. 2, 1876. See Boase and Courtney, *Bibl. Corn.* vol. iii. p. 1085; *Royal Inst. of Cornwall Rep.*, 1877, p. xli.; *Brit. Archæol. Assoc. Journ.* vol. xxxii. pp. 423, 536. 1876.

Jenner (Henry). Descriptions of Cornish MSS. I. The Borlase Manuscript. (*Royal Inst. of Cornwall Journ.*, vol. xix. pp. 162–176. 1913.)

Nicholls (Jasper). Index to Cornish Transcripts (of Parish Registers) at Exeter and Bodmin. (*Royal Inst. of Cornwall Journ.*, vol. xix. pp. 90–136. 1912.)

Whitaker (William). List of Works on the Geology, Mineralogy, and Palæontology of Cornwall. (*Royal Inst. of Cornwall. Journ.*, vol. v. pp. 61–110. 1874.)

Trimen (Henry). Botanical Biblio. of the British Counties. Cornwall. (*Journ. of Botany*, vol. xii. p. 68. 1874.)

Christy (Miller). Biblio. Note on Cornish Birds. (*The Zoologist*, Ser. 3, vol. xiv. p. 250, 1890, and reprinted in pamph., 1891, p. 9.) **Mammals.** (*The Zoologist*, Ser. 3, vol. xvii. p. 177. 1893.) **Reptiles.** (*Ibid.*, p. 242. 1893.) **Fishes.** (*Ibid.*, p. 252. 1893.)

Anderson (John P.). Book of Brit. Topo., 1881. Cornwall, pp. 68–74.
Gatfield (George). Guide to Heraldry. 1892. Cornwall, pp. 128–130.
Sims (Richard). Manual for the Genealogist. 1861. Cornwall, pp. 163, 202, 231.
Upcott (William). English Topo., 1818. Cornwall, vol. i. pp. 76–107, 599.
Smith (Alfred Russell). Catal. of Topo. Tracts, &c., 1878. Cornwall, pp. 43–47, 459.
Gough (Richard). Brit. Topo., 1780. Cornwall, vol. i. pp. 265–276.
Bandinel (Bulkeley). Catal. of Books bequeathed to Bodleian Library by Richard Gough, 1814. Cornwall, pp. 90–92.

BODMIN.

Archdeaconry Court Records at Bodmin, described by Rev. W. AGO (*Truro Diocesan Kalendar*, 1882, p. 69.)

FALMOUTH.

Borough Records, 1660, etc., at Town Clerk's Office, Falmouth. (*Local Records Comm. Rep.*, 1902, App. III. p. 56.)

LAUNCESTON.

Borough Records, 1245, etc., at Guildhall, Launceston. (*Local Records Comm. Rep.*, App. III. p. 62.)

Corporation Records, see *ante.* Hist. MSS. Comm. Reports.

Launceston Priory. Notes from MSS. in the Bodl. Lib., translated and abstracted by Otho B. Peter. (*Royal Inst. of Cornwall. Journ.*, vol. xviii. pp. 197–218. 1910.)

LISKEARD.

Borough Records, 1328, etc., with MS. Index, at Town Clerk's Office, Liskeard. (*Local Records Comm. Rep.*, 1902, App. III. p. 76.)

LOSTWITHIEL.

Borough Records, with a MS. List, at Municipal Buildings, Lostwithiel. (*Local Records Comm. Rep.*, 1902, App. III. p. 62.)

Corporation Records, see *ante* Hist. MSS. Comm. Reports.

CORNWALL (continued).

MARAZION.

Lach-Szyrma (W. S.). Notes on the Borough Records of the Towns of Marazion, Penzance, and St. Ives. (*Brit. Archæol. Assoc. Journ.*, vol. xxviii. pp. 354–370. 1882.)

PENRYN.

Borough Records, 1652, etc., at Penryn. (*Local Records Comm. Rep.*, 1902, App. III. p. 66.)

PENZANCE.

Lach-Szyrma (W. S.). Notes on the Borough Records, see *ante* Marazion.

REDRUTH.

Old Redruth Papers. (*Royal Inst. of Cornwall. Journ.*, vol. xviii. pp. 246–248. 1910.)

ST. IVES.

Lach-Szyrma (W. S.). Notes on the Borough Records, see *ante* Marazion.

Records of the Borough of St. Ives. By 'Porthminster.' With Index, principally of subjects. (*The Western Antiquary*, vol. v. pp. 33, 78, 199. 1885–86.)

SALTASH.

Borough Records, 1575, etc., at the Guildhall, Saltash. (*Local Records Comm. Rep.*, 1902, App. III. p. 68.)

TRURO.

Borough Records, 1130, etc., at Municipal Buildings, Truro. (*Local Records Comm. Rep.*, 1902, App. III. p. 72.)

Diocesan Records, 14th Cent., etc., at Diocesan Registry, Exeter. (*Local Records Comm. Rep.*, 1902, App. III. p. 106.)

CUMBERLAND.

HINDS (James Pitcairn). BIBLIOTHECA JACKSONIANA. Published for the Carlisle Public Library Committee by Titus Wilson. List of maps, p. 121. Kendal, 1909.

Sparke (Archibald). Tullie House (Carlisle Free Library), Carlisle: and what it contains. (*Northern Counties Mag.*, vol. ii. pp. 140–151. 1901.)

Sanderson (T.). Biblio. Hist. of Westmorland and Cumberland. 2 vols. (A Collection of printed and MS. extracts in the Jackson Collection.)

Ferguson (Richard Saul). Hist. of Cumberland. 1890. Bibliography, pp. 289–297.

—— **MS. Catal. of Papers, etc., referring to Cumberland in the Old Series,** vols. i.–iv. and **New Series,** vols. i. and ii. of the '*Archæol. Æliana.*' (In Carlisle Public Library.)

—— **Notes on the Heraldic Visitations of Cumberland and Westmorland.** (*Cumb. and Westm. Antiq. and Archæol. Soc. Trans.*, vol. ii. pp. 20–27. 1876.)

—— **On the Collection of Chap-Books in the Bibliotheca Jacksoniana,** with some Remarks on the Hist. of Printing in Carlisle, Whitehaven, Penrith, etc. (*Cumb. and Westm. Antiq. and Archæol. Soc. Trans.*, vol. xiv. pp. 1–120. 1895.)

CUMBERLAND (continued).

Ferguson (Richard Saul). On the Chap-Books in the Bibl. Jacksoniana in Tullie House, Carlisle. (*Archæol. Journ.*, vol. lii. pp. 292–335. 1895.)

——— **On some Additions to the Collection of Chap-Books in the Bibl. Jacksoniana.** (*Cumb. and Westm. Antiq. and Archæol. Soc. Trans.*, vol. xvi. pp. 56–79. 1900.)

——— **The Denton Manuscripts.** (*Cumb. & Westm. Antiq. & Archæol. Soc. Trans.*, vol. xiii. pp. 218–223. 1895.)

Biblio. of the Writings of Richard Saul Ferguson. (*Cumb. and Westm. Antiq. and Archæol. Soc. Trans.*, vol. xvi. pp. xiii.–xx. 1900; also *Archæol. Æliana*, Ser. 3. vol. x. pp. 314–317. 1913.)

Ferguson (R. S.) and Cowper (H. S.). An Archæol. Survey of Cumberland, Westmorland, and of Lancashire North-of-the-Sands. (*Archæologia*, vol. liii. pp. 485–538. 1893, and reprinted separately.) Biblio. and Topog. Index, pp. 488–520.

Catal. of a Collection of Books, Pamphlets, and Prints relating to the Counties of Cumberland and Westmorland, offered for sale by Charles Thurnam and Sons, Carlisle. [1913.]

Index to the Trans. of the Cumberland and Westmorland Antiq. and Archæol. Soc., Vols. I.–VII., compiled by W. B. Arnison. Kendal. 1885.

Catalogue-Index to the Trans. of the Cumberland and Westmorland Antiq. and Archæol. Soc., Vols. I.–XVI., 1866–1900, compiled by Archibald Sparke. Kendal. 1901.

Index to the Trans. of the Cumberland and Westmorland Association, Vols. I.—XI. (*Transactions*, no. xi. pp. 153–167. 1886.)

Curwen (J. F.). An Index to the Heraldry of Cumberland and Westmorland. (*Cumb. and Westm. Antiq. and Archæol. Soc. Trans.*, New Ser. vol. vi. pp. 204–236. 1906.)

Sparke (Archibald). A Biblio. of the Dialect Literature of Cumberland and Westmorland, and Lancashire North of the Sands. 1907.

Jackson (William). A List of Books illustrating English Dialects.—Cumberland. (*Papers and Pedigrees relating to Cumberland, etc.*, vol. ii. pp. 256–276. 1892.) Reprinted from English Dialect Soc., Ser. A. no. 2, p. 28.

——— **Anderson's Cumberland Ballads.** (*Papers and Pedigrees relating to Cumberland, etc.*, vol. i. p. 76–79. 1892.)

Allison (Sir R. A.). The History and Ballads of the Border. (*Cumb. Assoc. Trans.*, no. iv. pp. 61–88, 1879.)

A List of Private Acts, etc., Cumberland. 1913. Stevens & Sons. London.

Nightingale (B.). The Ejected of 1662 in Cumberland and Westmorland. (*Univ. of Manchester Publications*, no. xii. 1911.) Principal Authorities consulted, vol. i. pp. xvii.–xxiv. Bibliography, vol. ii. pp. 1409–1423.

Gross (Charles). Biblio. of Brit. Municipal Hist. (*Harvard Hist. Studies*, vol. v. 1897.) Cumberland, pp. 92, 93.

Davenport (Frances G.). List of Printed Materials for Manorial Hist. 1894. Biblio. Note on Cumberland Manorial Hist., p. 40.

Dove (Patrick Edward). Domesday Studies. 1891. Domesday Biblio. Cumberland, vol. ii. p. 673.

Lyell (Arthur H.). Biblio. List of Romano-British Remains. 1912. Cumberland, pp. 8–15.

Macklin (Herbert Walter). Monumental Brasses. London: Geo. Allen & Co., 1913. Biblio. Note on Cumberland Brasses, with a List, pp. 139 and 151.

Special Cumberland Collections are in the Lancaster Public Library, and in the Carlisle Public Library.

CUMBERLAND (*continued*).

Hist. MSS. Reports. Cumberland Collections.

Graham, Sir F. U., at Netherby ...	5th Rep. p. xi. ; 6th Rep. p. xii. and App. pp. 322–344.
Lonsdale, Earl of, at Lowther Castle and Whitehaven Castle	13th Rep. pp. 32–35, and App. VII.
Muncaster, Lord, at Muncaster Castle...	10th Rep. p. 15, and App. IV. pp. 223–298.
Le Fleming, Mr. S. H., at Rydal Hall, co. Westmorland	12th Rep. pp. 38, 39, and App. VII.
Carlisle, Dean and Chapter of	2nd Rep. p. xiii. and App. pp 123–125.
——— Diocesan Registry of	9th Rep. p. ix. and App. I. pp. 177–197.
——— Corporation of	9th Rep. p. ix. and App. I. pp. 197–203.

County Records, 1688, etc., with MS. Index, at Court House, Carlisle. (*Local Records Comm. Rep.*, 1902, App. III. p. 16.)

Hill's MS. Collections for Westmorland and Cumberland. List of Contents of the 9 vols. (*Cumb. & Westm. Antiq. & Archæol. Soc. Trans.*, vol. ix. pp. 14–28. 1888.)

Wilson (Rev. James). Calendar of the Original Deeds at Tullie House, Carlisle. I. Latin. (*Cumb. & Westm. Antiq. & Archæol. Soc. Trans.* New Ser. vol. xiv. pp. 63–82. 1914.)

Whitaker (William). A List of Works relating to the Geology of Cumberland and Westmorland. (*Cumb. & Westm. Assoc. Trans.*, no. vii. pp. 13–39. 1882.)

Trimen (Henry). Botanical Biblio. of the British Counties. Cumberland. (*Journ. of Botany*, vol. xii. p. 183. 1874.)

Christy (Miller). Biblio. Note on Cumberland Birds. (*The Zoologist*, Ser. 3, vol. xiv. p. 250, 1890, and reprinted in pamph., 1891, p. 10.) **Mammals.** (*The Zoologist*, Ser. 3, vol. xvii. p. 177, 1893.) **Reptiles.** (*Ibid.* p. 242, 1893.) **Fishes.** (*Ibid.* p. 253, 1893.)

Anderson (John P.). Book of Brit. Topo., 1881. Cumberland, pp. 74–79.
Gatfield (George). Guide to Heraldry. 1892. Cumberland, pp. 130, 131.
Sims (Richard). Manual for the Genealogist. 1861. Cumberland, pp. 163, 203, 231, 232.
Upcott (William). English Topo., 1818. Cumberland, vol. i. pp. 108–135, 600–605.
Smith (Alfred Russell). Catal. of Topo. Tracts, etc., 1878. Cumberland, pp. 49–52, 459.
Gough (Richard). Brit. Topo., 1780. Cumberland, vol. i. pp. 277–291.
Bandinel (Bulkeley). Catal. of Books bequeathed to Bodleian Lib. by Richard Gough, 1814. Cumberland, pp. 93, 94.

CARLISLE.

Ferguson (R. S.) and Nanson (W.). Some Municipal Records of the City of Carlisle. Cumb. & Westm. Antiq. & Archæol. Soc. 1887.

Murray (David). 'Museums.' Glasgow. 1904. Biblio. Note on Carlisle Museums, vol. ii. p. 165.

Carlisle Cathedral Records, 1400, etc. at Carlisle Cathedral. (*Local Records Comm. Rep.*, 1902, App. III. p. 110.)

Carlisle, Archdeaconry of, Ecclesiastical Records, 13th Cent. etc. at Chapter Buildings, Carlisle. (*Local Records Comm. Rep.*, 1902, App. III. p. 120.)

Ferguson (R. S.). An attempt to trace the missing Episcopal Registers of the See of Carlisle. (*Cumb. & Westm. Antiq. & Archæol. Soc. Trans.*, vol. vii. pp. 295–299. 1884.)

——— **The Parish Registers of St. Mary's and St. Cuthbert's, Carlisle.** (*Ibid.* vol. ii. pp. 347–354. 1876.)

CUMBERLAND (*continued*).

Dixon (Rev. R. W.). The Chapter Library of Carlisle. (*Cumb. & Westm. Antiq. & Archæol. Soc. Trans.*, vol. ii. pp. 312–336. 1876.)

Brown (James Walter). Carlisle in Ballad and Story. Carlisle, 1912.

KESWICK.

Murray (David). 'Museums.' Glasgow. 1904. Biblio. Note on Crosthwaite Museum, Keswick, vol. ii. p. 306.

Crosthwaite (J. Fisher). Peter Crosthwaite, the Founder of Crosthwaite's Museum, Keswick. (*Cumberland Assoc. Trans.*, no. iii. pp. 151–164. 1878.)

KIRKANDREWS-UPON-ESK.

Ferguson (R. S.). The Registers and Account Books of Kirkandrews-upon-Esk. (*Cumb. & Westm. Antiq. & Archæol. Soc. Trans.*, vol. viii. pp. 280–306. 1886.)

WESTWARD.

Wilson (Rev. James). The Early Registers of the Parish of Westward. (*Cumb. & Westm. Antiq. & Archæol. Soc. Trans.*, vol. xiii. pp. 103–117. 1895.)

DENBIGHSHIRE.

Hist. MSS. Comm. Reports. Denbighshire Collection.
Myddelton-Biddulph, Col., at Chirk Castle. 2nd. Rep. p. xi. and App. p. 73.

Myddelton Deeds at Chirk Castle. (Powys-Land Club. *Montgomeryshire Collections*, vol. xxix. pp. 57–67. 1895.)

Palmer (A. N.). Early Books Printed in Wrexham. (*Hist. of the Town of Wrexham*, App. II. pp. 253–255. 1893.)

Gross (Charles). Biblio. of Brit. Municipal Hist. (*Harvard Hist. Studies*, vol. v. 1897.). Denbighshire, p. 206.

Lyell (Arthur H.). Biblio. List of Romano-British Remains. 1912. Denbighshire, p. 144.

Trimen (Henry). Botanical Biblio. of the British Counties. Denbighshire. (*Journ. of Botany*, vol. xii. p. 158. 1874.)

Christy (Miller). Biblio. Note on Birds. (*Catal. of Local Lists of British Birds.* 1891, p. 10.)

Anderson (John P.). Book of Brit. Topo., 1881. Denbighshire, p. 347.
Gough (Richard). Brit. Topo., 1780. Denbighshire, vol. ii. p. 525.

DERBYSHIRE.

Luxmore (J. S.). Derbyshire Bibliography. (MSS., Books, Maps, Views, etc.). (*Notts. & Derbyshire Notes & Queries*, vol. i. pp. 127, 146, 156, 188; vol. iv. pp. 119, 137. 1893 and 1896.)

—— **Derbyshire References in 'Notes & Queries.'** (*Notts. & Derbyshire Notes & Queries*, vol. v. pp. 69, 92, 121. 1897.)

Index to the Journal of the Derbyshire Archæol. and Nat. Hist. Soc., Vols. I.–XXV., 1879–1903. Compiled by the Hon. Frederick Strutt. [1912.]

Bateman (Thomas). Descriptive Catal. of the Antiquities and Miscellaneous Objects preserved in the Museum at Lomberdale House, Derbyshire. Bakewell, 1855.

DERBYSHIRE (continued).

Index to the Visitation of Derbyshire, 1663-1664. Privately Printed. F. A. Crisp. 1887.

Pedes Finium. A Calendar of the Fines for the County of Derby, from their Commencement in the Reign of Richard I. (*Derbyshire Archæol. & Nat. Hist. Soc. Journ.*, vols. vii.-xv., xvii., xviii., 1885-1896.)

Bemrose (William). Derbyshire and other Horn-Books. (*Derbyshire Archæol. & Nat. Hist. Soc. Journ.*, vol. xxx. pp. 297-308. 1908.)

Sitwell (Sir George). Pocket Almanacks at Renishaw, 1671-1721. (*Derbyshire Archæol. & Nat. Hist. Soc. Journ.*, vol. xii. pp. 193-227. 1890.)

Wallis (Alfred). A Sketch of the Early Hist. of the Printing Press in Derbyshire. (*Derbyshire Archæol. & Nat. Hist. Soc. Journ.*, vol. iii. pp. 137-156. 1881.)

A List of Private Acts, etc., Derbyshire, 1913. Stevens & Sons, London.

Gross (Charles). Biblio. of Brit. Municipal Hist. (*Harvard Hist. Studies*, vol. v. 1897.) Derbyshire, p. 93. Derby, pp. 206-77.

Davenport (Frances G.). List of Printed Materials for Manorial Hist. 1894. Biblio. Note on Derbyshire Manorial Hist., p. 40.

Dove (Patrick Edward). Domesday Studies. 1891. Domesday Biblio. Derbyshire, vol. ii. pp. 673, 674.

Lyell (Arthur H.). Biblio. List of Romano-British Remains. 1912. Derbyshire, pp. 15-16.

Macklin (Herbert Walter). Monumental Brasses. London: Geo. Allen & Co. 1913. Biblio. Note on Derbyshire Brasses, with a List, pp. 139 and 151, 152.

Murray (David). 'Museums.' Glasgow, 1904. Biblio. Note on Derby Museum, vol. ii. p. 205.

Special Derbyshire Collections are in the Buxton Museum and Public Library, the Chesterfield Public Library, the Derby Public Library (the 'Devonshire' Collection), and the New Mills Public Library.

Hist. MSS. Comm. Reports. Derbyshire Collections.

Devonshire, Duke of, at Bolton Abbey and Hardwicke Hall	3rd Rep. pp. xiv. xv. and App. pp. 36-45.
Cowper, Earl (Coke MSS.), at Melbourne	11th Rep. p. 10; 12th Rep. pp. 34, 35, and App. I.-III.
FitzHerbert, Sir William, at Tissington	13th Rep. pp. 35, 36 and App. VI. pp. 1-185.
Chandos-Pole-Gell, Mr. H., at Hopton Hall	9th Rep. p. xvii. and App. II. pp. 384-403.

County Records, with Printed and MS. Indexes, at County Buildings, Derby. (*Local Records Comm. Rep.*, 1902, App. III. p. 16.)

Wolley MS. Collections for the Hist. of Derbyshire in the Brit. Museum. Add. MSS. 6666-6718. Index, Add. MS. 6699.

The Wolley Manuscripts.—An Analysis of the First Five Volumes. By J. Charles Cox. (*Derbyshire Archæol. & Nat. Hist. Soc. Journ.*, vol. xxxiii. pp. 131-190. 1911.)—An Analysis of Volumes Six to Ten. (*Ibid.* vol. xxxiv. pp. 81-132. 1912.)—An Analysis of the Last Forty-Two Volumes. (*Ibid.* vol. xxxv. pp. 171-206. 1913.)

Suckling's Collections for Derbyshire, 1821-1839, in the Brit. Museum. Add. MSS. 18478; 18479. Index, Add. MS. 18491.

Pegge's Collections for Derbyshire in the College of Arms.

Cox (Rev. J. Charles). Calendar of the Records of the County of Derby. London, 1899.

DERBYSHIRE (continued).

Cox (Rev. J. Charles). Notes on the Churches of Derbyshire. Biblio. Notes on MS. Collections relating to the County, see Introduction, vol. i. 1875.

Jeayes (Isaac Herbert). Descriptive Catal. of Derbyshire Charters in Public and Private Libraries, and Muniment Rooms. 1906. Index of Owners and Sources, pp. 485, 486.

Carrington (W. A.). Deeds, etc., Enrolled, County of Derby. (*Derbyshire Archæol. & Nat. Hist. Soc. Journ.*, vol. xxiv. pp. 57–67. 1902.)

——— **Records of the County of Derby.** (*Derbyshire Archæol. & Nat. Hist. Soc. Journ.*, vol. xxiii. pp. 63–76. 1901.)

Bowles (C. E. B.). Some Old Charters and Deeds. (*Derbyshire Archæol. & Nat. Hist. Soc. Journ.*, vol. xxxiv. pp. 61–74. 1912.)

——— **The Derby Municipal Muniments.** (*Ibid.* vol. xxvi. pp. 173–176. 1904.)

Cox (Rev. J. Charles). Ancient Documents relating to Tithes in the Peak. (*Derbyshire Archæol. & Nat. Hist. Soc. Journ.*, vol. v. pp. 129–164. 1883.)

——— **Documents relative to the Sequestration of the Derbyshire Estates of Philip, First Earl of Chesterfield.** (*Ibid.* vol. xi. pp. 107–119. 1889.)

Kerry (Rev. Charles). Gleanings from the Assize Rolls for Derbyshire preserved in the Record Office, London. (*Derbyshire Archæol. & Nat. Hist. Soc. Journ.*, vol. xviii. pp. 94–117. 1896.)

Trimen (Henry). Botanical Biblio. of the British Counties. Derbyshire. (*Journ. of Botany*, vol. xii. p. 179. 1874.)

Linton (W. R.). Flora of Derbyshire. 1903. Publications, MSS., etc., quoted in the '*Flora*,' arranged chronologically as a Record of Botanical Investigation in the County, pp. 28–44.

Christy (Miller). Biblio. Note on Derbyshire Birds. (*The Zoologist*, Ser. 3, vol. xiv. p. 251, 1890; and reprinted in pamph., 1891, p. 11.) **Mammals.** (*The Zoologist*, Ser. 3, vol. xvii. p. 177, 1893.) **Reptiles.** (*Ibid.* p. 242, 1893.) **Fishes.** (*Ibid.* p. 253, 1893.)

Anderson (John P.). Book of Brit. Topo., 1881. Derbyshire, pp. 79–85.
Gatfield (George). Guide to Heraldry. 1892. Derbyshire, pp. 131, 132.
Sims (Richard). Manual for the Genealogist. 1861. Derbyshire, pp. 164, 203, 232.
Upcott (William). English Topo., 1818. Derbyshire, vol. i. pp. 136–145, 606, 607.
Smith (Alfred Russell). Catal. of Topo. Tracts, etc., 1878. Derbyshire, pp. 54–56, 460.
Gough (Richard). Brit. Topo., 1780. Derbyshire, vol. i. pp. 289–298.
Bandinel (Bulkeley). Catal. of Books bequeathed to Bodleian Lib. by Richard Gough, 1814. Derbyshire, pp. 95–99.

ASHBURNE.

Jourdain (Rev. Francis). Charters connected with the Church of Ashburne. (*Derbyshire Archæol. & Nat. Hist. Soc, Journ.*, vol. xiii. pp. 52–107. 1891.)

BAKEWELL.

Holland (W. R.). The Greaves Parchments. (*Derbyshire Archæol. & Nat. Hist. Soc. Journ.*, vol. xiii., pp. 220–223. 1891.)

BELPER.

Derry (T. R.). Some Notes on Old Belper and Old Belper Books. (*Derbyshire Archæol. & Nat. Hist. Soc. Journ.*, vol. xii. pp. 1–23. 1890.)

BREADSALL.

Kerry (Rev. Charles). Early Charters of Breadsall. (*Derbyshire Archæol. & Nat. Hist. Soc. Journ.*, vol. xvi. pp. 157–182. 1894.)

DERBYSHIRE (*continued*).

CHAPEL-EN-LE-FRITH.

Bunting (W. B.). Some Early Chapel-en-le-Frith Charters. (*Derbyshire Archæol. & Nat. Hist. Soc. Journ.*, vol. xxviii. pp. 180–185. 1906.)

CHESTERFIELD.

Borough Records, 1100, etc., with Printed Calendar, at Municipal Hall, Chesterfield. (*Local Records Comm. Rep.*, 1902, App. III. p. 50.)

DERLEY ABBEY.

Kerry (Rev. Charles). Derley Abbey Charters preserved at Belvoir. (*Derbyshire Archæol. & Nat. Hist. Soc. Journ.*, vol. xvi. pp. 14–43. 1894.)

DRAKELOWE.

Jeayes (Isaac H.). Catal. of Charters and Muniments preserved by Sir Robert Gresley at Drakelowe. (See '*Gresley Charters*,' by A. W. Whatmore, in '*Notts. & Derbyshire Notes & Queries*,' vol. iv. p. 1, 2. 1896.)

HARDWICK.

Catal. of the Pictures at Hardwick Hall; in the possession of the Duke of Devonshire. By Lord Hawkesbury. (*Derbyshire Archæol. & Nat. Hist. Soc. Journ.*, vol. xxv. pp. 103–158. 1903.)

HEMINGTON.

Kerry (Rev. Charles). Hemington Church, with the more Ancient of the Hemington Deeds. (*Derbyshire Archæol. & Nat. Hist. Soc. Journ.*, vol. xii. pp. 139–161. 1890.)

MELBOURNE.

The Coke Papers at Melbourne Hall. (*Derbyshire Archæol. & Nat. Hist. Soc. Journ.*, vol. xi. pp. 54–67. 1889.) See also *ante* Hist. MSS. Comm. Reports.

REPTON.

Old Deeds in the Parish Chest of St. Wystan's, Repton, transcribed and translated by E. G. (*Derbyshire Archæol. & Nat. Hist. Soc. Journ.*, vol. ix. pp. 1–18. 1887.)

Cox (Rev. J. Charles). Early Deeds of Repton School. (*Derbyshire Archæol. & Nat. Hist. Soc. Journ.*, vol. xxxii. pp. 87–104. 1910.)

DEVONSHIRE.

DAVIDSON (James). BIBLIOTHECA DEVONIENSIS, a Catalogue of the Printed Books relating to the County of Devon. Exeter, 1852. Supplement, 1862.

Bellamy (John Cremer). An Alphabetical List of all Works relating to the Counties of Devon and Cornwall. (*A Thousand Facts in the Histories of Devon and Cornwall*, 1850, pp. 51–59.)

Dredge (Rev. John Ingle). A Few Sheaves of Devon Bibliography. (*Devon. Assoc. Rep. & Trans.*, vol. xxi. pp. 498–548; vol. xxii. pp. 324–356; vol. xxiv. pp. 476–526; vol. xxv. pp. 552–601; vol. xxviii. pp. 547–605; vol. xxxi. pp. 331–355. 1889–99.)

Adams (Maxwell). An Index to the Printed Literature relating to North Devon. (*Devon. Assoc. Rep. & Trans.*, vol. xxxiv. pp. 344–393. 1902.)

DEVONSHIRE (continued).

Rowe (J. Brooking). Presidential Address before the Devonshire Assoc., 1882. Appendix A.—List of some of the MSS. relating to Devon, pp. 73–85; Appendix B.—List of Histories of Towns, Parishes, etc., pp. 86–91. (*Devon. Assoc. Rep. & Trans.*, vol. xiv. pp. 33–91. 1882.)

Index (Classified) to Reports and Transactions of the Devonshire Assoc., vols. i.–xvii. 1862–85. Plymouth. 1886.

Guide to the Reports and Transactions of the Devonshire Assoc., First Series, vols. i.–xxx. By H. G. H. Shaddick. Plymouth. 1909.

Wright (W. H. K.). Plymouth Free Public Library. Index-Catal. of the General Reference Library, including the Devon and Cornwall Collections. 1892.

—— **A Plea for Devonshire Bibliography.** 1885.

—— **The Progress of Devonshire Bibliography.** (*Devon. Assoc. Rep. & Trans.*, vol. xxiii. pp. 376–388. 1891.)

—— **Devonian Literature: Its Special Wants.** (*Devon. Assoc. Rep. & Trans.*, vol. xiv. pp. 525–528. 1882.)

—— **Summary of Recent Devonian Literature.** Read at Second Annual Meeting of the United Devon Assoc. 1901.

—— **National Armada Tercentenary Commemoration, Plymouth.** Catal. of Loan Collection of Relics, Portraits, etc. 1888.

—— **Drake in History, Song, and Story.** (*Devonian Year Book*, 1914, pp. 36–63.)

Tapley-Soper (H.). Some Recent Devonshire Literature. (*The London Devonian Year Book*, 1910, pp. 144–146; 1911, pp. 117–123; 1912, pp. 112–114; 1913, pp. 105–106; 1914, pp. 114–117.)

Brushfield (T. N.). The Literature of Devonshire up to the year 1640. Privately printed, 1893.

—— **Presidential Address before the Devonshire Assoc., 1893.** Appendix A.—List of Principal Works referred to, pp. 113–152; Appendix B.—List of Devonshire Authors to 1640, pp. 153–158. (*Devon Assoc. Rep. & Trans.*, vol. xxv. pp. 25–158. 1893.)

—— **Extinct Devonshire Periodicals.** (*The Western Antiquary*, vol. ix. pp. 102–105, 181–183; vol. x. pp. 53–55; vol. xi. pp. 71–73. 1890–91.)

—— **The Broadside Ballads of Devonshire and Cornwall.** (*The Western Antiquary*, vol. vi. pp. v.–xiii. 1886.)

—— **Biblio. of Sir Walter Ralegh** (reprinted from *The Western Antiquary*). Plymouth, 1886. Second Edn. Exeter, 1908.)

—— **Biblio. of the 'History of the World,' and of the 'Remains of Sir Walter Ralegh'** (reprinted from *The Library Chronicle*). London, 1886.

—— **Raleghana. Pt. VI. 'The History of the World,' by Sir Walter Ralegh.** A Biblio. Study. (*Devon. Assoc. Rep. & Trans.*, vol. xxxvi. pp. 181–218. 1904.)

—— **Biblio. of Andrew Brice, and Remarks on the Early Hist. of Exeter Newspapers.** 1888. Privately printed.

—— **Richard Isacke and his 'Antiquities of Exeter.'** 1893.

—— **The Biblio. of Rev. George Oliver, D.D., of Exeter.** (*Devon Assoc. Rep. & Trans.*, vol. xvii. pp. 266–276. 1885.)

Collections of Jeremiah Milles, D.D., Dean of Exeter, in the Bodleian Library, Oxford. See Macray (W. D.) '*Annals*,' 1890, p. 345.

DEVONSHIRE (continued).

Friend (Rev. Hilderic). Literary Guides and Charts. (*Bygone Devonshire*, pp. 239–249. 1898.)

Troup (Mrs. F. B.) and Dredge (Rev. John Ingle). Biog. Sketch of Rev. Christopher Jelinger, M.A., with Biblio. Notes. (*Devon Assoc. Rep. & Trans.*, vol. xxxii. pp. 249–270. 1900.)

Index Catal. to the Library of the Plymouth Institution (contains many Devon entries). (*Plymouth Inst. Ann. Rep. & Trans.*, vol. xi. pp. 315–384. 1894.)

Catal. of the Davidson Collection of Pamphlets, etc., in the Library at the Athenæum, Plymouth. (*Plymouth Inst. Ann. Rep. & Trans.*, vol. xi. pp. 385–504. 1894.)

List of Libraries in Devonshire. (*The Devonian Year Book*, 1914, pp. 137–138.)

Devonshire Collections are to be found in Public Libraries at Plymouth, Torquay, and Swansea.

Dredge (Rev. John Ingle). Devon Booksellers and Printers in the Seventeenth and Eighteenth Centuries. (*The Western Antiquary*, vol. v. pp 1–8, 25–32. 1885.) Also privately printed and issued separately, 1885. Supplementary Paper, No. 1. (*The Western Antiquary*, vol. v. pp. 112–114, 119–123. 1885.)

——— No. 2. (*Ibid.* vol. vi. pp. 97–100, 121–124, 153–156. 1886.)

——— No. 3. (*Ibid.* vol. x. pp. 9–12, 34–37, 103–105, 126–128, 151–154. 1890-91.)

Worth (R. N.). Notes on the Hist. of Printing in Devon. (*Devon. Assoc. Rep. & Trans.*, vol. xi. pp. 497–515. 1879.)

——— **Notes on the Ancient Recorded Topo. of Devon.** (*Devon. Assoc. Rep. & Trans.*, vol. xvii. pp. 345–366. 1885.)

Shelly (John). List of Books, etc., written in, or relating to the Dialects of Devon. (*Plymouth Inst. Ann. Rep. & Trans.*, vol. iii. pp. 145–151. 1868.)

Catal. of a Loan Exhibition of Portraits of Worthies connected with Devon and Cornwall. Exeter. 1873.

Boase (George C.). Devonshire Bibliography: The Rev. Nathaniel Carpenter, born at Northleigh, 7 Feb. 1588–89, died 1628 or 1634. (*The Western Antiquary*, vol. ix. pp. 214, 215. 1890.)

Lane (Charles). Biblio. of Joanna Southcott. (*Devon. Assoc. Rep. & Trans.*, vol. xliv. pp. 757–809. 1912.)

Sydney (William). Biblio. Note on Devonshire Newspapers. (*The Western Antiquary*, vol. ix. pp. 228, 229, 1890.)

Wainwright (Thomas). An Index to the Names of Persons found in the Monumental Inscriptions in Devonshire Churches. (*Devon Assoc. Rep. & Trans.*, vol. xxxvi. pp. 522–541. 1904.)

Prowse (Arthur B.). Index to Personal Names in Westcote's 'View of Devonshire in 1630,' and his 'Devonshire Pedigrees,' 1845. (*Devon Assoc. Rep. & Trans.*, vol. xxvii. pp. 443–485. 1895.)

——— **Index to Risdon's 'Survey of Devon,' Personal Names.** (*Devon Assoc. Rep. & Trans.*, vol. xxvi. pp. 419–450. 1894.)

Gross (Charles). Biblio. of Brit. Municipal Hist. (*Harvard Hist. Studies*, vol. v. 1897.) Devonshire, p. 93. Barnstaple, p. 162. Devonport, p. 207. Exeter, p. 231. Plymouth, p. 366. Tavistock, p. 403. Totnes, p. 407.

Davenport (Frances G.). List of Printed Materials for Manorial Hist. 1894. Biblio. Note on Devon Manorial Hist., pp. 40–41.

Dove (Patrick Edward). Domesday Studies. 1891. Domesday Biblio. Devon, vol. ii. p. 674.

Lyell (Arthur H.). Biblio. List of Romano-British Remains. 1912. Devonshire, pp. 16–17.

DEVONSHIRE (continued).

Macklin (Herbert Walter). Monumental Brasses. London: Geo. Allen & Co. 1913. Biblio. Note on Devon Brasses, with a List, pp. 140, 152–153.

Hist. MSS. Comm. Reports. Devonshire Collections.

Coffin, Mr. J. R. Pine, at Portledge, N. Devon	4th Rep. p. xix. and App. pp. 374–379; 5th Rep. p. xiv. and App. pp. 370–386.
Devon, Earl of, at Powderham Castle...	3rd Rep. p. xv. and App. p. 216; 9th Rep. App. II. pp. 403–406.
Ellacombe, Rev. H. T., at Clyst St. George	5th Rep. p. ix. and App. pp. 323–329.
Fortescue, Earl, at Castle Hill, South-molton	3rd Rep. p. xv. and App. pp. 220–221.
Prideaux, Mr. R. W., at Dartmouth ...	5th Rep. App. pp. 423–426.
Somerset, Duke of, at Maiden Bradley, Wilts	15th Rep. App. VII. pp. 1–151.
Alwington Parish...	5th Rep. p. xvi. and App. p. 597.
Barnstaple Corporation	9th Rep. p. x. and App. I. pp. 203–216.
Dartmouth Corporation	5th Rep. p. xvi. and App. pp. 597–606.
Exeter, Bishop of...	17th Rep, pp. 112–115; Various Collections, vol. iv. pp. 13–32.
——— Dean and Chapter of	17th Rep. pp. 115–120; Various Collections, vol. iv. pp. 33–95.
Hartland Parish	4th Rep. p. xix. and App. p. 428; 5th Rep. p. xvi. and App. 571–575.
Parkham Parish	4th Rep. p. xviii. and App. pp. 468–469.
Plymouth Corporation	9th Rep. p. xiii. and App. I. pp. 262–284; 10th Rep. p. 14, and App. IV. pp. 536–560.
Totnes Corporation	3rd Rep. p. xx. and App. pp. 341–350.

Reports on Devonshire Records, by a Committee of the Devon Association. Edited by J. R. Chanter, R. W. Cotton, and J. Brooking-Rowe. (*Devon Assoc. Rep. & Trans.*, vols. xxi.–xxxiv. 1889–1902.)

Chanter (J. R.). Report on the Harding Collection of Manuscripts, Records, and Hist., Eccles., Heraldic, & Antiq. Documents relating to Devon & Cornwall. (*Devon Assoc. Rep. & Trans.*, vol. xx. pp. 49–68. 1888.)

Dymond (Robert) of Exeter. MS. Notes in 13 vols. presented to the Exeter Public Library. (See *Devon & Cornwall Notes & Queries*, vol. vi. p. 191. 1911.)

Levien (Edward). Devonshire Unpublished Manuscripts in the Brit. Museum. (*Brit. Archæol. Assoc. Journ.*, vol. xviii. pp. 134–145. 1862.)

Granville (Rev. Roger) and Mugford (W. E.). Abstracts of the Existing Transcripts of the Lost Parish Registers of Devon, 1596–1644. Vol. I. A–Bra. Exeter, 1908.

Reichel (Rev. Oswald J.). Extracts from the Pipe Rolls of Henry II. relating to Devon, with an Appendix from Testa de Nevil. (*Devon Assoc. Rep. & Trans.*, vol. xxix. pp. 453–509. 1897.)

Whale (Rev. T. W.). Index to 'Domesday' Analysis (Devon), vol. xxviii., and 'Testa de Nevill' Tax Roll (Devon), vol. xxx. (*Devon Assoc. Rep. & Trans.*, vol. xxxiv. pp. 289–324. 1902.)

Trimen (Henry). Botanical Biblio. of the British Counties. Devonshire. (*Journ. of Botany*, vol. xii. p. 69. 1874.)

Whitaker (William). List of Works on the Geology, Mineralogy, and Palæontology of Devon. (*Devon. Assoc. Rep. & Trans.*, vol. iv. pp. 330–352. 1870.) Supplementary List. (*Ibid.* vol. v. pp. 404–415. 1872.)

DEVONSHIRE (continued).

Pengelly (William). Notes on Notices of the Geology and Palæontology of Devonshire. Pts. i.-xii. (*Devon. Assoc. Rep. & Trans.*, vol. vi.-xvii. 1874-85.)

——— **The Literature of Kent's Cavern, Torquay, prior to 1859.** Pts. i.-v. (*Ibid.* vol. ii. pp. 468-522; vol. iii. pp. 191-482; vol. iv. pp. 467-490; vol. x. pp. 141-181; vol. xvi. pp. 189-434. 1868-71, 78, 84.)

——— **The Literature of the Caverns, near Yealmpton.** (*Ibid.* vol. iv. pp. 81-105. 1870.)

——— **The Literature of the Oreston Caverns, near Plymouth.** (*Ibid.* vol. v. pp. 249-316. 1872.)

——— **The Literature of the Caverns of Anstey's Cove, Torquay.** (*Ibid.* vol. vi. pp, 61-69. 1873.)

——— **The Literature of the Caverns and Fissures near Chudleigh.** (*Ibid.* vol. vi. pp. 46-60. 1873.)

——— **The Literature of the Caverns of Buckfastleigh.** (*Ibid.* vol. vi. pp. 70-72. 1873).

Julian (Mrs. Hester Forbes). William Pengelly, the Founder of the Devonshire Association. (*Devon. Assoc. Rep. & Trans.*, vol. xliv. pp. 157-191; vol. xlv. pp. 423-444. 1912-13.)

Christy (Miller). Biblio. Note on Devonshire Birds. (*The Zoologist*, Ser. 3, vol. xiv. p. 251, 1890; and reprinted in pamph., 1891, p. 11.) **Mammals.** (*The Zoologist*, Ser. 3, vol. xvii. p. 178. 1893.) **Reptiles.** (*Ibid.* p. 243. 1893.) **Fishes.** (*Ibid.* p. 253. 1893.)

Anderson (John P.). Book of Brit. Topo., 1881. Devon, pp. 85-93.

Gatfield (George). Guide to Heraldry. 1892. Devon, pp. 132-134.

Sims (Richard). Manual for the Genealogist. 1861. Devon, pp. 203, 204, 233.

Upcott (William). English Topo., 1818. Devon, vol. i. pp. 146-172, 607.

Smith (Alfred Russell). Catal. of Topo. Tracts, etc. 1878. Devon, pp. 57-69, 460.

Gough (Richard). Brit. Topo., 1780. Devon, vol. i. pp. 299-318.

Bandinel (Bulkeley). Catal. of Books bequeathed to Bodleian Lib. by Richard Gough, 1814. Devon, pp. 100-104.

BARNSTAPLE.

Borough Records, 1261, etc., with MS. Index, at North Devon Athenæum, Barnstaple. (*Local Records Comm. Rep.*, 1902. App. III. p. 46.)

Corporation Records, see *ante* Hist. MSS. Comm. Reports.

Chanter (J. R.) and Wainwright (Thomas). The Barnstaple Records. Reprinted from the *North Devon Journal*, Jan. 9, 1879-May 5, 1881; and *North Devon Herald*, Jan. 9, 1879-Apr. 21, 1881. 2 vols. 1900.

——— **Sketches of the Literary Hist. of Barnstaple,** with list of Books Printed at Barnstaple. 1886.

BUCKLAND FILLEIGH.

Reichel (Rev. O. J.). Batch of Old Deeds relating to Buckland Filleigh, with an Index. (*Devon. Assoc. Rep. & Trans.*, vol. xli. pp. 241-255. 1909.)

CREDITON.

Davidson (J. B.). On some Ancient Documents relating to Crediton Minster. (*Devon. Assoc. Rep. & Trans.*, vol. x. pp. 237-254. 1878.)

——— **On some further Documents relating to Crediton Minster.** (*Ibid.* vol. xiv. pp. 247-277. 1882.)

DEVONSHIRE (continued).

DARTMOOR.

Rowe (S.). Perambulation of Dartmoor. 3rd Edn. 1896. Biblio. of Dartmoor Literature, pp. 485–498.

Crossing (William). A Contribution towards a Biblio. of Dartmoor. Reprinted from *Weekly Mercury*, Nov. 10, 1883. (*The Western Antiquary*, vol. iii. pp. 131-132. 1883.)

Prowse (A. B.). An Index of References to Dartmoor contained in the Devonshire Assoc. Trans., Vols. I.-XXX. (*Devon Assoc. Rep. & Trans.*, vol. xxxvii. pp. 482 567 1905.)

Dymond (Robert). Hist. Documents relating to Dartmoor. (*Devon. Assoc. Rep. & Trans.*, vol. xi. pp. 371-382. 1879.)

DARTMOUTH.

Borough Records, Hen. III., etc., with MS. Index, at Dartmouth. (*Local Records Comm. Rep.*, 1902, App. III. p. 52.)

Corporation Records, see *ante* Hist. MSS. Comm. Reports.

Windeatt (E.). John Flavell: a Notable Dartmouth Puritan and his Bibliography. (*Devon. Assoc. Rep. & Trans.*, vol. xliii. pp. 172–189. 1911.)

EXETER.

Adams (Maxwell). An Index to the Printed Literature relating to the Antiquities, Hist., & Topo. of Exeter. (*Devon. Assoc. Rep. & Trans.*, vol. xxxiii. pp. 270–308. 1901.)

Bibliography of Exeter. (*Hist. Assoc. Leaflet*, No. 9. 1908.)

Borough Records, Inventories, etc., from reign of William I., with MS. and Printed Indexes, at Exeter. (*Local Records Comm. Rep.*, 1902, App. III. p. 34.)

Whale (Rev. T. W.). Analysis of the Exon 'Domesday.' (*Devon. Assoc. Rep. & Trans.*, vol. xxviii. pp. 391–463. 1896.)

Wright (Thomas). The Municipal Archives of Exeter. (*Brit. Archæol. Soc. Journ,*, vol. xviii. pp. 306–317. 1862.)

Exeter City Muniments. Printed from 'A Calendar of the Records and Muniments belonging to the Corporation, preserved at the Guildhall,' compiled by Stuart A. Moore, 1863–70. (*Notes and Gleanings*, vols. ii.-v. 1889–92.)

Oliver (Rev. George). Hist. of the City of Exeter. 1861. Appendix. Tables of Acts of Parliament, Cathedral and Parochial Registers, Charters, etc. **Index,** by J. S. Attwood. 1884.

——— **Monasticon Dioecesis Exoniensis,** being a Collection of Records, etc., illustrating the Ancient, Conventual and Collegiate Foundations, etc. 1846–54. **Index,** by J. S. Attwood [n.d.].

——— **Lives of the Bishops of Exeter and a Hist. of the Cathedral.** 1861. Appendix. Charters of City and Diocese, etc. **Index,** by J. S. Attwood. 1887.

Ecclesiastical Records, see *ante* Hist. MSS. Comm. Reports.

Reynolds (Herbert). A Short Hist. of the Ancient Diocese of Exeter. 1895. App. B. Episcopal Registers, etc.; App. C. Documents with Chapter Clerk; App. G. Documents with Town Clerk.

Edmonds (Rev. Canon). The Formation and Fortunes of Exeter Cathedral Library. (*Devon. Assoc. Rep. & Trans.*, vol. xxxi. pp. 25–50. 1899.)

Bibliographies of Andrew Brice, Richard Isacke, and Rev. George Oliver, see *supra*, Devonshire.

Allnutt (W. H.). English Provincial Presses. Earliest Printing at Exeter. (*Bibliographica*, vol. ii. pp. 288, 294, 298. 1896.)

Tapley-Soper (H.). Exeter Printers, Booksellers, and Libraries. (*Book-Auction Records*, vol. v. pt. 2, pp. xxi.-xxiii. 1908.)

DEVONSHIRE (*continued*).

Murray (David). 'Museums.' Glasgow, 1904. Biblio. Note on Exeter Museum, vol. ii. p. 234.

KINGSBRIDGE.

Hingston-Randolph (F. C.). Ancient MSS. in Kingsbridge Church. (*The Western Antiquary*, vol. vi.–xi. 1886–91.)

LUSTLEIGH.

The Private Press of the Rev. W. Davy at Lustleigh, 1795–1807, see Macray, *Annals of the Bodl. Lib. Oxford.* 1890, p. 337.

PLYMOUTH.

Borough Records, 1381, etc., with Printed Catalogue, at Municipal Buildings, Plymouth. (*Local Records Comm. Rep.*, 1902, App. III. p. 38.)

Corporation Records, see *ante* Hist. MSS. Comm. Reports.

Worth (R. N.). Calendar of the Plymouth Municipal Records. 1893.

——— **On the Plymouth Municipal Records.** (*Brit. Archæol. Assoc. Journ.*, vol. xxxix. pp. 110–118. 1883.)

——— **The Three Towns (Plymouth, Devonport, and Stonehouse) Bibliotheca:** A Catal. of Books, Pamphlets, Papers, etc., written by natives thereof; published therein; or relating thereto; with brief biographical notices. (*Plymouth Inst. Ann. Rep. & Trans.*, vol. iv. pp. 191–312. 1872.) Supplement. (*Ibid.* vol. iv. pp. 422–430. 1873.) Appendix. (*Ibid.* vol. vii. pp. 305–352. 1880.) Also issued separately.

List of Plymouth Municipal Records Printed. (*Notes & Queries*, Ser. 11, vol. v. p. 478. 1912.)

Halliwell-Phillipps (J. O.). A Brief Description of the Ancient and Modern MSS. preserved in the Plymouth Public Library. Privately Printed. London, 1853.

Rowe (J. Brooking). The Guides, Handbooks, etc., of the Three Towns. (*Plymouth Inst. Ann. Rep. & Trans.*, vol. vi. pp. 403–405. 1878.)

TAVISTOCK.

Worth (R. N.). Calendar of the Tavistock Parish Records. 1887.

Allnutt (W. H.). English Provincial Presses. Early Printing at Tavistock. (*Bibliographica*, vol. ii. pp. 29, 30. 1896.)

TORRINGTON (GREAT).

Borough Records, 1687, etc., at Great Torrington. (*Local Records Comm. Rep.*, 1902, App. III. p. 70.)

TOTNES.

Borough Records, 1230, etc., at Guildhill, Totnes. (*Local Records Comm. Rep.*, 1902, App. III. p. 70.)

Corporation Records, see *ante* Hist. MSS. Comm. Reports.

Windeatt (Edward). The Muniments of the Corporation of Totnes. (*Devon. Assoc. Rep. & Trans.*, vol. xxxii. pp. 400–406; vol. xxxiv. pp. 704–714. 1900–02.)

Dymond (Robert). Ancient Documents relating to the Civil Hist. of Totnes. (*Devon. Assoc. Rep. & Trans.*, vol. xii. pp. 192–203. 1880.)

Devonshire Bibliography.—Works by Totnes Worthies. (*The Western Antiquary*, vol. iii. p. 249. 1884.)

Watkin (Hugh R.). Charters of Totnes Priory. (*Torquay Nat. Hist. Soc. Journ.*, vol. i. pp. 271–273. 1914.)

DONEGAL.

Anderson (John P.). Book of Brit. Topo., 1881. Donegal, p. 430.

Gough (Richard). Brit. Topo., 1780. Donegal, vol. ii. pp. 788–790.

Bandinel (Bulkeley). Catal. of Books bequeathed to Bodleian Library by Richard Gough, 1814. Donegal, p. 377.

Christy (Miller). Biblio. Note on Donegal Birds. (*The Zoologist*, Ser. 3, vol. xiv. p. 267, 1890; and reprinted in pamph., 1891, p. 41.) **Mammals.** (*The Zoologist*, Ser. 3, vol. xvii. p. 215. 1893.)

DORSETSHIRE.

MAYO (CHARLES HERBERT). BIBLIOTHECA DORSETIENSIS; being a carefully compiled account of Printed Books and Pamphlets relating to the History & Topography of the County of Dorset. London, 1885. Lists of Newspapers, pp. 74–89; Maps, 100–103, 273; Printers, pp. 278–290.

Pope (A.). On the Topography & Chartology of Old Dorset, with an annotated list of Maps. 1575–1829. (*Dorset Nat. Hist. & Antiq. Field Club. Proc.*, vol. xxiv. pp. xxviii-xxxiv. 1903.)

Wilkinson (Rev. John). Parochial Histories of Wilts. & Dorset, with Heads of Information suggested. (*Wilts. Archæol. & Nat. Hist. Mag.*, vol. iv. pp. 253-266. 1858.) Also issued separately.

Index to the Proceedings of the Dorset Nat. Hist. & Antiq. Field Club. Vols. i.-xxvi. Dorchester, 1906.

Somerset & Dorset Articles & References in the 'Downside Review.' First Series. Vol. i.–xxv. 1880–1906. (*Som. & Dorset Notes & Queries*, vol. vii. pp. 284–287, 346; vol. viii. p. 214; vol. ix. pp. 215–216; vol. x. p. 247. 1901–07.)

Hutchins (John). The Hist. & Antiquities of the County of Dorset. Second Edition. 1796–1815.

Mr. A. M. Broadley of Bridport possesses a remarkable extra-illustrated copy of this Edition.

A Chronological List of the Works of Rev. William Barnes, B.D. (*Dorset Nat. Hist. & Antiq. Field Club. Proc.*, vol. viii. pp. xxvii.-xxxiii. 1887.)

Gross (Charles). Biblio. of Brit. Municipal Hist. (*Harvard Hist. Studies*, vol. v. 1897.) Dorsetshire, pp. 93–94. Bridport, p. 175. Dorchester, p. 209. Lyme Regis, p. 329. Shaftesbury, p. 387. Weymouth, p. 414.

Davenport (Frances G.). List of Printed Materials for Manorial Hist. 1894. Biblio. Note on Dorset Manorial Hist., p. 41.

Dove (Patrick Edward). Domesday Studies. 1891. Domesday Biblio. Dorset, vol. ii. pp. 675–676.

Macklin (Herbert Walter). Monumental Brasses. London: Geo. Allen & Co., 1913. Biblio. Note on Dorsetshire Brasses, with a List, pp. 140, 153.

Murray (David). 'Museums.' Glasgow. 1904. Biblio. Note on Pitt-Rivers Museum at Farnham, vol. ii. p. 237. See also 'The Museums at Farnham and at King John's House, Tollard Royal,' by Roach Le Schonix in '*The Antiquary*,' vol. xxx. pp. 166–171. 1894.

Lyell (Arthur H.). Biblio. List of Romano-British Remains. 1912. Dorsetshire, pp. 17–21.

Foster (J. J.). Biblio. and Index Notes on Roman Remains. Dorsetshire. (*The Archæol. Rev.*, vol iv. pp. 296–304. 1889.)

DORSETSHIRE (*continued*).

Hist. MSS. Comm. Reports. Dorsetshire Collections.

Bankes, Mr. Ralph, of Kingston Lacy	8th Rep. p. xiii. and App. pp. 208–213.
Digby, Mr. G. Wingfield, of Sherborne Castle	8th Rep. p. xiii. and App. pp. 213–226; 10th Rep. App. I. pp. 520–617.
Shaftesbury, Earl of, at St. Giles ...	3rd Rep. p. xi. and App. pp. 216–217.
Bridport Corporation	6th Rep. App. pp. 475–499.
Weymouth and Melcombe Regis Corporation...	5th Rep. p. xix. and App. pp. 575–590.

County Records, 1625, etc., with Printed & MS. Lists, at the Shire Hall, Dorchester. (*Local Records Comm. Rep.*, 1902, App. III. p. 16.)

Dorset Records. (A guide to Records and where kept.) (*Som. & Dorset Notes & Queries*, vol. viii. pp. 193–195. 1903.)

Sylvanus Morgan's Book of MS. Pedigrees, chiefly relating to Dorset, in possession of Mr. G. E. Solly, Wimborne. For list of Persons and Places mentioned see *Som. & Dorset Notes & Queries*, vol. xii. pp. 72–75. 1910.

Statute Merchant Bonds, Somerset & Dorset. By J. J. Hammond. (*Som. & Dorset Notes & Queries*, vol. x. pp. 327–330; vol. xi. pp. 9–12, 159–163, 256–260, 357–359; vol. xii. pp. 14–16, 66–68, 155–157, 205–208. 1907–11.)

Briefs relating to Dorset. (*Som. & Dorset Notes & Queries*, vol. viii. p. 35. 1903.)

Halliwell (J. O.). On the Municipal Archives of Dorset. (*British Archæol. Assoc. Journ.*, vol. xxviii. pp. 28–31. 1872.)

Fletcher (Canon J. M. J.). Chained Books in Dorset and elsewhere. (*Dorset Nat. Hist. & Antiq. Field Club. Proc.*, vol. xxxv. pp. 8–26. 1914.)

Trimen (Henry). Botanical Biblio. of the British Counties. Dorsetshire. (*Journ. of Botany*, vol. xii. p. 70. 1874.)

Christy (Miller). Biblio. Note on Dorsetshire Birds. (*The Zoologist*, Ser. 3, vol. xiv. p. 251, 1890; and reprinted in pamph., 1891, p. 12. **Mammals.** (*The Zoologist*, Ser. 3, vol. xvii. p. 179. 1893.) **Reptiles.** (*Ibid.* p. 243. 1893.) **Fishes.** (*Ibid.* p. 254. 1893.)

Anderson (John P.). Book of Brit. Topo., 1881. Dorsetshire, pp. 93–97.
Gatfield (George). Guide to Heraldry. 1892. Dorsetshire, pp. 134–135.
Sims (Richard). Manual for the Genealogist. 1861. Dorsetshire, pp. 165, 205, 233.
Upcott (William). English Topo., 1818. Dorsetshire, vol. i. pp. 170–200, 608.
Smith (Alfred Russell). Catal. of Topo. Tracts, etc., 1878. Dorsetshire, pp. 71–76, 461.
Gough (Richard). Brit. Topo., 1780. Dorsetshire, vol. i. pp. 319–328.
Bandinel (Bulkeley). Catal. of Books bequeathed to Bodleian Library by Richard Gough, 1814. Dorsetshire, pp. 105–108.

ASHMORE.

Watson (E. W.). Index to the Registers, 1651–1820, and Hist. of the Parish, 1890.

BEAMINSTER.

Hine (Richard). Inventory of Parish Books and Documents. ('*The Hist. of Beaminster*,' chap. xiii.)

BRIDPORT.

Borough Records, Hen. III. etc., at Town Hall, Bridport. (*Local Records Comm. Rep.*, 1902, App. III. p. 48.)

Corporation Records, see *ante* Hist. MSS. Comm. Reports.

DORSETSHIRE (*continued*).

Wainwright (Thomas). Bridport Corporation Records. (*Dorset Nat. Hist. & Antiq. Field Club Proc.*, vol. xi. pp. 97–108. 1890.)

——— **Bridport Records and Ancient Manuscripts.** Reprinted from the '*Bridport News.*' 1898–99.

DORCHESTER.

Borough Records, 1305, etc., with Printed Index, at Municipal Offices, Dorchester. (*Local Records Comm. Rep.*, 1902, App. III. p. 54.)

Halliwell (J. O.). On the Municipal Archives of Dorchester. See Mayo (C. H.). *Bibliotheca Dorsetiensis*, p. 150.

LYME REGIS.

Borough Records, 1284, etc., at the Guildhall, Lyme Regis. (*Local Records Comm. Rep.*, 1902, App. III. p. 64.)

MERLY.

Willett (Ralph). Description of the Library at Merly. 1785.

——— **Catal. of the Books in the Lib. of R. Willett, at Merly.** 1790.

SHAFTESBURY.

Borough Records, with MS. Index, at Town Hall, Shaftesbury. (*Local Records Comm. Rep.*, 1902, App. III. p. 68.)

Mayo (Charles Herbert). The Municipal Records of the Borough of Shaftesbury. Sherborne, 1889.

TRENT.

Harbin (Rev. E. H. Bates). Thomas Gerard of Trent. His Family and His Writings. (*Dorset Nat. Hist. & Antiq. Field Club. Proc.*, vol. xxxv. pp. 55–70. 1914.)

WEYMOUTH AND MELCOMBE REGIS.

Corporation Records, see *ante* Hist. MSS. Comm. Reports.

Moule (H. J.). Descriptive Catal. of the Charters, Minute Books, & other Documents of the Borough of Weymouth & Melcombe Regis, 1252 to 1800. Weymouth, 1883.

DOWN.

Crone (John S.). Ulster Bibliography. Down. (*Ulster Journ. of Archæol.*, vol. xii. pp. 35–39, 57–62; vol. xiii. pp. 105–108. 1906–7.)

Dix (Ernest Reginald McClintock). List of Books, Pamphlets, Newspapers, etc., printed in Newry, 1764–1810. (*Ulster Journ. of Archæol.*, vol. xiii. pp. 116–119, 170–173; vol. xiv. pp. 95–96; vol. xv. pp. 19, 184–185. 1907–9.)

——— **Ulster Bibliography. Newry Printing, with a List.** (*Ibid.* vol. ix. pp. 69–71. 1903.)

——— **The First Printing Presses in Armagh and Newry.** (*Ibid.* vol. xvi. p. 46. 1910.)

DOWN (continued).

Crossle (F. C.). Notes on the Literary Hist. of Newry, with lists of Printers, etc. Newry, 1897.

Latimer (Rev. W. T.). Newry Printing, with a List. (*Ulster Journ. of Archæol.*, vol. vii. pp. 175–176. 1901.) This is additional to Crossle.

——— **Ulster Bibliography. Downpatrick Printing, with a List, 1754–1800.** (*Ibid.* vol. vii. pp. 172–173. 1901.)

——— **Hillsborough Printing, with a List, 1786–1800.** (*Ibid.* vol. vii. 173–174. 1901.)

Lett (Canon H. W.). Maps of the Mountains of Mourne. (*Ibid.* vol. viii. pp. 133–137. 1902.)

Hist. MSS. Comm. Report. Down Collection.

Lord de Ros ... ... 4th Rep. p. xiv. and App. 317–325.

Christy (Miller). Biblio. Note on Down Birds. (*The Zoologist*, Ser. 3, vol. xiv. p. 267. 1890; and reprinted in pamph., 1891, p. 41.) **Mammals.** (*The Zoologist*, Ser. 3, vol. xvii. p. 215. 1893.) **Reptiles.** (*Ibid.* p. 251. 1893.) **Fishes.** (*Ibid.* p. 263. 1893.)

Anderson (John P.). Book of Brit. Topo., 1881. Down, p. 431.

Gough (Richard). Brit. Topo., 1780. Down, vol. ii. pp. 791-792.

Bandinel (Bulkeley). Catal. of Books bequeathed to Bodleian Lib. by Richard Gough, 1814. Down, p. 377.

DUBLIN.

Gilbert (Sir John T.) and **Gilbert (Rosa Mulholland, Lady). Calendar of Ancient Records of Dublin in the Possession of the Municipal Corporation of that City.** Vols. i.–xvi. Dublin, 1889–1913.

Dix (Ernest Reginald McClintock). The Earliest Dublin Printing, with List of Books, Proclamations, etc., printed in Dublin prior to 1601. (1551-1600.) Dublin, 1901.

——— **List of Books, Tracts, Broadsides, etc., printed in Dublin in the 17th Century, 1601-1700,** with Introduction and Notes by C. W. Dugan. 4 parts. Dublin, 1898-1905. **Supplement of Additions.** Dublin, 1912.

——— **Catal. of Early Dublin Printed Books belonging to E. R. McC. Dix.** Second Edition. 1900.

——— **The Earliest Dublin Printers and the Company of Stationers of London.** (*Biblio. Soc. Trans.*, vol. vii. pp. 75–85. 1904.)

——— **Humfrey Powell, the First Dublin Printer.** (*Royal Irish Acad. Proc.*, vol. xxvii. sect. C. pp. 213–216. 1908.)

——— **Early Printing in Dublin. John Francton; an early Dublin Printer and his Works.** (*New Ireland Rev.*, vol. ix. pp. 36–42. 1898.)

——— **The Ornaments used by John Francton, Printer, at Dublin.** (*Biblio. Soc. Trans.*, vol. viii. pp. 221–227. 1907.)

——— **Initial Letters used by John Francton, Printer at Dublin.** (*The Irish Book Lover*, vol. iii. p. 59. 1911.)

——— **The Earliest Printing in Dublin, in the Irish, Latin, Greek, Hebrew, French, Italian, Saxon, Welsh, Syriac, Armenian, and Arabic Languages.** (*Royal Irish Acad. Proc.*, vol. xxviii. sect. C. pp. 149–156. 1910.)

DUBLIN (continued).

Dix (Ernest Reginald McClintock). William Kearney, the Second Earliest known Printer in Dublin. (*Royal Irish Acad. Proc.*, vol. xxviii. sect. C. pp. 157–161. 1910.)

—— **Note upon the leaves of the First Book printed in Dublin discovered in the Academy.** (*Royal Irish Acad. Proc.*, vol. xxvii. sect. C. pp. 404–406. 1909.)

—— **The First Printing of the New Testament in English at Dublin.** (*Royal Irish Acad. Proc.*, vol. xxix. sect. C. pp. 180–185. 1911.)

—— **A Dublin Almanack of 1612.** (*Royal Irish Acad. Proc.*, vol. xxx. sect. C. pp. 327–330. 1913.)

—— **The Earliest Periodical Journals published in Dublin.** (*Royal Irish Acad. Proc.*, vol. xxii. pp. 33–35. 1900.)

—— **Rare Ephemeral (Dublin) Magazines of the Eighteenth Century.** (*The Irish Book Lover*, vol. i. pp. 71–73. 1910.)

—— **Eighteenth Century (Dublin) Newspapers.** (*The Irish Book Lover*, vol. i. pp. 39–41. 1909.)

—— **Tables relating to some Dublin Newspapers of the 18th Century,** shewing what volumes, etc., of each are extant, and where access to them can be had in Dublin. 1910.

Plomer (Henry R.). John Francton and his Successors, with additional Note by A. G. (*The Irish Book Lover*, vol. iii. pp. 109–112. 1912.)

Folds (G.). Specimen of National Typography, exhibiting the execution of the Press of Ireland. Dublin, 1833.

Conmey (P. J.). An Old Dublin Printing Office. (G. Folds, afterwards G. Drought's). Dublin, 1898.

Flood (W. H. Grattan). Music-Printing in Dublin from 1700 to 1750. (*Soc. Antiq. Irel. Journ.*, vol. xxxviii. pp. 236–240. 1908.)

McCready (C. T.). Dublin Bibliography; historical and topographical. Dublin, 1892.

Brindley (L. H.). A Study of some Old (Dublin) Newspapers. (*New Ireland Rev.*, vol. xvi. pp. 110–121. 1901.)

Power (John). List of Irish Periodical Publications (chiefly Literary) from 1729 to the Present Time. 1866.

A List of Books and Pamphlets written by the Members of the National Literary Society, Dublin. (*Nat. Lit. Soc. Journ.*, vol. i. pp. 112–132. 1900.)

Wilde (Sir W. R. W.). A Descriptive Catal. of the Antiquities, etc., in the Museum of the Royal Irish Academy, illustrated. 2 pts. Dublin, 1857–61.

Murray (David). 'Museums.' Glasgow, 1904. Biblio. Note on Dublin Museums, vol. ii. pp. 217–219.

Ryan (Michael J.). Some Notes on the Libraries and Book Trade of Dublin. (*Book-Auction Records*, vol. iv. pt. 4, pp. xlv.–xlix. 1907.)

Cosgrave (E. MacDowel). A Contribution towards a Catal. of Engravings of Dublin up to 1800. (*Soc. Antiq. Irel. Journ.*, vol. xxxv. pp. 95–109, 363–376. 1905.)

—— **A Contribution towards a Catal. of Nineteenth-Century Engravings of Dublin.** (*Soc. Antiq. Irel. Journ.*, vol. xxxvi. pp. 400-419; vol. xxxvii. pp. 41-60. 1906–07.)

Seymour (Rev. St. John). Old Dublin Caricatures. (*Soc. Antiq. Irel. Journ.*, vol. xxxvii. pp. 69-73. 1907.

DUBLIN (*continued*).

Hist. MSS. Comm. Reports.	**Dublin Collections.**
Bayly, Mr. J. W., at Finglas	1st Rep. p. xii. and App. p. 128.
Charlemont, Earl of (MSS. in possession of Roy. Irish Acad.)	1st Rep. p. xii. and App. pp. 126, 127; 12th Rep. p. 52 and App. X.; 13th Rep. p. 56 and App. VIII.
Lyons, Dr. R. D., of Dublin (Archbishop King's Collection)	1st Rep. p. xiii.; 2nd Rep. p. xxi. and App. pp. 231-257.
Talbot de Malahide, Lord, at Malahide Castle	1st Rep. p. xii. and App. p. 128; 8th Rep. p. xviii. and App. pp. 493-499.
Dublin, Corporation of	1st Rep. App. p. 129.
——— Royal Irish Academy	13th Rep. p. 56; 15th Rep. p. 45 and App. III. pp. 1-296.
——— Trinity College	4th Rep. p. xxiv. and App. pp. 588-599; 8th Rep. p. xix. and App. pp. 572-624.
——— See of	10th Rep. p. 43 and App. V. pp. 204-219.
——— College of Irish Franciscans ...	4th Rep. p. xxiv. and App. pp. 599-613.
——— Franciscan Convent, Merchants' Quay	17th Rep. pp. 153-159; and a vol. 1906.
——— Jesuits' Archives	10th Rep. p. 44 and App. V. pp. 340-379.

Abbott (T. K.). Catal. of the MSS. in the Library of Trinity Coll., Dublin, to which is added, a List of the Fagel Collection of Maps in the same Library. Dublin, 1900.

Hardiman (James). A Catal. of Maps, Charts, Plans, etc., in the Library of Trinity College. (*Royal Irish Acad. Trans.*, vol. xiv. pt. 2, pp. 57-77. 1825.)

The Franciscans and their Library. (Merchants' Quay, Dublin.) By O. O'B. (*The Irish Book Lover*, vol. iv. pp. 3-5, 21-24. 1912.) See also *ante* Hist. MSS. Comm. Reports. A systematic Inventory of the MSS. in the Library is being completed by Father O'Reilly.

Kelly (Denis H.). MS. Catal. of the Irish Historical MSS. in Marsh's Library, Dublin. 1864. See Auction Sale Catal. of D. H. Kelly. 1875.

Scott (John Russell). Catal. of the MSS. remaining in Marsh's Library, Dublin, edited by Newport J. D. White. 1913.

Duff (E. Gordon). Notes on a Visit to Archbishop Marsh's Library, Dublin. (*Edinb. Biblio. Soc. Pubns.*, vol. vi. pp. 133-140. 1906.)

Special Collections containing Books, MSS., etc., relating to Dublin, are in the Library of the late Sir John Gilbert at the Public Library, North Strand; in the Library of the Royal Irish Academy; in the National Library of Ireland; and in the Library of Trinity College.

Bernard (J. H.). Calendar of Documents contained in the cartulary commonly called '*Dignitas Decani*' of St. Patrick's Cathedral. (*Royal Irish Acad. Proc.*, vol. xxv. sect. C. pp. 481-507. 1905.)

Berry (Henry F.). Existing Records and Properties of the old Dublin City Guilds. (*Soc. Antiq. Irel. Journ.*, vol. xxxv. pp. 338-341. 1905.)

Christy (Miller). Biblio. Note on Dublin Birds. (*The Zoologist*, Ser. 3, vol. xiv. p. 267, 1890; and reprinted in pamph. 1891, p. 41.) **Mammals.** (*The Zoologist*, Ser. 3, vol. xvii. p. 216. 1893.) **Fishes.** (*Ibid.* p. 263. 1893.)

Anderson (John P.). Book of Brit. Topo., 1881. Dublin, pp. 431-434.

Gough (Richard). Brit. Topo., 1780. Dublin, vol. ii. pp. 793-801.

Bandinel (Bulkeley). Catal. of Books bequeathed to Bodleian Lib. by Richard Gough, 1814. Dublin, pp. 378-380.

DUMBARTONSHIRE.

Hist. MSS. Comm. Report. Dumbartonshire Collection. Hamilton, Miss, at Barns and Cochno 8th Rep. p. xvii. and App. pp. 308–310.

Livingstone (Matthew). Guide to the Public Records of Scotland. 1905. Dumbartonshire, p. 173.

Turnbull (William B.). Scottish Parochial Registers. 1849. List of Dumbartonshire Registers, pp. 42–45.

Anderson (John P.). Book of Brit. Topo., 1881. Dumbartonshire, p. 384.

Bandinel (Bulkeley). Catal. of Books bequeathed to Bodleian Library by Richard Gough. 1814. Dumbartonshire, p. 356.

Lyell (Arthur H.). Biblio. List of Romano-British Remains. 1912. Dumbartonshire, pp. 137–138.

Trimen (Henry). Botanical Biblio. of the British Counties. Dumbartonshire. (*Jour. of Botany*, vol. xii. p. 237. 1874.)

Christy (Miller). Biblio. Note on Dumbartonshire Mammals. (*The Zoologist*, Ser. 3, vol. xvii. p. 210. 1893.)

A Special Local Collection is at the Dumbarton Free Public Library.

DUMFRIESSHIRE.

Maxwell (Sir Herbert). Hist. of Dumfries and Galloway. The County Histories of Scotland, 1896. List of Books relating to Dumfries and Galloway. pp. 363–399 ; List of Principal Maps, pp. 400–401.

Hist. MSS. Comm. Reports. Dumfriesshire Collections.

Buccleuch and Queensberry, Duke of, at Drumlanrig Castle	15th Rep. pp. 43, 44 and App. VIII. ; 16th Rep. pp. 117–122 and vol. ii. 1903.
Hope-Johnstone, Mr. J. J., at Raehills House	15th Rep. p. 45 and App. IX.

Livingstone (Matthew). Guide to the Public Records of Scotland. 1905. Dumfriesshire, pp. 114, 175.

Turnbull (William B.). Scottish Parochial Registers. 1849. List of Dumfriesshire Registers, pp. 45–51.

Gladstone (Hugh S.). The Hist. of the Dumfriesshire & Galloway Nat. Hist. & Antiq. Soc., 1862-1912. (*Transactions*, Third Ser., vol. i. pp. 15–39. 1913.)

Collections of the Dumfriesshire Nat. Hist. & Antiq. Soc. described. (*Soc. Antiq. Scot. Proc.*, vol. xxii. p. 412. 1888.)

Shirley (G. W.). Old Public Libraries in Dumfries. (*Dumfriesshire & Galloway Nat. Hist. & Antiq. Soc. Trans.*, vol. xviii. pp. 39–44 ; vol. xix. p. 176. 1906, 1908.)

Cairns (Rev. James). Some Old Documents relating to Dumfries. (*Dumfriesshire & Galloway Nat. Hist. & Antiq. Soc. Trans.*, vol. ix. pp. 99–107. 1894.)

Stewart (William). The Rae Press at Kirkbride and Dumfries, with a Hand List. (*Edinb. Biblio. Soc. Pubns.*, vol. vi. pp. 107–115. 1906.)

Shirley (G. W.). Mr. Peter Rae, Printer, with a Biblio. of issues from the Rae Press at Kirkbride and Dumfries. (*Glasgow Biblio. Soc. Records*, vol. i. pp. 216–235. 1914.)

Lyell (Arthur H.). Biblio. List of Romano-British Remains. 1912. Dumfriesshire, p. 138.)

DUMFRIESSHIRE (continued).

Trimen (Henry). Botanical Biblio. of the British Counties. Dumfriesshire. (*Jour. of Botany*, vol. xii. p. 234. 1874.)

Gladstone (Hugh S.). The Birds of Dumfriesshire. 1910. Biblio., pp. xlix.–lxiii.

Christy (Miller). Biblio. Note on Dumfriesshire Birds. (*The Zoologist*, Ser. 3, vol. xiv. p. 263, 1890; and reprinted in pamph., 1891, p. 32.)

A Special Dumfries Collection is at the Dumfries Museum.

Anderson (John P.). Book of Brit. Topo., 1881. Dumfriesshire, p. 385.

Bandinel (Bulkeley). Catal. of Books bequeathed to Bodleian Lib. by Richard Gough, 1814. Dumfriesshire, p. 357.

ANNAN.

Burgh Records, 1538, etc., at Town Hall, Annan. (*Local Records Comm. Rep.*, 1902, App. III. p. 88.)

Miller (Frank). Annan: Its Historical and Literary Associations. (*Dumfriesshire & Galloway Nat. Hist. & Antiq. Soc. Trans.*, vol. vi. pp. 240–246. 1890.)

LOCHMABEN.

Burgh Records, 1770, etc., at Lochmaben. (*Local Records Comm. Rep.*, 1902, App. III. p. 96.)

THORNHILL.

Murray (David). 'Museums.' Glasgow. 1904. Biblio. Note on Thornhill Museum, vol. iii. p. 211.)

DURHAM.

An Address to the Public, relative to the compiling a complete Civil and Ecclesiastical Hist. of the County of Durham. [By G. Allan.] Darlington, 1774.

Thompson (Henry). A Reference Catal. of Books relating to the Counties of Durham and Northumberland; Historical and Topographical. Pt. 1. Newcastle-on-Tyne, 1888.

Lapsley (G. T.). The County Palatine of Durham. (*Harvard Hist. Studies*, vol. viii. 1900.) Appendix III.—The Records of the Palatinate, pp. 327–337. Appendix IV.—Bibliography, pp. 338–346.

Taylor (George). A Memoir of Robert Surtees in his '*Hist. & Antiquities of the County Palatine of Durham*,' vol. iv. pp. 1–98. 1840.

——— New Edition, with additions, by Rev. James Raine. Surtees Society. 1852.

Denham (M. A.). A Classified Catal. of the Antiquarian Tomes, Tracts, and Trifles. 1859.

Catal. of the Library of the Literary and Philos. Soc. of Newcastle-upon-Tyne. 1903. List of Local Collection relating to the County of Durham, pp. 616–628.

Catal. of the Library of the Soc. of Antiq. of Newcastle-upon-Tyne, inclusive of the MSS. Prints, Maps, etc. Contains many Durham items. 1896.

Catal. of Books and Tracts on Genealogy and Heraldry in the Central Public Libraries, Newcastle-on-Tyne. By Basil Anderson. 1910. Contains many Durham items.

Fawcett (J. W.). Some Contributions to a Biblio. of Durham. (*Sunderland Pub. Lib. Circular.* July, 1905, etc.)

Faber (R. S.). Some Durham Book-Lovers. (*Biblio. Soc. Trans.*, vol. viii. pp. 77–83. 1907.)

DURHAM (*continued*).

Catal. of the MS. Library of Sir Cuthbert Sharp connected with the County of Durham. Privately Printed, 1829.

A List of Durham (County) Booksellers. (*Notes & Queries*, Ser. 10, vol. vi. p. 443. 1906.)

A List of Private Acts relating to the County of Durham. 1913. London: Stevens & Sons.

Murray (David). 'Museums.' Glasgow, 1904. Biblio. Note on Museum in Durham Cathedral Library, vol. ii. p. 221.

Botfield (B.). Catalogues of the Library of Durham Cathedral at various periods, from the Conquest to the Dissolution. (Surtees Society, vol. vii. 1838.)

List of Reprinted Rare Tracts chiefly illustrative of the History of the Northern Counties. 4 vols. Newcastle, 1843. See Lowndes (W. T.) '*Bibliographer's Manual*,' 1871, App. pp. 271–275.

Dibdin (Rev. T. F.). Books at Durham. (*Northern Tour*, 1838, vol. i. pp. 286–291.)

——— **Account of George Allan's Press.** (*Biblio. Decameron*, 1817, vol. iii. p. 452.)

Martin (John). The Darlington Press, with illustration. (*Biblio. Catal. of Books Privately Printed*, 1834, vol. ii. pp. 317–346.)

Lowndes (Wm. Thomas). List of Publications of the Darlington Press of George Allan. (*Bibliographer's Manual*, 1871, App. pp. 200–216.)

Brockett (J. T.). A Catal. of Books and Tracts printed at the private press of George Allan of Darlington. Newcastle, 1818.

Darlington Private Press. Collectanea, etc. (of this curious Collection of the productions of George Allan's Private Press. 1774–79.

Allan (Robert Henry). The Life of the late George Allan, Esq., F.S.A., to which is added a Catal. of Books and Tracts printed at his Private Press at Blackwell Grange, in the County of Durham. Sunderland, 1829.

Gross (Charles). Biblio. of Brit. Municipal Hist. (*Harvard Hist. Studies*, vol. v. 1897.) Durham County, pp. 94–95. Sunderland, pp. 401–402.

Davenport (Frances G.). List of Printed Materials for Manorial Hist. 1894. Biblio. Note on Durham Manorial Hist., pp. 41–44.

Dove (Patrick Edward). Domesday Studies. 1891. Domesday Biblio. Durham, vol. ii. p. 676.

Lyell (Arthur H.). Biblio. List of Romano-British Remains. 1912. Durham, pp. 21–22.

Macklin (Herbert Walter). Monumental Brasses. London: Geo. Allen & Co., 1913. Biblio. Note on Durham Brasses, with a List, p. 153.

Special Collection of Local Literature at Sunderland Public Library, and a Collection of Durham Books at the West Hartlepool Public Library.

Hist. MSS. Comm. Report. Durham Collection.

Ushaw, College of St. Cuthbert ... 1st Rep. p. xi. and App. p. 91.

County Records, etc., 1616, etc., with MS. Lists, at Durham. (*Local Records Comm. Rep.*, 1902, App. III. p. 16.)

List of Records of the Palatinates of Chester, Durham, and Lancaster, etc., preserved in the Public Record Office. (*Public Record Office. Lists & Indexes*, No. xl. 1914.)

Durham Cathedral Records, 7th Cent., etc., with MS. Indexes, at Durham. (*Local Records Comm. Rep.*, 1902, App. III., p. 108.)

The Allan MSS. in Durham Cathedral Library contain a valuable Collection of Papers relating to the County of Durham.

DURHAM (continued).

A Collection of Deeds relating to Northumberland and Durham, formerly belonging to Mr. James Coleman, are now in the Central Public Libraries at Newcastle-upon-Tyne.

Brown (William). Deeds from Burton Agnes, relating to the Counties of Durham and Northumberland. (*Archæol. Aeliana*, Ser. 3, vol. vii. pp. 29-48. 1911.)

Durham Records. Indexes to Persons and Places mentioned in Kellawe's Register. (30th Ann. Rep. Dep. Keeper of Public Records, pp. 99-120. 1869.)

Welford (Richard). Records of the Committees for Compounding, etc., with Delinquent Royalists in Durham and Northumberland during the Civil War, 1643 60. Bibliography, pp. 460-461. Surtees Society Pubns., vol. cxi. 1905.

Wood (H. M.). List of Parochial and Non-Parochial Registers relating to the Counties of Durham and Northumberland. Durham & Northumb. Par. Reg. Soc., No. 26. 1912.

Trimen (Henry). Botanical Biblio. of the British Counties. Durham. (*Jour. of Botany*, vol. xii. p. 181. 1874.)

Christy (Miller). Biblio. Note on Durham Birds. (*The Zoologist*, Ser. 3, vol. xiv. p. 252, 1890; and reprinted in pamph., 1891, p. 12.) **Mammals.** (*The Zoologist*, Ser. 3, vol. xvii. p. 179. 1893.) **Reptiles.** (*Ibid.* p. 243. 1893.) **Fishes.** (*Ibid.* p. 254. 1893.)

Anderson (John P.). Book of Brit. Topo., 1881. Durham, pp. 97-101.

Gatfield (George). Guide to Heraldry. 1892. Durham, pp. 135-136.

Sims (Richard). Manual for the Genealogist. 1861. Durham, pp. 165, 205, 233.

Upcott (William). English Topo., 1818. Durham, vol. i. pp. 201-222, 609-614.

Smith (Alfred Russell). Catal. of Topo. Tracts, etc. 1878. Durham, pp. 77-84, 461.

Gough (Richard). Brit. Topo., 1780. Durham, vol. i. pp. 329-342.

Bandinel (Bulkeley). Catal. of Books bequeathed to Bodleian Lib. by Richard Gough. 1814. Durham, pp. 109-112.

AUCKLAND.

Archdeaconry of Auckland. Ecclesiastical Records, 1567, etc., at Bishop Wearmouth. (*Local Records Comm. Rep.*, 1902, App. III. p. 118.)

DARLINGTON.

For the Private Printing Press of George Allan at Blackwell Grange, see *supra*.

GAINFORD.

Index to the First Volume of the Parish Registers of Gainford, 1560-1784. Parts 1-3. 1889-90.

HARTLEPOOL.

Borough Records, 1592, etc., at Town Hall, Hartlepool. (*Local Records Comm. Rep.*, 1902, App. III. p. 58.

SOUTH SHIELDS.

Borough Records, 1830, etc., with MS. Index. (*Local Records Comm. Rep.*, 1902, App. III. p. 40.)

SUNDERLAND.

Wood (H. M.). Family Notices from the 'Newcastle Courant,' 1745-1800, relating to Sunderland and District. (Sunderland Antiq. Soc. *Antiq. of Sunderland*, vol. xiii. 1913.)

Murray (David). 'Museums.' Glasgow, 1904. Biblio. Note on Museum at Sunderland, vol. iii. p. 201.

EDINBURGHSHIRE.

Aldis (**Harry G.**). **A List of Books printed in Scotland before 1700,** including those printed furth of the Realm for Scottish Booksellers; with brief notes on the Printers and Stationers. (*Edinb. Biblio. Soc. Pubns.*, vol. vii. 1904.) List of Printers, Booksellers, and Stationers, pp. 105–124.

Scott (James W.). A Biblio. of Edinburgh Periodical Literature. (*Scottish Notes & Queries*, vols. v.-ix. 1891–96.)

Couper (W. J.). The Edinburgh Periodical Press, being a Biblio. Account of the Newspapers, Journals, and Magazines issued in Edinburgh from the earliest times to 1800, with copious indices, etc. 2 vols. 1908.

——— **A Biblio. of Edinburgh Periodical Literature.** (*Scottish Notes & Queries*, Ser. 2, vols. ii.-viii. 1901-07.) Based on the MS. Collections of J. W. Scott.

Norrie (William). Edinburgh Newspapers, Past and Present. 1891.

Grant (**James**). **Edinburgh Past and Present Newspapers.** (*The Newspaper Press*, 1872.)

The Edinburgh Newspapers. (*Fraser's Mag.*, vol. xvii. pp. 559–571. 1838.)

General Index and Index of Illustrations to the Proceedings of the Soc. of Antiquaries of Scotland. Vol. i.-xxiv. 1851-90. Edinb., 1892.

Watson (Charles B. B.). Notes on the Early Hist. of the Soc. of Antiq. of Scotland, etc. (*Soc. of Antiq. Scot. Proc.*, vol. xlv. pp. 250–264. 1911.)

Catal. of the Printed Books in the Library of the Society of Writers to H.M. Signet in Scotland, with Supplement and List of MSS. 2 vols. 1871, 1882.

——— A Second Supplement, 1882–87, with a Subject-Index to the whole Catal. 1891.

Dickson (**W. K.**). **The Signet Library.** (*Booklovers' Mag.*, vol. vi. pp. 1–13. 1907.)

Burton (John Hill). The Book Hunter, etc., with Memoir of the Author by his Widow. New Edn., 1882. For Edinburgh Book Clubs, see Pt. III., pp. 243–310; and Book-Club Literature, Pt. IV., pp. 311–417.

Literary and Philosophical Societies of Edinburgh during the Nineteenth Century. (*Eclectic Mag.*, New York, vol. xxiv. pp. 565–570. 1851.) Reprinted from '*Hogg's Instructor*.'

Hutton (**Laurence**). **The Literary Landmarks of Edinburgh.** (*Harper's New Monthly Mag.*, New York, vol. lxxxii. pp. 609–633. 1891.)

Millar (**J. H.**). **Edinburgh in Literature.** (*Bookman*, London, vol. xxxi. pp. 247–251. 1907.)

Johnston (Geo. P.). The First Edition of Hume of Godscroft's History, printed by Evan Tyler, with list of MSS. and Printed Editions. (*Edinb. Biblio. Soc. Pubns.*, vol. iv. pp. 149–171. 1900–01.)

Napier (**John**). b. at Merchiston, near Edinburgh, 1550; died 4 Apr. 1617. **Biblio. of the Various Editions of Napier's Works,** by William Rae Macdonald in '*The Construction of the Wonderful Canon of Logarithms*, pp. 101–169. Edinb. and Lond., 1889.

Riddell Papers: a Catal. of the Annotated Books and MSS. of the late John Riddell, Advocate. Ed. by James Maidment. 1863.

Stevenson (T. G.). Biblio. List of the various Pubns., by James Maidment, from 1817 to 1859. 1859.

The Biblio. of James Maidment, Esq., Advocate, Edinb., from 1817 to 1878, with Notices of the Sale of his Library. 1883.

EDINBURGHSHIRE (*continued*).

Dibdin (Rev. T. F.). Edinburgh Libraries and Printing. (*Northern Tour*, 1838, vol. ii. pp. 591–644.)

Scottish Univ. Libraries. Lists of Printed Catalogues. Edinburgh (*Aberdeen Univ. Lib. Bull.*, vol. i. pp. 403–404. 1912.)

Lists of Fifteenth Century Books in Edinburgh Libraries.

University Library. By F. C. Nicholson.
Advocates' Library. By W. K. Dickson and Miss J. M. G. Barclay.
Signet Library. By John Philip Edmond.
U.F. Church College Library. By W. Cowan.
The Crawford Library, Royal Observatory. By G. P. Johnston.
Library of the Royal Coll. of Physicians. By T. H. Graham.
St. Mary's Cathedral Library.
The Scottish Episcopal Church Theological Hall.
The Forbes Library in the Theological Hall.
The Library of the Church of Scotland.
The Public Library.

(*Edinb. Biblio. Soc. Pubns.*, vol. ix. pp. 93–199. 1912–13.) Also published separately. A review by J. C. Ewing appeared in '*The Scottish Hist. Review*,' vol. xi. pp. 297–298. 1914.

Dickson (W. K.). The Printed Catalogues of the Advocates' Library. (*Edinb. Biblio. Soc. Pubns.*, vol. ix. pp. 51–55. 1913.)

—— **The Advocates' Library.** (*Juridical Rev.*, vol. xiv. pp. 1–16, 113–128, 214–227. 1902.)

Smail (Adam). The Edinburgh Circulating Library. A historical retrospect. (*The Scots Mag.*, New Ser., vol. xxiv. pp. 382–386. 1899.)

—— **The Edinburgh Circulating Library and its Contents in 1781.** (*Ibid.* New Ser., vol. xxv. pp. 55–58. 1900.)

Dickson (Robert) and **Edmond (John Philip). Annals of Scottish Printing** from the Introduction of the Art in 1507 to the beginning of the Seventeenth Century. Cambridge, 1890.

Edmond (John Philip). Biblio. Gleanings, 1890–93: being additions and corrections to the 'Annals of Scottish Printing.' (*Edinb. Biblio. Soc. Pubns.*, vol. i, No. 17. 1893–94.)

Dickson (Robert). Introduction of Printing into Scotland. Aberdeen, 1885. (Contains valuable information about Edinburgh Printing.)

—— **Early Scottish Typography**; a series of articles. (*The Printer's Register*, 1876–78.)

—— **Who was Scotland's First Printer?** London, 1881.

Smail (Adam). Some Notes on Scottish Printing and the Libraries and Book Trade of Edinburgh. (*Book-Auction Records*, vol. v. Pt. I. pp. i.–v. 1907.)

Cowan (William). Andro Hart and his Press, with handlist of Books. (*Edinb. Biblio. Soc. Pubns.*, vol. i. No. 12. 1892–93.)

Aldis (Harry G.). Thomas Finlason and his Press, with a handlist of Books. (*Edinb. Biblio. Soc. Pubns.*, vol. i. No. 20. 1893–94.)

Axon (William E. A.). On an unrecorded issue of the Aberdeen Press of Edward Raban in 1627. With a handlist of the production of his Presses at Edinburgh, etc. (*Soc. of Antiq., Scot. Proc.*, vol. xliii. pp. 24–33. 1909.)

Gibb (John S.). James Watson, Printer: Notes on his Life and Work, with a handlist of Books and Pamphlets printed by him, 1697–1722. (*Edinb. Biblio. Soc. Pubns.*, vol. i. No. 1. 1890–91.)

EDINBURGHSHIRE (*continued*).

Tawse (George). James Watson, the Edinburgh Printer. (*The Bibliographer*, vol. ii. pp. 124–130. 1882.)

Couper (W. J.). James Watson, King's Printer, 1664-1722. Privately Printed. Glasgow, 1910. Reprinted from '*The Scottish Hist. Review*,' vol. vii. pp. 244–262. 1910.

——— **Watson's Preface to the 'History of Printing,' 1713,** with Introduction and Notes. Edinburgh, Darien Press. Reprinted from '*The Library*,' Ser. 3, vol. i. pp. 424–436. 1910.

——— **Scottish Rebel Printers.** Edinb. 1912. Privately Printed.

Collection of the Wills of Printers & Booksellers in Edinburgh between the years 1577 & 1687. (*Bannatyne Miscellany*, vol. ii. pp. 185–296. 1836.)

Edmond (John Philip). Notes on the Inventories of Edinburgh Printers, 1577–1603. (*Edinb. Biblio. Soc. Pubns.*, vol. i. No. 15, 1892–3.)

Inventory of Worke done for the State by His Majesty's Printer (Evan Tyler) in Scotland, 1642-47. Edinb. 1815.

Dobson (W. T.). Hist. of the Bassandyne Bible, the first printed in Scotland, with Notices of the Early Printers in Edinburgh. Edinb. 1887.

Cowan (William). The Holyrood Press, 1686-88, with a Bibliography. (*Edinb. Biblio. Soc. Pubns.* vol. vi. pp. 83–100. 1904.)

Dobson (W. T.) and **Carrie (W. L.). The Ballantyne Press and its Founders, 1796-1908,** with a Biblio. Edinb. 1909. See also the '*Scotsman*,' 15th Sept. 1886.

The Hist. of the Ballantyne Press & its connection with Sir Walter Scott, issued at the Centenary of Sir Walter Scott in 1871.

Johnston (George P.). The First Book printed by James Ballantyne: being '*An Apology for Tales of Terror*,' etc. (*Edinb. Biblio. Soc. Pubns.*, vol. i. No. 19. 1893–94.) Note to a Paper entitled '*The First Book printed by James Ballantyne.*' (*Ibid.* vol. ix. p. 90. 1913.)

Constable (Thomas). Archibald Constable & his Literary Correspondents. 1873. Edinburgh Booksellers of the End of the 18th Century, vol. i. pp. 1–33. Edinburgh Booksellers of the Period, vol. i. App. pp. 533–540.

Macleod (R. D.). The Early Scottish Typefounders. Scottish Library Assoc., 12 May, 1909.

Thin (James). Reminiscences of Booksellers & Bookselling in Edinb. in time of William IV. Privately Printed, 1905.

Nichols (John). List of Scottish Booksellers & of Scottish Book Auctions. (*Literary Anecdotes*, vol. iii. pp. 689–693. 1812.)

Edinburgh Booksellers. Petition for the free exercise of the trade of Printing. To the Right Honourable the Lords of His Majesties Most Honourable Privy Council, the Petition of the Book-sellers of Edinburgh, for Themselves, and the Rest of the Booksellers of the Kingdom. Edinb. 1696 (?) s. sh. fol.

Cowan (William). The Biblio. of the Book of Common Order. (*Edinb. Biblio. Soc. Pubns.*, vol. i. No. 3. 1890–91.)

——— **A Biblio. of the Book of Common Order & Psalm Book of the Church of Scotland, 1556-1644.** (*Edinb. Biblio. Soc. Pubns.*, vol. x. pp. 53–100. 1913.) A review by J. C. Ewing appeared in '*The Scottish Hist. Review*,' vol. xi. pp. 297, 298. 1914.

Lee (John), D.D. Memorial for the Bible Societies in Scotland, containing Remarks on the Complaint of his Majesty's Printer against the Marquess of Huntly & others. With Appendix of Original Papers. Edinb. 1824.

EDINBURGHSHIRE (continued).

Hist. MSS. Comm. Reports. Edinburghshire Collections.

Dalrymple, Mr. Charles, at Newhailes	4th Rep. p. xxii. and App. pp. 529–533.
Dundas, Mr. Robert, at Arniston, Gorebridge	3rd Rep. p. xxiv. and App. pp. 414–416.
Elphinstone, Lord, at Carberry Tower, Musselburgh	9th Rep. p. xviii. and App. II. pp. 182–229.
Jamieson, Mr. G. Auldjo (Breadalbane MSS.)	4th Rep. p. xxii. and App. pp. 511–514.
Lothian, Marquess of, at Newbattle ...	1st Rep. pp. x., xii. and App. pp. 14, 116; 17th Rep. pp. 45–51; and a vol. 1905.
Morton, Earl of, at Dalmahoy	2nd Rep. p. xviii. and App. pp. 183–185.
Stair, Earl of, at Oxenfoord, Dalkeith	2nd Rep. p. viii. and App. pp. 188–191.
Torpichen, Lord, at Calder House ...	2nd Rep. p. xix. and App. p. 196.
Wauchope, Mr. Andrew, at Niddrie, Merchell	4th Rep. p. xxiii. and App. pp. 537, 538.
Edinburgh, City of	1st Rep. App. p. 126.
——— University of (MSS. in the Library)	1st Rep. p. xii. and App. p. 121.
——— Advocates' Library	1st Rep. App. pp. 123–125.
——— Library of the Roman Catholic Bishop	1st Rep. p. xii. and App. p. 120.

Burgh Records, 1143, etc., with Printed Index, at Municipal Buildings, Edinburgh. (*Local Records Comm. Rep.*, 1902, App. III. p. 92.)

Anderson (John). Calendar of the Laing Charters, 854-1837. Edinburgh, 1899.

Stevenson (T. G.). Notices of David Laing, with chronological list of publications issued under his editorial superintendance, from 1815 to 1878. Edinb. 1878. See also Catal. of Lib. of D. Laing, 3 pts. 1879–80.

List of Manuscript Books & Miscellaneous Papers in the Collection of D. Laing. 1888 (?).

Goudie (Gilbert). David Laing, LL.D. A Memoir of his Life & Literary Work. Printed for Private Circulation. 1913. Biblio. pp. 152–234.

Murray (David). David Laing, Antiquary & Bibliographer. (*Scottish Hist. Rev.*, vol. xi. pp. 345–369. 1914.)

Drummond (William). A Brief Account of the Hawthornden MSS. in possession of the Soc. of Antiquaries, etc. By David Laing. 1831–32.

——— **Auctarium Bibliothecæ Edinburgenæ sive Catalogus Librorum quos Guilielmus Drummondus** ab Hawthornden Bibliothecæ D. D. Q., Anno 1627. Edin. hæredes And. Hart, 1627. Reprinted, 1815.

Turnbull (W. B. D. D.). Catal. of MSS. relating to Genealogy & Heraldry preserved in the Library of the Faculty of Advocates at Edinburgh. London, 1852.

Nichols (John Gough). Notice of the late W. B. D. D. Turnbull, with an Account of his Literary Labours. 1864.

Livingstone (Matthew). Guide to the Public Records of Scotland. 1905. Edinburghshire, pp. 109, 175, 204.

Turnbull (William B.). Scottish Parochial Registers. 1849. List of Edinburghshire Registers, pp. 52-60, 160.

Gross (Charles). Biblio. of Brit. Municipal Hist. (*Harvard Hist. Studies*, vol. v. 1897.) Edinburghshire, pp. 223–230.

Thomson (Thomas). List of the Protocol Books of the City of Edinburgh, with extracts. (*Soc. of Antiq. Scot. Proc.*, vol. v. pp. 141-164. 1865.)

EDINBURGHSHIRE (continued).

——— **List of the Protocol Books,** with some notice of the other Records of the Borough of Canongate and Regality and Barony of Brochton, Edinburgh, with extracts. (*Soc. of Antiq. Scot. Proc.*, vol. ii. pp. 354–368. 1859.)

Laing (David). A Note on the Subject of Protocol Books as connected with Public Records. (*Soc. of Antiq. Scot. Proc.*, vol. ii. pp. 350–353. 1859.)

——— **Preface to the Breviarium Aberdonense** (printed at Edinburgh in 1509–10 by Walter Chapman). Appeared separately, 1855.

——— **Inventory of the Original Documents in the Archives of George Heriot's Hospital, Edinburgh.** Printed for the Governors. 1857.

Way (Albert). Catal. of Antiquities, Works of Art, and Historical Scottish Relics exhibited during the Meeting of the Archæol. Institute at Edinb., 1856, comprising Notices of the Portraits of Mary, Queen of Scots, collected on that occasion. 1859.

Murray (David). 'Museums.' Glasgow, 1904. Biblio. Note on Edinburgh Museum, vol. ii. pp. 224–227.

Catal. of the National Museum of Antiquities of Scotland. Soc. of Antiq. Scot. Edinb., 1892.

Lyell (Arthur H.). Biblio. List of Romano-British Remains, 1912. Midlothian, p. 139.

Cowan (William). The Early Views and Plans of Edinburgh. (*Edinb. Biblio. Soc. Pubns.*, vol. ix. pp. 37–49. 1909.)

Wilson (Sir Daniel). Memorials of Edinburgh in the Olden Time. 1872. App. II. pp. 424–427. Ancient Maps and Views of Edinburgh.

Watson (W. F.). Edinburgh: its houses and its noted inhabitants, chiefly those of the 17th and 18th Centuries. Catal. of original drawings, engravings, etc., selected from the private collection of W. F. Watson. 1865.

Williamson (Peter). Reprint of the first published Directory for the City of Edinb., 1773–74. 1889.

There is a large Collection of MSS. relating to the Hist. of Scot. and of early Scottish Printed Books in the Advocates' Library; a Special Topographical and Historical Collection in the Signet Library, and about 11,000 works on Archæology in the Library of the Soc. of Antiquaries of Scotland.

Trimen (Henry). Botanical Biblio. of the British Counties. Edinburghshire. (*Jour. of Botany*, vol. xii. p. 235. 1874.)

Christy (Miller). Biblio. Notes on Edinburghshire Birds. (*The Zoologist*, Ser. 3, vol. xiv. p. 264, 1890; and reprinted in pamph., 1891, p. 35.) **Mammals.** (*The Zoologist*, Ser. 3, vol. xvii. p. 212. 1893.) **Fishes.** (*Ibid.* p. 261. 1893.)

Anderson (John P.). Book of Brit. Topo., 1881. Edinburghshire, pp. 386–391.

Bandinel (Bulkeley). Catal. of Books bequeathed to Bodleian Lib. by Richard Gough, 1814. Edinburghshire, p. 357.

MUSSELBURGH.

Burgh Records, 1450, etc., at Town Hall, Musselburgh. (*Local Records Comm. Rep.*, 1902, App. III. p. 96.)

ELGIN OR MORAY.

Hist. MSS. Comm. Report. Elgin Collection.

Cumming, Sir W. Gordon Gordon,
at Gordonstoun ... ... 6th Rep. p. xix. and App. pp. 681-688.

Rampini (Charles). A Hist. of Moray & Nairn. The County Histories of Scotland. 1897. List of Books relating to Moray and Nairn, pp. 417–429.

ELGIN OR MORAY (continued).

Livingstone (Matthew). Guide to the Public Records of Scotland. 1905. Elgin, pp. 124, 176.

Turnbull (William B.). Scottish Parochial Registers. 1849. List of Elgin Registers, pp. 60–64, 161.

A Private Press at Elgin, 1822. See Macray. '*Annals of the Bodl. Lib.*,' 1890, p. 338.

Anderson (Peter John). Inventories of Ecclesiastical Records of North-Eastern Scotland. Elgin, pp. 268, etc. New Spalding Club, vol. vi. Miscellany, vol. i. 1890.

Inventories of Northern Records. III. The Sheriff Court of Moray. By G. M. Hossack. (*Scottish Notes & Queries*, vol. xi. p. 184. 1898.)

Anderson (Joseph) and **Black (Geo. F.). Report on Local Museums in Scotland.** Elgin Museum. (*Soc. of Antiq. Scot. Proc.*, vol. xxii. p. 341. 1888.)

Gross (Charles). Biblio. of Brit. Municipal Hist. (*Harvard Hist. Studies*, vol. v. 1897.) Elgin, pp. 133, 231.

Lyell (Arthur H.). Biblio. List of Romano-British Remains. 1912. Elgin, p. 139.

Trimen (Henry). Botanical Biblio. of the British Counties. Elgin. (*Jour. of Botany*, vol. xii. p. 236. 1874.)

Christy (Miller). Biblio. Note on Elgin Birds. (*Catal. of Local Lists of British Birds*, London, 1891, pp. 32, 36.) **Mammals.** (*The Zoologist*, Ser. 3, vol. xvii. p. 212. 1893.)

Anderson (John P.). Book of Brit. Topo., 1881. Elgin, pp. 391-392.

Gough (Richard). Brit. Topo., 1780. Elgin, vol. ii. pp. 685-686.

FORRES.

Burgh Records, 1496, etc., with MS. Index, at Court House, Forres. (*Local Records Comm. Rep.*, 1902, App. III. p. 92.)

ESSEX.

[A General Bibliography was commenced about 1892 by a Committee of Essex *literati*, under the name of the Essex Bibliographical Committee, and Mr. W. H. Dalton was engaged to execute the bulk of the work. In 1902 it was stated that the material was almost complete. Apparently nothing further was done. See *The Essex Review*, vol. i. p. 10, 1892, and vol. xi. p. 246. 1902.]

Catal. of Books, Maps, and MSS. relating to, or connected with the County of Essex, and collected by Augustus Cunnington. A contribution towards the Biblio. of the County. Braintree, 1902. Privately Printed.

Walford (Edward). The Biblio. of Essex. (*The Antiquarian Mag. & Bibliographer*, vol. i. pp. 72–78, 283. 1882.)

Round (J. H.). Books bearing on Essex History. (*Essex Archæol. Soc. Trans.*, New Ser., vol. xiii. pp. 12–24. 1913.)

Fitch (E. A.). Historians of Essex. (*The Essex Review*, vols. ii.–ix. 1893–1900.) Also issued separately.

Moon (Z.). Essex Literature. Catal. of Books published in, or relating to the County of Essex. Leyton District Council Pub. Libraries. Leyton, 1900.

——— **Index to the Biographical Hist. of Essex.** (*Leyton Library Mag.*, vol. ii. No. 8. 1900.)

Dalton (W. H.). Catal. of the Books, Pamphlets, Periodicals, MSS., & Scrap Collections in the Library of the Essex Archæol. Society. Colchester, 1895.

ESSEX (continued).

General Index to the Transactions of the Essex Archæol. Society, vols. i.-v. 1858-73, & New Series, vols. i.-v. 1878-95. Colchester, 1900.

Catal. of the Library of George Scott, Esq., of Woolston Hall, containing curious articles in Local History and MSS. 1781.

Clark (Rev. Andrew). Notes on Libraries in Essex. Bodl. Lib. MSS. 33389-90.

Catal. of the Colchester Public Library, compiled by Geo. Rickwood, 1912. (Contains Essex & Colchester items.)

Avery (John). Reference List of Plates, Maps, etc., relating to Essex, appearing in the 'Gentleman's Magazine.' (*The Essex Review*, vol. iii. pp. 132-134. 1894.)

Brierley (Geo. H.). East Anglia, in the 'Annual Register,' 1758-1790. (*The East Anglian*, Ser. 2, vol. iii. pp. 116, 127, 137, 156, 285; vol. iv. pp. 310, 349; vol. v. p. 24. 1889-93.)

Jackson (George). Essex in Literature. (*The Essex Review*, vol. viii. pp. 145-166. 1899.)

Gould (I. C.). Essex in Drayton's Poly-olbion. (*Essex Archæol. Soc. Trans.*, New Ser., vol. v. pp. 63-64. 1895.)

East Anglia in Fiction. (*The East Anglian*, Ser. 2. vol. iv. pp. 308, 339; vol. vi. p. 116; vol. vii. p. 62. 1892-97.)

Gould (I. L. and B. M.). An Anthology of Essex, edited by C. Fell Smith. 1911. Index of Authors, pp. 257-268.

List of Private Acts relating to the County of Essex. London: Stevens & Sons, *circa* 1912.

List of Essex Poll Books. (*The Essex Review*, vol. i. pp. 57, 119. 1892.)

[A large Collection of Poll Books is in the Library of the Essex Archæol. Soc.]

Gross (Charles). Biblio. of Brit. Municipal Hist. (*Harvard Hist. Studies*, vol. v. 1897.) Essex, p. 95. Colchester, pp. 198-200. Saffron Walden, p. 381. Harwich, p. 254.

Davenport (Frances G.). List of Printed Materials for Manorial History. 1894. Biblio. Note on Essex Manorial History, pp. 44-45.

Dove (Patrick Edward). Domesday Studies. 1891. Domesday Biblio. Essex, vol. ii. p. 677.

Lyell (Arthur H.). Biblio. List of Romano-British Remains. 1912. Essex, pp. 23-28. Colchester, pp. 24-26. Chelmsford, p. 23.

Price (John E.). List of Roman Remains in Essex, with Biblio. Notes. (*The Archæol. Rev.*, vol. ii. pp. 96-102. 1888.)

Macklin (Herbert Walter). Monumental Brasses. London: George Allen & Sons, 1913. Biblio. Note on Essex Brasses, with a List, pp. 140, 154-157.

Deedes (Cecil) and **Walters (H. B.). The Church Bells of Essex.** 1909. Biblio. of Essex Literature and other Records, pp. xiii.-xix.

Allnutt (W. H.). English Provincial Presses. Earliest Printing in Essex. (*Bibliographica*, vol. ii. p. 305. 1896.)

Peddie (R. A.). Notes on Provincial Printers & Booksellers. Essex. (*The Library World*, vol. vii. pp. 57-60. 1904.)

Plomer (Henry R.). Charles Clark's Private Press at Great Totham Hall. (*Some Private Presses of the Nineteenth Century, in 'The Library,'* New Ser., vol. i. pp. 417-418. 1900.)

ESSEX (continued).

Lowndes (Wm. Thomas). List of Publications of the Great Totham Press. (*Bibliographer's Manual*, 1871. App. pp. 216–217.)

Eyton (J. Walter K.). List of Publications of the Great Totham Press. (*Sale Catal. of his Library of Privately Printed Books.* Sotheby's, 1848, pp. 46–47, 212.)

Plomer (Henry R.). Private Press of the Rev. Frederick Nolan, at Prittlewell. (*Some Private Presses of the Nineteenth Century, in 'The Library,'* New Ser., vol. i. p. 417. 1900.)

Special Essex Collections are in the Carnegie Free Lib. at Grays, the Leyton Public Lib., the Shoreditch Public Lib., London, the Walthamstow Public Lib., and the Stratford Central Lib. at West Ham. The Collections of E. J. Sage on the Romford and Barking District are in the Stoke Newington Public Lib., London.

Hist. MSS. Comm. Reports. Essex Collections.

Braybrooke, Lord, at Audley End ...	8th Rep. p. xii. and App. pp. 277–296.
Chisenhale-Marsh, Mr. T., at Gaynes Park	3rd Rep. p. xvii. and. App. p. 274.
Lennard, Sir T. Barrett, at Belhus ...	13th Rep. App. IV. pp. 365–377; 16th Rep. p. 116; Various Collections, vol. iii. pp. 155–255.
Lowndes, Mr. G. A., at Barrington Hall	5th Rep. p. xi.; 7th Rep. p. xiv. and App. pp. 537–589.
Majendie, Mr. Lewis, at Hedingham Castle	5th Rep. p. ix. and App. pp. 321–323.
Round, Mr. James, at Birch Hall ...	14th Rep. pp. 38–39 and App. IX. pp. 267–366.
County Records, at Chelmsford ...	10th Rep. p. 27 and App. IV. pp. 466–513.

County Records, 1556, etc., with MS. Index, at Shire Hall, Chelmsford. (*Local Records Comm. Rep.*, App. III. p. 18; and *Reports on the Public Records*, 1800, p. 268.)

The MSS. of the Custos Rotulorum and Justices of the Peace of the County of Essex, at the Shire Hall, Chelmsford. (*Essex Archæol. Soc. Trans.*, New Ser., vol. iii. pp. 185–191. 1889.)

The MS. Collections of Jekyll, Powell, and Suckling for Essex, are in the British Museum. (See Pedigrees of Gentry.)

Jekyll's Collections in Brit. Mus. Add. MSS. 19985–89; Harl. MSS. 3960, 4723, 5185, 5186, 5192, 5195, 6677, 6678, 6684, 6685, 6832, 7017.

Powell (Rev. D. T.). Essex Collections in Brit. Mus. Add. MSS. 17460, 17461.

Suckling's Collections in Brit. Mus. Add. MSS. 18476, 18479, 18482, 18486, 18488. Index, Add. MS. 18491.

Propert (Charles K.). Collections relating to Essex in Brit. Mus. 11 vols. Add. MSS. 33520–33530.

Strangeman (James). Geneal. & Hist. Collections relating to Essex in the Brit. Mus. Add. MS. 5937.

King (H. W.). James Strangman, Esq., of Hadleigh, an Eminent Essex Antiquary of the time of Elizabeth and James I. (*Essex Archæol. Soc. Trans.*, vol. ii. pp. 139–146. 1861.)

Nicholl (John). MS. Collections for Essex Archæology, Architecture, Genealogy, Heraldry, also **H. W. King's MS. Collections** are in the Library of the Essex Archæol. Soc.

Laver (Henry). The King Bequests. Notes on the MSS. bequeathed to the Essex Archæol. Soc. by H. W. King. (*Essex Archæol. Soc. Trans.*, New Ser., vol. v. pp. 65–68. 1895.)

ESSEX (*continued*).

Macray (W. D.). Holman, Ouseley, & Jekyll Collections in the Bodleian Lib. See '*Annals of the Bodleian*,' 1890, pp. 238–239. Catalogue in 2 vols. printed in 1862 and 1878, with a full Index.

Madden (Sir. F.). Note on Essex MSS. Collections of Jekyll, Ouseley, etc. (*Notes & Queries*, Ser. 1, vol. xii. pp. 454–455. 1855.)

Christy (Miller). The Rev. John Ouseley, 1645–1708, an Early Historian of Essex. (*The Essex Review*, vol. xxi. pp. 132–141. 1912.) Also reprinted. Some of Ouseley's MSS. are in the Bodleian Lib., where is also what appears to be Ouseley's own manuscript Catal. of his MSS.

King (H. W.). The Morant and Astle MSS. and other Hist. & Topog. Collections relating to Essex. (*Essex Archæol. Soc. Trans.*, vol. ii. pp. 147–154. 1861.)

Earle (Joseph Sim). A Collection of Topographical drawings, engravings, etc., relating to Essex is in the Library of the Soc. of Antiquaries, London.

Rickwood (George). List of Deeds recently acquired by the Colchester Public Library. (*Essex Archæol. Soc. Trans.*, New Ser., vol. xiii. pp. 140–142. 1913.)

Waller (W. C.). Some Essex Manuscripts: being an Account of those belonging to W. S. Chisenhale-Marsh, Esq., of Gaynes Park. (*Essex Archæol. Soc. Trans.*, New Ser., vol. v. pp. 200–225; vol. vi. pp. 101–121. 1895–97.)

East Anglians in Early Hebrew Deeds. (*The East Anglian*, Ser. 2, vol. iv. pp. 340, 358; vol. v. pp. 7, 37, 57, 84, 101, 121, 148, 167. 1892–93.)

Records of Manor Lands in Essex. ('*Descriptive Catal. of the Original Charters & Muniments of Battle Abbey*,' on Sale by Thomas Thorpe, Bedford St., London. 1835.)

[Essex MSS.] Catal. of a Collection of Books, Historical Documents, etc., to be sold by Messrs. Puttick & Simpson, London. Dec. 17th, etc., 1885. Essex County Documents, pp. 62–69.

Shadwell (C. L.). Calendar of Deeds relating to the Foundation for St. Antony's Exhibitions in Exeter College. (Over 140 Deeds relate to lands in Essex.) Privately printed.

Laver (Henry). The Mammals, Reptiles, & Fishes of Essex.—List of Authorities, pp. 125–127. (*Essex Field Club. Special Memoirs*, vol. iii. 1898.)

Christy (Miller) and Thresh (Miss May). A Hist. of the Mineral Waters & Medicinal Springs of the County of Essex,—Biblio. of Works treating of Essex Mineral Springs, pp. 6–10. (*Essex Field Club. Special Memoirs*, vol. iv. 1910.)

Christy (Miller). The Birds of Essex.—Chronological List of Works quoted. App. B, pp. 293–296. (*Essex Field Club. Special Memoirs*, vol. ii. 1890.)

——— **Biblio. Note on Essex Birds.** (*The Zoologist*, Ser. 3, vol. xiv. p. 252. 1890; and reprinted in pamph., 1891, p. 13.) **Mammals.** (*The Zoologist*, Ser. 3, vol. xvii. p. 179. 1893.) **Reptiles.** (*Ibid.* p. 243. 1893.) **Fishes.** (*Ibid.* p. 254. 1893.)

Anderson (John P.). Book of Brit. Topo., 1881. Essex, pp. 101-106.
Gatfield (George). Guide to Heraldry. 1892. Essex, pp. 136-138.
Sims (Richard). Manual for the Genealogist. 1861. Essex, pp. 166, 205, 206, 233.
Upcott (William). English Topo., 1818. Essex, vol. i. pp. 223-245, 615.
Smith (Alfred Russell). Catal. of Topo. Tracts, etc. 1878. Essex, pp. 85-98.
Gough (Richard). Brit. Topo., 1780. Essex, vol. i. pp. 343-369.
Bandinel (Bulkeley). Catal. of Books bequeathed to Bodleian Library by Richard Gough 1814. Essex, pp. 113-117.

ESSEX (*continued*).

COLCHESTER.

Borough Records, 1255, etc., with a Printed Calendar, at Colchester Castle. (*Local Records Comm. Rep.*, 1902, App. III. p. 52.)

The Charters and Letters Patent granted to the Borough, by Rich. I. and succeeding Sovereigns. By Isaac Herbert Jeayes. Printed by order of the Borough. Colchester, 1904.

Harrod (Henry). Repertory of the Records and Evidences of the Borough of Colchester. Colchester, 1865.

——— **Report on the Records of the Borough of Colchester.** 1865.

——— **Calendar of the Court Rolls of the Borough of Colchester.** 1865.

Morant's Collections relating to Colchester are in the Brit. Mus. Stowe MSS. 834–842.

Ecclesiastical Records of the Archdeaconry of Colchester, at the Registrar's Office, Chelmsford. (*Local Records Comm. Rep.*, 1902, App. III. p. 126.)

Lyell (Arthur H.). Biblio. List of Romano-British Remains. 1912. Colchester, pp. 24–26.

Murray (David). 'Museums.' Glasgow, 1904. Biblio. Note on Colchester Museum, vol. ii. pp. 183, 303.

A Catal. of Books on Archæology & Nat. History, presented to the Colchester Museum by the Rev. Henry Jenkins. 1870.

A Catal. of the Harsnett Library at Colchester, compiled by G. Goodwin. Privately Printed. London, 1888.

BARKING.

King (H. W.). Notes on the Registers of the Parish of Barking. (*Essex Archæol. Soc. Trans.*, vol. ii. pp. 122–133. 1860.)

CHELMSFORD.

Murray (David). 'Museums.' Glasgow, 1904. Biblio. Note on Chelmsford Museum, vol. ii. p. 174.

CHINGFORD.

Epping Forest Museum described. (*Nature*, vol. 53, p. 16. 1895.)

A short Account of the Epping Forest Museum. (*Essex Field Club. Museum Leaflets*, No. 1. 1895.)

HARWICH.

Borough Records, 1619, etc., with MS. Index, at the Guild Hall, Harwich. (*Local Records Comm. Rep.*, 1902, App. III. p. 58.)

MALDON.

Borough Records, 1204, etc., at the Moot Hall, Maldon. (*Local Records Comm. Rep.*, 1902, App. III. p. 66.)

SAFFRON WALDEN.

Borough Records, 1300, etc., with MS. list, at Town Hall, Saffron Walden. (*Local Records Comm. Rep.*, 1902, App. III. p. 68.)

An Abridged Catal. of the Saffron Walden Museum. 1845. Not published.

ESSEX (continued).

Murray (David). 'Museums.' Glasgow, 1904. Biblio. Note on Museums of Richard, Lord Braybrooke, at Audley End and Saffron Walden, vol. iii. pp. 51, 149.

TILTEY.

Waller (W. C.). Records of Tiltey Abbey. An Account of some preserved at Easton Lodge. (*Essex Archæol. Soc. Trans.*, New Ser., vol. viii. pp. 353–362; vol. ix. pp. 118–121. 1902–4.)

WALTHAM ABBEY.

Winters (W.). Historical Notes on some ancient MSS. formerly belonging to the monastic Library at Waltham Holy Cross. (*Roy. Hist. Soc. Trans.*, vol. vi. pp. 203–266. 1877.)

Littler (Edmund). Notes upon some Plans and Drawings illustratiev of the Antiquities of the Abbey and Town of Waltham Abbey. (*Essex Archæol. Soc. Trans.*, vol. ii. pp. 41–55. 1859.)

FERMANAGH.

Dix (Ernest Reginald McClintock). Printing in Enniskillen, 1798–1825, with a List. (*The Irish Book Lover*, vol. ii. pp. 185–186. 1911.) **Additional Note,** by J. S. C. (*Ibid.* vol. v. p. 147. 1914.)

Anderson (John P.). Book of Brit. Topo., 1881. Fermanagh, p. 434.

Gough (Richard). Brit. Topo., 1780. Fermanagh, vol. ii. p. 802.

Gross (Charles). Biblio. of British Municipal Hist. (*Harvard Hist. Studies*, vol. v. 1897.) Fermanagh, p. 120.

Belmore (Earl of). Ancient Maps of Enniskillen and its environs. (*Ulster Journ. of Archæol.*, vol. ii. pp. 218–243. 1896.)

FIFESHIRE.

Mackay (Æneas J. G.). List of Books relating to Fife and Kinross. Edinb. Biblio. Soc. Pubns., vol. iii. pp. 1–30. 1899. List of Maps of Fife and Kinross, p. 30. List of the Cupar Press of Tullis and of Westwood, pp. 25–29.

——— **A short Note on the Local Presses of Scotland;** with a List of Books relating to Fife, and a special List of those printed at Cupar-Fife. Edinb. Biblio. Soc. Pubns., vol. iii. pp. 33–35. 1899.

——— **A History of Fife and Kinross.** The County Histories of Scotland. 1896. List of Books relating to Fife & Kinross, pp. 361–389.

Beveridge (Erskine). A Biblio. of Works relating to Dunfermline and the West of Fife, including publications of Writers connected with the District. Edinb. Biblio. Soc. Pubns., vol. v. 1901.

Lyell (Arthur H.). Biblio. List of Romano-British Remains. 1912. Fifeshire, p. 139.

Laing (David). The Poetical Works of Sir David Lyndsay, of the Mount (Fifeshire). Biblio. with facsimiles of the title-pages of the chief Editions, vol. iii. pp. 222–298. Edinburgh, 1879.

Special Collections for Dunfermline and Fife are at the Pittencrieff House Museum, and at the Carnegie Public Lib. in Dunfermline.

FIFESHIRE (continued).

Hist. MSS. Comm. Reports. Fifeshire Collections.

Bethune, Sir John, at Kilconquhar ...	5th Rep. p. xxi. and App. pp. 623–626.
Glasgow, Earl of, at Crawford Priory	3rd Rep. p. xxiii. and App. p. 405; 8th Rep. p. xvii. and App. pp. 304–308.
Moray, Earl of, at Donybristle ...	6th Rep. p. xvii. and App. pp. 634–673.
Rosslyn, Earl of, at Dysart House, Kirkcaldy	2nd Rep. p. xviii. and App. pp. 191, 192.
Rothes, Henrietta, Countess of, at Leslie House	4th Rep. p. xx. and App. pp. 492–511.
Wemyss, Mr. R. G. E., at Wemyss Castle	3rd Rep. p. xxv. and App. pp. 422–423.
St. Andrew's University	2nd Rep. p. xx. and App. pp. 206–209.

Livingstone (Matthew). Guide to the Public Records of Scotland. 1905. Fifeshire, p. 176. Dunfermline, pp. 39, 132, 193.

Turnbull (William B.). Scottish Parochial Registers. 1849. List of Fifeshire Registers, pp. 64–76, 161.

Gross (Charles). Biblio. of Brit. Municipal Hist. (*Harvard Hist. Studies*, vol. v. 1897.) Fifeshire, p. 132. Dunfermline, p. 220.

Trimen (Henry). Botanical Biblio. of the British Counties. Fifeshire. (*Jour. of Botany*, vol. xii. p. 235. 1874.)

Christy (Miller). Biblio. Note on Fifeshire Birds. (*Catal. of Local Lists of Brit. Birds*, 1891, p. 32). **Mammals.** (*The Zoologist*, Ser. 3, vol. xvii. p. 210. 1893.)

Anderson (John P.). Book of Brit. Topo., 1881. Fifeshire, pp. 392–394.

Bandinel (Bulkeley). Catal. of Books bequeathed to Bodleian Lib. by Richard Gough, 1814. Fifeshire, p. 360.

CUPAR.

Burgh Records, with MS. Index, at Town Clerk's Office, Cupar. (*Local Records Comm. Rep.*, 1902. App. III. p. 90.)

Charters and other Muniments belonging to the Royal Burgh of Fife, 1363-1595. Translated from the originals by George Home, Edinburgh, in 1812. Cupar-Fife, 1882.

DUNFERMLINE.

Burgh Records, 1473, etc., at Dunfermline. (*Local Records Comm. Rep.*, 1902. App. III. p. 90.)

Beveridge (Erskine). A Biblio. of Works relating to Dunfermline and the West of Fife, see *ante*.

Couper (W. J.). The Millers of Haddington, Dunbar, and Dunfermline. A Record of Scottish Bookselling. London, 1914. Books printed and published by the Millers at the Dunfermline Press, pp. 301–312.

KINGHORN.

Burgh Records, at Town House, Kinghorn. (*Local Records Comm. Rep.*, 1902, App. III. p. 94.)

KIRKCALDY.

Burgh Records, 1663, etc., at Town House, Kirkcaldy. (*Local Records Comm. Rep.*, 1902, App. III. p. 94.)

LINDORES.

Dickson (Thomas). Notice of the Register of Lindores Abbey, in the Library at Caprington Castle, Ayrshire. (*Soc. of Antiq. Scot. Proc.*, vol. xx. pp. 148–159. 1886.)

FIFESHIRE (*continued*).

PITTENWEEM.

Burgh Records, 16th cent., etc., at Pittenween. (*Local Records Comm. Rep.*, 1902, App. III. p. 98.)

ST. ANDREWS.

University Records, see *ante* Hist. MSS. Comm. Reports.

Scottish Univ. Libraries. Lists of Printed Catalogues. St. Andrews. (*Aberdeen Univ. Lib. Bull.*, vol. i. p. 401. 1912.)

Anderson (Joseph) and Black (Geo. F.). Reports on Local Museums in Scotland. St. Andrews' University Museum. (*Soc. of Antiq. Scot. Proc.*, vol. xxii. p. 345. 1888.)

Axon (William E. A.). On an unrecorded issue of the Aberdeen Press of Edward Raban in 1627. With a handlist of the production of his Presses at Edinburgh, St. Andrews, etc. (*Soc. of Antiq. Scot. Proc.*, vol. xliii. pp. 24–33. 1909.)

FLINTSHIRE.

Hist. MSS. Comm. Reports. Flintshire Collections.

Cooke, Mr. P. B. Davies, at Owston Hall, nr. Doncaster	6th Rep. p. xv. and App, pp. 418, 426.
Dod, Mr. Whitehall, at Llanerch, St. Asaph	3rd Rep. p. xviii. and App. pp. 258–260.
Kenyon, Lord, at Gredington Hall, Flints.	14th Rep. pp. 31-36 and App. IV.
Mostyn, Lord, at Mostyn Hall ...	1st Rep. p. x. and App. p. 44; 4th Rep. App. pp. 347-363; Welsh MSS. in MSS. in the Welsh Language, vol. i.
Puleston, Sir Richard, at Worthenbury	2nd Rep. p. xi. and App. pp. 65–68.
Puleston, the Rev. Sir T. G., at Worthenbury Rectory, Wrexham	15th Rep. pp. 39, 40, and App. VII. pp. 307-343.

St. Asaph. Cathedral Records, at St. Asaph. (*Local Records Comm. Rep.*, 1902, App. III. p. 114.)

Catal. of the Books in the St. Asaph Cathedral Library, arranged by Rev. W. Morton. 1878.

List of Flintshire Illustrations in the 'Archæologia Cambrensis,' 1884–1900. See Alphabetical Index by F. Green, 1902, p. 102.

Gross (Charles). Biblio. of Brit. Municipal Hist. (*Harvard Hist. Studies*, vol. v. 1897.) Flintshire, p. 236.

Lyell (Arthur H.). Biblio. List of Romano-British Remains. 1912. Flintshire, p. 144.

Trimen (Henry). Botanical Biblio. of the British Counties. Flintshire, p. 158.

Christy (Miller). Biblio. Note on Flintshire Birds. (*Catal. of Local Lists of British Birds*, London, 1891, p. 14.)

Anderson (John P.). Book of Brit. Topo., 1881. Flintshire, p. 348.

Gough (Richard). Brit. Topo., 1780. Flintshire, vol. ii. p. 528.

FORFARSHIRE.

Hist. MSS. Comm. Reports. Forfarshire Collections.

Airlie, Earl of, at Cortachy Castle ...	2nd Rep. p. xvii. and App. pp. 186–188.
Dalhousie, Earl of, at Brechin Castle	1st Rep. p. xii. and App. pp. 117–119; 2nd Rep. pp. ix., xvii. and App. p. 186.
——, at Panmure Castle	1st Rep. p. xii. and App. pp. 117–119; 2nd Rep. pp. ix., xvii. and App. p. 186.

FORFARSHIRE (continued).

Hist. MSS. Comm. Reports. Forfarshire Collections (*continued*).

Erskine, Mr. A. J. Kennedy, at Dun	5th Rep. p. xxi. and App. pp. 633-644
Guthrie, Mr. John, of Guthry ...	2nd Rep. p. xix. and App. pp. 197, 198.
Southesk, Earl of, at Kinnaird Castle	7th Rep. p. xvi. and App. pp. 716-726.
Strathmore & Kinghorn, Earl of, at Glamis Castle	2nd Rep. p. xviii. and App. p. 185 ; 14th Rep. p. 49 and App. III. pp. 174-190.
Montrose, Royal Burgh of	2nd Rep. p. xx. and App. pp. 205-206.

County Council Records, 1740, etc., at Forfar. (*Local Records Comm. Rep.*, 1902, App. III. p. 82.)

Anderson (Peter John). Inventories of Ecclesiastical Records of North-Eastern Scotland. Forfarshire, pp. 238, etc. New Spalding Club, vol. vi. *Miscellany*, vol. i. 1890.

Livingstone (Matthew). Guide to the Public Records of Scotland. 1905. Forfarshire, p. 176.

Turnbull (William B.). Scottish Parochial Registers, 1849. List of Forfarshire Registers, pp. 77-85, 162.

Gross (Charles). Biblio. of Brit. Municipal Hist. (*Harvard Hist. Studies*, vol. v. 1897.) Forfarshire, p. 132. Dundee, pp. 217-220.

Barrington (Michael). Grahame of Claverhouse, Viscount Dundee. (1648-1689). London, 1911. Biblio., pp. 416-432.

Special County Collection for Forfarshire in the Arbroath Public Library.

Trimen (Henry). Botanical Biblio. of the British Counties. Forfarshire. (*Journ. of Botany*, vol. xii. p. 236. 1874.)

Christy (Miller). Biblio. Note on Forfarshire Birds. (*Catal. of Local Lists of British Birds*, London, 1891, p. 32.) **Mammals.** (*The Zoologist*, Ser. 3, vol. xvii. p. 210. 1893.) **Reptiles.** (*Ibid.* p. 249. 1893.) **Fishes.** (*Ibid.* p. 261. 1893.)

Anderson (John P.). Book of Brit. Topo., 1881. Forfarshire, pp. 394-395.

Gough (Richard). Brit. Topo., 1780. Forfarshire, vol. ii. pp. 692-693.

Bandinel (Bulkeley). Catal. of Books bequeathed to Bodleian Library by Richard Gough, 1814. Forfarshire, p. 361.

ARBROATH.

Burgh Records, 1491, etc.. with MS. Index, at Town House, Arbroath. (*Local Records Comm. Rep.*, 1902, App. III. p. 88.)

M'Bain (J. M.). Biblio. of Arbroath Periodical Literature, etc. (*Scottish Notes & Queries*, vol. ii. pp. 66, 84, 105, 119, 133 ; vol. iii. p. 42. 1888-89.) Also issued separately.

Hay (George). Hist. of Arbroath. 1899. List of Authorities, pp. vii.-x.

Anderson (Joseph). Reports on Local Museums in Scotland. Arbroath Museum. (*Soc. of Antiq. Scot. Proc.*, vol. xxii. p. 372. 1888.)

DUNDEE.

Burgh Records, 1292, etc., with Printed Index, at Dundee. (*Local Records Comm. Rep.*, 1902, App. III. p. 90.)

Charters, Writs, & Public Documents of the Royal Burgh of Dundee, the Hospital and Johnston's Bequest, 1292-1880. App. Inventory of Charters, etc., in the Town Repositories, 1879. Dundee, 1880.

Abstract or Inventory of Charters and Other Writings belonging to the Corporation of Weavers of the Royal Burgh of Dundee. 1881.

FORFARSHIRE (continued).

Lamb (A. C.). Biblio. of Dundee Periodical Literature. (*Scottish Notes & Queries*, vols. iii. & iv. *passim;* vol. vi. p. 107; vol. ix. p. 27; Ser. 2, vol. vi. pp. 90, 103; vol. vii. p. 134. 1889–1906.)

Maclauchlan (John). A brief Guide to the 'Old Dundee' historical Collection formed by A. C. Lamb. Dundee, 1901.

Mr. A. C. Lamb presented a collection of local books to the Dundee Free Library.

Duncan (James). The Albert Inst. of Literature, Science, & Art: Its Libraries, Museums, & Fine Art Galleries. Brit. Assoc. Dundee. 1912. (*Handbook & Guide to Dundee*, pp. 183–188.)

Jenkinson (F. J. H.). Note on a volume from the Library of the Dominicans of Dundee. Edin. Biblio. Soc. Pubns., vol. vi. pp. 181–184. 1906.

Murray (David). 'Museums.' Glasgow. 1904. Biblio. Note on Dundee Museums, vol ii. p. 221.

MONTROSE.

Burgh Records, 1275, etc., with MS. Index, at Town House, Montrose. (*Local Records Comm. Rep.*, 1902, App. III. p. 96.)

Burgh Records, see *ante* Hist. MSS. Comm. Reports.

Anderson (Joseph). Reports on Local Museums in Scotland. Montrose Museum. (*Soc. of Antiq. Scot. Proc.*, vol. xxii. p. 401. 1888.)

Low (J. G.) and (W.). Biblio. of Montrose Periodicals. (*Scottish Notes & Queries*, vol. iii. pp. 5, 23, 40, 57, 74, 76, 88, 112, 124; vol. iv. p, 55; vol. ix. p. 27; Ser. 2, vol. viii. p. 77. 1889–1906.)

GALLOWAY.

[*See also* KIRCUDBRIGHT *and* WIGTOWNSHIRE.]

Maxwell (Sir Herbert E.). Hist. of Dumfries and Galloway. The County Histories of Scotland. 1896. List of Books relating to Dumfries and Galloway, pp. 363–399. List of Principal Maps, pp. 400–401.

Murray (Thomas). Literary Hist. of Galloway from the Earliest Period to the Present Time, with an Appendix. 1822.

——— **Autobiographical Notes,** now first printed from the original MSS., with notes and a Biblio., by J. A. Fairley. 1912.

Gladstone (Hugh S.). The Hist. of the Dumfriesshire & Galloway Nat. Hist. & Antiq. Soc., 1862–1912. (*Transactions*, Third Ser., vol. i. pp. 15–39. 1913.)

The Special Collection of the Society is at the Ewart Public Library, Dumfries.

Gross (Charles). Biblio. of Brit. Municipal Hist. (*Harvard Hist. Studies*, vol. v. 1897.) Galloway, p. 132.

Biblio. of Historical Monuments, etc., in the Co. of the Stewartry of Kirkcudbright, in Inventory of Monuments, etc., in Galloway. (*Hist. Monuments (Scot.) Comm. Rep.*, pp. xix.–xx. 1914.)

Maxwell (Sir Herbert E.). Studies in the Topography of Galloway. 1887.) Authorities quoted, pp. xi.–xiii.

Harper (M. M'L.). The Bards of Galloway: A Collection of Poems, Songs, Ballads, etc., by Natives of Galloway. 1889. Notes, Biog., & Biblio., pp. 242–262.

GALWAY.

Falkiner (C. Litton). A List of Printed Books & Documents relating to Ireland which contain information relative to the Hist. of the County or City of Galway. (*Galway Archæol. & Hist. Soc. Journ.*, vol. 2, pp. 100–102. 1902.)

Coleman (James). Bibliographia Conaciensis: a list of Books relating to Connaught. **Galway,** pp. 29–31, 33, 239. (*Galway Archæol. & Hist. Soc. Journ.*, vol. v. 1908.)

Index to the Journal of the Galway Archæol. & Hist. Society, vols. i.–vii. Compiled by M. Bradshaw & J. Dowie. Dublin, 1913.

Catal. of the Exhibit of the Galway Archæol. & Hist. Soc. in the Archæological Section at the Galway Exhibition, 1908. By M. Redington. (*Galway Archæol. & Hist. Soc. Journ.*, vol. v. pp. 178–192. 1908.)

Gross (Charles). Biblio. of Brit. Municipal Hist. (*Harvard Hist. Studies*, vol. v. 1897.) Galway, p. 237.

Dix (Ernest Reginald McClintock). A brief Note on Galway Printing. (*Galway Archæol. & Hist. Soc. Journ.*, vol. iv. p. 62. 1905.)

—— **Local Printing in Galway, 1754–1804.** (*Dublin Penny Journ.*, 7 Jan., 1905.)

—— **Printing in Galway, 1754–1820,** with a List. (*The Irish Book Lover*, vol. ii. pp. 50–55. 1910.) **1801–25,** with a List. (*Ibid.* vol. iv. pp. 59–61. 1912.)

—— **Galway Song Books.** Biblio. (*Galway Archæol. & Hist. Soc. Journ.*, vol. iv. pp. 178–179. 1906.)

—— **Early Loughrea Printing.—Earliest Loughrea Printing, 1765–1800.** (*Galway Archæol. & Hist. Soc. Journ*,, vol. iv. pp. 110–112; vol. v. pp. 194–195. 1905–08.)

—— **Printing in Loughrea, 1766–1825,** with a List. (*The Irish Book Lover*, vol. ii. pp. 151–152. 1911.)

—— **Printing in Tuam, 1795–1810,** with a List. (*Dublin Penny Journ.*, 3 Dec., 1904.) **1774–1825,** with a List. (*The Irish Book Lover*, vol. ii. pp. 101–102. 1911.)

Catal. of the Library of University College, Galway. Compiled by V. Steinberger. 1913.

Notes on the Pictorial Map of Galway. By W. F. Trench, C. L. Falkiner, M. J. Blake, etc. Index by Rev. J. McErlean. (*Galway Archæol. & Hist. Soc. Journ.*, vol. iv. pp. 41–48, 133–160. 1905–06.)

Nolan (J. P.). The References for Political Changes of Property, Co. Galway. (*Galway Archæol. & Hist. Soc. Journ.*, vol. iii. pp. 37–43. 1903.)

Index to the References to National & Ancient Monuments in Co. Galway, contained in the Annual Reports of the Office of Public Works, Ireland, between the years 1875 and 1909. By Olive Creery. (*Galway Archæol. & Hist. Soc. Journ.*, vol. vii. pp. 120–125. 1911.)

Hist. MSS. Comm. Reports. Galway Collection.
Galway, Town Archives ... ... 10th Rep. p. 45 and App. V. pp. 380–520.

Trench (W. F.) and Lawson (T. Dillon). On the Corporation Books of Galway. (*Galway Archæol. & Hist. Soc. Journ.*, vol. i. pp. 132–136. 1901.)

Fahey (Very Rev. J.). The Galway Hist. MSS. and how they were discovered. (*Galway Archæol. & Hist. Soc. Journ.*, vol. i. pp. 85–89. 1901.)

Hardiman (James). Hist. of the Town & County of Galway. Appendix. Principal Charters and other Original Documents. Dublin, 1820.

Coleman (James). Memoir of James Hardiman, Librarian of Queen's Coll., Galway, 1849–55. (*Galway Archæol. & Hist. Soc. Journ.*, vol. vi. pp. 180–181. 1910.)

Anderson (John P.). Book of Brit. Topo., 1881. Galway, p. 434.

Gough (Richard). Brit. Topo., 1780. Galway, vol. ii. p. 802.

GLAMORGANSHIRE.

Hist. MSS. Comm. Reports. Glamorganshire Collection.
Cardiff Free Library (The Philipps MSS.) ... ... Welsh MSS., vol. ii. pts. 1 and 2.

County Records, 1719, etc., with MS. list, at Glamorgan County Offices. (*Local Records Comm. Rep.*, 1902. App. III. p. 28.)

County Records at Cardiff. (*Local Records Comm. Rep.*, 1902, p. 236.)

Cartæ et Alia Munimenta quæ ad Dominium de Glamorgan pertinent, etc., 1102–1689. Curante Geo. T. Clark. Dowlais, etc., 1885–93. 4 vols.

Cartæ et alia Munimenta quæ ad Dominium Glamorgancia pertinent, 447–1721. Collected by Geo. T. Clark. Edited by Godfrey L. Clark. Cardiff, 1910. 6 vols. Index in vol. vi.

'Cadrawd' (T. C. Evans). John Walters and the First Printing Press in Glamorganshire. (*Welsh Biblio. Soc. Journ.*, vol. i. pp. 83–89. 1911.)

List of Glamorganshire Illustrations in the 'Archæologia Cambrensis,' 1884–1900. See Alphabetical Index by F. Green, 1902, p. 103.

Lyell (Arthur H.). Biblio. List of Romano-British Remains. 1912. Glamorganshire, p. 144.

Gross (Charles). Biblio. of Brit. Municipal Hist. (*Harvard Hist. Studies*, vol. v. 1897.) Glamorgan, p. 238. Cardiff, p. 187. Neath, p. 341. Swansea, pp. 402–403.

Trimen (Henry). Botanical Biblio. of the British Counties. Glamorganshire. (*Journ. of Botany*, vol. xii. p. 156. 1874.)

Christy (Miller). Biblio. Note on Glamorganshire Birds. (*The Zoologist*, Ser. 3, vol. xiv. p. 262, 1890; and reprinted in pamph., 1891, p. 14.) **Mammals.** (*The Zoologist*, Ser. 3, vol. xvii. p. 179. 1893.) **Reptiles.** (*Ibid.* p. 244. 1893.) **Fishes.** (*Ibid.* p. 254. 1893.)

Anderson (John P.). Book of Brit. Topo., 1881. Glamorganshire, pp. 349-350.

Gough (Richard). Brit. Topo., 1780. Glamorganshire, vol. ii. p. 501.

Bandinel (Bulkeley). Catal. of Books bequeathed to Bodleian Lib. by Richard Gough, 1814. Glamorganshire, p. 333.

CARDIFF.

Borough Records, 1338, etc., with MS. Indexes, at Town Hall & Free Library, Cardiff. (*Local Records Comm. Rep.*, 1902, App. III. p. 32.)

Records in Public Library, 12th cent., etc. (*Local Records Comm. Rep.*, 1902, App. III. p. 136.) See also *ante* Hist. MSS. Comm. Reports.

Cardiff Records: being Materials for a Hist. of the County Borough from the earliest times. Edited by J. H. Matthews. General Index by Mary Petherbridge, vol. vi. pp. 1–362. 6 vols. Cardiff, 1898–1911.

Murray (David). 'Museums.' Glasgow. 1904. Biblio. Note on Cardiff Museum, vol. ii. p. 165.

LLANDAFF.

Cathedral Records, 1573, etc., at Llandaff. (*Local Records Comm. Rep.*, 1902, App. III. p. 112.)

A Digest of the Parish Registers within the Diocese of Llandaff prior to 1836, with Index to Transcripts to 1812, and Inventories of Act Books since 1575. 5 vols. Cardiff, 1905–14.

GLAMORGANSHIRE (continued).

NEATH.

Borough Records, 1397, etc., with MS. Index, at Town Clerk's Office, Neath. (*Local Records Comm. Rep.*, 1902, App. III. p. 66.)

Francis (George G.). Original Charters and Materials for a Hist. of Neath and its Abbey. 1845. Not published.

PENRICE.

Descriptive Catal. of the Penrice & Margam Abbey MSS. in the possession of Miss Talbot, of Margam, with introduction and notes by W. de Gray Birch. First and Second Series, 1893–94. Privately Printed.

SWANSEA.

Francis (George G.). Charters granted to Swansea. 1867. Not published. List of Statutes, pp. 157–163.

Murray (David). 'Museums.' Glasgow, 1904. Biblio. Note on Swansea Museum, vol. iii. p. 202.

GLOUCESTERSHIRE.

HYETT (Francis Adams) and **BAZELEY (William). THE BIBLIOGRAPHER'S MANUAL OF GLOUCESTERSHIRE LITERATURE.** 3 vols. Gloucester, 1895–7. 8vo. List of Gloucestershire Printers, vol. ii., pp. 394–400. An admirable work, arranged under Parishes.

Mr. Hyett is supplementing this work by one on Biographical Collectanea.

Phelps (J. D.). Collectanea Glocestriensia, or a Catal. of Books, Tracts, Coins, &c., relating to the County of Glos. in the possession of John Delafield Phelps, Chavenage House. London, 1842.

Austin (Roland). Gloucester Public Library. Catal. of MSS., Books, Pamphlets, etc., relating to the City and County of Glos. . . . . deposited [by C. H. Dancey] in the Glos. Public Library. 1911.

The Glos. Public Lib. has a special collection of Glos. literature and a County Photographic Record.

Bristol and Glos. Archæol. Soc. Catal. of the Books, Pamphlets, and MSS. in the Library of the Soc., 1898.

Index to the Transactions of the Bristol and Glos. Archæol. Soc. Vols. i.–xx. 1876–97. Glos. 1900.

Index to Papers in the Transactions of the Bristol and Glos. Archæol. Soc. Vols. xxi.–xxx. 1898–1907. Compiled by R. Austin. (*Trans.*, vol. xxxiii. pp. 78–95. 1910.)

Glos. Papers in 'Archæol. Journ. of Royal Archæol. Instit.' Vol. i.–xli., 1845–84. (*Glos. Notes & Queries*, vol. iii. pp. 288–292. 1886.)

Glos. Papers in 'Journ. of British Archæol. Assoc.' Vol. i.–xl., 1845–84. (*Glos. Notes & Queries*, vol. iii. pp. 279–282. 1886.)

Austin (Roland). Some Gloucestershire Books and their Writers, with introduction by F. A. Hyett. Glos., 1911.

Way (Albert). Catal. of the Museum formed at Gloucester during the meeting of the Archæol. Institute. 1860.

GLOUCESTERSHIRE (continued).

Gross (Charles). Biblio. of Brit. Municipal Hist. (*Harvard Hist. Studies*, vol. v., 1897.) Gloucestershire, p. 96. Bristol, pp. 176-181, 431. Cirencester, pp. 196-197. Gloucester, pp. 247-249. Tewkesbury, p. 404.

Davenport (Frances G.). List of Printed Materials for Manorial Hist. 1894. Biblio. Note on Glos. Manorial Hist., pp. 45-46.

Dove (Patrick Edward). Domesday Studies. 1891. Domesday Biblio. Glos., vol. ii. p. 677.

Lyell (Arthur H.). Biblio. List of Romano-British Remains. 1912. Gloucestershire, pp. 28-36.

Biblio. Note on Roman Remains, Glos. (*The Archæol. Review*, vol. i. pp. 115-117. 1888.)

Macklin (Herbert Walter). Monumental Brasses. London, Geo. Allen & Co., 1913. Biblio. Note on Glos. Brasses, with a List, pp. 140 and 157-158.

Murray (David). 'Museums.' Glasgow, 1904. Biblio. Note on Glos. Museum, vol. ii. pp. 259, 303.

Williams (T. W.). Glos. Mediæval Libraries. (*Bristol & Glos. Archæol. Soc. Trans.*, vol. xxxi. pp. 78-195. 1908.)

List of Glos. Biographies (A-C only) **in the D. N. B. Vols. i.-x.** (*Glos. Notes & Queries*, vol. iv. pp. 614-619. 1890.) No more published.

Bellows (John). Printer and Author, 1831-1902. Letters and Memoir, edited by his wife. London. 1904. Appendix. A List of J. Bellows' Writings.

The Private Press. A Study in Idealism. Printed by C. R. Ashbee at Broad Campden, Glos. 1909.

Chubb (Thomas). A Descriptive Catal. of the Printed Maps of Glos., 1577-1911. With Biog. Notes. Bristol, 1913. (*Bristol & Glos. Archæol. Soc. Trans.*)

John Washbourn's book 'Bibliotheca Gloucestrensis,' is not a bibliography, but a reprint of local Civil War Tracts.

Jackson (Mrs. F. Nevill). Some Account of a Portrait Collection of Gloucestershire Worthies. (*Glos. Notes & Queries*, vol. x. pp. 17-22. 1913.)

Hunter (A. A.). Portraits of the Bishops of Gloucester. (*Bristol and Glos. Archæol. Soc. Trans.*, vol. xxxv. pp. 139-142. 1912.)

Austin (Roland). List of Gloucestershire Poll Books. (*Notes & Queries*, Ser. 10, vol. x. p. 124. 1908.)

Glos. Genealogy. Heralds' Visitations and Heraldic Collections. (*Glos. Notes & Queries*, vol. iii. pp. 350-351. 1886.)

Were (F.). Index to the Heraldry in Bigland's 'Gloucestershire.' (*Bristol and Glos. Archæol. Soc. Trans.*, vol. xxviii. pp. 147-510. 1905.)

Hist. MSS. Comm. Reports. Gloucestershire Collections.

Lord Fitzhardinge, at Berkeley Castle ...	4th Rep. p. xiv. and App. pp. 364-367.
Captain S. Grove, of Taynton, nr. Gloucester...	5th Rep. p. x. and App. pp. 360, 361.
Duke of Beaufort, at Badminton	12th Rep. p. xii. and App. IX. pp. 1-115.
Bristol, Dean and Chapter	1st Rep. App. p. 97.
Gloucester Corporation	12th Rep. p. 46 and App. IX. pp. 400-529.
——— Dean and Chapter	12th Rep. p. 47 and App. IX. pp. 397-399.
Woodchester Monastery, nr. Stroud ...	2nd Rep. p. xiii. and App. pp. 146-149.

County Records. 1660, etc., with MS. Indices, at the Shire Hall, Gloucester. (*Local Records Comm. Rep.*, 1902, App. iii. p. 18.)

GLOUCESTERSHIRE (continued).

Borough Records, 1155, etc., with Printed Index, at Guildhall, Glos. (*Local Records Comm. Rep.*, 1902, App. iii. p. 42.)

Hyett (F. A.). Catal. of the MSS. in the British Museum relating to the County of Glos. and the City of Bristol. (*Bristol and Glos. Archæol. Soc. Trans.*, vol. xx. pp. 161–221. 1896–7.)

—— **Suggestions for increasing the utility of County Bibliographies.** (*Biblio. Soc. Trans.*, vol. iii. pp. 27–40. 1896.)

Glos. References in the Bodleian Library. (*Glos. Notes & Queries*, vol. vi. pp. 117–120, 149–151, 170–171; vol. vii. pp. 81–83, 168–173. 1895–96.)

Glos. Deeds. (*Glos. Notes & Queries*, vol. v. pp. 185–187, 346–351; vol. vi. pp. 7, 8, 75–76. 1892–94.)

List of Anglo-Saxon Charters, A.D. 680–966. (*Glos. Notes & Queries*, vol. iii. pp. 331–333, 604–605; vol. v. p. 40. 1886–91.)

Selections from Calendars of State Papers (Domestic) **relating to Glos.** (*Glos. Notes & Queries*, vol. iii. pp. 389–395, 466–475; vol. iv. pp. 253–260, 627–638. 1886–89.)

Extracts from the MS. Calendars of Close Rolls, Hen. III. (*Glos. Notes & Queries*, vol. iv. pp. 425–429, 1889.)

Stevenson (W. H.). Cal. of Records of the Corporation of Glos. Issued under the authority of the Corporation. Glos., 1893. Abstract of Royal Charters and Letters, 1155–1672, pp. 3–69; Abstract of Local Deeds and Charters, 1175–1667, pp. 70–454; Rolls, Council Books, etc., 1272 to the present time, pp. 455–66. A valuable work, well edited.

Jeayes (Isaac H.) Descriptive Catal. of Charters and Muniments at Berkeley Castle. 1892.

Sherborne House, Northleach. Catal. of the Charters, Rolls, etc. Privately printed. 1900.

Smyth (John). The Smyth of Nibley Papers, 1613–1674. (*New York Pub. Lib. Bull.*, vol. i. pp. 186–190. 1897.)

Cooke (J. H.). The Berkeley MSS. and their Author, John Smyth. N.D.

Glos. Cathedral Records, from 11th cent., with MS. Index, at Glos. (*Local Records Comm. Rep.*, 1902, App. III. p. 110.)

Bazeley (W.). Documents relating to Glos. Cath. Lib. (*Records of Glos. Cath.*, vol. ii. pp. 156–164. Glos. Cathedral Soc., 1883–84.)

Glos. Entries in Exeter Episcopal Registers. (*Glos. Notes & Queries*, vol. viii. pp. 11–13. 1901.)

Brown (L. E. G.). On some Glos. Manuscripts now in Hereford Cathedral Library. (*Bristol and Glos. Archæol. Soc. Trans.*, vol. xxvii. pp. 172–210. 1904.)

Glos. Parish Registers, 1538–1812. Arranged under Parishes from *Par. Reg. Abstract*, 1833. (*Glos. Notes & Queries*, vol. i. pp. 185–187; vol. iii. pp. 97–116. 1881–83.)

Glos. Parish Registers. (With a Chronological List.) By SIDNEY J. MADGE. (*Glos. Notes & Queries*, vol. ix. pp. 105–106, 164–175. 1902.)

Extracts from Parish Registers in Glos. By Rev. F. BROWN. (*Glos. Notes & Queries*, vol. ii. pp. 433, 536, 592, 644; vol. iii. pp. 3, 51, 67, 87, 141, 217, 236, 256, 410. 1884–87.)

Conder (E.). Some [Biblio.] Notes on the Visitations of Glos. (*Bristol and Glos. Archæol. Soc. Trans.*, vol. xxviii. pp. 124–130. 1905.)

GLOUCESTERSHIRE (continued).

Hall (J. M.).—Parliamentary Survey of Church Livings, 1649-50, Co. Glos. (*Glos. Notes & Queries*, vol. ii. pp. 214-222. 1884.)

Bigland's MS. Collections in College of Arms.

Trimen (Henry). Botanical Biblio. of the British Counties. Gloucestershire. (*Journ. of Botany*, vol. xii. p. 112. 1874.)

Christy (Miller). Biblio. Note on Glos. Birds. (*The Zoologist*, Ser. 3, vol. xiv. p. 253, 1890; and reprinted in pamph., 1891, p. 14.) **Mammals.** (*The Zoologist*, Ser. 3, vol. xvii. p. 180. 1893.) **Reptiles.** (*Ibid.* p. 244. 1893.) **Fishes.** (*Ibid.* p. 254. 1893.)

Anderson (John P.). Book of Brit. Topo., 1881. Gloucestershire, pp. 106-114.
Gatfield (George). Guide to Heraldry. 1892. Gloucestershire, pp. 138-139.
Sims (Richard). Manual for the Genealogist. 1861. Gloucestershire, pp. 166, 206, 207, 233.
Upcott (William). English Topo., 1818. Gloucestershire, vol. i. pp. 246-275, 616.
Smith (Alfred Russell). Catal. of Topo. Tracts, etc., 1878. Gloucestershire, pp. 99-105.
Gough (Richard). Brit. Topo., 1780. Gloucestershire, vol. i. pp. 371-386.
Bandinel (Bulkeley). Catal. of Books bequeathed to Bodleian Lib. by Richard Gough, 1814. Gloucestershire, pp. 118-122.

BRISTOL.

Hyett (F. A.) and **Bazeley (W.). The Biblio. Manual of Glos. Literature.** Vol. III., Bristol. List of Bristol Printers, pp. 339-344.

Borough Records, at Bristol. (*Local Records Comm. Rep.*, 1902, App. III. p. 118.)

Latimer (John). Calendar of Charters of the City and County of Bristol. 1909.

Seyer (Samuel). The Charters and Letters Patent granted to the Town and City of Bristol. 1812.

Birch (Walter de Gray). Original Documents relating to Bristol and the Neighbourhood. (*Brit. Archæol. Assoc. Journ.*, vol. xxxi. pp. 289-305. 1875.)

Bickley (F. B.). A Cal. of Deeds chiefly relating to Bristol, collected by G. W. Braikenridge. Edinb. 1899.

Faber (R. S.). Catal. of the Library at Clevedon and Bath, collected by G. W. Braikenridge. 1894.

Beaven (A. B.). Bristol Lists, Municipal and Miscellaneous. Bristol, 1899.

Bristol Municipal Public Library. Catal. of Local Literature. (Preparing.)

List of Books in the 'Bristol Library' of the Bristol and Glos. Archæol. Soc. (*Transactions*, vol. xxix. pp. 198-204; vol. xxx. pp. 292-295. 1906-07.)

Murray (David). 'Museums.' Glasgow, 1904. Biblio. Note on Bristol Museums, vol. ii. p. 141.

Catal. of Antiquities exhibited at the Annual Meeting of the Archæol. Inst. at Bristol, 1851. (*Memoirs, etc., of the Archæol. Instit. Bristol*, 1851, pp. lvii.-xcv.)

Index to the Proceedings of the Clifton Antiq. Club. Vol. i.-vii., 1884-1912. Exeter, 1911.

Archdeaconry Records at various places. (*Local Records Comm. Rep.*, 1902, App. III. p. 18.)

Consistory Court Records at Bristol. (*Local Records Comm. Rep.*, 1902, App. III. p. 244.)

Dean and Chapter Records, see *ante* Hist. MSS. Comm. Reports.

GLOUCESTERSHIRE (continued).

Ancient Bristol Documents. (*Clifton Antiq. Club. Proc.*, vols. i.-vii. 1884–1911.)

Winship (G. P.). Cabot Bibliography. Lond. 1900. (Cabot was a native of Bristol.)

Hyett (F. A.) and Bazeley (W.). Chattertoniana. Reprinted from *The Biblio. Manual of Glos. Literature*, with additions. 1914.

Barker (W. R.). A Catal. of the Autograph MSS. and other Remains of Thomas Chatterton, now in the Bristol Museum. 1907.

Pritchard (John E.). Catal. of Exhibition of Old Bristol Maps, Plans, Coinage, etc. (*Bristol and Glos. Archæol. Soc. Trans.*, vol. xxix. pp. 61–80. 1906.)

George (William). The Date of the First Authentic Plan of Bristol. (*Bristol and Glos. Archæol. Soc. Trans.*, vol. iv. pp. 296–300. 1879–80.)

Wells (C.). A List of Bristol Booksellers and Printers. (*Notes & Queries*, Ser. 11, vol. ii. pp. 23–24. 1910.)

Hutton (Stanley). Bristol: Its Libraries and its Booksellers. (*Book-Auction Records*, vol. iv. pt. 2, pp. xv.-xix. 1907.)

Tovey (Charles). A Free Library for Bristol, with a Hist. of the City Library, its Founders and Benefactors. 1855.

Mathews (E. R. Norris). A Survey of the Bristol Public Libraries. (*The Library Assoc. Record*, vol. ii. pt. 2, pp. 641–650. 1900.)

——— **Hist. of the Public Library in Bristol.** 1896.

——— **Early Printed Books and MSS. in the City Reference Library, Bristol.** 1899.

——— **A Few Words about Public Libraries and Museums** [at **Bristol**]. 1892.

Taylor (John). Earliest Free Libraries in England [at **Bristol**]. 1886.

Allnutt (W. H.). English Provincial Presses—Earliest Printing at Bristol. (*Bibliographica*, vol. ii. pp. 32, 286–288, 297. 1896.)

Hyett (F. A.). Notes on the First Bristol and Glos. Printers. (*Bristol and Glos. Archæol. Soc. Trans.*, vol. xx. pp. 38–51. 1895–6.)

Special Collections at the Bristol Municipal Public Libraries are the Bristol, Stuckey Lean, Heylin, and Clake Collections.

CHELTENHAM.

Ward (John). The Cheltenham College Museum described. (*The Antiquary*, vol. xxviii. p. 57. 1893.)

A local Collection at the Cheltenham Public Library.

CIRENCESTER.

Fuller (Rev. E. A.). Cirencester Documents. (*Bristol and Glos. Archæol. Soc. Trans.*, vol. xx. pp. 114–126. 1895–6.)

Murray (David). 'Museums.' Glasgow, 1904. Biblio. Note on Cirencester Museum, vol. ii. p. 180.

Lyell (Arthur H.). Biblio. List of Romano-British Remains. 1912. Cirencester, p. 30.

Norris (Herbert E.). The Booksellers and Printers of Cirencester. 1912.

A local Collection at the Bingham Public Library, Cirencester.

HADDINGTONSHIRE, OR EAST LOTHIAN.

Hist. MSS. Comm. Report. Haddingtonshire Collection.
Stuart, Mr. A. C., at Eaglescarnie ... 8th Rep. p. xvii. and App. pp. 310-315.

County Council Records, 1319, etc., at Haddington. (*Local Records Comm. Rep.*, 1902, App. III. p. 82.)

Charters and Writs concerning the Royal Burgh of Haddington, 1318-1543. Transcribed and Translated by J. G. Wallace-James. 1895.

Thomson (Thomas). A Description of the Oldest Council Books and other Records of the Town of Haddington. (*Soc. of Antiq. Scot. Proc.*, vol. ii. pp. 384-420. 1859.)

Livingstone (Matthew). Guide to the Public Records of Scotland. 1905. Haddingtonshire, p. 175.

Turnbull (William B.). Scottish Parochial Registers. 1849. List of Haddingtonshire Registers, pp. 85-89.

Couper (W. J.). The Millers of Haddington, Dunbar, and Dunfermline. A Record of Scottish Bookselling. London, 1914. Books printed and published at the East Lothian Press, pp. 278-300.

Macfie (R. A. Scott). A Biblio. of Andrew Fletcher of Saltoun. (1653-1716.) (*Edinb. Biblio. Soc. Pubns.*, vol. iv. pp. 117-148. 1901.)

Trimen (Henry). Botanical Biblio. of the British Counties. Haddingtonshire. (*Jour. of Botany*, vol. xii. p. 235. 1874.)

Christy (Miller). Biblio. Note on Haddingtonshire Birds. (*The Zoologist*, Ser. 3, vol. xiv. p. 263, 1890; and reprinted in pamph., 1891, p. 32.) **Mammals.** (*The Zoologist*, Ser. 3, vol. xvii. p. 211. 1893.)

Anderson (John P.). Book of Brit. Topo., 1881. Haddingtonshire, pp. 395-396.

Gough (Richard). Brit. Topo., 1780. Haddingtonshire, vol. ii. p. 694.

Bandinel (Bulkeley). Catal. of Books bequeathed to Bodleian Lib. by Richard Gough 1814. Haddingtonshire, p. 361.

DUNBAR.

Burgh Records, 1587, etc., with MS. list, at Dunbar. (*Local Records Comm. Rep.*, 1902, App. III. p. 90.)

NORTH BERWICK.

Burgh Records, 1539, etc., at North Berwick. (*Local Records Comm. Rep.*, 1902, App. III. p. 96.)

HAMPSHIRE AND THE ISLE OF WIGHT.

GILBERT (H. M.) and GODWIN (G. N.). BIBLIOTHECA HANTONIENSIS: A LIST OF BOOKS RELATING TO HAMPSHIRE, including Magazine references, etc. Southampton, 1891. List of Books and Periodicals containing references to Hampshire, pp. i.-xxxv.; List of Hampshire Newspapers, by F. E. Edwards, pp. xxxvii.-xliii.; List of Works on the Natural Hist. and Geology of Hampshire, pp. xlv.-lxiii.

Wilson (Rev. Sumner). Supplementary Hampshire Bibliography: List of Hampshire Topography not in Biblio. Hantoniensis. (*Hants. Field Club. Papers & Proc.*, vol. iii. pp. 303-316. 1898.) Also issued separately.

HAMPSHIRE AND THE ISLE OF WIGHT (*continued*).

Davis (Rev. R. G.). A Second Supplement to Hampshire Bibliography. (*Hants. Field Club. Papers & Proc.*, vol. v. pp. 127–136, 229–239. 1905–06.)

Cope (Rev. Sir W. H.). A List of Books relating to Hampshire in the Library at Bramshill (afterwards bequeathed to the Hartley Inst., Southampton.) Wokingham, 1879.

Index to the Victoria Hist. of Hampshire and the Isle of Wight. London: Constable & Co. 1914.

Gilbert (Owen). Notes on Recent Publications concerning Hampshire. (*Hants. Field Club. Papers & Proc.*, vol. v. pp. 241–243; vol. vi. *passim.* 1906–10.)

Edwards (F. A.). Early Hampshire Printers. (*Hants. Field Club. Papers & Proc.*, vol. ii. pp. 110–134. 1891.) Also issued separately.

——— **A List of Hampshire Booksellers & Printers.** (*Notes & Queries*, Ser. 10, vol. v. pp. 415, 481–483; vol. vi. pp. 31–32. 1906.)

——— **The Early Newspaper Press of Hampshire.** (Reprinted from the '*Hampshire Independent.*') 1889.

——— **A List of Hampshire Newspapers.** (*The Hampshire Antiquary*, vol. i. pp. 94–97. 1891.) See also vol. ii. pp. 77–78. 1892.

Gross (Charles). Biblio. of Brit. Municipal Hist. (*Harvard Hist. Studies*, vol. v. 1897.) Hampshire, pp. 96–97. Southampton, p. 393. Winchester, p. 417. Portsmouth, p. 370.

Davenport (Frances G.). List of Printed Materials for Manorial History. 1894. Biblio. Note on Hampshire Manorial History, p. 46.

Dove (Patrick Edward). Domesday Studies. 1891. Domesday Biblio., Hampshire, vol. ii. p. 678.

Lyell (Arthur H.). Biblio. List of Romano-British Remains. 1912. Hampshire, pp. 36–43. Silchester, pp. 40–41.

Macklin (Herbert Walter). Monumental Brasses. London: Geo. Allen & Co., 1913. Biblio. Note on Hampshire Brasses, with a List, pp. 140, 158–161.

Catal. of Antiquities exhibited at the Ann. Meeting of the Archæol. Institute, at Winchester, 1845. (*Proceedings of the Archæol. Inst., Winchester*, 1845, pp. xxxix.–liv.)

Transactions of the Brit. Archæol. Assoc. at its Second Annual Congress, at Winchester, 1845, with an Account of the Exhibitions. London, 1846.

Hist. MSS. Comm. Reports. Hampshire & Isle of Wight Collections.

Cope, Rev. Sir William, at Bramshill	3rd Rep. p. xvi. and App. pp. 242–244.
Hare, Mr. Theodore J., of Borden Wood	14th Rep. pp. 37–38 and App. IX. pp. 200–266.
Jervoise, Mr. F. H. T., at Herriard Park	17th Rep. p. 122; Various Collections, vol. iv. pp. 140–174.
Kingsmill, Mr. Andrew, at Sydmonton Court	15th Rep. App. X. pp. 173–174.
Mildmay, Sir H., at Dogmersfield Park	5th Rep. p. viii. and App. p. 307.
Montagu of Beaulieu, Lord, at Beaulieu	16th Rep. pp. 59–62, and a vol. 1900.
Portsmouth, Earl of, at Hurstbourne Park	8th Rep. p. xix. and App. pp. 60–92.
Wodehouse, Mr. Edmund R. ...	13th Rep. pp. 48–50 and App. IV. pp. 405–494.
Carisbrooke Parish	6th Rep. p. xiv. and App. p. 499.
Petersfield Corporation	10th Rep. p. 23.
Southampton Corporation	11th Rep. pp. 29–33 and App. III. pp. 1–444.
——— God's House at (MSS. at Queen's Coll., Oxford)	6th Rep. App. pp. 551–569.
Winchester Corporation	6th Rep. App. pp. 595–605.

HAMPSHIRE AND THE ISLE OF WIGHT (*continued*).

Suckling's MS. Collections for Hampshire are in the Brit. Museum. Add. MSS. 18478, 18479, 18482, 18488–18490. Index, Add. MS. 18491.

Other Collections relating to Hampshire in the Brit. Museum are: Stowe MS. 845, and Add. MS. 14296, Collections of William Pavey; Add. MSS. 33278–33285 and Add. MS. 24788, Collections of Sir Frederick Madden, and John Latham's Collections for a Hist. of Romsey, Add. MSS. 26774–26780.

Hampshire Parish Registers. Brief Biblio. Notes, with a List. (*The Hampshire Antiquary*, vol. ii. pp. 38, 97, 98. 1892.)

Williams (J. F.). The Early Churchwardens' Accounts of Hampshire. (With Biblio. Notes.) 1913.

Summary List of Records in the possession of His Majesty's Commissioners of Woods and Forests relating to the New Forest. (*Local Records Comm. Rep.*, 1914, vol. ii. pt. 2, p. 251.

Report of an Inspection of the Records of the Admiralty and War Office, at Portsmouth, Jan., 1911. (*Local Records Comm. Rep.*, 1914, vol. ii. pt. 2, pp. 185–187.)

Trimen (Henry). Botanical Biblio. of the British Counties. Hampshire. (*Journ. of Botany*, vol. xii. p. 71. 1874.)

Boulger (G. S.). Botanical Biblio. of the South-Eastern Counties. Hampshire. (*South-Eastern Union of Scientific Societies. Trans.*, vol. iv. pp. 45–46. 1899.)

Townsend (Frederick). Flora of Hampshire, including the Isle of Wight. Second Edn. 1904. Principal Works & Authorities, pp. xxvi.–xxxiv.

Whitaker (William). List of Books on the Geology of Hampshire. (*Winchester & Hants. Scientific Soc. Proc.* 1873.)

Kelsall (J. E.) and Munn (P. W.). The Birds of Hampshire and the Isle of Wight. 1905. Biblio., pp. xx.–xxvi.

Christy (Miller). Biblio. Note on Hampshire Birds. (*The Zoologist*, Ser. 3, vol. xiv. p. 253, 1890; and reprinted in pamph., 1891, p. 14.) **Mammals.** (*The Zoologist*, Ser. 3, vol. xvii. p. 180. 1893.) **Reptiles.** (*Ibid.* p. 244. 1893.) **Fishes.** (*Ibid.* p. 254. 1893.)

Anderson (John P.). Book of Brit. Topo., 1881. Hampshire, pp. 114–125.

Gatfield (George). Guide to Heraldry. 1892. Hampshire, pp. 139–140.

Sims (Richard). Manual. 1861. Hampshire, pp. 166, 207, 233–234.

Upcott (William). English Topo., 1818. Hampshire, vol. i. pp. 276–320, 617–621.

Smith (Alfred Russell). Catal. of Topo. Tracts, etc., 1878. Hampshire, pp. 107–109.

Gough (Richard). Brit. Topo., 1780. Hampshire, vol. i. pp. 387–408.

Bandinel (Bulkeley). Catal. of Books bequeathed to Bodleian Library by Richard Gough. 1814. Hampshire, pp. 123–127.

ANDOVER.

Titheridge (W. H. W.). A Catal. of the Records, Deeds, and Muniments and Writings belonging to the Corporation of Andover, with Report and Table of Contents. 1837. (In MS. at Andover.)

BASINGSTOKE.

Borough Records, with MS. Index, at Town Hall, Basingstoke. (*Local Records Comm. Rep.*, 1902, App. III. p. 46.)

Baigent (F. J.) and Millard (J. E.). A Hist. of the Ancient Town and Manor of Basingstoke. 1889. Calendars of Documents, pp. 593–687.

CHRISTCHURCH.

Borough Records, Edw. I. etc., with MS. Index, at Town Hall, Christchurch. (*Local Records Comm. Rep.*, 1902, App. III. p. 50.)

HAMPSHIRE AND THE ISLE OF WIGHT (continued).

CRONDAL.

Baigent (F. J.). A Collection of Records and Documents relating to the Hundred & Manor of Crondal. Appendix: Catal. of Documents in the possession of the Dean & Chapter of Winchester, pp. 481-497. Hampshire Record Soc. 1891.

ELVETHAM.

MS. Catal. of Elvetham Charters, in the possession of F. H. Gough-Calthorpe, with Index to names of Persons and Places.

LYMINGTON.

Borough Records, 1609, etc., at Town Clerk's Office, Lymington. (*Local Records Comm. Rep.*, 1902, App. III. p. 64.)

St. Barbe (Charles). Records of the Corporation of the Borough of New Lymington. 1848. (Contains List of Town Books, Schedule of Deeds, Papers, etc.)

PETERSFIELD.

Corporation Records, see *ante* Hist. MSS. Comm. Reports.

PORTSMOUTH.

Gates (William G.). Illustrated Hist. of Portsmouth. 1900. Biblio. of Portsmouth, pp. 713-715.

ROMSEY.

Liveing (H. G. D.). Records of Romsey Abbey. 1906. App. C. 'John Latham and his Collections for a Hist. of Romsey,' pp. 330-331.

Latham (John). Collections for a Hist. of Romsey. 7 vols. Brit. Mus. Add. MSS. 26774-26780.

ROPLEY.

Kirkby (T. F.). The Charters of the Manor of Ropley. (*Archæologia*, Ser. 2, vol. viii. pp. 227-236. 1902.)

SELBORNE.

Macray (W. Dunn). Calendar of Charters & Documents relating to Selborne and its Priory, preserved in Magdalen Coll., Oxford. 2 vols. Hampshire Record Soc. 1891-94.

Watt (Hugh Boyd). A List of Bibliographies of the Writings of Gilbert White. (*The Selborne Mag.*, vol. xx. pp. 198-201. 1909.) Also issued separately.

Sherborn (C. Davies). Biblio. of White's Hist. of Selborne. (*The Nat. Hist. and Antiquities of Selborne*, ed. by R. Bowdler Sharpe, vol. ii. pp. 347-364. 1900.)

SILCHESTER.

Lyell (Arthur H.). Biblio. List of Romano-British Remains. 1912. Silchester, pp. 40-41.

SOUTHAMPTON.

Borough Records, with MS. Index, at Municipal Offices, Southampton. (*Local Records Comm. Rep.*, 1902, App. III. p. 40.)

Gidden (H. W.). The Charters of the Borough of Southampton. 2 vols. Southampton Record Soc. 1909-10. Description of the Charters, vol. ii. App. I. pp. 206-211.

HAMPSHIRE AND THE ISLE OF WIGHT (continued).

Wright (Thomas). Report on the Municipal Records of Winchester & Southampton. (Brit. Archæol. Assoc. Trans. at Winchester, 1845, pp. 28-39.

Vaux (W. S. W.). Some Notices of Records preserved amongst the Corporation Archives at Southampton. (*The Archæol. Journ.*, vol. iii. pp. 229-233. 1846.)

Indexes to the Southampton Court Leet Records, 1550-1624. Southampton Record Soc. 1908.

Hearnshaw (F. J. C.). The Records of Southampton. (*South-Eastern Union of Scientific Societies. Trans.*, 1909, pp. 11-14.)

Corporation Records, see *ante* Hist. MSS. Comm. Reports.

Rogers (W. H.). A Southampton Atlas: A Collection of Old Maps & Plans of Southampton. Southampton Record Soc. 1907.

Davies (Rev. T. L. O.). An Old Southampton Newspaper. (The Hampshire Chronicle.) (*Hants. Field Club. Papers & Proc.*, vol. vi. pp. 1-28. 1907.)

Relics of Old Southampton: Memorial volume of the Loan Exhibition of Local Antiquities held in the Hartley University Coll. 1904. Edited by F. J. C. Hearnshaw. 1904. The Borough Documents & other Local MSS., pp. 30-32; Maps & Plans of Old Southampton, pp. 35-36; Old Guide Books, etc., pp. 37-38; Prints, pp. 45-48; Literature in Southampton, pp. 123-132.

A Special Local Collection is in the Public Library, and one of Local Paintings and Drawings in the Art Gallery, Southampton. The latter has a printed Catal. The Tudor House Museum (Historical & Antiquarian) at Southampton has no printed Catal.

SYDMONTON.

Kingsmill (Andrew). The MSS. of Andrew Kingsmill, at Sydmonton Court, being ancient deeds relating to Hampshire and Berkshire. (*Hist. MSS. Comm. 15th Rep.*, App. X. pp. 173-174. 1899.)

TITCHFIELD.

Titchfield Abbey Documents. Edited by the Rev. G. W. W. Minns. Announced by the Hampshire Record Soc., 1895, as in the Press.

WELLOW.

Empson (C. W.). Index to the Registers of Baptisms, Marriages, & Burials of the Parish of Wellow. 1889.

WINCHESTER.

Borough Records, & St. John's Hospital Documents, etc., Hen. II. etc., with Printed Index, at the Guildhall, Winchester. (*Local Records Comm. Rep.*, 1902, App. III. p. 74.)

Wright (Thomas). Report on the Municipal Records of Winchester and Southampton. (Brit. Archæol. Assoc. Trans. at Winchester, 1845, pp. 28-39.)

Shenton (F. K. J.). Winchester (Corporation) Records. (*Gentleman's Mag.*, vol. viii. pp. 163-184. 1872.)

Corporation Records, see *ante* Hist. MSS. Comm. Reports.

Winchester Cathedral Records, 10th cent., etc., with MS. Indexes, at Winchester. (*Local Records Comm. Rep.*, 1902, App. III. p. 108.)

Documents relating to the Foundation of the Chapter of Winchester, 1541-47. Edited by G. W. Kitchin and F. T. Madge. Hampshire Record Soc. 1889.

Documents relating to the Hist. of the Cathedral Church of Winchester in the seventeenth century. By W. R. W. Stephens and F. T. Madge. Hampshire Record Soc. 1897.

HAMPSHIRE AND THE ISLE OF WIGHT (continued).

Deedes (Cecil). Report on the Muniments of the Bishopric of Winchester, preserved in the Consistory Court in Winchester Cathedral. Winchester, 1912.

Fearon (W. A.) and Williams (J. F.). Parish Registers and Parochial Documents of the Archdeaconry of Winchester. 1909.

Gunner (W. H.). Catal. of Books belonging to the College of St. Mary, Winchester, in the reign of Henry VI. (*The Archæol. Journ.*, vol. xv. pp. 59–74. 1858.)

Vaughan (John). Winchester Cathedral Close, its Historical and Literary Associations. London, 1914. Part II. chap. vi. Bishop Morley's Library.

A Catal. of Charters, etc., exhibited during the Celebration of the 700th Anniversary of the Mayoralty, 1884. Winchester, 1884.

Holgate (C. W.). Winchester Long Rolls, 1653-1721. Winchester, 1899. Biblio. Introduction, pp. ix.–xcii. Description of Rolls, App. I. pp. 165–187. Lists of other Schools, App. III. pp. 191–201. **1723-1812.** Winchester, 1904. Notes on Long Rolls, App. I. pp. 286–319.

ISLE OF WIGHT.

Davis (Rev. R. G.). Bibliotheca Vectensis, a preliminary Catal. of Books relating to the Isle of Wight (to 1894). 1895.

Note on the Public Records of the Isle of Wight. (*Local Records Comm. Rep.*, 1914, vol. ii. pt. 2, p. 115.)

Index to Births, Marriages, and Deaths in a number of Isle of Wight parishes, compiled by J. C. Burrows, B.A., of Gainsborough, Shide, Isle of Wight.

Plomer (Henry R.). E. V. Utterson's Private Press at Beldornie House, Ryde. (*Some Private Presses of the Nineteenth Century*, in '*The Library.*' New Ser., vol. i. pp. 418–419. 1900.)

Lowndes (Wm. Thomas). List of Publications of the Beldornie Press. (*Bibliographer's Manual*, 1871, App. p. 199.)

Eyton (J. Walter K.). List of Reprints of Rare Poetical Tracts, at the Beldornie Press. (*Sale Catal. of his Library of Privately Printed Books*, Sotheby's, 1848, p. 199.)

12 to 16 copies only were issued of each of the Tracts.

Lyell (Arthur H.). Biblio. List of Romano-British Remains. 1912. Roman Villa at Brading, p. 37.

Trimen (Henry). Botanical Biblio. of the British Counties. Isle of Wight. (*Journ. of Botany*, vol. xii. p. 71. 1874.)

Boulger (G. S.). Botanical Biblio. of the South-Eastern Counties. Isle of Wight. (*South-Eastern Union of Scientific Societies. Trans.*, vol. iv. p. 46. 1899.)

Christy (Miller). Biblio. Note on Isle of Wight Birds. (*Catal. of Local Lists of British Birds*, London, 1891, p. 14.) **Mammals.** (*The Zoologist*, Ser. 3, vol. xvii. p. 185. 1893.) **Reptiles.** (*Ibid.* p. 248. 1893.) **Fishes.** (*Ibid.* p. 259. 1893.)

HEBRIDES.

Anderson (John P.). Book of Brit. Topo., 1881. **Hebrides,** pp. 367–370. 452.

Gough (Richard). Brit. Topo., 1780. **Hebrides,** vol. ii. pp. 732–736.

Bandinel (Bulkeley). Catal. of Books bequeathed to Bodleian Lib. by Richard Gough. 1814. **Hebrides,** p. 366.

Biblio. of the Western Islands and Principal Antiquities of Scotland. (*Soc. Antiq. Irel. Journ.*, vol. xxix. pp. 144–145. 1899.)

Trenholme (Rev. E. C.). The Story of Iona. 1909. Biblio. pp. 165–168.

HEBRIDES (continued).

Beveridge (Erskine). Ancient Maps of North Uist and Descriptions recorded by Early Travellers in that Island. (*North Uist: Its Archæology and Topography*, pp. 332–336. 1911.)

Smith (G. Gregory). The Book of Islay. Documents illustrating the History of the Island. 1895. Privately printed. Descriptions of the Islands from various sources, App. II. pp. 474–483.

Goodrich-Freer (A.). Outer Isles. 1902. (Biblio. references in Preface.)

Macdonald (Archibald). Some Hebridean Singers and their Songs. (*Gaelic Soc. of Inverness. Trans.*, vol. xv. pp. 255–279; vol. xvi. pp. 253–266. 1890–91.)

Trimen (Henry). Botanical Biblio. of the British Counties. Hebrides. (*Journ. of Botany*, vol. xii. p. 237. 1874.)

Christy (Miller). Biblio. Note on St. Kilda Birds. (*The Zoologist*, ser. 3, vol. xiv. p. 265, 1890; and reprinted in pamph., 1891, p. 38.)

——— **Biblio. Note on Isle of Skye Birds.** (*The Zoologist*, Ser. 3, vol. xiv. p. 265, 1890; and reprinted in pamph., 1891, p. 33.)

Special Collection of Isle of Lewis Literature at Stornoway Public Library.

HEREFORDSHIRE.

Allen (John), Jun. Bibliotheca Herefordiensis, or a Descriptive Catal. of Books, Pamphlets, Maps, Prints, etc., relating to the County of Hereford. Hereford, 1821. Maps, Plans, & Prints, pp. 73–92. Portraits, pp. 93–98. Acts of Parliament, 99–117.

Havergal (F. T.). Fasti Herefordenses, and other Antiquarian Memorials of Herefordshire. 1869. List of Books, Pictures, Maps, etc., relating to the Hist. and Antiquities of the City and County of Hereford, pp. 205–214. List of MSS. at the Brit. Museum, pp. 215–218.

Catal. of the Reference Department of the City of Hereford Free Public Library, by J. Cockcroft. 1901. Special Collection of Herefordshire Books, etc., fully Indexed at pp. 203–276.

Bodenham (Frederick). Bibliographer's Manual of Herefordshire Literature. 1890.

Robinson (Charles J.). Materials for a Hist. of Herefordshire. (*Archæol. Journ.*, vol. xxxiv. pp. 425–430. 1877.)

Index to the Transactions of the Woolhope Naturalists' Field Club, 1852–82, compiled by Rev. F. T. Havergal, 1888. **Index, 1883–92,** compiled by W. H. Banks, 1894. Later Indexes issued at short intervals.

Catal. of the Literary Collections relating to Herefordshire, the property of the late Thomas Bird, Esq., consisting of Books, MSS., Portraits, Views, Maps, Pedigrees, etc., sold by auction, 8th March, 1837.

Beach (F. N.). Literary Haunts and Shrines of Herefordshire. (*Book-Auction Records*, vol. v. pt. 4, pp. lv.–lviii. 1908.)

Gross (Charles). Biblio. of Brit. Municipal Hist. (*Harvard Hist. Studies*, vol. v. 1897.) Herefordshire, p. 97. Hereford, pp. 256–257. Leominster, p. 276.

Davenport (Frances G.). List of Printed Materials for Manorial Hist. 1894. Biblio. Note on Herefordshire Manorial Hist., p. 47.

Dove (Patrick Edward). Domesday Studies. 1891. Domesday Biblio. Herefordshire, vol. ii. p. 679.

Lyell (Arthur H.). Biblio. List of Romano-British Remains. 1912. Herefordshire, pp. 43–44.

Murray (David). 'Museums.' Glasgow, 1904. Biblio. Note on Hereford Museum, vol. ii. p. 284.

HEREFORDSHIRE (continued).

An Archæol. Survey of Herefordshire. Part I. by Rev. J. O. Bevan and F. Haverfield. 1896. Biblio. and Topog. Index, pp. 8–13. **Part II.** Mediæval Period, by James Davies and Rev. J. O. Bevan. 1897. Biblio. and Topog. Index, pp. 10–37. (Woolhope Naturalists' Field Club and Soc. of Antiq., London.)

Hist. MSS. Comm. Reports. Herefordshire Collection.

Boycott, The Misses, at Hereford ...	10th Rep. p. 4 and App. IV. pp. 210–223.
Money-Kyrle, Major, at Homme House, Much Marcle	17th Rep. pp. 120–121; Various Collections, vol. iv. pp. 96–139.
Webb, Rev. T. W., of Hardwick Vicarage, co. Hereford	7th Rep. p. xv. and App. pp. 681–693.
Hereford Corporation...	13th Rep. pp. 50–51 and App. IV. pp. 283–353.

County Records, 1615, etc., with MS. Index at the Shire Hall, Hereford. (*Local Records Comm. Rep.*, 1902, App. III. p. 18.)

Macray (W. D.). Catal. of, and Index to MS. Papers, Proclamations and other Documents selected from the Municipal Archives of the City of Hereford. (1894.)

Black (W. H.) and Hills (G. M.). The Hereford Municipal Records and the Customs of Hereford. (*Brit. Archæol. Assoc. Journ.*, vol. xxvii. pp. 453–488. 1871.)

Collins (William). Modern Hereford, with Special Reference to the Development of its Municipality. 1911. List of Acts of Parliament, in part ii. pp. 36–38.

Hereford Cathedral Records, 1228, etc., with MS. Index, at Hereford. (*Local Records Comm. Rep.*, 1902, App. III. p. 112.)

Capes (W. W.). Charters and Records of Hereford Cathedral. [840–1421.] Biblio. Introduction. (Cantilupe Society. 1908.)

Leigh (Rev. the Hon. J. W.). Some Archives and Seals of Hereford Cathedral, with a List. (*Woolhope Naturalists' Field Club Trans.*, 1901, pp. 107–121.)

James (M. R.). The Library of the Grey Friars of Hereford. (Brit. Soc. of Franciscan Studies. '*Collectanea Franciscana*,' vol. i. pp. 114–123, 154, 155. 1914.)

Trimen (Henry). Botanical Biblio. of the British Counties. Herefordshire. (*Journ. of Botany*, vol. xii. p. 155. 1874.)

Christy (Miller). Biblio. Note on Herefordshire Birds. (*The Zoologist*, Ser. 3, vol. xiv. p. 253, 1890; and reprinted in pamph., 1891, p. 15.) **Mammals.** (*The Zoologist*, Ser. 3, vol. xvii. p. 180. 1893.) **Reptiles.** (*Ibid.* p. 244. 1893.) **Fishes.** (*Ibid.* p. 255. 1893.)

Anderson (John P.). Book of Brit. Topo., 1881. Herefordshire, pp. 125-127.
Gatfield (George). Guide to Heraldry. 1892. Herefordshire, pp. 141-142.
Sims (Richard). Manual. 1861. Herefordshire, pp. 167, 207-208, 234.
Upcott (William). English Topo., 1818. Herefordshire, vol. i. pp. 321-332, 622.
Smith (Alfred Russell). Catal. of Topo. Tracts, etc. 1878. Herefordshire, pp. 117-120, 463.
Gough (Richard). Brit. Topo., 1780. Herefordshire, vol. i. pp. 409-418.
Bandinel (Bulkeley). Catal. of Books bequeathed to Bodleian Library by Richard Gough, 1814. Herefordshire, pp. 128-129.

LEOMINSTER.

Borough Records, 1553, etc., at Town Hall, Leominster. (*Local Records Comm. Rep.*, 1902, App. III. p. 62.)

UPTON BISHOP.

Havergal (Rev. F. T.). Records, Historical and Antiquarian, of the Parish of Upton Bishop. 1883. List of Books and Documents, pp. 55–56. Registers, pp. 56-65. Parish Account Books, pp. 65–70.

HERTFORDSHIRE.

[A Bibliography for Hertfordshire under the title 'Bibliotheca Hertfordiensis,' and also a National Portrait Catalogue of the County, were taken in hand some years ago by the East Herts. Archæological Society, and by the St. Albans and Herts. Architectural and Archæological Society. Apparently the work was not completed, although much progress was made.]

Catal. of the 'Lewis Evans' Collection of Books and Pamphlets relating to Hertfordshire in the Hertfordshire County Museum, St. Albans, compiled by H. R. Wilton Hall. 2 parts. St. Albans, 1906, '08.

'The best and only Bibliography of the County in existence. I possess a large number of items which are not recorded in these Catalogues, for I have, in a desultory fashion, been collecting Herts. books, pamphlets, and extracts, for nearly 20 years. I possess, in addition, much material in MS. volumes, which I have extracted from the Public Record Office Publications and elsewhere.'—W. B. Gerish. Bishop's Stortford, 1914.

An Index to the Transactions of the St. Albans and Hertfordshire Architectural and Archæological Soc. 1884–1894. St. Albans, 1898.

A List of Papers read before the St. Albans and Herts. Archit. & Archæol. Soc., from its Foundation in 1845. By H. R. Wilton Hall. (*Trans.*, New Ser., vol. ii. pp. 104–114. 1905.)

''Tis Sixty Years Since.' A Sketch of the St. Albans & Herts. Archit. & Archæol. Soc. By H. R. Wilton Hall. (*Trans.*, New Ser., vol. ii. pp. 123–146. 1912.)

Gerish (W. B.). A Notable County History. An Account of a remarkable 'Grangerized' copy of Clutterbuck's Hertfordshire, illustrated by and for John Morice, F.S.A. (*East Herts. Archæol. Soc. Trans.*, vol. i. pp. 169–171. 1900.)

Andrews (W. F.). The Topographical Collections of a Hertfordshire Archæologist. (*East Herts. Archæol. Soc. Trans.*, vol. i. pp. 159–167. 1900.)

A Quarterly Biblio. of Middlesex and Hertfordshire. (*Middlesex and Herts. Notes and Queries*, vols. i.–iv. 1895–98.)

Norden (John). Speculi Britaniæ Pars. A Description of Hartfordshire, 1598. Reprint, with Biography and Biblio. of Norden's Works, by W. B. Gerish. 1903.

The Hertfordshire Historians. John Norden, 1548-1626 (?). A Biography, with a Biblio., by W. B. Gerish. Ware, 1903.

—— **Sir Henry Chauncy, 1632-1719, Author of 'The Historical Antiquities of Hertfordshire,' 1700.** A Biography with Biblio. Notes, by W. B. Gerish. London, 1907.

Fordham (Sir H. G.). Hertfordshire Maps; A Descriptive Catal. of the Maps of the County, 1579–1900. Hertford, 1907. Reprinted from *Herts. Nat. Hist. Soc. Trans.*, vol. xi. pts. 1, 6; vol. xii. pt. 5. 1902–07.)

—— **Supplement.** Hertford, 1914. Reprinted from *Herts. Nat. Hist. Soc. Trans.*, vol. xv pt. 2. 1914.

Hertfordshire Portraits, Maps and Plans, Newspaper Cuttings, etc., in the Herts. County Museum, St. Albans, with Special MS. Catalogues.

Description of a Collection of Local Sketches (Herts. Topography) at Essendon Place in 1898, made about 1797 by a Schoolmaster of Tewin, named Pridmore, in 9 vols. (*St. Albans and Herts. Archit. & Archæol. Soc. Trans.*, New Ser., vol. i. pp. 29–33. 1898.)

Boyle (Mary Louisa). Biographical Catal. of the Portraits at Panshanger. London, 1885.

Evans (John). An Archæol. Survey of Hertfordshire. (*Archæologia*, vol. liii. pp. 245–262, 1892, and reprinted separately.) Biblio. and Topog. Index, pp. 252–262.

HERTFORDSHIRE (continued).

Gross (Charles). Biblio. of Brit. Municipal Hist. (*Harvard Hist. Studies*, vol. v. 1897.) Hertfordshire, p. 97. Hertford, p. 258. St. Albans, pp. 382-383.

Davenport (Frances G.). List of Printed Materials for Manorial History. 1894. Biblio. Note on Herts. Manorial History, p. 47.

Dove (Patrick Edward). Domesday Studies. 1891. Domesday Biblio. Herts., vol. ii. pp. 679-680.

Lyell (Arthur H.). Biblio. List of Romano-British Remains. 1912. Herts., pp. 45-46.

An Inventory of the Historical Monuments in Hertfordshire. 1910. (*Royal Comm. on Hist. Monuments—England.*)

Gerish (W. B.). Hertfordshire Monumental Inscriptions. A List of Parishes and Transcribers. (*The Register of English Monumental Inscriptions*, vol. ii. pp. 85-89. 1914.)

——— **A Record of Monumental Inscriptions in Hertfordshire,** with a List of Parishes and Transcribers. (*East Herts. Archæol. Soc. Trans.*, vol. v. pp. 191-196. 1913.)

The Transcripts in 13 vols. with Indexes of about 70,000 names are at the Hon. Secretary's House at Bishop's Stortford.

Macklin (Herbert Walter). Monumental Brasses. London: George Allen & Co., 1913. Biblio. Note on Herts. Brasses, with a List, pp. 140, 159-161.

The Late Rev. Henry Fowler's Papers (relating chiefly to St. Albans and Hertfordshire) with a List, by H. R. Wilton Hall. (*St. Albans & Herts. Archit. & Archæol. Soc. Trans.*, New Ser., vol. i. pp. 398-402. 1903.)

An Almanack Maker. Henry Andrews, of Royston. (*Herts. Illust. Review*, vol. i. p. 231. 1893.)

The Ashendene Private Printing Press of St. John Hornby. List of Issues. (*The Revival of Printing. A Biblio. Catal. of Works issued by the Chief Modern English Presses*, with an Introduction by Robert Steele, 1912, pp. 45-48.)

Biblio. of the Rye House Plot. (*Notes and Queries*, Ser. 9, vol. i. pp. 212, 372; vol. ii. pp. 34, 175. 1898.)

Fordham (Sir H. G.). On Local Museums. (*Herts. Nat. Hist. Soc. Trans.*, vol. i. pp. 215-220. 1881.)

Hopkinson (John). The Formation and Arrangement of Provincial Museums. (*Herts. Nat. Hist. Soc. Trans.*, vol. i. pp. 193-214. 1881.)

Special Topographical Collections relating to Hertfordshire are in the County Museum and at the St. Albans Public Library.

Hist. MSS. Comm. Reports. Hertfordshire Collections.

Baker, Mr. W. R., at Bayfordbury ...	2nd Rep. p. xi. and App. pp. 69-72.
Harvey, Mr. John, of Ickwell Bury ...	1st Rep. p. x. and App. pp. 62-63; 2nd Rep. App. pp. 89-91.
Salisbury, Marquess of, at Hatfield ...	3rd Rep. p. xii. and App. pp. 147-180; 4th Rep. p. xii, and App. pp. 199-227; 5th Rep. p. vii. and App. pp. 261-294; 6th Rep. App. pp. 250-277; 7th Rep. p. xiii. and App. pp. 182-196; 12th Rep. pp. 23-34; 13th Rep. pp. 26-31; 14th Rep. pp. 16-23; 15th Rep. pp. 21-27; 16th Rep. pp. 48-56; 17th Rep. pp. 28-34; and vols. i.-xii. (1306-1603).
Verulam, Earl of, at Gorhambury ...	17th Rep. pp. 51-54, and a vol. 1906.
Hertford Corporation	14th Rep. App. VIII. pp. 158-164.
St. Albans Corporation	5th Rep. p. xviii. and App. pp. 565-568.

HERTFORDSHIRE (continued).

County Records, 1620, etc., with MS. and Printed Lists, at the Shire Hall, Hertford, and at the Court House, St. Albans. (*Local Records Comm. Rep.*, 1902, App. III. p. 18.)

Borough Records, 1304, etc., at Hertford. (*Local Records Comm. Rep.*, 1902, App. III. p. 60.)

Records in Public and Private Custody. (*Local Records Comm. Rep.*, 1902, App. III. p. 132.)

Johnston (C. E.). Some Hertfordshire Deeds from the Phillipps Sale, 1913. Chauncy Deeds. (*East Herts. Archæol. Soc. Trans.*, vol. v. pp. 139–142. 1913.)

List of Hertfordshire Non-Parochial Registers. (*The Herts. Genealogist*, vol. i. pp. 182–184. 1895.)

Tancock (Rev. O. W.). The Old Parish Registers of Hertfordshire, with a List arranged under Parishes. (*Midd. and Herts. Notes and Queries*, vol. iii. pp. 7, 59, 140, 178; vol. iv. pp. 24, 62, 135, 170. 1897–98.)

Andrews (W. F.). The Parish Registers of St. Andrew, Hertford. (*East Herts. Archæol. Soc. Trans.*, vol. v. pp. 148–169. 1913.)

Whitaker (William). List of Works on the Geology of Hertfordshire to 1873. (*Watford Nat. Hist. Soc. Trans.*, vol. i. pp. 78–82. 1876.) **1874–83, by John Hopkinson.** (*Herts. Nat. Hist. Soc. Trans.*, vol. iii. pp. 165–172. 1885.)

Pryor (A. R.) and Jackson (B. D.). A Flora of Hertfordshire. Herts. Nat. Hist. Soc. 1887. Biblio., pp. xxxvii.–lviii.

Trimen (Henry). Botanical Biblio. of the British Counties. Hertfordshire. (*Journ. of Botany*, vol. xii. p. 108. 1874.)

Christy (Miller). Biblio. Note on Hertfordshire Birds. (*The Zoologist*, Ser. 3, vol. xiv. p. 254, 1890; and reprinted in pamph., 1891, p. 15.)

Anderson (John P.). Book of Brit. Topo., 1881. Herts., pp. 128-131.

Gatfield (George). Guide to Heraldry. 1892. Herts, pp. 142-143.

Sims (Richard). Manual. 1861. Herts., pp. 167, 208-209, 234.

Upcott (William). English Topo., 1818. Herts., vol. i. pp. 333-347, 623-626.

Smith (Alfred Russell). Catal. of Topo. Tracts, etc., 1878. Herts., pp. 121-126, 463.

Gough (Richard). Brit. Topo., 1780. Herts., vol. i. pp. 419-434.

Bandinel (Bulkeley). Catal. of Books bequeathed to Bodleian Lib. by Richard Gough, 1814. Herts., pp. 130-133.

BENGEO.

Mansel-Pleydell (Rev. J. C. M.) Bengeo Old Church Plate and Old Registers. (*St. Albans and Herts. Archit. & Archæol. Soc. Trans.*, pp. 47–50. 1886.)

BISHOP'S STORTFORD.

Glasscock (J. L.). The Records of St. Michael's Parish Church, Bishops Stortford. 1882. Catalogue of Papers, etc., pp. ix.–xii.

MELDRETH.

Palmer (W. M.) Meldreth Parish Records. Royston. 1896.

ST. ALBANS.

Gibbs (Arthur Ernest). The Corporation Records of St. Albans. 1890.

Corporation Records, see *ante* Hist. MSS. Comm. Reports.

Black (W. H.) On the Town Records of St. Albans. (*Brit. Archæol. Assoc. Journ.*, vol. xxvi. pp. 143–149. 1870.)

List of St. Albans Municipal Records Printed. (*Notes & Queries*, Ser. 11, vol. vi. p. 91. 1912.)

HERTFORDSHIRE (continued).

Archdeaconry Records, 16th cent. etc., with Printed Index, at St. Albans Abbey and Chelmsford. (*Local Records Comm. Rep.*, 1902, App. III. p. 126.)

Hall (H. R. Wilton). Records of the Old Archdeaconry of St. Albans; A Calendar of Papers, 1575-1637. St. Albans and Herts. Archit. and Archæol. Soc. 1908.

Gibbs (A. E.). List of Transcripts of Registers for the Archdeaconry of St. Albans. (*The Herts. Genealogist*, vol. i. pp. 30-32. 1895.)

Blades (William). Some Account of the Typography at St. Albans in the 15th century. London. 1860.

—— **The Printer at St. Albans.** (*The Book-Worm*, vol. i. pp. 169-172. 1866.)

—— **The Schoolmaster-Printer of St. Albans.** (*The Antiquary*, vol. i. pp. 28-30. 1880.)

—— **The Book of St. Albans, printed at St. Albans, in 1486,** with an Introduction. 1901.

Scott (Edward). Who was the Schoolmaster Printer of St. Albans? (*The Athenæum*, 1878, vol. i. pp. 541, 763; vol. ii. pp. 497, 623.)

Allnutt (W. H.). English Provincial Presses—Early Printing at St. Albans. (*Bibliographica*, vol. ii. pp. 24-25. 1896.)

Kitton (F. G.). Notes on Engravings of St. Albans Abbey. (*The Antiquary*, vol. xxxi. pp. 43-52. 1895.)

SAWBRIDGEWORTH.

Gerish (W. B.). Dr. Charles Wade (an Antiquary whose Collections towards a History of Sawbridgeworth are in the possession of Mr. Gerish), with a List of Dr. Wade's Papers in the Sawbridgeworth Collections. (*East Herts. Archæol. Soc. Trans.*, vol. ii. pp. 210-213. 1905.)

TRING.

Murray (David). 'Museums.' Glasgow, 1904. Biblio. Note on Tring Museum, vol. iii. p. 219.

HUNTINGDONSHIRE.

['My MS. Bibliography of Huntingdonshire is formed of quarto sheets arranged alphabetically, of the Books, etc., I have or want, and many biographical notes. It consists of many thousand pages. I want to arrange it for the Press and make it a standard work on the Bibliography of the County.'—H. E Norris. Cirencester. 1914.]

Norris (Herbert E.). Catal. of the Huntingdonshire Books collected by H. E. Norris. Printed by John Bellows of Gloucester for Private Circulation. Cirencester, 1895.

King (Charles). Bibliotheca Huntingdoniensis: a contribution to a Huntingdonshire Bibliography, with Biographical Notices of Authors connected either by birth, residence or an official capacity with that County. (A MS. in possession of H. E. Norris.)

Norris (Herbert E.). Lists of the Booksellers and Printers of St. Ives, St. Neots, and Huntingdon. (*Notes & Queries*, Ser. 10, vol. viii. p. 201; vol. xii. p. 164; Ser. 11, vol. vi. p. 207; viii. p. 44. 1907-13.)

—— **The First Huntingdon Printer: John Jenkinson, 1768-1807.** (*Hunts. County News*, 14 Feb. 1903, and reprinted in *Hunts. Post*, 29 Aug. 1903.)

—— **Robert Edis. 1802-1880. A Huntingdon Printer.** (At present in MS. only.)

—— **Thomas Lovell, Printer at Huntingdon,** with a list of Books printed by him. (At present in MS. only.)

HUNTINGDONSHIRE (continued).

Norris (Herbert E.). Andrew Page Wood and his Son, Alfred Wood, Huntingdon Printers. (At present in MS. only.)

—— **List of Articles on Hunts. Printers.** (*Notes & Queries*, Ser. 10, vol. ii. p. 12. 1904.)

—— **Hunts. Privately Printed Books,** unpublished copies and limited editions. (At present in MS. only.)

—— **Hunts. Book Collectors.** (At present in MS. only.)

—— **On the Earliest Circulating Libraries of Hunts.** (*St. Neots Advertiser*, 14 Apr. 1904.)

—— **Hunts. Book Clubs,** with a list. (*Notes & Queries*, Ser. 11, vol. ix. p. 461. 1914.)

—— **Biblio. of Hunts. Newspapers.** (At present in MS. only.)

—— **The First Hunts. Newspaper.** (*Hunts. County News*, 8 Nov. 1902.)

—— **Index to Newspaper Articles on Hunts.** (At present in MS. only.)

—— **Hunts. Book-plates and Book-labels.** (At present in MS. only.)

—— **Dedications of some Hunts. Books.** (At present in MS. only.)

—— **Catalogues of Engraved Prints, Views, Portraits and Water Colour Drawings.** (At present in MS. only.)

—— **The Earliest Photographs of Hunts.** (*Notes & Queries*, Ser. 11, vol. viii. p. 405. 1913.)

—— **Huntingdonshire Broadsides.** (At present in MS. only.)

—— **Hunts. Poll Books.** (*Notes & Queries*, Ser. 11, vol. ii. p. 183. 1910.)

—— **List of the Principal items in Medland's Collections of Auction Catalogues, Bills, etc.** (At present in MS. only.) Mr. Medland was formerly an auctioneer at St. Neots.

—— **The Hunts. Feast in London.** (*Hunts. County News*, 15 Aug. 1903.)

Gross (Charles). Biblio. of Brit. Municipal Hist. (*Harvard Hist. Studies*, vol. v. 1897.) Huntingdon, p. 261.

Davenport (Frances G.). List of Printed Materials for Manorial Hist. 1894. Biblio. Note on Hunts. Manorial Hist. pp. 47–48.

Dove (Patrick Edward). Domesday Studies. 1891. Domesday Biblio. Hunts., vol. ii. p. 680.

Lyell (Arthur H.). Biblio. List of Romano-British Remains. 1912. Hunts., p. 46.

Macklin (Herbert Walter). Monumental Brasses. London: Geo. Allen & Co., 1913. Biblio. Note on Hunts. Brasses, with a List, pp. 161, 140.

—— **The Brasses of Huntingdonshire.** (*Monumental Brass Soc. Trans.*, vol. iii. pp. 144–182. 1898.)

Boyle (Mary Louisa). Biographical Notices of the Portraits at Hinchingbrook. London, 1876.

Hist. MSS. Comm. Reports. Huntingdonshire Collections.

Duke of Manchester, at Kimbolton...	1st Rep. p. x. and App. pp. 12, 13; 8th Rep. App. II. pp. 1–140.
Tillard, Mr. P. E., at the Holme, Godmanchester	15th Rep. p. 42, and App. X. pp. 78–91.

Griffith (Edward). A Collection of Ancient Records relating to the Borough of Huntingdon. London, 1827.

Archdeaconry of Huntingdon Records, at the Archdeaconry Office, Huntingdon. (*Local Records Comm. Rep.*, 1902, App. III. p. 120.)

HUNTINGDONSHIRE (continued).

Cole (Rev. W.). Collection of MSS., many relating to Hunts. in the Brit. Museum, in 92 vols. numbered. Add. MSS. 5798–5887. Gen. Index to the first forty-six vols. Add. MS. 5801. Other Indexes are at Add. MSS. 5799 and 5800.

Gray (George J.). Index to the Contents of the Cole MSS. in the British Museum. Bowes & Bowes. Cambridge, 1912.

Heraldic and Topographical Collections for the County of Huntingdon of Sir Robert Cotton in the Brit. Museum. Lans. MS., 921.

Suckling's Collections for Huntingdonshire, 1821-1839, in the Brit. Museum. Add. MS. 18479. Index, Add. MS. 18491.

Christy (Miller). Biblio. Note on Hunts. Birds. (*The Zoologist*, Ser. 3, vol. xiv. p. 254, 1890; and reprinted in pamph., 1891, p. 15.) **Mammals.** (*The Zoologist*, Ser. 3, vol. xvii. p. 180. 1893.) **Reptiles.** (*Ibid.* p. 244. 1893.) **Fishes.** (*Ibid.* p. 255. 1893.)

Anderson (John P.). Book of Brit. Topo., 1881. Hunts., pp. 131–132.

Gatfield (George). Guide to Heraldry. 1892. Hunts., p. 143.

Sims (Richard). Manual. 1861. Hunts., pp. 167, 209, 234.

Upcott (William). English Topo., 1818. Hunts., vol. i. pp. 348–349.

Smith (Alfred Russell). Catal. of Topo. Tracts, etc. 1878. Hunts., pp. 127–128.

Gough (Richard). Brit. Topo., 1780. Hunts., vol. i. pp. 435–440.

Bandinel (Bulkeley). Catal. of Books bequeathed to Bodleian Lib. by Richard Gough, 1814. Hunts., pp. 134–135.

KIMBOLTON.

Norris (Herbert E.). Kimbolton Printers. (At present in MS. only.)

LITTLE GIDDING.

Ferrar (Michael Lloyd). The Limerick-Huntingdon Ferrars. Privately printed, 1903. Appendix, Biblio. of the Ferrars, pp. 20–25.

Mayor (J. E. B.). Nicholas Ferrar. (*Cambridge in the Seventeenth Century*, Pt. 1.) 1855. Biblio., Appendix, pp. 289–384.

Skipton (H. P. K.). The Life and Times of Nicholas Ferrar. 1907. Biblio. Notes of Ferrar material.

Norris (Herbert E.). Biblio. Note on Little Gidding Nunnery pamphlet. (The Arminian Nunnery, etc. 1641.) (*Notes & Queries*, Ser. 11, vol. viii. p. 445. 1913.)

RAMSEY.

Birch (Walter de Gray). Historical Notes on the MSS. belonging to Ramsey Abbey. (*Brit. Archæol. Assoc. Journ.* New Ser., vol. v. pp. 229–242. 1899.)

Norris (Herbert E.). Ramsey Printers. (*Ramsey Herald*, 20 Apr. 1904, and *Hunts. County News*, 23 Apr. 1904.)

——— **Ramsey Printers.** (At present in MS. only.)

ST. IVES.

Norris (Herbert E.). St. Ives and the Printing Press. 1889. Reprinted from the '*Hunts County Guardian.*

——— **The St. Ives Mercury.** (*Fenland Notes & Queries*, vol. i. pp. 71–72, 1889; and *Notes & Queries*, Ser. 11, vol. ii. p. 481. 1910.)

——— **St. Ives Booksellers and Printers,** see *ante*.

ST. NEOTS.

Norris (Herbert E.). Notes on St. Neots Printers, past and present. Reprinted from the *St. Neots Advertiser*, 4 May, 1901.

HUNTINGDONSHIRE (continued).

Norris (Herbert E.). Letter on 'Notes on St. Neots Printers.' (*St. Neots Advertiser*, 29 June, 1901.)

—— **A few additional Notes on St. Neots Printers.** (*St. Neots Advertiser*, Sept. 1903.)

—— **David Richard Tomson** (1826–1910), **Printer at St. Neots.** (At present in MS. only.)

—— **The First Directory for St. Neots, 1792.** *St. Neots Advertiser* Office, 1911.

—— **Booksellers and Printers of St. Neots**, see *ante*.

—— **The Contemporary Pamphlets of the Battle of St. Neots.** (*St. Neots Advertiser*, 2 Sept. 1910.)

WARBOYS.

Norris (Herbert E.) Biblio. of the Witches of Warboys. (At present in MS. only.)

INVERNESS-SHIRE.

Noble (John). Miscellanea Invernessiana, with a Bibliography of Inverness Newspapers and Periodicals, edited by John Whyte, and Appendix by William Mackay. 1902. Biblio., pp. 185–230.

—— **Biblio. of Inverness Newspapers and Periodicals.** (*Scottish Notes & Queries*, vol. i. pp. 168, 191; vol. ii. pp. 10, 24, 39, 51. 1888.)

Lees (J. Cameron). A History of County of Inverness. The County Histories of Scotland, 1897. List of Books and Maps relating to or published in Inverness-shire, by William Mackay, pp. 355–367.

Livingstone (Matthew). Guide to the Public Records of Scotland, 1905. Inverness-shire, pp. 121, 177.

Turnbull (William B.) Scottish Parochial Registers, 1849. List of Inverness Registers, pp. 89–93.

Mitchell (Alexander). Inverness Kirk-Session Records, 1661-1800. Inverness, 1902. Account of Kirk-Session Library, in Pt. 3, pp. 189–206.

Gross (Charles). Biblio. of Brit. Municipal Hist. (*Harvard Hist. Studies*, vol. v. 1897.) Inverness, p. 261.

Barron (James). The Northern Highlands in the Nineteenth Century. Newspaper Index and Annals (from the '*Inverness Journal*,' and the '*Inverness Courier*,') 1800–56. 3 vols. Inverness. 1903–13.

Murray (David). 'Museums.' Glasgow, 1904. Biblio. Note on Inverness Museum, vol. ii. p. 297.

Anderson (Joseph) and Black (G. F.). Report on Local Museums in Scotland. Inverness Museum. (*Soc. of Antiq. Scot. Proc.*, vol. xxii. p. 354. 1888.)

Mackintosh (Charles Fraser-). An Old Map of Inverness-shire. (*Antiquarian Notes*, First Series, 1865, pp. 295–298.

List of Books in the Library of the Gaelic Soc. of Inverness. (*Trans.*, vol. xxv. 1907.)

Trimen (Henry). Botanical Biblio. of the British Counties. Inverness-shire. (*Journ. of Botany*, vol. xii. p. 236. 1874.)

Christy (Miller). Biblio. Notes on Inverness-shire Birds. (*Catal. of Local Lists of Brit. Birds*, 1891, p. 34.) **Mammals.** (*The Zoologist*, Ser. 3, vol. xvii. p. 211. 1893.) **Reptiles.** (*Ibid.* p. 249. 1893.)

Anderson (John P.). Book of Brit. Topo., 1881. Inverness-shire, p. 396.

ISLE OF MAN.

HARRISON (WILLIAM). BIBLIOTHECA MONENSIS: a Bibliographical Account of Works relating to the Isle of Man. (Manx Soc. Pubns., vol. viii. 1861.) New Edition. (*Ibid.* vol. xxiv. 1876.)

—— **The Old Historians of the Isle of Man.** (Manx Soc. Pubns., vol. xviii. 1871.)

Train (Joseph). An Historical and Statistical Account of the Isle of Man. 2 vols. 1845. Vol. i. Bibliographical Notes in Introduction; vol. ii. Manks Periodical Press, pp. 381-382.

List of Isle of Man Records Printed. (*Notes & Queries*, Ser. 11, vol. v. p. 74. 1912.)

Some Account of the Manx Society. (*The Manx Note Book*, vol. ii. pp. 174-179. 1886.)

Bailey (John E.). The First Book Printed in Manks. (*Isle of Man Nat. Hist. & Antiq. Soc. Journ.*, vol. i. p. 88. 1890.)

Moore (A. W.) Manx Literature. (*Isle of Man Nat. Hist. & Antiq. Soc. Journ.*, vol. i. pp. 110-115. 1890.)

—— **A Hist. of the Isle of Man.** 1900. List of Authorities, vol. ii. pp 981-988.

Caine (W. Ralph Hall). Isle of Man. 1909. Manx Books, pp. 193-204. Manx Histories, pp. 205-211. The Newspaper Press, pp. 212-219.

Jeffcott (J. M.). Archibald Cregeen, the Manx Lexicographer. (*Notes & Queries*, Ser. 7, vol. x. pp 181-183, 1890; and *Isle of Man Nat. Hist. & Antiq. Soc. Journ.*, vol. i. pp. 302 304. 1890.)

Black (George F.). List of Books in the New York Public Library relating to the Isle of Man. (*Bulletin of the New York Public Lib.*, vol. xv. pp. 756-768. 1911).

Douglas Public Library. Catal. of the Lending & Reference Departments. 1890. Isle of Man Books, etc., pp. 185-190, 357-360.

Special Isle of Man Collection at the Douglas Public Library. Mr. G. W. Wood, of London, has a Collection of Manx Books, MSS., Maps, Prints, etc., of 'unrivalled completeness.'

A List of Principal MSS. at Knowsley, relating to the Isle of Man, examined by P. M. C. Kermode and A. W. Moore in 1896 and 1897. (*Isle of Man Nat. Hist. & Antiq. Soc. Journ.*, vol. iii. pp. 297-303. 1898.)

Quine (Rev. John). The Manx Domesday Book. (*Isle of Man Nat. Hist. & Antiq. Soc. Journ.*, vol. iii. pp. 92-95. 1895.)

Trimen (Henry). Botanical Biblio. of the British Counties. Isle of Man. (*Journ. of Botany*, vol. xii. p. 183. 1874.)

Christy (Miller). Biblio. Note on Isle of Man Mammals. (*The Zoologist*, Ser. 3, vol. xvii. p. 181. 1893.) **Reptiles.** (*Ibid.* p. 245. 1893.) **Fishes.** (*Ibid.* p. 255. 1893.)

Anderson (John P.). Book of Brit. Topo., 1881. Isle of Man, pp. 28-30, 446.

KIRK MICHAEL.

Savage (Rev. E. B.). Notes on the Parish Registers of Kirk Michael. (*Isle of Man Nat. Hist. & Antiq. Soc. Journ.*, vol. i. pp. 3-10. 1889.)

ISLE OF WIGHT.

See HAMPSHIRE AND THE ISLE OF WIGHT.

KENT.

SMITH (JOHN RUSSELL). BIBLIOTHECA CANTIANA: A BIBLIOGRAPHICAL ACCOUNT OF WHAT HAS BEEN PUBLISHED ON THE HISTORY, TOPOGRAPHY, ANTIQUITIES, CUSTOMS, AND FAMILY GENEALOGY OF THE COUNTY OF KENT, with Biographical Notes. 1837.

Contents.—I. Historians of the County. II. Principal Maps of the County. III. Heraldic Visitations, with reference to the MSS. in the British Museum and other places. IV. Tracts printed during the Civil War and Commonwealth, 1640-60. V. A Chronological List of all the Local, Personal, and Private Acts of Parliament (upwards of 600), which have been passed on the County, from Edward I. to Queen Victoria. VI. Works relative to the County in general. VII. Particular Parishes, Seats, Customs, and Family Genealogy, in alphabetical order. The work also comprises a notice of every Paper that has been written on the County, and published in the *Philosophical Transactions of the Royal Society, Gentleman's Magazine, Archæologia, Vetusta Monumenta, etc.*

J. Russell Smith's own copies (2) of '*Bibl. Cantiana,*' interleaved with copious notes and letters, are in the British Museum. The present Vicar of Wateringbury (1914) has a specially fine copy, and Mr. F. W. Cock, of Appledore, has two copies, with ample material for a new edition.

——— **Bibliotheca Cantiana: A Catal. of a valuable and interesting Collection of Books and MSS. relative to the Co. of Kent, collected while writing a Biblio. History of that County.** London, 1837.

Rye (W. B.). Notes on J. R. Smith's Bibliotheca Cantiana. (*Archæol. Cantiana*, vol. xvii. pp. 409-410. 1887.)

Henshall (S.). Specimens and Parts of an Early Hist. of the Co. of Kent. 1798.

Streatfeild (Rev. Thomas). Excerpta Cantiana: being the Prospectus of a Hist. of Kent, preparing for publication. [1836.]

Larking (Rev. L. B.). Memoir of the Rev. Thomas Streatfeild (of Chart's Edge), and Proposals for printing his 'Hist. of Kent,' with a list of plates. Privately printed. [1861.]

The Rev. Lambert Blackwell Larking. (In Memoriam.) (*Archæol. Cantiana*, vol. vii. pp. 323-329. 1868.)

Robertson (W. A. Scott). Memoir of Philipot, the Herald and Antiquary. (*Archæol. Cantiana*, vol. x. pp. lxxxvi.-xcv. 1876, and *Kentish Archæology*, vol. i. 1876.)

Hasted (Edward). Anecdotes of the Hasted Family, with Account of Edward Hasted, by R. Cooke. (*Archæol. Cantiana*, vol. xxvi. pp. 267-294. 1904.)

Letters of Edward Hasted to Thomas Astle (relating to his Hist. of Kent), with references to Deeds and a List. (*Archæol. Cantiana*, vol. xxvii. pp. 136-166. 1905.)

General Index to vols. i.-xviii. 1858-89, of the Archæologia Cantiana. Kent Archæological Soc. Compiled by Rita Fox, and edited by W. A. Scott Robertson. (*Archæol. Cantiana*, vol. xix. 1892.)

Catal. of the Kent Archæological Society's Collections at Maidstone. By George Payne. (*Ibid.* vol. xix. 1892.)

Catal. of Books in the Library of the Maidstone Museum, Chillington House. 1886. Kentish items, pp. 110-121.

A MS. Catal. of Kentish Books to date is in the Museum.

Sale Catalogues of the Topographical Drawings and Prints, Portraits, Library, and MSS. of Thomas Fisher, F.S.A. (including many Kentish items, also a copy of Hasted's 'Kent,' with original drawings and additional prints by Thomas Fisher). Sold by Auction by Southgate & Son, London, Mar. 15, 1837, and by Evans, London, May 30, 1837.

KENT (continued).

Robertson (W. A. Scott). Publications relating to Kentish Archæology. (*Archæol. Cantiana*, vol. xv. pp. 369-381, 1883; reprinted in *Kentish Archæology*, vol. vi. 1884.) Also issued separately.

Notices of Books (relating to Kent). By W. A. Scott Robertson and others. (*Archæol. Cantiana*, vol. xviii. pp. 451-454, 1889, and vol. xxv. pp. 299-308. 1902.)

Notices of New Books relating to Kent. (Assoc. of Men of Kent and Kentish Men, *Year Book*, 1910, p. 49; 1911, p. 44; 1912, pp. 43-45.)

List of Books in the Library of County Literature of the Assoc. of Men of Kent and Kentish Men. (*Year Book*, 1907, pp. 37-39; 1909, p. 37; 1910, p. 37.)

Allnutt (W. H.). English Provincial Presses—Earliest Printing of Canterbury. (*Bibliographica*, vol. ii. pp. 41-45, 300. 1896.)

Plomer (Henry R.). Sir Egerton Brydges' Private Press at Lee Priory. (*Some Private Presses of the Nineteenth Century*, in '*The Library*,' New Ser., vol. i. pp. 409-414. 1900.)

A Catal. of all the Works printed at the Private Press at Lee Priory in Kent from its commencement in July 1813 till its termination in Jan. 1823. Printed by John Warwick, Brooke St., Holborn, London. 1823.

Eyton (J. Walter K.). Publications of the Lee Priory Press. (*Sale Catal. of his Library of Privately Printed Books*, Sotheby's, 1848, pp. 109-114.)

Lowndes (Wm. Thomas). List of Publications of the Lee Priory Press, at Ickham, near Canterbury. (*Bibliographer's Manual*, 1871, App. pp. 218-225.)

Martin (John). Lee Priory Press, with illustration. (*Biblio. Catal. of Books Privately Printed*, 1834, vol. i. pp. 379-404, 533.)

Dibdin (Rev. T. F.). Account of the Lee Priory Press. (*Biblio. Decameron*, 1817, vol. iii. pp. 457-468.)

Catal. of the Sale of Library, etc., at Lee Priory, Aug. 1834, with specimens of the original Wood Cuts engraved for the purpose of illustrating the several works from the Lee Priory Press.

Jubilee of the 'Kentish Express and Ashford News,' July 14, 1855—July 15, 1905. History of the Paper. Ashford, 1905.

Freeman (Rowland). An Account of the Huggett Copy of Lewis's 'Hist. of Thanet'; with a narrative of circumstances which took place between Mr. J. Boys, Solicitor, of Margate, and R. Freeman, of Minster in Thanet, relating to that copy. Canterbury, 1809. A Reply by John Boys, 1809. An Answer to the Reply, by R. Freeman, 1810. Remarks by Daniel Jarvis, 1810. An Answer to Jarvis, 1810.

Payne (George). An Archæol. Survey of Kent. (*Archæologia*, vol. li. pp. 447-468, 1888, and reprinted separately, 1889.) Biblio. and Topog. Index, pp. 451-468.

The Archæol. Section of the South Eastern Union of Scientific Societies has in hand 'Material for a Topographical Index of West Kent,' supplementing this Archæol. Survey.

Hannen (Hon. Henry). An Account of a Map of Kent, dated 1596. (*Archæol. Cantiana*, vol. xxx. pp. 85-92. 1914.)

MS. Catal. of Pictures referring to Kent in the Royal Academy, 1769-1782. (In Maidstone Museum.)

A List of Private Acts, etc., relating to the County of Kent. Stevens & Sons, *circa* 1912.

Gross (Charles). Biblio. of Brit. Municipal Hist. (*Harvard Hist. Studies*, vol. v. 1897.) Kent, p, 98. Canterbury, pp. 185-187. Dover, pp. 209-210. Maidstone, pp. 333-334. Rochester, p. 379.

KENT (continued).

Davenport (Frances G.). List of Printed Materials for Manorial Hist. 1894. Biblio. Note on Kent Manorial Hist., p. 48.

Dove (Patrick Edward). Domesday Studies. 1891. Domesday Biblio., Kent, vol. ii. pp. 680–681.

Lyell (Arthur H.). Biblio. List of Romano-British Remains. 1912. Kent, pp. 47–53.

Macklin (Herbert Walter). Monumental Brasses. London: Geo. Allen & Co., 1913. Biblio. Note on Kentish Brasses, with a List, pp. 141, 161–165.

Special Topographical and Local Collections for Kent are in the Public Libraries at Canterbury, Maidstone, Folkestone, Woolwich, and Lewisham, in the Lambeth Palace Library, and also at St. Augustine's College, Canterbury. Collections of Local and County Antiquities are in the Maidstone Museum and in the Rochester Museum.

Hist. MSS. Comm. Reports. Kentish Collections.

De la Warr, Earl, at Knole Park, Sevenoaks	3rd Rep. p. xv. and App. pp. 217–220; 4th Rep. p. xiii. and App. pp. 276–317.
De L'Isle and Dudley, Lord, at Penshurst	3rd Rep. p. xvi. and App. pp. 227–233.
Filmer, Sir Edmund, at East Sutton Park	3rd Rep. p. xvi. and App. p. 246.
Hothfield, Lord	11th Rep. p. 23, and App. VII. pp. 81–90.
Mackeson, Mr. H. B., at Hythe ...	2nd Rep. p. xi. and App. pp. 91–92.
Sackville, Lord, at Knole	7th Rep. p. xiii. and App. pp. 249–260.
Wilson, Sir J. Maryon, at Charlton House	5th Rep. p. viii. and App. p. 305.
Wykeham-Martin, Mr. P., at Leeds Castle	6th Rep. p. xiv. and App. pp. 465–468.
Canterbury, Black Book of the Archdeacon of	6th Rep. App. p. 498.
——— Dean and Chapter of... ...	5th Rep. p. xii. and App. pp. 426–462; 8th Rep. p. xiv. and App. pp. 315–355; 9th Rep. p. viii. and App. I. pp. 72–129; 16th Rep. pp. 99, 100; Various Collections, vol. i. pp. 205–281.
——— Corporation of...	9th Rep. p. ix. and App. I. pp. 129–177.
Faversham Corporation	6th Rep. App. pp. 500–511.
Folkestone Corporation	5th Rep. p. xvi. and App. pp. 590–592.
Fordwich Corporation...	5th Rep. App. pp. 606–608.
Hythe Corporation	4th Rep. p. xviii. and App. pp. 429–439.
——— Hospital of St. Bartholomew	4th Rep. App. pp. 511–522.
Lydd Corporation	5th Rep. p. xvii. and App. pp. 516–533.
New Romney Corporation	4th Rep. p. xviii. and App. pp. 439–442; 5th Rep. p. xvii. and App. pp. 533–554; 6th Rep. App. pp. 540–545.
Rochester Corporation	9th Rep. p. viii. and App. I. pp. 286–289.
——— Bridge, Wardens of	9th Rep. p. viii. and App. I. pp. 285–286.
Sandwich Corporation	5th Rep. p. xviii. and App. pp. 568–571.
Tenterden Corporation	6th Rep. App. pp. 569–572.

County Records, 1595, etc., with MS. Index, at the Sessions House, Maidstone. (*Local Records Comm. Rep.*, 1902, App. III. p. 18.)

Hasted (Edward). MS. Collections for Kent in the Brit. Museum. 62 vols. Add. MSS. 5478–5539, 16631. List of MSS. etc., relating to Kent by Hasted, Add. MS. 5513. Alphabetical Index to Hasted's Hist. of Kent, Add. MSS. 5517–5519. Gen. Index to Hasted's MSS. relating to Kent, Add. MSS. 5536–5537.

KENT (continued).

Collections to illustrate Hasted's Hist. of Kent. (18th and 19th cent.) 33 vols. Brit. Mus. Add. MSS. 32353–32375.

Philipot's Collections for Kent in the Brit. Museum. Lans. MSS. 267–269, 276.

Suckling's Collections for Kent in the Brit. Museum, 1821–39. Add. MSS. 18484, 18485, 18490. Index, Add. MS. 18491.

Austen (Thomas). Collectanea Cantiana, or Hints and Helps towards a Natural History of the County of Kent. 2 vols. 1759, 1767. Brit. Mus. Add. MSS. 24269, 24270. Catal. of Printed Books and MSS. relating to the Hist. of Kent, at end of vol. i.

Larking (J. W. and Rev. L. B.). Collections, historical and topographical, relating to the County of Kent. 32 vols. Brit. Mus. Add. MSS. 34147–34178. Relates chiefly to the Family of Twysden of East Peckham.

Alexander (W.). Collections for Hist. of Kent. Brit. Mus. Add. MSS. 8836–8838.

Streatfeild (Rev. Thomas). Collections for a Parochial Hist. of Kent Brit. Mus. Add. MSS. 33878–33929.

Thorpe (Dr. John). Collections relating to Kent in Library of Soc. of Antiquaries. MSS. 156–201, 204.

Somner's Collections relating to Kent in the Library of Canterbury Cathedral.

Collections of the Rev. John Lewis, of Margate, relating to Kent, in the Bodleian Library, including a Catal. of MS. Books to be consulted in order to prepare a History of the Co. of Kent. MS. Gough. Kent. 14.

Collection of Kent Deeds in the possession of the Soc. of Genealogists, London.

Catal. of the Heralds' Visitations, with references to other valuable Genealogical and Topographical MSS. in the Brit. Mus. (relating to Kent). MS. Second edition. Printed for James Taylor, London. n.d.

Pegge (Dr. Samuel). A Catalogue Alphabetical of Kentish Authors and Worthies, consisting of voluminous notes, genealogical and bibliographical, with Indexes. Bodleian Lib. MS. Gough. Kent. 8.

Records of Manor Lands, etc., in Kent. (*Descriptive Catal. of the Original Charters & Muniments of Battle Abbey*, on Sale by Thomas Thorpe, Bedford St., London. 1835.)

Descriptive Catal. of Documents belonging to the Kent Archæological Soc. at Chillington House, Maidstone. (*Archæol. Cantiana*, vol. xxv. pp. 256–298. 1902.)

Ancient Deeds and Seals belonging to Lord De L'Isle and Dudley, at Penshurst and Robertsbridge Abbey. Summary of a Paper read before Soc. of Ant. 1914. (*Brit. Archæol. Assoc. Journ.* New Ser. vol. xx. pp. 146–147. 1914.)

Kershaw (S. W.). Lambeth Palace Library, and its Kentish Memoranda. (*Archæol. Cantiana*, vol. ix. pp. 176–188. 1874.)

——— **Kentish Annals in Lambeth Library.** (*Ibid.* vol. xxix. pp. 206–216. 1911.)

Knocker (Herbert W.). A Kentish Register. Details of a Scheme for a Register of Old Deeds relating to Kent. (*Ibid.* vol. xxx. pp. lxxvi.–lxxxviii. 1914.)

Buckland (W. E.). Kent Records. The Parish Registers and Records in the Diocese of Rochester. A Summary of information collected by the Eccles. Records Committee of the Rochester Diocesan Conference. Part I. Introduction. Part II. Inventory of all volumes of Registers of the Parishes in the Diocese of Rochester, and Lists of Accounts of Churchwardens, Accounts of Overseers, Vestry Minute Books, Terriers, Inventories, Tithe Maps and Awards, etc. Kent Archæol. Soc. 1912.

KENT (continued).

Notes on Kent Parish Registers, with a List of those published. (Assoc. of Men of Kent and Kentish Men, *Year Book*, 1907, p. 12; 1910, p. 52.)

Catal. of Books and MSS., many of which were in the celebrated Library at Surrenden, formed by Sir Edward Dering, the first Bart., and his Son and Successor, the Second Bart., also **Books and Tracts formerly in the Library of Sir Roger Twysden,** Bart., the Historian and Antiquary. Sold by Puttick & Simpson, June 8-12, 1858.

Catal. of 300 Deeds and Charters from the famous Surrenden Library formed by Sir Edwd. Dering, in the reign of Chas. I. Sold by auction by Puttick & Simpson, July 10-13, 1861.

Catal. of a Further Portion of the Collection of Deeds and Charters from the Surrenden Library. Sold by Puttick & Simpson, Feb. 4-7, 1863.

Catal. of the Fourth and concluding portion of the famous Dering Collection of Deeds and Charters, formed by Sir Edwd. Dering, sold by auction by Puttick & Simpson, July 13-15, 1865.

On the Surrenden Charters. By Rev. L. B. Larking. (*Archæol. Cantiana*, vol. i. pp. 50-65. 1858.)

The Rev. L. B. Larking compiled elaborate Calendars of the entire Dering Collection of Deeds and Charters, which largely relates to Kentish Parishes.

De Vaynes (Julia H. L.). The Kentish Garland. (Contains reprints of rare single-sheet ballads) with additional notes by J. W. Ebsworth. 2 vols. Hertford. 1881-82.

Trimen (Henry). Botanical Biblio. of the British Counties. Kent. (*Journ. of Botany*, vol. xii. p. 72. 1874.)

Boulger (G. S.). Botanical Biblio. of the South-Eastern Counties. Kent. (*South-Eastern Union of Scientific Societies. Trans.*, vol. iv. pp. 47-49. 1899.)

Hanbury (F. J.) and Marshall (E. S.). Flora of Kent. 1899. List of Books Quoted or Consulted, pp. lxxix.-lxxxiii.

Ticehurst (N. F.). A Hist. of the Birds of Kent. 1909. Biblio. pp. xxv.-xxix.

Christy (Miller). Biblio. Note on Kentish Birds. (*The Zoologist*, Ser. 3, vol. xiv. p. 254, 1890; and reprinted in pamph., 1891, p. 15.) **Mammals.** (*The Zoologist*, Ser. 3, vol. xvii. p. 180. 1893.) **Reptiles.** (*Ibid.* p. 244. 1893.) **Fishes.** (*Ibid.* p. 255. 1893.)

Anderson (John P.). Book of Brit. Topo., 1881. Kent, pp. 132-150.
Gatfield (George). Guide to Heraldry. 1892. Kent, pp. 143-148.
Sims (Richard). Manual. 1861. Kent, pp. 168, 209-211, 235.
Upcott (William). English Topo., 1818. Kent, vol. i. pp. 350-454, 627-636.
Smith (Alfred Russell). Catal. of Topo. Tracts, etc., 1878. Kent, pp. 131-166.
Gough (Richard). Brit. Topo., 1780. Kent, vol. i. pp. 441-492.
Bandinel (Bulkeley). Catal. of Books bequeathed to Bodleian Lib. by Richard Gough, 1814. Kent, pp. 136-150.

BOUGHTON MONCHELSEA.

Calendar of Ancient Deeds presented to the Kent Archæol. Soc., by Charles Marchant (chiefly relating to Boughton Monchelsea). 1904. (*Archæol. Cantiana*, vol. xxvii. pp. 167-176. 1905.)

CANTERBURY.

Borough Records, from reign of Hen. II., at the Guildhall, Canterbury. (*Local Records Comm. Rep.*, 1902, App. III. p. 30.)

Corporation Records, see *ante* Hist. MSS. Comm. Reports.

Wright (Thomas). On the Municipal Archives of the City of Canterbury. (*Archæologia*, vol. xxxi. pp. 198-211. 1846.)

—— **The Archives of Canterbury.** (*Proceedings of the Brit. Archæol. Assoc. at Canterbury*, 1844, pp. 316-328.)

KENT (continued).

Plomer (Henry R.). A short Account of the Records of Canterbury. 1892.

Canterbury Cathedral Records, A.D. 838, etc., with MS. Index, at Canterbury. (*Local Records Comm. Rep.* 1902. App. III. pp. 108, 118.

Ecclesiastical Records, see *ante* Hist. MSS. Comm. Reports.

Powell (Rev. D. T.). Collections relating to Canterbury and the Co. of Kent in Brit. Museum. Add MS. 17733.

Boggis (R. J. E.). A Hist. of St. Augustine's Monastery, Canterbury. 1901. The Historians, p. 129. The Library, p. 186. List of Authorities, pp. 195–196.

Woodruff (Rev. C. E.). A Catal. of the MS. Books in the Library of Christ Church, Canterbury. 1911. Somner Collection, pp. 42–48.

James (M. R.). The Ancient Libraries of Canterbury and Dover. The Catalogues of the Libraries of Christ Church Priory, and St. Augustine's Abbey, at Canterbury, and of St. Martin's Priory at Dover. 1903.

Woodruff (Rev. C. E.) and Danks (W.). Memorials of the Cathedral and Priory of Christ Church in Canterbury. 1912. The Library, pp. 377–404.

Cowper (J. M.) Our Parish Books, and what they tell us: Holy Cross, Westgate, Canterbury. 2 vols. 1885.

Cozens (Walter). Old Canterbury. 1906. Ancient City Plans, pp. 92–118.

Sands (Harold). An Old Map of Canterbury. (*Archæol. Cantiana*, vol. xxxv. pp. 250–254. 1902.)

Murray (David). 'Museums.' Glasgow, 1904. Biblio. Note on Canterbury Museums, vol. ii. p. 163.

COBHAM.

Stephens (F. G.). On the Pictures at Cobham Hall. (*Archæol. Cantiana*, vol. xi. pp. 160–188. 1877.)

DEPTFORD.

Report on the Old Records of the Parish of St. Paul, Deptford, by the Town Clerk, 1906.

Report and List of Records at Deptford Dockyard. (*Local Records Comm. Rep.*, 1914, vol. ii. pt. 2, pp. 184–185.)

DOVER.

Borough Records, Henry III., etc., with MS. Index, at Town Hall, Dover. (*Local Records Comm. Rep.*, 1902, App. III, p. 54.)

Knocker (Edward). On the Municipal Records of Dover. (*Archæol. Cantiana*, vol. x. pp. cxxxiv.–cl. 1876.)

——— **A Lecture on the Archives of Dover.** 1879.

——— **The Archives of the Borough of Dover.** (*Brit. Archæol. Assoc. Journ.*, vol. xl. pp. 1–14. 1884.)

Sims (Richard). Dover Records in the British Museum. (*Brit. Archæol. Assoc. Journ.*, vol. xl. pp. 129–132. 1884.)

Statham (S. P. H.) The History of the Castle, Town, and Port of Dover. 1899. Biblio., pp. xi.–xiii.

——— **Dover Charters and other Documents in the possession of the Corporation of Dover (from 1227 to 1569).** 1902. List of Town Records, pp. xxi.–xxiii.

KENT (continued).

Report of Inspections of certain Records of the Cinque Ports at Dover, Romney, and Rye, Nov. 1911, July 1912, Aug. 1913. (*Local Records Comm. Rep.*, 1914, vol. ii. pt. 2, pp. 165–166.)

James (M. R.). The Ancient Libraries of Canterbury and Dover, 1903, see *ante* Canterbury.

Murray (David). 'Museums.' Glasgow, 1904. Biblio. Note on Dover Museum, vol. ii. p. 210.

FAVERSHAM.

Borough Records, Hen. 3, etc., at Town Hall, Faversham. (*Local Records Comm. Rep.*, 1902, App. III. p. 56.)

Corporation Records, see *ante* Hist. MSS. Comm. Reports.

Giraud (Francis F.). Municipal Archives of Faversham, 1304–1324. (*Archæol. Cantiana*, vol. xiv., pp. 185–205. 1882.)

—— **Faversham Town Charters.** (*Archæol. Cantiana*, vol. ix. pp. lxii.–lxx. 1874.)

Cowper (J. M.). Notes from the Records of Faversham, 1560–1600. (*Royal Hist. Soc. Trans.*, vol. i. pp. 218–238. 1875.)

FOLKESTONE.

Borough Records, 1313, etc., at Town Hall, Folkestone. (*Local Records Comm. Rep.*, 1902, App. III. p. 58.)

Corporation Records, see *ante* Hist. MSS. Comm. Reports.

FORDWICH.

Woodruff (Rev. C. E.). Fordwich Municipal Records. (*Archæol. Cantiana*, vol. xviii. pp. 78–102. 1889.)

Corporation Records, see *ante* Hist. MSS. Comm. Reports.

GOUDHURST.

Hill (R. H. Ernest). MSS. relating to Goudhurst and Neighbourhood. (*Archæol. Cantiana*, vol. xxviii. pp. 10–27. 1909.)

GRAVESEND.

Some Extracts from Gravesend Corporation Records, by a 'Shrimp.' (*The Invicta Magazine*, vol. i. pp. 40–42, 92–93. 1908.)

GREENWICH.

Nunn (F. W.). A list of Books, Pamphlets, Views, etc., relating to Greenwich in the British Museum (and elsewhere). (*Greenwich Anti Soc. Trans.*, vol. i. pp. 75–100, 155–158, 223–243. 1910–12.)

Stone (John M.). Greenwich History as told by Venetian Records. (*Greenwich Antiq. Soc. Trans.*, vol. i. pp. 190–201. 1912.)

HYTHE.

Corporation and other Records, see *ante* Hist. MSS. Comm. Reports.

LESNES ABBEY.

Mandy (W. H.). Collections for Lesnes Abbey. (*Woolwich District Antiq Soc. Ann. Rep.* vol. xvii. pp. 104–107. 1912.)

KENT (continued).

LYDD.

Corporation Records, see *ante* Hist. MSS. Comm. Reports.

Records of Lydd, translated and transcribed by A. Hussey and M. M. Hardy, and edited by Arthur Finn. Ashford, 1911. Biblio. Notes in Introduction.

Lydd Records, by Henry Stringer, Town Clerk. (*Archæol. Cantiana*, vol. xiii. pp. 250–255. 1880.)

MAIDSTONE.

Borough Records, 1500, etc., at Town Hall, Maidstone. (*Local Records Comm. Rep.*, 1902, App. III. p. 66.)

List of Maidstone Municipal Records Printed. (*Notes & Queries*, Ser. 11, vol. v. p. 74. 1912.)

Records in Maidstone Public Library and Museum, 14th cent., etc., with MS. Indices. (*Local Records Comm. Rep.*, 1902, App. III. p. 134.)

A Guide to the Collections in the Museum and Bentlif Art Gallery, with Notes on the Hist. of Chillington Manor House. 1909.

The Reference Library contains a Special Collection of Works relating to Kent generally, including the Topog. Drawings, etc., by Edward Pretty, Dr. T. Charles, and Edward Hughes.

Catal. of Books in the Library of the Maidstone Museum, 1886.

A MS. Catal. of Kentish Books to date is in the Museum.

Kershaw (S. W.). On MSS. and Rare Books in the Maidstone Museum. (*Archæol. Cantiana*, vol. xi. pp. 189–198. 1877.)

Gilbert (Walter B.). The Accounts of the Corpus Christi Fraternity, and Papers relating to the Antiquities of Maidstone. 1865. (Reprinted from '*Maidstone Journal.*') Ancient Deeds relating to Maidstone, pp. 67–86.

Monckton (Herbert). Notes from the Parish Registers of Maidstone. (*Archæol. Cantiana*, vol. xxix. pp. 319–322. 1911.)

MALLING.

Fielding (Rev. C. H.). Memories of Malling and its Valley. 1893. Biblio. Notes on the Registers, pp. 145–220.

NEW ROMNEY.

Corporation Records, see *ante* Hist. MSS. Comm. Reports.

List of New Romney Municipal Records Printed. (*Notes & Queries*, Ser. 11, vol. vi. p. 91. 1912.)

Salisbury's (Edward) Report on the Records of New Romney, with Schedule. (*Archæol. Cantiana*, vol. xvii. pp. 12–33. 1887.)

ORLESTONE.

Lightfoot (W. J.). Notes from the Parochial Registers of Orlestone, and Index to Reg. of Baptisms. (*Archæol. Cantiana*, vol. ii. pp. 89–94. 1859.)

QUEENBOROUGH.

Woodruff (Rev. C. E.). Notes on the Municipal Records of Queenborough. (*Archæol. Cantiana*, vol. xxii. pp. 169–185. 1897.)

List of Queenborough Municipal Records Printed. (*Notes & Queries*, Ser. 11, vol. vi. p. 91. 1912.)

RICHBOROUGH.

Lyell (Arthur H.). Biblio. List of Romano-British Remains. 1912. Richborough, p. 52.

KENT (continued).

ROCHESTER.

Corporation Records, see *ante* Hist. MSS. Comm. Reports.

Blencowe (R. W.). Rochester Records. (*Archæol. Cantiana*, vol. ii. pp. 73–84. 1859.)

Burtt (Joseph). On the Archives of Rochester. (*Archæol. Cantiana*, vol. vi. pp. 108–119. 1866.)

List of Rochester Municipal Records Printed. (*Notes & Queries*, Ser. 11, vol. vi. p. 91. 1912.)

Rochester Cathedral Records. 12th cent., etc., at Rochester. (*Local Records Comm. Rep.*, 1902, App. III. p. 114.)

Archdeaconry Records, 1504, etc., at Rochester. (*Local Records Comm. Rep.*, 1902, App. III. p. 124.)

Buckland (W. E.). Kent Records. The Parish Registers and Records in the Diocese of Rochester. A Summary of information collected by the Eccles. Records Committee of the Rochester Diocesan Conference. Kent. Archæol. Soc. 1912.

Shindler (Thomas). The Registers of the Cathedral Church of Rochester, 1657–1837. Privately Printed. Canterbury, 1892. Biblio. Notes in Introduction.

Fielding (Rev. C. H.). The Records of Rochester. 1910. Notes on Episcopal and Parish Registers, pp. 589–605.

Index to the Monumental Inscriptions in the 'Registrum Roffense.' Privately Printed by F. A. Crisp. 1885.

MS. Collection relating to the Diocese of Rochester in Library of Soc. of Antiquaries, London, consisting of Extracts from Testamentary and Parochial Registers, Transcripts of Deeds, etc.

A Catalogue of Books and Engravings connected with the Hist. and Antiquities of Rochester and Chatham, copied from the 'Bibliotheca Cantiana.' 1837. (A MS. in Brit. Mus. Library.)

Rye (W. B.). Collections for a Hist. of Rochester and the Neighbourhood, comprising an interleaved copy of 'The Hist. & Antiquities of Rochester and its Environs.' Second Edn., with copious MS. notes, letters, cuttings, illustrations, pamphlets, etc. 3 vols. 1817–87. (In British Museum Library.)

SANDWICH.

Borough Records, 1300, etc., with MS. List, at the Guildhall, Sandwich. (*Local Records Comm. Rep.*, 1902, App. III. p. 68.)

Corporation Records, see *ante* Hist. MSS. Comm. Reports.

List of Sandwich Municipal Records Printed. (*Notes & Queries*, Ser. 11, vol. vi. p. 92. 1912.)

TENTERDEN.

Corporation Records, see *ante* Hist. MSS. Comm. Reports.

TRULEGH.

Phillipps (Sir Thomas). Charters relative to the Priory of Trulegh in Kent. (*Archæologia*, vol. xxv. pp. 146–150. 1834.)

TUNBRIDGE WELLS.

Mr. A. M. Broadley, of Bridport, has a fine Collection of Prints, etc., relating to Tunbridge Wells.]

KENT (*continued*).

WALMER.

Elvin (Rev. C. R. S.). Records of Walmer. London. 1890. The Parish Registers, pp. 119–129.

WAREHORNE.

Lightfoot (W. J.). Notes on Warehorne Church, with Indices to the Parochial Registers of Warehorne and Newenden. (*Archæol. Cantiana*, vol. iv. pp. 97–112. 1861.)

WOOLWICH,

Vincent (W. T.). A Woolwich Bibliography; A Schedule of Woolwich Books. (*Woolwich District Antiquarian Soc. Ann. Reports*, vols. 7–19. 1902–14.)

Mr. W. T. Vincent has a large Collection of Books, Prints, and Drawings relating to Woolwich and District.

—— **Local Historiography (relating to Woolwich).** (*Woolwich District Antiquarian Soc. Ann. Rep.*, vol. xiv. pp. 55–78. 1909.)

General Index to vols. i. to xvii., 1895–1911, of the Ann. Reports of the Woolwich District Antiquarian Society. (In vol. xvii.)

A Survey and Record of Woolwich and West Kent. Edited by C. H. Grinling, T. A. Ingram, and B. C. Polkinghorne. (South-Eastern Union of Scientific Societies.) Woolwich, 1909. Biblio. of Works on Geology of District, by W. Whitaker and R. H. Chandler, pp. 25-30. List of Woolwich Celebrities, by W. T. Vincent, pp. 462–464.

The Archæol. Section of the South-Eastern Union of Scientific Societies has in hand 'Material towards a Biblio. of the Archæology of Woolwich and West Kent,' which may be published in a future edition of the '*Survey*.' It is also proposed to compile Lists of Celebrities, Portraits, Prints. etc., illustrating the District.

Norman (William). Woolwich Parish Registers and Vestry Books. (*Woolwich District Antiq. Soc. Ann. Rep.* vol. ii. pp. 43–61. 1897.)

Mandy (W. H.). Documents relating to Plumstead, described in 'The Manor of Plumstead in the XIIIth and XIVth Centuries,' and in 'Early Days of Plumstead.' (*Woolwich District Antiq. Soc.*, vol. xvii. pp. 36–63; vol. xix. pp. 33–49. 1912–14).

KERRY.

Coleman (James). Bibliographia Kerriensis. A List of the Topographical and other separately published Works relating to the County of Kerry. (*Kerry Archæol. Mag.*, vol. i. pp. 38–44. 1908.)

King (Jeremiah). King's History of Kerry. Liverpool. 1908. Kerry Biblio. (from King's '*Irish Bibliography*'), vol. i. pp. 121–125.

Macalister (R. A. Stewart). Studies in Irish Epigraphy. Pts. I. and II. Kerry. 1897, 1902. (With Biblio. references.)

Dix (Ernest Reginald McClintock). List of Newspapers, Pamphlets, etc., printed in the Town of Tralee, from earliest date to 1820. (*Kerry Archæol. Mag.* vol. i. pp. 280–284, 1910.)

—— **Printing in Tralee, 1801-1830,** with a List. (*The Irish Book Lover*, vol. iv. pp. 149–150. 1913.)

—— **Local Printing. Tralee. 1774-1850.** (*Kerry Evening Star*, 4 June, 1906.)

Anderson (John P.). Book of Brit. Topo., 1881. Kerry, pp. 435-436.

Gough (Richard). Brit. Topo., 1780. Kerry, vol. ii. p. 803.

Bandinel (Bulkeley). Catal. of Books bequeathed to Bodleian Lib. by Richard Gough, 1814. Kerry, p. 380.

KILDARE.

Hist. MSS. Comm. Report. Kildare Collections.

Drogheda, Marquess of, at Moore Abbey, Monasterevin ... ... 9th Rep. p. xix. and App. II. pp. 293–330.
Leinster, Duke of, at Carton, Maynooth ... ... 9th Rep. p. xix. and App. II. pp. 263–293.

Macalister (R. A. Stewart). Studies in Irish Epigraphy. Pt. I. Kildare. 1897. (With Biblio. references.)

Paintings and Drawings of Places in the County Kildare, lent to the Picture Gallery of the Dublin Int. Exhib. 1907. (*Co. Kildare Archæol. Soc. Journ.* vol. v. pp. 465–466. 1908.)

Ballads and Poems of the County Kildare, with descriptions, etc. (*Co. Kildare Archæol. Soc. Journ.*, vol. v. pp. 55, 101, 200, 275, 348, 457 ; vol. vi. pp. 101, 175, 240, 347, 415, 494. 1906–11.)

Chamney (W.). Some Old Kildare Book-Plates. (*Co. Kildare Archæol. Soc. Journ.*, vol. vii. pp. 281-287. 1914.)

Anderson (John P.). Book of Brit. Topo., 1881. Kildare, p. 436.
Gough (Richard). Brit. Topo., 1780. Kildare, vol. ii. p. 804.

KILKENNY.

Hist. MSS. Comm. Reports. Kilkenny Collections.

Ormonde, Marquess of, at Kilkenny Castle ... ... 2nd Rep. p. xxi. and App. pp. 209, 210 ; 3rd Rep. p. xxv. and App. pp. 425–430 ; 4th Rep. p. xxiv. and App. pp. 539–573 ; 6th Rep. App. pp. 719–780 ; 7th Rep. p. xvii. and App. pp. 737–834 ; 8th Rep. p. xviii. and App. pp. 499–552 ; 9th Rep. p. xix. and App. II. pp. 126–181 ; 10th Rep. p. 42 and App. V. pp. 1–106 ; 14th Rep. p. 51 and App. VII. ; 15th Rep. p. 46 ; 16th Rep. pp. 122–132 ; 17th Rep. pp. 139–143 ; Ormonde MSS., vols. i., ii. & Index to vols. i., ii. ; New Ser., vols. i.–iv.
Kilkenny Corporation... ... ... 1st Rep. App. pp. 129, 130.
Ossory, Archives of the See of ... 10th Rep. p. 44 and App. V. pp. 219–265.
Rothe's Register of the Antiquities and Statutes of Kilkenny ... 2nd Rep. p. xxi. and App. pp. 257–262.

Prendergast (John P.). Missing Records. No. 1. Records of the Kilkenny Confederate Assembly, 1642–50. (*Kilkenny Archæol. Soc. Trans.*, vol. i. pp. 420–427. 1851.)

Prim (John G. A.). Missing Records. No. 2. Muniments of the Corporation of Kilkenny. (*Ibid.* vol. i. pp. 427-432. 1851.)

—— **Documents connected with the City of Kilkenny Militia in the Seventeenth and Eighteenth Centuries.** (*Kilkenny & South-East of Irel. Archæol. Soc. Proc.*, vol. iii. pp. 231–274. 1856.)

Graves (Rev. James). The Records of the Ancient Borough Towns of the County of Kilkenny. (*Kilkenny & South-East of Irel. Archæol. Soc. Journ.*, vol. iv. pp. 84–93. 1858.)

Carrigan (Rev. William). The Hist. and Antiquities of the Diocese of Ossory. 4 vols. Dublin, 1905. Principal Authorities Consulted, vol. i. pp. xxi.–xxv.

KILKENNY (*continued*).

Watters (**Patrick**). **Original Documents connected with Kilkenny.** (*Roy. Hist. & Archæol. Assoc. of Irel. Journ.*, vol. xii. pp. 532–543. 1874.)

Coleman (**James**). **Local Printing at Kilkenny, 1640–1893.** (*Waterford & South-East of Irel. Archæol. Soc. Journ.*, vol. i. pp. 186–192; vol. ii. pp. 60–64. 1898–99.)

Dix (**Ernest Reginald McClintock**). **Irish Provincial Printing prior to 1701. Biblio. Note on Kilkenny Printing.** (*The Library.* New Ser., vol. ii. p. 344. 1901.)

—— **Printing in the City of Kilkenny in the Seventeenth Century, 1642–49.** (*Royal Irish Academy Proc.*, vol. xxxii., sect. C., pp. 125–137. 1914.)

—— **A very rare Kilkenny-printed Proclamation, and William Smith, its Printer.** (*Royal Irish Academy Proc.*, vol. xxvii., sect. C., pp. 209–212. 1908.)

Gross (**Charles**). **Biblio. of Brit. Municipal Hist.** (*Harvard Hist. Studies*, vol. v. 1897.) Kilkenny, pp. 266–267.

Hogan (**John**). **Map of the City of Kilkenny,** constructed from Rocque's Survey, 1757, the Ordnance Survey, 1841, and from Personal Inspection. (*Kilkenny & South-East of Irel. Archæol. Soc. Proc.*, vol. vi. pp. 350–355. 1861.)

Anderson (John P.). Book of Brit. Topo., 1881. Kilkenny, p. 437.

Gough (Richard). Brit. Topo., 1780. Kilkenny, vol. ii. p. 804.

Bandinel (Bulkeley). Catal. of Books bequeathed to Bodleian Library by Richard Gough, 1814. Kilkenny, p. 380.

GOWRAN.

Prim (**J. G. A.**). **Ancient Documents relative to the Town of Gowran.** (*Roy. Hist. & Archæol. Assoc. of Irel. Journ.*, vol. x. pp. 231–240. 1869.)

Watters (**Patrick.**) **Documents connected with the ancient Corporation of Gowran, 1608–44,** edited by J. G. A. Prim. (*Roy. Hist. & Archæol. Assoc. of Irel. Journ.*, vol. xi. pp. 535–552. 1871.)

KINCARDINESHIRE.

JOHNSTONE (**JAMES FOWLER KELLAS**). **BIBLIOGRAPHY OF THE SHIRES OF ABERDEEN, BANFF, AND KINCARDINE.** New Spalding Club.

Robertson (**Alexander W.**). **Hand-List of Biblio. of the Shires of Aberdeen, Banff, and Kincardine.** New Spalding Club. 1893.

Local Bibliography. (*Scottish Notes & Queries*, vols. viii.–xi. 1895–98.)

Watt (**James Crabb**). **The Mearns of Old. A Hist. of Kincardine from the Earliest times to the Seventeenth Century.** Edinb. 1914. List of Authorities, pp. xxiii.–xxiv. List of References in Proc. Soc. Antiq. Scot., and Catal. Nat. Mus. at Edinb., pp. xxv.–xxxvii. Cartography of The Mearns, pp. xlii.–xlviii.

Jervise (**Andrew**). **Memorials of Angus and the Mearns.** 2 vols. 1885. List of Authorities, vol. i. pp. xxxv.–xli.

Aitken (**G. A.**). **Biblio. of the Writings of John Arbuthnot,** (B. Arbuthnot, N.B.) in '*Life and Works of John Arbuthnot*,' 1892, pp. 176–188.

References to Kincardineshire in Acts of Parliament of Scotland. ('*Aberdeen Journal*' *Notes & Queries*, vol. ii. pp. 133, 134, 141. 1909.)

KINCARDINESHIRE (continued).

Hist. MSS. Comm. Reports. Kincardineshire Collections.

Arbuthnott, John, Viscount, at Arbuthnott Castle	8th Rep. p. xvii. and App. pp. 297–308.
Burnett, Sir James Horn, at Crathes Castle	2nd Rep. p. xix. and App. p. 197.
Monboddo, Lord, at Monboddo ...	4th Rep. p. xxii. and App. pp. 518–521; 6th Rep. p. xviii. and App. pp. 673–681.

Inventories of Northern Records. II. The Sheriff Court of Kincardine. By G. M. Hossack. (*Scottish Notes & Queries*, vol. xii. pp. 168, 169. 1899.)

Turnbull (William B.). Scottish Parochial Registers, 1849. List of Kincardineshire Registers, pp. 93–95.

Trimen (Henry). Botanical Biblio. of the British Counties. Kincardineshire. (*Journ. of Botany*, vol. xii. p. 236. 1874.)

Christy (Miller). Biblio. Note on Kincardine Birds. (*Catal. of Local Lists of British Birds*, 1891, p. 35.)

Anderson (John P.). Book of Brit. Topo., 1881. Kincardineshire, p. 397.

Gough (Richard). Brit. Topo., 1780. Kincardineshire, vol. ii. p. 697.

Bandinel (Bulkeley). Catal. of Books bequeathed to Bodleian Lib. by Richard Gough, 1814. Kincardineshire, p. 361.

KING'S COUNTY.

Hist. MSS. Comm. Report. King's County Collection.

Rosse, Earl of, at Birr Castle, Parsonstown	1st Rep. p. xii. and App. p. 127; 2nd Rep. p. xx. and App. pp. 217–223.

Macalister (R. A. Stewart). Studies in Irish Epigraphy. Pt. II. King's County. 1902. (With Biblio. references.)

Dix (Ernest Reginald McClintock. Local Printing. Birr, 1775-1892. (*Leinster Reporter.* 7 Sept. 1901, and 22 Aug. 1903.)

——— **Printing in Birr, or Parsonstown, 1775-1825, with a List.** (*The Irish Book Lover*, vol. iii. pp. 177–179. 1912.)

Anderson (John P.). Book of Brit. Topo., 1881. King's County, p. 437.

KINROSS SHIRE.

Mackay (Æneas J. G.). List of Books relating to Fife and Kinross. Edinb. Biblio. Soc. Pubns., vol. iii. pp. 1–30. 1899. List of Maps of Fife & Kinross, p. 30.

——— **A History of Fife and Kinross.** The County Histories of Scotland. 1896. List of Books relating to Fife & Kinross, pp. 361–389.

Simpkins (J. E.). Examples of Printed Folk-Lore concerning Fife, with some notes on Clackmannan and Kinross-shire. (*County Folk-Lore*, vol. vii. Folk-Lore Soc., 1914.) List of Authorities, pp. xix.-xxxv.

The Blairadam Private Press at Cleish. For some books printed there, see Beveridge, '*Biblio. of Works relating to Dunfermline and the West of Fife.*' (Edinb. Biblio. Soc. Pubns. vol. v. 1901.)

Turnbull (William B.). Scottish Parochial Registers. 1849. List of Kinross-shire Registers, pp. 96, 97.

Trimen (Henry). Botanical Biblio. of the British Counties. Kinross shire. (*Journ. of Botany*, vol. xii. p. 235. 1874.)

KINROSS-SHIRE (continued).

Christy (Miller). Biblio. Note on Kinross-shire Mammals. (*The Zoologist*, Ser. 3, vol. xvii. p. 211. 1893.)

Anderson (John P.). Book of Brit. Topo., 1881. Kinross-shire, p. 397.
Gough (Richard). Brit. Topo., 1780. Kinross-shire, vol. ii. p. 698.
Bandinel (Bulkeley). Catal. of Books bequeathed to Bodleian Lib. by Richard Gough, 1814. Kinross-shire, p. 362.

KIRKCUDBRIGHTSHIRE.

Hist. MSS. Comm. Reports. Kirkcudbright Collections.

Selkirk, Earl of, at St. Mary's Isle ... 4th Rep. p. xxiii. and App. pp. 516–518.
Witham, Mr. & Mrs. Maxwell, at Kirkconnell ... ... 5th Rep. p. xx. and App. pp. 650–654.
Kirkcudbright, Burgh of ... ... 4th Rep. p. xxiii. and App. pp. 538–539.

County Council Records, 1600, etc., at Kirkcudbright. (*Local Records Comm. Rep.*, 1902, App. III. p. 84.)

Burgh Records, 17th cent., etc., with MS. Index, at Town Hall, Kirkcudbright. (*Local Records Comm. Rep.*, 1902, App. III. p. 94.)

Turnbull (William B.). Scottish Parochial Registers. 1849. List of Kirkcudbright Registers, pp. 97–101.

Biblio. of Historical Monuments, etc., in the Co. of the Stewartry of Kirkcudbright, in '*Fifth Report and Inventory of Monuments, etc., in Galloway*,' vol. ii. pp. xix–xx. Hist. Monuments (Scot.) Commission. 1914.

Anderson (Joseph) and Black (Geo. F.). Report on Local Museums in Scotland. Kirkcudbright Museum. (*Soc. of Antiq. Scot. Proc.*, vol. xxii. p. 398. 1888.)

Trimen (Henry). Botanical Biblio. of the British Counties. Kirkcudbrightshire. (*Journ. of Botany*, vol. xii. p. 234. 1874.)

Christy (Miller). Biblio. Note on Kirkcudbright Birds. (*Catal. of Local Lists of British Birds*, London, 1891, p 35). **Mammals.** (*The Zoologist*, Ser. 3, vol. xvii. p. 211. 1893.) **Reptiles.** (*Ibid.* p. 250. 1893.)

Anderson (John P.). Book of Brit. Topo., 1881. Kirkcudbright, p. 398.
Gough (Richard). Brit. Topo., 1780. Kirkcudbright, vol. ii. p. 698.
Bandinel (Bulkeley). Catal. of Books bequeathed to Bodleian Lib. by Richard Gough, 1814. Kirkcudbright, p. 362.

LANARKSHIRE (Chiefly GLASGOW).

[Glasgow items have not been separately grouped, but are included with those for the County generally.]

Murray (David). Bibliography: Its Scope and Methods, with a View of the Work of a Local Bibliographical Society. Opening Presidential Address, Glasgow Biblio. Soc. 1912. (*Records*, vol. i. pp. 1–105. 1914.) The Printing Press in Glasgow, pp. 65–77. Local Bibliography, pp. 78–80. Biblio. of Glasgow, pp. 81-96. Some Glasgow Bibliographers, pp. 97–105.

Records of the Glasgow Bibliographical Society. Vol. I. Sess. 1912–1913. Glasgow, 1914. Contents:
Constitution and Rules, pp. vii–viii.
Bibliography: Its Scope and Methods, by David Murray, pp. 1–105.
On 'The Protestation of the Generall Assemblie of the Church of Scotland,' made at Glasgow in November, 1638, by William Stewart, pp. 106–117.
The Campbeltown Declaration of 1685, by Rev. W. J. Couper, pp. 118–124.
Biblio. of the Chap-Books attributed to Dougal Graham, by J. A. Fairley, pp. 125–215.
Mr. Peter Rae, Printer, by G. W. Shirley, pp. 216–235.

LANARKSHIRE (*continued*).

Records of the Glasgow Bibliographical Society. Vol. II. Book of the Foulis Exhibition comprising Catalogue, President's Opening Address and Descriptive Account. Glasgow, 1913. Contents:

Catalogue of The Foulis Exhibition held in the Univ. of Glasgow, April 1913.

Robert & Andrew Foulis and the Glasgow Press, with some account of The Glasgow Academy of the Fine Arts, by David Murray.

Descriptive Account of The Foulis Exhibition (reprinted from 'The Library,' July 1913).

The objects of the Glasgow Biblio. Soc. are thus expressed in the Constitution and Rules:—II. The object of the Society is to encourage and stimulate the study of Bibliography in all its branches, but with special attention to the Bibliography of Scotland, and particularly of Glasgow and the West.

The Society seeks to attain this object so far as concerns Glasgow and the West:

I. By the preparation and reading of papers giving (1) Lists of authors, printers, publishers, booksellers, and bookbinders; and of illustrations, manuscripts and printed books. (2) Histories and bibliographies of authors, printers, presses, publishers, booksellers, book-auctions, institutions, libraries, periodicals and individual books. (3) Bibliographies of special movements in religion, politics, science, letters, art, commerce, etc.

II. By the exhibition, at the meetings, of manuscripts, books, broadsides, etc.

Catal. of Stirling's and Glasgow Public Library. By Thomas Mason. 1888. Glasgow items, pp. 211–221. **Supplementary Catal. 1888–96.** By W. J. S. Paterson. 1897. Glasgow items, pp. 49–51.

Catal. of the Books in the Library of the Faculty of Procurators in Glasgow, with Index of Subjects. By John Muir. Glasgow, 1903. Glasgow items, pp. 285–294. **Supplement to Catal. 1903–09.** Glasgow, 1909. Glasgow items, pp. 60–66.

Catal. of Books in the Library of the Philosophical Soc. of Glasgow, to which is added Catal. of Books in the Library of the Architectural Section. Glasgow, 1883. Glasgow and District items, pp. 61–68.

Catal. of the Books in the Library of the Inst. of Accountants and Actuaries in Glasgow, compiled by J. M. Mitchell. Glasgow, 1906 (contains numerous Glasgow items).

Catal. of Books in the Library of the Natural History Soc. of Glasgow, 1883.

Hill (William Henry). Reference Catal. of Books, Pamphlets and Plans, etc., relating to Glasgow, in the Library at Barlanark. Glasgow, 1905.

The Book of Bishop's Castle and Handbook of the Archæological Collection, Inter. Exhib. Glasgow, 1888. Glasgow Literature, pp. 135–144. Glasgow Maps, Views, etc., pp. 159–170.

The Memorial Catal. of the Old Glasgow Exhib. 1894. [Exhibition illustrative of Old Glasgow.] Published by the Glasgow Inst. of the Fine Arts. 1896.

Portraits, by J. O. Mitchell, pp. xv–xx, with a List, pp. 473–480.

Views, Maps and Plans, by William Young, pp. xxi–xxiii.

Charters and MSS., by Robert Renwick, pp. xxiv–xxvi.

Glasgow Printers, Publishers and Booksellers, by David Robertson, pp. xxx–xxxii.

List of Newspapers, Periodicals, etc. 1713–1855, pp. 469–472.

Mitchell (John Oswald). Old Glasgow Essays. 1905. Biblio. of Author's Writings on local Glasgow Hist., pp. v–viii. 'Old Glasgow' Exhib. Portraits, pp. 268–303.

Renwick (Robert). Glasgow Memorials. 1908. List of Authorities, pp. ix–xii.

Index to 'Glasgow Past and Present.' [By Robert Reid and others.] Second Edition. 3 vols. 1884. Index compiled by David Robertson. Glasgow, 1884.

Gough (Richard). Correspondence as to his Materials for Biblio. of Lanarkshire. (In the Mitchell Library, Glasgow.)

LANARKSHIRE (continued).

Notices of William Euing (1788-1874), Book Collector, in Mason. *Public & Private Libraries of Glasgow*, 1885, p. 176; Dickson, *Notes on Hist. of Glasgow Univ. Lib.*, 1888, pp. 72–87; and Dickson, *Roy. Soc. of Edinb. Proc.*, vol. viii. p. 491.

Catal. of a Rare and Valuable Library of Works in Early Englishand Scottish History, Ballads, Songs, and Chap Books,—the Property of a well-known Collector (James Barclay Murdoch, 1831-1906). Glasgow, 1870.

There were other Sales: Edinburgh, Mar. & Apr. 1907; Glasgow, Apr. 1907, and London, June 1907. See Mason's '*Public and Private Libraries of Glasgow*,' 1885, p. 333, and '*Hist. of the Geol. Soc. of Glasgow*,' 1908, p. 241.

Couper (W. J.). Biblio. of the Glasgow Periodical Press. (Preparing.)

Chronological and Biblio. Catal. of Literary Periodical Works published in Glasgow during the present century. 1801-26. (*The Ant.*, Glasgow, pp. 289–296. 1827.)

Grant (James). Past and Present Glasgow Newspapers. (*The Newspaper Press, its Origin*, etc., 1872, pp. 457–472.)

Graham (M.). The Early Glasgow (Newspaper) Press. Glasgow, 1906.

Kilpatrick (James A.). Literary Landmarks of Glasgow. 1898.

Indexes to 'The Glasgow Herald' issued in separate volumes since 1907.

Centenary of 'The Glasgow Herald.' Proceedings at the Celebration in Glasgow and London, Jan. 27, 1882, with notes on the Hist. of the Newspaper.

Guild (J. Wyllie). Early Glasgow Directories. (*Glasgow Archæol. Soc. Trans.*, vol. ii. pp. 199–203. 1883.)

Many of the valuable Glasgow Directories, formerly in Mr. Guild's possession, are now (by his gift) in the Lib. of the Inst. of Accountants of Glasgow, of which a Catalogue is printed.

Jones's Directory for 1789, Reprint with introduction by James MacLehose, its Publisher, with Manuscript Notes on Early Glasgow Directories, etc., by the late John Buchanan. 1866. (Exhibit at Old Glasgow Exhibition, 1894.) See also *Notes & Queries*, Ser 6, vol. ix. pp. 73, 434. 1884.

Strang (John). Glasgow and its Clubs. (Contains many Biblio. and Literary allusions). Glasgow, 1856.

Catal. of the Water Color Drawings of 'Glasgow in the forties,' by William Simpson, with explanatory notes. 1900.

Catal., descriptive and historical, of the Pictures and Sculpture in the Corporation Galleries of Art, Glasgow, compiled by James Paton. Glasgow, 1898.

Murray (David). 'Museums.' Glasgow, 1904. Biblio. Note on Glasgow Museums, vol. ii. p. 257.

Gross (Charles). Biblio. of Brit. Municipal Hist. (*Harvard Hist. Studies*, vol. v. 1897.) Lanarkshire, p. 132.

Lyell (Arthur H.). Biblio. List of Romano-British Remains. 1912. Lanarkshire, p. 139.

Murray (David). The Printing Press in Glasgow. (*Glasgow Biblio. Soc. Records*, vol. i. pp. 65–77. 1914.)

——— **Printing in Glasgow, 1638-1742.** Lists of issues of various Glasgow Printers from George Anderson to Robert Urie. (*Glasgow Biblio. Soc. Records*, vol. ii. *Catal. of The Foulis Exhibition*, pp. 5–10. 1913.)

A paper on Robert Urie, by Dr. H. A. M'Lean, is to be published in the '*Records of the Glasgow Biblio. Soc.*'

——— **Some Early Grammars and other School Books in use in Scotland,** more particularly those printed at or relating to Glasgow. (From Proceedings Roy. Philos. Soc. of Glasgow.) 2 pts. 1905-06.

LANARKSHIRE (*continued*).

Macvean (Duncan). Hist. of Glasgow Printing, 1638–1740. (Appended to his Edition of M'Ure's '*View of the City of Glasgow*,' pp. 367–372. 1830.)

Couper (W. J.). The Origins of Glasgow Printing. (Reprinted from the '*Scottish Typographical Journal*.') Privately printed. Edinb., 1911.

Stewart (William). Early Glasgow Printers. (*Glasgow Herald*, 18 Apr., 1903.)

Aldis (Harry G.). List of Glasgow Printers, Booksellers, etc. (*A List of Books printed in Scotland before* 1700. Edinb. Biblio. Soc. Pubns., vol. vii. p. 106. 1904.)

Smail (Adam). Some Notes on the Early Printers, Publishers, and Booksellers of Glasgow, and Remarks on its Public and Private Libraries. (*Book-Auction Records*, vol. v. pt. 3, pp. xxxv.–xl. 1908.)

Mr. David Murray possesses 'a fair collection of Glasgow, and another of Scottish Catalogues.'

Memorial of the Printers and Booksellers of Glasgow addressed to the House of Commons, April 25, 1774.

Information anent His Majestie's Printers in Scotland, and Answers for James Anderson, His Majesty's Printer, and Agnes Campbell, his mother, to the petition of Robert Saunders, Printer in Glasgow. (*The Spottiswoode Miscellany*, vol. i. pp. 295–310.) The Spottiswoode Soc., 1844.

The Rev. W. J. Couper read a paper on 'Robert Sanders, Printer in Glasgow, 1661-1694,' with a Bibliography, before the Glasgow Biblio. Soc. in Jan., 1914. Mr. Couper has in preparation a list of the productions of the Sanders press.

Murray (David). Robert and Andrew Foulis, and the Glasgow Press, with some account of the Glasgow Academy of the Fine Arts. Glasgow : J. MacLehose & Sons, 1913. Also issued in '*Glasgow Biblio. Soc. Records*, vol. ii. *Book of The Foulis Exhibition*.' 1913.

Catal. of The Foulis Exhibition held in the University of Glasgow. April, 1913. (*Glasgow Biblio. Soc. Records*, vol. ii. *Book of The Foulis Exhibition*. 1913.) The Foulis Press, pp. 11–19. The various Catalogues issued by the Foulis firm are also described.

Macleod (R. D.). The Foulis Press. (*The Library*, Ser. 3, vol. i. pp. 172–189. 1910.)

Ferguson (John). The Brothers Foulis and Early Glasgow Printing. (*The Library*, vol. i. pp. 81–96. 1889.) Also issued separately.

Duncan (William James). Notices and Documents illustrative of the Literary Hist. of Glasgow during the greater part of last century. Maitland Club, 1831, and reprint, 1886. Hist. of Printing in Glasgow, pp. 1–48. Catal. of Books printed by R. & A. Foulis, pp. 49–80.

MacGeorge (Andrew). Old Glasgow. 3rd Edn., 1888. Literary History, pp. 278–285 (includes accounts of Glasgow Printers, The Foulises, The First Directory, Newspapers, etc.).

Wallace (Andrew). A Popular Sketch of the Hist. of Glasgow. 1882. Biblio. Notes on Printing and Newspapers, pp. 57–60.

A Catalogue of Books To be sold by way of Auction in the Coffee-House of Glasgow upon the 17 day of June, etc. [1712]. Printed in the year 1712. A reprint. (*Glasgow Archæol. Soc. Trans.*, vol. ii. pp. 313-335. 1883.)

Duncan (A. and J.). Specimens of Types and Inventory of Printing Materials belonging to the University Printing Office of Glasgow. . . . offered for sale by private bargain. n.d.

Regulations for the Bookbinders Society, Glasgow, 1797.

Regulations for the Company of Stationers of Glasgow, 1817.

LANARKSHIRE (*continued*).

Aird (**Andrew**). **Reminiscences of Editors, Reporters, and Printers [in Glasgow] 1830-1890.** Glasgow, 1891

——— **Letterpress Printing in Glasgow during the last fifty years.** 1882.

Dibdin (**Rev. T. F.**). **Glasgow Libraries and Printing.** (*Northern Tour*, 1838, vol. ii. pp. 661–779.)

Murray (**David**). **Account of Chap-Books issued at Glasgow, with List of Glasgow Publishers and Booksellers engaged in the Chap-Book business,** in Presidential Address on 'Bibliography.' (*Glasgow Biblio. Soc. Records*, vol. i. pp. 55–58, 86–89. 1914.)

Halliwell-Phillipps (**J. O.**). **Some Account of a Singular and Unique Collection of Early Penny Merriments and Histories printed at Glasgow, 1695–98.** [London], 1864. 25 copies printed.

Catal. of the Culter Maynes Library. Edinburgh, 1869.

'Adam Sim, of Culter Maynes (1805-1868), a Glasgow citizen, had a Collection of Penny Ballads with Motherwell's autograph.'—David Murray.

Murray (**David**). **'Museums.'** Glasgow, 1904. Biblio. Note on Collection of Adam Sim, at Coulter, vol. iii. p. 176.

MacGregor (**George**). **The Collected Writings of Dougal Graham,** with Biog. & Biblio. Introduction, and a Sketch of the Cheap Literature of Scotland. Glasgow, 1883. 2 vols.

Fairley (**John A.**). **Dougal Graham. 'Skellat' Bellman of Glasgow and his Chap-Books.** Hawick, 1908.

——— **Biblio. of the Chap-Books attributed to Dougal Graham.** (*Glasgow Biblio. Soc. Records*, vol. i. pp. 125–215. 1914.)

The Glasgow Ballad Society was formed in 1876 for the Study of Ballads and Ballad Literature. Three vols. have been issued of Ballads and Poems by the Members, 1885-1908.

Ewing (**J. C.**). **Brash and Reid. Their Collection of Poetry.** (*Glasgow Herald*, 16 & 23 Apr., 1910.) A few copies reprinted in slips.

Brash and Reid were Booksellers, in Trongate, and were also Publishers. To their labours the bibliomaniac is indebted for some rather scarce and curious publications. In 1800 they issued 'A Catal. of Books on Sale.'

Mason (**Thomas**). **Public and Private Libraries of Glasgow:** a Bibliographical Study. 1885.

Descriptive Handbook of the Glasgow Corporation Public Libraries, with plans and illustrations. Issued on the occasion of the laying of the Memorial Stone of the New Mitchell Library by Dr. Andrew Carnegie, and of the Annual Conference of the Library Assoc. at Glasgow, 1907. Glasgow, 1907.

Barrett (**F. T.**). **Glasgow Libraries.** British Assoc. Handbook, pp. 163–174. Glasgow, 1901.

Notes on Glasgow Libraries (by various authorities). (*The Library Assoc. Record*, vol. ix. pp. 549-567. 1907.)

Brief Notices of Glasgow and its Libraries. Prepared for American Librarians. Glasgow, 1897.

Stirling (**Walter**). **'Deed of Mortification'** by Walter Stirling, Merchant in Glasgow, of a Fund for establishing a public library for the benefit of the Inhabitants of Glasgow. Glasgow: A. Duncan & R. Chapman. 1791.

Catal. of the Library of James Bogle (**1804-55**). Glasgow, 1856.

James Bogle gave to Stirling's Library a valuable Collection of Local Tracts and Pamphlets. A Notice of Bogle, by John Buchanan, appeared in the '*Glasgow Herald*,' 11 May, 1855.

LANARKSHIRE (continued).

Murray (David). A Plea for Stirling's Library. An Address at the Anniversary Meeting, 10 Apr., 1894, with a Note on the copy of Cranmer's Bible in Stirling's Library. Glasgow, 1894.

Stirling's and Glasgow Public Library. Its story from the Minute Books. (*Report of the Proceedings at the Centenary Meeting*, 1891. Appendix A, pp. 29–52.)

The New Mitchell Library, Glasgow. (*The Builder*, vol. 101, pp. 569–571. 1911.)

Munimenta Alme Universitatis Glasguensis. Records of the Univ. of Glasgow from its Foundation till 1727. (Maitland Club.) 4 vols. 1854. Tables of Records in vols. i.–iii. The Library and Early Catalogues, vol. iii. pp. xxvi.–xxxvi.

Dickson (William Purdie). The Glasgow University Library. Notes on its history, arrangement, and aims. 1888.

——— **The Glasgow University Library—Its Growth by Donations.** (*The Library*, vol. viii. pp. 381–393. 1896.)

Galbraith (James Lachlan). The Curator of Glasgow University Library (William Purdie Dickson). Glasgow, 1909.

Scottish Univ. Libraries. Lists of Printed Catalogues. Glasgow. (*Aberdeen Univ. Lib. Bull.*, vol. i. pp. 401–403. 1912.)

Books Published by James MacLehose from 1838 to 1881, and by James MacLehose to 1905. Presented to the Library of the Univ. of Glasgow. Glasgow, 1905.

Included in the gift is a Collection of 1121 pamphlets and prints, many of them relating to the Univ. of Glasgow, published by James MacLehose and by James MacLehose & Sons, publishers to the Univ. 60 vols. 1841-1905.

Young (John). Address on the Hunterian Library. (*Essays and Addresses*, 1904, pp. 119–142.)

Catal. of the MSS. in the Library of the Hunterian Museum in the Univ. of Glasgow. By John Young and P. Henderson Aitken. 1908.

The Glasgow Univ. Lib. contains the finest, if not the most extensive Library in Scotland. It possesses many Special Collections, including a unique set of Glasgow pamphlets, in 118 volumes, bequeathed about 1847 by John Smith, bookseller, Secretary of the Maitland Club. This Collection includes political manifestoes, election squibs, placards, tracts, ballads, and chap-books. The Library also contains eleven vols. of MS. Letters relative to the Stained Glass Windows of the Cathedral, by Charles Heath Wilson.

Index to the Proceedings of the Philosophical Soc. of Glasgow, vol. i.–xx. 1841–89. Glasgow, 1892.

Anderson (P. J.). List of Glasgow University Periodicals. (*Notes & Queries*, Ser. 7, vol. iv. p. 69; Ser. 8, vol. ix. p. 453. 1887, 96.)

Special Glasgow and other Collections are in the Glasgow University Library, the Mitchell Library, Stirling's Library, Baillie's Institution (including the Books and Pamphlets belonging to the Glasgow Archæol. Soc.).

Hist. MSS. Comm. Reports. Lanarkshire Collections.

Cochrane, Mr. A. D. R. Baillie-, at Lamington	5th Rep. p. xx. and App. p. 632.
Hamilton, Duke of, at Hamilton Palace	1st Rep. p. xii. and App. pp. 112–116; 11th Rep. pp. 38–42, and App. VI. pp. 1–261.
Murray, Mr. A. Erskine, at Glasgow	6th Rep. p. xviii. and App. pp. 709–712.
Glasgow, Corporation of	1st Rep. App. p. 126.
,, University of	3rd Rep. p. xxv. and App. pp. 423–425.

LANARKSHIRE (continued).

County Council Records, at Lanark. (*Local Records Comm. Rep.*, 1902. App. III. p. 84.)

Burgh Records, 1488, etc., at Lanark. (*Local Records Comm. Rep.*, 1902. App. III. p. 94.)

Burgh Records, 1446, etc., with Printed Index, at City Chambers, Glasgow. (*Local Records Comm. Rep.*, 1902. App. III. p. 92.)

Corporation Records, see *ante.* Hist. MSS. Comm. Reports.

Marwick (Sir James D.) and Renwick (Robert). Charters and other Documents relating to the City of Glasgow, 1175–1707. Glasgow, 1894–1906. 2 vols. in 3. Scottish Burghs Record Society.

'Extracts from the Records of the Burgh of Glasgow, 1573-1759,' edited by Sir J. D. Marwick and R. Renwick, in 6 vols., have also been issued by this Society and the Corporation, also 'Burgh Records of the City of Glasgow, 1573-1581,' by the Maitland Club in 1832, with an Index in 1834.

Smith (John). Index to a Private Collection of Notices entitled Memorabilia of the City of Glasgow, selected from the Minute Books of the Burgh, 1587-1750. Maitland Club. Glasgow, 1836.

The City of Glasgow and its Records. (*The Scottish Review*, vol. xxxii. pp. 249–271. 1898.)

Inventory of the Records of the City of Glasgow. Glasgow, 1881.

Livingstone (Matthew). Guide to the Public Records of Scotland. 1905. Lanarkshire, pp. 122, 178. Glasgow, pp. 118, 179, 193.

Turnbull (William B.). Scottish Parochial Registers. 1849. List of Lanarkshire Registers, pp. 102–108.

Catal. of Books belonging to the Cathedral Church of Glasgow, taken in the year 1432, from the Chartulary of Glasgow, with notes and observations on the preceding Catal. of Books. (*Archæol. Scotica*, vol. ii. pp. 328–349. 1822.) Soc. of Antiq. of Scotland.

Dillon (John). Inventory of the Ornaments, Reliques, Jewels, Vestments, Books, etc., belonging to the Cathedral Church of Glasgow, 1432, with observations on the Catal. of Books. Glasgow, 1831. Maitland Club.

Dowden (John). The Inventory of Ornaments, Jewels, Relicks, Vestments, Service Books, etc., belonging to the Cathedral Church of Glasgow in 1432, illustrated from various sources, and more particularly from the Inventories of the Cathedral of Aberdeen. (*Soc. of Antiq. Scot. Proc.*, vol. xxxiii. pp. 280–329. 1899.)

Trimen (Henry). Botanical Biblio. of the British Counties. Lanarkshire. (*Journ. of Botany*, vol. xii. p. 234. 1874.)

Christy (Miller). Biblio. Note on Lanarkshire Birds. (*The Zoologist*, Ser. 3, vol. xiv. p. 264, 1890; and reprinted in pamph. 1891, p. 35.) **Mammals.** (*The Zoologist*, Ser. 3, vol. xvii. p. 212. 1893.) **Reptiles.** (*Ibid.* p. 250. 1893.)

Anderson (John P.). Book of Brit. Topo., 1881. Lanarkshire, pp. 398-401.

Bandinel (Bulkeley). Catal. of Books bequeathed to Bodleian Library by Richard Gough, 1814. Lanarkshire, p. 362.

RUTHERGLEN.

Burgh Records, 1324, etc., at Rutherglen. (*Local Records Comm. Rep.*, 1902, App. III. p. 98.)

LANCASHIRE.

[As many bibliographical works relating to this county include Cheshire as well, reference should be made under both 'Lancashire' and 'Cheshire.']

FISHWICK (HENRY). THE LANCASHIRE LIBRARY, A BIBLIOGRAPHICAL ACCOUNT OF BOOKS ON TOPOGRAPHY, BIOGRAPHY, HISTORY, ETC., RELATING TO THE COUNTY PALATINE, including an Account of Lancashire tracts, etc., printed before the year 1720. London, 1875.

Folkard (Henry Tennyson). Lancashire Books. A List of Books and Pamphlets relating to the County Palatine of Lancaster preserved in the Reference Department of the Wigan Free Public Library. 1898. 25 copies only printed, detached from the General Catalogue.

Sutton (Albert). Bibliotheca Lancastrensis: A Catal. of Books (on sale) on the Topography and Genealogy of Lancashire. (With Biblio. & Biog. Notes, etc.) Manchester, 1913.

Biblio. of Lancs. and Cheshire Publications during 1876. (*Manchester Lit. Club. Papers*, vol. iii. pp. 261–302. 1877.) Also issued separately.

Biblio. of Lancs. and Cheshire Antiquities, 1889. By Ernest Axon. (*Lancs. & Cheshire Antiq. Soc. Trans.*, vol. vii. pp. 327–332. 1890.)

Biblio. of Lancs. and Cheshire Antiquities, 1890. By Ernest Axon. (*Ibid.* vol. viii. pp. 195–204. 1891.)

Biblio. of Lancs. and Cheshire Antiquities, 1891, and Subject-Index to Biblio. of Local Antiquities, 1889–91. By Ernest Axon. (*Ibid.* vol. ix. pp. 217–221. 1892.)

Biblio. of Lancs. and Cheshire Antiquities, 1892, and Subject-Index. By Ernest Axon. (*Ibid.* vol. x. pp. 230–236. 1893.

Biblio. of Lancs. and Cheshire Antiquities and Biography, with Subject-Indexes, 1893–99. By John Hibbert Swann. (*Ibid.* vol. xii. p. 148; vol. xiii. p. 201; vol. xiv. p. 212; vol. xv. p. 229; vol. xvi. p. 188; vol. xvii. p. 271. 1895–1900.)

Biblio. of Lancs. and Cheshire Antiquities, and Biographical Publications, 1900–03, and Subject-Indexes. By Norman Hollins. (*Ibid.* vol. xviii. pp. 165–176; vol. xix. pp. 276–287; vol. xx. pp. 265–275; vol. xxi. pp. 224–233. 1901–03.)

Local Bibliography of Lancashire (chiefly relating to Early Printing in various Towns), by W. H. Allnutt, W. A. Abram, H. Fishwick, & others. (*Local Gleanings relating to Lancs. & Cheshire*, ed. by J. P. Earwaker, vols. I., II. *passim.* 1875–78.)

Madeley (Charles). Warrington Municipal Museum. Catal. of the Reference Library. 1898. Lancashire items, pp. 177–180. **Supplement,** 1908, pp. 62–64.

List of Books, Tracts, MSS., etc., relating to Lancashire History. (*The Cheshire & Lancs. Hist. Collector*, vol. ii. pp. 7, 36, 57, 87. 1855.)

Rondeau (J. B.). Manuscript Collections towards a Bibliography of Lancashire and Cheshire. (In Wigan Free Library.)

Bibliotheca Chethamensis. Vols. i.–iv. 1791–1862. Vol. v. **Index,** 1863. Vol. vi. **Catal. of the Books and MSS. added 1863–1881,** including the Collection of John Byrom, and all the MSS. 1883.

Catal. of the MSS. and Printed Books bequeathed to Owen's College, Manchester, by the late James Prince Lee, D.D., Lord Bishop of Manchester. 1870.

The Bishop Lee Lib. contains many MSS. and Books relating to Lancs.

LANCASHIRE (continued).

Robson (John). The Materials for the Hist. of the Two Counties (Lancs. and Cheshire) **and the Mode of Using Them.** (*Hist. Soc. Lancs. & Cheshire Proc.*, vol. v. pp. 199–217; *Trans.*, vol. vii. pp. 99–114; vol. x. pp. 47–58. 1853–58.)

Winstanley (R.). Sale Catal. of Works relating to Lancs. and Cheshire. (Collected by Thomas Heywood.) Manchester, 1835.

Sale Catal. of the Library of James Crossley, F.S.A., Stocks House, Cheetham, 12–19 May, 1884. Manchester, F. Thompson, 1884.

Sutton (Charles William). Rough List of Lancashire County and Local Histories in the Manchester Free Reference Library. Manchester, 1885.

——— **A List of Lancashire Authors,** with brief Biog. and Biblio. Notes. Manchester Literary Club, 1876.

J. Eglinton Bailey's copy of the above in the Brit. Museum contains a very large number of additions in his handwriting.

——— **Lancashire and Cheshire Archæology:** A List of Contributions from some Archæological Journals. Manchester, 1881 (reprinted from '*The Palatine Note-book*,' 1881).

——— **Special Collections of Books in Lancs. and Cheshire.** (Paper read before Library Assoc., 1899.) Aberdeen, 1900. A précis appeared in '*Lib. Assoc. Record*,' vol. i. pt. 2, pp. 627–628. 1899.

Some of the Lancs. Private Collections mentioned are the following:—Samuel H. Brooks, H. T. Crofton, William Farrer, Henry Fishwick, W. Fergusson Irvine, Arthur G. Leigh, Robert Muschamp, William Ormerod, Giles Shaw, and Joseph Whitehead.

Nodal (J. H.). Special Collections of Books in Lancs. and Cheshire. (*Lib. Assoc. of the U. K. Trans.*, 1879, pp. 54–60, and App. III. and *Manchester Lit. Club. Papers*, vol. vi. pp. 31–57. 1880.)

Madeley (C.). Limits of Local Collections in the Town Libraries of Lancs. and Cheshire. (*Manchester Lit. Club. Papers*, vol. vi. pp. 300–303. 1880.)

Fishwick (Henry). Quaker Lancashire Literature of the Seventeenth Century. (*Lancs. & Cheshire Antiq. Soc. Trans.*, vol. v. pp. 105–116. 1887.)

Catal. of the Books and MSS. belonging to the late John Leyland, at the Leyland Free Lib. & Museum, Hindley. By H. T. Folkard. Wigan, 1896. Privately Printed. (Special Collections of Views, Portraits, Newspaper-cuttings, etc., relating to Lancs.)

General Index to the Remains, Historical and Literary, published by the Chetham Soc., vols. i.–xxx. and vols. xxxi.–cxiv. Manchester, 1863 and 1893. (Contains numerous Lancs. items.)

Index to the Transactions of the Hist. Soc. of Lancs. and Cheshire, vols. i.–li., 1849–1900, in vol. liv., 1902, compiled by F. C. Beazley, and **Rough Index to Papers and Communications,** vols. lii.–lxi. in vol. lxi. 1909.

Catal. of the Library and Museum of the Hist. Soc. of Lancs. and Cheshire, arranged by H. Ecroyd Smith, Liverpool. 1876. (Lancs., Liverpool, Manchester, etc., Books, Pamphlets, Maps, etc.)

Catal. of the Museum of the Hist. Soc. of Lancs. and Cheshire, compiled by R. T. Bailey and R. Gladstone. (*Hist. Soc. Lancs. and Cheshire, Trans.*, vol. lxv. pp. 222–239. 1914.)

Index to the Titles of Local Papers in the Trans. of the Hist. Soc. of Lancs. and Cheshire, 1848–81, by J. Cooper Morley. (Palatine Note-book, vol. ii. pp. 266–268. 1882.)

Indexes to the Transactions of the Lancs. and Cheshire Antiq. Soc., vols. i.–x. in vol. x. 1892; vols. xi.–xx. in vol. xx. 1902; and vols. xxi.–xxx. in vol. xxx. 1912.

LANCASHIRE (continued).

Table of Contents and Index to Publications of the Manchester Literary Club, compiled by C. W. Sutton, pp. 1–139, and **Catalogue of the Library of the Manchester Literary Club,** compiled by W. R. Credland, pp. 143–235. Manchester Lit. Club. 1903.

List of Publications of the Record Soc. for the Publication of Original Documents relating to Lancs. and Cheshire (issued in the '*Annual Reports*').

Nodal (J. H.). List of Books and Pamphlets by Members (Past & Present) **of the Manchester Literary Club.** (*Manchester Lit. Club. Trans.*, vol. i. Appendix. 1875.)

The Spenser Society, Manchester. Final Report of the Council, with Lists of Works issued by the Society. 1894.

Credland (W. R.). The Work of the Spenser Society. (*Manchester Lit. Club. Papers*, vol. xi. pp. 117–123, 1885; vol. xxviii. p. 478, 1902; *Manchester Quarterly*, vol. iv. pp. 117–123, 1885; vol. xxi. p. 478. 1902.)

Sutton (C. W.). Some Early Lancashire Authors. (*Memorials of Old Lancashire*, vol. ii. pp. 44–64. 1909.)

Milner (G.). Lancashire Writers. (*Manchester Lit. Club. Proc.*, 1873–74, pp. 29–32.)

Case (Robert H.). Lancs. & Cheshire in English Literature up to about 1700. (*Hist. Soc. Lancs. & Cheshire. Trans.*, vol. lvii. pp. 96–119. 1906.)

Nodal (J. H.). Lancashire in Fiction. (*Manchester Lit. Club. Papers*, vol. v. pp. 261–262. 1879.)

Folkard (H. T.). Portraits and Portraiture. A List of Engraved Portraits and Photographs (including Lancs.) in the Reference Department of the Wigan Free Public Library. Wigan, 1907.

Rylands (J. P.). Notes on Book-Plates (Ex-Libris), with special reference to Lancs. and Cheshire Examples. (*Hist. Soc. Lancs. & Cheshire. Trans.*, vol. xl. pp. 1–76. 1890.) See also lists in '*The Palatine Note-book*,' vol. i. p. 31, 1881, and '*Manchester Notes & Queries*,' vol. vii. pp. 240, 242, 245, 247, 249. 1888.)

Bateman (C. T. Tallent-). Hist. Notes on a Collection of Lancs. and Cheshire Autographs. (*Lancs. & Cheshire Antiq. Soc. Trans.*, vol. i. pp. 53–58. 1884.)

'The Lancashire Journal,' 1738-39. (*Palatine Note-book*, vol. ii. pp. 205–207. 1882.)

Wightman (H.). Official List of Newspapers issued in Lancs., Yorks., & Cheshire. Liverpool, 1887.

Bailey (James). Lancashire Periodicals. Biblio. Notes. (*Manchester City News Notes & Queries*, vol. v. pp. 121–122. 1883.)

Axon (William E. A.). Select List of Works relating to Bibliography, Natural History, History, Topography, etc., of Lancashire. 1877. (MS. in Wigan Free Library.)

—— **Provincial Biblio. in relation to Lancashire and Cheshire.** (*Manchester Lit. Club. Papers*, vol. iii. pp. 183–186. 1877.) Also issued separately.

—— **The Literature of the Lancashire Dialect.** A Biblio. Essay. London, 1870.

—— **A Bibliographical List of Books illustrating the Lancashire Dialect** (reprinted from English Dialect Soc. Pubns., with additions). (*Manchester Lit. Club. Papers*, vol. ii. Appendix. 1875.)

LANCASHIRE (continued).

Axon (William E. A.). Some Old Lancashire Ballads, Broadsides, and Chapbooks. (*Lancashire Gleanings*, 1883, pp. 329-335.)

——— **Curiosities of Street Literature.** (*Lancashire Gleanings*, 1883, pp. 145-150.)

——— **The Libraries of Lancashire and Cheshire.** (*Lib. Assoc. of the U.K. Trans.*, 1879, pp. 47-53; *Manchester Lit. Club. Papers*, vol. vi. pp. 21-30. 1880.) Also issued separately.

——— **On Lancashire Antiquarian Societies.** (*Lancs. & Cheshire Antiq. Soc. Trans.*, vol. xxi. pp. 212-218. 1903.)

——— **Biblio. List of the Writings of John Harland, F.S.A.** (1806-1868.) (*The Reliquary*, vol. ix. pp. 90-93. 1868.)

——— **In Memoriam. J. E. Bailey, F.S.A.**, with a Biblio. List. (*Manchester Lit. Club. Papers*, vol. xiv. pp. 297-306, 1888; *Manchester Quarterly*, vol. vii. pp. 297-306. 1888.)

——— **The Library of Richard Brereton of Ley, 1557.** (*Lancs. & Cheshire Antiq. Soc. Trans.*, vol. xi. pp. 103-112. 1894.

——— **Biblio. of the Writings of Mrs. Elizabeth Cleghorn Gaskell, Author of 'Mary Barton,' and of her Husband, the Rev. William Gaskell, M.A.** (*Manchester Lit. Club. Papers*, vol. xxi.; *Manchester Quarterly*, vol. xiv. Appendix. 1895.)

——— **and Axon (Ernest). Henry Ainsworth, the Puritan Commentator** (1571-1622 or 1623), with Biblio. (*Lancs. & Cheshire Antiq. Soc. Trans.*, vol. vi. pp. 42-57. 1888.) Also reprinted 1889.

List of some of the Writings of William E. A. Axon, in 'Report of the Presentation of a Testimonial to W. E. A. Axon,' 18 July, 1878. Manchester, 1878.

Axon (Ernest). List of Writings of John Eglinton Bailey. (*Lancs. & Cheshire Antiq. Soc. Trans.*, vol. vi. pp. 129-150. 1888.)

——— **Henry Ainsworth** (1571-1622 or 1623): **His Birthplace and His Death.** (*Palatine Note-book*, vol. v. pp. 1-3. 1885.) Also issued separately.

Formby (Thomas) and Axon (Ernest). List of the Writings of W. Thompson Watkin. (*Lancs. & Cheshire Antiq. Soc. Trans.*, vol. vi. pp. 173-178. 1888.) Also issued separately. 1889.

Sutton (C. W.). List of W. Thompson Watkin's Writings. (*Manchester Notes & Queries*, vol. vii. pp. 200-202. 1888.)

Herford (Rev. Brooke). In Memoriam. John Harland. 1868. Privately printed.

Christie (R. C.). A Biblio. of the Works written and edited by Dr. John Worthington. Chetham Soc. New Ser., vol. xiii. 1888.

Sutton (C. W.). Richard Heyrick (1600-67) **and Richard Hollinworth** (1607-56). Biblio. Notes. (*Lancs. & Cheshire Antiq. Soc. Trans.*, vol. vii. pp. 134-141. 1889.) Also issued separately. 1890.

Dredge (John Ingle). Samuel Bolton, D.D. (b. at Manchester, 1607; d. 1654). A Bibliography. (*Lancs. & Cheshire Antiq. Soc. Trans.*, vol. vi. pp. 67-73. 1889.)

Sparke (Archibald). Henry Fishwick, 1835-1914. An Obituary Notice. (*Notes & Queries*, Ser. 11. vol. x. p. 279. 1914.)

Bailey (J. Eglinton). Thomas Bell, of Lancashire & Yorkshire, Anti-Romanist Writer, with a Biblio. (Reprinted from '*Notes & Queries*,' Nov. 27 & Dec. 4, 1880.) Not published.

LANCASHIRE (continued).

Wilkinson (T. T.). An Account of the Life and Writings of Henry Buckley (1811-56). (*Hist. Soc. Lancs. & Cheshire, Trans.*, vol. xv. pp. 115-128. 1863.)

—— **An Account of the Life and Writings of John Henry Swale** (b. 1775, d. 1837) **of Liverpool.** (*Hist. Soc. Lancs. & Cheshire, Trans.*, vol. vii. pp. 143-164; vol. x. pp. 169-182. 1855, 1858.)

Nodal (J. H.) and Milner (G.). A Glossary of the Lancashire Dialect. Manchester Lit. Club. 1875-82. List of Authorities, pp. xi.-xv.

A Collection of Lancashire Dialect Pamphlets, etc., is in Wigan Free Public Library.

Briscoe (J. P.). The Literature of Tim Bobbin [*i.e.* John Collier]; being a chronologically arranged list of the various editions. Manchester. 1872.

Halliwell-Phillipps (J. O.). The Palatine Anthology: A Collection of Ancient Poems and Ballads relating to Lancs. and Cheshire, to which is added The Palatine Garland, being a selection of Ballads and Fragments, supplementary to The Palatine Anthology. London, 1850.

Harland (John). Ballads and Songs of Lancashire, chiefly older than the 19th cent. Second edition. 1875.

Derby (Thomas). Folk Songs of Lancs. (*Manchester Lit. Club. Papers*, vol. xxxix. pp. 79-99. 1913.)

Langton (Robert). The Black-Letter Ballads in the Free Reference Library, Manchester. (*Lancs. & Cheshire Antiq. Soc. Trans.*, vol. ii. pp. 21-27. 1885.)

Early Lancashire and Cheshire Printers. (Brief notes.) (*Manchester City News Notes & Queries*, vol. i. pp. 300, 310. 1878.)

Abram (W. A.). Obituaries of Lancashire Printers and Booksellers, 1796-1848 (from '*Preston Guardian*' Local Sketches. May 22, 1880.) (*Lancs. & Cheshire Antiq. Notes*, vol. ii. pp. 57-58. 1886.)

Christie (R. C.). The Old Church and School Libraries of Lancs. A Paper read at the Liverpool Meeting of the Lib. Assoc. 1883. (*Lib. Assoc. of the U. K. Trans. & Proc.*, 1883, pp. 45-57.)

—— **The Old Church and School Libraries of Lancs.** Chetham Soc. New Ser., vol. vii. 1885.

Binns (Thomas). Collection of Maps, Plans, Charts, Views, Portraits, and MS. and Printed Documents serving to illustrate the Hist. of Lancs., especially Liverpool and Neighbourhood: begun by Thomas Binns of Liverpool, *circa* 1820, and continued by the Libraries Committee of the Corp. of Liverpool. (In the Reference Lib. of the Liverpool Free Public Libraries.)

Harrison (William). Early Maps of Lancashire and their Makers. (*Lancs. & Cheshire Antiq. Soc. Trans.*, vol. xxv. pp. 1-31. 1907.)

Gillow (Joseph). Lord Burghley's Map of Lancashire, 1590, with Notes. (*Catholic Rec. Soc. Miscellanea*, vol. iv. pp. 162-222. 1907.)

List of Private Acts relating to the County of Lancashire. London: Stevens & Sons, *circa* 1912.

Gross (Charles). Biblio. of Brit. Municipal Hist. (*Harvard Hist. Studies*, vol. v. 1897.) Lancashire, pp. 98-99. Liverpool, pp. 280-285. Manchester, pp. 335-338. Lancaster, pp. 270, 271.

Davenport (Frances G.). List of Printed Materials for Manorial History. 1894. Biblio. Note on Lancashire Manorial History, pp. 48-49.

Dove (Patrick Edward). Domesday Studies. 1891. Domesday Biblio. Lancashire, vol. ii. pp. 681-682.

LANCASHIRE (*continued*).

Lyell (Arthur H.). Biblio. List of Romano-British Remains. 1912. Lancashire, pp. 54–55.

Cowper (H. S.). An Archæol. Survey of Lancashire North-of-the-Sands. (*Archæologia*, vol. liii. 1893, and reprinted separately.) Biblio. and Topog. Index, pp. 531–538.

Harrison (William). An Archæol. Survey of Lancashire. Soc. of Antiq. London. 1896.

Macklin (Herbert Walter). Monumental Brasses. London: George Allen & Co. 1913. Biblio. Note on Lancs. Brasses, with a List, pp. 141, 165.

A Classified Catal. of the Works on Architecture and the Allied Arts in the principal Libraries of Manchester and Salford, with alphabetical Author list and Subject Index. Edited for the Joint Architectural Committee of Manchester, by Henry Guppy. 1909. Lancashire items, pp. 79–81.

Special Topographical Collections for the County of Lancashire are in the Public Libraries at Wigan, Bury, Rochdale, St. Helens, Accrington, Manchester (The Free Reference Lib. & Chetham's Lib.), Warrington (Municipal Museum), Chester, and other places. Local Collections are in the Public Libraries at Ashton-under-Lyne, Blackburn, Bootle, etc. For other Local Collections see note under the respective Towns.

Hist. MSS. Comm. Reports. Lancashire Collections.

Beamont, Mr. W., of Orford Hall, Warrington	4th Rep. p. xv. and App. p. 368.
Ellesmere, Earl of (Bridgewater Trust), at Walkden	11th Rep. p. 24 and App. VII. pp. 126–167.
ffarington, Miss, of Worden Hall ...	6th Rep. p. xiii. and App. pp. 426–448.
FitzGerald, Sir Gerald, at Thurnham Hall	3rd Rep. p. xvi. and App. pp. 246, 247; 5th Rep. App. p. 321.
Hulton, Mr. W. W. B., at Hulton Park	12th Rep. p. 40 and App. IX. pp. 165–178.
Kenyon, Lord, at Gredington Hall, Flints.	14th Rep. pp. 31–36 and App. IV.
Raffles, Mr. T. Stamford, at Liverpool	6th Rep. p. xvi. and App. pp. 468–475.
Towneley, Colonel, at Towneley Hall, Burnley	4th Rep. p. xvi. and App. pp. 406–416, 613.
Manchester, Chetham's Library ...	2nd Rep. App. p. 156.
Stonyhurst College	2nd Rep. p. xiii. and App. pp. 143–146; 3rd Rep. p. xxi. and App. pp. 334–341; 10th Rep. p. 25 and App. IV. pp. 176–199.

County Records, 1710, etc., with MS. Index, at County Offices, Preston. (*Local Records Comm. Rep.*, 1902, App. III. p. 18.)

Public Record Office. Duchy of Lancaster. Calendar of Rolls of the Chancery of the Co. Palatine, Rolls of Fines, Letters Close and Patent, and Charters of 29 Edw. III. (*Deputy Keeper Public Records*, 32 *Ann. Rep.*, 1871, pp. 331–365.) **Henry IV.** (*Ibid.* 33 *Ann. Rep.*, 1872, pp. 1–42; 37 *Ann. Rep.*, 1876, pp. 172–179.)

—— **Calendar of Royal Charters. William II. to Richard II.** (*Ibid.* 31 *Ann. Rep.*, 1870, pp. 1–42.) **Henry I. to Henry VI.** (*Ibid.* 35 *Ann. Rep.*, 1874, pp. 1–41; 36 *Ann. Rep.*, 1875, pp. 161–205.)

—— **Calendar of Lancaster Inquisitions Post Mortem, etc.** (*Ibid.* 39 *Ann. Rep.*, 1878, pp. 532–562.)

—— **Calendar of Patent Rolls. 4 Richard II. to 21 Henry VII.** (*Ibid.* 40 *Ann. Rep.*, 1879, pp. 521–545.)

LANCASHIRE (continued).

Public Record Office. Calendar of Privy Seals of the Co. Palatine. Richard II. (*Ibid.* 43 *Ann. Rep.*, 1882, pp. 363–370.)

——— **Inventory of the Accounts of the Ministers and Particular Receivers, Edward I. to George III.** (*Ibid.* 45 *Ann. Rep.*, 1884, pp. 1–152.)

——— **Inventory of Court Rolls, Henry III. to George IV.** (*Ibid.* 43 *Ann. Rep.*, 1882, pp. 206–362.)

——— **Inventory and Lists of Documents transferred from the Duchy of Lancaster Office, Lancaster Place, to the Public Record Office, 1868.** (*Ibid.* 30 *Ann. Rep.*, 1869, pp. 1–43.)

——— **List of the Records of the Duchy of Lancaster preserved in the Public Record Office.** (*Lists and Indexes.* No. 14. 1901.)

——— **A Calendar of the Lancs. Assize Rolls preserved in the Public Record Office.** Transcribed and calendared by Col. John Parker. (*Record Soc. for Lancs. and Cheshire*, vols. xlvii., xlix. 1904–5.)

A Calendar of the Duchy of Lancaster Inquisitions Post Mortem. By Ethel Stokes. (*Genealogical Mag.*, vols. ii.–iv. 1899–1900.)

Selby (Walford D.). Lancs. and Cheshire Records in the Public Record Office, London. 2 vols. (*Record Soc. for Lancs. and Cheshire*, vols. vii., viii. 1882–83.)

List of Records of the Palatinates of Chester, Durham, and Lancaster, preserved in the Public Record Office. (*Lists and Indexes*, No. XL. 1914.)

The Charters of the Duchy of Lancaster, translated and edited by Sir William Hardy. 1845. Chronological List of Contents, pp. v.–xx.

Account of the Public Records in the Duchy of Lancaster, etc., with a Table with dates of Records and where kept. (Gregson (Matthew.) *Portfolio of Fragments relative to the Hist., etc., of the Co. Pal. & Duchy of Lancaster*, 1817, pp. 123–129.)

Extracts relating to Lancs. from the 'Calendarium Rotulorum Chartarum' (Calendar of the Charter Rolls, 1199–1483), **the 'Cal. Inquis. ad quod Damnum' and the 'Cal. Inquis. Post Mortem.'** (*Ibid.* pp. 51–120.)

Official Lists of the Duchy and Co. of Lancaster from the Earliest Times to the Present Day, by W. R. Williams. 1901. Privately Printed.

A Calendar of Lancs. & Cheshire Exchequer Depositions by Commission, 1558–1702. Edited by C. Fishwick. (*Record Soc. for Lancs. & Cheshire Publications*, vol. xi. 1885.)

Beamont (William). An Account of the Rolls of the Honour of Halton, part of Her Majesty the Queen's Duchy of Lancaster, being the substance of a Report on the removal of the Records from Halton Castle, in Cheshire, to the office of the Public Records, London. Warrington, 1879.

Report of an Inspection of the Records of the Palatinate Courts at Preston and Lancaster. (*Local Records Comm. Rep.*, 1914, vol. ii. pt. 2, p. 141.)

Harland (John). 'Mamecestre.' 3 vols. 1861–62. Chetham Soc. vols. liii., lvi., lviii. Lancashire Town Charters, vol. i. pp. 178–207.

Crofton (H. T.). Lancashire & Cheshire Coal-mining Records. (*Lancs. & Cheshire Antiq. Soc. Trans.*, vol. vii. pp. 26–73. 1890.)

Evans (George Eyre). Record of the Provincial Assembly of Lancs. & Cheshire (with lists of Non-Parochial Registers, and Biblio. Notes to Biographies and Places). Manchester, 1896.

LANCASHIRE (*continued*).

Shaw (W. A.). Materials for an Account of the Provincial Synod of the Co. of Lancaster, 1646-1660. Manchester, 1890. Privately Printed.

Holt (Emily S.). Collectanea, or What the Records Say: Lancashire Notes. (*Old South-East Lancashire*, vol. i. pp. 44–49, 129–133. 1880.)

List of MS. Collections in Reports of the Royal Hist. MSS. Comm. relating to Lancs. & Cheshire. (*Manchester Lit. Club. Papers*, vol. v. p. 57. 1880.)

The Owen MSS. (in the Free Reference Library, Manchester), by Ernest Axon. (*Lancs. & Cheshire Antiq. Soc. Trans.*, vol. xvii. pp. 48–63. 1899.)

Index to the Owen MSS., compiled by Ernest Axon. (Manchester Public Free Libraries. *Occasional Lists.* No. 6. 1900.)

Raines's MS. Collections for Lancs., 44 vols.; **Piccope's MS. Collections**, 21 vols.; and **Kuerden's MS. Collections**, 2 vols. (in Chetham's Library, Manchester).

Other vols. of Kuerden's Lancs. Collections are in the College of Arms, London, and a vol. is in the Harleian Collection at the Brit. Museum.

Randle Holmes' Collections, Brit. Mus. Harl. MSS. 2042, 2085, 2112; **William John Roberts' Collections**, Brit. Mus. Add. MSS. 22642–22658; **Lysons' Collections**, Brit. Mus. Add. MS. 9458; **Suckling's Collections**, 1821–39, Brit. Mus. Add. MSS. 18478, 18479; **Norris Papers**, Brit. Mus. Add. MSS. 36924–36927; **Upcott's Topog. Collections**, Brit. Mus. Add. MS. 5922; **John Hopkinson's Collections**, 1671, Brit. Mus. Add. MS. 26741.

Other Lancs. Collections in the Brit. Mus. are Harl. MSS. 1926, 2219, 7386.

The Watson MSS. (chiefly relating to Lancs. and Cheshire) in the Bodleian Lib., Oxford.

Beamont MSS. relating to Families in South Lancs. & Cheshire (in Warrington Museum Reference Library).

Gregson (Matthew). MS. Collections of Lancashire, taken from Records, etc., with Title-pages dated 1822, in 6 vols. See Catal. Historical Exhibition, Liverpool, 1907, p. 159.

MS. Collections relating to Lancs. (in Leeds Subscription Lib.), by F. R. Atkinson. (*The Cheshire & Lancs. Hist. Collector*, vol. ii. pp. 43-45. 1855.)

Earwaker (J. P.). Notes on some Early Deeds, Pedigree Rolls, etc., relating to Cheshire & Lancs. (*Manchester Lit. Club. Papers*, vol. ix. pp. 176–193, 1883; *Manchester Quarterly*, vol. ii. pp. 176–193. 1883.)

Rylands (W. H.). Some Lancs. & Cheshire Heraldic Documents. (*Hist. Soc. Lancs. & Cheshire, Trans.*, vol. lxiii. pp. 178–219. 1912.)

Maclean (Sir John). Parish Registers in the County of Lancaster. An Epitome. (*Lancs. & Cheshire Hist. & Geneal. Notes*, vol. i. pp. 311, 322, 338, 344, 360, 386, 409, 411; vol. ii., pp. 9, 16, 20. 1879–80.)

Brierley (Henry). Notes on Lancs. Parish Registers. (*Memorials of Old Lancashire*, ed. by H. Fishwick & P. H. Ditchfield, vol. ii. pp. 191–203. 1909.)

Moore Collection. A Calendar of that part of the Collection of Deeds and Papers of the Moore Family, of Bankhall, co. Lancs., now in the Liverpool Public Library. By J. Brownbill. With an Appendix containing a Calendar of a further portion of the same Collection, now in the Univ. of Liverpool School of Local Hist. and Records. By Kathleen Walker. (*Record Soc. of Lancs. & Cheshire*, vol. lxvii. 1913.) See also Hist. MSS. Comm., 10th Rep., Pt. iv. pp. 59–146, Capt. Stewart's MSS., in which are described many of the Moore documents.

LANCASHIRE (continued).

Morton (T. N.). The Family of Moore of Liverpool. Rough Lists of their Paper Records. (*Hist. Soc. of Lancs. & Cheshire, Trans.*, vol. xxxviii. pp. 149–158. 1886.) MS. Lists are also at the Liverpool Public Library. Selections by T. N. Morton were issued in the '*Hist. Soc. of Lancs. & Cheshire, Trans.*' vols. xxxix. pp. 159–174; vol. xl. pp. 177–182, 1887–88; and by R. Stewart-Brown in vol. lxi. pp. 203–211. 1909.

Radcliffe (R. D.). Schedule of Deeds & Documents, the property of Col. Thomas Richard Crosse, preserved in the Muniment Room at Shaw Hill, Chorley, co. Lancs. (*Hist. Soc. Lancs. & Cheshire, Trans.*, vol. xli. pp. 209–226; vol. xlii. pp. 275–295; vols. xliii., xliv. pp. 330–352; vol. xlv. pp. 221–246. 1889–93.)

Earwaker (J. P.). An Account of the Charters, Deeds, and other Documents, now preserved at Agecroft Hall, co. Lancs. 1199–1811. (*Lancs. & Cheshire Antiq. Soc. Trans.*, vol. iv. pp. 199–220. 1886.)

Powell (Rev. Edward). Ancient Charters preserved at Scarisbrick Hall. (*Hist. Soc. Lancs. & Cheshire, Trans.*, vol. xlviii. pp. 259–294; vol. xlix. pp. 185–230. Index, pp. 242–250. 1896–98.)

Bold Deeds. A Collection of 218 Charters relating to the Bold Estate, with Calendar and transcriptions. (In Warrington Museum.)

Sibson Papers. Correspondence, Memoranda, etc., of the Rev. E. Sibson (an Antiquary), Vicar of St. Thomas', Ashton-in-Makerfield. 34 vols. (In Warrington Museum.)

The Culcheth Deeds. A List, by J. P. Rylands, of Abstracts by William Beamont, of Warrington. (*Lancs. & Cheshire Hist. & Geneal. Notes*, vols. i.–iii. *passim.* 1878–83.)

Wheldon (J. A.) and Wilson (A.). The Flora of West Lancs. Liverpool, 1907. List of Authorities for Details, Books and Herbaria consulted, and MS. Contributions, pp. 120–124.

Trimen (Henry). Botanical Biblio. of the British Counties. Lancashire. (*Journ. of Botany*, vol. xii. p. 180. 1874.)

Christy (Miller). Biblio. Note on Lancs. Birds. (*The Zoologist*, Ser. 3, vol. xiv. p. 254, 1890; and reprinted in pamph., 1891, p. 16.) **Mammals.** (*The Zoologist*, Ser. 3, vol. xvii. p. 180. 1893.) **Reptiles.** (*Ibid.* p. 244. 1893.) **Fishes.** (*Ibid.* p. 255. 1893.)

Anderson (John P.). Book of Brit. Topo., 1881. Lancs., pp. 150–164.
Gatfield (George). Guide to Heraldry. 1892. Lancs., pp. 148–151.
Sims (Richard). Manual. 1861. Lancs., pp. 168, 211, 212, 235.
Upcott (William). English Topo., 1818. Lancs., vol. i. pp.455–480, 637–639.
Smith (Alfred Russell). Catal. of Topo. Tracts, etc., 1878. Lancs., pp. 167–180.
Gough (Richard). Brit. Topo., 1780. Lancs., vol. i. pp. 493–508.
Bandinel (Bulkeley). Catal. of Books bequeathed to Bodleian Library by Richard Gough, 1814. Lancs., pp. 151–156.

BOLTON.

Sparke (Archibald). Bibliographia Boltoniensis; being a Biblio., with Biog. details of Bolton Authors, and the Books written by them from 1550 to 1912; Books about Bolton; and those Printed and Published in the Town from 1785 to date. Manchester, 1913.

Scholes (James C.). Bolton Bibliography, and Jottings of Book-Lore; with Notes on Local Authors and Printers. Manchester, 1886.

Waite (James K.). List of Bolton Authors and their principal Works. (*Manchester Lit. Club. Papers*, vol. v. pp. 29–32. 1879.)

LANCASHIRE (continued).

Biblio. Notes on Bolton Books. (*Local Gleanings relating to Lancs. & Cheshire*, ed. by J. P. Earwaker, vol. i. pp. 21, 27, 30. 1875.)

Axon (W. E. A.). Bolton and its Free Library. (*Manchester Lit. Club. Papers*, vol. v. pp. 18–29. 1879.)

A Collection of Bolton Books, locally printed or by local authors, is at the Bolton Public Library.

BURNLEY.

Wilkinson (T. T.). Hist. of the Parochial Church of Burnley, its Endowments, Records, etc. 1856. The Records described, pp. 51–53.

BURY.

Butterworth (James). An Hist. and Topog. Description of the Town and Parish of Bury. Manchester, 1829. Reprinted by Albert Sutton, Manchester, 1902, with Memorial Introduction and Bibliography (of James Butterworth) added.

Biblio. Notes on Bury Books. (*Local Gleanings relating to Lancs. & Cheshire*, ed. by J. P. Earwaker, vol. i. pp. 21, 71; vol. ii. pp. 58, 298. 1875–78.)

CLITHEROE.

Borough Records, 1263, etc., at Town Hall, Clitheroe. (*Local Records Comm. Rep.*, 1902, App. III. p. 50.)

Harland (John). Ancient Charters and other Muniments of the Borough of Clitheroe. Printed for the Corporation of Clitheroe. 1851.

——— **On some ancient Charters and Grants to the Borough of Clitheroe.** (*Brit. Archæol. Assoc. Journ.*, vol. vi. pp. 425–437. 1851.)

Farrer (William). The Court Rolls of the Honor of Clitheroe, in the Public Record Office, and at Clitheroe Castle. 2 vols. 1897, 1912.

GARSTANG.

Hughes (T. Cann). Notes on the 'Garstang Trust' and their Records. (*Lancs. & Cheshire Antiq. Soc. Trans.*, vol. xxx. pp. 164–177. 1912.)

HAWKSHEAD.

Cowper (H. S.). Hawkshead: Its Hist., Archæology, Folklore, Dialect, etc. 1899. Biblio. Notes on Dialect, Parish Books, and a Schedule of Documents.

HEYWOOD.

Green (John Albert). Biblio. of the Town of Heywood. 1902. List of Newspapers, etc., pp. 99–102. Maps and Plans, p. 113.

Heywood Miscellanea. The Collection of the late James Turner relating to the Town of Heywood. 1850-1904. (On sale by Albert Sutton, Manchester.)

HINDLEY.

Collection of Newspaper Cuttings and other matters relating to Hindley, formed by John Leyland. 2 vols. 1872–80. (In Leyland Free Library an Museum, Hindley.)

LANCASHIRE (*continued*).

LANCASTER.

Borough Records, 1193, etc., with MS. Index, at Lancaster Town Hall. (*Local Records Comm. Rep.*, 1902, App. III. p. 60.)

Archdeaconry Records, at Registrar's Office, Lancaster. (*Ibid.* 1902, App. III. p. 122.)

Roper (W. O.). The Charters of Lancaster. (*Hist. Soc. Lancs. & Cheshire, Trans.*, vol. xxxv. pp. 1–14. 1886.)

Biblio. Notes on Lancaster Books, by W. H. Allnutt, and others. (*Local Gleanings relating to Lancs. & Cheshire*, ed. by J. P. Earwaker, vol. i. pp. 31, 71, 233; vol. ii. p. 58. 1875–77.)

Warburton's MS. Collections relating to Lancaster. (In the College of Arms, London.)

Fleury (Cross). Hist. Notes on the Ancient Borough of Lancaster. 1891. Biblio. Notes on Lancaster Books, Maps, etc., pp. 515, 532. List of Authorities, p. 583.

'Old Lancaster' Exhibition of Historical and Antiquarian Objects of Interest connected with Lancaster. July–Aug., 1908. (Nearly 300 Deeds, Documents, Maps, MSS., etc., were exhibited.)

A Special Local Collection is in the Lancaster Public Library.

LEIGH.

Stanning (J. H.). Old Documents relating to Leigh. [1882.] Not published.

Lists of Old Leigh Documents. (*Lancs. & Cheshire Hist. & Geneal. Notes*, vols. ii. and iii. *passim.*)

Bailey (John E.). The Grammar School of Leigh and its Library. (Reprinted from '*The Leigh Chronicle.*') 1879.

—— **The Library of Leigh Grammar School.** (*Manchester Lit. Club. Papers*, vol. v. pp. 256–257. 1879.)

Worsley (James E.). The Hist. of the Parish Church of St. Mary, at Leigh. 1870. Appendix. List of Old Deeds.

LIVERPOOL.

Cowell (Peter). Liverpool Prints and Documents: Catal. of Maps, Plans, Views, Portraits, Memoirs, Literature, etc., in the Reference Lib. of the Liverpool Public Libraries, relating to Liverpool, and serving to illustrate its history, biography, etc., from the earliest times. 1908.

Mott (Albert J.). On Books published in Liverpool, with a Chronological Catal. of Books published in Liverpool up to 1850. (*Hist. Soc. Lancs. & Cheshire. Trans.*, vol. xiii. pp. 103–166. 1861.)

Palmer (John). MS. Biblio. of Liverpool Literature before 1820, compiled about 1820. (See Catal. Hist. Exhib. Liverpool, 1907, p. 161.)

Mott's Biblio. was based on this.

Dawson (Thomas). The Pamphlet Literature of Liverpool, with a Catalogue. (*Hist. Soc. Lancs. & Cheshire. Trans.*, vol. xvii. pp. 73–138. 1865.)

Jaggard (William). Liverpool Literature. A descriptive Biblio. of Old Deeds, Codices, Maps, and Printed Literature, etc. 1905.

Catal. of the Liverpool Library, Lyceum, Bold Street. Liverpool, 1889. Liverpool entries, pp. 267–271.

LANCASHIRE (*continued*).

An Index to the Proceedings of the Literary and Philosophical Soc. of Liverpool. Vols. i.-lxii., compiled by A. W. Newton. Liverpool, 1912.

Picton (Sir James A.). Historic Notices of the Old Philosophical and Lit. Soc. of Liverpool. (*Lit. & Philos. Soc. of Liverpool. Proc.*, vol. xxix. pp. 341–349. 1875.)

Catal. of the Historical Exhibition held at the Walker Art Gallery, 1907, in connection with the 700th Centenary of the Foundation of Liverpool. Liverpool, 1907. Views of Liverpool, pp. 80–141. Liverpool Charters, Books, etc., pp. 142–180. Newspapers, Periodicals, Directories and Maps, pp. 181–195. Portraits, pp. 202–222. Book-Plates, pp. 223–234.

Foundation of Liverpool. Historical Exhibition of Liverpool Antiquities. 1907.

Binns (Thomas). Collection of Maps, Plans, Charts, Views, Portraits, and MS. and Printed Documents serving to illustrate the History of Lancs., especially Liverpool and Neighbourhood, see *ante* p. 119.

Brown (R. Stewart-). Maps and Plans of Liverpool and District, by the Eyes Family of Surveyors. (*Hist. Soc. Lancs. & Cheshire. Trans.*, vol. lxii. pp. 143–174. 1911.)

—— **The Herdman Drawings of Old Liverpool.** (*Ibid.* vol. lxiii. pp. 5–18. 1912.)

The Liverpool Athenæum has a good collection of Local Maps, Plans, etc.

Picton (Sir James A.). Forged and Authentic Maps of Old Liverpool. A Biblio. Note. (*Lit. & Philos. Soc. of Liverpool. Proc.*, vol. xxvii. p. lxx. 1873.)

Morley (J. Cooper). The Newspaper Press and Periodical Literature of Liverpool. (Reprinted from the '*Liverpool Weekly Mercury*.') 1887.

List of Liverpool Periodicals, by J. Cooper Morley and W. M. (*Palatine Note-Book*, vol. ii. pp. 122–123, 201–202. 1882.) See also *Hist. Soc. of Lancs. & Cheshire. Trans.*, vol. xvii. pp. 131–135. 1865.

Picton (Sir James A.). Gleanings from Old Liverpool Newspapers, a hundred years ago. (*Hist. Soc. Lancs. & Cheshire. Trans.*, vol. vi. pp. 109–126. 1854.)

—— **Hist. and Curiosities of the Liverpool Directory.** (*Hist. Soc. Lancs. & Cheshire. Trans.*, vol. xxix. pp. 9–32. 1877.) Also issued separately.

Shaw (George T.). Hist. of the Liverpool Directories, 1766-1907, with a List. (*Hist. Soc. Lancs. & Cheshire. Trans.*, vol. lviii. pp. 113–162. 1907.)

—— **and (I.). Liverpool's First Directory.** (Reprint from Gore's Directory, 1766. Street Directory, 1766, and Hist. of Liverpool Directories, 1766-1907.) 1907.

Cowell (Peter). The Origin and Hist. of some Liverpool Libraries. (*Lib. Assoc. of the U.K. Trans. & Proc.*, 1883, pp. 31–39.)

—— **Liverpool Public Libraries. A History of Fifty Years.** (Liverpool, 1903.)

May (G. S. William). Literature and Libraries in Liverpool. (*Book-Auction Records*, vol. vi. pt. 3. 1909.)

Shaw (George T.). Liverpool Public Libraries. Descriptive Handbook. (Prepared for Ann. Meeting of Lib. Assoc. at Liverpool.) 1912.

Macintyre (P.). Hist. Sketch of the Liverpool Library. (*Hist. Soc. Lancs. & Cheshire. Trans.*, vol. ix. pp. 235–244. 1857.)

A Catal. of the Books, printed and in manuscript, bequeathed by the late Thomas Glazebrook Rylands, of Highfields, Thelwall, Cheshire, to the Library of University College, Liverpool, compiled by John Sampson. 1900.

LANCASHIRE (continued).

Aspinall (J.). Roscoe's Library, or, Old Books and Old Times. Liverpool, 1853.

Catal. of the Library and Prints of William Roscoe, sold by Mr. Winstanley. 2 vols. Liverpool, 1816.

Murray (David). 'Museums.' Glasgow, 1904. Biblio. Note on Liverpool Museums, vol. ii. pp. 335–336.

Picton (J. A.). Sir James A. Picton. A Biography. 1891. Chap. xi. Historian of Liverpool.

Borough Records, 1551, etc., at Municipal Buildings, Liverpool. (*Local Records Comm. Rep.*, 1902, App. III. p. 36.)

Borough and other Records in Public and Private Custody. (*Ibid.* 1902, App. III. p. 248.)

Picton (Sir James A.). Report on the Records and Documents relating to the City of Liverpool, now in the possession of the Corporation. 1881.

——— **Notes on the Charters of the Borough (now City) of Liverpool.** (*Hist. Soc. Lancs. & Cheshire. Trans.*, vol. xxxvi. pp. 53–128. 1884.)

Two vols. of Selections from the Municipal Archives, extracted and annotated by Sir James A. Picton, were issued in 1883 and 1886.

Morton (T. N.). A Concise Account of the Charters, Muniments, and other Records of the Corporation of Liverpool in 1897. (*Hist. Soc. Lancs. & Cheshire. Trans.*, vol. xlix. pp. 71–86. 1898.)

Charters of Liverpool. The Appendix to the '*Report of the Commissioners on Municipal Corporations*,' at the Inquiry held at Liverpool, 1833, contains the Charters in full, with translations.

A Hist. of Municipal Government in Liverpool, from the earliest times to the Municipal Reform Act of 1835. Pt. I. A Narrative Introduction (containing Biblio. Notes on Charters), by Ramsay Muir; Pt. II. A Collection of Charters, by Edith M. Platt. (Univ. of Liverpool School of Local Hist., etc. Vol. I. 1906.)

Liverpool Vestry Books, 1681-1834, edited by Henry Peet. Univ. of Liverpool School of Local History and Records. 1912. Vol. II. Introduction on the Eccles. & Miscell. Records.

Brooke (Richard). Liverpool as it was during the last quarter of the eighteenth century, 1775 to 1800. Liverpool, 1853. List of Acts of Parliament, pp. 442–450.

Lumby (J. H.). Chester, Birkenhead, and Liverpool, in the Patent and Close Rolls of the Three Edwards, with an Index of References. (*Hist. Soc. Lancs. & Cheshire. Trans.*, vol. liv. pp. 45–72. 1902.)

——— **Chester and Liverpool in the Patent Rolls** of Richard II. and the Lancastrian and Yorkist Kings. (*Hist. Soc. Lancs. & Cheshire. Trans.*, vol. lv. pp. 163–187. 1903.)

Report of an Inspection of the Records of the Liverpool Court of Passage, Jan. 1913. (*Local Records Comm. Rep.*, 1914, vol. ii. pt. 2, pp. 164–165.)

Holt (John). MS. Collections for a Hist. of Liverpool. (In Liverpool Public Library.)

Mayer (Joseph). A Collection of MS. and Printed Materials relating to Liverpool. (In Liverpool Public Library.)

'A Catal. of Books and Papers concerning the Town of Liverpool, with a list of an illustrative Collection of Maps, Views, Portraits, etc., preserved in the Library of the Athenæum, 1833.' Copied from the original MS. by W. Roscoe Jones, Librarian. (In Brit. Museum. Add. MS. 22647.) See also '*Hist. of the Athenæum, Liverpool*, 1798–1898,' by G. T. Shaw and W. F. Wilson. 1898.

Another Liverpool Collection in the Brit. Mus. is Add. MS. 22645. There are also 40 to 50 Liverpool Deeds there among the Aston Hall Charters.

LANCASHIRE (*continued*).

The Moore Charters and Documents relating to Liverpool. Report to City Council. First Part, Jan. 1889, by Sir James Picton. No Second Part issued. See also *ante* p. 122 for other entries relating to the Moore Collection.

Peet (Henry). An Inventory of the Plate, Register Books, etc., of the Two Parish Churches in Liverpool, with a Catal. of the Ancient Lib. in St. Peter's Church. 1893.

Diocese of Liverpool. Collection and Custody of Local Ecclesiastical Records. Report of Committee on Local Ecclesiastical Records, 1910, with lists of Parish Registers, with dates, etc., Churchwardens' Accounts, etc. (Lancs. Par. Reg. Soc. xxxv. 1909. *The Earliest Registers of the Parish of Liverpool,* 1660–1704. Appendix.) Also issued separately.

Special Liverpool Collections are at the Liverpool Free Public Library, the Liverpool Library, and the Athenæum, Liverpool, and the T. G. Rylands Collection, and the Library of the Liverpool Lit. & Philos. Soc. at the Liverpool Univ. Library.

MANCHESTER.

Sutton (Charles W.). Manchester Bibliography, 1880-87. (*Manchester Lit. Club. Papers,* vol. vii.-xiv. 1881-88.)

Harland (John). 'Mamecestre.' 3 vols. 1861-62. Chetham Soc. vols. liii. lvi. lviii. Biblio. Notes on Histories of Manchester, in Introduction to Vol. III.

Bailey (John Eglinton). John Whitaker, the Historian of Manchester. (*Manchester Lit. Club. Papers,* vol. iii. pp. 148–180. 1877.)

Harland (John). Collectanea relating to Manchester and its Neighbourhood at various periods. 2 vols. Chetham Soc. vols. lxviii. lxxii. 1866–67.

Vol. I. Maps or Plans of Manchester, pp. 88-118.
The Oldest Manchester Directories, pp. 119-166.
Thomas Barritt (the Antiquary), of Manchester, and his MSS., pp. 240-258.
Vol. II. Brief Notes on Manchester Newspapers, pp. 102-115.
An Old Manchester Newspaper, Orion Adams's 'Weekly Journal,' 1752, pp. 115-120.
The 'Lancashire Mag. or Manchester Mus.,' pp. 120-123.
Local Broadsides, pp. 124-130.

Shaw (W. A.). Manchester, Old and New. 3 vols. [1895.] Chap. viii. Biblio. Notes on Manchester Printing Clubs, and Newspapers.

Biblio. Notes on Manchester Books, with a List of Manchester Printers of the 18th century. By J. P. Earwaker, W. H. Allnutt, and others. (*Local Gleanings relating to Lancs. & Cheshire,* ed. by J. P. Earwaker, vol. i. pp. 54, 62, 67, 177. 1875.)

Table of Contents and Index to Publications, and Catal. of the Library, of the Manchester Literary Club, etc., see *ante* p. 117.

Swann (John H.). Hist. of the Manchester Literary Club. (*Manchester Lit. Club. Papers,* vol. xxviii. p. 443. 1902; *Manchester Quarterly,* vol. xxi. p. 443. 1902.)

—— **Manchester Lit. Club: Some Notes on its History, 1862-1908.** Manchester, 1908. (Reprinted from the '*Manchester City News.*')

Hardwick (Charles). The Review Club, a Precursor of the Manchester Lit. Club. (*Manchester Lit. Club. Papers,* vol. xi. pp. 344–353. 1885; *Manchester Quarterly,* vol. iv. pp. 344–353. 1885.)

Clegg (James). List of Manchester Associations, Artistic, Literary, Professional, and Scientific. (*Directory of Secondhand Booksellers,* 1914, pp. 512–517.)

Hunter (J. Weir). The Clubs of Old Manchester. (*Manchester Lit. Club. Papers,* vol. ii. pp. 1–32. 1876.)

LANCASHIRE (*continued*).

Axon (William E. A.). Handbook of the Public Libraries of Manchester and Salford. 1877.

—— **The Book Rarities of the Manchester Free Library.** (*Manchester Lit. Club. Trans.*, vol. i. pp. 76–84. 1875.) Also issued separately.

—— **Botanical Books in the Manchester Free Library, with Additions.** Oldham, 1879–81.

—— **What was the first Book printed in Manchester?** (*Lancs. & Cheshire Antiq. Soc. Trans.*, vol. iv. pp. 13–15. 1886.)

—— **In Memoriam 'Bibliothecarius Chethamensis.' (Thomas Jones B.A., F.S.A., Chetham's Librarian.)** (*Manchester Lit. Club. Papers*, vol. ii. pp. 59–65. 1876.)

Sutton (Charles W.). The Libraries of Manchester. 1902.

—— **Manchester Libraries and Booksellers.** (*Book-Auction Records*, vol. vi. pt. 4, pp. lxv.–lxxi. 1909.)

Hist. and Descriptive Accounts of the Manchester Libraries visited by the Library Association, 1879. (*Trans. & Proc. Second Ann. Meeting Library Assoc.*, pp. 113–129. 1880.)

Croston (James). The First Free Library (Prestwich's) in Manchester. 1878.

Biblio. of Humphrey Chetham and his Hospital, with List of Catalogues, in '*Life of Humphrey Chetham*,' by F. R. Raines and C. W. Sutton, vol. i. App. ix. pp. 353–363. Chetham Soc., New Ser., vols. xlix., L. 1903.

Halliwell-Phillipps (J. O.). A Catal. of Proclamations, Broadsides, Ballads, and Poems, presented to The Chetham Lib. by James O. Halliwell. Printed for Private Circulation. Liverpool, 1851.

Chetham's Library, see *ante* Hist. MSS. Comm. Reports.

Kay (J. Taylor). Owens College Library. A Note for the Conference of Librarians. Manchester, 1879.

—— **Notes on the Library of Owens College.** (Reprinted from '*Owens College Mag.*' 1891.)

—— **Book Rarities of Owens College Library.** (*Manchester Lit. Club. Papers*, vol. vii. pp. 321–322. 1881.)

Lockhart (Joseph C.). John Owens, the Founder of the College. Biog. Notice. (*Manchester Lit. Club. Papers*, vol. iv. pp. 135–144. 1878.)

Guppy (Henry). Some Famous Libraries. The John Rylands Lib., Manchester. (*The Bibliophile*, vol. ii. pp. 62, 137, 205. 1908.)

—— **The John Rylands Library, Manchester.** (*The Library Assoc. Record*, vol. i. pt. 2, pp. 564–571. 1899.)

—— **The John Rylands Library, Manchester.** A brief historical description of the Library and its Contents. 1914. List of Publications of the Library, pp. 63–68.

Catal. of the Printed Books and Manuscripts in the John Rylands Library. Preface by E. Gordon Duff. 3 vols. Manchester, 1899.

Catal. of Books in the John Rylands Library printed in England, Scotland and Ireland, and of Books in English printed abroad to end of 1640. Manchester, 1895.

The John Rylands Library has issued a Bulletin since 1903.

Credland (W. R.). The Althorp Library. (Purchased for Manchester by Mrs. John Rylands.) (*Manchester Lit. Club. Papers*, vol. xix. pp. 135–147, 1893; *Manchester Quarterly*, vol. xii. pp. 135–147. 1893.)

Bailey (J. Eglinton). The Old 'English Library' of Manchester Church. (From '*Notes & Queries*,' Ser. 5, vol. viii. 1877.)

LANCASHIRE (*continued*).

Botfield (Beriah). Notes on the Cathedral Libraries of England. 1849. **Manchester,** pp. 328–329.

Earwaker (J. P.). Notes on the Early Booksellers and Stationers of Manchester prior to 1700. (*Lancs. & Cheshire Antiq. Soc. Trans.*, vol. vi. pp. 1–26. 1888.)

Manchester Booksellers. By Joseph Johnson, J. T. Slugg, and others. (*City News Notes & Queries*, vol. ii. pp. 67–68, 76, 82, 100, 236. 1879.)

Slugg (Josiah T.). Reminiscences of Manchester Fifty Years Ago. ('*City News' Notes & Queries*, vols. ii. and iii. 1879–80.) Also issued separately, 1881. Contains chapters on Booksellers and Printers, Newspapers, etc.

Ford's Catalogue of Books, 1805. An Account of a Catal. of Books on sale by William Ford, a Manchester Bookseller and Collector, 1805. (*Palatine Note-book*, vol. ii. pp. 269–272. 1882.)

Earwaker (J. P.). Biblio. Note on Ford, the Manchester Bookseller. (*Local Gleanings relating to Lancs. & Cheshire*, ed. by J. P. Earwaker, vol. i. pp. 38, 52, 70. 1875.)

Old Manchester Newspapers. Biblio. Notes, with Lists. (*City News Notes & Queries*, vols. iv.–vii. 1882–88, *passim.*)

Nodal (J. H.). Manchester Periodicals. Biblio. Notes and Lists. (*City News Notes & Queries*, vols. i., iii., v. 1878–83, *passim.*)

——— **and Heywood (Abel), Jun. Newspapers and Periodicals: Their Circulation in Manchester.** (*Manchester Lit. Club. Papers*, vol. ii. pp. 32–58. 1876)

Raffald (Elizabeth). The Manchester Directory for the year 1772. A reprint with a Biblio. Preface.

Roeder (C.). Maps and Views of Manchester. (*Lancs. & Cheshire Antiq. Soc. Trans.*, vol. xxi. pp. 153–171. 1904.)

Views of Manchester and the Neighbourhood, with Notices of the Artists. (From a MS. of Thomas Baker, 1869.) (*Palatine Note-book*, vol. iii. pp. 53, 87, 116, 121, 162, 234. 1883.)

Maps of Manchester. Lists. (*City News Notes & Queries*, vol. iv. pp. 124–125, 132. 1881.)

Lists of Works issued by various Manchester Printers (in MS.), 10 vols., n.d. On sale by Albert Sutton, Manchester. See '*Bibliotheca Lancastrensis*,' 1913, p. 52.

Early Manchester Printers. Biblio. Notes. (*Manchester Notes & Queries*, vol. vii. 1888, *passim.*)

Slatter (Henry). The Typographical Association. A Fifty Years' Record, 1849–99, edited by Richard Hackett. Manchester, 1899.

The Priory Press, Manchester. Private Printing Press of Walter Arthur Copinger, at The Priory, Greenheys, Manchester. See art. Copinger in *Dict. Nat. Biog.* for a list of Books printed.

Sutton (Charles W.). Biblio. Note on the Writings of 'Doctor' Thomas Deacon, of Manchester, 1719–1747, and of his opponent, the Rev. J. Owen, of Rochdale. Manchester, 1879.

List of Manchester Municipal Records Printed. (*Notes & Queries*, Ser. 11, vol. v. p 74. 1912.)

Murray (David). 'Museums.' Glasgow, 1904. Biblio. Note on Manchester Museums, vol. iii. p. 11.

Borough Records, 1301, etc., with MS. Index, at Town Hall, Manchester. (*Local Records Comm. Rep.*, 1902, App. III. p. 36.)

LANCASHIRE (*continued*).

Harland (John). Court Leet Records of the Manor of Manchester in the Sixteenth Century. Chetham Soc., vol. lxiii. 1864.

—— **Continuation of the Court Leet Records, etc., 1586–1602.** *Ibid.* vol. lxv. 1865.

The Court Leet Records of the Manor of Manchester. (*Palatine Note-book*, vol. i. pp. 187–190. 1881.)

Earwaker (J. P.). The Early Deeds relating to the Manor of Manchester, now in the possession of the Corporation. (*Brit. Archæol. Assoc. Journ.*, New Ser., vol. i. pp. 49–57. 1895.)

Esdaile (George). The Charters of Manchester and Salford. (*Lancs. & Cheshire Antiq. Soc. Trans.*, vol. v. pp. 242–248. 1887.)

Manchester Cathedral Records, 15th cent., etc., at Manchester. (*Local Records Comm. Rep.*, 1902, App. III. p. 112.)

Manchester Diocesan Records, at the Registry, Manchester. (*Local Records Comm. Rep.*, 1902, App. III. p. 104.)

Barritt (Thomas). A Collection of Antiquarian Memoranda, principally relating to Manchester and vicinity. Chetham Library MS. 8026.

An account of Thomas Barritt and his MSS. is contained in '*Collectanea relating to Manchester*,' by John Harland, vol. i. pp. 240–258.

Special Collections for Manchester are at the Free Reference Library, at Chetham's Library, and at the Portico Library, in Manchester. A large Local Collection is in the Library of the Manchester Literary Club.

MUCH WOOLTON.

Gladstone (Robert). Early Charters of the Knights Hospitallers relating to Much Woolton, near Liverpool, with an Index. (*Hist. Soc. Lancs. & Cheshire. Trans.*, vol. liv. pp. 173–196, 233–235. 1904.)

OLDHAM.

Borough Records, at Town Hall, Oldham. (*Local Records Comm. Rep.*, 1902, App. III. p. 44.)

Biblio. Lists of Books relating to Oldham, by Giles Shaw and W. Mackie. (*Local Notes & Gleanings*, ed. by Giles Shaw, vol. i. pp. 35, 52, 59, 61 ; vol. ii. p. 48 ; vol. iii. p. 10. 1886–89.)

Mellor (C.). An Oldham Literary Club in 1847. (*Manchester Lit. Club. Papers*, vol. xix. pp. 440–443. 1893.)

Shaw (Giles). Sketch of the Life of James Butterworth, with a Biblio. 1909.

—— **Edwin Butterworth: His Life and Labours,** with a Biblio. (*Lancs. & Cheshire Antiq. Soc. Trans.*, vol. xxii. pp. 61–72. 1904.) Published separately, 1905.

Hollinhead (J.). List of the Works of James and Edwin Butterworth. (*Local Notes & Gleanings*, ed. by Giles Shaw, vol. i. pp. 204–210, 229-337. 1886–87.)

The Oldham Free Public Library has a Local Collection, including a large number of MSS. of James and Edwin Butterworth, the Local Historians. A Local Collection is also at the Lyceum Library.

ORMSKIRK.

Roberts (William John). Collectanea relative to the Hist. and Antiquities of the Parish of Ormskirk. 1819. (In British Museum, Add. MS. 22648.)

Papers relating to the Parish of Ormskirk, found by E. A. Baldwin Mordaunt, in Skelmersdale, 1902, with a description of each document, and Index of Persons and Places. (In British Museum, Add. MS. 36876.)

LANCASHIRE (*continued*).

PENDLE HILL.

McKay (**James**). **Pendle Hill in History and Literature.** 1888. (Contains various Biblio. Notes.)

PENWORTHAM.

Hulton (**W. A.**). **Documents relating to the Priory of Penwortham and other Possessions in Lancs. of the Abbey of Evesham.** Chetham Soc. vol. xxx. 1853.

PRESTON.

Borough Records, 1199, etc., at Town Hall, Preston. (*Local Records Comm. Rep.*, 1902, App. III. p. 38.)

Biblio. Notes on Preston Books, by W. H. Allnutt, and others. (*Local Gleanings relating to Lancs. & Cheshire*, ed. by J. P. Earwaker, vol. i. pp. 37, 43; vol. ii. p. 230. 1875–78.)

Dobson (**William**) **and Harland** (**John**). **A Hist. of Preston Guild.** Preston, n.d. Description of the Charters, pp. 78–87.

Lingard (**John**). **The Charters granted by different Sovereigns to Preston.** (A complete set with translations.) Preston, 1821.

Smith (**Tom C.**). **Records of The Parish Church of Preston in Amounderness.** 1892. Extracts from the Parish Registers, with Biblio. Notes, pp. 81–229.

List of Preston Municipal Records Printed. (*Notes & Queries*, Ser. 11, vol. v. p. 478. 1912.)

Abram (**W. A.**). **Index to the Local and Topographical Sketches in 'The Preston Guardian' from 1874 to 1881.** 2 parts. 1882.

A Local Collection is at the Free Public Library, Preston.

PRESTWICH.

Kidson (**J. H.**). **The Patron Saint of Prestwich, and the Old Deeds of the Church.** 1885.

RIBCHESTER.

Smith (**Tom C.**) **and Shortt** (**Jonathan**). **The Hist. of the Parish of Ribchester.** 1890. Biblio. Notes on the Registers, and the Parish Library, pp. 189–204, 214–219.

RIXTON.

Schedule of Deeds relating to the Manors of Rixton and Glazebrook (made 1786). Transcript, 1886. (MS. in Warrington Museum Ref. Library.) See also under Warrington.

ROCHDALE.

Fishwick (**Henry**). **The Biblio. of Rochdale,** as illustrated by the Books in the local Free Public Lib. (*Manchester Lit. Club. Papers*, vol. vi. pp. 233–253. 1880.) Also issued separately.

Rochdale Parish Church Registers. MS. Index to the Registers from 1582 to 1801, compiled by Henry Brierley, Hon. Sec. Lancs. Parish Reg. Soc. 45 vols.

March (**H. Colley**). **The Writings of Oliver Ormerod** (b. at Rochdale, 1811), **with a Memoir of the Author.** Rochdale, 1901.

A Special Collection of Rochdale Books is at the Rochdale Free Public Library, and another at the Pioneers' Co-operative Library in Rochdale.

LANCASHIRE (*continued*).

ST. HELENS.

Borough Records, with MS. Index, at Town Hall, St. Helens. (*Local Records Comm. Rep.*, 1902, App. III. p. 38.)

A Special Local Collection is at the Public Library, St. Helens.

SALFORD.

Borough Records, 1150, etc., at Town Hall, Salford. (*Local Records Comm. Rep.*, 1902, App. III. p. 40.)

Makinson (C.). On the Ancient Court Records of the Borough of Salford. (*Brit. Archæol. Assoc. Journ.*, New Ser., vol. i. pp. 314–326. 1895.)

The Portmote or Court Leet Records of Salford, transcribed and edited by J. G. de T. Mandley. 2 vols. Chetham Soc., New Ser., vols. xlvi. xlvii. 1902. (Biblio. Notes in Preface.)

Esdaile (George). The Charters of Manchester and Salford. (*Lancs. & Cheshire Antiq. Soc. Trans.*, vol. v. pp. 242–248. 1887.)

Bailey (J. Eglinton). The First Charter of Salford. Manchester, 1882.

List of Salford Municipal Records Printed. (*Notes & Queries*, Ser. 11, vol. vi. p. 91. 1912.)

Axon (William E. A.). Handbook of the Public Libraries of Manchester and Salford. 1877.

Murray (David). 'Museums.' Glasgow, 1904. Biblio. Note on Salford Museum, vol. iii. p. 155.

SOUTHPORT.

Cheetham (F. H.). Some Old Books on Southport. (*Hist. Soc. Lancs. & Cheshire. Trans.* vol. lx. pp. 105-139. 1909.)

A Local Collection is at the Atkinson Free Library, Southport.

STANDISH.

Earwaker (J. P.). Charters and Deeds relating to the Standish Family of Standish and Duxbury, co. Lancs. Manchester, n.d.

STONYHURST.

Stonyhurst College MSS. See *ante* Hist. MSS. Comm. Reports.

TURTON.

French (Gilbert J.). Biblio. Notices of the Church Libraries at Turton and Gorton, bequeathed by Humphrey Chetham. Chetham Soc. vol. xxxviii. 1855.

WARRINGTON.

Borough Records, with Printed & MS. Indexes, at the Museum, Warrington. (*Local Records Comm. Rep.*, 1902, App. III. p. 72.)

Kendrick (J.), Jun. Catal. of Books, etc., connected with Warrington, *circa* 1880. (MS. in Warrington Museum.)

Madeley (Charles). Warrington Municipal Museum. Catal. of the Reference Library, 1898, and **Supplement,** 1908.

Axon (William E. A.). Book Rarities of the Warrington Museum. 1878.

Murray (David). 'Museums.' Glasgow, 1904. Biblio. Note on Warrington Museum, vol. iii. pp. 259–260.

Nodal (J. H.). The Jackson Collection at the Warrington Library. Warrington, 1877.

LANCASHIRE (continued).

Hadfield (Charles). The Jackson Collection at the Warrington Library. A List of some of the Rare and Curious Books. 1877.

Kendrick (J.), Jun. List of Contents of 'Local Notes, Queries, and Replies,' in the 'Warrington Guardian,' 1868-84. (MS. in Warrington Museum.)

Dr. James Kendrick, of Warrington (b. 1809, d. 1882), with a List of his Works. (*Palatine Note-book*, vol. ii. pp. 113-116. 1882.)

Rylands (W. Harry). Booksellers and Stationers in Warrington, 1639 to 1657, with the full list of the contents of a Stationer's Shop there in 1647. (*Hist. Soc. Lancs. & Cheshire. Trans.*, vol. xxxvii. pp. 67-115. 1885.)

Kendrick (James). Eyres' Warrington Press and its Local Association, —The Eyres' Printing Press at Warrington. A series of Articles in the '*Warrington Guardian*,' Jan.-May, 1881.

W. Eyres printed numerous Chap-Books.

——— **Biblio. Note on some Warrington Chap-Books** (printed by William Ashton) **of the last Century.** (*Local Gleanings relating to Lancs. & Cheshire*, ed. by J. P. Earwaker, vol. i. pp. 139-140. 1876.)

Tempest (Mrs. Arthur Cecil). Schedule of Deeds, chiefly relating to Warrington, late the property of the Mascys of Rixton, now preserved in the Muniment Room, at Broughton Hall, in Craven. (*Hist. Soc. Lancs. and Cheshire. Trans.*, vol. xl. pp. 156-176. 1883.) See also under Rixton.

The Library of John Fitchett Marsh, late of Warrington. (*Palatine Note-book*, vol. ii. pp. 168-172. 1882.)

A Large Local Collection is at the Municipal Museum, Warrington.

WARTON.

Roper (W. O.). The Missing Hist. of Warton, by John Lucas. (*Hist. Soc. Lancs. & Cheshire. Trans.*, vol. xxxviii. pp. 159-169. 1889.)

WIGAN.

Folkard (H. T.). Wigan Bibliography. A Local Catal. of Wigan Printed Books and Pamphlets, and the Works of Authors connected with Wigan and the District, in the Reference Department of the Wigan Free Public Library. 1886. List of Wigan Directories, Maps, Newspapers, Printers, etc., pp. 25-27.

Lea (Edith). Wigan Local Catalogue. A Catal. of the Works of Wigan Authors, and of Books Printed in, or Relating to Wigan. (*Wigan Public Library Quarterly Record*, vol. ii. nos. 13-16. 1913-14.) In progress.

Folkard (H. T.). Wigan Free Public Library: Its Rise and Progress. A List of some of its Treasures, with an Account of the Celebration of the Twenty-first Anniversary of its Opening. 1900.

Biblio. Notes on Wigan Books, by W. H. Allnutt, John Leyland, and others. (*Local Gleanings relating to Lancs. & Cheshire*, ed. by J. P. Earwaker, vol. i. pp. 53, 62, 124, 233; vol. ii. p. 57. 1875-77.)

Borough Records, 1250, etc., with Printed Index, at the Free Public Library, Wigan. (*Local Records Comm. Rep.*, 1902, App. III. p. 42.)

A Large Wigan Collection is at the Wigan Free Public Library. Wigan has had the great good fortune to enjoy the liberal patronage of one of the most gifted and princely book Collectors who has ever lived. The late Lord Crawford presented to the Wigan Free Library valuable MSS. and Printed Books, including the De Bry Collection, the Masonic Collection, and Collections of Civil War Tracts, Papal Bulls, Caricatures, etc. Lord Crawford's matchless Collections are housed at Haigh Hall, and the Catalogues of his Library are themselves most valuable possessions. For list of these Catalogues, see Folkard, 'Catal. of the Wigan Library,' under Lindsay.

LEICESTERSHIRE.

Kirkby (C. V.). Leicester Free Public Libraries. Catal. of Books, Pamphlets, Maps, Views, MSS., etc., relating to Leicestershire, in the Central Reference Library. 1893.

Additions to the 'Leicestershire Department' of the Leic. Free Libraries are issued in the yearly Reports.

Nichols (John). History of Leicestershire. 4 vols. 1795–1815. The following Indexes were issued:—

Index to the Names in the First Vol., by Joseph Strutt, pp. 1–28.

General Index to the First Vol., by Joseph Strutt, pp. 1–113.

Index to the Arms & General Index to the Pedigrees in the Four Vols., by Barak Longmate, pp. 1–11.

Personal Index to the Second, Third, & Fourth Vols., by J. P. Malcolm, pp. 13–86.

Local & Miscellaneous Index to the Second, Third, and Fourth Vols., & Supplementary Index, by J. P. Malcolm, pp. 1–25.

——— **Notices from the 'Gentleman's Mag.' upon the 'Hist. and Antiquities of Leicestershire.'** (Bibliotheca Topographica Britannica, vols. vii., viii. 1790.) London, 1791.

Brief Memoirs of John Nichols, with list of his Publications. London, 1804.

12 copies only printed, by John Nichols. See also the Memoir by Alexander Chalmers in the '*Gentleman's Mag.*' Dec. 1826. For an account of the fire which destroyed the stock of his '*Hist. of Leics.*' see '*Gentleman's Mag.*' 1808, vol. i. p. 99.

Letters of John Nichols, Historian, to John Ward, of Hinckley, during the compilation of a portion of the 'Hist. of Leics.,' with biog. notice. (*Leics. & Rutland Notes & Queries*, vol. ii. pp. 16, 59, 134, 221, 247, 310; vol. iii. pp. 101, 287. 1893–95.)

John Throsby, Historian of Leicester (b. 1740, d. 1803), **with list of Works,** by Sempronius. (*Leics. & Rutland Notes & Queries*, vol. i. pp. 126–128. 1891.)

Catal. of the Books, Pamphlets, Drawings, etc., in the Library of the Leicestershire Archit. & Archæol. Soc. (*Leics. Archit. & Archæol. Soc. Trans.*, vol. vi. pp. 83–85. 1885.)

A Brief Notice of the Work of the Leics. Archit. & Archæol. Soc. during the Fifty Years of its existence. (*Leics. Archit. & Archæol. Soc. Trans.*, vol. ix. pp. 252–257. 1905.)

A Catal. of Leicestershire Antiquities at the Jubilee Meeting of the Leics. Archit. & Archæol. Soc., 1905, compiled by H. H. Peach. (*Leics. Archit. & Archæol. Soc. Trans.*, vol. x. pp. 28–35. 1905.)

Indexes to the Reports and Papers of the Associated Architectural Societies, etc. (includes 'Leics. Archit. & Archæol. Soc.'). Vols. i.–viii. (1850–66); vols. ix.–xiv. (1867–78); vols. xv.–xix. (1879–88); and vols. xx.–xxv. (1889–1900). Lincoln, 1867–1905.

Horwood (A. R.). Classified Biblio. of Principal Works on the Geology, Botany, Palæontology, Zoology, and Archæology of Leicestershire. (*A Guide to Leicester and District*, 1907, pp. 386–420.) Brit. Assoc. for Advancement of Science.

Nuttall (G. Clarke). Guide to Leicester and Neighbourhood. Brit. Medical Assoc. Leicester, 1905. Biblio., pp. 189–192.

Johnson (Mrs. T. Fielding). Glimpses of Ancient Leicester in Six Periods. London, 1906. List of Works Consulted, pp. xiv–xv.

Thompson (James). The Herrick Portraits in the Guild Hall, Leicester. (*Leics. Archit. & Archæol. Soc. Trans.*, vol. ii., pp. 43–54. 1866.)

Fulleylove (John). Catal. of a Collection of Drawings of Leicester and Neighbourhood. Leicester, 1892.

LEICESTERSHIRE (continued).

Herne (Frank S.). The Libraries of Leicester. (*Book-Auction Records,* vol. vi. pt. 2, pp. xxv.-xxix. 1909.)

—— **Hist. of the Town Library, and of the Permanent Library, Leicester.** 1891.

—— **The Town Library, Leicester.** (*Leic. Lit. & Philos. Soc. Trans.*, 1893, pp. 249-261.)

Catal. of the Old Town Hall Library, Leicester, by C. Deedes, and others. Oxford, 1907.

Notes on the Leicester Town Library, by James Thompson, and others. (*Notes & Queries,* Ser. 3, vol. ii. p. 5, 50, 94 ; vol. xi. p. 225. 1862 & 1867.)

The Press and the Book-shop in Leicester. (*Leics. & Rutland Notes & Queries,* vol. iii. pp. 293–295. 1895.)

Herne (Frank S.). An Old Leicester Bookseller (Sir Richard Phillips). (*Leic. Lit. & Philos. Soc. Trans.*, 1893, pp. 65–73.)

The Oldest Local Bookseller. (Note on Francis Ward.) (*Leics. & Rutland Notes & Queries,* vol. i. p. 129. 1891.)

A Leicestershire Bibliophile. (John Moore, b. 1646.) *Leics. & Rutland Notes & Queries,* vol. iii. pp. 18–19. 1895.)

A Bookish Family. (John Brown (b. 1755) and John Garle Browne, Early Leicester Printers and Publishers.) *Leics. & Rutland Notes & Queries,* vol. iii. pp. 127–179. 1895.)

Gross (Charles). Biblio. of Brit. Municipal Hist. (*Harvard Hist. Studies,* vol. v. 1897.) Leicestershire, p. 99. Leicester, pp. 273–276.

Davenport (Frances G.). List of Printed Materials for Manorial Hist. 1894. Biblio. Note on Leics. Manorial Hist., p. 50.

Dove (Patrick Edward). Domesday Studies. 1891. Domesday Biblio. Leics. vol. ii. p. 682.

Lyell (Arthur H.). Biblio. List of Romano-British Remains. 1912. Leics., pp. 56–60.

Macklin (Herbert Walter). Monumental Brasses. London: Geo. Allen & Co., 1913. Biblio. Note on Leics. Brasses, with a List, p. 166.

Murray (David). 'Museums.' Glasgow, 1904. Biblio. Note on Leicester Museum, vol. ii. p. 322.

County Folk-Lore. Vol. i. Leicestershire and Rutland, edited by C. J. Billson. (With List of Authorities.) Folk-Lore Soc. Pubns. vol. xxxvii. 1895.

A List of Private Acts, etc., relating to the County of Leic. Stevens & Sons, *circa* 1914.

Special Topographical Collections for Leicestershire are in the Central Reference Library of the Leicester Free Public Libraries, and in the Library of the Leics. Archit. & Archæol. Soc.

Hist. MSS. Comm. Reports. Leicestershire Collections.

Braye, Lord, at Stanford Park ...	10th Rep. p. 21 and App. VI. pp. 104–252.
Collis, Mrs., of Leicester	2nd Rep. p. xiii. and App. pp. 76, 77.
Peake, Mr. F. (The Neville Family, of Holt)	2nd Rep. p. xii. and App. pp. 92–97 ; 3rd Rep. p. xvii. and App. pp. 277–280.
Rutland, Duke of, at Belvoir ...	1st Rep. p. x. and App. pp. 10–12 ; 12th Rep. pp. 13–23 and Vols. I., II. (App. IV., V.) ; 14th Rep. pp. 6–11 and Vol. III. (App. I.) ; 17th Rep. pp. 19–25 ; and Vol. IV. (1905).
Leicester Corporation	8th Rep. p. xvi. and App. pp. 403–441.

LEICESTERSHIRE (continued).

County Records, from reign of Jas. II., with MS. List, at the Castle, Leicester. (*Local Records Comm. Rep.*, 1902, App. III. p. 20.)

Borough Records, 14th cent., etc., at Town Hall, Leicester. (*Local Records Comm. Rep.*, 1902, App. III. p. 36.)

Bateson (Mary). Records of the Borough of Leicester. 3 vols. London, 1899–1905. (Tables of Records and Lists of Documents in each vol.)

Jeaffreson (J. Cordy). An Index to the Ancient Manuscripts of the Borough of Leicester. 1878.

Kelly (William). Ancient Records of Leicester. (*Leic. Lit. & Philos. Soc. Rep.*, 1855, pp. 31–103.)

Also incorporated in Kelly's 'Notices illustrative of the Drama, etc., in Leicester, 1865.

Biblio. Note on The Ancient Records of Leicester. (*Assoc. Archit Soc. Reports & Papers*, vol. xiv. pp. lxiii.–lxvi., 1877.)

Return as to Parish Documents ordered to be made by the Leics. County Council, Nov. 5, 1895.

Thompson (James). The Rolls of the Mayors of Leicester. (*Leics. Archit. & Archæol. Soc. Trans.*, vol. iv. pp. 280–293. 1878.)

——— **On the Archives of the Borough of Leicester.** (Brit. Archæol. Assoc. Trans., Winchester, 1845, pp. 70–84. 1846.)

Lysons (Rev. S.). Collections for Leicestershire, Brit. Mus. Add. MS. 9458.

Powell's Topographical Collections for Leicestershire, Brit. Mus. Add. MS. 17462.

Suckling's Collections for Leicestershire, 1821–39, Brit. Mus. Add. MS. 18481. Index, Add. MS. 18491.

Upcott W.). Topographical Collections for Leicestershire, Brit. Mus. Add. MS. 15922. Other Brit. Mus. Collections are at Add. MSS. 41533–41542.

Leicestershire Topographical MSS. in the British Museum (from the Class Catal. of MSS.). (*Leics. Archit. & Archæol. Soc. Trans.*, vol. vi. pp. 159–167. 1890.)

Fletcher (W. G. Dimock). Some Unpublished Documents relating to Leics., preserved in the Public Record Office, and the Brit. Museum. Leics. Archit. and Archæol. Soc. (In *Assoc. Archit. Soc. Reports & Papers*, vol. xxiii. pp. 213–252, 392–436; vol. xxiv. pp. 234–277. 1895–97.)

——— **Notes on Leics. MSS. in the Public Record Office, and our National Libraries.** (*Leics. Archit. & Archæol. Soc. Trans.*, vol. v. pp. 324–341. 1882.)

——— **Documents relating to Leics., preserved in the Episcopal Registers at Lincoln.** Leics. Archit. & Archæol. Soc. (In *Assoc. Archit. Soc. Reports & Papers*, vol. xxi. pp. 277–329; vol. xxii. pp. 109–150, 227–365. 1892–94.)

Deeds relating to Leics., in possession of G. F. Tudor Sherwood (a brief list). (*Leics. & Rutland Notes & Queries*, vol. ii. pp. 159–162, 199–201. 1893.)

Foster (C. W.). Index to the Bishops' Transcripts of Parish Registers in the Registry of the Archdeacon of Leicester, 1561 to 1700, also a List of Leics. Parish Registers prior to 1890, compiled by H. Hartopp. Leicester, 1909.

Hartopp (Henry). Parish Registers of Leicestershire, with a Digest of the Registers, and a Table of the Early Transcripts. (*Leics. Archit. & Archæol. Soc. Trans.*, vol. viii. pp. 391–424. 1899.)

Beasley (J. A. L.). Parish Registers and Records. (*Ibid.* vol. x. pp. 259–274. 1909.)

LEICESTERSHIRE (continued).

Parish Registers in Leicestershire. Biblio. Note by 'Sempronius.' (*Leics. & Rutland Notes & Queries*, vol. i. pp. 22–26, 104. 1891.)

Owen (Rev. T. W.). The Parish Registers of S. Nicholas, Leicester. (*Leics. Archit. & Archæol. Trans.*, vol. vi. p. 344; vol. vii. pp. 31, 195, 227, 298. 1888–92.)

Hartopp (Henry). The Ancient Parish Registers of Leicester. (*Leics. & Rutland Notes & Queries*, vol. i. pp. 65, 99, 141, 193, 241; vol. ii. p. 22. 1891–93.)

Fletcher (W. G. Dimock). Two Leics. Parish Registers. (Shackerstone and Somerby.) (*Leics. Archit. & Archæol. Soc. Trans.*, vol. v. pp. 232–284. 1881.)

Trimen (Henry). Botanical Biblio. of the British Counties. Leics. (*Journ. of Botany*, vol. xii. p. 178. 1874.)

The Flora of Leicestershire, compiled by F. T. Mott, and others. Issued by the Leicester Lit. & Philos. Soc. 1886. List of Works relating to the Botany of Leics., p. xv.

Christy (Miller). Biblio. Note on Leics. Birds. (*The Zoologist*, Ser. 3, vol. xiv. p. 255, 1890; and reprinted in pamph., 1891, p. 17.) **Mammals.** (*The Zoologist*, Ser. 3, vol. xvii. p. 181. 1893.) **Reptiles.** (*Ibid.* p. 245. 1893.) **Fishes.** (*Ibid.* p. 255. 1893.)

Anderson (John P.). Book of Brit. Topo., 1881. Leics., pp. 164-167.

Gatfield (George). Guide to Heraldry. 1892. Leics., pp. 151-152.

Sims (Richard). Manual. 1861. Leics., pp. 169, 212, 235, 236.

Upcott (William). English Topo., 1818. Leics., vol. i. pp. 481-557, 630.

Smith (Alfred Russell). Catal. of Topo. Tracts, etc., 1878. Leics., pp. 181-186.

Gough (Richard). Brit. Topo., 1780. Leics., vol. i. pp. 509-518.

Bandinel (Bulkeley). Catal. of Books bequeathed to Bodleian Lib. by Richard Gough, 1814. Leics., pp. 157-160.

CHURCH LANGTON.

Hanbury (William). Plan for a Public Library at Church Langton. 1760.

EVINGTON.

North (Thomas). Notes on Evington Parish Registers. (*Leics. Archit. & Archæol. Soc. Trans.*, vol. iv. pp. 319–320. 1878.)

FRISBY-ON-THE-WREAKE.

North (Thomas). The Parish Registers of Frisby-on-the-Wreake. (*Leics. Archit. & Archæol. Soc. Trans.*, vol. v. pp. 26–29. 1879.)

LOUGHBOROUGH.

Fletcher (W. G. Dimock). The Parish Registers of Loughborough. (Reprinted from 'The Reliquary' for Private Circulation.) London, 1873.

MARKET HARBOROUGH.

Stocks (J. E.) and Bragg (W. B.). Market Harborough Parish Records, to 1530. Biblio. Notes. London, 1890.

Biblio. Note on William Harrod, a Local Historian. (*Leics. & Rutland Notes & Queries*, vol. iii. p. 48. 1895.)

Stocks (J. E.). On Ancient Charters and other Documents lately discovered at Market Harborough. (*Assoc. Archit. Soc. Reports & Papers*, vol. xvi. pp. 284–290. 1882.)

LEICESTERSHIRE (*continued*).

MELTON MOWBRAY.

List of Melton Mowbray Municipal Records Printed. (*Notes & Queries*, Ser. 11, vol. v. p. 74. 1912.)

MISTERTON.

Bradbrook (W.). Extracts from, and Notes on the Parish Registers of Misterton. (*Assoc. Archit. Soc. Reports & Papers*, vol. xxvi. pp. 449–457. 1902.)

NOSELEY.

Hartopp (H.). Some Unpublished Documents relating to Noseley. (*Assoc. Archit. Soc. Reports & Papers*, vol. xxv. pp. 431–458; vol. xxvi. pp. 276–320. 1900–01.)

SAXELBY.

North (Thomas). The Parish Records of Saxelby. (*Leics. Archit. & Archæol. Soc. Trans.*, vol. v. pp. 100–108. 1880.)

SOUTH CROXTON.

Fletcher (W. G. Dimock). The Parish Registers of South Croxton. (*Leics. & Archit. & Archæol. Soc. Trans.*, vol. vi. pp. 29–31. 1884.)

LEINSTER.

[The Province of Leinster comprises the Counties of Carlow, Dublin, Kildare, Kilkenny, King's County, Longford, Louth, Meath, Queen's County, Westmeath, Wexford, and Wicklow (*q. v.*). No separate Bibliography of Leinster as a Province so far exists.]

LEITRIM.

Coleman (James). Bibliographia Conaciensis: a list of Books relating to Connaught. Leitrim, p. 32. (*Galway Archæol. and Hist. Soc. Journ.*, vol. v. 1907–08.)

O'Hanlon (John). List of Materials for the Hist. & Topography of the Co. of Leitrim in the Ordnance Survey Records. (*Kilkenny & South-East of Irel. Archæol. Soc. Journ.*, vol. ix. pp. 218–219. 1867.)

Anderson (John P.). Book of Brit. Topo., 1881. **Leitrim,** p. 437.

Bandinel (Bulkeley). Catal. of Books bequeathed to Bodleian Lib. by Richard Gough. 1814. **Leitrim,** p. 380.

LIMERICK.

Coleman (James). Limerick and Clare Bibliography. A List of the Topog. and Hist. Works relating to the Counties Limerick and Clare. (*Limerick Field Club. Journ.*, vol. iii. pp. 139–141. 1907.)

——— **Limerick's Early Printed Books and Newspapers.** (*Ibid.* vol. i. No. 3, pp. 31–35; No. 4, pp. 45–47. 1899–1900.)

A further List of Limerick-Printed Books, etc., contributed by Messrs. Dix, Buckley, Coleman and Fogerty. (*Ibid.* vol. ii. pp. 136–137. 1902.)

The Rev. T. Lee, P. P. of Croom, has a special Collection of Limerick-Printed Books.

LIMERICK (continued).

Buckley (James). Some Account of the Earliest Limerick Printing. (*Cork Hist. & Archæol. Soc. Journ.*, vol. viii. pp. 195–200. 1902.) Also printed separately.

Dix (Ernest Reginald McClintock). List of Books, Pamphlets, Newspapers, etc., printed in Limerick from the earliest period to 1800. Limerick, 1907. Second edition. Limerick, 1912. (Irish Bibliography, No. V.)

—— **Early Printing in Limerick. Printing in Limerick prior to 1801.** Supplementary List. (*North Munster Archæol. Soc. Journ.*, vol. i. pp. 194–195, 269–271. 1910–11.)

—— **Will of a Limerick Printer of the 18th century.** (Andrew Welsh.) (*Ibid.* vol. ii. pp. 44–46. 1911.)

—— **The Earliest Limerick Newspaper.** (*Limerick Field Club Journ.*, vol. iii. pp. 248–250. 1908.)

Madden (R. R.). Biblio. Note on Limerick Newspapers. (*Hist. of Irish Periodical Literature*, 1867, vol. ii. pp. 202–206.)

Early Printing in Limerick and Ennis. (*Irish Book-Lover*, vol. iii. pp. 157–158. 1912.)

O'Hanlon (John). Index of Materials for the Hist. & Topography of the Co. of Limerick in the Irish Ordnance Survey Records, and in the Royal Irish Academy. (*Kilkenny & South-East of Irel. Archæol. Soc. Journ.*, vol. viii. pp. 422–424. 1866.)

Lenihan (Maurice). Limerick; its Hist. and Antiquities. 1886. Biblio. Notes (with a List of Authorities) in Preface, and a List of Charters, in Appendix, pp. 739–740.)

A Collection of Newspaper Cuttings, Placards, Ballads, etc., relating to Limerick Politics, etc., 1819–80 (in the Brit. Museum). Includes a MS. copy of corrections, by Ralph Ousley, of Ferrar's 'Hist. of Limerick' and a Prospectus of Lenihan's 'Hist. of Limerick.'

Gross (Charles). Biblio. of Brit. Municipal Hist. (*Harvard Hist. Studies*, vol. v. 1897.) Limerick, p. 119.

Macalister (R. A. Stewart). Studies in Irish Epigraphy. Part II. Biblio. of Limerick Epigraphy. 1902.

The Limerick Philosophical and Literary Society. Notes by J. G. Barry. (*Limerick Field Club. Journ.*, vol. i. No. 4, pp. 36–39. 1900.)

Hist. MSS. Comm. Reports. Limerick Collections.

Emly, Lord, of Tervoe	8th Rep. p. xviii. and App. pp. 174–208; 14th Rep. p. 52 and App. IX. pp. 155–199.
Limerick, The Black Book of ...	3rd Rep. p. xxvi. and App. p. 434.
,, Corporation of	1st Rep. App. pp. 131–132.

The Black Book of Limerick, with Introduction and Notes. Edited by James MacCaffrey. 1907. Some references to Limerick in the Papal and State Papers, pp. ci.–cvii. General Index to the Items contained in the Manuscript, pp. cviii.–cxx.

Miscellaneous Papers chiefly relating to the City and County of Limerick, 15th to 19th cent. (In Brit. Museum. Add. MS. 31888.)

Limerick's Historical Documents. Biblio. Note by J. C. (*Limerick Field Club. Journ.*, vol. i. No. 3, pp. 38–39. 1899.)

Anderson (John P.). Book of Brit. Topo., 1881. Limerick, p. 438.

Gough (Richard). Brit. Topo., 1780. Limerick, vol. ii. pp. 805–806.

Bandinel (Bulkeley). Catal. of Books bequeathed to Bodleian Lib. by Richard Gough, 1814. Limerick, p. 380.

LINCOLNSHIRE.

CORNS (A. R.). BIBLIOTHECA LINCOLNIENSIS. A CATALOGUE OF THE BOOKS, PAMPHLETS, ETC., RELATING TO THE CITY AND COUNTY OF LINCOLN, PRESERVED IN THE REFERENCE DEPARTMENT OF THE CITY OF LINCOLN PUBLIC LIBRARY. Lincoln, 1904. List of Maps, Prints, etc. pp. 245–260.

Recent Additions to 'The Collection of Lincolnshire Literature' are printed in the City of Lincoln Public Library Quarterly Record, 1910, etc.

Materials for a Complete List of Lincolnshire Topographical Books, partly compiled by Jos. Phillips of Stamford. (*Lincs. Notes & Queries*, Supplement, vols. i., ii. 1888–90.) Pp. 1–32 only printed.

The Bibliography of Lincolnshire and the Great County History. Lincolnshire Books in the Thirlestaine House Collection (formed by Sir Thomas Phillipps). (*Old Lincolnshire*, vol. i. pp. 9–14. 1883.)

Grange (Ernest L.). A List of Civil War Tracts and Broadsides relating to the County of Lincoln. Horncastle, 1889.

Indexes to the Reports and Papers of the Associated Architectural Societies, etc. (includes the 'Lincoln Diocesan Architectural Soc.'). Vols. i.–viii. (1850–66); vols. ix.–xiv. (1867–78); vols. xv.–xix. (1879–88); and vols. xx.–xxv. (1889–1900), Lincoln, 1867–1905.

Willson (Edward James), Antiquary and Architect, b. at Lincoln, 1787, d. 1854. **Collection of Prints, Drawings, and Scrap Books relating to Lincs. in the Library of the Soc. of Antiquaries, London.**

Catal. of Collection of Books, Prints, etc., of the late E. J. Willson, of the Minster Yard. Lincoln, 1854.

Smith (J. J.). Architectural Drawings of Lincoln Cathedral in Norman Times. (*Assoc. Archit. Soc. Reports & Papers*, vol. xxviii. pp. 95–98. 1905.)

Descriptive Catal. of 'The Jackson Collection' at the Sheffield Public Lib., compiled by T. Walter Hall and A. H. Thomas. 1914. (Lincs. entries, pp. 204–205.)

Catal. of a Collection of Books, Historical Documents, etc., to be sold by Messrs. Puttick & Simpson, London, Dec. 17th, etc., 1885. (Lincs. items, pp. 88–97.)

A Collection of Topographical and Antiquarian Extracts from Newspapers, etc., relating to Lincs., collected and arranged by E. B. Drury. 4 vols. (In City of Lincoln Public Library.)

Biblio. Notes on the Hist. of 'The Stamford Mercury,' by Herbert E. Norris and others. (*Notes & Queries*, Ser. 11, vol. vii. pp. 365, 430, 471; vol. viii. p. 37. 1913.)

Corns (A. R.). Lincolnshire Libraries and Literature. (*Book-Auction Records*, vol. vii. pt. 3, pp. xli.–xlv. 1910.)

Dibdin (Thomas Frognall). Books at Lincoln. (*Northern Tour*, 1838, vol. i. pp. 104–119.)

—— **The Lincolne Nosegay.** Here Begyneth a Littel Tome and hath to name The Lincolne Nosegay: beynge a brefe table of certaine Bokes in the possession of Maister Thomas Frognall Dibdin, Clerk, which Bookes Be To be Sold to him who shal gyue the most for ye same. W. Bulmer, London, 1811.)

Thirty-six copies printed. Reprinted in Botfield's 'Cathedral Libraries,' pp. 272-279. The Contents of 'The Lincolne Nosegay' are the cream of the Library of Michael Honeywood (1597-1681), Dean of Lincoln, and were obtained by Dibdin as the outcome of a visit to Lincoln Cathedral. The Books described passed into the Libraries of Lord Spencer and Richard Heber. See Dibdin's 'Biblio. Decameron,' vol. iii. pp. 261-262; 'Northern Tour,' vol. i. pp. 105-106; and the 'Dict. Nat. Biog.'

LINCOLNSHIRE (*continued*).

Sympson (E. M.). The Lincoln Stock Library. (1813-1909.) (*Lincs. Notes & Queries*, vol. xii. pp. 97-106. 1912.)

Lincs. Topographical Society. A Selection of Papers relative to the Co. of Linc. read before the Society, 1841-42. Lincoln, 1843. Biblio. Notes in Opening Address, by E. J. Willson, pp. 3-13; Advantage of Recording the Discovery of Local Antiquities, by W. A. Nicholson, pp. 87-90.

Catal. of the Museum of Antiquities formed for the Annual Meeting of the Royal Archæol. Institute at Lincoln, 1848. (*Memoirs, etc., of the Archæol. Inst.*, 1850, pp. xxvii.-lvii.)

A List of Books and Papers in the Lincoln Public Library relating to Saint Hugh, Bishop of Lincoln, 1186-1200. (*City of Lincoln Pub. Lib. Quarterly Record*, July 1912, pp. 14-15.)

Jeans (Rev. G. E.). A List of the Sepulchral Brasses in Lincolnshire. (*Lincs. Notes & Queries.* Supplement, vols. i.-iv. 1888-95.) Also issued separately, 1895.

Macklin (Herbert Walter). Monumental Brasses. London : Geo. Allen & Co., 1913. Biblio. Note on Lincs. Brasses, with a List, pp. 141, 166-168.

Gross (Charles). Biblio. of Brit. Municipal Hist. (*Harvard Hist. Studies*, vol. v. 1897.) Lincolnshire, p. 99. Lincoln, pp. 278-279.

Davenport (Frances G.). List of Printed Materials for Manorial Hist. 1894. Biblio. Note on Lincs. Manorial Hist., pp. 50-51.

Dove (Patrick Edward). Domesday Studies. 1891. Domesday Biblio. Lincs., vol. ii. p. 682.

Lyell (Arthur H.). Biblio. List of Romano-British Remains. 1912. Lincs., pp. 60-65.

Price (J. E.). Biblio. and Index Notes on Roman Remains. Lincolnshire. (*The Archæol. Review*, vol. iii. pp. 175-184. 1889.)

County Folk-Lore, vol. v. Examples of Printed Folk-Lore concerning Lincolnshire, with List of Authorities. Collected by Mrs. Gutch and Mabel Peacock. Folk-Lore Soc., vol. lxiii. 1908.

A List of Private Acts, etc., relating to Lincolnshire. Stevens & Sons, London, *circa* 1914.

Special Topographical Collections for Lincolnshire are at the Lincoln Public Library and the Grimsby Public Library.

Hist. MSS. Comm. Reports. Lincolnshire Collections.

Ancaster, Earl of, at Grimsthorpe ...	13th Rep. p. 31 and App. VI. pp. 203-261; 17th Rep. pp. 41-54, and a vol. 1907.
Lindsey, Earl of, at Uffington ...	14th Rep. pp. 28-29 and App. IX. pp. 367-457.
Underwood, Mr. C. F. Weston, of Somerby Hall	10th Rep. p. 9 and App. I. pp. 199-520.
Great Grimsby Corporation	14th Rep. pp. 41-44 and App. VIII. pp. 237-291.
Lincoln, Dean & Chapter of... ...	12th Rep. p. 45 and App. IX. pp. 553-572.
——— Bishop's Registry	12th Rep. App. IX. pp. 573-579.
——— Probate Registry	12th Rep. App. IX. p. 573.
——— Corporation	14th Rep. pp. 39-41 and App. VIII. pp. 1-120.

County Records, 1600, etc., with MS. Index, at the Sessions House, Spalding, and at Lincoln Castle. (*Local Records Comm. Rep.*, 1902, App. III. p. 20.)

LINCOLNSHIRE (continued).

Borough Records, from Hen. III. at Corporation Offices, Lincoln. (*Local Records Comm. Rep.*, 1902, App. III. p. 36.)

Birch (Walter de Gray). Catal. of the Royal Charters and other Documents, with List of Books belonging to the Corporation of Lincoln, 1904. Lincoln, 1906. (Also issued in *Lincs. Notes & Queries*, vol. x. pp. 88, 107, 145, 167, 218, 250; vol. xi. pp. 19, 62, 94, 123. 1908-10.)

—— **The Royal Charters of the City of Lincoln, Henry II. to William III.** Cambridge, 1911. (Biblio. Notes in Introduction.)

List of Lincoln Municipal Records Printed. (*Notes & Queries*, Ser. 11, vol. iv. p. 132. 1911.)

Lincolnshire Records in the Public Record Office. (*Lincs. Notes & Queries*, vol. v. pp. 13, 76, 94, 111. 1896–98.)

Lincolnshire Charters in the 'More Collection.' (*Lincs. Notes & Queries*, vol. i. pp. 99–104. 1888.)

Boyd (W.). Calendar of all Enrolments on the Close Rolls, temp. Hen. VII. relating to the Co. of Linc. (*Assoc. Archit. Soc. Reports & Papers*, vol. xxiii. pp. 260–273. 1896.)

A List of Assize Rolls of Divers Counties, including the Co. of Lincoln, with a List of Coroner's Rolls. (*Lincs. Notes & Queries*, vol. v. pp. 107–112. 1897.)

A Calendar of Lincs. Exchequer Lay Subsidies in the Public Record Office, by Alfred C. E. Welby. (*Lincs. Notes & Queries*, vol. ix. pp. 119, 171–179, 205–209. 1906–07.)

Gibbons (Alfred). List of Lincs. Manorial Court Rolls, with places of deposit. (*Lincs. Notes & Queries*, vol. i. pp. 44–46. 1888.)

Gervase Holles' MS. Collections for Lincs. in the Brit. Museum. Lansd. MS. 207, A–F. Add. MS. 6118.

Cole (R. E. G.). Observations on Gervase Holles' Lincolnshire Notes, 1634-1642. (*Assoc. Archit. Soc. Reports & Papers*, vol. xxxi. pp. 378–420. 1912.)

Ralph Bigland's Parochial Collections relating to Lincs. in the Brit. Museum. Add. MSS. 34141.

R. W. Eyton's Collections for a Hist. of the County of Lincoln, in the Brit. Museum (19th cent.). Add. MSS. 31929, 31930.

W. Upcott's Topog. Collections relating to Lincs. in the Brit. Museum. Add. MS. 15922.

Lysons' Collections for Lincs. in the Brit. Museum. Add. MS. 9458.

Powell's Topog. Collections for Lincs. in the Brit. Museum. Add. MS. 17462.

Suckling's Collections for Lincs. (1821–39) in the Brit. Museum. Add. MSS. 18478, 18479. Index. Add. MS. 18491.

Cole MSS. in the Brit. Museum. For Lincs. entries see 'Index to the Contents of the Cole MSS.' by G. J. Gray, 1912, pp. 101–102. Other smaller Lincs. Collections in the Brit. Museum are: Add. MSS. 24804–24808; Add. MSS. 47660, 47661; Add. MS. 8938; Harl. MS. 6289.

Lord Boston's Muniments relating to South Lincolnshire (at Hedsor, Bucks.), with copy of W. J. Hardy's Report (1884) and a descriptive Calendar. (*Lincs. Notes & Queries*, vol. xiii. pp. 9–30, 51–63, 78–93. 1914.)

Larken's Collections relating to Lincs. in the College of Arms. For an account of this Collection see Preface to '*Lincolnshire Pedigrees*,' ed. by A. R. Maddison, vol. i. 1902.

LINCOLNSHIRE (continued).

'Collectanea Lincolniensia.' A MS. Collection in the Library at Burton Hall (Lord Monson). Materials collected by Lord Monson, assisted by Arthur Staunton Larken, sometime Richmond Herald, for a Genealogical Hist. of Lincs.

Banks (Sir Joseph). Lincolnshire Topographical Collection. 1784 (A MS.). See '*Lincs. Notes & Queries*,' vol. i. p. 5. 1888.

Collections relating to Lincs. Families (18th Cent.) **in Queen's College. Oxford.** MS. lxxxv.

Grange (Ernest L.). Lincs. Parish Registers. A List of those Printed or Transcribed. (*Lincs. Notes & Queries*, vol. v. pp. 86-87. 1897.)

Smith (W. H.). A Few Notes on Lincs. Parish Registers. (A MS. in City of Lincoln Public Library.)

Lincoln Cathedral Records, 12th cent., etc., with Printed Index, at Lincoln. (*Local Records Comm. Rep.*, 1902, App. III. p. 112.)

Lincoln Episcopal Records, 1571–1584. Edited by C. W. Foster. Lincoln Record Society, 1912, and Canterbury and York Soc. London, 1913. Index of Lincolnshire, pp. 435–440.

Lincoln Cathedral Charters, translated by W. O. Massingberd, with Notes. (*Assoc. Archit. Soc. Papers*, vol. xxvi. pp. 18–96, 321–369 ; vol. xxvii. pp. 1–91. 1901–3.)

Apthorp (G. F.). A Catal. of the Books and MSS. in the Library of Lincoln Cathedral. Lincoln, 1859.

Maddison (A. R.). Catal. of MSS. belonging to Lincoln Cathedral in the Fifteenth Century. (*Assoc. Archit. Soc. Reports & Papers*, vol. xxiii. pp. 348–353. 1896.)

——— **Lincoln Cathedral Library.** (*The Library*, vol. iv. pp. 306–313. 1892.)

——— **Dean Honeywood's Library.** (*The Lib. Assoc. Record*, vol. iv. pp. 390–393. 1902.)

Wickenden (J. Frederic). Contents of the Muniment Room of Lincoln Cathedral. (*The Archæol. Journ.*, vol. xxxviii. pp. 309–315. 1881.)

Botfield (Beriah). Notes on the Cathedral Libraries of England. 1849. **Lincoln,** pp. 268–296.

Lincs. Parish Registers: Col. Chester's Transcript, with a List of Lincs. references from Marshall's List of Parish Registers, 1891. (*Lincs. Notes & Queries*, vol. ii. pp. 241–245. 1891.)

Registry of Deeds relating to the Fens called Bedford Level, 15 Car. II. See S. R. Scargill-Bird. '*Guide to Documents in the Public Record Office*,' 1908, p. 23.)

Fordham (Sir H. G.). Descriptive List of the Maps of the Great Level of the Fens, 1604–1900. (*Studies in Carto-Bibliography*, 1914, pp. 61–83.)

Wheeler (W. H.). Books relating to the Hist. of the Fens of South Lincolnshire. (*A Hist. of the Fens of South Lincolnshire*, 1897, Appendix II.).

Trimen (Henry). Botanical Biblio. of the British Counties. Lincs. (*Journ. of Botany*, vol. xii. p. 178. 1874.)

Burton (F. M.). Biblio. of Papers, etc., relating to Lincolnshire Geology published 1819-93. (*Linc. Nat. Union*, vol. i. pp. 19–23.)

Whitaker (W.) and **Dalton (W. H.). List of Books, etc., relating to the Geology of Lincs.** (*Memoirs of the Geol. Survey, S.W. Lincs.*, by A. J. Jukes-Browne, 1885, pp. 164–176.)

Sheppard (Thomas). List of Works on Lincolnshire Boulders. (*The Naturalist*, 1896, p. 373.)

LINCOLNSHIRE (continued).

Christy (Miller). Biblio. Note on Lincs. Birds. (*The Zoologist*, Ser. 3, vol. xiv. p. 255, 1890; and reprinted in pamph., 1891, p. 17.) **Mammals.** (*The Zoologist*, Ser. 3, vol. xvii. p. 181. 1893.) **Reptiles.** (*Ibid.* p. 245. 1893.) **Fishes.** (*Ibid.* p. 255. 1893.)

Anderson (John P.). Book of Brit. Topo., 1881. Lincs., pp. 167-173.

Gatfield (George). Guide to Heraldry. 1892. Lincs., pp. 152-154.

Sims (Richard). Manual. 1861. Lincs., pp. 169, 212-213, 236.

Upcott (William). English Topo., 1818. Lincs., vol. i. pp. 558-580, 640-642.

Smith (Alfred Russell). Catal. of Topo. Tracts, etc. 1878. Lincs., pp. 187-193.

Gough (Richard). Brit. Topo., 1780. Lincs., vol. i. pp. 519-536.

Bandinel (Bulkeley). Catal. of Books bequeathed to Bodleian Lib. by Richard Gough, 1814. Lincs., pp. 161-167.

BOSTON.

Borough Records, Henry VIII., etc., at Mayor's Parlour, Boston. (*Local Records Comm. Rep.*, 1902, App. III. p. 48.)

CROWLAND.

English (H. S.). A Light on the Historians and on the History of Crowland Abbey. London, 1868. Also forms vol. i. of the Author's 'Crowland and Burgh.' 3 vols. 1871.

GAINSBOROUGH.

Gurnhill (James). A Monograph on the Gainsborough Parish Registers. 1890.

GOKEWELL.

Lowe (F. Pyndar). On Some Charters relating to the Nunnery of Gokewell. (*Assoc. Archit. Soc. Reports & Papers*, vol. iii. pp. 102-108. 1854.)

GRIMSBY.

Borough Records, 1227, etc., at Municipal Offices, Grimsby. (*Local Records Comm. Rep.*, 1902, App. III. p. 34.)

Corporation Records, see *ante* Hist. MSS. Comm. Reports.

Shaw (Rev. George). Old Grimsby. 1897. Biblio. pp. 246-251.

HORNCASTLE.

Hudson (J. Clare) and Boyd (William). Records of Ancient Horncastle. (*Lincs. Notes & Queries*, vols. iii.-v. 1892-98, *passim.*)

INGOLDMELLS.

Maddison (A. R.). Manor of Ingoldmells-cum-Addlethorpe Court Rolls. (*Assoc. Archit. Soc. Reports & Papers*, vol. xxi. pp. 176-190. 1892.)

LANGTON-BY-SPILSBY.

Massingberd (W. O.). Some Ancient Records relating to the Manor of Langton-by-Spilsby. (*Assoc. Archit. Soc. Reports & Papers*, vol. xxii. pp. 157-173. 1894.)

LOUTH.

Goulding (R. W.). Louth Old Corporation Records. (1551-1836.) Louth, 1891.

Chronicon Abbatie de Parco Lude. The Chronicle of Louth Park Abbey, with Appendix of Documents, ed. by Rev. Edmund Venables. Lincs. Record Soc. vol. i. 1891.

LINCOLNSHIRE (continued).

SPALDING.

Moore (William). The Gentlemen's Society at Spalding; its Origin and Progress. London, 1851.

—— **The Gentlemen's Society at Spalding, with notices of the researches and labours of the earliest Lincolnshire Antiquarians.** (*Archæol. Institute. Proc. Memoirs at Lincoln*, 1848, pp. 82–89.)

Nichols (John). An Account of the Gentlemen's Soc. at Spalding. (*Bibliotheca Topographica Britannica*, vol. iii. 1784.)

Reliquiæ Galeanæ; or Miscellaneous Pieces by Roger and Samuel Gale, with an Account of the Literary Soc. at Spalding. (*Ibid.* vol. iii. 1781.)

Perry (Marten). Spalding Gentlemen's Society. (*Bygone Lincolnshire*, ed. by William Andrews, vol. ii. pp. 215–225. 1891.)

—— **Spalding Gentlemen's Society.** (*Memorials of Old Lincolnshire*, ed. by E. M. Sympson, pp. 319–339. 1911.)

Catal. of the Books, MSS., Pamphlets, and Tracts in the Library of the Spalding Gentlemen's Soc., revised by M. Perry, R. Hollis, T. A. Stoodley. Spalding, 1893.

STAMFORD.

Borough Records, at Town Hall, Stamford. (*Local Records Comm. Rep.*, 1902, App. III. p. 70.)

Harrod, the Topographer. Note by Justin Simpson. (*Leics. and Rutland Notes & Queries*, vol. iii. pp. 185–187. 1895.)

LINLITHGOWSHIRE.

Hist. MSS. Comm. Reports. Linlithgowshire Collections.

Dalyell, Sir R. A. O., at The Binns	9th Rep. p. xix. and App. II. pp. 230–238.
Dundas, Mr. James, at Dundas Castle, Dalmeny	3rd Rep. p. xxiv. and App. pp. 413–414.

County Council Records, 15th cent., etc., at Linlithgow. (*Local Records Comm. Rep.*, 1902, App. III. p. 84.)

Burgh Records, 1389, etc., with MS. List, at Town Hall, Linlithgow. (*Local Records Comm. Rep.*, 1902, App. III. p. 96.)

Gross (Charles). Biblio. of Brit. Municipal Hist. (*Harvard Hist. Studies*, vol. v. 1897.) Linlithgowshire, p. 279.)

Turnbull (William B.). Scottish Parochial Registers. 1849. List of Linlithgowshire Registers, pp. 108–110.

Bisset (Alex. M.). The Poets and Poetry of Linlithgowshire. An Anthology of the County. Paisley, 1896.

Chalmers (James). Notices of the Life of William Hamilton of Bangour, and a chronological List of his Poems. (*Archæologia Scotia, or Trans. Soc. Antiq. Scot.*, vol. iii. pp. 255–266. 1831.)

Trimen (Henry). Botanical Biblio. of the British Counties. Linlithgowshire. (*Journ. of Botany*, vol. xii. p. 235. 1874.)

Christy (Miller). Biblio. Note on Linlithgowshire Birds. (*The Zoologist*, Ser. 3, vol. xiv. p. 264, 1890; and reprinted in pamph., 1891, p. 35.) **Mammals.** (*The Zoologist*, Ser. 3, vol. xvii. p. 212. 1893.)

Anderson (John P.). Book of Brit. Topo., 1881. Linlithgowshire, p. 401.

Gough (Richard). Brit. Topo., 1780. Linlithgowshire, vol. ii. p. 704.

Bandinel (Bulkeley). Catal. of Books bequeathed to Bodleian Lib. by Richard Gough, 1814. Linlithgow, p. 362.

LONDON.

[Entries under Middlesex should also be consulted.]

Kingsford (**Charles L.**). **Chronicles of London.** Oxford, 1905. Biblio. Notes on Early Chronicles in Introduction.

——— **English Historical Literature of the Fifteenth Century.** Oxford, 1913. Chap. IV. The Chronicles of London, pp. 70–112.

——— **A Survey of London, by John Stow,** reprinted from the text of 1603, With Introduction and Notes. 2 vols. Oxford, 1908. Biblio. of Stow's Works and an Account of Stow's Collections and MSS., pp. lxxxii.–xciii.

Norman (**Philip**). **Notes concerning various 17th and 18th Century Writers in London Topography,** including the Continuators of Stow's Survey, and their Publications. (*The Home Counties Mag.*, vol. x. pp. 187–202. 1908.)

Downes (**Thomas**). **Copious Index to Pennant's Account of London.** London, 1814. Among fine copies of Pennant's London, extra-illustrated, is the one sold at the Bessborough Sale from the Library of Lord Bessborough. A similar copy is at the Soane Museum, Lincoln's Inn Fields. Another is the magnificent 'Croll' copy in the Print Department at the Brit. Museum.

Index to the 'London' volumes of the General Catalogue of the Library of the British Museum.

This is a separate volume placed with the 'London' Catalogues in the Reading Room. A Key to the arrangement of the Catalogues is at the beginning of the first volume of these Catalogues which include official and other Documents relating to London, and all Institutions connected with it, also anonymous works relating in any way to the City of London.

Subject-Index of the London Library, St. James's Square, with Appendix and Synopsis of Headings. By C. T. Hagberg Wright. London, 1909. London entries, pp. 665–670.

Catal. of the Library of the Peabody Institute of the City of Baltimore. 5 vols. 1883–92. London entries, vol. iii. pp. 2601–2612.

Second Catal. of the Library of the Peabody Institute, including additions since 1882. 8 vols. 1896–1905. London entries, vol. v. pp. 2849–2877.

Bibliotheca Lindesiana. Catal. of the Printed Books preserved at Haigh Hall, Wigan. Compiled for James Ludovic Lindsay, 26th Earl of Crawford. 1910. London entries, vol. iii. pp. 5541–5577.

Index to the Orders in Council, Proclamations, Royal Commissions of Inquiry, etc., in the 'London Gazette,' 1830-1883, by Alexander Pulling. London, 1885.

Index to the 'Archæological Journal' of the Royal Archæological Institute of Great Britain, vols. i.–xxv. 1844–68. London, 1878.

General Index to the 'Journal of the British Archæological Association,' vols. i.-xxx., 1845-74. London, 1875; **vols. xxi.-xlii., 1875-86, and to 'Collectanea Archæologica,' vols. i., ii., and the separate vols. for the Winchester and Gloucester Congresses.** London, 1887.

Index to the 'Archaeologia' of the Royal Soc. of Antiquaries of London, vols. i.-xv. 1770-1806. London, 1809; **vols. xvi.-xxx. 1812-44.** London, 1844. **Index to vols. I.-L. 1770-1887.** London, 1889.

Index to the 'Proceedings' of the Royal Soc. of Antiquaries of London. First Series, vols. i.-iv. 1843-59 (in vol. iv.) **Second Series, vols. i.-xx. 1859-1905,** with Classified List of Illustrations. London, 1908.

Thirty-six Years' Work of the London and Middlesex Archæol. Society, by Charles Welch. (Contains lists of articles, etc., in the '*Transactions.*') (*London & Midd. Archæol. Soc. Trans.* New Ser. vol. i. pp. 1–12. 1892, and *The London & Middlesex Notebook*, ed. by W. P. W. Phillimore, pp. 1–8. 1892.)

LONDON (*continued*).

Catal. of the Guildhall Library of the City of London, with additions to June, 1889. London, 1889. London entries, pp. 545–571. The following Extra-Illustrated copies of London Topographical Works are in the Guildhall Library :—

Lysons' Hist. of London. 13 vols.
Thomson's Chronicles of London Bridge. 5 vols.
Allen's Hist. of London, with MS. Index. 17 vols.
Brayley, Nightingale, & Brewer's Hist. of Lond. & Middlesex. 21 vols.

As regards the Guildhall Library, one may reasonably wonder why no better Catalogue exists, and why, considering that this Library is maintained by the richest Corporation in the World, nothing is done towards compiling an adequate Bibliography of London, or in issuing a Bulletin.

Gross (Charles). Biblio. of Brit. Municipal Hist. (*Harvard Hist. Studies*, vol. v. 1897.) **London entries,** pp. 286–325.

Dove (Patrick Edward). Domesday Studies. 1891. **Domesday Biblio. of London,** vol. ii. p. 683.

Davenport (Frances G.). List of Printed Materials for Manorial Hist. 1894. Biblio. Note on London Manorial Hist., p. 51.

Macklin (Herbert Walter). Monumental Brasses. London : Geo. Allen & Co., 1913. Biblio. Note on London Brasses, with a List, pp. 141, 168–169.

Gomme (G. Laurence). The Literature of Local Institutions. London, 1886. Biblio. of London Municipal Government, pp. 122–134.

Welch (Charles). Notes on London Municipal Literature, with Lists of Authorities. A Scheme for the Biblio. of London. (*Biblio. Soc. Trans.*, vol. ii. pp. 49–80. 1894.)

——— **Hist. of the Monument, with a brief account of the Great Fire of London.** 1893. Views, Bibliography, and Authorities, pp. 89–116.

Huck (Thomas W.). Account of a Scheme for a Biblio. of London. (*The Library*, Ser. 3, vol. iii. pp. 38–54. 1912.)

Prideaux (W. F.). Note on the Bibliography of London. (*Notes & Queries*, Ser. 11, vol. v. pp. 343–344. 1912.)

A Quarterly Biblio. of Middlesex (including London) and Hertfordshire. (*Midd. & Herts. Notes & Queries*, vols. i.–iv. *passim*, 1895–98; *The Home Counties Mag.*, vol. i. pp. 82–83. 1899.)

Biblio. of London. (The Historical Assoc. Leaflet, No. 14. 1908).

Upcott (William). Manuscript Materials for the Biblio. of London. A MS., on Sale by Alfred Russell Smith, giving the full titles and collations of the articles and what Library they are in. See 'Catal. of Topog. Tracts,' etc. 1878, p. 238.

Tyrrell (Edward). Catal. of the Valuable and Singularly Curious Library of Edward Tyrrell, late City Remembrancer, to be Sold by Auction, April 4–8, 1864, by Sotheby's, London. (A valuable London Collection.)

Gregory (Samuel). Catal. of the Curious Collections illustrating the Hist. of the Corporation of the City of London, formed by the late Samuel Gregory, to be Sold by Auction, March 10 & 11, 1859, by Sotheby's, London.

Catal. of an extensive Collection of Books and Tracts relating to London and its Suburbs, to be Sold by Auction, April 29 & 30, 1872, by Sotheby's, London.

Catal. of Books relating to London and Environs including a portion of the Library of the late John E. Gardner. On Sale by Francis Edwards, Bookseller, London, October, 1912.

LONDON (*continued*).

List of a Collection of Tracts relating to London and Westminster, issued between 1638 and 1783. (*A Catal. of the Lib. of the London Institution*, 1835, vol. i. pp. 353–357.)

Oldys (William). MS. Catal. of Books and Pamphlets relating to the City of London, its Laws, Customs, etc., and of every thing that has happened in London, from 1521 to 1759. See 'Memoir of William Oldys,' ed. by W. J. Thoms, 1862, p. xlvii., and Gough 'British Topography,' 1780, vol. i. pp. li., 567–761.

Rawlinson (Richard). The English Topographer. London, 1720. **London,** pp. 117–154.

This book though much out of date is still valuable for London.

A List of Books on London and Suburbs contained in the West Ham Public Libraries. (*West Ham Library Notes*, ed. by A. Cotgreave, vol. vi. p. 55—vol. viii. p. 3. 1901–03.) Also issued as Public Library Hand-List No. 6. 1903.

MS. List of Books on London Topography in the Special Collection at the Kensington Public Library.

Daniell (W. V.). Catal. of 1000 Books, Pamphlets and Maps illustrating the Hist. and Topography of Greater London. 1899.

Boynton (Percy H.). London in English Literature. Chicago, 1913. Bibliographies of Chaucer's London, p. 33; Milton's London, pp. 91–92; Dryden's London, pp. 121–123; Addison's London, pp. 151–152; Johnson's London, pp. 190–191; Lamb and Byron's London, pp. 217–218; Dickens's London, pp. 247–248; Contemporary London, pp. 247–248; and an Appendix containing lists of Novels illustrating London Life.

Webb (Sidney and Beatrice). The History of Trades Unionism. London, 1911. **Biblio. by R. A. Peddie,** pp. 499–543. **Biblio. Notes** in Preface.

Cunningham (William). The Growth of English Industry and Commerce. Cambridge, 1910. **List of Authorities,** vol. i. pp. 657–681. **Biblio. Index,** vol. iii. pp. 943–998.

London Statutes. A Collection of Public Acts relating specially to the Administrative County of London, and of Local and Personal Acts affecting the Powers and Duties of the London County Council, 1750–1907. Prepared by G. L. Gomme and Seager Bury. 2 vols. 1907.

A List of Private Acts, Enclosures, Settlements, Estates, Railways, etc., relating to the County of London. Stevens & Sons, London. 1913.

Special Topographical Collections for London are at the Guildhall Library, the Bishopsgate Institute, and in the Public Libraries of Westminster, Camberwell, Kensington, Finsbury, Shoreditch, Leyton, and West Ham.

Special Local Collections are in the Public Libraries at Battersea, Bermondsey, Finsbury, Fulham, Hackney, Hammersmith, Islington, Shoreditch, Southwark, and Stoke Newington.

Hist. MSS. Comm. Reports. London and Middlesex Collections.

Aitken, Mr. G. A.	12th Rep. App. IX. pp. 334–342.
Buccleuch, Duke of, at Drumlanrig Castle	15th Rep. pp. 43, 44 and App. VIII.; and vol. ii. (1903).
——— at Montagu House	16th Rep. pp. 29–47; and vol. i. (1903), vol. ii. pts. i. and ii. (1899).
Bute, Marquess of, at Mountstuart ...	3rd Rep. pp. xiii., xxii. and App. pp. 202–209, 402, 403; 5th Rep. p. xix. and App. pp. 617–620.
Bradford, Earl of, at Belgrave Square	2nd Rep. p. ix. and App. p. 30.
Calthorpe, Lord, at Grosvenor Square	2nd Rep. p. x. and App. pp. 39–46.
Colchester, Lord	3rd Rep. p. xi.; 4th Rep. p. xiv. and App. pp. 344–347.

LONDON (*continued*).

Hist. MSS. Comm. Reports (*continued*).

Dasent, Sir George W.	6th Rep. p. xiii. and App. pp. 407–418.
Dilke, Sir Charles W., at Sloane St., London...	2nd Rep. p. xvi. and App. p. 63.
Egmont, Earl of, at St. James's Palace	7th Rep. p. xiii. and App. pp. 232–249; 17th Rep. pp. 143–153; and vol. i. (1905).
Fitz-Gibbon, Mr. A.	3rd Rep. p. xxvi. and App. pp. 431–432.
Jersey, Earl of, at Osterley Park ...	8th Rep. p. xi. and App. pp. 92–101.
Lansdowne, Marquess of, at London...	2nd Rep. p. viii.; 3rd Rep. p. xii. and App. pp. 125–147; 4th Rep. p. xii.; 5th Rep. p. vii. and App. pp. 215–260; 6th Rep. p. xi. and App. pp. 235–243.
Lefroy, Mr. T. E. P.	1st Rep. p. ix. and App. p. 56.
Malet, Sir Alexander, at Queensberry Pl., Kensington	5th Rep. p. viii. and App. pp. 308–321; 7th Rep. p. xiii. and App. pp. 428–433.
Morrison, Mr. Alfred, of Fonthill House, Wilts....	9th Rep. p. xvii. and App. II. pp. 406–493.
Northumberland, Duke of, at Alnwick Castle	3rd Rep. p. xii. and App. pp. 45–125; 5th Rep. p. xi.; 6th Rep. p. xi. and App. pp. 221–233.
Peake, Mr. Frederick, of Bedford Row, London...	2nd Rep. p. xii. and App. pp. 92–97; 3rd Rep. p. xvii. and App. pp. 277–280.
Prescott, Mrs., of Oxford Square, London...	2nd Rep. p. xii. and App. pp. 97–99.
Ranyard, Mr. A. C., of Lincoln's Inn	5th Rep. p. x. and App. pp. 404–405.
Smith, Mr. Philip V., of Lincoln's Inn	12th Rep. p. 42 and App. IX. pp. 343–374.
Spencer, Earl, at Spencer House, St. James's	2nd Rep. p. ix. and App. pp. 12–20.
Torrens, Mr. W. T. M., of London ...	2nd Rep. p. xv. and App. pp. 99–100.
Zetland, Earl of	1st Rep. p. xi. and App. p. 44.
London: House of Lords	6th Rep. p. viii. and App. pp. 1–221; 8th Rep. p. viii. and App. pp. 101–174.
——— Westminster Abbey	1st Rep. App. p. 94; 4th Rep. p. xi. and App. pp. 171–199.
——— Dean and Chapter of St. Paul's	9th Rep. p. viii. and App. I. pp. 1–72.
——— Queen's Anne's Bounty Office	8th Rep. App. pp. 632–635.
——— Roman Catholic Chapter of, ...	5th Rep. pp. 463–470.
——— Roman Catholic Archbishopric of Westminster	5th Rep. p. xii. and App. pp. 470–476.
——— Royal College of Physicians ...	8th Rep. p. xiv. and App. pp. 226–235.
——— Inner Temple	2nd Rep. p. xv. and App. pp. 151–156; 11th Rep. p. 36 and App. VII. pp. 227–308.
——— Trinity House	8th Rep. p. xiv. and App. pp. 235–262.
——— Royal Institution	17th Rep. pp. 103–109; and vol. i. (1904), vol. ii. (1906).
——— Rev. Dr. Williams's Library ...	3rd Rep. p. 365.
Lambeth Palace	6th Rep. p. xiv. and App. pp. 522–524.
Southwark, Roman Catholic Bishopric of	3rd Rep. p. xxi. and App. pp. 233–237.

A Guide to the Reports on Collections of MSS. issued by the Hist. MSS. Comm. Part I. Topographical. 1914. See 'London' entries in this valuable Index, pp. 133–136.

LONDON (*continued*).

County Records, 1557, etc., with Printed Index, at County Hall, London. (*Local Records Comm. Rep.*, 1902, App. III. p. 20.)

Borough Records, with various Local Authorities. (*Ibid.* pp. 78–81.)

Middlesex County Records. Sessions' Rolls, 3 Edw. VI.—4 Jas. II. Edited by J. Cordy Jeaffreson. Index by A. T. Watson. 4 vols. Middlesex County Records Soc. 1886–1892.

Middlesex County Records. Calendar of the Sessions Books, 1689 to 1709. By W. J. Hardy. Index by M. D. Brakspear. London, 1905.

The Middlesex County Records. (A description of the Records at the Guildhall, Westminster, the County Offices of Middlesex.) (*The Home Counties Mag.*, vol. v. pp. 307–309. 1903.)

List of London and Middlesex Municipal Records Printed. (*Notes and Queries*, Ser. 11. vol. v. p. 74. 1912.)

Report on the Records of the Lord Chamberlain's Office. (*Local Records Comm. Rep.*, 1914, vol. ii. pt. 3, pp. 79–80.)

Report of an Inspection of the Records of the Metropolitan Water Board. (*Ibid.* vol. ii. pt. 2, p. 196.)

Report on Metropolitan Water Board Collections. (*Ibid.* vol. ii. pt. 3, pp. 89–90.)

Report on Thames Conservancy Records. (*Ibid.* vol. ii. pt. 3, pp. 85–87.)

Norman (Philip). Abstracts of Documents relating to London from early Chancery Proceedings, and from the Court of Requests. (*The London Topog. Record*, vol. vi. pp. 65–89. 1909.)

Phillipps (Sir Thomas). 1489 Cartæ Antiquæ in the Tower. Index of those which are printed. Second edition. Privately printed. Middle Hill, 1846.

Hardy (T. Duffus). Description of Close Rolls in the Tower of London. Privately Printed. 1833.

Report of an Inspection of the Records at the Tower of London. (*Local Records Comm. Rep.*, 1914, vol. ii. pt. 2, pp. 179–180.)

MSS. Collections relating to London in the British Museum, see 'Classed Catalogue of Topographical MSS.' in MS. Department.

Burtt (Joseph). Public Record Office. (*Old London. Papers read at the London Congress of the Archæol. Institute*, 1866, pp. 241–260.

Trimen (Henry). Botanical Biblio. of the British Counties. London. (*Journ. of Botany*, vol. xii. p. 109. 1874.)

Whitaker (William). Guide to the Geology of London and the Neighbourhood. Biblio. of Geol. Survey Pubns. relating to London, pp. 95–96. (*Memoirs of the Geol. Survey of the U.K.* 1901.)

Boulger (G. S.). Botanical Biblio. of the South-Eastern Counties. London and Middlesex. (*South-Eastern Union of Scientific Societies. Trans*, vol. iv. p. 49. 1899.)

Christy (Miller). Biblio. Note on London Birds. (*The Zoologist*, Ser. 3, vol. xiv. p. 255, 1890; and reprinted in pamph., 1891, p. 17.)

Anderson (John P.). Book of Brit. Topo., 1881. London, pp. 178–213.

Gatfield (George). Guide to Heraldry. 1892. London, pp. 154–162.

Sims (Richard). Manual. 1861. London, pp. 169, 213–214, 236.

Upcott (William). English Topo., 1818. London, vol. ii. pp. 605–930, 1473–1481.

Smith (Alfred Russell). Catal. of Topo. Tracts, etc., 1878. London, pp. 195–260.

Gough (Richard). Brit. Topo., 1780. London, vol. i. pp. 567–760, Westminster, pp. 761-783, Southwark, pp. 784–786.

Bandinel (Bulkeley). Catal. of Books bequeathed to Bodleian Lib. by Richard Gough, 1814. London, pp. 176-224, Westminster, pp. 225-230, Southwark pp. 231-232.

Hoare (Sir R. Colt). Catal. of the Stourhead Lib. co. Wilts. 1840. London & Westminster, pp. 254–297.

LONDON (*continued*).

CORPORATION RECORDS.

Guildhall Documents.

'There is not one man outside the Guildhall who knows anything about my Calendar and admirable **Index of 40,000 Deeds** that has been made, and the Corporation has not yet printed a line of it.'

'There is a Report drawn up as to what classes of Records there are, and what the dates are of the Records in the Town Clerk's office, in the Chamberlain's office, and in the Comptroller's office. It is printed and accessible, but not for sale, but it can be seen at the Guildhall Library, and I daresay at the British Museum.'

Evidence of R. R. Sharpe before the Royal Commission on Public Records. Report, 1914, part iii. pp. 57 and 59.

Report to the Court of Common Council from the Library Committee, on the Corporation Records, 16 Dec., 1869, and a Further Report, 24 Nov., 1870. These two Reports describe the Records of the Corporation.

List of Papers and Documents printed for the use of the Members of the Corporation of London, Acts and Reports of the Court of Common Council from the year 1606 to the year 1849.

A List of Works printed by the Corporation of London since 1863. (*Notes & Queries*, Ser. 10, vol. viii. pp. 122–123. 1907).

Gross (Charles). Biblio. of Brit. Municipal Hist. (*Harvard Hist. Studies*, vol. v. 1897.) London Corporation Records, pp. 287–289.

Freshfield (Edwin). A Discourse on some Unpublished Records of the City of London. 1887. Privately Printed.

Overall (William Henry and Henry Charles). Analytical Index to the Series of Records known as the Remembrancia, preserved among the archives of the City of London. 1878.

—— **Analytical Indexes to vols. ii. (1593-1609) and viii. (1613-1614) of the Series of Records known as the Remembrancia, 1580-1664.** London, 1870.

Hugo (Thomas). 'The Liber Albus,' and other Records of the Corporation of London. (*London & Midd. Archæol. Soc. Trans.*, vol. i. pp. 245–258. 1860.)

Munimenta Gildhallæ Londoniensis; Liber Albus, Liber Custumarum, et Liber Horn, edited by H. T. Riley. 3 vols. 1859–62. **Index to 'Liber Albus,'** vol. iii. pp. 477–520.

Birch (Walter de Gray). The Historical Charters and Constitutional Documents of the City of London. Revised edition, 1887. List of Charters and Documents, pp. xlv.–xlviii.

Thomson (R.). Historical Charters and Constitutional Documents of the City of London, with an Introduction and Notes, by an Antiquary. 1884.

Calendar of Letter-Books preserved among the Archives of the Corporation of the City of London at the Guildhall, edited by R. R. Sharpe. 11 vols. 1899–1912. Letter-Books A to L issued up to the present.

Calendar of Coroners' Rolls of the City of London, 1300-1378, edited by R. R. Sharpe. London, 1913.

Alchin (William Turner). Indexes to Records of the Corporation of London, see 'Notes on London Municipal Literature,' by Charles Welch. (*Biblio. Soc. Trans.*, vol. ii. p. 52. 1895.)

Orridge (B. R.). The Corporation of London and their Records. (*Macmillan's Mag.*, vol. xx. pp. 562–567. 1869.)

LONDON (*continued*).

LIVERY COMPANIES.

Hazlitt (W. Carew). The Livery Companies of the City of London. London, 1892. Biblio. Notes *passim.*

Unwin (George). List of MS. Sources for the Hist. of the Industrial Companies of London during the Sixteenth and Seventeenth Centuries. (*Industrial Organization in the 16th and 17th Centuries*, 1904, pp. 253–262.) A Preliminary Survey of the material in the State Papers and the MSS. in the Brit. Museum.

——— **List of Sources for the Hist. of the Existing London Companies.** (*Gilds and Companies of London*, 1908, pp. 372–385.)

Welch (Charles). Biblio. of the Livery Companies of London. (*The Library*, vol. ii. pp. 301–307. 1890.) Also issued separately.

——— **Coat-Armour of the London Livery Companies,** with a Biblio. List of Authorities. London, 1914.

List of Books on Livery Companies in the Library of the British Museum. See Brit. Mus. General Catalogue under London.

Rhodes (A.). List of Records Printed of London Livery Companies. (*Notes & Queries*, Ser. 11, vol. iv. pp. 391–392, 451–453. 1911.)

Gross (Charles). Biblio. of Brit. Municipal Hist. (*Harvard Hist. Studies*, vol. v. 1897.) London Livery Companies, pp. 304–314.

Bakers' Hall and the Muniments of the Company (from Notes by various Writers). (*Lond. & Midd. Archæol. Soc. Trans.*, vol. iii. pp. 55–66. 1866.)

The Muniments of the Vintners' Company, by John Gough Nichols. (*Ibid.* vol. iii. pp. 432–447. 1870.)

The Stationers' Company, see under **Printers and Booksellers.**

PAGEANTS.

Fairholt (F. W.). Lord Mayors' Pageants: being Collections towards a Hist. of these Annual Celebrations, with Specimens of the Descriptive Pamphlets published by the City Poets. 2 parts. Percy Society. London, 1843–44.

——— **The Civic Garland: a Collection of Songs from London Pageants.** Percy Soc. London, 1845.

Catal. of a Collection of Works on Pageantry, bequeathed to the Soc. of Antiquaries by F. W. Fairholt. London, 1869. London Pageants, pp. 31–33.

Nichols (John Gough). Accounts of Fifty-five Royal Processions and Entertainments in the City of London, Biblio. List of Lord Mayors' Pageants. 1831.

Hazlitt (W. Carew). Biblio. of Pageants and the rarer Literature connected with Livery Companies, up to 1700. (*The Livery Companies of the City of London*, 1892.)

Records of London Pageants, etc. (*Local Records Report*, 1914, pt. iii. pp. 98–99.)

Gatfield (George). List of Books upon Ceremonials, Processions and Tournaments. (*Guide to Heraldry, etc.*, 1892, pp. 268–283.)

ARCHÆOLOGY, ETC.

Catal. of London Antiquities in the Guildhall Museum, with introduction by Charles Welch. 1903.

LONDON (*continued*).

Tite (Sir William). A Descriptive Catal. of the Antiquities found in the Excavations at the New Royal Exchange, preserved in the Museum of the Corporation of London. 1848.

Smith (C. Roach). Catal. of the Museum of London Antiquities, etc. 1854.

A Catal. of the Antiquities and Works of Art exhibited at Ironmongers' Hall, May 1861. 4 parts. London & Middlesex Archæol. Soc., 1863–69.

Lyell (Arthur H.). Biblio. List of Romano-British Remains. 1912. **London,** pp. 65–86.

Price (J. E.). Biblio. and Index Notes on Roman Remains. London. (*The Archæol. Review*, vol. i. pp. 274–278, 355–361. 1888.)

Murray (David). List of Catalogues and other Publications relating to London Museums. ('*Museums*,' Glasgow, 1904, vol. ii. pp. 338–357.)

ECCLESIASTICAL.

St. Paul's Cathedral.

St. Paul's Cathedral Records, from the 12th cent., with MS. Index, at St. Paul's Cathedral. (*Local Records Comm. Rep.*, 1902, App. III. p. 108.)

Archdeaconry Records, 1678, etc., at St. Paul's Cathedral. (*Ibid.* p. 118.)

Dean and Chapter of St. Paul's Records, see *ante* Hist. MSS. Comm. Reports.

A List of the Muniments in the Registry of the Lord Bishop of London in the Cathedral Church of St. Paul. (*Local Records Comm. Rep.*, 1914, vol. ii. pt. 2, p. 93.)

Notes on the Ecclesiastical Registers of London. By Rev. G. L. Hennessy. (*St. Paul's Ecclesiological Soc. Trans.*, vol. iv. pp. 331–339. 1900.)

Index to the Visitation of London, 1593, ed. by Sir Thomas Phillipps Privately Printed. Middlehill, 1840.

Simpson (W. Sparrow). S. Paul's Cathedral Library. A Catal. of Bibles, Rituals, and Rare Books; Works relating to London and especially to S. Paul's Cathedral, including a large Collection of Paul's Cross Sermons; Maps, Plans, and Views of London, and of S. Paul's Cathedral. London, 1893.

—— **Documents illustrating the Hist. of S. Paul's Cathedral.** Camden Soc. New Ser. xxvi. London, 1880. App. A. List of Indulgences. App. B. Note on the Tracts, English, French, & Latin, on the Burning of the Spire in 1561.

Botfield (Beriah). Notes on the Cathedral Libraries of England. 1849. **St. Paul's Cathedral,** pp. 297–327.

Keynes (Geoffrey). Biblio. of the Works of Dr. John Donne, Dean of St. Paul's. Baskerville Club. Cambridge, 1914. List of Printers of Donne's Works, 1607–1719, p. 161.

Welch (Charles). St. Paul's Cathedral and its early Literary Associations (with a List of Printers and Booksellers to 1556). (*Lond. & Midd. Archæol. Soc. Trans.*, New Ser. vol. i. pp. 74–114. 1892.)

Ashpitel (Arthur). The Original Drawings of Sir Christopher Wren for St. Paul's Cathedral. (*Lond. & Midd. Archæol. Soc. Trans.*, vol. iii. pp. 39–51. 1866.)

Lethaby (W. R.). Wren's Drawings of Old St. Paul's at All Souls College, Oxford. (*The Lond. Topog. Record*, vol. v. pp. 136–137. 1908.) Reproductions were also issued by the London Topog. Soc.

Westminster Abbey.

Westminster Abbey Records, A.D. 692, etc., with MS. Indexes, at Westminster. (*Local Records Comm. Rep.*, 1902, App. III. p. 116.)

LONDON (*continued*).

Westminster Abbey Records, see *ante* Hist. MSS. Comm. Reports.

Hart (W. H.). The Library of Westminster Abbey. (*Lond. & Midd. Archæol. Soc. Trans.*, vol. ii. pp. 81–87. 1860.)

Botfield (Beriah). Notes on the Cathedral Libraries of England. 1849. **Library of the Dean and Chapter of Westminster,** pp. 430–464.

Catal. of MSS. in Westminster Abbey. By J. Armitage Robinson and Montague R. James. (*Notes and Documents relating to Westminster Abbey*, No. 1, 1909.)

WESTMINSTER ARCHBISHOPRIC.

Westminster Archbishopric (Roman Catholic) Records, see *ante* Hist. MSS. Comm. Reports.

CHURCHES.

List of Articles on the 'City Churches,' in the 'City Press,' 1896-97. (*Midd. & Herts. Notes & Queries*, vol. iii. p. 203. 1897.)

CITY PARISHES.

Hallen (A. W. C.). An Account of the Old Registers of St. Botolph, Bishopsgate. 1886. (Reprinted from 'The City Press.')

Bell (Walter George). Wardmote Inquest Registers of St. Dunstan's-in-the-West. (*Lond. & Midd. Archæol. Soc. Trans.*, New Ser. vol. iii. pp. 56–70. 1914.)

Freshfield (Edwin). Some Remarks upon the Book of Records and Hist. of the Parish of St. Stephen, Coleman St. (*Archæologia*, vol. l. pp. 17–57. 1887.)

Christie (James). Notes on the Records, and Hist. of the Parish of St. Michael, Wood St. (*Lond. & Midd. Archæol. Soc. Trans.*, New Ser. vol. i. pp. 267–282. 1900.)

White (J. G.) The Ancient Records and Antiquities of the Parishes of St. Swithin, London Stone, and St. Mary Bothaw. (*Ibid.* New Ser. vol. i. pp. 183-209. 1898.)

INSTITUTIONS.

BANK OF ENGLAND.

Stephens (Thomas A.). A Contribution to the Biblio. of the Bank of England. London, 1897.

STREETS.

Piccadilly and Haymarket. Mr. A. M. Broadley has made a remarkable Collection of Prints, Maps, Plans, etc., illustrating the History of Piccadilly and the Haymarket.

Whitehall. Explanation of the Plan of Whitehall, by Walter L. Spiers. (*The London Topog. Record*, vol. vii. pp. 56–66. 1912.)

INNS OF COURT.

A Calendar of the Inner Temple Records, edited by F. A. Inderwick and W. Page. 3 vols. London, 1896–1901.

Inner Temple Records, see *ante* Hist. MSS. Comm. Reports.

A Calendar of the Middle Temple Records, edited by C. H. Hopwood. London, 1903.

Middle Temple Records, edited by C. H. Hopwood. Minutes of Parliament of the Middle Temple. 1501–1703. Translated and edited by C. T. Martin. 4 vols. London, 1904–05. Index of Persons and Places in vol. iv.

LONDON (*continued*).

VIEWS, MAPS, PLANS, ETC.

A Catal. of Maps, Plans, and Views of London, Westminster, and Southwark, collected and arranged by Frederick Crace [now in the British Museum]. Edited by John Gregory Crace. London, 1878.

The Gardner Collection. Catal. of the famous Collection of London Topography formed by John Edmund Gardner. First Portion. To be Sold by Auction by Sotheby's. London, May 23–27, 1910.

The most remarkable Collection of Topographical Prints and Drawings in existence, excelling all others in every possible direction. The above Sale never took place as the Collection was privately purchased about April, 1910 by Major Sir E. F. Coates, M.P., of Tayle's Hill, Ewell, Surrey. The Catal. of the First Portion was the only one issued. For a note on the Collection, see '*The Connoisseur*,' vol, xxvi. pp. 117–118, 1910. A selection from the Collection was included in the Exhibition at the Opening of the New Library at the Guildhall, 1872, and formed part of the Catalogue. A few copies of the section were issued as a separate pamphlet.

Pepys's Collection of Prints and Drawings relating to London and Westminster, and Environs, in Magdalene College, Cambridge. 1700. Index to Collection by W. Cornforth. 1811. A Copy of the Index is now Bodleian MS. 30734.

Lethaby (W. R.). Pepys's London Collection. (*The London Topog. Record*, vol. ii. pp. 66–69. 1903.)

'Pepys was the first person who began to collect Prints and Drawings to illustrate the History of the City of London.' This Collection is in the Pepysian Lib. Vol. i. comprises Maps and Views. Vol. ii. is mainly relating to Pageants, Coronations, Street Cries, etc. For a Note on the Collection, see H. B. Wheatley's '*Samuel Pepys and the World he lived in*,' 1889, p. 92.

Holbert Wilson Collection. Catalogue of the First and Second Portions of the Collection of Engravings and Drawings relating to the Architecture, History, and Social History of London, formed by James Holbert Wilson. Sold by Sotheby's. May and Nov., 1898. The Collection was formed previous to 1865.

Bagford (John). Biblio. Notes on Maps and Views of London, in 'Letter relating to the Antiquities of London,' 1715. (Leland's *Collectanea*, 1770, vol. i. pp. lxxx.–lxxxvi.) See also Richard Gough's 'British Topography,' 1780, vol. i. p. 743.

Fancourt (H.). Collectors of Old London. (*The Home Counties Mag.*, vol. v. pp. 129–134. 1903.)

Mitton (G. E.). Maps of Old London. (Reproductions and descriptions of early Maps.) 1908.

Overall (W. H.). On the Early Maps of London. (*Soc. Antiq. Lond. Proc.*, Ser. 2, vol. vi. pp. 81–99. 1874.)

Catal. of the MS. Maps, Charts and Plans, and of the Topographical Drawings in the British Museum. Middlesex (including London) items, vol. ii. pp. 1–52. 1844.

Catal. of Maps, Views, etc., in the Library of the British Museum. See section London in the Brit. Mus. Map Catalogue.

Catal. of Maps, Prints, Drawings, etc., forming the Geographical and Topographical Collection in the King's Library, Brit. Museum. 1829. London entries, pp. 187–209.

Catal. of Sculpture, Paintings, Engravings, etc., belonging to the Corporation, together with Books not included in the Catal. of the Guildhall Library. 2 vols. London, 1867–68.

Vol. II.—**Maps, Plans, etc., of London, Westminster, and Southwark.**

LONDON (*continued*).

A Catal. of Engraved Portraits, Topographical Drawings and Prints, etc., exhibited at Opening of New Library and Museum of the Corporation, Nov., 1872, ed. by W. H. Overall, with an Historical Account of the Ancient and Modern Library at the Guildhall, by W. S. Saunders. London, 1872.

A large section of the Catal. is occupied with a Selection of Topog. Views, etc., of London, Westminster, and Southwark from the Collection of John Edmund Gardner, see *ante* p. 156.

Catal. of Exhib. of Maps, Views and Plans of London, exhibited at Drapers' Hall, London, March 1905, by Bernard Gomme. (*The London Topog. Record*, vol. iv. pp. 113–140. 1907.)

Catal. of an Exhib. of Engravings and Drawings of London in the Reigns of the Georges, with prefatory note by H. B. Wheatley, held at the Fine Art Soc., London, Feb., 1904. London, 1904.

Catal. of Drawings of Old London, issued by the Archæol. Institute. London, 1893.

Topographical Soc. of London. General Report and Handbook to Views and Maps published by them, 1880-87.

——— **Index to the Various Articles and Illustrations in the London Topographical Record, vols. i.–viii.** (*The London Topog. Record*, vol. ix. pp. 57–76. 1914.

——— **Notes on London Views** (reproduced by the Society), by Philip Norman. (*Ibid.* vol. viii. pp. 94–102. 1913.) The London Topog. Soc, have issued numerous facsimiles of Early London Views and Maps.

Drawings of New and Old London Bridge, and of Southwark Bridge, by E. W. Cooke, R.A. Notes by Philip Norman. (*Ibid.* vol. ix. pp. 1–14. 1914.)

Scott's Pictures of the River Side. (*The Builder*, June 15, 1895.)

Price (F. G. Hilton). Signs of Old London. With Biblio. Notes. (*The London Topog. Record*, vols. ii.–iv. *passim.* 1903–08.)

Wilson (James Holbert). Catal. of Pictorial Records of London, past and present. Privately Printed. London, n.d. The Holbert Wilson Collection was sold at Sotheby's in 1898, see *ante* p. 156.

An Engraving of London in 1510. Note by S. C. Cockerell. (*The London Topog. Record*, vol. i. p. 51. 1900.)

Notes upon Norden and his Map of London, 1593, by Henry B. Wheatley. (*Ibid.* vol. ii. pp. 42–65. 1903.) Originally appeared in Harrison's 'Description of England in Shakspere's Youth,' Part I. App. III. pp. lxxxix.–cvi. New Shakspere Society. 1877.

Notes on Visscher's View of London, 1616, by T. F. Ordish. (*Ibid.* vol. vi. pp. 39–64. 1909.)

Hollar's Map. Notes by W. R. Lethaby and Rhys Jenkins. (*Ibid.* vol. ii. pp. 109–110. 1903.)

Ogilby and Morgan's Map of London, 1677. Facsimile Reproduction, with Ogilby's description 'London Survey'd,' edited (with a lexicographical Index) by Charles Welch. London and Middlesex Archæol. Soc. 1895.

Morden and Lea's Plan of London, 1682, by Walter L. Spiers. (*The London Topog. Record*, vol. v. pp. 117–135. 1908.)

A Few Words about John Ogilby and his Topographical Publications, by Philip Norman. (*Ibid.* vol. viii. pp. 93–94. 1913.)

Notes on Vertue's edition of Agas's Map of London, by William Martin. (*Soc. Antiq. Lond. Proc.* Ser. 2, vol. xxii. pp. 535–539. 1909.) A reproduction of the Map attributed to Ralph Agas, *circa* 1560–1570, was issued by the London Topog. Soc.

LONDON (continued).

Rocque's Plan of London, 1746, by Henry B. Wheatley. (*The London Topog. Record*, vol. ix. pp. 15–28. 1914.)

Notes on Kensington Turnpike Trust Plans (Solway's Plan of the Road from Hyde Park Corner to Counter's Bridge. 1811). By Col. W. F. Prideaux. (*Ibid.* vol. iii. pp. 21–63 ; vol. v. pp. 138–144. 1906–08.)

PRINTERS AND BOOKSELLERS.

[The first six entries following this paragraph give clues to the output of the London Press from 1457 to 1711. If these works are used in connection with Bigmore and Wyman's 'Biblio. of Printing,' and the 'Catal. of the Blades Library at the St. Bride's Foundation' (compiled by its accomplished Librarian, Robert Alexander Peddie) as full information as possible will be obtained until the date of the regular publication of systematic Catalogues of London Books.]

Duff (E. Gordon). A Century of the English Book Trade, 1457-1557. London, Bibliographical Soc., 1905.

A Dictionary of Printers and Booksellers in England, Scotland, and Ireland, etc., 1557-1640. By H. G. Aldis and others. Gen. Editor, R. B. McKerrow. Index of Addresses, etc., of London Printers, pp. 321–335. London, Bibliographical Soc., 1910.

Plomer (Henry R.). A Dictionary of the Booksellers and Printers who were at work in England, Scotland, and Ireland, from 1641 to 1667. London. Bibliographical Soc., 1907.

Arber (Edward). A Transcript of the Registers of the Company of Stationers of London, 1554-1640. 5 vols. (vol. v. Index). Privately Printed. London, 1875–94.

A Transcript of the Registers of the Worshipful Company of Stationers from 1640 to 1708, by G. E. Briscoe Eyre. 3 vols. London. The Roxburghe Club. London, 1913. Privately Printed.

Arber (Edward). The Term Catalogues, 1668 to 1711. London, 1903–06. Privately Printed. A Contemporary Biblio. of English Literature, compiled from Lists issued by the Booksellers of London.

——— **Contemporary Printed Lists of Books produced in England.** (*Bibliographica*, vol. iii. pp. 173–191. 1897.)

——— **A List, based on the Registers of the Stationers' Company, of 837 London Publishers between 1553 and 1640.** Birmingham, 1890. An advance Issue of the List that appeared later in vol. v. of Arber's 'Transcript of the Registers of the Stationers' Company.' The latter List was increased to 847 Publishers.

——— **An Index to the Mechanical Producers of English Books,** and of Persons and Places connected with them and with the Company of Stationers, 1553–1640. (*A Transcript of the Registers of the Company of Stationers*, vol. v. pp. 216–276.)

Caxton Celebration, 1877. Catalogue of the Loan Collection of Antiquities, Curiosities, and Appliances connected with the Art of Printing. Edited by G. Bullen. 1877.

A copy in the Brit. Museum Library is in 8 quarto vols. inlaid and interleaved with special title-pages, containing the correspondence, prospectuses, circulars, portraits, photographs, facsimiles, newspaper cuttings, etc., relating to the Exhibition, formed by William Blades.

Bigmore (E. C.) and Wyman (C. W. H.). A Biblio. of Printing. 3 vols. London, 1880–86. A good annotated Dictionary of Printers, with their marks and other valuable information.

Ames (Joseph) and Herbert (William). Typographical Antiquities. 3 vols. London, 1785–90.

LONDON (continued).

An Index to Dibdin's Edition of the 'Typographical Antiquities,' first compiled by Joseph Ames, with some references to the intermediate edition by William Herbert. London, Bibliographical Soc., 1899.

Aldis (H. G.). The Book Trade, 1557-1625, with a Bibliography. (*The Cambridge Hist. of English Literature*, ed. by A. W. Ward and A. R. Waller, vol. iv. pp. 378–414, and pp. 544–549. 1909.)

——— **Book Production and Distribution, 1625-1800, with a Bibliography.** (*Ibid.* vol. xi. pp. 311–342, and pp. 466–470. 1914.)

——— **Catalogues of Books produced in England.** (*Ibid.* vol. xi. pp. 470–471. 1914.)

Growoll (A.). Three Centuries of English Book Trade Bibliography. New York. The Dibdin Club. 1903. (Contains valuable lists of English Book Catalogues.)

Peddie (R. A.). Catal. of the Blades Library at the St. Bride's Foundation, London. 1915.

A MS. Index to some London and Provincial Printers and Booksellers from the earliest period. (In the Typographical Library of the St. Bride Foundation, London.) Compiled by R. A. Peddie.

Eames (Wilberforce). A List of the Catalogues, etc., published for the English Book Trade from 1595 to 1902. (*Three Centuries of English Book Trade Bibliography*, by Growoll, pp. 101–173. 1903.)

Duff (E. Gordon). The Printers, Stationers and Bookbinders of London and Westminster in the Fifteenth Century. A Series of Four Lectures delivered at Cambridge, 1899. Privately Printed, 1899.

——— **The Printers, Stationers and Bookbinders of London, from the year 1500 to the year 1535.** A Series of Lectures at Cambridge, 1904. London, 1904.

——— **The Printers, Stationers and Bookbinders of Westminster and London from 1476 to 1535.** The Sandars Lectures, 1899 and 1904. Cambridge, 1906.

——— **The Introduction of Printing into England and the Early Work of the Press, with a Biblio. by E. G. D. and A. R. W.** (*The Cambridge Hist. of English Literature*, vol. ii. pp. 310–331 and pp. 483–486. 1908.)

McKerrow (R. B.). Printers' and Publishers' Devices in England and Scotland, 1485-1640. London, Bibliographical Soc., 1913. (*Illustrated Monographs.* No. XVI.)

Reed (Talbot Baines). A List of Books and Papers on Printers and Printing. London and Westminster, pp. 13–14. n. d.

List of Books Printed in London in the three years preceding the Great Fire of London, in which many of the copies are presumed to have been destroyed. See Catal. of Library of Rev. Philip Bliss. Part II. Sold by Sotheby's in Aug. 1858.

Negus (Samuel). A Compleat and Private List of all the Printing-houses in and about the Cities of London and Westminster, together with the Printers' names, what Newspapers they print and where they are to be found, also an Account of the Printing-houses in the several Corporation Towns in England. Printed by William Bowyer in White Friars, 1724.

Nichols (John). Literary Anecdotes of the Eighteenth Century. 1813. See vol. vii. (Index) pp. 336–337, under Printers, etc.

Bibliotheca Pepysiana: A Descriptive Catal. of the Library of Samuel Pepys. Part II. Early Printed Books to 1558. London, 1914. Index of London Printers, pp. 74–79.

LONDON (*continued*).

Rivington (Charles Robert). The Records of the Worshipful Company of Stationers (with lists of Royal Printers, Univ. of Oxford and Cambridge Printers, Printers to the City of London, etc.) (*Lond. & Midd. Archæol. Soc. Trans.*, vol. vi. pp. 280–340. 1882.)

—— **The Stationers' Company.** (*Ibid.* New Ser. vol. ii. pp. 119–136. 1909.)

—— **The Records of the Worshipful Company of Stationers.** Second Edn. Edinb., 1893. See Arber (Edward). A Transcript of the Registers of the Stationers' Company, vol. v.

—— **Notes on the Stationers' Company.** (*The Library*, New Ser. vol. iv. pp. 355–366. 1903.)

—— **Stationers' Company, 1403-1903.** A short account of the Worshipful Company of Stationers. Presented to guests at celebration of the 500th Anniversary of Foundation. 1903.

Welch (Charles). A Brief Hist. of the Worshipful Company of Stationers. London, 1880.

Nichols (John Gough). Notices of the Stationers' Company, their Hall, Pictures and Plate. (*Lond. & Midd. Archæol. Soc. Trans.*, vol. ii. pp. 37–61. 1861.) Also reprinted for Private Circulation, 1861.

Collier (J. Payne). Extracts from the Registers of the Stationers' Company of Works entered for publication between 1557 and 1587. 2 vols. The Shakespeare Soc. London, 1848–49.

Company of Stationers. The Orders, Rules, and Ordinances made by the Master, etc., of the Mystery of Stationers of London. 1678 and 1692.

—— **Order by the Lord Chancellor and Lords Justices endorsing the by-law of the Company with reference to the placing of imprints on all books, pamphlets, etc.** London, 1681.

—— **At a Court held at Stationers-Hall on Friday the 22nd day of Msy, 1685** (giving particulars as to the various authorities for licensing books).

—— **The Charter and Grants of the Company of Stationers, now in force.** London, 1741.

—— **The Stationers' Charters, etc.** (*Luckombe's Hist. of Printing*, 1770. pp. 175–212.)

—— **Stationers' Hall, July 11, 1894.** A Programme, with historical notes on the Company.

—— —— **July 8, 1897.** A Programme, with details of the Hall.

Duff (E. Gordon). The Stationers at the Sign of the Trinity in St. Paul's Churchyard, 1506-1539. (*Bibliographica*, vol. i. pp. 93–113, 175–193. 1895.)

Peet (W. H.). Biblio. of Bookselling. (*The Romance of Book-Selling*, by F. A. Mumby, pp. 432–470. 1910.) Reprinted with additions from '*Notes & Queries*.' Ser. 10, vol. i. pp. 81, 142, 184, 242, 304, 342. 1904.)

Plomer (Henry R.). The Booksellers of London Bridge. (*The Library*, New Ser., vol. iv. pp. 28–46. 1903.)

—— **The Long Shop in the Poultry.** (An Old City Printing-House.) (*Bibliographica*, vol. ii. pp. 61–80. 1896.)

Thomson (Richard). Chronicles of London Bridge. London, 1827. Biblio. Note on Books printed and sold on London Bridge, pp. 374–382.

Bookselling on London Bridge. (*Walford's Antiquarian Mag.*, vol. xii. pp. 21–27. 1887.)

LONDON (*continued*).

Ashbee (E. W.) and others. London Signs of Booksellers and Printers. (*The Bibliographer*, vol. ii. pp. 112, 143, 174; vol. iii. pp. 45, 67, 94; vol. iv. p. 76. 1882–83.)

Francis (John C.). Jubilee of 'The City Press.' (*Notes & Queries*, Ser. 10, vol. viii. pp. 81, 103, 122, 142. 1907.)

BALLADS, CHAPBOOKS, ETC.

[See also Appendix, '**England**—General,' for Bibliographies of Ballads, many of which relate to London.]

The Ballad Society was founded in London by F. J. Furnivall in 1868, to publish and render accessible the rare and large stores of Street Ballads in the Public and Private Collections of the Country. It was intended to deal first with the 'Pepysian Collection' at Cambridge, but this was not done. The most important publications (some of which contain copious Indices) issued during its existence were :—

The Roxburghe Ballads (in Brit. Mus.), ed. by William Chappell and J. Woodfall Ebsworth. Vol. i. has a list of Ballad Printers, etc.; vol. viii. William Thackeray's List of Ballads, 1685. 9 vols. 1869–99.

The Bagford Ballads (in Brit. Mus.) ed. by J. Woodfall Ebsworth. 3 vols. 1876–78.

Ballads from MSS., ed. by F. J. Furnivall and W. R. Morfill. 2 vols. 1868–73.

Large numbers of the Ballads relate to incidents connected with the history of London.

Pepys's Collection of English Broadside Ballads at Magdalene College, Cambridge. For description and arrangement see H. B. Wheatley's '*Samuel Pepys and the World he lived in*,' 1889, p. 91, also C. H. Hartshorne, '*Book Rarities of the Univ. of Cambridge*,' 1829, pp. 258–260.

Many of the Pepysian Ballads are printed in the Ballad Society's 'The Roxburghe Ballads,' ed. by J. W. Ebsworth.

Ballads, etc., principally relating to the City of London, 1659-1711. A Collection in the King's Library of the British Museum, see King's Lib. Catalogue under 'Poetae Anglici' in vol. iv. pp. 484–487. 1828.

A Collection of Ballads chiefly printed in London by J. Catnach, J. Pitts, H. P. Such, and others, mostly between 1800 and 1870. Collected by the Rev. Sabine Baring Gould. With MS. Indexes. 10 vols. (In British Museum.) The British Museum Library is rich in Collections of Ballads, for which see the General Catalogue under the heading Ballads. For an Account of the Catnach Ballads see '*The Hist. of the Catnach Press*,' by C. Hindley. 1886.

Bibliotheca Lindesiana. Catal. of Collection of English Ballads of the XVIIth and XVIIIth centuries; printed for the most part in black letter. 1890. Compiled for James Ludovic Lindsay, 26th Earl of Crawford. Privately Printed. List of Printers and Publishers and of Booksellers who sold Ballads, pp. 535–545.

Collmann (Herbert L.). Ballads and Broadsides, chiefly of the Elizabethan Period and Printed in Black Letter, most of which were formerly in the 'Heber Collection,' and are now in the Library at Britwell, Bucks. The Roxburghe Club, 1912.

Alphabetical List of Black Letter Ballads and Broadsides, known as 'The Heber Collection,' in the possession of S. Christie-Miller, of Britwell, Bucks. London, 1872. Consists largely of London Ballads.

Lemon (Robert). Catal. of a Collection of Broadsides (Ballads, etc.) in the possession of the Soc. of Antiquaries of London. 1866. The Collection is largely relating to London.

LONDON (continued).

Rimbault (E. F.). Old Ballads illustrating the Great Frost of 1683-4 and the Fair on the River Thames. London. Percy Society, vol ix. 1844.

Mackay (Charles). A Collection of Songs and Ballads relative to the London Prentices and Trades; and to the Affairs of London generally, during the Fifteenth, Sixteenth, and Seventeenth Centuries. London. Percy Society, vol. i. 1841.

Halliwell (J. O.). Notices of Fugitive Tracts and Chap-Books printed at Aldermary Churchyard, Bow Churchyard, etc. London. Percy Society, vol. xxix. 1849.

Fairholt (F. W.). The Civic Garland. A Collection of Songs from London Pageants. London. Percy Society, vol. xix. 1845.

Hazlitt (W. Carew). A General Index to Hazlitt's Handbook and his Bibliographical Collections (1867–1889), by G. J. Gray. 1893. Contains references to the rarer fugitive literature relating to London.

Routh (Harold V.). London and the Development of Popular Literature, with Biblio. of Street Literature, Ballads, Street Songs, Broadsides, and Popular Ditties. (*The Cambridge Hist. of English Literature*, vol. iv. pp. 316–363 and pp. 514–536.)

NEWSPAPERS, ETC.

Catal. of the London Newspapers in the British Museum Library. 2 vols. (Arranged under Titles.) Newspapers before 1700 are not included in this Catal., but are in the Catal. of Periodical Publications.

Catal. of the Burney Collection of Early London Newspapers in the British Museum. (MS. in the Newspaper Room.) 1603–1817. 2 vols.

Grant (James). The Newspaper Press, its Origin, Progress, and Present Position. 3 vols. 1871–72. Vol. III. The Metropolitan Weekly and Provincial Press.

Williams (Joseph Batterson). A Hist. of English Journalism to the foundation of the Gazette. London, 1908. Catal. of Periodicals, Newspapers, etc., from 1641 to 1666, pp. 218–265.

Nichols (John). Biblio. Notes on Newspapers. (*Literary Anecdotes of the Eighteenth Century.* Index, vol. vii. p. 286. 1813.)

Besant (Sir Walter). List of 18th Century London Newspapers. (*The Survey of London: London in the Eighteenth Century*, 1902, pp. 393–394.)

LIBRARIES.

Rye (R. A.). The Libraries of London. A Guide for Students. Published by the Univ. of London. Second Edn. London, 1910.

Oldys (William). Of London Libraries; with Anecdotes of Collectors of Books, Remarks on Booksellers, and of the first Publishers of Catalogues (probably joint production of John Bagford and William Oldys). Reprinted in '*Memoir of William Oldys, Norroy King-at-Arms, with his Diary,*' etc., edited by W. J. Thoms. London, 1862. (Reprinted from '*Notes & Queries.*')

Bagford (John). An Account of several Libraries in and about London. (*The Monthly Miscellany: or Memoirs of the Curious.* London, vol. ii. pp. 167–182. 1708.)

Cannons (H. G. T.). List of Articles on London Libraries. (*Biblio. of Library Economy*, 1910, pp. 129–130.)

LONDON (*continued*).

Welch (Charles). The Guildhall Library and its Work. 1893. Catalogues of the Library & Museum, pp. 43–44. List of the Special Collections, pp. 45–52. The Card Catalogue, pp. 52–53. List of Works published by the Library Committee, pp. 54–55.

Milman (W. H.). Some Account of Sion College, and of its Library. (*Lond. & Midd. Archæol. Soc. Trans.*, vol. vi. pp. 53–122. 1883.)

Spilsbury (W. H.). Lincoln's Inn and its Library. (*Lond. & Midd. Archæol. Soc. Trans.*, vol. iv. pp. 445–466. 1874.)

WESTMINSTER.

A Catal. of Westminster Records deposited at the Town Hall, with introductory Essay, by J. E. Smith. 1900.

Early Plans of Part of the Palace of Westminster, 1593. (*Home Counties Mag.*, vol. v. pp. 1–4. 1903.)

CHELSEA.

Reports of Inspections of the Records of the Royal Hospital, Chelsea, July and Oct. 1913. (*Local Records Comm. Rep.*, 1914, vol. ii. pt. 2, p. 181.)

Beaver (Alfred). Memorials of Old Chelsea. London, 1892. Biblio. pp. 389–402.

Catal. of Books, Portraits, etc., of, or relating to, Sir Thomas More, collected by Alfred Cock. Presented to the Guildhall Library. 1903.

DULWICH.

Warner (George F.). Catal. of the MSS. and Muniments of Alleyn's College of God's Gift at Dulwich. London, 1881.

EALING.

Jackson (Edith). Annals of Ealing. 1898. Biblio. of the Geology of the District, pp. 335–340.

FINCHLEY.

Passmore (W. B.). Note upon the Parish Registers of Finchley. (*Middlesex and Herts. Notes & Queries*, vol. iv. pp. 200–203. 1898.)

FULHAM.

Fèret (Charles James). Fulham, Old and New. 3 vols. London. 1900. List of Views, etc. pp. 289–291. Biblio. pp. 296–304.

HACKNEY.

Hugo (Thomas). A Calendar of Records, belonging or relating to the Rectory, Church, and Parish of West Hackney. London, 1872.

Catalogue of the Tyssen Library, Hackney. A Collection of Books, MSS, Maps, Plans, Prints, etc., relating to, or connected with Hackney and its Vicinity, originally formed by John Robert Daniel Tyssen. Compiled by J. T. Whitehead. London, 1888.

HAMPSTEAD AND HIGHGATE.

Barratt (Thomas J.). The Annals of Hampstead. 3 vols. 1912. Biblio. of Hampstead and of Accessions to Hampstead in various branches of Literature, vol. iii. pp. 320–343.

LONDON (continued).

Newton (**Ernest Edward**). **An Annotated Catal. of the Bell-Moor Collection of Hampsteadiana,** comprised in 16 vols., folio, in the possession of Thomas J. Barratt, 1912. Privately Printed. The Bell-Moor Collection is the largest in existence relating to Hampstead.

Marshall (**Miss L.**). **Hist. of the Hampstead Library, 1833–1898.** (*The Hampstead Annual.* 1898, pp. 22–31.)

Munich (**Charles J.**). **The Hampstead Antiquarian and Historical Society.** A brief Sketch. (*Ibid.* 1898, pp. 136–139.)

A Special Collection of Books and Records relating to Hampstead is in the Reference Room of the Hampstead Subscription Library. Important Local Collections for Highgate are those of George Potter and Ambrose Heal. The Literary and Scientific Institute, Highgate, has a Collection of Prints and Drawings.

ISLINGTON.

Islington Public Libraries. Select Catalogue and Guide. A Classified List of the Books on all Subjects. 1910. Islington Books, pp. 640–641.

Catal. of a Collection of Prints, Drawings and Photographs of Ancient and Modern Islington, issued in connexion with an Exhibition held at the West and North Libraries. 1907.

LAMBETH.

Lambeth Palace Records, see *ante* Hist. MSS. Comm. Reports.

ST. MARTIN-IN-THE-FIELDS.

Mason (**Thomas**). **Catal. of Books and Documents belonging to the Royal Parish of St. Martin-in-the-Fields.** London, 1895.

ST. PANCRAS.

Percival Collection. A Collection illustrative of the Parish of St. Pancras, formed by Richard Percival, comprising engraved Views and Portraits, cuttings from books and newspapers, 1729–1830. 2 vols. (In British Museum Library.)

Ambrose Heal Collection of Local Literature, bequeathed by Ambrose Heal to the Borough of St. Pancras, to be deposited at the Town Hall. See 'Notes and Queries,' Ser. 11, vol. ix. p. 235. 1914.

List of Books relating to St. Pancras, by various writers. (*Notes & Queries,* Ser. 11. vol. ix. pp. 191, 235, 312. 1914.)

List of Old Deeds in the Public Record Office relating to St. Pancras. (*St. Pancras Notes & Queries,* 1900–01, pp. 132–138.)

Weatherley (**Rev. Charles Thomas**). **Collections for a Hist. of Old St. Pancras Church.** (*Ibid.* 1900, pp. 106–107.)

List of Drawings and Prints in the Crace Collection in the Brit. Museum, relating to St. Pancras. (*Ibid.* 1899, pp. 81–82.)

List of Local Views, etc., from 'A Catal. of the MS. Maps, Views, etc., in the Brit. Museum,' vol. ii. pp. 34–35. 1844. (*Ibid.* 1900, pp. 125–126.)

List of Local Prints and Drawings in the King's Library Collection at the Brit. Museum. (*Ibid.* 1902, pp. 201–202.)

A List of Local Water-colour Drawings by John Wykeham Archer in the Archer Collection at the Brit. Museum. (*Ibid.* 1899, p. 104.)

SOUTHWARK.

Southwark Bishopric Records, see *ante* Hist. MSS. Comm. Reports.

LONDONDERRY.

Hist. MSS. Comm. Reports. Londonderry Collection.
Derry, Diocesan Library ... ... 8th Rep. pp. 639, 640.

Unpublished Hist. MS. Collections relating to the County of Derry. A Biblio. Note. (*Ulster Journ. of Archæol.*, vol. xv. p. 185. 1909.)

O'Hanlon (John). Index of Materials for the Hist. & Topography of the Co. of Londonderry in the Irish Ordnance Survey Records, and in the Royal Irish Academy. (*Kilkenny & South-East of Irel. Archæol. Soc. Journ.*, vol. vii. p. 313. 1863.)

Dix (Ernest Reginald McClintock). List of Books, Pamphlets, Newspapers, etc., printed in Londonderry, prior to 1801. Dundalk, 1911. (Irish Bibliography, no. vii.)

—— **Ulster Bibliography. Derry Printing, with a List, 1689-1800.** (*Ulster Journ. of Archæol.*, vol. vii. pp. 132–136, 174; vol. viii. p. 24; vol. ix. p. 71. 1901–3.)

—— —— **Coleraine Printing, with a List, 1794-1800.** (*Ibid.* vol. xiii. pp. 22–23. 1907.)

Crone (John S.). Ulster Bibliography. Derry. (*Ibid.* vol. x. pp. 151–156; vol. xi. pp. 27–32. 1904–5.)

—— **Early Printing in Derry.** (*Irish Book-Lover*, vol. iii. pp. 112–113. 1912.)

Eakin (J. H.). Journals and Journalism in Derry. (*Ibid.* vol. i. pp. 161–162. 1910.)

Gross (Charles). Biblio. of Brit. Municipal Hist. (*Harvard Hist. Studies*, vol. v. 1897.) **Londonderry,** p. 325.

Christy (Miller). Biblio. Note on Londonderry Mammals. (*The Zoologist*, Ser. 3, vol. xvii. p. 216. 1893.)

Anderson (John P.). Book of Brit. Topo., 1881. Londonderry, p. 438.
Gough (Richard). Brit. Topo., 1780. Londonderry, vol. ii. p. 807.
Bandinel (Bulkeley). Catal. of Books bequeathed to Bodleian Lib. by Richard Gough, 1814. Londonderry, p. 381.

LONGFORD.

Coleman (James). Biblio. of the Counties of Louth, Meath, Westmeath, and Longford. (*Co. Louth Archæol. Journ.*, vol. ii. pp. 24–26. 1908.)

Hist. MSS. Comm. Reports. Longford Collection.
Granard, Earl of, at Castle Forbes... 2nd Rep. p. xx. and App. pp. 210–217; 3rd Rep. p. xxvi. and App. pp. 430–431.

O'Hanlon (John). Index of Materials for the Hist. & Topography of the Co. of Longford in the Irish Ordnance Survey Records, and in the Royal Irish Academy. (*Kilkenny and South-East of Irel. Archæol. Soc. Journ.*, vol. vi. p. 321. 1861.)

Anderson (John P.). Book of Brit. Topo., 1881. Longford, p. 439.

LOUTH.

Coleman (James). Biblio. of the Counties of Louth, Meath, Westmeath, and Longford. (*Co. Louth Archæol. Journ.*, vol. ii. pp. 24–26. 1908.)

Dix (Ernest Reginald McClintock). List of Books, Pamphlets, and Newspapers, printed in Droghedain the 18th century (1728-1800). Dundalk, 1904. Second edition. Dundalk, 1911. (Irish Bibliography, No. III.)

—— **Supplementary List.** (*Dublin Penny Journ.*, vol. iii. p. 455. 1904.)

LOUTH (continued).

Dix (Ernest Reginald McClintock). List of Books, Pamphlets, Newspapers, etc., printed in Drogheda from 1801 to 1825 inclusive. (*Irish Book-Lover*, vol. iv. pp. 1–3. 1912.)

—— **Drogheda Printing.** (*Drogheda Argus*, 4 Jan. 1902.)

—— **Dundalk Printing from the Earliest Period. 1782-1897.** (*Dundalk Herald*, 5 July, 1902, and *Dundalk Examiner*, 31 Jan. 1903.)

—— **Printing in Dundalk, with a List, 1801-1825.** (*Irish Book-Lover*, vol. v. pp. 46, 58, 78. 1913.)

—— **Earliest Printing in the County Louth.** (*Co. Louth Archæol. Journ.*, vol. i. no. 1. pp. 52–53. 1904.)

—— **Some Dundalk Song Books.** (*Ibid.* vol. i. no. 4. pp. 62–63. 1907.)

Gogarty (Rev. Fr.). Early Printing in the County Louth. (*Ibid.* vol. i. no. 2. pp. 25–31. 1905.)

The Origin of the Drogheda 'Argus.' (*Ibid.* vol. i. no. 4, p. 103. 1907.)

Some Local Sheet Ballads. (*Ibid.* vol. i. no. 4, p. 64. 1907.)

A New Private Press (of Rev. Guy W. C. L'Estrange, Rector of Charlestown, nr. Ardee.) (*Irish Book-Lover*, vol. v. p. 67. 1913.)

O'Hanlon (John). Index of Materials for the Hist. and Topography of the County Louth in the Irish Ordnance Survey Records, and in the Royal Irish Academy. (*Kilkenny & South-East of Irel. Archæol. Soc. Journ.*, vol. v. p. 97. 1858.)

On the Ordnance Survey Papers relating to County Louth, by James MacCarte. (*Co. Louth Archæol. Journ.*, vol. i. no. 2, pp. 74–76; vol. ii. p. 442; vol. iii. p. 110. 1905–12).

John D'Alton's MS. Materials for a Hist. of Co. Louth, by James MacCarte. (*Ibid.* vol. i. no. 1, p. 60. 1904.)

Moynagh (S. H.). Notes on some of the Old Dundalk Charters. (*Soc. Antiq. Irel. Journ.*, vol. xxxviii. pp. 232–235. 1908.)

Leslie (James B.). Hist. of Kilsaran. Dundalk, 1908. List of Authorities, pp. xi.–xiv.

Anderson (John P.). Book of Brit. Topo., 1881. Louth, p. 439.
Gough (Richard). Brit. Topo., 1780. Louth, vol. ii. p. 811.
Bandinel (Bulkeley). Catal. of Books bequeathed to Bodleian Lib. by Richard Gough. 1814. Louth, p. 382.

MAN (ISLE OF).

[*See* Isle of Man.]

MAYO.

Coleman (James). Bibliographia Conaciensis: a list of Books relating to Connaught. Mayo, pp. 31, 34. (*Galway Archæol. and Hist. Soc. Journ.*, vol. v. 1907–08.)

Hist. MSS. Comm. Reports. Mayo Collection.
O'Donnell, Sir Richard, at Newport. 4th Rep. p. xxiv. and App. pp. 584–588.

O'Hanlon (John). Index of Materials for the Hist. & Topography of the County of Mayo in the Irish Ordnance Survey Records, and in the Royal Irish Academy. (*Kilkenny & South-East of Irel. Archæol. Soc. Journ.*, vol. ix. p. 212. 1867.)

MAYO (continued).

Macalister (R. A. Stewart). Studies in Irish Epigraphy. Part I. Biblio. of Mayo Epigraphy. 1897.

The Achill Press, with a List, by R. S. Maffett, and an additional Note, by J. S. Crone. (*Irish Book-Lover*, vol. ii. pp. 65–68; vol. iii. pp. 29-30. 1910–11.)

Blake (Martin J.). A Map of part of the County of Mayo in 1584, with notes thereon and an account of its Author. (*Galway Archæol. & Hist. Soc. Journ.*, vol. v. pp. 145–158. 1908.)

Christy (Miller). Biblio. Notes on Mayo Birds. (*The Zoologist*, Ser. 3. vol. xiv. p. 267. 1890; and reprinted in pamph., 1891, p. 42.)

Anderson (John P.). Book of Brit. Topo., 1881. Mayo, p. 440.
Gough (Richard). Brit. Topo., 1780. Mayo, vol. ii. p. 813.
Bandinel (Bulkeley). Catal. of Books bequeathed to Bodleian Lib. by Richard Gough, 1814. Mayo, p. 382.

MEATH.

Coleman (James). Biblio. of the Counties of Louth, Meath, Westmeath, and Longford. (*Co. Louth Archæol. Journ.*, vol. ii. pp. 24–26. 1908.)

Hist. MSS. Comm. Reports. Meath Collections.

Balfour, Mr. B. R. T. at Townley Hall, Drogheda	10th Rep. p. 22, and App. VI. pp. 252-258; 13th Rep. p. 56.
Fingall, Earl of, at Fingall, Killeen Castle	10th Rep. pp. 42, 43, and App. V. pp. 107–204.
Gormanston, Viscount, at Gormanston Castle	4th Rep. p. xxiv. and App. pp. 573–584,

O'Hanlon (John). Index of Materials for the Hist. & Topography of Meath in the Irish Ordnance Survey Records, and in the Royal Irish Academy. (*Kilkenny & South-East of Irel. Archæol. Soc. Journ.*, vol. v. p. 42. 1858.

Dix (Ernest Reginald McClintock). Printing in Trim, with a List, 1835-60. (*Irish Book-Lover*, vol. i. pp. 63, 77, 78, 107. 1910.)

Anderson (John P.). Book of Brit. Topo., 1881. Meath, p. 440.
Gough (Richard). Brit. Topo., 1780. Meath, vol. ii. p. 814.
Bandinel (Bulkeley). Catal. of Books bequeathed to Bodleian Lib. by Richard Gough, 1814. Meath, p. 382.

MERIONETHSHIRE.

Hist. MSS. Comm. Reports. Merionethshire Collection.

Wynne, Mr. W. W. E. at Peniarth	2nd Rep. p. xii., and App. pp. 103–106; Welsh MSS. vol. i. part ii.

County Records, at County Hall, Dolgelley. (*Local Records Comm. Rep.*, 1902. App. III. p. 28.)

Wynne (W. W. E.). Catal. of the Hengwrt MSS. at Peniarth. (*Archæol. Cambrensis*, Ser. 3, vol. xv. pp. 210, 352; Ser. 4, vol. i. pp. 73, 323; vol. ii. p. 101. 1869–71.) 'Selections from the Hengwrt MSS.,' by Canon Robert Williams, 2 vols. were issued in 1876–80.

Owen (Aneurin). List of the Hengwrt MSS. (*The Cambrian Journ.* Ser. 2, vol. ii. pp. 276–296. 1859.)

The Hengwrt Library of Printed Books. (*Welsh Biblio. Soc. Journ.*, vol. i, pp. 76–83, 123–128. 1911–12.)

MERIONETHSHIRE (continued).

List of Merionethshire Illustrations in the 'Archæologia Cambrensis,' 1884–1900. See Alphabetical Index by F. Green, 1902, p. 105.

Lyell (Arthur H.). Biblio. List of Romano-British Remains, 1912. **Merioneth,** p. 145.

Trimen (Henry). Botanical Biblio. of the British Counties. Merioneth. (*Journ. of Botany*, vol. xii. p. 157. 1874.)

Christy (Miller). Biblio Note on Merionethshire Birds. (*Catal. of Local Lists of British Birds*, 1891, p. 17.)

Anderson (John P.). Book of Brit. Topo., 1881. Merionethshire, p. 354.

Gough (Richard). Brit. Topo., 1780. Merionethshire, vol. ii. p. 533.

HARLECH.

Wynne (W. W. E.). Documents relating to the Town and Castle of Harlech. (*Archæol. Cambrensis*, vol. i. pp. 246–267; vol. iii. pp. 49–55. 1846–48.)

MIDDLESEX.

[Entries under London should also be consulted.]

Middlesex County Records. Sessions' Rolls, 3 Edw. VII.—4 Jas. II. Edited by J. Cordy Jeaffreson. Index by A. T. Watson. 4 vols. Middlesex County Records Soc. 1886–1892.

Middlesex County Records. Calendar of the Sessions Books, 1689 to 1709. By W. J. Hardy. Index by M. D. Brakspear. London, 1905.

County Records, 1549, etc., at the Guildhall, Westminster. (*Local Records Comm. Rep.*, 1902, App. III. p. 22.)

The Middlesex County Records. (A description of the Records at the Guildhall, Westminster, the County Offices of Middlesex.) (*The Home Counties Mag.*, vol. v. pp. 307–309. 1903.)

Hist. MSS. Comm. Reports, see *ante* London.

List of Middlesex Municipal Records Printed. (*Notes & Queries*, Ser. 11, vol. v. p. 74. 1912.)

Registry of Deeds for the County of Middlesex. (Amalgamated by 54 and 55 Vict. c. 64, with the Land Registry, established in 1875.) See S. R. Scargill-Bird, 'Guide to Documents in the Public Record Office,' 1908, p. 24.

Descriptive Catal. of 'The Jackson Collection' at the Sheffield Public Library, compiled by T. Walter Hall and A. H. Thomas. 1914. **Middlesex items,** pp. 248–250.

A Quarterly Biblio. of Middlesex and Hertfordshire. (*Midd. & Herts. Notes & Queries*, vols. i.–iv. *passim*, 1895–98; *The Home Counties Mag.*, vol. i. pp. 82–83. 1899.)

Gross (Charles). Biblio. of Brit. Municipal Hist. (*Harvard Hist. Studies*, vol. v. 1897. **Middlesex items,** pp. 286–325.)

Dove (Patrick Edward). Domesday Studies. 1891. Domesday Biblio. of Middlesex, vol. ii. p. 683.

Davenport (Frances G.). List of Printed Materials for Manorial Hist. 1894. Biblio. Note on Middlesex Manorial Hist. p. 51.

Macklin (Herbert Walter). Monumental Brasses. London: Geo. Allen & Co., 1913. Biblio. Note on Middlesex Brasses, with a List, pp. 144, 168–169.

Catal. of the MS. Maps, Charts and Plans, and of the Topographical Drawings in the British Museum. 1844. **Middlesex,** vol. ii. pp. 1–52.

MIDDLESEX (continued).

A List of Private Acts relating to the County of Middlesex. Stevens & Sons, London, *circa* 1912.

Trimen (Henry) and Dyer (W. T. Thiselton). Flora of Middlesex. 1869. Biblio. pp. 3–10.

Trimen (Henry). Botanical Biblio. of the British Counties. Middlesex. (*Journ. of Botany*, vol. xii. p. 109. 1874.)

Boulger (G. S.). Botanical Biblio. of the South-Eastern Counties. Middlesex. (*South-Eastern Union of Scientific Societies. Trans.*, vol. iv. p. 49. 1899.)

Christy (Miller). Biblio. Note on Middlesex Birds. (*The Zoologist*, Ser. 3, vol. xiv. p. 255. 1890; and reprinted in pamph., 1891, p. 17.)

Anderson (John P.). Book of Brit. Topo., 1881. Middlesex, pp. 173–177.

Gatfield (George). Guide to Heraldry. 1892. Middlesex, pp. 162–164.

Sims (Richard). Manual. 1861. Middlesex, pp. 169, 214–215, 236.

Upcott (William). English Topo., 1818. Middlesex, vol. ii. pp. 581–604, 1471–1472.

Smith (Alfred Russell). Catal. of Topo. Tracts, etc. 1878. Middlesex, pp. 195–205, 255–260.

Gough (Richard). Brit. Topo., 1780. Middlesex, vol. i. pp. 537–566.

Bandinel (Bulkeley). Catal. of Books bequeathed to Bodleian Lib. by Richard Gough, 1814. Middlesex, pp. 168–175.

Hoare (Sir R. Colt). Catal. of the Stourhead Lib. co. Wilts. 1840. Middlesex, pp. 298–310.

BRENTFORD.

Turner (Fred. Alfred). Brentford: Literary & Hist. Sketches. 1898. Biblio. pp. 44–73.

Calendar to a volume entitled the 'Brentford Journal,' being a Record of the Proceedings at Petty Sessions, held at Brentford. 1651–1714. (The original Journal owned by W. J. Stracey Clitherow, of Boston House, Brentford.)

A Special Collection of Local Literature is at the Brentford Free Public Library.

CHISWICK.

Weitenkampf (Frank). A Biblio. of the Works of William Hogarth and of the Publications relating to them. (*Harvard Univ. Library, Bibliographical Contributions*, vol. ii. no. 37. 1890.)

HARROW.

Cooper (W. Durrant). The Parish Registers of Harrow-on-the-Hill, with special reference to the Families of Bellamy and Page. (*Lond. & Midd. Archæol. Soc. Trans.*, vol. i. pp. 285–298. 1860.)

Murray (David). Biblio. Note on Harrow Museums. ('*Museums*,' Glasgow, 1904, vol. ii. p. 279.)

PINNER.

Hogg (Edward). Pinner Church Records. (*Midd. & Herts. Notes & Queries*, vol. i. pp. 99–100. 1895.)

TWICKENHAM.

Eyton (J. Walter K.). Catal. of complete set of Works privately printed at the Strawberry Hill Press. (*Sale Catal. of his Library of Privately Printed Books*, Sotheby's, 1848, pp. 182–188, 214.)

Lowndes (Wm. Thomas). List of Publications of the Strawberry Hill Press. (*Bibliographer's Manual*, 1864, Appendix, pp. 237–245.)

MIDDLESEX (continued).

Martin (John). The Strawberry Hill Press. (*Biblio. Catal. of Books Privately Printed*, 1834, pp. 487–513.)

Baker (George). Catal. of Books, Poems, Tracts, and small detached Pieces, printed at the Press at Strawberry Hill. 1810. 20 copies only privately printed.

Kirgate (Thomas). The Strawberry Hill Printer, Catal. of his Collection of Books, Prints, etc., with the Supplement, forming 11 Days' Sale. 1810.

Dibdin (Rev. T. F.). Strawberry Hill Press. (*Biblio. Decameron*, 1817, vol. iii. p. 448.)

Murray (David). Biblio. Note on Strawberry Hill Press. ('*Museums*,' Glasgow, 1904, vol. iii. p. 257.)

Havens (M. A.). Horace Walpole and the Strawberry Hill Press, 1757-89. Canton, Pa, 1901.

Dobson (Austin). Horace Walpole, with an Appendix containing a list of Books printed at the Strawberry Hill Press. London, 1910.

Wheatley (Henry B.). The Strawberry Hill Press. (*Bibliographica*, vol. iii. pp. 83–98. 1897.)

MONAGHAN.

Dix (Ernest Reginald McClintock). Ulster Bibliography. Monaghan. (*Ulster Journ. of Archæol.*, vol. vii. pp. 102–108, 137 ; vol. viii. p. 171 ; vol. xi. p. 48. 1901–5.)

——— **List of Books, Pamphlets, and Newspapers, printed in Monaghan, in the Eighteenth Century, 1770–1800.** Dundalk, 1906. Second edition. Dundalk, 1911. (Irish Bibliography, No. IV.)

——— **Printing in Monaghan in the First Half of the 19th century, 1801–1850.** (*Northern Standard*, 17 Aug., 1901 ; 2 May, 1903 ; 9 June, 1906.)

——— **Printing in Monaghan, 1801–1825, with a List.** (*Irish Book-Lover*, vol. iv. pp. 200–202 ; vol. v. pp. 2, 3, 26, 27. 1913.)

O'Hanlon (John). Index of Materials for the Hist. and Topography of the County of Monaghan in the Irish Ordnance Survey Records, and in the Royal Irish Academy. (*Kilkenny & South-East of Irel. Archæol. Soc. Journ.*, vol. viii. p. 24. 1864.)

The Lough Fea Library, by J. S. Crone. (*Irish Book-Lover*, vol. v. pp. 23–25. 1913), and by R. S. Maffett. (*Ibid.* vol. v. pp. 60–61. 1913.) See also 'Library Catalogue at Lough Fea,' by E. P. Shirley. 1872.

Gross (Charles). Biblio. of British Municipal Hist. (*Harvard Hist. Studies*, vol. v. 1897.) Monaghan, p. 340.

Anderson (John P.). Book of Brit. Topo., 1881. Monaghan. p. 440.

Gough (Richard). Brit. Topo., 1780. Monaghan, vol. ii. p. 815.

MONMOUTHSHIRE.

Blackwell (Henry). Biblio. of Local and County Histories relating to Wales and Monmouth. (*Old Welsh Chips*, 1888, pp. 138, 171, 198, 224.)

Haines (W.). Notes on the Biblio. of Monmouthshire. (*The Library*, vol. viii. pp. 239–247. 1896.)

Bradney (Col. J. A.). Rare and Early-Printed Books relating to Monmouthshire. (*Welsh Biblio. Soc. Journ.*, vol. i. pp. 169–180. 1914.)

MONMOUTHSHIRE (continued).

Cardiff Free Libraries. Catal. of Printed Literature in the Welsh Department, by John Ballinger and J. I. Jones. 1898. **Monmouthshire items,** pp. 327–333.

Monmouth Borough Records, at Shire Hall, Monmouth. (*Local Records Comm. Rep.*, 1902, App. III. p. 66.)

List of Monmouth County Records Printed. (*Notes & Queries*, Ser. 11, vol. v. p. 74. 1912.)

Memorandum on the Records of the Crown Lordships or Manors in Wales and Monmouthshire. (*Local Records Comm. Rep.*, 1914, vol. ii. pt. 2, pp. 259–260.)

Gross (Charles). Biblio. of Brit. Municipal Hist. (*Harvard Hist. Studies*, vol. v. 1897.) Monmouthshire entries, p. 340.

James (Lemuel J. Hopkin). The Llanover Manuscripts. (*Welsh Biblio. Soc. Journ.*, vol. i. pp. 180–183. 1914.)

List of Monmouthshire Illustrations in the 'Archæologia Cambrensis,' 1884-1900. See Index by F. Green, 1902, p. 106.

Haines (W.). Notes on Charles Heath, of Monmouth, Author, Printer, Publisher, *circa* 1788–1831. (*Welsh Biblio. Soc. Journ.*, vol. i. pp. 145–151. 1913.)

Lyell (Arthur H.). Biblio. List of Romano-British Remains, 1912. **Caerleon and Caerwent,** pp. 86–88.

Lee (John Edward). Isca Silurum, or an Illustrated Catal. of the Museum of Antiquities at Caerleon. 1862. **Supplement,** 1868.

Murray (David). 'Museums.' Glasgow, 1904. Biblio. Note on the Caerleon Museum, vol. ii. p. 153.

Macklin (Herbert Walter). Monumental Brasses. London: Geo. Allen & Co., 1913. Biblio. Note on Monmouthshire Brasses, with a List, p. 169.

Martin (John). The Private Press at Raglan Castle. (*Biblio. Catal. of Books Privately Printed*, 1854, p. xvi.)

Trimen (Henry). Botanical Biblio. of the British Counties. Monmouthshire. (*Journ. of Botany*, vol. xii. p. 155. 1874.)

Anderson (John P.). Book of Brit. Topo., 1881. Monmouthshire, pp. 213–216.

Gatfield (George). Guide to Heraldry. 1892. Monmouthshire, p. 164.

Upcott (William). English Topo., 1818. Monmouthshire, vol. ii. pp. 931–942.

Gough (Richard). Brit. Topo., 1780. Monmouthshire, vol. i. pp. 787–792.

Bandinel (Bulkeley). Catal. of Books bequeathed to Bodleian Lib. by Richard Gough, 1814. Monmouthshire, pp. 233–234.

MONTGOMERYSHIRE.

Hist. MSS. Comm. Reports. Montgomeryshire Collections.
Powis, Earl of, at Powis Castle, Welshpool. 10th Rep. p. 18 and App. IV. pp. 378–399. Welsh MSS. vol. ii. pt. I.

County Records, at Town Hall and at Powysland Museum, Welshpool. (*Local Records Comm. Rep.*, 1902, App. III. p. 28.)

Records in Public and Private Custody. (*Ibid.* p. 132.)

Montgomeryshire Records. Extracts from the Reports of the Deputy Keeper of the Records, as to the arrangement and removal of Montgomeryshire Records from Welshpool, Chester, and elsewhere, including the Reports of Thomas Morgan, William Henry Black, and others, with Summaries or Digests of Exchequer Depositions, Inquisitions Post Mortem, Lay Subsidies, etc. Transcribed by Edward Rowley Morris. (*Collections Hist. & Archæol. relating to Mont.*, vol. xxix.–xxxvii. 1895–1913.)

MONTGOMERYSHIRE (continued).

Hancock (Thomas W.). Parish Registers in Montgomeryshire, with lists. (*Ibid.* vol. xv. pp. 235–248. 1882.)

Thomas (Ven. David Richard). A Terrier of the Registers, Church Plate, and Documents in the Archdeaconry of Montgomery. (*Ibid.* vol. xxxiv. pp. 213–221. 1906.)

Index to the Collections Historical and Archæological relating to Montgomeryshire, vol. i.–xxviii. 1868–94. The Powys-Land Club. London, 1895.

Classified List of Articles, presented to the Powys-land Museum and Library, with the names of the donors. (*Collections Hist. & Archæol. relating to Mont.*, vol. vii. pp. xli.–lxxvi. 1874.) Additional lists issued from time to time.

Williams (Richard). Materials for a 'Topographicon' of Montgomeryshire. (An alphabetical List of Places mentioned in Ancient Welsh Authors, with references to the works in which they occur.) (*Collections Hist. & Archæol. relating to Mont.*, vol. ii. pp. 173–184, 353–366; vol. iii. pp. 215–230; vol. iv. pp. 185–200; vol. v. pp. 89–108. 1869–72.)

Portraits connected with Montgomeryshire, at Wynnstay, Llangedwyn, Peniarth, Powis Castle, and at other places. A List. (*Ibid.* vol. v. pp. 149–152; vol. vi. pp. 147–154, 341–346. 1872–73.)

Montgomeryshire Newspapers, Biblio. Notes, by R. Williams and A. R. (*Ibid.* vol. v. pp. 393–394; vol. x. pp. 426–428. 1872, 1877.)

Williams (Richard). Mercator's and Speed's Maps and Descriptions of Montgomeryshire. (*Ibid.* vol. xvii. pp. 305–310. 1884.)

Lyell (Arthur H.). Biblio. List of Romano-British Remains. 1912. Montgomeryshire, p. 146.

Trimen (Henry). Botanical Biblio. of the British Counties. Montgomeryshire. (*Journ. of Botany*, vol. xii. p. 157. 1874.)

Anderson (John P.). Book of Brit. Topo., 1881. Montgomeryshire, p. 351.
Gough (Richard). Brit. Topo., 1780. Montgomeryshire, vol. ii. p. 534.
Bandinel (Bulkeley). Catal. of Books bequeathed to Bodleian Lib. by Richard Gough, 1814. Montgomeryshire, p. 337.

NEWTOWN.

A Biblio. of Robert Owen, the Socialist, 1771–1858. Preface by A. J. H. The Welsh Biblio. Soc. and The National Library of Wales. Aberystwyth, 1914.

Bibliographies of Robert Owen are also contained in the Lives by Podmore, Davies, and Hutchins, in the Cardiff Pub. Lib. Journ., vol. iii. and in Lockwood's 'New Harmony.'

WELSHPOOL.

Borough Records, 1340, etc., at Town Clerk's Office, Welshpool. (*Local Records Comm. Rep.*, 1902, App. III. p. 72.)

Howell (Abraham). Printed Statement of the Result of an Examination and Inquiry respecting the Books, etc., relating to the Borough of Pool, April, 1865.

Catal. of the Registers in the Parish Chest, Welshpool, in the year 1819. (*Collections Hist. & Archæol. relating to Mont.*, vol. xv. pp. 310–311. 1882.)

An article on the Welshpool Registers, with slight extracts, by Mary Newill Owen, is in vol. 36 of the same 'Collections.'

MORAY. [*See* Elgin or Moray.]

MUNSTER.

[The Province of Munster consists of the Counties of Clare, Cork, Kerry, Limerick, and Waterford, which should also be consulted.]

Hist. MSS. Comm. Report. Munster Collection.
The Geraldine Earls of Desmond.
(Memoirs) ... ... 3rd Rep. p. xxvi. and App. p. 431.

The Early Irish MSS. of Munster. (*Cork Hist. & Archæol. Journ.*, Ser. 2, vol. xiv. pp. 83–92. 1908.)

O'Hanlon (John). Index of Materials for the Hist. & Topography of Munster in the Irish Ordnance Survey Records, and in the Royal Irish Academy. (*Kilkenny & South-East of Irel. Archæol. Soc. Journ.*, vol. viii. p. 418. 1866.)

The Poets and Poetry of Munster. A Selection of Irish Songs by the Poets of the last Century, with Poetical Translations by James Clarence Mangan. With Biographical Sketches of the Authors. Edited by C. P. Meehan. Third edition. Dublin, n.d.

NAIRNSHIRE.

Hist. MSS. Comm. Report. Nairnshire Collection.
Cawdor, Earl, at Cawdor Castle ... 2nd Rep. pp. viii. xvii. and App. pp. 31, 193.

Rampini (Charles). A Hist. of Moray and Nairn. The County Histories of Scotland, 1897. List of Books relating to Moray and Nairn, pp. 417–429.

Livingstone (Matthew). Guide to the Public Records of Scotland. 1905. Nairnshire, p. 176.

Turnbull (William B.). Scottish Parochial Registers. 1849. List of Nairnshire Registers, p. 111.

Anderson (Peter John). Inventories of Ecclesiastical Records of North-Eastern Scotland. Presbytery of Nairn, pp. 283–287. New Spalding Club, vol. vi. Miscellany, vol. i. 1890.

Gross (Charles). Biblio. of Brit. Municipal Hist. (*Harvard Hist. Studies*, vol. v. 1897. Nairnshire, p. 133.)

Anderson (John P.). Book of Brit. Topo., 1881. Nairnshire, pp. 401-402.
Gough (Richard). Brit. Topo., 1780. Nairnshire, vol. ii. p. 705.

NORFOLK.

RYE (WALTER). AN INDEX TO NORFOLK TOPOGRAPHY. Index Soc. Pubns., vol. x. London, 1881.

A Valuable Account of Collections and Collectors relating to the County, pp. viii.–xxix.

Catal. of the L'Estrange Papers, pp. xvii.–xxii. Among Collections Indexed in the Work are the Kerrich MSS. in the Brit. Mus., the Le Neve Collections in the Bodleian Lib. and in the Brit. Mus., and Tanner's Collections.

—— **An Index to Norfolk Pedigrees and Continuation of Index to Norfolk Topography.** Norwich, 1896.

—— **An Index Rerum to Norfolk Antiquities.** Norwich, 1899. App. I. Reprint of 'Fifty Norfolk MSS.,' with descriptions of Fifty Additions, pp. 91–100.

NORFOLK (*continued*).

Rye (**Walter**). **A Short Calendar of the Topographical and Genealogical Books and MSS. in the Free Library at Norwich.** (*The Norfolk Antiq. Miscellany*, Ser. 2, pt. 2, pp. 10–54. 1907.) Also issued as 'A Catal. of the Topographical and Antiquarian Portions of the Free Library at Norwich,' 1908.

——— **Catal. of Local Biographies.** 1908.

——— **Catal. of Portraits referring to Norfolk and Norwich Men, in the Free Lib. at Norwich.** 1908.

List of Publications, Papers, Indexes, and Contributions to various Periodicals, etc., 1866 to 1910, by Walter Rye. See Rye's 'Calendar of Norwich Deeds Enrolled, etc.,' 1910, pp. 161–166.

Bibliotheca Norfolciensis. A Catal. of the Writings of Norfolk Men and of Works relating to the County of Norfolk, in the Library of J. J. Colman, at Carrow Abbey, Norwich (**now at Crown Point**). Compiled by John Quinton. Norwich, 1896. List of Maps, pp. 318–319.

Woodward (**Samuel**). **The Norfolk Topographer's Manual: being a Catal. of the Books and Engravings hitherto published in relation to the County:** by the late Samuel Woodward; the whole revised and edited by W. C. Ewing. London, 1842. List of Directories, pp. 5–6, 36–37; Maps, pp. 23–24.

Appendix I. List of Original Drawings, Engravings, Etchings and Deeds, etc., inserted in a copy of Blomefield's Hist. of Norfolk, in the Library of Dawson Turner.

" II. Short Notices of such of the Contents of the Harleian, Cottonian, Lansdowne, and other MSS. in the Brit. Museum as refer to Norfolk.

" III. List of the Chartularies as far as they are known to exist, of Norfolk Monasteries.

" IV. List of Drawings, etc., in the Brit. Museum relating to Norfolk.

Catal. of Engravings, Etchings, and Original Drawings and Deeds, etc., collected towards the Illustration of the Topography of Norfolk, and inserted in a copy of Blomefield's Hist. of that County, in the Library of Dawson Turner, at Yarmouth. 1841. Privately Printed. The work was also issued as Appendix I. to 'The Norfolk Topographer's Manual,' see above.

Catal. of the Principal Part of the Library of Dawson Turner, removed from Yarmouth. Sold by Auction by Sotheby's, London, March 7, and five following days, and March 17, and six following days. 1853.

Catal. of the Remaining Portion of the Library of Dawson Turner. Sold by Auction by Puttick & Simpson, London, May 16, & seven following days, 1859.

Catal. of the Manuscript Library of Dawson Turner, formerly of Yarmouth, comprising upwards of 40,000 Autograph Letters, the unique copy of Blomefield's Hist. of Norfolk, containing about 7000 Drawings, Engravings, etc. Sold by auction by Puttick and Simpson, London, June 6, & four following days, 1859. A Description of the MS. Collection is at pp. i.–xix., and one of Blomefield's 'Norfolk,' at pp. 289–294 of the Catalogue.

Blomefield (**Francis**). **An Essay towards a Topographical Hist. of Norfolk.** 11 vols. 1805–10. Appended to a copy of the above in the MS. Department at the Brit. Museum are 39 vols. containing Drawings, Engravings, Portraits, etc., collected and annotated by Dawson Turner, 1810–57, with a Catal. in 2 vols. 1835 & 1848. General Indexes are in vol. xi. of the original work.

Index Nominum; being an Index of Christian and Surnames (**with Arms**) **mentioned in Blomefield's Hist. of Norfolk,** by John Nurse Chadwick. King's Lynn, 1862.

An Index to the Names of the Manors mentioned in Blomefield's Norfolk. (Octavo edn.), by Walter Rye. (*Norf. Antiq. Misc.*, vol. ii. pp. 285–304. 1883.)

NORFOLK (continued).

A General Index to the first Ten Volumes of Norfolk Archæology, 1847-1888, with an Index to the Illustrations. Edited by C. R. Manning. Norfolk & Norwich Archæological Soc. Norwich, 1891.

Rye (Walter). The Norfolk and Norwich Archæol. Society. (*Norf. Antiq. Misc.*, Ser. 2, vol. i. pt. 1, pp. 167–172. 1906.)

Index to the Transactions of the Norfolk & Norwich Naturalists' Soc., 1869-1908. (In Trans. vol. viii. pt. 5. 1909.)

Norfolk Annals. A Chronological Record of Remarkable Events in the Nineteenth Century. Vol. 1. 1801-51. Compiled from the files of the 'Norfolk Chronicle,' by Charles Mackie. Norwich, 1901.

Descriptive Catal. of 'The Jackson Collection' at the Sheffield Public Library, compiled by T. Walter Hall and A. H. Thomas. 1914. Norfolk entries, p. 206.

Dove (Patrick Edward). Domesday Studies. 1891. Domesday Biblio. Norfolk, vol. ii. p. 684.

Catal. of Antiquities exhibited at the Annual Meeting of the Archæological Institute at Norwich, 1847. (*Memoirs, etc., of the Archæol. Inst. Norwich*, 1847, pp. xxiii.-lvi.

Catal. of Antiquities found principally in East Anglia, in the Norwich Castle Museum. Edited by Walter Rye. Compiled by Frank Leney. Norwich, 1909. Biblio., pp. ix.-x.

Lyell (Arthur H.). Biblio. List of Romano-British Remains. 1912. **Norfolk,** pp. 88–90.

Allnutt (W. H.). English Provincial Presses. Earliest Printing at Norwich, 1566 ?-1580. (*Bibliographica*, vol. ii. pp. 150-154. 1896.)

Norgate (F.). Anthony de Solemne, the First Printer at Norwich, 1565-1580. (*Notes & Queries*, Ser. 9, vol. vii. pp. 241–242. 1901.)

Biblio. Notes on Anthony Solempne, Printer at Norwich in 1570. (*Norfolk Archæology*, vol. i. p. 20; vol. v. pp. 79–80. 1847, 1859.)

Early Printers and Printing in Norwich. (*Norf. & Norw. Notes & Queries*, vol. i. pp. 34, 61, 305, 308–314. 1898.)

Biblio. Notes on Printing in Norwich, and Private Printing Presses. (*Ibid.* Ser. 2, pp. 194, 216, 221, 231. 1901.)

Biblio. Notes on Early Printers at Norwich. (*The East Anglian*, vol. i. pp. 150, 252, 281, 303. 1861–63.)

Blomefield's Printing Press at Fersfield. (*Norfolk Archæology*, vol. ii. pp. 212–215. 1849.)

Farrell (F. J.). Yarmouth Printing and Printers. Gt. Yarmouth. 1912.

Nall (John Greaves). An Etymological and Comparative Glossary of the Dialect and Provincialisms of East Anglia. London, 1866. Biblio. Notes on East Anglian Writers, pp. 463–473.

Rye (Walter). A Glossary of Words used in East Anglia, founded on that of Forby, with corrections and additions. English Dialect Soc. London, 1895. Biblio. of Books on Dialect of East Anglia, in Preface, pp. viii.-x.

——— **Ballads, Songs, and Rhymes.** (*Songs, Stories, and Sayings of Norfolk.* Norwich, 1897.)

Halliwell (J. O.). The Norfolk Anthology. A Collection of Poems, Ballads, and Rare Tracts relating to the County of Norfolk. Privately printed at Brixton Hill, 1852.

Glyde (John). The Norfolk Garland: A Collection of Ballads and Songs of the People of Norfolk. London, 1872.

NORFOLK (continued).

Smith Collection of Prints, Drawings, Maps, etc., relating to Norfolk and Norwich. Presented to the Norwich Public Library by Walter Rye, with 2 vols. of Indexes. Detailed lists by Walter Rye and Harry Brittain in 'A Rough Catal. of Maps relating to Norwich and Norfolk.' (Norf. Antiq. Miscellany, Ser. 2, pt. 1, pp. 114–142. 1906.)

Biblio. Notes on Old Maps of Norfolk. (*Eastern Counties Collectanea*, vol. i. pp. 9, 16, 47, 186. 1872–73.) See also 'Bibliotheca Norfolciensis,' 1896, for List of Maps at Carrow Abbey, pp. 318–319.

Rye (Walter). An Index to the Localities occurring on the Ordnance Map of Norfolk, and in Bryant's Map of Norfolk. (*Norf. Antiq. Misc.*, vol. ii. pp. 305–319. 1883.) Incorporated in Rye's 'Index to Norfolk Topography.'

Rye (Walter). A Short Calendar of the Feet of Fines for Norfolk. Rich. I. to Rich. III. 2 pts. Norwich, 1885, 1886.

—— **Rough Indexes Nominum to the Feet of Fines for Norfolk, Hen. VIII., Edw. VI., and Mary.** (*Norf. Antiq. Misc.*, vol. ii. pp. 195–216. 1883.)

—— **Calendar of Norfolk Fines Enrolled, 1507-16.** List of Norfolk Names from the Indices in the Public Record Office. (*The East Anglian*, vol. ii. pp. 183–185. 1865.)

An Index to the Visitation of Norfolk, 1664, with an Introduction by C. H. Athill, edited by C. H. E. White. Reprinted from 'East Anglian Notes and Queries.' Ipswich, 1885.

Le Strange (Hamon). Norfolk Official Lists, from the Earliest Period to the Present Day. Norwich, 1890. Biblio. Notes on Norfolk Archives in Introduction.

Macklin (Herbert Walter). Monumental Brasses. London: Geo. Allen & Co., 1913. Biblio. Note on Norfolk Brasses, with a List, pp. 141, 169–173.

Gross (Charles). Biblio. of Brit. Municipal Hist. (*Harvard Hist. Studies*, vol. v. 1897.) Norfolk, p. 100. Norwich, pp. 350–354. King's Lynn (Lynn Regis), pp. 330–332. Yarmouth, pp. 424–426.

Davenport (Frances G.). List of Printed Materials for Manorial Hist. 1894. Biblio. Note on Norfolk Manorial Hist., pp. 51–52.

List of Norfolk Municipal Records Printed. (*Notes & Queries*, Ser. 11, vol. v. p. 298. 1912.)

Special Topographical Collections for Norfolk are in the Norwich Public Library and the Yarmouth Public Library.

Hist. MSS. Comm. Reports. Norfolk Collections.

Bedingfeld, Sir Henry, at Oxburgh ...	3rd Rep. p. xvi. and App. pp. 237–240.
Buxton, Miss, of Shadwell Court ...	16th Rep. pp. 105–107; Various Collections, vol. ii. pp. 227–288.
Ffolkes, Sir W. H. B., at Hillington Hall	3rd Rep. p. xvi. and App. pp. 247–248.
Frere, Mr. G. E., of Roydon Hall ...	7th Rep. p. xiv. and App. pp. 518–537.
Gurney, Mr. J. H., at Keswick Hall ...	12th Rep. p. 39, and App. IX. pp. 116–164.
Hare, Sir Thomas, at Stow Hall ...	3rd Rep. p. xvi. and App. pp. 250–252.
Ketton, Mr. R. W., at Felbrigg Hall ...	12th Rep. p. 40, and App. IX. pp. 179–226.
Leicester, Earl of, at Holkham ...	9th Rep. pp. xvi.–xx. and App. II. pp. 340–375; 17th Rep. pp. 126–129; Various Collections, vol. iv. pp. 313–325.

NORFOLK (continued).

Hist. MSS. Comm. Reports. Norfolk Collections (*Continued*)

le Strange, Mr. Hamon S., at Hunstanton Hall	3rd Rep. p. xvii. and App. pp. 271–274; 11th Rep. p. 23, and App. VII. pp. 93–118.
Lothian, Marquess of, at Blickling Hall	1st Rep. pp. x., xii. and App. pp. 14, 116; 17th Rep. pp. 45–51; and a vol. 1905.
Manning, Rev. C. R., Rector of Diss...	10th Rep. p. 26, and App. IV. pp. 458–463.
Rye, Mr. Walter (Gawdy Papers) ...	10th Rep. p. 13, and App. II.
Stafford, Lord, at Cossey Hall... ...	10th Rep. p. 25, and App. IV. pp. 152–168.
Townshend, Marquess, at Raynham Hall	11th Rep. pp. 13–19, and App. IV.
Hunstanton Parish	9th Rep. App. I. p. 358.
King's Lynn Corporation	11th Rep. pp. 33–36, and App. III. pp. 145–247.
Norwich, Bishop's Registry	1st Rep. App. pp. 86, 87.
——— Corporation	1st Rep. App. pp. 102–104.
——— Dean & Chapter of	1st Rep. App. pp. 87–89.
Yarmouth, Great, Corporation... ...	9th Rep. p. xv. and App. I. pp. 299–324.

County Records, 1532, etc., with MS. Indexes, at the Shirehouse, Norwich. (*Local Records Comm. Rep.*, 1902, App. III. p. 26.)

Norfolk Records, Vol. I., being a Collection of Record-References derived from the Official MS. Indexes preserved in the Public Record Office. Edited by Walford D. Selby. Norf. & Norw. Archæol. Soc. Norwich, 1886.

——— **Vol. II., being an Index to Four Series of Norfolk Inquisitions. the Tower Series, the Chancery or Rolls Series, the Exchequer Series, the Wards and Liveries, or Court of Wards Series.** Edited by Walter Rye. Norf. & Norw. Archæol. Soc. Norwich, 1892.

A Short Catal. of the Records of the County of Norfolk preserved in the Shirehall, Norwich, 1904.

Rye (**Walter**). **A Catal. of Fifty of the Norfolk MSS. in the Library of Walter Rye, at Winchester House, Putney.** Privately printed, 1889. This was reprinted with descriptions of Fifty additional MSS., in 'An Index Rerum to Norfolk Antiquities,' 1899, pp. 91–100, by Walter Rye, and also in his 'Calendar of Norwich Deeds Enrolled,' 1910, pp. 167–172.

——— **Norfolk Genealogy and Heraldry.** Notes on Collections of Norfolk MSS. (*Norf. Antiq. Misc.*, vol. iii. pp. 168–176. 1887.)

——— **The Unpublished Material for a Hist. of the County of Norfolk.** (*Archæol. Journ.*, vol. xlvii. pp. 164–169. 1890.)

——— **MSS. relating to Norfolk in the Harleian and Cottonian Libraries.** (*The East Anglian*, vol. ii. pp. 330–331, 336–338. 1866.)

——— **MSS. in the Public Record Office relating to Norfolk.** (*Norfolk Archæology*, vol. vii. pp. 136–152. 1872.)

——— **Index Nominum to Norfolk Deeds Enrolled in the Common Pleas, 1504–1629,** from the Indices in the Public Record Office. (*The East Anglian*, vol. ii. pp. 251–255. 1865.)

Hart (**Rev. Richard**). **Analysis of the Harleian MS. Cod. 4756** (**bound up with Cod. 1101 and Cod. 5823**) **and a Part of the Index of Cod. 1109.** (*Norf. Archæology*, vol. iii. pp. 40–51; vol. iv. pp. 292–295. 1852, 1855.)

Tingey (**J. C.**). **A Calendar of Deeds enrolled within the County of Norfolk.** (*Ibid.* vol. xiii. pp. 33–92, 125–191, 241–292. 1898.)

NORFOLK (continued).

MS. Catal. of Norfolk Charters in the possession of F. H. Gough-Calthorpe, at Elvetham, Hants., with Index of Persons and Places, *circa* 1880.

Neve (Peter Le) and others. **Collections for a Hist. of Norfolk, in the Brit. Museum.** 5 vols. Add. MSS. 8839–8843. Some of Le Neve's MSS. are in the Lib. of Walter Rye. Other vols. are among the Gough MSS. in the Bodleian Library. For an account of the Collections, see Rye's 'Index of Norfolk Topography.' Preface, p. x., and also a note in 'Memoirs of the Life of Thomas Martin, of Palgrave,' in 'Norfolk Archæology,' vol. xv. p. 254. 1904.

Calendar of Correpondence and Documents relating to the Family of Oliver Le Neve, of Witchingham, Norfolk, 1675-1743, by the late Francis Rye. Edited with Introduction by Walter Rye. Norwich, 1895. Biblio. Notes on Peter Le Neve, Preface, p. xvi.

Suckling's Collections for Norfolk, 1821-1839, in the Brit. Museum. Add. MSS. 18476, 18477, 18479–18482. Index, Add. MS. 18491.

Collectanea Thomæ Gibbonsii, Arm., Historiam Familiarum tam Norfolciensium quam Suffolciensium illustrantia. Brit. Mus. Harl. MSS. 970–972.

Upcott's Topographical Collections for Norfolk, in the Brit. Museum. Add. MS. 15925.

Powell's Topographical Collections for Norfolk, in the Brit. Museum. Add. MS. 17462.

Lysons (Rev. S.). Collections for Norfolk, in the Brit. Museum. Add. MS. 9459.

Kempe's Heraldical & Historical Collections relating to Norfolk, in the Brit. Museum. Harl. MS. 901.

Collections for a Hist. of Norfolk, probably by the Rev. Charles Parkin, in the Brit. Museum. Add. MS. 8844.

List of the MS. Collections made by Anthony Norris, towards the illustration of the Topography of Norfolk. Privately Printed, 1842. The Norris MSS. are in the Library of Walter Rye. See the List in Rye's 'Catal. of Fifty Norfolk MSS.' 1889; reprinted in his 'Index Rerum to Norfolk Antiquities,' 1899, and also in his 'Calendar of Norwich Deeds Enrolled,' 1910.

Bibliotheca Martiniana. Catal. of Library of the late Antiquary, Thomas Martin, of Palgrave, issued by Martin Booth and John Berry. A reprint of the Entries relating to Norfolk. (*Norf. Antiq. Misc.*, vol. iii. pp. 394–401. 1887.)

Memoirs of the Life of Thomas Martin, of Palgrave, in Suffolk, with an Account of the disposal and disposition of his large and valuable Collections of MSS., Printed Books, Papers, Pictures, etc., by John Fenn. 1784. (*Norfolk Archæology*, vol. xv. pp. 233–266. 1904.)

Tom Martin's MSS. List of MSS. formerly belonging to Tom Martin, the Palgrave Antiquary. (*East Anglian Miscellany*, 1914, pp. 49–50.) Many of Martin's MSS. are in the Lib. of Walter Rye.

A Catal. of the Library of John Ives (a writer on Norfolk Antiquities) sold by Baker & Leigh, London. Mar. 3–10, 1777. (Includes important MSS. and Books relating to Norfolk.)

Cockerell (Sydney C.). The Gorleston Psalter: A MS. of the beginning of the 14th cent. in the Library of C. W. D. Perrins, described in relation to other East Anglian Books of the period. London, 1907.

NORFOLK (continued).

Report on the Records of the District Registry of the High Court of Justice and County Court Registry in Norwich, and on the District Registries of the Courts of Survey and Wreck for Norfolk. (*Local Records Comm. Rep.*, 1914, vol. ii. pt. 2, pp. 140–141.)

Trimen (Henry). Botanical Biblio. of the British Counties. Norfolk. (*Journ. of Botany*, vol. xii. p. 110. 1874.)

A Flora of Norfolk, by Members of the Norf. and Norwich Naturalists' Soc. Edited by W. A. Nicholson. London, 1914. List of Authorities, pp. 41–43.

Harrison (W. Jerome). A Biblio. of Norfolk Glaciology, including the Cromer Cliffs, with the forest-bed series. Reprinted from the 'Glacialists' Mag.' 1897.

Christy (Miller). Biblio. Note on Norfolk Birds. (*The Zoologist*, Ser. 3, vol. xiv. p. 256, 1890; and reprinted in pamph., 1891, p. 18.) **Mammals.** (*The Zoologist*, Ser. 3, vol. xvii. pp. 181–182. 1893.) **Reptiles.** (*Ibid.* p. 245. 1893.) **Fishes.** (*Ibid.* p. 256. 1893.)

Anderson (John P.). Book of Brit. Topo., 1881. Norfolk, pp. 216–224.
Gatfield (George). Guide to Heraldry. 1892. Norfolk, pp. 161–167.
Sims (Richard). Manual. 1861. Norfolk, pp. 170, 215–216, 237.
Upcott (William). English Topo., 1818. Norfolk, vol. ii. pp. 943–1002, 1482–1488.
Smith (Alfred Russell). Catal. of Topo. Tracts, etc., 1878. Norfolk, pp. 259–272.
Gough (Richard). Brit. Topo., 1780. Norfolk, vol. ii. pp. 1–36.
Bandinel (Bulkeley). Catal. of Books bequeathed to Bodleian Lib. by Richard Gough, 1814. Norfolk, pp. 235–242.

NORWICH.

Rye (Walter). An Attempt at a General Index to the Topography of the City of Norwich. (*Norfolk Antiq. Miscellany*, vol. i. pp. 437–460. 1877.)

—— **Works relating to the Hist. and Topography of Norwich.** (*Catal. of the Topographical & Antiquarian Portions of the Free Lib. at Norwich*, 1908, pp. 31–42.)

Stephen (George A.). Guide to the Study of Norwich; a select Biblio. of the principal Books, Pamphlets, and Articles on Norwich in the Norwich Public Library, 1914. The Norwich Public Library has a large Local Collection of Books, Pamphlets, Engravings and Maps.

Borough Records, from about 1160, etc., with Printed Catalogue, at the Castle Museum, Norwich. (*Local Records Comm. Rep.*, 1902, App. III. p. 36.)

'Repertory.' A Catal. of the Muniments in the City Record Room, made in 1848 by Goddard Johnson. (A MS. in the possession of the Corp. of Norwich.)

Hudson (William) and Tingey (J. C.). Revised Catal. of the Records of the City of Norwich. 1898. Called 'revised' because in 1848 a MS. Catal. was compiled. Indexes to this Catal., by Walter Rye, are printed in his 'Calendar of Norwich Deeds Enrolled, etc.' 1898, pp. 151–159. Abstracts of the principal Deeds, by Hudson and Tingey, were published under the title, 'The Records of the City of Norwich,' 2 vols. in 1906 & 1910.

Borough Records, see Hist. MSS. Comm. Reports, p. 177.

Blomefield (Francis). Original Collections for the Hist. of Norwich, arranged according to districts, with original Deeds dating from Edw. III. Sold by Sotheby's, Apr. 27–May 2, 1903. See 'Catal. of MSS. of Sir Thomas Phillipps, of Middle Hill, Worcs.,' p. 110. Included in the Sale were other Norfolk Documents from the Collections of Sir John Fenn, Peter Le Neve, Francis Blomefield, and Thomas Martin.

NORFOLK (continued).

Rye (Walter). Calendar of Norwich Deeds Enrolled, etc., 1377-1504. Norwich, 1910. Includes 'Indexes to the Revised Catal. of the Records of the City of Norwich,' by Hudson and Tingey, 1898, pp. 151–159; 'List of Publications, Papers, etc., by Walter Rye, 1866 to 1910,' with Lists of his MS. Indexes to various MSS. and Printed Works and to the Norris MSS., pp. 161–165, and a 'List of MSS. left by Walter Rye in his Will to the Corporation of Norwich,' pp. 167–172.

——— **A Short Calendar of the Deeds relating to Norwich enrolled in the Court Rolls of that City; 1285-1306.** Norf. & Norw. Archæol. Soc. Norwich. 1903.

——— **Norwich Deeds enrolled in the Court Rolls of that City. A Calendar of 1307-1341.** Norf. & Norw. Archæol. Soc. Norwich, 1915.

——— **Catal. of Norwich Corporation Documents.** 1908.

Enfield (William). Collection relating to Norwich purchased by J. J. Colman in 1878. See Preface to 'Bibliotheca Norfolciensis,' 1896.

Arderon's Collections for Norwich 1745-60, in the Brit. Museum. Add. MS. 27966. A Biog. Note on William Arderon and his MSS. in 'The East Anglian,' vol. ii. pp. 239, 260. 1865.

Norwich Cathedral Records, 13th cent., etc., with MS. Index, at Norwich. (*Local Records Comm. Rep.*, 1902, App. III. p. 112.)

Norwich Archdeaconry Records, 1584, etc., with MS. Indexes, at Registrar's Office, Norwich. (*Ibid.* App. III. p. 124.)

Botfield (Beriah). Notes on the Cathedral Libraries of England. 1849. **Norwich,** pp. 330-347.

List of Norwich Municipal Records Printed. (*Notes & Queries*, Ser. 11, vol. v. p. 298. 1912.)

Hudson (William). Leet Jurisdiction in the City of Norwich during the XIIIth. and XIVth. centuries. Selden Society, vol. v. London, 1892. Local MSS. and Books referred to, mostly in the possession of the Corporation of Norwich, p. lxxxiv.

Murray (David). List of Catalogues, etc., relating to Norwich Museums. ('*Museums*,' Glasgow, 1904, vol. iii. p. 57.)

Botfield (Beriah). Notes on the Public Library of Norwich, and the Library at Blickling Hall. Philobiblon Soc. (*Biblio. & Hist. Miscellanies*, vol. i. no. 22. 1854.)

Euren (A. D.). Books and Bookmen of Norwich. (*Book-Auction Records*, vol. x. pt. 2, pp. xxi.–xxix. 1913.)

Bensly (W. T.). Early Maps of Norwich. (*The Streets & Lanes of the City of Norwich*, by John Kirkpatrick, edited by William Hudson.) Norf. & Norw. Archæol. Soc. 1889.

A Collection of Lantern Slides of Old Norwich Engravings and Etchings formed by Jabez Algar is in the Library of the Society.

Catal. of the Pictures, Drawings, Etchings, etc. (Norfolk and Norwich Painters and Scenery) in the Picture Gallery of the Norwich Castle Museum. 4th edn. Norwich, 1909.

Catal. of the Portraits and Paintings (Norfolk & Norwich People) in St. Andrew's Hall, and other Public Buildings. Norwich, 1905.

EAST DEREHAM.

Wise (Thomas James). A Biblio. of the Writings in prose and verse of George Henry Borrow (born at East Dereham, 1803). Privately printed. London, 1914.

Thomas (Philip Edward). George Borrow; the Man and his Books. London, 1912. Biblio., pp. 323–333.

NORFOLK (*continued*).

GREAT YARMOUTH.

Borough Records, from reign of King John, at the Town Hall, Gt. Yarmouth. (*Local Records Comm. Rep.*, 1902, App. III. p. 34.)

Corporation Records, see Hist. MSS. Comm. Reports, p. 177.

Harrod (Henry). Repertory of Deeds and Documents relating to the Borough of Great Yarmouth. 1855.

——— **Notes on the Records of the Corporation of Great Yarmouth.** (*Norfolk Archæology*, vol. iv. pp. 239–266. 1855.)

Teniswood (C. G. H.). Charters relating to the government of Great Yarmouth. (*Brit. Archæol. Assoc. Journ.*, vol. xxxvi. pp. 273-290. 1880.)

Nall (John Greaves). Biblio. Notes on Corbridge's and Buck's Old Views of Yarmouth, in '*Glossary of the Dialect of East Anglia,*' see *ante*, p. 175.

Collection relating to Gt. Yarmouth in the Brit. Museum, made by Dawson Turner, of Pamphlets, Broadsides, etc., published chiefly during 1830–62. 9 vols. Yarmouth, 1732-1862.

HUNSTANTON.

Parish Records, see Hist. MSS. Comm. Reports, p. 177.

KING'S LYNN (LYNN REGIS).

Corporation Records, see Hist. MSS. Comm. Reports, p. 177.

Harrod (Henry). Report on the Deeds and Records of the Borough of King's Lynn. 1874.

Bulwer (James). Notice of a MS. Volume among the Records of the Corporation of Lynn. (*Norfolk Archæology*, vol. vi. pp. 217–251. 1864.)

List of King's Lynn Municipal Records Printed. (*Notes & Queries*, Ser. 11, vol. v. p. 73. 1912.)

The Charters of Lynn Regis. (*The Pedigree Register*, vol. ii. pp. 97–100. 1911.)

MERTON.

Crabbe (George). Report on the Muniments at Merton Hall. (*Norfolk Antiq. Miscellany*, vol. ii. pp. 553–629; vol. iii. pp. 1–114, 1883, 1887.)

THETFORD.

Hunt (A. Leigh). Analysis of Ancient Maps and Plans of Ancient Thetford. (*The Capital of the Ancient Kingdom of East Anglia.* 1870, pp. 462–469.)

BROADS. (Norfolk)

Rye (Walter). A Biblio. of the Broads. (*Songs, Stories, and Sayings of Norfolk*, 1897. App. II. pp. 154–160.)

——— **List of Books on the Broads.** (*A Catal. of the Topog. and Antiq. Portions of the Free Lib. at Norwich*, 1908, pp. 12–13.)

NORTHAMPTONSHIRE.

TAYLOR (JOHN). BIBLIOTHECA NORTHANTONENSIS: A BIBLIOGRAPHICAL ACCOUNT OF WHAT HAS BEEN WRITTEN, OR PRINTED, RELATING TO THE HISTORY, TOPOGRAPHY, ANTIQUITIES, FAMILY HISTORY, CUSTOMS, ETC., OF NORTHAMPTONSHIRE, INCLUDING A LIST OF WORTHIES AND AUTHORS, AND THEIR WORKS. Northampton, *circa* 1869.

The following is a description by John Taylor of this almost unique work when announced in 1868.

CONTENTS.

I. Historians of the County.
II. Principal Maps.
III. Heraldic Visitations, and Reference to Genealogical and MSS. Collections in the Principal Public and Private Libraries.
IV. Tracts printed during the Civil War and Commonwealth, 1640–1660.
V. Acts of Parliament – Local, Personal, and Private, from Edwd. I. to Victoria.
VI. Calendar of State Papers.
VII. Blue Books.
VIII. Books relative to the County in General.
IX. Newspapers and Books printed in the County.
X. Books relative to particular Towns, Parishes, Seats, Families, Customs, and Historical Events, in alphabetical order.
XI. Authors and Worthies, in alphabetical order, with Lists of their Works.
XII. Explanation of the References to the Works referred to throughout the volume.
XIII. Index of Places and Subjects.
XIV. Index of Persons.

Of this valuable book only Six Copies were printed and but Three offered for sale. One is in the Public Lib. at Northampton, another in the Public Lib. at Kettering, and a third in the Public Lib. at Peterborough—the remaining copies are in private hands. Taylor issued his 'Bibliotheca' in parts, but did not complete it in this form.

The copy in the Northampton Public Library, which by the courtesy of Mr. Reginald W. Brown, the Librarian, I have been able to consult, is a 'laid-down copy,' the material for which was acquired for £25, and a Supplement was bought later for a further outlay of £5. The entries are kept up-to-date. The arrangement of the titles is done with great skill and consists of Two main Classifications under

NORTHAMPTONSHIRE PARISHES.

NORTHAMPTONSHIRE AUTHORS.

There are also minor headings under such subjects as

Acts of Parliament.
Americana.
Books printed in Northamptonshire.
Brasses.
Calendars of State Papers.
Civil War Tracts.
Drawings.
Eleanor Crosses.
Engravings, Views, and Maps.
Heraldic Visitations.
Northants. Sales and Book Catalogues.
Portraits.
Quakers.
Sporting.

It is doubtful whether any other County can shew so useful a work as this one of John Taylor's. The regret is that so few copies were printed. The work occupied the compiler his whole life. He began in 1868 the publication of a specimen of what he proposed to issue, and this was called

NORTHAMPTONSHIRE (continued).

Taylor (John). Bibliotheca Northantonensis: A Bibliographical Account of what has been published on the Topography, Antiquities, Customs, Family History, etc., of Northamptonshire, with an Account of its Worthies and Authors, and Lists of their Works. Northampton, Oct., 1868, pp. 55.

CONTENTS.

Historians of the County.
Principal Maps of the County.
Books relative to particular towns, parishes, families, etc.

—— **Catal. of a Special Collection of Printed Books relating to the Hist. of the Co. of Northants, in General, 1800–1883,** collected by John Taylor. Northampton, 1884.

John Taylor collected Bibliographical information on a most extensive scale. He could only obtain possession of a comparatively small number of the books he had notes upon. His Collections were obtained by purchase and are now in the Northampton Public Library. The Collection of Northamptonshire Authors was bought in 1876, and a further Collection was purchased by Public Subscription in 1885. Further valuable work by John Taylor was a compilation of a

—— **MS. Index to the Topography of Northamptonshire, begun by John Taylor, and continued by the Staff of the Public Lib. at Northampton.**

Various works by John Taylor of smaller magnitude are as follows:

—— **A Calendar of Papers of the Tresham Family, of the reigns of Elizabeth and James I. 1580–1605, preserved at Rushton Hall, Northamptonshire.** Northampton, 1871. Reprinted in 'Tracts relating to Northants.' Second Series. 1881.

—— **Schedule of Deeds, etc., belonging to Brington Charity Estate, etc.** Northampton, 1876. Reprinted in 'Tracts relating to Northants.' Second Series. 1881.

—— **Index Locorum. Baker's Hist. of Northamptonshire.** Northampton, 1867. Reprinted in 'Tracts relating to Northants.' First Series. 1876.

—— **Memorials of the Rev. John Dod, Rector of Fawsley, Northants, 1624-1645,** with Appendix containing Bibliographical List of the Writings of John Dod, and References to Biographical Notices of him, etc. Northampton, 1881. Reprinted in 'Tracts relating to Northants.' Second Series. 1881.

Antiquarian Memoranda. (A Collection of items relating to Northants. History found in various Public Libraries when compiling his 'Bibliotheca.') The Biblio. Titles are:

No. I. Fawsley and the Mar-Prelate Press.
III. Northamptonshire Notes from Nichols, 1812.
VI. References to Northamptonshire MSS. in Brit. Museum.
XV. Rockingham Castle MS. 1655.
XX. MS. Maps, Charts, and Plans, in Brit. Museum.
XXVIII. Bridges' 'Northamptonshire.'
XXXIII. MSS. of John Cole.
XXXVII. Gunton's Peterborough.
XXXVIII. A Dicey Chap Book.

—— **Northampton Book Circular** was begun before 1861 and continued to 1884, or probably later. It contains much valuable information.

A brief Biography of John Taylor appeared in 'Northamptonshire Notes and Queries,' New Series, vol. I. pp. 13–16. 1905.

Among Bibliographical Reprints by John Taylor are

Gough (Richard). Northamptonshire Topography: an Historical Account of what has been done for Illustrating the Topographical Antiquities of the County of Northants.

NORTHAMPTONSHIRE (continued).

Nichols (J. Bowyer). Hist. & Geneal. Notes relating to Northamptonshire, from 'Collectanea Topographica et Genealogica' and 'Excerpta Historica.' Northampton, 1879. Reprinted in 'Tracts relating to Northants.' Second Series. 1881.

The Huth Library. A Catal. of the Printed Books, Manuscripts, Autograph Letters, and Engravings, collected by Henry Huth, with Collations and Bibliographical Descriptions. Books relating to the Hist. of Northants, or written by Natives or Residents in the County. Northampton, 1881. Reprinted in 'Tracts relating to Northants.' Second Series. 1881.

In addition to the Taylor Collection in the Northampton Public Library there is another local library, collected and catalogued independently on the sheaf system, with special headings for such subjects as

Acts of Parliament.
Enclosure Acts.
Newspapers.
Northamptonshire Catalogues, including Sale Catalogues.

Indexes to the Reports and Papers of the Associated Architectural Societies, etc. (includes the Northampton Architectural Soc., now called Northampton and Oakham Architectural and Archæological Soc.). Vols. i.–viii. (1850–66); vols. ix.–xiv. (1867–78); vols. xv.–xix. (1878–88); and vols. xx.–xxv. (1889–1900). Lincoln, 1867–1905.

Catal. of Books belonging to the Northampton Architectural Soc. Issued in 'Reports and Papers of the Assoc. Archit. Societies,' vol. i. pp. vi.–viii. lxii., 1850, and in later vols.

General Index to the Journal of the Northamptonshire Natural History Soc. and Field Club, with list of Illustrations. Vols. I.-X. 1880 to 1900.

List of Northamptonshire References in the Four volumes of the New Series of the 'Miscellanea Genealogica et Heraldica' 1870-1883. (*Northamptonshire Notes & Queries*, vol. ii. pp. 209–210. 1887.)

Northamptonshire Topography. An Unique Collection of upwards of 1300 volumes and tracts relative to Family Hist., Customs, Hist. Events, Antiquities, Civil Wars, Royal Visits, etc., in Northamptonshire, many privately printed. 1600–1868. On Sale for Eighty Guineas, see John Taylor's 'Northampton Book Circular,' New Ser., no. 23. 1868. The Collection was made from the Libraries of George Baker, Samuel Deacon, T. O. Gery, and from other sources.

Catal. of the Lib. of the late William Upcott, sold by Evans, New Bond St., 15 June, 1846. Northamptonshire Collections, pp. 66–69.

Sweeting (W. D.). Bibliography of the River Nene. (*Northants. Notes & Queries*, vol. vi. pp. 185–192. 1895.)

Matthew Holbeche Bloxam. Biographical Account, with List of his Works relating to Northants, and a List of References to Northants in the various editions of 'The Principles of Gothic Ecclesiastical Architecture.' By J. T. Page. (*Northants. Notes & Queries*, vol. iii. pp. 124–136, 203. 1889–90.)

Dryden (Sir Henry). A Catal. of the Collection of Drawings, Plans, Notes on Churches, Houses, and various Archæological matters made by the late Sir Henry E. L. Dryden, of Canons Ashby, Northants, presented to the Corporation of Northampton by Miss Alice Dryden (with a valuable Subject-Index). Northampton, 1912.

NORTHAMPTONSHIRE (continued).

Clarke's Drawings of Gentlemen's Seats in Northamptonshire, reproduced from the vols. in the possession of the Northampton and Oakham Archit. and Archæol. Soc., with descriptions, etc., by Christopher A. Markham, and a short biog. notice of George Clarke. (*Northants. Notes & Queries*, New Ser., vol. iv. pp. 1, 33, 100, 1912–13, and continued in subsequent vols.)

Lectures on the History and Literature of Northampton. Edited by John Taylor, the Younger.

Eastman (Rev. P. M.). An hour among the Echoes of Northampton Castle, with an Appendix of Documents, pp. 35–49. Second edn. London & Northampton, 1879.

Goadby (Rev. J. Jackson). The Baptists and Quakers in Northamptonshire, 1650–1700. Appendix, contains List of Authorities, Notes on Quaker Tracts, and Biblio. List of Works on the Baptists, with References to Northants. Northampton, 1882.

George (T. J.). An Archaeological Survey of Northants. Soc. of Antiq. Lond. 1904. Biblio. and Topog. Index, pp. 9–21.

Markham (Christopher A.). Domesday Book, Northamptonshire. An Account, with Biblio. of Domesday Books for Northants. Northampton Archit. Soc. (*Assoc. Archit. Soc. Reports & Papers*, vol. xix. pp. 126–139. 1887.)

Dove (Patrick Edward). Domesday Studies. 1891. Domesday Biblio. of Northants, vol. ii. p. 684.

Lyell (Arthur H.). Biblio. List of Romano-British Remains. 1912. **Northants,** pp. 90–94.

Macklin (Herbert Walter). Monumental Brasses. London: Geo. Allen & Co., 1913. Biblio. Note on Northants. Brasses, with a List, pp. 141, 173–175.

Gross (Charles). Biblio. of Brit. Municipal Hist. (*Harvard Hist. Studies*, vol. v. 1897.) Northants., pp. 100–101. Northampton, p. 349. Peterborough, p. 365.

Davenport (Frances G.) List of Printed Materials for Manorial Hist. 1894. Biblio Note on Northants. Manorial Hist., p. 52.

Murray (David). 'Museums.' Glasgow, 1904. Biblio. Note on Northampton Museum, vol. iii. p. 57.

List of Acts of Parliament relating to the County and Borough of Northampton, and the Soke of Peterborough. 1322 to 1907, etc. (*Northants. Notes & Queries.* New Ser., vol. i. pp. 54, etc. 1905.) Continued in later vols.

Curiosities of Northamptonshire Printing. Short descriptions of rare specimens of Northants. Typography, principally Dicey Chap Books. (*Northants. Notes & Queries*, vol. ii. pp. 184–189, 265–268; vol. v. p. 240. 1887, 1893.)

Biblio. Notes on the Dicey Press, by W. D. Sweeting and others. (*Northants. Notes & Queries*, vol. vi. pp. 73–74, 176, 236–237. 1895.)

The Old Dicey Press, Northampton. (*The Northampton Mercury*, 22 Dec., 1899.)

Biblio. Notes on the Dicey Chap Books and Broadsheets. (In '*Hist. of "The Northampton Mercury,"* 1720–1901.' (Mercury Extra. No. 10. pp. 33–36.)

See also *ante*, p. 183, John Taylor's 'Antiquarian Memoranda.'

'The Northampton Mercury,' 1720-1901. A Popular and Illustrated Hist. of 'The Northampton Mercury' from the early part of the Eighteenth to the commencement of the Twentieth Century. Mercury Extra. No. 10. 1901. Reprinted from the 'Mercury.'

MS. Index to 'The Northampton Mercury' from 1720 up to about 1850. (In the Northampton Public Lib.)

NORTHAMPTONSHIRE (continued).

Biblio. Note on Vol. I. of 'The Northampton Mercury,' 1720, by J. L. Cherry. (*Northants. Notes & Queries*, vol. i. pp. 225–227. 1885.)

The First Issue of 'The Northampton Mercury.' (*The Northampton Mercury*, 19 July, 1901.)

Norris (Herbert E.). Local Newspaper History. (*Ibid.* 1 Dec., 1899.)

Biblio. Notes on 'The Northampton Miscellany,' 1720-21, by J. L. Cherry. (*Northants. Notes & Queries*, vol. i. p. 153; vol. iii. pp. 211–212. 1885, 1890.)

'The Northamptonshire Journal,' 1741. Biblio. Note by J. T. (*Ibid.* vol. i. p. 215. 1885.)

The Private Press of the Rev. Thomas R. Brown at Southwick, Northants. See W. D. Macray, 'Annals of the Bodleian Lib.,' 1890, p. 337.

Northants. Printers and Newspapers. Mr. Reginald W. Brown, the Librarian of the Northampton Public Library, who has shown great civility and rendered much assistance with these Northants. entries, is engaged in preparing a List.

Celebrated Northamptonshire Booksellers. I. Thomas Payne. (*Northants. Notes & Queries*, vol. i. pp. 65–67. 1884.) **II. John Simco,** with a list of Books relating to the County, in his Sale Catal., by Evans, Pall Mall, 1824; a list of Prints and Drawings from Sotheby's Catal.; a list of Drawings illustrative of Bridges' 'Hist. of Northants,' &c. (*Ibid.* vol. ii. pp. 162–169. 1887.)

Mundy (Percy D.) Northamptonshire Book-Plates. (*Northants. Notes & Queries*, New Ser. vol. iv. pp. 120–123, 206–207. 1913–14.)

Northamptonshire Characters and Caricatures. Compiled from a Series of Prints in the possession of John Taylor, by F. T. (*Ibid.* vol. ii. pp. 67–74. 1886.)

Special Topographical Collections for Northants are at the Northampton Public Lib., including John Clare's Library, and the Dryden Collection of MS. Notes, Drawings, etc.

Hist. MSS. Comm. Reports. Northamptonshire Collections.

Clarke-Thornhill, Mr. T. B., of Rushton Hall ...	16th Rep. pp. 112–116. Various Collections, vol. iii. pp. 1–154.
Corbet, Sir Walter O., of Acton Reynald, Salop ...	15th Rep. App. X. pp. 66–77.
Dryden, Sir Henry, at Canons Ashby	2nd Rep. p. xi. and App. pp. 63–64.
Exeter, Marquess of, at Burghley House	6th Rep. p. xi. and App. pp. 234–235.
Gunning, Sir Henry ...	3rd Rep. p. xviii. and App. pp. 248–250.
Isham, Sir Charles, at Lamport Hall ...	3rd Rep. p. xviii. and App. pp. 252–254.
Knightley, Sir Rainald, at Fawsley Park ...	3rd Rep. p. xix. and App. p. 254.
Northampton, Marquess of ...	3rd Rep. p. xvii. and App. p. 209.
Sackville, Mrs. Stopford—of Drayton House, Thrapston ...	9th Rep. pp. xx., xxi. and App. III. pp. 1–150; 16th Rep. p. 110, and vol. i. 1904.
Westmorland, Earl of, at Apethorpe ...	10th Rep. p. 2, and App. IV. pp. 1–59.
Higham Ferrers Corporation ...	12th Rep. p. 47, and App. IX. pp. 530–537.
Peterborough, Dean and Chapter of ...	12th Rep. p. 45, and App. IX. pp. 580–585.

County Records, from Reign of Queen Elizabeth, with MS. Index, at County Offices, Northampton. (*Local Records Comm. Rep.*, 1902, App. III. p. 22.)

Borough Records, Richard I., etc., with MS. Indexes, at Town Hall, Northampton. (*Ibid.* 1902, App. III. p. 36.)

NORTHAMPTONSHIRE (continued).

The Records of the Borough of Northampton. 2 vols. Vol. i. edited by C. A. Markham, vol. ii. edited by J. Charles Cox. Published by the Corporation. 1898. Schedule of Public, Private, and Local Acts of Parliament, pp. 435–448.

Mr. Stuart A. Moore compiled a MS. Calendar of the Archives and Muniments in 1864.

List of Northampton Municipal Records Printed. (*Notes & Queries*, Ser. 11, vol. v. p. 298. 1912.)

Hartshorne (C. H.). Historical Memorials of Northampton. 1848. Schedule of Municipal Archives, pp. 101–110.

Bridges (John). MS. Collections relating to Northants. in the Bodleian Lib. See List in Madan 'Summary of the Western MSS. in the Bodl. Lib.' vol. iii. pp. 642–651, and Whalley's Preface to Bridges' 'Hist. of Northants.' 1791, vol. i.

Lee (Henry). MS. Collections relating to the Antiquities of Northampton, 1715. (Among the Bridges' MSS. in the Bodl. Lib.)

Upcott's Topographical Collections for Northants., in the Brit. Museum. Add. MS. 15925.

Suckling's Collections for Northants., 1821–39, in the Brit. Museum. Add. MS. 18481.

Lysons (Rev. S.). Collections for Northants. in the Brit. Museum. Add. MS. 9459.

List of Charters relating to Northants, compiled from the first and second volumes of the 'Cartularium Saxonicum,' by Walter de Gray Birch, 1885–87. (*Northants. Notes & Queries*, vol. iii. p. 65. 1888.)

List of Cartularies of Monasteries in Northants. (from Index to Cartularies now or formerly existing, since the Dissolution of Monasteries, by Sir Thomas Phillipps. Middle Hill Press, 1839). (*Northants. Notes & Queries*, vol. i. pp. 72–73. 1884.)

A Chest of Old MSS. Broadsides, from the old Manor House of Kibworth Harcourt, co. Leics. A Rough List of those relating to Northants, by Rev. W. D. Sweeting. (*Ibid.* vol. i. pp. 94–96. 1884.)

Elliott (H. L.). The Parish Registers of Northampton and the Neighbourhood. (*Assoc. Archit. Soc. Reports & Papers*, vol. vi. pp. 200–219. 1862.) Also issued separately. Extracts from various Northants. Parish Registers, with slight Biblio. Notes are in the 'Northants. Notes & Queries,' vol. ii. etc.

Eunson (Henry J.). List of Works on the Geology, Mineralogy, and Palæontology of Northamptonshire. (*Northants. Nat. Hist. Soc. Journ.* vol. iv. pp. 178–189. 1886.)

Roebuck (W. D.) and Taylor (John W.). Biblio. of Works and Papers relating to the Mollusca of Northamptonshire. (*Ibid.* vol. iv. pp. 108–112. 1886.)

Trimen (Henry). Botanical Biblio. of the British Counties. Northants. (*Journ. of Botany*, vol. xii. p. 111. 1874.)

Christy (Miller). Biblio. Note on Northants Birds. (*The Zoologist*, Ser. 3, vol. xiv. p. 257, 1890 ; and reprinted in pamph., 1891, p. 20.) **Mammals.** (*The Zoologist*, Ser. 3, vol. xvii. p. 182. 1893.) **Reptiles.** (*Ibid.* p. 246. 1893.) **Fishes.** (*Ibid.* p. 256. 1893.)

Anderson (John P.). Book of Brit. Topo., 1881. Northants., pp. 224–229.

Gatfield (George). Guide to Heraldry. 1892. Northants., pp. 167–168.

Sims (Richard). Manual. 1861. Northants., pp. 170, 216, 217, 237.

Upcott (William). English Topo., 1818. Northants., vol. ii. pp. 1003–1027.

Smith (Alfred Russell). Catal. of Topo. Tracts, etc., 1878. Northants., pp. 273–280.

Gough (Richard). Brit. Topo., 1780. Northants., vol. ii. pp. 37–52.

Bandinel (Bulkeley). Catal. of Books bequeathed to Bodleian Library by Richard Gough. 1814. Northants., pp. 243–246.

NORTHAMPTONSHIRE (continued).

ALTHORP.

Dibdin (Thomas Frognall). Ædes Althorpianæ; or an Account of the Mansion, Books, and Pictures at Althorp. To which is added a Supplement to the Bibliotheca Spenceriana. 2 vols. 1822.

The various other bibliographical works by Dibdin relating to Lord Spencer's Library should be consulted. The Spencer Library was, with some unimportant exceptions, bought in 1892 by Mrs. Rylands, and removed to Manchester to form 'The John Rylands Library.'

BRACKLEY.

Macray (W. Dunn). Calendar of the Collection of Brackley Deeds at Magdalen College, Oxford. 1867. Copy made by the Rev. Richard Ussher, Vicar of Westbury, Brackley, and published in the 'Buckingham Advertiser,' 1908–1909. Six Copies only reprinted.

DAVENTRY.

Borough Records, 1595, etc., at Moot Hall, Daventry. (*Local Records Comm. Rep.*, 1902, App. III. p. 54.)

FAWSLEY.

Pierce (William). An Historical Introduction to the Marprelate Tracts. London, 1908. The Secret Press at Fawsley House, p. 156. A Select Marprelate Bibliography, pp. 322–332.

Allnutt (W. H.). English Provincial Presses. The Marprelate Press, 1588-89. (*Bibliographica*, vol. ii. pp. 172–180. 1896.)

Arber (Edward). An Introductory Sketch to the Martin Marprelate Controversy, 1588-90. English Scholar's Library. No. VIII. London, 1880. Biblio. of the General Controversy, pp. 17–18. A Chronological List of Works on the Controversy, pp. 197–200.

Wilson (J. Dover). The Marprelate Controversies, with a Biblio. (*The Cambridge Hist. of Eng. Literature*, vol. iii. pp. 537–546. 1909.)

FOTHERINGHAY.

Scott (John). A Biblio. of Works relating to Mary, Queen of Scots, 1544-1700. Edinburgh Biblio. Soc. 1896.

HIGHAM FERRERS.

Corporation Records. See *ante* Hist. MSS. Comm. Reports.

Borough Records, 1300, etc., at Town Hall, Higham Ferrers. (*Local Records Comm. Rep.*, 1902, App. III. p. 60.)

The Charters of Higham Ferrers. Biblio. Notes by M. A. P. (*Northants. Notes & Queries*, vol. vi. pp. 87–88, 180, 234. 1894–95.)

KINGSTHORPE.

Kingsthorpiana, or Researches in a Church Chest, being a Calendar of Old Documents now existing in the Church Chest of Kingsthorpe, edited by J. H. Glover. London, 1883.

LAMPORT.

Graves (R. E.). The Isham Books. (*Bibliographica*, vol. iii. pp. 418–429. 1897.)

The Isham Reprints. Biblio. Notes by J. T. (*Northants. Notes & Queries*, vol. v. pp. 26–28. 1892.)

The Isham Reprints. Edited by Charles Edmonds, with Biblio. Prefaces. Nos. I.–IV. London, 1870–95.

NORTHAMPTONSHIRE (continued).

A Lamport Garland from the Library of Sir Charles Edmund Isham, comprising Four Unique Works hitherto Unknown. Edited by Charles Edmonds, with Biblio. Introductions. The Roxburghe Club. London, 1881.

Sale Catal. of a Portion of the Library of Sir Charles Isham, of Lamport Hall. Sold by Puttick & Simpson, 15 July, 1874.

PETERBOROUGH.

Dean and Chapter of Peterborough Records. See *ante* Hist. MSS. Comm. Reports.

Liber Niger of Peterborough: a Register of Charters and other Documents relating to the Abbey, including a Chronicle from 1192 to 1294. (MS. 60 in Lib. of Soc. of Antiquaries, London.)

English (H. S.). Crowland and Burgh (now Peterborough), a Light on the Historians and on the Hist. of Crowland Abbey. 3 vols. London, 1871.

Dibdin (Thomas Frognall). Books at Peterborough. (*Northern Tour*, 1838, vol. i. pp. 1–40.)

Botfield (Beriah). Notes on the Cathedral Libraries of England. 1849. **Peterborough,** pp. 369–383.

Irvine (J. T.). Engravings in Gunton's Peterborough. Notes relative to Etchings of Peterborough Cathedral given in Dean Patrick's publication of the Rev. Symon Gunton's History, 1686. (*Northants. Notes & Queries*, vol. ii. pp. 216–219. 1887.)

A Special Collection of Local Books, Prints, etc., is at the Peterborough Museum, and a Collection of Fenland Literature at the Peterborough Public Library.

NORTHUMBERLAND.

Thompson (Henry). A Reference Catal. of Books relating to the Counties of Durham and Northumberland, divided into Parishes, etc. Part I. Historical and Topographical. 1888. No further part was issued.

Fawcett (J. W.). Some Contributions to a Biblio. of Durham and Northumberland. (*Sunderland Public Library Circular*, vol. iii. pp. 67–70. July, 1905.) Only the first instalment was issued.

Anderton (Basil), Librarian of the Public Library, Newcastle-upon-Tyne. **On Planning a Printed Catalogue of Local Literature.** (*The Lib. Assoc. Record*, vol. xv. pp. 542–552, 635–639. 1913.)

Peddie (Robert Alexander). List of Books printed in Northumberland and Durham, with an Index to Pictorial Illustrations of Newcastle appearing in Books, Magazines, etc., to the end of the 19th Century. Presented by the Compiler to the Soc. of Antiquaries of Newcastle-upon-Tyne.

'The Thomas Bell Library.' The Catal. of 15,000 volumes of Scarce and Curious Printed Books, and Unique MSS. collected by Thomas Bell, 1797–1860, sold by Auction at Newcastle-upon-Tyne, 15 Oct. 1860. (Contains a valuable list of Books, etc., relating to Northumberland.) The following are some of the grouped items in the Catalogue:—

Reprints and other Publications by John Bell, of Newcastle (mostly Ballads, etc.), pp. 17–18.
Works of Thomas and John Bewick, pp. 27–30.
Works relative to the Coal Trade, pp. 66–68.
Bell's Genealogical and Biographical Collections, pp. 109–114.
Works relating to Newcastle, pp. 169–175.
Newcastle Typog. Soc. (a complete set), pp. 176–178.
Books relating to the County of Northumberland, pp. 181–183.
Books relating to the Dukes and Earls of Northumberland, pp. 184–185.
Poll Books of Newcastle and Northumberland, pp. 196–197.

NORTHUMBERLAND (continued).

Catal. of 'The Thomas Bell Collection' of Curious Prints, Fine Drawings, etc., and other Illustrations of Antiquarian and Topographical Research, sold by Auction at Newcastle-upon-Tyne, Nov. 5, 1860.

Large Paper copies of the two preceding Catalogues of the Thomas Bell Collection are in the British Museum Library, bound together in a volume formerly belonging to his son, John Gray Bell, with his MS. notes and the items marked which he bought with their prices. Interspersed throughout are Newspaper Cuttings, Views, etc., and at the end a Collection of Memoranda by Thomas Bell relating to the purchase of many of the books.

Hodgson (John). A Hist. of the County of Northumberland. 6 vols. London, 1820–40. Part III. vol. I. is mainly devoted to Charters, Rolls, etc., with Calendars, etc.

Gibson (William Sidney). A Memoir of Northumberland. London, 1860. Biblio. Notes on Northumberland Books, Appendix, pp. 71–77.

——— **An Hist. Memoir of Northumberland.** London, 1862. Biblio. Notes on the Literary Worthies of Northumberland, chap. xi. pp. 117–123.

A History of Northumberland, issued under the direction of the Northumberland County History Committee. Vols. i.–x. (all yet published). Newcastle-upon-Tyne, 1893–1914. Appendices to various vols. contain Lists of Deeds, etc.

General Index to the 'Archaeologia Aeliana,' vols. i. to iv. 1822–55, and New Series, vols. i. to xvi. 1857–1894, and to the 'Proceedings,' vol. i. 1855–57, and New Series, vols. i. to v. 1883–1892, of the Soc. of Antiquaries of Newcastle-upon-Tyne. Edited by Robert Blair. South Shields, 1896–97.

A Classified Catal. of Papers from 'Archaeologia Aeliana,' 1813–1913, by John Crawford Hodgson. (*Archaeol. Aeliana*, Centenary vol., Ser. 3, vol. x. pp. 334–376. 1913.)

Biographies of Contributors to the Literature of the Soc. of Antiquaries of Newcastle-upon-Tyne, with Bibliographies of their Writings in the Society's Publications and elsewhere. By Richard Welford and J. C. Hodgson. (*Ibid.* Ser. 3, vol. x. pp. 109–333. 1913.)

A Catal. of the Library belonging to the Soc. of Antiquaries of Newcastle-upon-Tyne, inclusive of the MSS., Drawings, Prints and Maps. 1896.

A Hist. of the Newcastle Soc. of Antiquaries, 1813 to 1913. (*Archaeol. Aeliana*, Centenary vol. Ser. 3, vol. x. pp. 1–5. 1913.) The Society's Museum, by R. O. Heslop, p. 13. The Society's Library, by C. Hunter Blair, p. 26.

Catal. of the Library of the Literary and Philosophical Soc. of Newcastle-upon-Tyne, with Author and Subject Indexes. 1903. Local Collection of Works relating to Northumberland, Durham, and Berwick-on-Tweed, pp. 587–616. Works relating to the Newcastle Lit. and Philos. Soc. pp. 629–632.

The Hist. of the Lit. and Philos. Soc. of Newcastle-upon-Tyne, 1793–1896, by Robert Spence Watson. London, 1897. The Library of the Soc. pp. 173–201. List of Lectures, 1803–1896, pp. 339–366.

Catal. of Books and Tracts on Genealogy and Heraldry in the Central Public Libraries, Newcastle-upon-Tyne. Preface by Basil Anderton. 1910.

General Index to vols. i. to v. 1887–1891 of 'The Monthly Chronicle of North-Country Lore and Legend.' Newcastle-upon-Tyne.

Richardson (Moses Aaron). The Local Historian's Table Book, of Remarkable Occurrences, Historical Facts, Traditions, Legendary and Descriptive Ballads, connected with the Counties of Newcastle-upon-Tyne, Northumberland and Durham. 8 vols. London, 1841–46. Biblio. Notes are scattered throughout the Work. The Legendary Division in 3 vols. contains Ballads, etc., with Biblio. Notes.

NORTHUMBERLAND (continued).

Hodgkin (Thomas). Suggestions for a New County Hist. of Northumberland. (*Archaeol. Aeliana*, Ser. 2, vol. xv. pp. 54–63. 1893.)

Catal. of the Private Library of John Trotter Brockett, of Newcastle, sold by Sotheby's, Dec. 8, etc. 1823. (Contains a unique Collection of the Works of Bewick, and also Newcastle Reprints and Privately Printed Publications.)

Catal. of the Choice and Valuable Library of John Trotter Brockett, sold by Sotheby's, June 16, etc. 1843. (Contains a Collection of Brockett's Works, and also Works edited by him.)

Gross (Charles). Biblio. of Brit. Municipal Hist. (*Harvard Hist. Studies*, vol. v. 1897.) Northumberland, pp. 101–102. Newcastle-upon-Tyne, pp. 343–347. Morpeth, pp. 340–341. Alnwick, pp. 156–157.

Davenport (Frances G.). List. of Printed Materials for Manorial Hist. 1894. Biblio. Note on Northumberland Manorial Hist., pp. 52–54.)

Macklin (Herbert Walter). Monumental Brasses. London: Geo. Allen & Co. 1913. Biblio. Note on Northumberland Brasses, with a List, p. 175.

Lyell (Arthur H.). Biblio. List of Romano-British Remains. 1912. Northumberland, pp. 94–101.

Hodgkin (Thomas). The Literary Hist. of the Roman Wall. (*Archaeol. Aeliana*, Ser. 2, vol. xviii. pp. 83–108. 1896.

For a Biblio. of the Roman Wall, see Lyell, pp. 100–101, in preceding entry. A Collection of Drawings of the Roman Wall is in the Lang Art Gallery and Museum at Newcastle.

County Folk-Lore, vol. iv. Examples of Printed Folk-Lore concerning Northumberland, with List of Authorities. Collected by M. C. Balfour and Edited by N. W. Thomas. Folk-Lore Soc., vol. liii. 1903.

Heslop (R. Oliver). A Biblio. List of Works illustrative of the Dialect of Northumberland. English Dialect Soc., No. 80. London, 1896.

A List of Private Acts relating to the County of Northumberland. Stevens & Sons, London, *circa* 1912.

Carr-Ellison (Ralph). List of Papers contributed to various Publications (many relating to Northumberland). (*Berwickshire Naturalists' Club. Proc.* vol. x. pp. 514–516. 1884.)

Wilson (William). Notes on the Early Literature of Flodden Field. (*Ibid.* vol. x. pp. 517–522. 1884.)

Welford (Richard). Early Newcastle Typography, 1639-1800. (*Archaeol. Aeliana*, Ser. 3. vol. iii. pp. 1–134. 1907.) Also issued separately The following are the group headings.

Books printed in Newcastle, 1639-1800, pp. 55-117.
Undated Newcastle Books, pp. 118-120.
Early Newcastle Chap Books, without date, etc., pp. 121-123.
Undated Newcastle Broadsides, pp. 124-125.
Early Book Auctions in Newcastle, p. 126.
Newcastle Newspapers and Magazines published during the 18th cent., p. 127.
Newcastle Printers, Booksellers, etc., 1639-1800, pp. 128-129.
Printers, Booksellers, Stationers, etc., from Newcastle Directories, pp. 130-133.

—— **Supplementary List.** (*Archaeol. Aeliana*, Ser. 3, vol. iv. pp. 147–153. 1908.) Also issued separately.

Hinde (John Hodgson). On Early Printing in Newcastle. (*Ibid.* Ser. 2, vol. vi. pp. 225–230. 1865.)

Clephan (James). Early Printing in Newcastle. (*Ibid.* Ser. 2, vol. vii. pp. 267–271. 1876.)

Early Printers on the Tyne. Biblio. Notes by James Clephan, and others. (*Monthly Chron. of North-Country Lore*, vol. i. pp. 314–318. 1887.)

NORTHUMBERLAND (continued).

Peddie (Robert Alexander). A List of the issues of the Press in Newcastle-upon-Tyne, 1639-1800. [Typewritten MS. in the Blades Library at the St. Bride's Foundation, London.] 1900.

——— **Newcastle Printing, 1639-1800.** (A List of Books, etc., on Newcastle Printing, not in the British Museum.) (*The Newcastle Weekly Chronicle.*)

Allnutt (W. H.). English Provincial Presses. Earliest Printing at Newcastle and Gateshead. (*Bibliographica*, vol. ii. pp. 280-281, 290-293, 298. 1896.)

Anderton (Basil). Notes on some of the Printers and Libraries of Newcastle-upon-Tyne. (*Book-Auction Records*, vol. vii. pt. 1, pp. i.-xii. 1909.)

A Collection of Newspaper cuttings relating to local Printing, transcripts of titlepages, etc., by Bell and Longstaffe. (In Reference Library of the Newcastle-upon-Tyne Pub. Lib.)

Brockett (James Trotter). Hints on the propriety of establishing a Typographical Society in Newcastle upon Tyne. Newcastle, Printed for Emerson Charnley. 1818.

Martin (John). List of Publications Issued by the Newcastle Typographical Soc. 1817, etc. (*Biblio. Catal. of Books Privately Printed*, 1834, pp. 419-440.)

Eyton (J. Walter K.). A Complete List of Publications of the Newcastle Typog. Soc. (*Sale Catal. of his Library of Privately Printed Books*, Sotheby's, 1848, pp. 136-140.)

Lowndes (William Thomas). List of Newcastle-on-Tyne Typographical Society's Publications, 1817-57. (*The Bibliographer's Manual.* 1864. Appendix, pp. 159-164.)

Dibdin (Thomas Frognall). Books at Newcastle. (*Northern Tour*, 1838, vol. i. pp. 383-400.)

Burman (C. C.). An Account of the Art of Typography as practised at Alnwick. Alnwick, 1896.

The Darlington Private Press of George Allan. See entries under Durham, p. 55.

Hugo (Thomas). The Bewick Collector. A Descriptive Catal. of the Works of Thomas and John Bewick, with Appendix of Portraits, etc. 2 vols. London, 1866-68. The Edington Collection in the Tynemouth Public Lib., which illustrates the History of Engraving in England during the last century, includes an entire volume devoted to the Bewicks.

——— **Bewick's Woodcuts. Impressions of upwards of two thousand wood blocks, engraved, for the most part, by Thomas and John Bewick,** with an Introduction, a descriptive Catal. of the Blocks, and a List of the Books and Pamphlets illustrated. London, 1870. For other books with Bewick impressions, see *passim* in the next entry.

Anderton (Basil) and Gibson (W. H.). Catal. of the Bewick Collection (Pease Bequest) in the Newcastle-upon-Tyne Public Library. Newcastle, 1904. Lists of Bewick Collections, pp. 54-59, Bewick Catalogues, pp. 60-68, Sale Catalogues of various Collections, pp. 69-73.

——— **Concerning the Book-Plates of Thomas Bewick, with Lists of Books with Bewick Illustrations, and Bookplates.** (*Fragrance among Old Volumes*, 1910, pp. 44-74.)

Catal. of Edwin Pearson's Collection of Books and Wood Engravings by T. and J. Bewick. 1868.

NORTHUMBERLAND (continued).

Stephens (F. G.). Notes on a Collection of Drawings and Woodcuts by Thomas Bewick, exhibited at the Fine Art Society's Rooms, 1880; also a complete list of all works illustrated by Thomas and John Bewick, with their various editions. 1881.

Impressions of a numerous collection of ancient Wood Cuts in George Angus's Printing-office, Newcastle-upon-Tyne, which have ornamented Old Ballads, Songs, Histories, Wonderful Tales, etc. 1825. See p. 58 of 'Catal. of the Bewick Collection (Pease Bequest) in the Newcastle Public Lib.'

Reprints of Rare Tracts and Imprints of Antient MSS., etc., chiefly illustrative of the Hist. of the Northern Counties, and Printed at the Press of M. A. Richardson, Newcastle. 1843–49. 7 vols. (Biblio. Notes, and Titles and Tables of Contents to the last Four volumes completing the Series.) See Lists in Lowndes' 'Bibliographers' Manual,' 1864, Appendix, pp. 271–275, and 'Catal. of Lib. of Soc. of Antiquaries of Newcastle-upon-Tyne,' 1896, pp. 78–80.

Bell (Thomas). Local Poetry, Songs, and Ballads. (Chiefly cuttings, with hawker's Ballads, and others in MS.) **relating to the Town and County of Newcastle-upon-Tyne, or incidents connected therewith,** collected by Thomas Bell. 1780–1830. 2 vols. (In British Museum Library.)

Bell (John), Jun. Rhymes of Northern Bards, being a curious Collection of Old and New Songs and Poems peculiar to Newcastle, Northumberland, and Durham. Newcastle, 1812.

Crawhall (Joseph). The Newcastle Fishers' Garlands. A Collection of Right Merrie Garlands for North Country Anglers, continued to this present year. Newcastle-on-Tyne, 1864.

—— **A Beuk o' Newcassel Sangs.** Newcastle-on-Tyne, 1888.

Northumbrian Minstrelsy. A Collection of the Ballads, Melodies, Small-Pipe tunes of Northumbria, edited by J. Collingwood Bruce and J. Stokoe. Soc. of Antiq. Newcastle-upon-Tyne. 1882. For other Books of Garlands, see *ante*, p. 192, 'Catal. of the Bewick Collection (Pease Bequest) in the Newcastle Public Lib.,' by Anderton and Gibson.

A Collection of Chap-books relating principally to Northumberland and Durham. 230 chap-books in 6 vols. Presented to the Sunderland Public Lib. by Mr. John Moore of Beckenham, Kent.

Watson (Robert Spence). Ballads of Northumberland. (*Lectures delivered to the Lit. & Philos. Soc. Newcastle-upon-Tyne*, 1898, pp. 69–92.)

A Right Pleasaunt Book of Histories, collected by William Garret, Newcastle. [A Collection of Chap-books of various dates with printed title-page prefixed to each vol.] 5 vols. Newcastle, 1818. (In Brit. Mus. Library.)

A Book of Wood-Cuts Cut and Printed by William Garret, Newcastle. 1820 (?).

Charnley (Emerson). Specimens of Early Wood Engraving, being impressions of wood-cuts from the Collection of Mr. Charnley. Newcastle-on-Tyne, 1858. 20 copies privately printed.

Specimens of Early Wood Engraving, being impressions of wood-cuts in the possession of William Dodd. Newcastle-upon-Tyne, 1862.

The Collection of impressions was afterwards purchased by Emerson Charnley.

Hindley (Charles). The Hist. of the Catnach Press; at Berwick-upon-Tweed, Alnwick, Newcastle-upon-Tyne, and Seven Dials. London, 1886.

—— **The Life and Times of James Catnach** (late of Seven Dials), Ballad Monger. London, 1878.

NORTHUMBERLAND (continued).

Books illustrated by Birket Foster (b. at North Shields, 1825) **and William Harvey** (b. at Newcastle-upon-Tyne, 1796). A valuable Collection in the Newcastle Public Lib. with typed Catalogues.

Vinycomb (John). Lambert, of Newcastle-upon-Tyne, as an Engraver of Book-Plates, with a List. (*Ex Libris Soc. Journ.* vol. v. pp. 29–33, 46, 71–72, 1895.) Issued separately in 1896, corrected and revised.

A List of Northumberland Booksellers. (*Notes & Queries*, Ser. 10, vol. vi. pp. 443–444. 1906.)

Early Booksellers on the Tyne, by James Clephan. (*Monthly Chron. of North-Country Lore*, vol. i. pp. 362–365, 412–415. 1887.) **Old Newcastle Booksellers,** by W. W. W. (*Ibid.* pp. 68–69.)

Special Topographical Collections for Northumberland, at Newcastle, are in the Public Library, and in the Libraries of the Soc. of Antiquaries, and the Lit. & Philos. Soc. A Bewick Collection (Pease Bequest) is in the Public Library, and another at the Lang Art Gallery and Museum.

Hist. MSS. Comm. Reports. Northumberland Collections.

Ainslie, Miss, at Berwick-upon-Tweed	2nd Rep. p. xii. and App. p. 68.
Brumell, Mr. F., at Morpeth ...	6th Rep. App. pp. 538–540.
Carr-Ellison, Mr. J. R., at Dunston Hill	15th Rep. pp. 40–41, and App. X. pp. 92–100.
The Delaval Family MSS.	13th Rep. p. 47, and App. VI. pp. 186–202.
Northumberland, Duke of, at Alnwick Castle	3rd Rep. p. xii. and App. pp. 45–125 ; 5th Rep. p. xi. ; 6th Rep. p. xi. and App. pp. 221–233.
Waterford, Louisa, Marchioness of, at Ford Castle	11th Rep. p. 22 and App. VII. pp. 58-81.
Berwick-upon-Tweed Corporation ...	3rd Rep. p. xxi. and App. pp. 308–309 ; 16th Rep. p. 93 ; Various Collections, vol. i. pp. 1–28.
Morpeth Corporation	6th Rep. App. pp. 526–538.

County Records, 1594, etc., with MS. Index at the Moothall, Newcastle-upon-Tyne. (*Local Records Comm. Rep.*, 1902, App. III. p. 22.)

Records in Public and Private Custody relating to Northumberland. (*Ibid.* App. III. p. 138.)

List of Northumberland Municipal Records Printed. (*Notes & Queries*, Ser. 11, vol. v. p. 298. 1912.)

The Brumell Collection of Charters. (In possession of the Soc. of Antiquaries of Newcastle-upon-Tyne.) Biblio. Note by J. C. Hodgson, with Catal. of Contents by Miss M. T. Martin. (*Archaeol. Aeliana*, Ser. 2, vol. xxiv. pp. 115–123. 1903.) See also *ante* Hist. MSS. Comm. Report.

Lysons (Rev. S.). Collections for Northumberland in the Brit. Museum. Add. MS. 9459.

Upcott (William). Topographical Collections for Northumberland in the Brit. Museum. Add. MS. 15925.

A Collection of Deeds relating to Northumberland and Durham, formerly belonging to James Coleman, in the Central Public Libraries at Newcastle-upon-Tyne.

Schedule of MSS. belonging to the late Dr. Hardy, and relating to Northumberland, arranged by J. C. Hodgson. (*Berwickshire Naturalists' Club. Proc.*, vol. xix. pp. 81–82. 1903.)

NORTHUMBERLAND (continued).

Hardy (Dr. James). List of Communications to the Proceedings of the Berwickshire Naturalists' Club, the Archaeologia Aeliana, the Tyneside Naturalists' Field Club Transactions, and other Publications. (*Berwickshire Naturalists' Club. Proc.*, vol. xvi. pp. 358–372. 1898.)

Martin (Miss M. T.). Index to Northumbrian Inquisitions Post Mortem, (*Soc. Antiq. Newcastle-upon-Tyne. Proc.*, Ser. 3, vol. ii. pp. 27–30. 1905.) Supplements the earlier lists in Hodgson's 'Hist. of Northumberland.'

Brown (William). Deeds from Burton Agnes, relating to the Counties of Durham and Northumberland. (*Archaeol. Aeliana*, Ser. 3, vol. vii. pp. 29–48. 1911.)

Craster (H. H. E.). The Marquess of Waterford's MSS. at Ford Castle. (*Soc. Antiq. Newcastle-upon-Tyne. Proc.*, Ser. 3, vol. ii., pp. 36–41. 1905.) See also *ante* Hist. MSS. Comm. Reports, p. 194.

Robinson (John). A Collection of Delaval Papers, at Ford Castle. (*Archaeol. Aeliana*, Ser. 2, vol. xv. pp. 125–143. 1892.) See also *ante* Hist. MSS. Comm. Reports, p. 194.

Welford (Richard). Records of the Committees for Compounding, etc., with Delinquent Royalists in Durham and Northumberland during the Civil War, 1643–60. Bibliography, pp. 460–461. Surtees Soc. Pubns. vol. cxi. 1905.

Wood (H. M.). List of Parochial and Non-Parochial Registers relating to the Counties of Durham and Northumberland. Durham & Northumb. Par. Reg. Soc., No. 26. 1912. The Society has also issued Transcripts of various Parish Registers in the County.

Biblio. of References to Geological Papers and Literature, relating to Northumberland and Durham. (In 'A History of Northumberland,' vol. i. pp. 417–418; vol. ii. p. 496; vol. iii. p. 314; vol. iv. p. 426; vol. v. p. 504; vol. viii. pp. 417–420. 1893–1907.) See *ante*, p. 190.

Trimen (Henry). Botanical Biblio. of the British Counties. Northumberland. (*Journ. of Botany*, vol. xii. p. 182. 1874.)

Christy (Miller). Biblio. Note on Northumberland Birds. (*The Zoologist*, Ser. 3, vol. xiv. p. 257, 1890; and reprinted in pamph., 1891, p. 20.) **Mammals.** (*The Zoologist*, Ser. 3, vol. xvii. pp. 182–183. 1893.) **Reptiles.** (*Ibid.* p. 246. 1893.) **Fishes.** (*Ibid.* p. 256. 1893.)

Anderson (John P.). Book of Brit. Topo., 1881. Northumberland, pp. 229–234.
Gatfield (George). Guide to Heraldry. 1892. Northumberland, p. 168–170.
Sims (Richard). Manual. 1861. Northumberland, pp. 170, 216–217, 237.
Upcott (William). English Topo., 1818. Northumberland, vol. ii. pp. 1028–1046, 1489.
Smith (Alfred Russell). Catal. of Topo. Tracts, etc. 1878. Northumberland, pp. 281–294.
Gough (Richard). Brit. Topo., 1780. Northumberland, vol. ii. pp. 53–69.
Bandinel (Bulkeley). Catal. of Books bequeathed to Bodleian Lib. by Richard Gough, 1814. Northumberland, pp. 247–249.

NEWCASTLE-UPON-TYNE.

Borough Records, 1640, etc., with MS. Indexes, at Town Hall, Newcastle-upon-Tyne. (*Local Records Comm. Rep.*, 1902, App. III. p. 36.)

Bell (John). Collections for a Hist. of the Municipal Government of the Borough Town and County of Newcastle-upon-Tyne, and the Conservancy of the River (consisting of Documents, MSS. and Extracts from Newspapers, etc., from 1733 to 1855). In the Newspaper Room at the British Museum.

List of Newcastle-upon-Tyne Municipal Records Printed. (*Notes & Queries*, Ser. 11, vol. v. pp. 297–298. 1912.)

NORTHUMBERLAND (continued).

An Index to the Hist. of Newcastle-upon-Tyne by John Brand. Compiled by William Dodd. Soc. of Antiq. Newcastle-upon-Tyne. 1881.

Boyle (John Roberts). Christopher Hunter's Copy of Bourne's Hist. of Newcastle, with List of MS. Documents in the volume. (*Archaeol. Aeliana*, Ser. 2, vol. xv. pp. 167–191. 1891.)

Adamson (E. H.). Henry Bourne, the Historian of Newcastle. (*Ibid.* Ser. 2, vol. xi. pp. 147–153. 1885.)

Welford (Richard). History of Newcastle and Gateshead. 3 vols. London, 1883–87. Biblio. Notes in Prefaces to each volume.

Local Muniments (relating to Newcastle and Environs). (*Archaeol. Aeliana*, Ser. 2, vol. xxiii. pp. 247–267; vol. xxiv. pp. 128–177; Ser. 3, vol. v. pp. 55–145. 1902–09.)

Sykes (John). A Collection of Publications relating to Newcastle-upon-Tyne and Gateshead. Newcastle, 1822–28. For a List, see *ante*, p. 192, 'Catal. of the Bewick Collection (Pease Bequest) in the Newcastle Public Lib.' by Anderton and Gibson.

List of John Fenwick's Privately Printed Publications, 1836–57 (mostly relating to Newcastle or the County). See *ante*, p. 189, 'Sale Catal. of the Thomas Bell Library,' 1860, pp. 98–99.

Memoir of Dr. Thomlinson, by W. Shand. (*Archaeol. Aeliana*, Ser. 2, vol. x. pp. 59–79. 1885.), and **Some Further Notices of Dr. Thomlinson, the Founder of the Thomlinson Library.** (*Ibid.* Ser. 2, vol. x. pp. 80–87. 1885.)

Welford (Richard). Art and Archaeology: The Three Richardsons, [Thomas Miles Richardson — Moses Aaron Richardson — George Bouchier Richardson.] (*Ibid.* Ser. 3, vol. iv. pp. 147-154. 1908.) Also issued separately.

Murray (David). Biblio. Note on Museums at Newcastle-upon-Tyne. ('*Museums*,' Glasgow, 1904, vol. iii. p. 51.)

Fox (George Townshend). Synopsis of the Newcastle Museum, late the Allan, formerly the Tunstall, or Wycliffe Museum, etc. In 'Memoirs of Marmaduke Tunstall and George Allan,' Newcastle, 1827.

The Catnach Press at Newcastle-upon-Tyne, see *ante*, p. 193.

The First Newcastle Directory, 1778, reproduced in facsimile with biblio. introduction by John Roberts Boyle. Newcastle, 1889.

Collections of Newspaper Cuttings, Broadsides, Ballads, etc., relating to Newcastle-upon-Tyne. (In Brit. Mus. Library.)

ALNWICK.

Skelly (George). Biblio. List of the Books and Pamphlets printed at Alnwick, with Biog. Notices of the Authors and Printers. A Paper read classifying the Publications of William Davison, Printer and Publisher at Alnwick, with a List of Topog. Prints, etc., by Davison. See 'Berwickshire Naturalists' Club. Proc.,' vol. x. p. 473. 1884. The Paper was not printed in the 'Proceedings.'

Burman (C. C.). An Account of the Art of Typography as practised at Alnwick. 1896.

The Catnach Press at Alnwick, see *ante*, p. 193.

Murray (David). Biblio. Note on Museum at Alnwick. ('*Museums*,' Glasgow, 1904, vol. iii. p. 57.)

BERWICK-UPON-TWEED.

Corporation Records, see *ante* Hist. MSS. Comm. Reports, p. 194.

The Catnach Press at Berwick-upon-Tweed, see *ante*, p. 193.

NORTHUMBERLAND (continued).

MORPETH.

Corporation Records, see *ante* Hist. MSS. Comm. Reports, p. 194.

List of Morpeth Municipal Records Printed. (*Notes & Queries*, Ser. 11, vol. v. p. 74. 1912.)

Fergusson (James). A Notice of some rare Books by Morpeth Authors, in the Lib. of the Morpeth Mechanics' Institution. (*Berwickshire Naturalists' Club. Proc.*, vol. ix. pp. 300–302. 1880.)

TYNEMOUTH.

Spence (Charles J.). Local Books in Public Libraries (with Biblio. Notes on Local Books, Newspapers, Printing Presses, Maps, Authors, etc.). (*Tynemouth Public Lib. Report*, 1902, pp. 9–17.)

A List of Books, etc., printed at, or relating to, North Shields and Tynemouth, and a Supplementary List. (*Ibid.* 1902, pp. 19–26; 1903, pp. 9-15.)

A Local Collection is at the Tynemouth Public Lib.

NOTTINGHAMSHIRE.

Nottinghamshire Collection. List of Books in the Reference Library of the Borough of Nottingham Free Public Libraries (Class List No. XIV.). Compiled under the direction of J. Potter Briscoe. Nottingham, 1890.

Part I. General Collections, pp. 1-65, 81-89.
„ II. Poll Books, pp. 66-68.
„ III. Directories and Annuals, pp. 68-70.
„ IV. Robin Hood Collection, pp. 70-71.
„ V. Corporation Reports, p. 71.
„ VI. Byron Collection, pp. 72-79.
„ VII. Kirke White Collection, p. 80.

Ward (James). A Descriptive Catal. of Books relating to Nottinghamshire in the Library of James Ward. Nottingham, 1892. **Supplementary Catalogue.** Nottingham, 1898. Privately Printed.

—— **Catal. of Books relating to the History, Bibliography, and Genealogy of Nottinghamshire.** Nottingham, 1913.

A List of Books and Pamphlets of Local Interest, either Printed or Published in, or relating to, Nottingham and Notts., or Written by Natives or Residents in the Town or County. (*Catal. of the Reference Department of the Nottingham Free Library*, by J. Potter Briscoe, 1872, pp. 34–48.)

A List of the Books and Pamphlets relating to the County, presented to the Library in 1867 by Martin Inett Preston, appeared in the Catalogue issued in 1868.

Briscoe (John Potter). Biblio. Note on Orange's Hist. of Nottingham. (*Notts. and Derbyshire Notes & Queries*, vol. v. pp. 62–63. 1897.)

—— **Chapters of Nottinghamshire History.** Nottingham, 1908. Two 18th Century Nottingham Directories, pp. 77–80. Old Nottingham Book Plates, pp. 112–113.

—— **Catal. of Portraits, Engravings, Books, Letters, and MSS. relating to Henry Kirke White, exhibited at the Centenary held in Nottingham, 21 Nov., 1906.** A Kirke White Collection is in the Nottingham Public Lib.

—— **Contributions towards Biblio. of Notts.** No. 1. 1888.

—— **A Biblio. of Pre-Norman Antiquities in Derbyshire and Notts. in the 'Archaeologia,' vols. i.-liii.** (*Notts. and Derbyshire Notes & Queries*, vol. ii. pp. 136–137. 1894.)

Herring (Paul). Notes on a Collection of Notts. Books. (*The Library*, vol. ii. pp. 338–340. 1890.)

NOTTINGHAMSHIRE (*continued*).

Godfrey (John Thomas). Notes on The Bibliography of Nottinghamshire. Nottingham, 1891. Privately Printed.

Some little known Notts. Books, by Thomas M. Blagg, and 'Bibl. Nott.' (*Notts. and Derbyshire Notes & Queries*, vol. v. pp. 65, 89, 105, 118, 152; vol. vi. pp. 43, 59. 1897–98.)

Descriptive Catal. of 'The Jackson Collection,' at the Sheffield Public Library, compiled by T. Walter Hall and A. H. Thomas. 1914. **Notts. items,** pp. 200–204.

Catal. of a Collection of Books, Historical Documents, etc., to be sold by Puttick & Simpson, London, Dec. 17th, etc., 1885. (Notts. items, pp. 70–85.)

Chicken (Rupert Cecil). An Index to Deering's 'Nottinghamia Vetus et Nova.' Nottingham, 1899.

Godfrey (John Thomas). Robert Thoroton, Physician and Antiquary. (The Historian of Nottingham.) 1890.

Blagg (Thomas M.). Dr. Robert Thoroton. (*Thoroton Soc. Trans.* 1890, vol. xii. pp. 50–55. 1908.)

Gross (Charles). Biblio. of Brit. Municipal Hist. (*Harvard Hist. Studies*, vol. v. 1897.) Notts., p. 102. Nottingham, pp. 354–356. Newark, pp. 377–378.

Dove (Patrick Edward). Domesday Studies. 1891. Domesday Biblio. Notts., vol. ii. p. 685.

Davenport (Frances G.). List of Printed Materials for Manorial Hist. 1894. Biblio. Note on Notts. Manorial Hist., p. 54.

Catal. of Antiquities and Historical Objects, etc., exhibited by the Thoroton Society, at the Exchange Hall, Nottingham, 1899 (includes Books, MSS., Newspapers, Views, Maps, etc.).

List of Exhibits of Local Antiquarian Interest in the Catal. of the Church Congress Exhibition at Nottingham, 1898, by D'Arcy Lever. (*Notts. and Derbyshire Notes & Queries*, vol. vi. pp. 22–24. 1898.)

Lyell (Arthur H.). Biblio. List of Romano-British Remains. 1912. **Notts.,** pp. 101–102.

Macklin (Herbert Walter). Monumental Brasses. London: Geo. Allen & Co., 1913. Biblio. Note on Notts. Brasses, with a List, p. 175.

Madge (Sidney). References to the Bells of Nottinghamshire. (*Notts. and Derbyshire Notes & Queries*, vol. iv. pp. 73–75, 85–87. 1896.)

Murray (David). 'Museums.' Glasgow, 1904. Biblio. Note on Nottingham Museums, vol. iii. p. 58.

Catal. of Engraved Portraits, Miniatures, etc., exhibited at Nottingham, 1900, compiled by John T. Godfrey and C. B. Stevenson. (*The Thoroton Soc. Trans.*, Supp. to vol. iv. 1900.) Also issued separately.

Catal. of Engravings of Nottinghamshire and Portraits of Nottinghamshire Worthies, lately in the possession of James Ward. 1914.

Hosiery, Lace, Embroidery, etc. List of Books in the Nottingham Free Public Libraries (and elsewhere), compiled by J. Potter Briscoe and S. J. Kirk. (Class List, No. XX.) Nottingham, 1896. 50 copies were issued separately with the title, 'A Contribution towards a Biblio. of Hosiery and Lace, etc.' 1896.

Pt. I. Works in the Reference Library.
,, II. Works in the Lending Library.
,, III. Works in other large Libraries which are not in the Nottingham Public Libraries.

NOTTINGHAMSHIRE (continued).

Cropper (Percy J.). Bibliotheca Nottinghamiensis. 1892. Biblio. Notes on Quaker Tracts in Introduction. Privately Printed.

Bibliotheca Piscatoria. (A contribution towards a Biblio. of Angling in Notts. and Derbyshire, by 'Biblio. Nott.') (*Notts. and Derbyshire Notes & Queries*, vol. v. pp. 6–8. 1897.)

Blagg (Thomas M.). Newark as a Publishing Town. A Series of Notes in 'The Newark Advertiser,' 1898. Revised and Reprinted.

Creswell (Samuel Francis). Collections towards the Hist. of Printing in Nottinghamshire. London, 1863. See also additional note by W. C. B. in 'Notes and Queries,' Ser. 10, vol. ix. pp. 205–206. 1908.

Briscoe (J. Potter). Nottinghamshire Facts and Fictions. Second Series. 1877. Pt. VII. **Ballads and Songs,** pp. 26–45.

Cropper (Percy James). The Nottinghamshire Printed Chapbooks, with Notices of their Printers and Vendors. Nottingham, 1892. See also 'The Nottingham-Printed Chap-books,' by P. J. C. in 'Notts. and Derbyshire Notes & Queries,' vol. ii. pp. 4–6, 1893.

Ritson (Joseph). Robin Hood. A Collection of all the Ancient Poems, Songs, and Ballads, now extant, relative to that Celebrated English Outlaw. London, 1885.

Robin Hood Literature in the Nottingham Free Public Reference Lib., by J. Potter Briscoe. (*Ye Nottingham Sette of Odde Volumes*, opuscula xi. 1898.)

Russell (John). Nottinghamshire Poets. (*Memorials of Old Nottinghamshire*, 1912, pp. 193–227.)

A Rare Map of Nottingham (Overton, 1714). Biblio. Note by A. Stapleton. (*Notts. and Derbyshire Notes & Queries*, vol. i. p. 199. 1893.)

Stevenson (William). Biblio. Notes on a Collection of Maps and Views of Nottingham in the Brit. Museum. (*Ibid.* vol. ii. pp. 138–140, 154–156. 1894.)

Briscoe (J. Potter) and others. Notts. Bookplates. (*Notts. and Derbyshire Notes & Queries*, vol. iii. *passim*; vol. iv. *passim*; vol. v. p. 167. 1895–97.)

Dent (T.). Notts. Libraries. Nottingham Artizans' Library. (*Notts. and Derbyshire Notes & Queries*, vol. v. pp. 71–72. 1897.)

A List of Private Acts relating to Nottinghamshire. Stevens & Sons. London, *circa* 1913.

A Special Topographical Collection for Nottinghamshire is in the Nottingham Free Public Library, and also Special Collections on Byron, Kirke White, Robin Hood, and Lace and Hosiery, see pp. 197, 198.

Hist. MSS. Comm. Reports. Nottinghamshire Collections.

Foljambe, Mr. F. J. Savile, at Osberton	15th Rep. pp. 35–39 and App. V.
Manvers, Earl, at Thoresby Park ...	9th Rep. p. xvi. and App. II. pp. 375–379.
Portland, Duke of, at Welbeck ...	13th Rep. pp. 13–26 and App. I. & II.; 14th Rep. pp. 11–16 and App. II.; 15th Rep. pp. 8–16 and App. IV.; 16th Rep. pp. 14–29; vol. v. (1899), vols. vi. and vii. (1901); 17th Rep. pp. 25–28, vol. viii. (1907).
Savile, Mr. Augustus W., at Rufford Abbey	11th Rep. p. 24 and App. VII. pp. 119–126.
Nottingham Corporation	1st Rep. App. pp. 105–106.
Newark Corporation	12th Rep. p. 47 and App. IX. p. 538.
Southwell Minster	12th Rep. p. 46 and App. IX. pp. 539–552.

NOTTINGHAMSHIRE (continued).

County Records, 1700, etc., with MS. Index, at the Shire Hall, Nottingham. (*Local Records Comm. Rep.*, 1902, App. III. p. 22.)

Borough Records, 1155, etc., with MS. Indexes, at the Guildhall, Nottingham. (*Ibid.* 1902, App. III. p. 38.)

Records of the Borough of Nottingham, 1155–1702. A Series of Extracts by W. H. Stevenson and W. T. Baker. Vols. 1–5. Nottingham, 1882–1900. Biblio. Notes in Introduction to each volume. Calendar of Charters, etc., 1399–1702, vol. ii. pp. 400–421; vol. iii. pp. 425–446; vol. iv. pp. 395–404; vol. v. pp. 409–421. See also 'Royal Charters granted to the Burgesses of Nottingham, 1155–1712,' with an Analytical Index. By W. H. Stevenson. 1890.

List of Nottingham Municipal Records Printed. (*Notes & Queries*, Ser. 11, vol. v. p. 298. 1912.)

Godfrey (John Thomas). Manuscripts relating to the County of Nottingham in the possession of James Ward, Nottingham. 1900.

Kaye's Notes relating to Notts. (18th cent.) in the Brit. Museum. Add. MSS. 18551–18553 a, b. 'References to Public Records relating to the Town and County of Nottingham,' by Sir Richard Kaye, is in the Bromley House Library, Nottingham.

Lysons' Collections for Nottinghamshire in the Brit. Museum. Add. MS. 9459.

Powell's Topog. Collections for Notts. in the Brit. Museum. Add. MS. 19915.

Upcott's Topog. Collections for Notts. in the Brit. Museum. Add. MS. 15925.

The Stretton Manuscripts: being Notes on the Hist. of Nottinghamshire, by William Stretton (of Lenton Priory), d. 1828, with an Introduction by J. T. Godfrey. Privately Printed, 1910.

Carr (J. W.). A Contribution to the Geology and Natural Hist. of Nottinghamshire. British Assoc. Nottingham, 1893. **Biblio. of Geology, by J. Shipman and J. W. Carr,** in Appendix.

——— **Biblio. of Nottinghamshire Botany.** (*Notts. and Derbyshire Notes & Queries*, vol. v. pp. 49–54. 1897.)

Trimen (Henry). Botanical Biblio. of the British Counties. Nottinghamshire. (*Journ. of Botany*, vol. xii. p. 179. 1874.)

Christy (Miller). Biblio. Note on Notts. Birds. (*The Zoologist*, Ser. 3, vol. xiv. p. 258, 1890; and reprinted in pamph., 1891, p. 22.)

Anderson (John P.). Book of Brit. Topo., 1881. Notts., pp. 235–238.
Gatfield (George). Guide to Heraldry. 1892. Notts., pp. 170–171.
Sims (Richard). Manual. 1861. Notts., pp. 171, 217, 237.
Upcott (William). English Topo., 1818. Notts., vol. ii. pp. 1047–1068, 1490.
Smith (Alfred Russell). Catal. of Topo. Tracts, etc. 1878. Notts., pp. 295–298.
Gough (Richard). Brit. Topo., 1780. Notts., vol. ii. pp. 71–78.
Bandinel (Bulkeley). Catal. of Books bequeathed to Bodleian Lib. by Richard Gough, 1814. Notts., pp. 250–251.

NEWARK.

Corporation Records. See *ante* Hist. MSS. Comm. Reports, p. 199.

RETFORD (EAST).

Borough Records, Henry III., etc., with MS. Index, at Town Clerk's Office, East Retford. (*Local Records Comm. Rep.*, 1902, App. III. p. 56.)

SOUTHWELL.

Southwell Minster Records. See *ante* Hist. MSS. Comm. Reports, p. 199.

ORKNEY AND SHETLAND.

Cursiter (James Walls). List of Books and Pamphlets relating to Orkney and Shetland, with Notes of those by Local Authors. Kirkwall, 1894.

Baikie (William Balfour). List of Books and Manuscripts relating to Orkney and Zetland, or in which these Islands are mentioned. Kirkwall, 1847.

List of Works respecting the Islands of Orkney and Shetland, forming a series of donations to the Soc. of Antiquaries of Scotland, by 'A. Z.' 1803–30. (*Archaeologia Scotica*, vol. iii. pp. 267–274. 1831.)

Biblio. of the Western Islands and Principal Antiquities of Scotland. (*Soc. Antiq. Irel. Journ.*, vol. xxix. pp. 144–145. 1899.)

Groat (Alexander G.). Thoughts on Orkney and Zetland, their Antiquities and capabilities of Improvement; with hints towards the formation of a Local Society for the Investigation and Promotion of these Objects; to which are annexed Extracts from curious Manuscripts, together with useful lists. Privately Printed. Edinb., 1831. Biblio. of Printed Books and MSS. pp. 37–47.

Tudor (J. R.). The Orkneys and Shetland. 1883. Biblio. pp. 671–679.

List of a Collection of Antiquities belonging to the Museum at Lerwick of the Shetland Literary and Scientific Society. (*Soc. Antiq. Scot. Proc.* vol. xvii. pp. 13–20. 1883.)

Goudie (Gilbert). Notice of Norwegian Documents relating to Shetland. (*Ibid.* vol. xiv. pp. 13–45. 1880.)

——— **Notice of Ancient Legal Documents (lay and ecclesiastical) preserved among the Public Records of Shetland,** with Appendix of Deeds. (*Ibid.* vol. xvi. pp. 181–203. 1882.)

Macfarlane (Walter). Geographical Collections relating to Scotland. Edited by Sir A. Mitchell and J. T. Clark. 3 vols. Edinburgh, 1906–08. Scottish History Soc., vols. li.–liii. Biblio. Notes on Orkney and Shetland in Preface to vol iii.

Examples of Printed Folk-Lore concerning the Orkney and Shetland Islands. Collected by G. F. Black and edited by N. W. Thomas. County Folk-Lore, vol. iii. (Folk-Lore Soc. Pubns. xlix. 1903.) Biblio., pp. ix.–xii.

The Dryden Collection relating to Orkney and Shetland, in the Brit. Museum. Add. MSS. 37329–37332.

A List of Books belonging to the Viking Club. 1906.

Kirkwall. Burgh Records, at Kirkwall. (*Local Records Comm. Rep.*, 1902, App. III. p. 94.)

County Council Records, at Kirkwall. (*Ibid.* 1902, App. III. p. 84.)

Gross (Charles). Biblio. of Brit. Municipal Hist. (*Harvard Hist. Studies*, vol. v. 1897.) Kirkwall, p. 269.

List of Orkney Municipal Records Printed. (*Notes & Queries*, Ser. 11, vol. v. p. 398. 1912.)

Turnbull (William B.). Scottish Parochial Registers. 1849. List of Orkney Registers, pp. 112–114. List of Shetland Registers, pp. 146–148.

Livingstone (Matthew). Guide to the Public Records of Scotland. 1905. Orkney and Shetland, pp. 32, 125, 178, 204.

Collection of Plans, Charts, etc., relating to the Orkney Islands, in the Brit. Museum. Add. MS. 38076.

Trimen (Henry). Botanical Biblio. of the British Counties. Orkney and Shetland. (*Journ. of Botany*, vol. xii. p. 237. 1874.)

ORKNEY AND SHETLAND (continued).

Christy (Miller). Biblio. Note on Orkney and Shetland Birds. (*The Zoologist*, Ser. 3, vol. xiv. pp. 264–265, 1890; and reprinted in pamph., 1891, pp. 36, 38.) **Mammals.** (*The Zoologist*, Ser. 3, vol. xvii. pp. 212, 214. 1893.) **Reptiles.** (*Ibid.* p. 250. 1893.) **Fishes.** (*Ibid.* pp. 261–262. 1893.)

Anderson (John P.). Book of Brit. Topo., 1881. Orkney and Shetland, p. 402-404.

Gough (Richard). Brit. Topo., 1780. Orkney and Shetland, vol. ii. pp. 724-731.

Bandinel (Bulkeley). Catal. of Books bequeathed to Bodleian Lib. by Richard Gough, 1814. Orkney and Shetland, pp. 365-366.

OXFORDSHIRE.

MADAN (FALCONER). OXFORD BOOKS. A BIBLIOGRAPHY OF PRINTED WORKS RELATING TO THE UNIVERSITY AND CITY OF OXFORD, OR PRINTED OR PUBLISHED THERE, with Appendices. 2 vols. Oxford, 1895, 1912.

Vol. I. The Early Oxford Press, 1468–1640. Biblio. Contents :—

A Chronological list of persons connected with Book-production at Oxford, 1180-1640. App. C. pp. 266-278.

Lists of Imprints and Tables of Oxford Printers and Publishers, 1585-1640. App. F. pp. 293-313.

Vol. II. Oxford Literature, 1450–1640, and 1641–1650. Biblio. Contents :—

Biblio. of First Book Printed at Oxford (1468). p. 2.

Periodicals issued at Oxford, 1641-1650. pp. 491-499.

A Chronological list of persons connected with Book-production at Oxford, 1180-1650. App. C. pp. 502-515.

Documents relating to the History of the Oxford Press, 1373-1637. App. D. pp. 515-530.

Devices, Ornaments, and Types of the Oxford Press, App. E. pp. 531-534.

Lists of Imprints, Tables of Printers and Publishers, etc., 1641-1650, with some earlier. App. F. pp. 534-542.

'"*The Early Oxford Press*," a bibliography of printing and publishing at Oxford "1468"-1640, was published in 1895, and confined itself entirely to books printed or published *at Oxford*. It was in fact a study of the earlier days of the greatest English press, rather than a view of the literature of Oxford. It was obvious that sooner or later a more interesting volume would suggest itself, which should add to the record of the Oxford Press a corresponding study of the books which concern Oxford, whether printed at Oxford or not.

'The second volume accordingly includes a bibliography of books about Oxford, wheresoever printed, and divides them theoretically into three classes:—books of primary importance, fully described; minor pieces, more summarily treated; and thirdly, a register of the Oxford Press.

'Pages 1-147 of the second volume are therefore a supplement to Volume I., adding to that work an account of books about Oxford *not* printed at Oxford, and giving a long series of running numbers (1-963) by which each book can be quoted (if desired) as "Oxford Books" or "Madan" number so-and-so. The opportunity has been taken to incorporate corrections and additions and to add brief annals of Oxford history for each year from 1450 to 1640.

'It is hoped that Vol. III. may cover 1651 to 1800.'—Extract from Preface to Vol. II.

The first vol. of 'Oxford Books' was also issued in 1895 by the Oxford Hist. Soc. (Publications, vol. xxix.) as a separate work under the title 'The Early Oxford Press, a Biblio. of Printing and Publishing at Oxford, "1468"-1640.'

—— **Specimen of a Biblio. of Books Printed at Oxford, 1468-1640,** shortly to be issued. (Biblio. Soc. Trans., vol. i. pp. 99-102. 1893.)

—— **A Chart of Oxford Printing, '1468'-1900, with Notes, etc.** Bibliographical Soc. (*Illustrated Monographs*, No. xii.) London, 1904. List of Oxford Printers and Publishers, pp. 27-37.

OXFORDSHIRE (continued).

Madan (Falconer). A Brief Account of the University Press at Oxford, with illustrations, together with a Chart of Oxford Printing. Oxford, 1908.

—— **Some Notes on the Oxford Press, with Special Reference to the Fluctuations in its Issues.** (*Biblio. Soc. Trans.*, vol. vii., pp. 1–3. 1904.) A Summary of a Paper read before the Biblio. Soc.

—— **The Oxford Press during the Civil War.** (*Ibid.* vol. ix. pp. 107–110. 1908.) A Summary of a Paper read before the Biblio. Soc.

—— **Some Curiosities of the Oxford Press.** (*The Library*, vol. i. pp. 154–160. 1889.)

—— **The Daniel Press (at Worcester House, Oxford), with a List of its Issues.** Privately Printed at The Philosopher Press, Wausau, Wisconsin, U.S.A. 1904. Reproduced from 'The Times,' 20 Feb. 1903. See also *infra*, p. 204.

—— **Rough List of Manuscript Materials relating to the Hist. of Oxford, contained in the Printed Catalogues of the Bodleian and College Libraries,** arranged according to subjects. Oxford, 1887.

—— **A Summary Catalogue of Western MSS. in the Bodleian Library at Oxford, which have not hitherto been catalogued in the Quarto Series.** Oxford, 1895, etc.

Vols. 3 to 6, pt. 1, only as yet issued. Descriptions of British Topographical Collections are included as well as those of Wood, Ballard, Rawlinson, etc., relating to Oxford and the County.

—— **The Daily Ledger of John Dorne, Bookseller in Oxford, 1520,** with Indexes of Books, Printers, etc. Oxford Hist. Soc. (*Collectanea*, Ser. 1, pp. 71–177. 1885.) On pp. 141–143 is reprinted a List of sixty-six books which Thomas Hunt, the Oxford Printer and Bookseller, had for sale in 1483. **Supplementary Note,** by F. Madan, with Notes on the former edition of Dorne's Day-book, by Henry Bradshaw. (*Ibid.* Ser. II. pp. 463–478. 1890.)

—— **A Biblio. of Dr. Henry Sacheverell (Fellow of Magdalen Coll., Oxford, 1701-13).** Reprinted from 'The Bibliographer,' vols. iii. and iv., 1883–84, with additions. Oxford, 1884.

Bliss (Rev. Philip). List of Books printed at Oxford, 1585-1857, arranged chronologically. (*Catal. of the Second and Remaining Portion of the Lib. of the Rev. Philip Bliss*, pp. 1–97. Sold by Sotheby's, Aug. 9th, etc., 1858.)

—— **List of Works illustrative of Oxford and Oxfordshire.** (*Ibid.* pp. 98-104.)

For a note on Bliss's 'Index of Notes and References of biographical, historical, and antiquarian matters,' in the Bodleian Lib., see Macray, 'Annals of the Bodleian,' 1890, p. 368.

A History of the Progress of the Art of Printing in the Univ. of Oxford (with a list of books printed up to 1709). Bagford Collection, Harl. MS. 5901, Brit. Museum.

Specimens of Oxford Printing in the Bagford Collection at the Brit. Museum, Harl. MS. 5929. See 'List of the Contents of the Bagford Collection,' by A. W. Pollard in 'Trans. Biblio. Soc.' vol. vii. p. 147, 1904.

Pollard (Alfred W.). A New Oxford Book of 1517. (*The Library*, New Ser. vol. x. pp. 212–213. 1909.)

Blades (William). The First Printing-Press at Oxford. (*The Antiquary*, vol. iii. pp. 13–17. 1881.)

OXFORDSHIRE (continued).

Bradshaw (Henry). A Half-Century of Notes on the Day-Book of John Dorne, bookseller in Oxford, 1520, as edited by F. Madan for the Oxford Hist. Soc. [Facsimile of Henry Bradshaw's MS.] Cambridge, 1886. See also *ante*, p. 203, for Madan's 'The Daily Ledger of John Dorne.'

Lindsay (T. M.). An Oxford Bookseller in 1520 (John Dorne), in Report of Stirling's and Glasgow Public Lib. Glasgow, 1907.

Burrows (Montagu). Linacre's Catal. of Books belonging to William Grocyn in 1520, followed by a Memoir of Grocyn. Oxford Hist. Soc. (*Collectanea*, Ser. II. pp. 319–380. 1890.)

Singer (S. W.). Some Account of the Book Printed at Oxford in 1468. London, 1812. See also *ante*, p. 202, 'Oxford Books,' by Madan, vol. ii.

Latham (H.). Oxford Bibles and Printing in Oxford. Oxford, 1870.

Allnutt (W. H.). English Provincial Presses. Early Printing at Oxford, 1478, etc. (*Bibliographica*, vol. ii. pp. 23, 127, 168. 1896.)

Hart (Horace). Notes on a Century of Typography at the University Press, Oxford, 1693-1794, with annotations & appendixes. Oxford, 1900.

—— **Charles, Earl Stanhope and the Oxford University Press.** Oxford Hist. Soc. (*Collectanea*, Ser. III. pp. 365–412. 1896.)

Hilton (R.). The Oxford University Press. (*The Caxton Mag.*, Sept.-Oct. 1901.)

The Private Printing Press (of Father Campion) at Stonor, 1581, by Thomas Edward Stonor. Philobiblon Soc. (*Biblio. & Hist. Misc.*, vol. i. No. 20. 1854.)

Allnutt (W. H.). English Provincial Presses. The Private Press at Stonor Park. (*Bibliographica*, vol. ii. pp. 163–165. 1896.)

Plomer (Henry R.). The Private Press of Dr. J. A. Giles at Bampton Vicarage, Oxon. (*Some Private Presses of the Nineteenth Century*, in '*The Library*,' New Ser., vol. i. pp. 421–422. 1900.) See also Macray, 'Annals of the Bodl. Lib., 1890,' p. 338.

The Daniel Press, Oxford. Check List of Publications. (*The Book-buyer*, New York, July 1900, p. 471.) See also *ante*, p. 203, Madan's 'The Daniel Press.'

Clark (Andrew). The Shirburn Ballads, 1585-1616, edited from the MS. in the Library of the Earl of Macclesfield at Shirburn Castle, Oxon., with Indexes. Oxford, 1907.

Pearson (Edwin). Banbury Chap Books and Nursery Toy Book Literature of the Eighteenth and Early Nineteenth Centuries, with impressions by Bewick and others. London, 1890.

Bell (C. F.). The Oxford Almanacks, a Bibliographical article. (*The Art Journal*, vol. lvi. pp. 241–247. 1904.)

Painton (Harry). Some Famous Oxford Bookshops. (*Oxford Journal Illustrated*, Jan. 28, 1914.) See also 'The Antiquary,' vol. l. p. 105. 1914.

Hewett (J. W.). On Paving Tiles, a Monumentarium, Bibliotheca Oxoniensis, and Extracts from Parish Registers, with a List of Books and Tracts relating to Oxfordshire. (*Archæol. Soc. of North Oxfordshire, Trans.*, 1853–55, pp. 89–100.)

Catal. of the Lib. of the late William Upcott, sold by Evans, New Bond St., 15 June, 1846. Oxfordshire Collections, pp. 69–78.

Haverfield (F. J.). Extracts from the 'Gentleman's Magazine' relating to Oxford, 1731-1800. Oxford Hist. Soc., vol. xvi. (*Collectanea*, Ser. II. pp. 417–448. 1890.)

OXFORDSHIRE (continued).

Index to Obituary and Biographical Notices in 'Jackson's Oxford Journal,' 1753–1853, compiled by E. A. B. Mordaunt. London, 1904. Pt. I. 1753–55, only issued.

Oxford City Millenary Exhibition, 1912. Catal. of a loan Collection of Antiquities, Pictures, Books, MSS., etc., illustrating the Hist. and Topog. of the City of Oxford. Oxford, 1912. Maps, Plans, Views, pp. 38–69. Books, Broadsides and MSS., pp. 70–73.

A Catal. of Antiquities, exhibited at the meetings of the Archæol. Soc. of North Oxfordshire. (*Transactions*, 1853–55, pp. 113–120.)

Murray (David). List of Catalogues and other Publications relating to the Museums of Oxford. ('*Museums*,' Glasgow, 1904, vol. iii. pp. 69–71.)

The Objects and Work of the Oxford Historical Society. May, 1911.

Gibson (Strickland). Early Oxford Bindings. (*Biblio. Soc. Illust. Monographs*, No. X.) Oxford, 1903.

—— **Some Notable Bodleian Bindings, 12th to 18th Cents.** Oxford, 1901–04.

Gross (Charles). Biblio. of Brit. Municipal Hist. (*Harvard Hist. Studies*, vol. v. 1897.) Oxfordshire, p. 102. Oxford, pp. 358–360.

Davenport (Frances G.). List of Printed Materials for Manorial Hist. 1894. Biblio. Note on Oxfordshire Manorial Hist., pp. 54–55.

Macklin (Herbert Walter). Monumental Brasses. London : Geo. Allen & Co. 1913. Biblio. Note on Oxfordshire Brasses, with a List, pp. 142, 175–177.

Oxford University Brass-Rubbing Society. The 'Journal' (1897–1900) contains Catalogues of Brasses in Churches, Colleges, etc., with Biblio. Notes.

Lyell (Arthur H.). Biblio. List of Romano-British Remains. 1912. Oxfordshire, pp. 102–105.

Dove (Patrick Edward). Domesday Studies. 1891. Domesday Biblio. of Oxfordshire, vol. ii. p. 685.

Smith (Lucy Toulmin). Parliamentary Petitions relating to Oxford in the Thirteenth, Fourteenth, and Fifteenth Centuries, with a List. Oxford Hist. Soc., vol. xxxii. (*Collectanea*, Ser. III. pp. 77–161. 1896.)

Shadwell (L. L.). Enactments in Parliament specially concerning the Universities of Oxford and Cambridge, the Colleges and Halls therein, and the Colleges of Winchester, Eton, and Westminster. 4 vols. Oxford Hist. Soc., vols. lviii.–lxi. Oxford, 1912. This work supersedes that by J. Griffiths, published in 1869.

Biblio. of Tractarianism. The Oxford Movement and the Church Crisis, by W. E. D. (*The Library Assoc. Record*, vol. i. pp. 324–330. 1899.)

Salter (H. E.). The Oxford Deeds of Balliol College. Oxford Hist. Soc., vol. lxiv. Oxford, 1913.

Madan (Falconer). Brief Annals of Brasenose College, with a List of Books relating to it. Oxford Hist. Soc., vol. lii. (*Brasenose College Quatercentenary Monographs*, vol. i. pp. 13–30. 1909.)

Gibson (Strickland). Some Oxford Libraries. London, 1914.

—— **Oxford Libraries.** (*Book-Auction Records*, vol. viii. pt. I. pp. i.–xix. 1910.)

Thomas (Ernest C.). The Libraries of Oxford, and the Uses of College Libraries. (*The Library Assoc. Trans. & Proc. at Oxford*, 1878, pp. 24–28.)

Macray (William Dunn). Annals of the Bodleian Library, Oxford, with a notice of the earlier Library of the University. Second Edition, enlarged, and continued from 1868 to 1880. Oxford, 1890.

OXFORDSHIRE (continued).

Clark (Andrew). A Bodleian Guide for visitors (containing a good history of the Library). Oxford, 1906.

Pietas Oxoniensis. In Memory of Sir Thomas Bodley and the Foundation of the Bodleian Library. Published for the Delegates of the Bodleian Tercentenary. October, 1902. The principal Contents are—

Sir Thomas Bodley, pp. 1-4.
The Oldest Lib. of the University, pp. 4-5.
Bishop Cobham's Lib., p. 5.
Duke Humfrey's Lib., pp. 6-7.
Sir Thomas Bodley and his Lib., pp. 7-15.
Chief Gifts to the Lib. after Bodley's Death, p. 21.
List of Librarians and Sub-Librarians, pp. 28-35.
Biblio. List of Printed Bodleian Lib. Catalogues, pp. 36-49.
Catalogues in course of Printing or Preparation, p. 50.

Tercentenary (of the Bodl. Lib.) Collection in the Bodleian Lib., 1902. See Madan. 'Summary Catal. of Western MSS. in the Bodleian,' vol. v. pp. 225-229.

The Bodleian Quarterly Record. Published for the Bodl. Lib. from April, 1914, etc. Vol. i. contains 'Humphrey Wanley and the Bodleian in 1697,' pp. 106-112 ; 'Bodley's Library in 1697,' pp. 136-140 ; 'Index to Duke Humphrey's Gifts to the Old Library of the University in 1439, 1441 and 1444,' pp. 131-135, and Biblio. Notes *passim.*

Nicholson (Edward W. B.). Bodley and the Bodleian, 1598-1898. Oxford, 1898.

——— **The Bodleian Library in 1882-1887.** A Report from the Librarian. Oxford, 1888. Description of, and Guide to the 'Subject-Catalogue of Printed Books,' pp. 31-32.

Tedder (Henry R.). E. W. B. Nicholson, Bodley's Librarian, 1882-1912. In Memoriam. Aberdeen, 1914.

Burgon (John William). Memoir of Henry Octavius Coxe (Bodleian Librarian, 1860-81), in 'Lives of Twelve Good Men,' 1891, pp. 307-320. See also 'Mr. Coxe's Work at the Bodleian,' by W. Dunn Macray, in 'Trans. Lib. Assoc. 4th & 5th Ann. Meeting,' pp. 13-16. 1884.

Botfield (Beriah). Notes on the Cathedral Libraries of England. 1849. **Christ Church, Oxford,** pp. 348-368.

Shadwell (C. L.). A Catal. of the Library of Oriel College in the year 1375. Oxford Hist. Soc. (*Collectanea*, Ser. I. pp. 57-70. 1885.)

Daniel (C. H. O.). Notes from a Catal. of Pamphlets (Civil War Period) in Worcester College. Oxford, 1874.

Oxford Historical Portraits. Illustrated Catalogues. Vol. i. (before 1625), vol. ii. (1625-1714), vol. iii. (after 1715). Oxford, 1904-06.

Poole (Mrs. Reginald Lane). Catal. of Portraits in the possession of the University, Colleges, City, and County of Oxford. Vol. i. The Portraits in the University Collections and in the Town and County Halls. Oxford, 1912. Only vol. i. as yet published. Also issued by the Oxford Hist. Soc. as Publication LVII.

Haverfield (Francis John). Brief Guide to the Portraits in Christ Church Hall, Oxford. 5th Edition. 1912.

Old Plans of Oxford, by Agas, Hollar and Loggan. A Portfolio of Reproductions of 15 Plans. Oxford Hist. Soc., vol. xxxviii. 1898.

Oxford Topography; an Essay by Herbert Hurst, forming a Companion volume to the Portfolio containing Agas's Map (1578-88) and other Old Plans of Oxford, with Index by George Parker. Oxford Hist. Soc., vol. xxxix. 1899.

OXFORDSHIRE (*continued*).

Firth (J. B.). The Minstrelsy of Isis. An Anthology of Poems relating to Oxford and all Phases of Oxford Life. London, 1908.

A Special Topographical Collection for Oxfordshire is in the Oxford Public Library.

Hist. MSS. Comm. Reports. Oxfordshire Collections.

Camoys, Lord, at Stonor Park ...	2nd Rep. p. xii. and App. p. 33.
Dillon, Viscount	2nd Rep. p. x. and App. pp. 31–33.
Dormer, Mr. C. Cottrell	2nd Rep. p. xi. and App. pp. 82–84.
Macclesfield, Earl of	1st Rep. p. ix. and App. pp. 34–40.
Macray, Rev. W. Dunn, at Ducklington	13th Rep. App. IV. pp. 507–508.
Marlborough, Duke of, at Blenheim Palace	8th Rep. p. x. and App. pp. 1–60.
Turner, Mr. W. H.	2nd Rep. App. pp. 101–102.
Ewelme Hospital...	8th Rep. p. xiv. and App. pp. 624–632; 9th Rep. App. I. pp. 216–222.
Oxford, Balliol College	4th Rep. p. xvii. and App. pp. 442–451.
——— Corpus Christi College... ...	2nd Rep. p. xiv. and App. p. 126.
——— Exeter College	2nd Rep. p. xiv. and App. pp. 127–130.
——— Jesus College	2nd Rep. p. xv. and App. p. 130.
——— Lincoln College	2nd Rep. p. xiv. and App. pp. 130–132.
——— Magdalen College	4th Rep. p. xix. and App. pp. 458–465; 8th Rep. App. pp. 262–269.
——— Merton College	6th Rep. App. pp. 545–549.
——— New College	2nd Rep. p. xiv. and App. pp. 132–136.
——— Oriel College	2nd Rep. p. xiv. and App. pp. 136–137.
——— Pembroke College	6th Rep. App. pp. 549–551.
——— Queen's College...	2nd Rep. p. xv. and App. pp. 137–142; 4th Rep. p. xvii. and App. pp. 451-458.
——— ——— God's House at Southampton, Records	6th Rep. App. pp. 551-569.
——— St. John's College	4th Rep. p. xvii. and App. pp. 465–468.
——— Trinity College	2nd Rep. p. xv. and App. p. 142.
——— University College	5th Rep. p. xv. and App. pp. 477–479.
——— Wadham College	5th Rep. p. xv. and App. pp. 479–481.
——— Worcester College	2nd Rep. p. xv. and App. p. 143.
Burford Corporation	16th Rep. pp. 94–95; Various Collections, vol. i. pp. 29–64.

County Records, 1690, etc., at the County Hall, Oxford, and Probate Court Records, 1801, etc., at the Probate Registry, Oxford. (*Local Records Comm. Rep.*, 1902, App. III. p. 26.)

List of Oxford Municipal Records Printed. (*Notes & Queries*, Ser. 11, vol. v. p. 398. 1912.)

Rogers (J. E. Thorold). Oxford City Documents. Financial and Judicial, 1268-1665. Oxford Hist. Soc., vol. xviii. 1891.

Anstey (Henry). Munimenta Academica, or Documents illustrative of Academical Life and Studies at Oxford. 2 vols. London, 1868. Catal. of the Books given to the University by Humphrey, Duke of Gloucester, vol. ii. pp. 758–772.

Calendar of Charters and Rolls preserved in the Bodleian Library. Edited by William Henry Turner, under the direction of H. O. Coxe. Oxford, 1878. **Oxfordshire items,** pp. 277–384, 660–662, 684.

'Selections from the Records of the City of Oxford, illustrating the Municipal History, 1509–1583,' edited by W. H. Turner, under the direction of R. S. Hawkins. Oxford, 1880, contains Biblio. Notes in Preface and an Analytical Table of Contents.

OXFORDSHIRE (continued).

Catalogi Codicum Manuscriptorum Bibliothecæ Bodleianæ. Oxford, 1845, 1853–1900.

Pars IV. **Thomas Tanner,** ed. by Alfred Hackman. 1859. Oxford references, pp. 1049–1056.

Pars V. **Richard Rawlinson,** ed. by W. Dunn Macray. 5 pts. 1862–1900.

Pars X. **Elias Ashmole,** ed. by W. H. Black. 1845.

Index to the Catal. of the MSS. of Elias Ashmole. By W. Dunn Macray. Oxford, 1866. This 'Ashmole' Cat. also forms Pars X. of the preceding 'Catalogi.'

A Descriptive, Analytical, and Critical Catal. of the MSS. bequeathed unto the Univ. of Oxf. by Elias Ashmole, also of some additional MSS. contributed by Kingsley, Lhuyd, Borlase, and others. By William Henry Black. Oxford, 1845.

Catalogi Librorum Manuscriptorum Angliæ et Hiberniæ in unum collecti, cum indice alphabetico, edited by Edward Bernard. Oxford, 1698.

Pt. I. relates to the Bodleian and Ashmolean. Pt. II. to the Oxford Colleges. A Life of Sir Thomas Bodley and a Hist. of the Bodleian are included in the work. For a list of the Collections then or now in the Bodleian which are catalogued in the volume, see *ante*, p. 206. 'Pietas Oxoniensis,' 1902, p. 39.

The Life and Times of Anthony Wood, Antiquary, of Oxford, 1632-1695, described by himself. Collected from his Diaries and other Papers, by Andrew Clark. Oxford Hist. Soc. Oxford, 1891–1900.

Vol. I. contains an important analysis with details of the MSS. available for the Life of Wood, and full notes on the Wood Collection of MSS. and Printed Books, including the Almanacs, Newspapers, Oxford Pamphlets, Chap-books, Ballads, Book-lists, Catalogues of Plays, etc. Vol. IV. has a Catal. of Wood's MS. Authorities, at pp. 87-312. Indexes (Biographical, Topographical, Academical, Matters, Words, Persons) form Vol. V.

Huddesford (William). Catalogus Librorum Manuscriptorum . . . . Antonii à Wood, being a minute Catal. of each particular contained in the MS. Collections of Anthony à Wood deposited in the Ashmolean Museum at Oxford. 1761. Reprinted by Sir Thomas Phillipps at the Middle Hill Press. 1824. For further descriptions of Anthony à Wood's Collections in the Bodleian, see also Macray, 'Annals of the Bodl. Lib., 1890,' pp. 365–366, and Madan, 'Summary Catal. of Western MSS. in the Bodleian,' vol. v. Preface, p. v. and pp. 86–93.

The Rawlinson Collections in the Bodleian Library. For an account of Richard Rawlinson and his Collections, see Macray, 'Annals of the Bodl. Lib., 1890,' pp. 231–251, and for items relating to Oxford in the Collection, see Madan, 'Summary Catal. of Western MSS. in the Bodleian,' vol. iii. Preface, p.ix. and pp. 120, etc.

Fletcher (W. Y.). The Rawlinsons and their Collections, with a List of the Thomas Rawlinson Sale Catalogues in the Bodleian Lib., by F. Madan. (*Biblio. Soc. Trans.*, vol. v. pp. 67–86. 1901.) A list of the Sale Catalogues of Thomas Rawlinson's books is in Dibdin's 'Bibliomania.'

The Ballard MS. Collection in the Bodl. Lib. For items relating to Oxford Topography, see Madan, 'Summary Catal. of Western MSS. in the Bodleian,' vol. iii. Preface, p. ix. and pp. 160–170.

The Gough Collection in the Bodl. Lib. For items relating to Oxfordshire, see Madan, 'Summary Catal. of Western MSS. in the Bodleian,' vol. iv. Preface, p. vii. and pp. 254–261. See also Biblio. Note on Richard Gough Collections (other than Books) in David Murray's 'Museums,' 1904, vol. ii. p. 263.

Thomas Delafield's MS. Collections for Oxfordshire in the Bodl. Lib., 3 vols See Macray, 'Annals of the Bodl. Lib., 1890,' p. 385.

OXFORDSHIRE (continued).

Turner's MS. Collections for Oxfordshire in the Bodl. Lib. See Madan, 'Summary Catal. of Western MSS. in the Bodleian,' Preface, vol. v. p. v. and pp. 545–547.

Upcott's Collections relating to the Hist. of Oxfordshire, in the Brit. Museum, 1644-1814. Add. MSS. 15930–15931.

Catal. of MSS. collected by the Rev. Philip Bliss, sold by Sotheby's, 21 Aug., 1858. Oxford and Oxfordshire items, pp. 22–23.

MS. Materials for the Topography of Oxfordshire, in the Library of the Soc. of Antiquaries, London, by Percy Manning. (*Berks., Bucks., & Oxon. Archæol. Journ.*, vol. ii. pp. 99-106. 1897.)

Oxford Barbers' Company Records, in the Bodl. Lib. See Madan, 'Summary Catal. of Western MSS. in the Bodleian,' vol. vi. Preface, and pp. 19–21.

Catalogus Codicum MSS. qui in Collegiis aulisque Oxoniensibus hodie adservantur. By H. O. Coxe. 2 vols. Oxford, 1852.

The Catalogue of each College has a separate pagination and Register. The second vol. has a full Index with numerous Oxford references.

Catal. of the Archives in the Muniment Rooms of All Souls' College, Oxford, prepared by Charles Trice Martin. London, 1877.

Catalogus Librorum Impressorum Bibl. Coll. B. Mariæ Magdalenæ in Academia Oxoniensi. By E. M. Macfarlane. 3 vols. Oxford, 1860-62. Oxfordshire References, vol. ii. pp. 679–686. List of Works by Authors connected with the College, entered separately in Appendix to vol. iii. See also Macray (W. Dunn), 'A Register of the Members of St. Mary Magdalen College, Oxford.' New Ser., 8 vols., 1894–1915, for details of works by members of the College.

Archdeaconry of Oxford Records, 1558, etc., with MS. Index, at the Bodl. Lib. Oxford. (*Local Records Comm. Rep.*, 1902, App. III. p. 124.) For a list see Madan, 'Summary Catal. of Western MSS. in the Bodleian,' vol. v. Preface, p. v. and pp. 157–184.

Diocesan Records, 1543, etc., at the Diocesan Registry, Oxford. (*Local Records Comm. Rep.*, 1902, App. III. p. 106.)

Christ Church Records, Hen. I., etc., with MS. Lists, at Oxford. (*Ibid.* 1902, App. III. p. 114.)

Faulkner (Charles). A Brief Hist. of Parish Registers, with Remarks on a few of the Registers in the North of Oxfordshire. (*Archæol. Soc. of N. Oxfordshire, Trans.*, 1853-55, pp. 101–111.)

Extracts from the Parish Registers of Oxfordshire, by Canon Oldfield, appeared in the 'Berks., Bucks., and Oxon. Archæol. Journal,' vols. xvi. xvii. 1910-11.

Bucks. and Oxon. Marriage Bonds, with a List, by G. F. Tudor Sherwood. (*Berks., Bucks., & Oxon. Archæol. Journ.*, vol. ii. pp. 52, 77, 117. 1896–97.)

Poole (Reginald Lane). A Lecture on the History of the University Archives, delivered at the Ashmolean Museum, 8 May, 1912, and printed with an Appendix, 'Inventory of Muniments in the Congregation House,' printed with corrections from Brian Twyne's 'Collectanea.' Oxford. 1912.

Günther (R. W. T.). Oxford Gardens. Oxford, 1912. Biblio. of the Botanic Garden 'Guide,' & list of Works and Prints relating to the Botanic Garden, pp. 181–187.

Trimen (Henry). Botanical Biblio. of the British Counties. Oxfordshire. (*Journ. of Botany*, vol. xii. p. 109. 1874.)

Aplin (Oliver V.). The Birds of Oxfordshire. Oxford, 1889. Biblio. of Birds of Oxfordshire, pp. 13–16.

Christy (Miller). Biblio. Note on Oxfordshire Birds. (*The Zoologist*, Ser. 3, vol. xiv. p. 258, 1890; and reprinted in pamph., 1891, p. 22.) **Mammals.** (*The Zoologist*, Ser. 3, vol. xvii. p. 183, 1893.) **Reptiles.** (*Ibid.* p. 246, 1893.) **Fishes.** (*Ibid.* p. 257, 1893.)

OXFORDSHIRE (continued).

Anderson (John P.). Book of Brit. Topo., 1881. Oxfordshire, pp. 238-245.
Gatfield (George). Guide to Heraldry. 1892. Oxfordshire, pp. 171-174.
Sims (Richard). Manual. 1861. Oxfordshire, pp. 171, 217-218, 238.
Upcott (William). English Topo., 1818. Oxfordshire, vol. iii. pp. 1069-1134, 1491-1493.
Smith (Alfred Russell). Catal. of Topo. Tracts, etc., 1878. Oxfordshire, pp. 299-317.
Gough (Richard). Brit. Topo., 1780. Oxfordshire, vol. ii. pp. 79-172.
Bandinel (Bulkeley). Catal. of Books bequeathed to Bodleian Lib. by Richard Gough. 1814. Oxfordshire, pp. 252-279.

BURFORD.

Corporation Records. See *ante* Hist. MSS. Comm. Reports, p. 207.

CHIPPING NORTON.

Borough Records, 1606, etc., at Chipping Norton. (*Local Records Comm. Rep.*, 1902, App. III. p. 50.)

DUCKLINGTON.

Macray (W. Dunn). An Index to the Registers in the Parish of Ducklington. (*North Oxon. Archæol. Soc. Trans.* 1880.) Oxford, 1881.

EWELME.

Ewelme Almshouse MSS. See *ante* Hist. MSS. Comm. Reports, p. 207.

HASELEY.

Thomas Delafield's MS. Collections for the Parish of Haseley, in the Bodleian Library. See Macray, 'Annals of the Bodl. Lib.,' 1890, p. 386.

WOODSTOCK.

Borough Records, Edw. IV., etc., with MS. List, at Town Hall, Woodstock. (*Local Records Comm. Rep.*, 1902, App. III. p. 74.)

PEEBLESSHIRE.

Douglas (Sir George). A Hist. of the Border Counties (Roxburgh, Selkirk, Peebles). The County Histories of Scotland. 1899. List of Books relating to Peeblesshire, pp. 465-470. List of Maps, pp. 471-472.

Hist. MSS. Comm. Reports. Peeblesshire Collections.

Hay, Mr. Robert Mordaunt, of Duns Castle, Berwickshire	Report on MSS. in various Collections, vol. v. pp. 1-71. 1909.
Stuart, Hon. H. C. Maxwell, at Traquair House	9th Rep. p. xviii. and App. II. pp. 241-262.

Burgh Records, 1362, etc., with Printed List, at Town Hall, Peebles. (*Local Records Comm. Rep.*, 1902, App. III. p. 96.) The Scottish Burgh Records Soc. issued in 1872, 'Charters and Documents relating to the Burgh of Peebles, with extracts from the Records of the Burgh, 1165-1710,' and in 1910, 'Extracts from the Records of the Burgh of Peebles, 1652-1714, with Appendix, 1367-1665.'

List of Peeblesshire Municipal Records Printed. (*Notes and Queries*, Ser. 11, vol. v. p. 478. 1912.)

Gross (Charles). Biblio. of Brit. Municipal Hist. (*Harvard Hist. Studies*, vol. v. 1897. Peeblesshire, p. 133. Peebles, p. 362.

Livingstone (Matthew). Guide to the Public Records of Scotland. 1905. Peeblesshire, pp. 126, 180.

PEEBLESSHIRE (continued).

Turnbull (William B.). Scottish Parochial Registers. 1849. List of Peeblesshire Registers, pp. 115–117.

Lyell (Arthur H.). Biblio. List of Romano-British Remains, 1912. Peeblesshire, p. 139.

Anderson (Joseph) and Black (Geo. F.). Report on Local Museums in Scotland. Peebles Museum. (*Soc. of Antiq. Scot. Proc.*, vol. xxii. pp. 333–337. 1888.)

Trimen (Henry). Botanical Biblio. of the British Counties. Peeblesshire. (*Journ. of Botany*, vol. xii. p. 234. 1874.)

Christy (Miller). Biblio. Note on Peeblesshire Birds. (*Catal. of Local Lists of British Birds*, 1891, p. 36.) **Mammals.** (*The Zoologist*, Ser. 3, vol. xvii. p. 213. 1893.) **Reptiles.** (*Ibid.* p. 250. 1893.) **Fishes.** (*Ibid.* p. 262. 1893.)

Anderson (John P.). Book of Brit. Topo., 1881. Peeblesshire, pp. 404–405.

Gough (Richard). Brit. Topo., 1780. Peeblesshire, vol. ii. p. 706.

Bandinel (Bulkeley). Catal. of Books bequeathed to Bodleian Lib. by Richard Gough, 1814. Peeblesshire, p. 363.

PEMBROKESHIRE.

Owen (Henry). A List of Printed Books relating to Pembrokeshire. Solva, Pemb., 1897.

——— **Index to Fenton's 'Historical Tour through Pembrokeshire.'** 1894. Reprinted in the 1903 edn. of the 'Historical Tour.'

Owen (George). The Description of Pembrokeshire. Edited by Henry Owen. Cymmrodorion Record Series, No. I. London, 1892. Biblio. Notes on George Owen in Preface to Part I.

'A Catal. of Books belonging to the Pembroke Society,' 1791, printed by William Wilmot. Biblio. Note by E. D. J. (*Welsh Biblio. Soc. Journ.*, vol. i. pp. 152–153. 1913.)

The Earliest Printers of Haverford, with a list of Books printed there, by H. E. H. James. (*Welsh Biblio. Soc. Journ.*, vol. i. pp. 114–118, 153–155. 1912-13.)

List of Pembrokeshire Illustrations in the 'Archæologia Cambrensis,' 1884-1900, see Alphabetical Index by F. Green, 1902, p. 107.

Vaughan (H. M.). Old Book Plates of West Wales. Pembrokeshire. (Hist. Soc. of West Wales. *West Wales Hist. Records*, vol. iv. pp. 177–192. 1914.)

Lyell (Arthur H.). Biblio. List of Romano-British Remains. 1912. **Pembrokeshire,** p. 146.

Davenport (Frances G.). List of Printed Materials for Manorial Hist. 1894. Biblio. Note on Pembrokeshire Manorial Hist., p. 64.

George Owen's MSS. in the Library of Sir Thomas Phillipps, of Middle Hill, including 'A Table to the Book of Pedigrees, intituled Penbrokeshire, 1601.' (*Archæol. Cambrensis*, New Ser., vol. v. pp. 33–41. 1854.)

St. David's Cathedral Records, at St. David's. (*Local Records Comm. Rep.*, 1902, App. III. p. 114.)

Summary of Ancient Records of the Diocese of St. David's preserved in the Registry at Carmarthen, including the St. David's Bishops' Registers, 1397–1825. (*Carmarthenshire Antiq. Soc. Trans.*, vol. i. pp. 81–82. 1905.)

Phillips (James). The Oldest Parish Registers in Pembrokeshire. (*Archæol. Cambrensis*, Ser. 6, vol. ii. pp. 115–127 ; vol. iii. pp. 298–318 ; vol. v. pp. 38–61. 1902–05.)

PEMBROKESHIRE (continued).

Index to a Volume of Pedigrees of Caermarthenshire, Cardiganshire, and Pembrokeshire, *circa* 1700, belonging to J. L. Philipps, of Dale, co. Pembroke. 1857. Privately Printed at Middle Hill Press.

An Index of Pedigrees of Caermarthenshire, Cardiganshire, and Pembrokeshire, in continuation of Lewis Dwnn, to about the years 1700–10. Privately Printed at Middle Hill Press. 1859.

Trimen (Henry). Botanical Biblio. of the British Counties. Pembrokeshire. (*Journ. of Botany*, vol. xii. p. 157. 1874.)

Christy (Miller). Biblio. Note on Pembrokeshire Birds. (*The Zoologist*, Ser. 3, vol. xiv. p. 262, 1890; and reprinted in pamph., 1891, p. 22.)

Anderson (John P.). Book of Brit. Topo., 1881. Pembrokeshire, p. 352.

Gough (Richard). Brit. Topo., 1780. Pembrokeshire, vol. ii. p. 512.

Bandinel (Bulkeley). Catal. of Books bequeathed to Bodleian Lib. by Richard Gough 1814. Pembrokeshire, p. 334.

PERTHSHIRE.

Urquhart (A. R.). Literature in Perth, with a Biblio. of Local Interest. (*Auld Perth*, edited by A. R. Urquhart, Perth. 1906.) Also reprinted with additions.

BIBLIO. CONTENTS.

Biblio. Note on Perth Printers, pp. 118-120.
Biblio. Note on Perthshire Newspapers and Magazines, pp. 121-123.
List of Library and Book Catalogues, etc., p. 173.
List of Magazines, Transactions, etc., pp. 173-175.
List of Directories, p. 176.
List of Guides and Maps, pp. 183-184.

Smith (D. Crawford). The Historians of Perth, and other Local and Topographical Writers, up to the end of the Nineteenth Century. Perth, 1906.

Note on the Biblio. of Perth, by J. B. T. (*Scottish Notes & Queries*, Ser. 2, vol. viii. p. 164. 1907.)

Murray (Katharine M.). Marchioness of Tullibardine. **A Military Hist. of Perthshire, 1660-1902.** 2 vols. Perth, 1908. List of Authorities, Printed Works, pp. 563–571. List of MSS., pp. 571–573.

Bridges (James). Letterpress Printing in Perth. A Lecture. 1892.

Minto (John A.). A Notable Publishing House, the Morisons of Perth. (*The Library*, New Ser., vol. i. pp. 254–263. 1900.) See also article with the same title in 'Perth Library and Museum Record,' vol. i. pp. 30-36, 1900; 'Notes on the Morisons' in Urquhart's 'Auld Perth,' pp. 118–119; and 'The Morisons, Printers, Booksellers, etc.,' in D. Crawford Smith's 'Historians of Perth,' pp. 77–109.

Memoranda of the Transactions of the Literary and Antiquarian Soc. of Perth, and of the Papers read at their meetings [includes List of Papers and Lists of Books, MSS., etc., presented to the Soc.] (*Transactions*, vol. i. pp. 9–19. 1827.)

An Account of the Foundation of the Leightonian Library. By Robert Douglas, Bishop of Dunblane. (Relates to Archbishop Leighton's Foundation at Dunblane.) (*The Bannatyne Miscellany*, vol. iii. pp. 227–272. 1855.)

Drummond P. R.). Perthshire Poets, 1800 to 1850. 1873.

——— **Perthshire in Bygone Days.** London, 1879.

BIBLIO. CONTENTS.

Personal Recollections of Perthshire Poets, pp. 255-452.
Perthshire Songs by Perthshire Men, pp. 453-492.
Perthshire Songs and their Authors, pp. 495-562.
Perthshire Ballads, pp. 565-580.
The Perthshire Drummond Ballads, pp. 583-628.

PERTHSHIRE (continued).

Ford (Robert). The Harp of Perthshire. A Collection of Songs, Ballads etc., chiefly by local Authors, with Explanatory Notes. Paisley, 1893.

Wilson (Rev. W.). The Trossachs in Literature and Tradition. 1908.

Lyell (Arthur H.). Biblio. List of Romano-British Remains. 1912. Perthshire, p. 140.

Murray (David). 'Museums.' Glasgow, 1904. Biblio. Note on the Museums at Perth, vol. iii. p. 102.

Anderson (Joseph) and Black (G. F.). Report on Local Museums in Scotland. Perth Museum. (*Soc. of Antiq. Scot. Proc.*, vol. xxii. pp. 337-341. 1888.)

Catal. of the Exhibition of Local Relics and Antiquities at the Sandeman Gallery, Jan. and Feb., 1903. Perth, 1903.

Bowick (James B.). Summary of a Hist. of the Sandeman Public Lib. (*The Dundee Advertiser*, 10 Nov., 1908.)

Gray (W. Forbes). An Ancient Scottish Library. [Innerpeffray Library.] (*The Scots Mag.*, vol. xxii. pp. 88-94. 1898.)

Special Topographical Collection for Perth and Perthshire, including the Library of Robert Scott Fittis, the Historian of Perth, is in the Sandeman Public Lib. at Perth.

Hist. MSS. Comm. Reports. Perthshire Collections.

Atholl, Duke of, at Blair Castle ...	7th Rep. p. xv. and App. pp. 703-716; 12th Rep. pp. 48-51 and App. VIII. pp. 1-75.
Barclay-Allardice, Mrs., at Loyal House	5th Rep. p. xx. and App. pp. 629-632.
Kinnaird, Lord, at Rossie Priory ...	5th Rep. p. xx. and App. pp. 620-621.
Kinnoull, Earl of, at Dupplin	4th Rep. p. xxiii. and App. pp. 514-515.
Maxwell, Sir J. M. Stirling-, at Keir House	10th Rep. pp. 34-37 and App. I. pp. 58-81.
Menzies, Sir Robert, at Castle Menzies	6th Rep. p. xviii. and App. pp. 688-709.
Moray, Mr. C. S. H. Drummond, at Ardoch, Abercairny, and Blair Drummond	3rd Rep. p. xxiii. and App. pp. 416-429; 10th Rep. p. 37 and App. I. pp. 81-199.
Murray, Sir Patrick Keith, at Ochtertyre	3rd Rep. p. xxiv. and App. pp. 408-413.
Rattray, Col. James, at Craighall ...	4th Rep. p. xxiii. and App. p. 536.
Rollo, Lord, of Duncrub Park, Dunning	3rd Rep. p. xxiii. and App. pp. 406-407.
Wharncliffe, Earl of, at Belmont ...	3rd Rep. p. xvi. and App. pp. 224-226; 4th Rep. p. xxiii. and App. p. 518; 5th Rep. p. xx. and App. pp. 621-622.
Perth, Royal Burgh of	5th Rep. p. xxi. and App. p. 655.
——— King James's Hospital ...	6th Rep. p. xix. and App. pp. 713-715.
Glenalmond, Trinity College	2nd Rep. p. xx. and App. pp. 203-205.

Burgh Records, 1210, etc., at City Chambers, Perth. (*Local Records Comm Rep.*, 1902, App. III. p. 96.)

County Council Records, 1650, etc., at County Buildings, Perth. (*Local Records Comm. Rep.*, 1902, App. III. p. 84.)

Records at Sandeman Public Library, 1210, etc. (*Local Records Comm. Rep.*, 1902, App. III. p. 134.)

List of Perthshire Municipal Records Printed. (*Notes and Queries*, Ser. 11, vol. v. p. 478. 1912.)

PERTHSHIRE (continued).

Marshall (David). Notes on the Record Room of the City of Perth. (*Soc. of Antiq. Scot. Proc.*, vol. xxx. pp. 274–291 ; vol. xxxiii. pp. 414-440. 1896–99.)

Anderson (Peter John). Inventories of Ecclesiastical Records of North-Eastern Scotland. Perthshire. New Spalding Club, vol. vi. Miscellany, vol. i. 1890.

Livingstone (Matthew). Guide to the Public Records of Scotland. 1905. Perthshire, p. 179.

Turnbull (William B.). Scottish Parochial Registers. 1849. List of Perthshire Registers, pp. 118–131.

Gross (Charles). Biblio. of Brit. Municipal Hist. (*Harvard Hist. Studies*, vol. v. 1897.) Perthshire, p. 134. Perth, pp. 363-364.

White (F. Buchanan White). Annals of the Perthshire Soc. of Natural Science, from its Foundation to 1881, with List of Papers published by the Society bearing on the Nat. Hist. of Perthshire and the Basin of the Tay, arranged systematically. (*Perthshire Soc. of Nat. Science. Proc.*, vol. iv. pp. lxxxii.–lxxxix. 1908.)

List of Papers, Notes, and Addresses communicated to the Perthshire Soc. of Nat. Science, by Dr. F. Buchanan White, with List of Publications issued by the Soc. compiled or edited by Dr. Buchanan White. (*Perthshire Soc. of Nat. Science. Proc.*, vol. ii. pp. lxii.-lxvi. 1898.)

White (F. Buchanan White). The Flora of Perthshire. Edited, with an Introduction and Life of the Author, and a List of his Scientific Publications, by J. W. H. Trail. Edinburgh, 1898.

Trimen (Henry). Botanical Biblio. of the British Counties. Perthshire. (*Journ. of Botany*, vol. xii. p. 235. 1874.)

Christy (Miller). Biblio. Note on Perthshire Birds. (*Catal. of Local Lists of British Birds*, 1891, p. 37.) **Mammals.** (*The Zoologist*, Ser. 3, vol. xvii. p. 213. 1893.)

Anderson (John P.). Book of Brit. Topo., 1881. Perthshire, pp. 405-407.

Gough (Richard). Brit. Topo., 1780. Perthshire, vol. ii. pp. 707-710.

Bandinel (Bulkeley). Catal. of Books bequeathed to Bodleian Lib. by Richard Gough, 1814 Perthshire, p. 363.

QUEEN'S COUNTY.

Hist. MSS. Comm. Reports. Queen's County Collection.

Dunne, Maj.-Gen. F. Plunket, at Brittas ... ... 2nd Rep. p. xx. and App. pp. 227–231

O'Hanlon (John). Index of Materials for the Hist. & Topography of Queen's County in tho Irish Ordnance Survey Records, and in the Royal Irish Academy. (*Kilkenny & South-East of Irel. Archæol. Soc. Journ.*, vol. iv. p. 192. 1856.)

Berry (Henry F.). Ancient Charters in the Liber Albus Ossoriensis. (With Biblio. Notes.) (*Royal Irish Acad. Proc.*, vol. xxvii. Sect. C. pp. 115–125. 1908.)

Lawlor (H. J.). Calendar of the Liber Ruber of the Diocese of Ossory, with an Index. (*Ibid.* vol. xxvii. Sect. C. pp. 159–208. 1908.) A Description and Calendar of the 'Liber Ruber,' by Sir John T. Gilbert is in the 10th Report, Hist. MSS. Comm. App. Pt. v. 1885.

Anderson (John P.). Book of Brit. Topo., 1881. Queen's County, p. 441.

Gough (Richard). Brit. Topo., 1780. Queen's County, vol. ii. p. 815.

Bandinel (Bulkeley). Catal. of Books bequeathed to Bodleian Lib. by Richard Gough, 1814. Queen's County, p. 383.

RADNORSHIRE.

Ballinger (John) and Jones (James Ifano). Catal. of the Welsh Department of the Cardiff Free Libraries. 1898. Radnorshire entries, pp. 411–412.

Gross (Charles). Biblio. of Brit. Municipal Hist. (*Harvard Hist. Studies*, vol. v. 1897.) Radnorshire, p. 103.

Lyell (Arthur H.). Biblio. List of Romano-British Remains. 1912. Radnorshire, p. 146.

Davenport (Frances G.). List of Printed Materials for Manorial Hist. 1894. Biblio. Note on Radnorshire Manorial Hist., p. 65.

List of Radnorshire Illustrations in the 'Archæologia Cambrensis,' 1884-1900, see Alphabetical Index by F. Green, 1902, p. 107.

Trimen (Henry). Botanical Biblio. of the British Counties. Radnorshire. (*Journ. of Botany*, vol. xii. p. 157. 1874.)

Anderson (John P.). Book of Brit. Topo., 1881. Radnorshire, p. 353.

Gough (Richard). Brit. Topo., 1780. Radnorshire, vol. ii. p. 519.

Bandinel (Bulkeley). Catal. of Books bequeathed to Bodleian Lib. by Richard Gough. 1814. Radnorshire, p. 335.

RENFREWSHIRE.

Metcalfe (William Musham). A History of Paisley, 600-1908. Paisley, 1909. Biblio. Note on Paisley Newspapers, pp. 422–424. List of Authors connected with Paisley and their Works, pp. 426–442.

The William Rowat Collection of Paisley Books, etc. (In Paisley Free Public Lib. and Museum.) There is another important Paisley Collection in the Library. The MS. of the famous Work by Robert Watt, 'Bibliotheca Britannica,' arranged and bound in 69 vols.—15 of Authors and 54 of Subjects is also in the Reference Dept. For an account of the Lib. & Museum, see the Report for 1907, pp. 7–12.

Semple (David). Popular Errors in Crawfurd and Semple's History of Renfrewshire (1782) reviewed and corrected. (With Biographies of George Crawfurd and William Semple, and Biblio. Notes on the 'History,' with an account of the preparation of an Index to it by the author.) Paisley, 1878.

Anderson (Joseph). and Black (George F.). Report on Local Museums in Scotland. Paisley Museum. (*Soc. of Antiq. Scot. Proc.*, vol. xxii. p. 406. 1888.)

The Harp of Renfrewshire. A Collection of Songs and other Poetical Pieces, with Biblio. and Biog. Notes, and a short Essay on the Poets of Renfrewshire. Originally published in 1819. 2 vols. Paisley, 1872–73.

Brown (Robert). The Paisley Poets. 2 vols. Paisley, 1890.

Hist. MSS. Comm. Reports. Renfrewshire Collections.

Glasgow, Earl of, at Hawkhead ... 3rd Rep. p. xxiii. and App. p. 405; 8th Rep. p. xvii. and App. pp. 304–308.

Stewart, Sir M. R. Shaw, at Greenock 4th Rep. p. xxiii. and App. p. 528.

Burgh Records, 1492, etc. at Renfrew. (*Local Records Comm. Rep.*, 1902, App. III. p. 98.) Transcripts of the Records, by W. M. Metcalfe, were published under the title 'Charters and Documents relating to the Burgh of Paisley (1163-1665) and Extracts from the Records of the Town Council (1594–1620).' Paisley, 1902.

List of Paisley Municipal Records Printed. (*Notes & Queries*, Series 11, vol. v. p. 478. 1912.)

RENFREWSHIRE (continued).

Gross (Charles). Biblio. of Brit. Municipal Hist. (*Harvard Hist. Studies*, vol. v. 1897.) Renfrewshire, p. 134. Paisley, pp. 361–362.

Livingstone (Matthew). Guide to the Public Records of Scotland. 1905. Renfrewshire, p. 179.

Turnbull (William B.). Scottish Parochial Registers. 1849. List of Renfrewshire Registers, pp. 131–134.

Hector (William). Selections from the Judicial Records of Renfrewshire. First and Second Series. Paisley, 1876–78. The Record Room and its Contents. Series I., pp. 9–12. Biblio. Notes in Preface to Series II.

Trimen (Henry). Botanical Biblio. of the British Counties. Renfrewshire. (*Journ. of Botany*, vol. xii. p. 234. 1874.)

Christy (Miller). Biblio. Note on Renfrewshire Birds. (*The Zoologist*, Ser. 3, vol. xiv. p. 264, 1890; and reprinted in pamph., 1891, p. 37.)

Anderson (John P.). Book of Brit. Topo., 1881. Renfrewshire, p. 408.

Gough (Richard). Brit. Topo., 1780. Renfrewshire, vol. ii. pp. 711-713.

Bandinel (Bulkeley). Catal. of Books bequeathed to Bodleian Lib. by Richard Gough, 1814 Renfrewshire, pp. 363-364.

GREENOCK.

Anderson (Joseph) and Black (Geo. F.). Report on Local Museums in Scotland. Greenock Museum. (*Soc. of Antiq. Scot. Proc.*, vol. xxii. p. 385. 1888.)

PAISLEY.

[Items relating to Paisley are included with those of the County generally.]

PORT GLASGOW.

Burgh Records, 1774, etc., at Port Glasgow. (*Local Records Comm. Rep.*, 1902, App. III. p. 98.)

ROSCOMMON.

Coleman (James). Bibliographia Conaciensis: a List of Books relating to Connaught. Roscommon. (*Galway Archæol. and Hist. Soc. Journ.*, vol. v. pp. 31–32, 34. 1907–08.)

O'Hanlon (John). List of Materials for the Hist. and Topography of the Co. of Roscommon in the Ordnance Survey Records. (*Kilkenny & South-East of Irel. Archæol. Soc. Journ.*, vol. ix. p. 106. 1867.)

Dix (Ernest Reginald McClintock). Printing in some Irish Provincial Towns in the Eighteenth Century. Athlone Printing, 1794–1800. (*Dublin Penny Journ.*, vol. iii. p. 184. 1904.)

—— **Earliest Printing in Athlone, with a List.** (*Irish Book Lover*, vol. ii. pp. 84–85. 1911.)

Hist. MSS. Comm. Report. Roscommon Collection.

O'Conor Don, The, at Clonalis ... 2nd Rep. p. xxi. and App. pp. 223–227; 8th Rep. p. xviii, and App. pp. 441–492.

Anderson (John P.). Book of Brit. Topo., 1881. Roscommon, p. 441.

Bandinel (Bulkeley). Catal. of Books bequeathed to Bodleian Lib. by Richard Gough. 1814. Roscommon, p. 383.

ROSS-SHIRE. [Ross and Cromarty.]

Hist. MSS. Comm. Report. Ross-shire Collection.
Ross, Mr. George, at Pitcalmie ... 6th Rep. p. xix. and App. pp. 715–719.

Burgh Records, 1455, etc., at Fortrose. (*Local Records Comm. Rep.*, 1902, App. III. p. 92.)

Livingstone (Matthew). Guide to the Public Records of Scotland. 1905. Ross-shire, pp. 39, 177.

Turnbull (William B.). Scottish Parochial Registers. 1849. List of Ross-shire Registers, pp. 135–139.

Trimen (Henry). Botanical Biblio. of the British Counties. Ross shire. (*Journ. of Botany*, vol. xii. p. 237. 1874.)

Christy (Miller). Biblio. Note on Ross and Cromarty Birds. (*The Zoologist*, Ser. 3, vol. xiv. pp. 263, 265. 1890; and reprinted in pamph., 1891, pp. 31, 37.) **Mammals.** (*The Zoologist*, Ser. 3, vol. xvii. pp. 210, 213. 1893.) **Reptiles.** (*Ibid.* pp. 249, 250. 1893.) **Fishes.** (*Ibid.* p. 261. 1893.)

Anderson (John P.). Book of Brit. Topo., 1881. Ross-shire, pp. 383, 409.
Gough (Richard). Brit. Topo., 1780. Ross-shire, vol. ii. p. 714.

ROXBURGHSHIRE.

Douglas (Sir George). A History of the Border Counties. (Roxburgh, Selkirk, Peebles.) The County Histories of Scotland. Edinb., 1899. List of Books relating to, or published in Roxburghshire, by James Sinton, pp. 432–457.

Goodfellow (J. Cumming). The Bibliography of Hawick. (*Hawick Archæol. Soc. Trans.* 1896.)

Sinton (James). Biblio. of Works relating to, or published in, Hawick, with an Appendix containing a List of Hawick Newspapers, Local Maps, and Music. (*Hawick Archæol. Soc. Trans.*, 1908, pp. 49–64.)

Indexes to the Trans. of the Hawick Archæol. Society, 1856-1906. With Historical Sketch, by J. J. Vernon. (*Transactions*, 1906, Supplement.)

James Wilson, Town Clerk of Hawick, Author of the 'Annals' and 'Memories' of Hawick, by W. E. Wilson. (*Hawick Archæol. Soc. Trans.*, 1907, pp. 18–20.)

Anderson (Joseph) and Black (Geo. F.). Report on Local Museums in Scotland. Hawick Museum. (*Soc. of Antiq. Scot. Proc.*, vol. xxii. p. 394. 1888.) **Jedburgh Museum.** (*Ibid.* vol. xxii. p. 380. 1888.) **Kelso Museum.** (*Ibid.* vol. xxii. p. 389. 1888.)

Robert Wilson, the Historian of Hawick, by R. Murray. (*Border Counties' Mag.*, vol. ii. pp. 73–77. 1881.)

Gross (Charles). Biblio. of Brit. Municipal Hist. (*Harvard Hist. Studies*, vol. v. 1897.) Roxburghshire, p. 135. Kelso, p. 265. Hawick, p. 255.

Lyell (Arthur H.). Biblio. List of Romano-British Remains. 1912. Roxburghshire, p. 140.

Black (George F.). Descriptive Catal. of Loan Collections of Prehistoric and other Antiquities from the Shires of Berwick, Roxburgh, and Selkirk. (*Soc. of Antiq. Scot. Proc.*, vol. xxviii. pp. 321–342. 1894.) Reprinted in the 'Hist. of the Berwickshire Naturalists' Club,' vol. xv. pp. 144–165. 1894.)

ROXBURGHSHIRE (continued).

Biblio. Note on 'An Apology for Tales of Terror,' the first book printed by James Ballantyne at Kelso in 1799. By George P. Johnston. (*Edinb. Biblio. Soc. Proc.*, vol. i. no. 19, 1893; vol. ix. p. 90, 1913.)

Hist. MSS. Comm. Reports. Roxburghshire Collections.

Douglas, Mr. James, at Cavers ...	7th Rep. p. xvi. and App. pp. 726–732.
Roxburghe, Duke of, at Floors Castle	14th Rep. pp. 46, 47, and App. III. pp. 1–55.
Rutherford, Mr. W. Oliver, at Edgerston	7th Rep. p. xvi. and App. pp. 735–737.

Hawick Burgh Records, 1640, etc., at Town Hall, Hawick. (*Local Records Comm. Rep.*, 1902, App. III. p. 94.)

Hawick Records in Public and Private Custody, relating to Hawick and District. (*Ibid.* 1902, App. III. p. 136.)

Jedburgh Records in Private and Public Custody. (*Ibid.* 1902, App. III. p. 136.)

Livingstone (Matthew). Guide to the Public Records of Scotland. 1905. Roxburghshire, p. 180.

Turnbull (William B.). Scottish Parochial Registers. 1849. List of Roxburghshire Registers, pp. 139–144.

Trimen (Henry). Botanical Biblio. of the British Counties. Roxburghshire. (*Journ. of Botany*, vol. xii. p. 234. 1874.)

Christy (Miller). Biblio. Note on Roxburghshire Mammals. (*The Zoologist*, Ser. 3, vol. xvii. p. 213. 1893.)

Anderson (John P.). Book of Brit. Topo., 1881. Roxburghshire, pp. 409-410.

Gough (Richard). Brit. Topo., 1780. Roxburghshire, vol. ii. pp. 715-717.

Bandinel (Bulkeley). Catal. of Books bequeathed to Bodleian Lib. by Richard Gough 1814. Roxburghshire, p. 364.

RUTLAND.

Hist. MSS. Comm. Report. Rutland Collection.

Finch, Mr. G. H., at Burley-on-the-Hill	7th Rep. p. xiv. and App. pp. 511–518; 8th Rep. App. p. 640.

Lysons' Collections for Rutland in the Brit. Museum. Add. MSS. 9459.

Upcott's Topographical Collections for Rutland in the Brit. Museum. Add. MSS. 15926.

Phillips (George). The Bibliography of Rutland. An article on Thomas Blore, the Historian of Rutland, and his Collections. (*The Rutland Mag.*, vol. i. pp. 54–61, 151. 1903–04.)

——— **Some Rutland Authors and their Books,** with remarks on Printers and Printing. (*Ibid.* vol. ii. pp. 53–61, 90–95, 216–221. 1905–06.)

——— **Biblio. Notes on Rutland Records.** (Quarter Sessions, Military, Ecclesiastical, etc.) (*Ibid.* vol. iv. pp. 43, 73, 102, 150, 181, 212, 250. 1909–10.)

Catal. of the Oakham Lending Library. 1900. List of Books relating to Rutland, pp. 41–44.

Harrod's Reprint of Wright's Rutland, with additions. A Biblio. Note. (*The Rutland Mag.*, vol. v. p. 151. 1912.) See also 'Leics. & Rutl. Notes & Queries,' vol. iii. pp. 48, 186. 1893–95.

Descriptive Catal. of 'The Jackson Collection' at the Sheffield Public Library, compiled by T. Walter Hall and A. H. Thomas. 1914. Rutland entries, p. 205.

RUTLAND (continued).

Dove (Patrick Edward). Domesday Studies. 1891. Domesday Biblio. Rutland, vol. ii. p. 686.

Davenport (Frances G.). List of Printed Materials for Manorial Hist. 1894. Biblio. Note on Rutland Manorial Hist., p. 55.

Lyell (Arthur H.). Biblio. List of Romano-British Remains. 1912. Rutland, p. 105.

County Folk-Lore. Vol. I. Leicestershire and Rutland, edited by C. J. Billson. (With List of Authorities.) (Folk-Lore Soc. Pubns., vol. xxxvii. 1895.)

A List of Private Acts, etc., relating to Rutland. Stevens & Sons, *circa* 1913.

Trimen (Henry). Botanical Biblio. of the British Counties. Rutland. (*Journ. of Botany*, vol. xii. pp. 178–179. 1874.)

Christy (Miller). Biblio. Note on Rutland Birds. (*The Zoologist*, Ser. 3, vol. xiv. p. 258, 1890, and reprinted in pamph., 1891, p. 22.) **Mammals.** (*The Zoologist*, Ser. 3, vol. xvii. p. 183. 1893.) **Reptiles.** (*Ibid.* p. 246. 1893.) **Fishes.** (*Ibid.* p. 257. 1893.)

A Topographical Collection for Rutland is in the Oakham Lending Lib.

Anderson (John P.). Book of Brit. Topo., 1881. Rutland, pp. 245-246.
Gatfield (George). Guide to Heraldry. 1892. Rutland, p. 174.
Sims (Richard). Manual. 1861. Rutland, pp. 172, 218, 238.
Upcott (William). English Topo., 1818. Rutland, vol. iii. pp. 1135-1139.
Smith (Alfred Russell). Catal. of Topo. Tracts, etc. 1878. Rutland, p. 319.
Gough (Richard). Brit. Topo., 1780. Rutland, vol. ii. pp. 173-174.
Bandinel (Bulkeley). Catal. of Books bequeathed to Bodleian Lib. by Richard Gough, 1814 Rutland, p. 280.

SELKIRKSHIRE.

Douglas (Sir George). A Hist. of the Border Counties. (Roxburgh, Selkirk, Peebles.) The County Histories of Scotland. 1899. List of Books relating to Selkirkshire, pp. 457–464.

Hist. MSS. Comm. Report. Selkirkshire Collection.

Hay, Mr. Robert Mordaunt, of Duns Castle, Berwickshire... ... ... Report on MSS. in various Collections, vol. v. pp. 1–71. 1909.

County Council Records, 1774, etc., at Selkirk. (*Local Records Comm. Rep.*, 1902, App. III. p. 86.)

Burgh Records, at Selkirk. (*Ibid.* 1902, App. III. p. 98.)

Memorandum on Selkirkshire Records, by T. Craig-Brown. (*Ibid.* 1902, App. III. p. 237.)

Gross (Charles). Biblio. of Brit. Municipal Hist. (*Harvard Hist. Studies*, vol. v. 1897.) Selkirkshire, p. 135.

Livingstone (Matthew). Guide to the Public Records of Scotland. 1905. Selkirkshire, p. 180.

Turnbull (William B.). Scottish Parochial Registers. 1849. List of Selkirkshire Registers, pp. 145–146.

Black (George F.). Descriptive Catal. of Loan Collections of Prehistoric and other Antiquities from the Shires of Berwick, Roxburgh, and Selkirk. (*Soc. of Antiq. Scot. Proc.*, vol. xxviii. pp. 321–342. 1894.) Reprinted in the 'History of the Berwickshire Naturalists' Club,' vol. xv. pp. 144–165. 1894.

SELKIRKSHIRE (*continued*).

Brown (Thomas Craig-). The Poetry of Selkirkshire. (*The Hist. of Selkirkshire, etc.*, 1886, vol. i. pp. 1–26.)

Angus (William). Ballads and Songs of Ettrick and Yarrow, with Biblio. notes. (*Ettrick and Yarrow*, 1894, pp. 159–215.)

Trimen (Henry). Botanical Biblio. of the British Counties. Selkirkshire. (*Journ. of Botany*, vol. xii. p. 234. 1874.)

Christy (Miller). Biblio. Note on Selkirkshire Mammals. (*The Zoologist*, Ser. 3, vol. xvii. p. 213. 1893.)

Anderson (John P.). Book of Brit. Topo., 1881. Selkirkshire, pp. 410-411.

Gough (Richard). Brit. Topo., 1780. Selkirkshire, vol. ii. p. 718.

Bandinel (Bulkeley). Catal. of Books bequeathed to Bodleian Lib. by Richard Gough, 1814. Selkirkshire, p. 361.

SHROPSHIRE.

Dukes (Thomas Farmer). An Account of the principal Books, MSS., Maps, Plans, and Views, illustrative of the History, Topography, Geology, and Antiquities of the County of Salop; with a List of published Portraits of Persons born within or connected with the County. Appendix to 'Antiquities of Shropshire, from an old MS. of Edward Lloyd, revised and enlarged from private and other MSS.,' by T. F. Dukes. Shrewsbury, 1844.

The Rev. R. W. Eyton's (the historian of Salop) copy in the Brit. Museum Library, contains his marginal notes and additions. Another copy which belonged to Thomas Farmer Dukes was sold at the disposal of his Library in 1850, containing a Collection of Ancient Deeds, Charters, etc., and Original Drawings, with MS. Indexes.

Catal. of Local Books and Pamphlets in the Shrewsbury Free Public Library, compiled by Harry T. Beddows, together with a Calendar of the MSS. (other than Charters and Deeds) preserved in the same Library, by W. G. Dimock Fletcher. Shrewsbury, 1903.

The following important Collections are among those entered in the foregoing Calendar of MSS.'—the MSS. of the Rev. Edward Williams (1762-1833), the Rev. Leonard Hotchkis (1691-1771), George Morris (1799-1859), Joseph Morris (1792-1860), the Rev. Canon Newling (1762-1838). Included in these and other collections are many from the Library of Sir Thomas Phillipps. A MS. Calendar of the Deeds and Charters in the Shrewsbury Public Lib., by W. G. D. Fletcher is stated, in the Introduction to the Catal., to be in preparation.

Shropshire Bibliography. Biblio. Notes by W. A. L. (*Salopian Shreds & Patches*, vol. v. p. 9–11.)

Walcott (Mackenzie E. C.). An Introduction to Sources of Salopian Topography. (*Shrop. Archæol. & Nat. Hist. Soc. Trans.*, vol. ii. pp. 297–316. 1879.)

Indexes of Names and Places in the First Series of the Transactions of the Shropshire Archæol. and Nat. Hist. Soc. MSS. in Shrewsbury Free Public Library. 5 vols.

Index of Papers published in the First and Second Series of the Trans. of the Shrop. Archæol. and Nat. Hist. Soc., vols. i.-xxiii., 1878-1900, compiled by R. E. Davies. (*Transactions*, Ser. 2, vol. xii. pp. 371–390. 1900.)

Index of Papers published in the Third Series of the Trans. of the Shrop. Archæol. and Nat. Hist. Soc., vols. i.-x., 1901-10, compiled by Flora A. Macleod. (*Transactions*, Ser. 3, vol. x., pp. xxvii.–xlii. 1910.)

List of Papers on Salopian Subjects from the Indices of the 'Journ. of the Brit. Archæol. Assoc.' (*Bye-gones*, vol. vi. p. 314. 1883.)

SHROPSHIRE (continued).

Lists of Documents and Papers relating to Shropshire in 'The Genealogist,' vols. 1-3, and New Ser. vols. 1-10, and in 'Miscellanea Genealogica et Heraldica,' New Ser. vols. 1-4, and Ser. II. vols. 1-5. (*Shrop. Notes & Queries*, New Ser. vol. iii. p. 123. 1894.)

A Collection of Newspaper Cuttings, etc., from Shrewsbury and Shropshire Newspapers, collected by Edward Edwards. 19 vols. (In Shrewsbury Public Library.)

Biblio. Notes on Thomas Phillips, the Historian of Shrewsbury. (*Shrop. Notes & Queries*, New Ser. vol. vi. pp. 19, 24, 30, 32, 38, 43. 1897.)

Henry Pidgeon's Contributions to the 'Gentleman's Magazine,' with a List. (*Ibid.* New Ser. vol. v. pp. 39-40. 1896.) Pidgeon was the Author of 'Memorials of Shrewsbury.'

General Index of Subjects and Places to the 'Antiquities of Shropshire,' by Robert William Eyton, 12 vols. 1854-60 (in vol. xii.). Biblio. Notes in Preface to vol. i. of the work.

The Rev. Robert William Eyton. An Account of his Life and Writings, with a List, by E. Chester Waters. (*Shrop. Archæol. & Nat. Hist. Soc. Trans.*, vol. x., pp. 1-9. 1887.)

A short Memoir of the late eminent Shropshire Genealogist and Antiquary, William Hardwicke, b. 1772, d. 1843, by Hubert Smith. Reprinted from 'The Salopian Illustrated Mag.' 1879.

William Cartwright, Nonjuror, and his Chronological Hist. of Shrewsbury, edited by William Phillips. (*Shrop. Archæol. & Nat. Hist. Soc. Trans.*, vol. xxxvii. pp. 1-70. 1914.)

Dove (Patrick Edward). Domesday Studies. 1891. Domesday Biblio. of Shropshire, vol. ii. p. 686.

Lyell (Arthur H.). Biblio. List of Romano-British Remains. 1912. Shropshire, pp. 105-107. Wroxeter (Uriconium), pp. 106-107.

Macklin (Herbert Walter). Monumental Brasses. London: Geo. Allen & Co., 1913. Biblio. Note on Shropshire Brasses, with a List, pp. 142, 178.

Gross (Charles). Biblio. of Brit. Municipal Hist. (*Harvard Hist. Studies*, vol. v. 1897). Shropshire, p. 103. Shrewsbury, pp. 389-392. Ludlow, pp. 327-329. Oswestry, p. 357. Wenlock, p. 412.

Davenport (Frances G.). List of Printed Materials for Manorial Hist. 1894. Biblio. Note on Shropshire Manorial Hist., p. 55.

Catal. of the Loan Exhibition of Shropshire Antiquities, Shrewsbury, 1898, compiled by H. R. H. Southam. (*Shrop. Archæol. & Nat. Hist. Soc. Trans.*, Ser. 2, vol. x. pt. iv. 1898.) Also issued separately. List of Portraits, Prints, Views, etc., pp. 45-76, 170-173. List of Books printed in and relating to Shropshire, Charters, Deeds, etc., pp. 77-90, 174-176.

Murray (David). 'Museums.' Glasgow, 1904. Biblio. Note on Shrewsbury Museum, vol. iii. p. 174.

Broadley (A. M.). The Royal Miracle. A Collection of Rare Tracts, Broadsides, etc., concerning the Wanderings of Charles II. after the Battle of Worcester. London, 1912. Biblio. of Books, Pamphlets, Broadsides, Ballads, etc., relating to Boscobel and other Places. App. X. pp. 303-326.

Mr. Broadley has an extra illustrated copy of 'The Royal Miracle' containing a fine 'Boscobel' Collection.

Blount (Thomas). Boscobel, or the Hist. of the Preservation of Charles II. after the Battle of Worcester, edited, with Biblio., by C. G. Thomas. 1894. Biblio. pp. xxv.-xxxiv.

SHROPSHIRE (continued).

A List of Private Acts, etc., relating to the Counties of Shropshire and Staffordshire. Stevens & Sons, London. 1913.

Salopian Printers. Biblio. Notes on Shropshire Printing & on the Early Press at Shrewsbury. (*Salopian Shreds & Patches*, vol. i.-x. 1874.)

The Printing Press in Shrewsbury. Biblio. Notes. (*Shrop. Notes & Queries*, New Ser. vol. viii. pp. 1, 3, 6. 1899.)

Prideaux (W. F.). John Bill, Queen's Printer (b. at Much Wenlock, bapt. 1576, d. 1630.) Reprinted from 'Notes & Queries.' (*Shrop. Notes & Queries*, New Ser. vol. vi. pp. 47–49, 51. 1897.)

Allnutt (W. H.). The King's Printer (Robert Barker and others) at Shrewsbury, 1642-43. (*The Library*, New Ser. vol. i. pp. 355–364. 1900.)

Early Printing at Ludlow. Biblio. Note by 'Typo.' (*Bye-gones*, vol. v. 1880–81, pp. 140, 216.)

The Private Printing Press of Charles Hulbert at Providence Grove, Shrewsbury. See obituary notice by C. H. Hulbert, extracted from the 'Shrewsbury Chronicle,' Nov. 6, 1857, in Charles Hulbert's 'Hist. & Description of the County of Salop.'

Biblio. Note on Wood-Engraving, Printing, etc., at Madeley. (*The Salopian Monthly Illustrated Journ.*, vol. i. no. 1. 1875.)

Shropshire Almanack Printers. Biblio. Notes. (*Salopian Shreds & Printers*, vol. ix. pp. 290, 299.)

Salopian Book Plates, with a List, by Rev. F. R. Ellis. (*Shrop. Archæol. & Nat. Hist. Soc. Trans.*, Ser. 3, vol. v. pp. 291-301. 1905.)

William Bowley, the Shrewsbury Engraver, by William Phillips. (*Ibid.* Ser. 3, vol. v. pp. 301-302. 1905.)

Shropshire Maps, Views, etc. Biblio. Notes. (*Salopian Shreds & Patches*, vol. iv. pp. 67, 86, 140; vol. vii. p. 236; vol. viii. p. 92; vol. x. pp. 8, 67, 81, 149, 171.)

List of Shropshire Prints in the 'Gentleman's Mag.,' 1731-1807. (*Shropshire Notes & Queries*, vol. ii. p. 178. 1886.)

List of Shropshire Illustrations in the 'Archæologia Cambrensis,' 1884-1900. See Alphabetical Index by F. Green, 1902, p. 108.

Salopian Journal and Courier of Wales, afterwards Eddowes's Journal. A Collection illustrating the History of this Newspaper, 1794-1853, is in the British Museum Library, consisting of specimen nos. indicating changes of printer, size, etc. letters, newspaper cuttings, etc,

Newspaper Press in the last Century to 1860, with Recollections of James Amphlett (sometime Editor of 'Eddowes's Journal'). 1860.

Salopian Books and Authors. Biblio. Notes by E. G. Salisbury and others, with lists from various sources. Reprinted with additions from Eddowes's 'Shrewsbury Journal.' (*Salopian Shreds & Patches*, vols. i.–x. *passim.* 1874–93.)

Beddows (Harry T.). MS. List of Shropshire Authors in the 'Dictionary of National Biography.' (In the Shrewsbury Public Library.) See also 'Notes on certain Names in the Dict. of Nat. Biog.' by Rev. Geo. W. Fisher, in 'Trans. Shrop. Archæol. Soc.' Ser. 2, vol. xi. pp. 10–15. 1899.

Adnitt (Henry W.). Biblio. of the Writings of Thomas Churchyard (b. at Shrewsbury, 1520, d. 1604.) (*Shrop. Archæol. & Nat. Hist. Soc. Trans.*, vol. iii. pp. 51–68. 1880.) Also issued separately.

SHROPSHIRE (*continued*).

Hiatt (Charles). The Literary Associations of Shropshire. Wellington, 1902.

Burne (Charlotte S.). Shropshire Folk-Lore. London, 1883. Ballads, Songs, and Rhymes connected with Shropshire, pp. 532–568.

Jackson (Georgina F.). Shropshire Word-Book. London, 1879–81. List of Authorities, pp. xcvi.–ciii.

Salopian Chap Books, Ballads, etc. Biblio. Notes. (*Salopian Shreds & Patches*, vols. i.–ix. *passim*, 1874–91.)

Biblio. Notes on the Booksellers of Shrewsbury, from 1696 to 1846, with a List. (*Shrop. Notes & Queries*, vol. vii. pp. 42, 43; vol. viii. pp. 12, 16, 18, 26. 1898–99.) See also Biblio. Notes in 'Salopian Shreds & Patches,' vols. i.–iii. *passim*, 1874, etc., on Shropshire Booksellers.

Hist. MSS. Comm. Reports. Shropshire Collections.

Cholmondeley, Mr. Reginald, of Condover Hall	5th Rep. p. x. and App. pp. 333–360.
Corbet, Mr. Richard, at Market Drayton	2nd Rep. p. ii. and App. p. 77.
Corbet, Sir Walter O., at Acton Reynald	15th Rep. p. 40, and App. X. pp. 66–77.
Dovaston, Mr. John, at West Felton...	13th Rep. App. IV. pp. 247–282.
Gatacre, Mr. E. Lloyd, at Gatacre ...	10th Rep. p. 20, and App IV. pp. 437–444.
Harlech, Lord, see J. R. Ormsby-Gore	
Kilmorey, Earl of, at Shavington ...	10th Rep. p. 17, and App. IV. pp. 358–374.
Lee, Mr. J. H., of Redbrook House, Whitchurch	3rd Rep. p. xvii. and App. pp. 267–268.
Leighton, Sir Baldwin, at Loton Park	2nd Rep. p. xi. and App. p. 64.
Leighton, Mr. Stanley, at Sweeny Hall, nr. Oswestry	10th Rep. p. 18, and App. IV. pp. 374–378.
More, Mr. R. Jasper, at Shipton Hall	10th Rep. p. 19, and App. IV. pp. 407–408.
Ormsby-Gore, Mr. J. R., at Brogyntyn	2nd Rep. p. xi. and App. pp. 84–88; 4th Rep. p. xv. and App. pp. 379–397.
Parkinson, Mr. J. L., at Ludford House, nr. Ludlow	10th Rep. p. 19, and App. IV. pp. 415–417.
Plowden, Mr. W. F., at Plowden ...	10th Rep. p. 19, and App. IV. p. 409.
Salwey, Mr. Alfred, at Overton ...	10th Rep. p. 19, and App. IV. pp. 409–415.
Walcot, Rev. John, at Bitterley Court	10th Rep. p. 19, and App. IV. pp. 418–420.
Bishop's Castle Corporation	10th Rep. p. 18, and App. IV. pp. 399–407.
Bridgnorth Corporation	10th Rep. p. 20, and App. IV. pp. 424–437.
Oswestry Corporation	10th Rep. p. 18.
Shrewsbury Corporation	15th Rep. pp. 42–43, and App. X. pp. 1–65.
Wenlock Corporation	10th Rep. p. 19, and App. IV. pp. 420–424.

Shropshire Records in Public and Private Custody. (*Local Records Comm. Rep.*, 1902. App. III. pp. 132, 250.)

Shrewsbury Borough Records, 1189, etc. with printed Index, at the Guildhall, Shrewsbury. (*Ibid.* 1902. App. III. p. 76.)

SHROPSHIRE (continued).

Calendar of the Muniments and Records of the Borough of Shrewsbury, compiled by the Records Committee. Shrewsbury, 1896.

Fletcher (W. G. Dimock). The Municipal Records of Shrewsbury. (*The Archæol. Journ.*, vol. li. pp. 283–292, 1894, and *Shrop. Archæol. & Nat. Hist. Soc. Trans.*, Ser. 2, vol. x. pp. 145–156, 1898.)

——— **Some Documents relative to the Battle of Shrewsbury.** (*Shrop. Archæol. & Nat. Hist. Soc. Trans.*, Ser. 2, vol. x. pp. 227–250. 1898). **Further Documents relative to the Battle of Shrewsbury.** (*Ibid.* Ser. 2, vol. xii. pp. 39–44. 1900.)

——— **Shropshire Topographical MSS. in the British Museum.** A Catalogue. (*Shrop. Archæol. & Nat. Hist. Soc. Trans.*, Ser. 2, vol. ii. pp. 76–104. 1890.)

——— **Shropshire Topographical and Genealogical MSS. preserved in the Bodleian Library, Oxford.** (*Ibid.* Ser. 2, vol. vii. pp. 79–93. 1895.)

——— **Shropshire Topographical and Genealogical MSS. in the William Salt Library at Stafford.** (*Ibid.* Ser. 2, vol. vii. pp. 94–96. 1895.)

——— **A Biblio. of Battlefield.** (*Ibid.* Ser. 3, vol. iii. pp. 273–283. 1903.)

Peele (E. C.) and Clease (R. S.). Interim Report of the Clerk and Deputy Clerk of the County Council of Salop upon certain Parish Documents, etc. (Ecclesiastical and Secular), inspected by them. [1901.]

——— **Shropshire Parish Documents. A Report to the Shropshire County Council.** [1903.] Abstracts of the Quarter Session Records, etc., have been issued under the title of 'Shropshire County Records,' 1638, etc., edited by Sir Offley Wakeman, R. Lloyd Kenyon, and others. 1901, etc.

Catal. of some miscellaneous Books and an interesting Collection of Historical MSS., Ancient Deeds, Grants, etc., chiefly relating to the County of Salop, the property of Thomas Farmer Dukes, of Shrewsbury. Sold by Sotheby's, 16 Dec. 1846.

Catal. of Antiquarian, Topographical, and miscellaneous Books forming the Library of Thomas Farmer Dukes, with his MS. and Printed Collections in illustration of the County of Salop. Sold by Sotheby's, 27 July, 1850.

Catal. of the Library and Heraldic and Historical MSS. belonging to William Noel Hill, Lord Berwick. Sold by Sotheby's, Apr. 26–May 10, 1843. Shropshire items (including the collection of Rev. E. Williams, formed with a view of publishing a History of Salop.), pp. 100–104.

Shropshire MSS. Biblio. Notes. (*Shrop. Notes & Queries*, New Ser. vol. i. pp. 41, 107; vol. iv. p. 64; vol. v. pp. 67–68, 71–72, 84; vol. vi. p. 60. 1892–97.)

Collections for Shropshire in the Lib. of the Soc. of Antiquaries, London. MS. 139.

The MS. Collections of the Rev. John Brickdale Blakeway for the Hist. of Shropshire in the Bodleian Lib., Oxford. 26 vols. See Macray, Annals of the Bodleian, 1890, p. 341. A List of Blakeway's Works with his Contributions to the 'Trans. of the Shrop. Archæol. Soc.' appeared in 'Notes & Queries,' Ser. 11, vol. xi. pp. 231, 286. 1915.

A Schedule of Sundorne Deeds, by W. P. (*Shrop. Notes & Queries.* New Ser. vol. iv. pp. 72, 74, 76, 79, 81, 83, 86, 87, 92. 1895.)

Hardwicke's MS. Collections for a Hist. of Shropshire. See *ante* 'Memoir of Hardwicke,' by Hubert Smith, 1879, pp. 36–37, for notes on this Collection.

SHROPSHIRE (continued).

Collections relating to Salop made in the 18th cent. by William Mytton, of Halston, and Edward Lloyd, of Trenewith, in the Brit. Museum. Add. MSS. 30311-30331.

The Rev. William Mytton's Collection of Materials for a Hist. of Shropshire. See List in Dukes' 'An Account of the principal Books, etc., of the County of Salop,' 1844, p. 220.

Collections by Edward Lloyd, of Trenewith, relating to Salop, in the Brit. Mus. Add. MSS. 30324, 30325 (includes a Calendar of the Records in the Tower relating to Shropshire, 1705–06, and a Calendar of Records in the Office of the Remembrancer of the Treasury, 1400–1660).

Collections on 'The Antiquities of the Co. of Salop, with the State thereof,' principally by Edward Lloyd about 1700, and by William Mytton, about 1730, 5 vols. with Indexes. A Transcript, corrected for the press by T. F. Dukes? (Brit. Mus. Add. MSS. 21019–21023.)

Lysons (Rev. S.). Collections for Shropshire, in the Brit. Mus. Add. MS. 9459.)

Upcott's Topographical Collections for Shropshire, in the Brit. Mus. Add. MS. 15926.

Dukes (T. F.) and Parkes (D.). Collections for a Hist. of Shropshire. Brit. Mus. Add. MSS. 21011–21025. Other Collections for the Co. of Salop in the Brit. Mus. are Harl. MSS. 1984, 5178, 5179, 5848, 7510, and Ashm. Lib. MS. 854.

The Morris MSS., with a List. (*The Cambrian Journ.*, 1860, pp. 290–294.) See also *ante* Beddows, pp. 32–33. 'The MSS. of George and Joseph Morris' in Shrewsbury Public Lib. Extracts from old Shropshire Deeds collected by George Morris in 'Trans. Shrop. Archæol. & Nat. Hist. Soc.,' vol. ix. pp. 171–192. 1886.

The MSS. of Sir Thomas Phillipps relating to Shropshire in the Shrewsbury Public Library. See *ante* Beddows, 'Catal. of Books in Shrewsbury Public Lib.,' 1903, p. 40.

The Early MSS. belonging to Shrewsbury School, by Stanley Leighton, including a Catal. by J. A. Herbert, a Report on the MSS., by F. G. Kenyon, and Dr. Butler's Catal. of the MSS. (*Shrop. Archæol. & Nat. Hist. Soc. Trans.*, Ser. 2, vol. ix. pp. 285–308. 1897.)

Ancient Deeds of St. Chad's Church, Shrewsbury. A List, with notes by William Phillips. (*Ibid.* Ser. 2, vol. iii. pp. 147–150. 1891.)

List of Shropshire Registers, Parochial and Non-Parochial, by W. G. Dimock Fletcher, in Chas. A. Bernau's 'Genealogical Directory,' Second Supp. pp. xxvi.–xxvii. 1910. See also 'Some Shropshire Parish Registers,' by Fletcher, in 'The Antiquary,' vol. xxxix. pp. 6–8. 1903.

Martin (Charles Trice). Catal. of the Archives in the Muniment Room of All Souls' College, Oxford. London, 1877. Documents relating to possessions of the College at Alberbury in Shropshire, pp. 1–18.

Whitaker (William) and Watts (W. W.). List of Works on the Geology, Mineralogy and Palæontology of Shropshire. (*Shrop. Archæol. & Nat. Hist. Soc. Trans.*, vol. xii. pp. 33–62. 1889.)

Christy (Miller). Biblio. Notes on Shropshire Birds. (*The Zoologist.* Ser. 3, vol. xiv. p. 258, 1890; and reprinted in pamph., 1891, p. 22.) **Mammals,** (*The Zoologist*, Ser. 3, vol. xvii. p. 183, 1893.) **Reptiles.** (*Ibid.* p. 246, 1893.) **Fishes.** (*Ibid.* p. 257, 1893.)

SHROPSHIRE (continued).

Anderson (John P.). Book of Brit. Topo., 1881. Salop., pp. 246-250.
Gatfield (George). Guide to Heraldry. 1892. Salop., pp. 175-177.
Sims (Richard). Manual. 1861. Salop., pp. 172, 218, 238.
Upcott (William). English Topo., 1818. Salop., vol. iii. pp. 1140-1145.
Smith (Alfred Russell). Catal. of Topo. Tracts, etc. 1878. Salop., pp. 321-327.
Gough (Richard). Brit. Topo., 1780. Salop., vol. ii. pp. 175-186.
Bandinel (Bulkeley). Catal. of Books bequeathed to Bodleian Lib. by Richard Gough. 1814. Salop., pp. 281-284.

BISHOP'S CASTLE.

Corporation Records. See *ante* Hist. MSS. Comm. Reports, p. 223.

The Manuscripts of the Corporation of Bishop's Castle. A List from the Hist. MSS. Comm. Report, by H. C. Maxwell Lyte. (*Shrop. Archæol. & Nat. Hist. Soc. Trans.*, vol. x. pp. 124–133. 1887.)

BRIDGNORTH.

Corporation Records. See *ante* Hist. MSS. Comm. Reports, p. 223.

The Manuscripts of the Corporation of Bridgnorth. A List from the Hist. MSS. Comm. Report, by H. C. Maxwell Lyte. (*Shrop. Archæol. & Nat. Hist. Soc. Trans.*, vol. x. pp. 139–156. 1887.)

BUILDWAS.

List of Records relating to Buildwas Abbey. See *ante* p. 220, Dukes, An Account, etc., Appendix, pp. lxii.-lxiv.

CHIRBURY.

Wilding (William). On a Library of Chained Books at Chirbury. (*Shrop. Archæol. & Nat. Hist. Soc. Trans.*, vol. viii. pp. 113-121. 1885.)

CLUN.

Salt (Thomas). A concise account of Ancient Documents relating to the Honour, Forest, and Borough of Clun. 1858.

—— **Ancient Documents relating to the Honour, Forest, and Borough of Clun.** (*Shrop. Archæol. & Nat. Hist. Soc. Trans.*, vol. xi. pp. 244–271. 1888.)

ELLESMERE.

Charters of Ellesmere, 1343-1656. (*Salopian Shreds & Patches*, vol. ix. 1891.)

LUDLOW.

Borough Records, 1283, etc., at Town Hall, Ludlow. (*Local Records Comm. Rep.*, 1902, App. III. p. 64.)

Charters of Ludlow. (*Salopian Shreds & Patches*, vol. viii. pp. 201–262. 1889.) For Abstracts from the 'Records of Ludlow,' see Shrop. Archæol. & Nat. Hist. Soc. Trans., vol. viii. pp. 203–228. 1885.

List of Ludlow Municipal Records Printed. (*Notes & Queries*, Ser. 11, vol. v. p. 73. 1912.)

MORE.

Clark-Maxwell (W. G.). On the Library of More Church, Salop. (*Shrop. Archæol. & Nat. Hist. Soc. Trans.*, Ser. 3, vol. vii. pp. 115-124. 1907.)

SHROPSHIRE (*continued*).

OSWESTRY.

Borough Records, 1262, etc., at the Guildhall, Oswestry. (*Local Records Comm. Rep.*, 1902, App. III. p. 66.) For 'The Records of the Corporation of Oswestry,' edited by Stanley Leighton, see 'Shrop. Archæol. & Nat. Hist. Soc. Trans.,' vols. ii.-vii. 1879-84. Extracts from the Records since the 16th cent. were published in 'Bye-gones,' 1876-1883. See also *ante* Hist. MSS. Comm. Reports, p. 223.

List of the Oswestry Charters. (*Bye-gones*, vol. iv. pp. 76, 83, 149, 154, 167; vol. vi. pp. 12, 301. 1878-82.)

List of Oswestry Municipal Records Printed. (*Notes & Queries*, Ser. 11, vol. v. p. 398. 1912.)

SHAVINGTON.

Harrod (Henry D.). The Muniments of Shavington, being a Catal. of the Deeds and Writings deposited in the Muniment Room of Shavington Hall, Salop. Shrewsbury, 1891.

TONG.

Botfield (Beriah). The Catal. of the Minister's Library in the Collegiate Church at Tong in Shropshire. (*Philobiblon Soc. Biblio. & Hist. Miscellanies*, vol. iii. no. 1. 1856.)

Auden (J. E.). Documents relating to Tong College. (*Shrop. Archæol. & Nat. Hist. Soc. Trans.*, Ser. 3, vol. viii. pp. 169-244. 1908.)

WENLOCK.

Corporation Records. See *ante* Hist. MSS. Comm. Reports, p. 223. For Extracts from the Records by H. F. J. Vaughan, see 'Shrop. Archæol. & Nat. Hist. Soc. Trans.,' Ser. 2, vol. vi. pp. 223-283. 1894. For Extracts from Old Registers and other Documents connected with the Wenlock Corporation, see 'The Salopian Monthly Illustrated Journal,' vol. 5, etc. 1877, etc.

The Manuscripts of the Corporation of Wenlock. A List from the Hist. MSS. Comm. Report, by H. C. Maxwell Lyte. (*Shrop. Archæol. & Nat. Hist. Soc. Trans.*, vol. x. pp. 134-138. 1887.)

List of Deeds relating to Wenlock Priory. See *ante* p. 220, Dukes, 'An Account,' etc. Appendix, pp. xlvii.-xlviii.

WROXETER.

Lyell (Arthur H.). Biblio. List of Romano-British Remains. 1912. Wroxeter (Uriconium), pp. 106-107.

SLIGO.

Coleman (James). Bibliographia Conaciensis: a List of Books relating to Connaught. Sligo. (*Galway Archæol. and Hist. Soc. Journ.*, vol. v. pp. 32, 34. 1907-08.)

O'Hanlon (John). List of Materials for the Hist. & Topography of the Co. of Sligo in the Ordnance Survey Records. (*Kilkenny & South-East of Irel. Archæol. Soc. Journ.*, vol. ix. p. 103. 1867.)

SLIGO (continued).

Dix (Ernest Reginald McClintock). Printing in some Irish Provincial Towns in the 18th cent. Sligo (1752-1800). (*Dublin Penny Journ.*, vol. iii. p. 360. 1904.)

——— **Earliest Printing in the Town of Sligo, with a List (1752-1800).** (*The Irish Book Lover*, vol. ii. pp. 21–24. 1910.) **Printing in Sligo during the 19th cent., with a List (1801-1899).** (*Ibid.* vol. vi. pp. 52–54, 69–71, 89–90. 1914-15.)

O'Rorke (Terence). Biblio. Notes on Sligo Newspapers. (*The Hist. of Sligo*, 1890, vol. ii. pp. 541–550.) See also Biblio. Note in W. G. Wood-Martin's 'Hist. of Sligo,' 1892, vol. iii. pp. 403-405.

Gross (Charles). Biblio. of Brit. Municipal Hist. (*Harvard Hist. Studies*, vol. v. 1897.) Sligo, p. 393.

Anderson (John P.). Book of Brit. Topo., 1881. Sligo, p. 441.

Gough (Richard). Brit. Topo., 1780. Sligo, vol. ii. p. 815.

Bandinel (Bulkeley). Catal. of Books bequeathed to Bodleian Lib. by Richard Gough. 1814. Sligo, p. 383.

SOMERSETSHIRE.

GREEN (EMANUEL). BIBLIOTHECA SOMERSETENSIS. A CATALOGUE OF BOOKS, PAMPHLETS, SINGLE SHEETS, AND BROADSIDES, IN SOME WAY CONNECTED WITH THE COUNTY OF SOMERSET. 3 vols. Taunton, 1902.

Vol. I. Bath Books, and General Introduction.
Vol. II. County Books. A—K. (Bath excepted.)
Vol. III. County Books. L—Z. (Bath excepted) and General Index.

HUMPHREYS (ARTHUR L.). SOMERSETSHIRE PARISHES. A HANDBOOK OF HISTORICAL REFERENCE TO ALL PLACES IN THE COUNTY. 2 vols. London, 1906. (Alphabetically arranged under Parishes.)

Baker (Arthur E.). Somerset Bibliography, including the Periodical Literature, 1896-1910. The Contents of the above prospective work will largely consist of items taken from the next entry. (Preparing for publication.)

Lists of Books and Magazine Articles relating to Somerset, written by Somersetshire Authors, or printed in the County, 1895 to 1913. By Edwin Pearce. (*Notes & Queries for Som. & Dorset*, vols. v.-xiv. 1896–1914.) Appears annually. For a few years previous to 1895, a similar list to the above was contributed yearly to 'The Somerset County Gazette,' by A. L. Humphreys.

General Index to the Somerset Archæological & Nat. History Society's Proceedings, vols. i. to xx. 1849-74. Edited by Rev. W. Hunt. **Indexes to the Record Books of the Dean and Chapter of the Cathedral Church of S. Andrew, Wells.** Edited by F. H. Dickinson. Bristol, 1876.

Index to Proceedings of the Som. Archæol. & Nat. Hist. Soc., vols. xxi.-xxv. 1875-94. Extracted and arranged by Emanuel Green. 1880. (Issued in Proceedings, vol. xxv.)

Index to vols. xxi.-xl. of the Proc. of the Som. Archæol. & Nat. Hist. Soc. Edited by F. T. Elworthy. (Issued in Proceedings, vol. xliv.) Taunton, 1898. The Society is contemplating the publication of a complete Index to the first 60 vols. of its 'Proceedings.'

SOMERSETSHIRE (continued).

Index-Catal. of the Library of the Som. Archæol. & Nat. Hist. Soc. By William Bidgood. Taunton, 1889. Additions to the Library are enumerated in the 'Proceedings' of the Society.

'The re-arrangement of the Library is being continued, a work upon which the Rev. E. H. Bates Harbin has bestowed a good deal of time. The most important gift has been the five volumes of Portraits and twelve volumes of Illustrations of general topographical interest relating to Somerset, presented by Mr. C. Tite. A search in this valuable series will be found indispensable for all students of Somerset History. The Pigott drawings, the Braikenridge extra-illustrated "Collinson," the Tite series, and the Pridham drawings of Fonts represent a mass of pictorial information of which any district might be proud, and such as few Counties can be fortunate enough to possess.' Report of Council of the Soc. in 'Proc.' vol. lx. p. 8. 1914.

Index to Collinson's History of Somerset (1791). Edited by F. W. Weaver and E. H. Bates, including a Supplemental Index to all the Armorial Bearings mentioned in the Work, by J. R. Bramble. Taunton, 1898.

An extra-illustrated copy of Collinson's History, in 14 vols., made by William Adlam, is in the Lib. of the Soc. of Antiquaries, London. A copy among the Phelps MSS. in the Brit. Museum, in 4 vols., is interleaved with MS. Notes by the Rev. William Phelps, one of the Somerset Historians.

New County History of Somerset. Proposals were issued some years ago, by a County History Committee, appointed by the Som. Archæol. Soc., and an important circular was circulated relating to the scheme.

Elliot (W. F.). A Collection of Books, Drawings, Engravings, illustrating the History, Topography, Antiquities, etc., of the County of Somerset, formed by W. F. Elliot, of Wilton, Taunton, in 63 vols., including many extra-illustrated copies of important Somerset County Histories, among which was Collinson's 'Hist. of Somersetshire,' 1791, with special title-pages, extended to 9 vols. by the addition of 690 drawings and 873 engravings, and a copious MS. Index. Also included was a Collection of Drawings, Engravings (many now rarely seen), and Papers, 1853, forming an Appendix to the same work; a set of the 'Proceedings of the Som. Archæol. Soc.,' 1849–54, inlaid to folio size, and extra-illustrated; a copy of Savage's 'Hist. of Taunton,' 1822, inlaid to folio size, and extra-illustrated, and other works. This remarkable collection was sold by Christie's on 14 July, 1897, and purchased by Messrs. Sotheran, who offered it for sale in its entirety; and issued a description.

A Guide to the Museum of the Som. Archæol. & Nat. Hist. Soc. in Taunton Castle, by William Bidgood. Taunton, 1879. Second edition. 1883.

Index to vols. i.–ix., 1867–1902, of the Proceedings of the Bath Nat. Hist. & Antiq. Field Club, by A. W. Jamieson. (*Proceedings*, vol. ix. pp. 317–323. 1901.)

Catal. of the Books of the Bath Nat. Hist. & Antiq. Field Club. 1906. (*Proceedings*, vol. xi. pp. 50–71. 1906. **Additions to Sept., 1909.** (*Ibid.* pp. 199–201. 1909.)

Bath and Somerset Bibliography. A Catal. of Books descriptive of Bath and Somerset, as well as Books printed in, or written by Bath or Somerset Men. With a Collection of Views, Portraits, Maps, illustrating the County, on Sale by B. & J. F. Meehan, Bath, *circa* 1890.

Somerset and Dorset Articles and References in the First Series of 'The Downside Review,' vols. i.–xxv. 1880–1906. (*Notes & Queries for Som. & Dorset*, vol. vii. pp. 284, 346; vol. viii. p. 214; vol. ix. p. 215; vol. x. p. 247. 1901–07.)

List of Publications of the Rev. Thomas Hugo. See 'Miscellaneous Papers,' by Rev. Thomas Hugo, London, 1878, pp. xv.-xvi.

SOMERSETSHIRE (continued).

Thomas Gerard of Trent, his Family and his Writings. By E. H. Bates Harbin. (*Dorset Nat. Hist. & Antiq. Field Club. Proc.*, vol. xxxv. pp. 55–70. 1914.) Gerard's 'The Particular Description of the County of Somerset,' 1633, edited by E. H. Bates, was reprinted by the Somerset Record Soc. as vol. xv. of their Publications in 1900, with a Biblio. Note in the Introduction.

Baker (Ernest E.). Calendar of a few Uncommon Volumes relating to the County of Somerset. 1900.

Dredge (John Ingle). The Biblio. of Richard Bernard (1567?-1641) of Batcombe (Som.). Horncastle, 1890.

Catal. of the Library at Claremont, Clevedon, and Royal Cres., Bath, collected by George Weare Braikenridge, arranged and described by R. S. Faber. 1894. Somerset items, pp. 155–173. A MS. Catal. of the Library of G. W. Braikenridge is in the Bristol Public Library.

Humphreys (Arthur L.). Some Sources of History for the Monmouth Rebellion and the Bloody Assizes. (*Som. Archæol. & Nat. Hist. Soc. Proc.*, vol. xxxviii. pt. ii. pp. 312–326. 1892.)

Collection of Prints, Broadsides, etc., relating to the Battle of Sedgmoor, is in the Private Library of Mr. A. M. Broadley at Bradpole, Dorset.

Gross (Charles). Biblio. of Brit. Municipal Hist. (*Harvard Hist. Studies*, vol. v. 1897.) Somersetshire, pp. 103-104. Bath, pp. 163–164. Wells, pp. 411–412.

Davenport (Frances G.). List of Printed Materials for Manorial Hist. 1894. Biblio. Note on Somerset Manorial Hist., pp. 55–57.

Dove (Patrick Edward). Domesday Studies. 1891. Domesday Biblio. Somerset, vol. ii. p. 687.

Lyell (Arthur H.). Biblio. List of Romano-British Remains. 1912. Somersetshire, pp. 108–117.

Macklin (Herbert Walter). Monumental Brasses. London: Geo. Allen & Co., 1913. Biblio. Note on Somerset Brasses, with a List, pp. 178–179.

Index to Monumental Brasses mentioned in the Proceedings of the Som. Archæol. & Nat. Hist. Soc., vols. i.-lii., compiled by H. St. George Gray. (*Proceedings*, vol. lii. pt. iii. pp. 167–170. 1906.)

The 'Walter Collection' of Antiquities in Taunton Castle Museum, described and enumerated by H. St. George Gray. (*Som. Archæol. & Nat. Hist. Soc. Proc.*, vol. xlviii. pt. ii. pp. 24–78. 1902.)

The 'Norris Collection' in Taunton Castle Museum, with a Biog. Notice of Hugh Norris, by H. St. George Gray. (*Ibid.* vol. li. pt. ii. pp. 136–159. 1905.)

The 'Stradling Collection' of Monmouth Relics, and Antiquities in Taunton Castle Museum, by H. St. George Gray. (*Ibid.* vol. xlviii. pt. i. pp. 81–87. 1902.)

Green (Emanuel). Biblio. Notes on Early Printing in Somerset, in Introduction to 'Bibliotheca Somersetensis,' pp. xxxiv.-xxxix., see *ante*, p. 228.

—— **On Some Somerset Chap-Books.** (*Som. Archæol. and Nat. Hist. Soc. Proc.*, vol. xxiv. pp. 50–66. 1878.)

Baker (Ernest E.). Somerset Chap-Books. (*Notes & Queries for Som. & Dorset*, vol. iv. pp. 13–14. 1894.)

Sharp (Cecil). Somerset Folk Songs. A Lecture. (*Somerset Men in London Assoc.*, 3rd Ann. Rep. pp. 7–8. 1903–4.)

Williams (Thomas Webb). Some Mediæval Libraries and Miscellaneous Notices of Books in Somerset prior to the Dissolution of the Monasteries. Som. Archæol. & Nat. Hist. Soc. Northern Branch. Bristol, 1897.

SOMERSETSHIRE (continued).

Chubb (Thomas). A Descriptive List of the Printed Maps of Somersetshire, 1575-1914. With Biographical Notes & Illustrations. Som. Archæol. & Nat. Hist. Soc. Taunton, 1914.

Hobhouse (Edmund), Bishop. **On a Map of Mendip.** (*Som. Archæol. & Nat. Hist. Soc. Proc.*, vol. xli. pp. 65–72. 1895.)

——— **Remarks on Domesday Map of Somerset, A.D. 1086.** (*Ibid.* vol. xxxv. pp. ix.–x. 1889.)

A Report on the Pigott Collection of Drawings (**of Churches, etc., relating to Somerset**). (*Som. Archæol. & Nat. Hist. Soc. Proc.*, vol. xxiii. pt. i. pp. 4–5. 1877.)

A Catal. of 'The Pigott Drawings' deposited in the Museum of the Som. Archæol. & Nat. Hist. Soc. (*Ibid.* vol. viii. pp. 149–190. 1858.)

A Photographic Survey of the County of Somerset, by F. J. Allen. (*Ibid.* vol. xxxvii. pt. ii. pp. 100–105. 1891.)

A Photographic Survey of the County of Somerset, by C. H. Bothamley. (*Ibid.* vol. xliii. pt. ii. pp. 166–171. 1897.)

Special Topographical Collections for Somerset are in the Library of the Som. Archæol. Soc. at Taunton Castle, including the 'Serel' and 'Tite' Collections. Others are in the Public Libraries at Bath, Weston-super-Mare, and Bristol. A special Local Collection is at the Taunton Public Library.

Hist. MSS. Comm. Reports. Somersetshire Collections.

Bouverie, Mr. Philip Pleydell, at Brymore, near Bridgwater	10th Rep. p. 22, and App. VI. pp. 82–98.
Carew, Col., at Crowcombe Court ...	2nd Rep. p. xiii. and App. pp. 74–76; 4th Rep. p. xv. and App. pp. 368–374.
Hood, Sir A. Acland, at St. Audries, Bridgwater	5th Rep. p. x.; 6th Rep. p. xii. and App. pp. 344–352.
Luttrell, Mr. G. F., at Dunster Castle	1st Rep. p. x. and App. pp. 56–57; 10th Rep. p. 23, and App. VI. pp. 72–81.
Macaulay, Col.	4th Rep. p. xv. and App. pp. 397–404.
Mildmay, Capt. H. G. St. John, at Hazelgrove House	7th Rep. p. xiv. and App. pp. 590–596.
Phelips, Mr. W., at Montacute House	1st Rep. p. ix. and App. pp. 57–58; 3rd Rep. p. xviii. and App. pp. 281–287.
Pyne, Rev. W., of Charlton Mackerel	9th Rep. p. xviii. and App. II. pp. 493–499.
Skrine, Mr. H. Duncan, at Claverton Manor	11th Rep. p. 24, and App. I. pp. 1–197.
Strachey, Sir Edward, at Sutton Court	6th Rep. p. xiv. and App. pp. 395-407.
Woodforde, Rev. A. J., at Ansford ...	9th Rep. p. xviii. and App. II. pp. 493–499.
Axbridge Corporation	3rd Rep. p. xx. and App. pp. 300–308.
Bridgwater Corporation...	1st Rep. App. p. 99; 3rd Rep. p. xix. and App. pp. 310–320.
Cheddar Parish	3rd Rep. p. xix. and App. pp. 329–331.
Glastonbury Corporation	1st Rep. App. p. 102.
Somerset County Records	3rd Rep. p. xix. and App. p. 333; 7th Rep. p. xv. and App. pp. 693–701.
Wells Almshouses	8th Rep. pp. 638-639.
——— Bishop's Registry	1st Rep. App. p. 92.
——— Corporation	1st Rep. App. pp. 106–108; 3rd Rep. p. xix. and App. p. 350.

SOMERSETSHIRE (*continued*).

Hist. MSS. Comm. Reports. Somersetshire Collections (*continued*).

Wells Dean and Chapter ... ... 1st Rep. App. p. 93; 3rd Rep. p. xix. and App. pp. 351–364; 10th Rep. pp. 28–29, and App. III.; 17th Rep. pp. 97–103, and vol. i. (1907), vol. ii. (1914).

——— Vicars Choral of... ... ... 3rd Rep. p. xix. and App. p. 364.

County Records, 1650, etc. with MS. Index, at the Shire Hall, Taunton. (*Local Records Comm. Rep.*, 1902, App. III. p. 22.)

Records in Public and Private Custody relating to Somerset. (*Ibid.* 1902, App. III. p. 138.)

Documents relating to Somerset in the Bodleian. (*Som. & Dor. Notes & Queries*, vol. xi. pp. 35–37. 1908.)

Somerset Archives at Lambeth Palace Library. (*Ibid.* vol. viii. pp. 169–172, 209–212. 1903.)

Somerset Documents at Stratford-on-Avon. MS. Calendar to Corporation Records. Div. XII. (*Ibid.* vol. viii. pp. 230–231. 1903.)

Deeds and other Papers relating to Somerset in possession of G. T. Tudor Sherwood. (*Ibid.* vol. ix. pp. 272–273. 1905.)

Public Records in the County of Somerset. Biblio. Note by Thomas Serel. (*Som. Archæol. & Nat. Hist. Soc. Proc.*, vol. xvii. pt. i. pp. 43–46. 1871.)

Phelps (Rev. William). Collections for a Hist. of Somersetshire, designed for issue in 4 vols., of which 2 vols. only were printed in 1836 and 1839. 17 vols. Brit. Mus. Add. MSS. 33820–33836.

Hugo (Rev. Thomas). Collections for various Parishes in the County of Somerset. 6 vols. Brit. Mus. Add. MSS. 30283–30288.

Lysons (Rev. S.). Collections for Somerset. Brit. Mus. Add. MS. 9459.

Powell's Topographical Collections for Somerset. Brit. Mus. Add. MS. 17463.

Upcott's Topographical Collections for Somerset. Brit. Mus. Add. MS. 15926.

Ellacombe (H. T.). Collections of MSS., Newspaper extracts, etc., relating to Local History, etc., 1512–1896. In Bristol Public Library. 15 vols. (Contains numerous Somerset items.)

Jefferies (C. T.). Collection of MSS., Newspaper and Magazine extracts, etc., relating to the Hist. of Bristol, 1573–1896. In Bristol Public Library. 16 vols. Vol. 15. Somerset MSS. Vol. 16. Bath Play-bills.

Fry (E. A.). A Description of the Rev. Frederick Brown's Collection of Manuscript Somerset Wills and Pedigrees, now preserved at Taunton Castle, with a list of names. (*Som. Archæol. & Nat. Hist. Soc. Proc.*, vol. lvii. pt. ii. pp. 86–90. 1911.)

Mr. Fry has also made a typewritten Index to the Testators in the Rev. F. Brown's Collection of Somerset Wills printed by F. A. Crisp in 6 vols., which now belong to the Som. Archæol. Soc. Humphreys' 'Somersetshire Parishes' embodies a complete Index to Brown's Somerset Wills.

Diocesan Records, etc., of Bath and Wells, at Wells, Taunton, etc. (*Local Records Comm. Rep.*, 1902. App. III. p. 104.)

SOMERSETSHIRE (continued).

Holmes (T. Scott). A Report to the Convocation of the Province of Canterbury on the Ecclesiastical Records of the Diocese of Bath and Wells, etc. Taunton, 1914.

Biblio. and Descriptive Notes in Introduction on The Ecclesiastical Records of the Registry of the Bishop of Bath and Wells, pp. ix.–x. The Registers, Charters, etc., of Wells Cathedral, pp. x.–xi. Records of the Archdeaconries of Wells, Taunton, and Bath, p. xii. The Parochial Registers of the Diocese, with lists of Somerset Parishes of which Bishop's Transcripts (printed or MS.) of the Registers are at Wells, pp. xii.–xxviii.

Hutton (Matthew). Catalogues of the Contents of the Episcopal Registers of the Diocese of Bath and Wells. (In the Brit. Museum, Harl. MSS. 6964–6968.)

Bates (Rev. E. H.). Dedications of the Churches of Somersetshire, with list of Biblio. references in the Records. (*Som. Archæol. & Nat. Hist. Soc. Proc.*, vol. li. pt. ii. pp. 105–135. 1905.)

Monday (Alfred J.). The County Records of Somerset. An Index to the Head Deeds and other Documents enrolled with the Custos Rotulorum of the County. (*Som. & Dor. Notes & Queries*, vol. xi. pp. 101–112, 146–156. 1908.)

List of a portion of a large Collection of Deeds and other Documents relating to Somerset. On Sale by F. Marcham, New Southgate, London.

Murray (Richard Paget). A List of Books and Pamphlets relating to the Flora of Somerset. (*The Flora of Somerset*, pp. xv.–xvii.) Som. Archæol. & Nat. Hist. Soc. Taunton, 1896. Also issued in the 'Proceedings' of the Soc.

Trimen (Henry). Botanical Biblio. of the British Counties. Somersetshire. (*Journ. of Botany*, vol. xii. p. 69. 1874.)

Swanton (E. W.). The Mollusca of Somerset. Som. Archæol. & Nat. Hist. Soc. Taunton, 1912. Biblio. pp. 84–85. Also issued in the 'Proceedings.'

Christy (Miller). Biblio. Note on Somersetshire Birds. (*The Zoologist*, Ser. 3, vol. xiv. p. 258, 1890; and reprinted in pamph., 1891, p. 23.) **Mammals.** (*The Zoologist*, Ser. 3, vol. xvii. pp. 183–184. 1893.) **Reptiles.** (*Ibid.* p. 246. 1893) **Fishes.** (*Ibid.* p. 257. 1893.)

Anderson (John P.). Book of Brit. Topo., 1881. Somersetshire, pp. 250–256.
Gatfield (George). Guide to Heraldry. 1892. Somersetshire, pp. 177–178.
Sims (Richard). Manual. 1861. Somersetshire, pp. 172, 219, 239.
Upcott (William). English Topo., 1818. Somersetshire, vol. iii. pp. 1146–1171.
Smith (Alfred Russell). Catal. of Topo. Tracts, etc. 1878. Somersetshire, pp. 329–348, 471.
Gough (Richard). Brit. Topo., 1780. Somersetshire, vol. ii. pp. 187–228.
Bandinel (Bulkeley). Catal. of Books bequeathed to Bodleian Lib. by Richard Gough, 1814. Somersetshire, pp. 285–293.

AXBRIDGE.

Corporation Records. See *ante* Hist. MSS. Comm. Reports, p. 231.

Hunt (Rev. William). On the Charters and Municipal Government of Axbridge. (*Som. Archæol. & Nat. Hist. Soc. Proc.*, vol. xv. pt. ii. pp. 6–20. 1869.)

BATH.

Green (Emanuel). Bibliotheca Somersetensis. 3 vols. 1902. **Vol. I. Bath Books.** See *ante* p. 228.

Shum (Frederick). A Catal. of Bath Books, being various Works on the Hot Mineral Springs of Bath from the 16th century to the 20th century, and an alphabetical List of Books, Pamphlets, and Tracts. Bath, 1913.

—— **Stray Notes on Bath Books.** (*Bath Nat. Hist. & Antiq. Field Club. Proc.*, vol. vii. pp. 179–185. 1892.)

—— **Early Bath Books.** A summary of a Paper read before the Biblio. Soc. (*Biblio. Soc. Trans.*, vol. v. pp. 6–7. 1899.)

SOMERSETSHIRE (continued).

Edwards (C. P.). Bath Bibliography. A List. (*The Bath Herald*, 2 Dec., 1876—10 Feb., 1877.) A Series also appeared in the 'Bath Chronicle' about the same period. See also article by C. P. Edwards in 'The Bibliographer,' vol. i. pp. 101–104. 1882.

Peach (R. E. M.). Collections of Books belonging to the City [Bath], with suggestions as to their amalgamation in a Public Library of Reference. [1893.]

——— **Old Bath Booksellers.** 1894.

——— **A Letter to R. S. Blaine on the several Collections of Books in the City [Bath].** 1889.

Bath and Somerset Bibliography. A Catal. of Books on Sale by B. & J. F. Meehan. See *ante* p. 229.

Freeman (Henry William). The Thermal Baths of Bath, their History, Literature, etc. London, 1888. Biblio. of the Mineral Waters of Bath, pp. ix.–xxiv.

Green (Emanuel). The Earliest Map of Bath. (*Bath Nat. Hist. & Antiq. Field Club. Proc.*, vol. vi. pp. 58–74. 1889.)

Biblio. Note on the Maps and Plans of Bath collected by C. P. Russell, the Librarian of the Royal Literary and Scient. Instn. (*Brit. Archæol. Assoc. Journ.*, vol. xiii. pp. 147–148. 1857.)

The Meehan Collection of Bath Prints, Drawings, Maps, etc., formed by J. F. Meehan. The Bath Town Council have taken steps towards acquiring the Collection for the City of Bath.

Lyell (Arthur H.). Biblio. List of Romano-British Remains. 1912. **Bath,** pp. 108–110.

Murray (David). 'Museums.' Glasgow, 1904. Biblio. Note on the Museum of the Royal Literary and Scientific Institution, Bath, vol. ii. pp. 103–104.

Green (Emanuel). Bath and Early Lithography. (*Bath Nat. Hist. & Antiq. Field Club. Proc.*, vol. viii. pp. 23–35. 1894.)

Lewis (Harold). The Beginnings of the Bath Newspaper Press. (*Ibid.* vol. v. pp. 8–21. 1885.)

Barbeau (Alfred). Life and Letters at Bath in the 18th century, with a preface by Austin Dobson. London, 1904. Biblio., pp. xvii.–xxxi. Authors at Bath, pp. 168–279.

Hunter (Joseph). The Connexion of Bath with the Literature and Science of England. 1853.

Monkland (G.). The Literature and Literati of Bath. 2 vols. Bath, 1854–55.

Bath Play-bills. A Collection is contained in vol. xvi. of the Jefferies Collection in the Bristol Public Library, see *ante* p. 232.

Peach (R. E. M.). The Bath Abbey Library, with notes thereon. Reprinted from the 'Bath Chronicle,' 1879. [Bath, 1879.]

King (Austin J.) and Watts (B. H.). The Municipal Records of Bath, 1189 to 1604. London [1885]. App. A. A Chronological List of Charters, etc.

——— **The Municipal Records of Bath.** (*Som. Archæol. & Nat. Hist. Soc. Proc.*, vol. xli. pt. ii. pp. 47–52. 1895.)

Hunt (Rev. W.). The Early Royal Charters of Bath. (*Ibid.* vol. xxii. pt. i. pp. 73–86. 1876.)

Poynter (James A.). Ancient Bath Charters. (*Ibid.* vol. xxii. pt. ii. pp. 1–9. 1876.)

SOMERSETSHIRE (continued).

Falconer (R. W.). List of Charters, etc., connected with the City of Bath. [1858.]

Archdeaconry of Bath Records. See Biblio. and Descriptive Note in T. Scott Holmes, *ante* p. 233.

A Collection of Prints, etc., relating to Ralph Allen (1694-1764), the Bath Philanthropist, in the possession of Mr. A. M. Broadley at Bradpole, Dorset.

BRUTON.

Talbot de Malahide (Lord). On the Charters of Bruton Priory. (*Som. Archæol. & Nat. Hist. Soc. Proc.*, vol. vii. pp. 72–81. 1857.)

CADBURY.

Biblio. of Cadbury Castle. (*Som. Archæol. & Nat. Hist. Soc. Proc.*, vol. lix. pt. ii. pp. 1–2. 1913.)

CHEDDAR.

Balch (Herbert E.). Wookey Hole, its Caves and Cave Dwellers. 1914. Historical References from Books, etc., to the Cave & Village, pp. 223–246.

CLEEVE.

Hugo (Rev. Thomas). On the Charters and other Archives of Cleeve Abbey. (*Som. Archæol. & Nat. Hist. Soc. Proc.*, vol. vi. pp. 17–73. 1855.) Reprinted with additions as 'The Charters and other hitherto inedited Archives of Cleeve, Clyve, or Clyff Abbey.' Taunton, 1856.

DOWNSIDE.

Among the Archives. A Calendar of Papers of St. Gregory's Monastery at Downside, by Dom John Gilbert Dolan. (*The Downside Review*, vols. ii.–vii. *passim.* 1883–88.)

An Index to the Writers and Principal Contents of 'The Downside Review,' vols. i. to xxv. 1880–1906. (*Ibid.* vols. xxvi. xxvii. 1907–08.)

The Downside Library, by Edmund Bishop. (*Ibid.* vol. v. pp. 256–264. 1886.)

The Downside Museum, by Dom J. C. Fowler. (*Ibid.* vol. iii. pp. 180-185. 1884.)

The Downside Picture Gallery, with list of Portraits, etc. (*Ibid.* vol. ii. pp. 162–166. 1883.)

Literary Output of the Century. (A Biblio. of Writings by the Monks of Downside.) By E. Cuthbert Butler, the Abbot of Downside. (*Ibid.* vol. xxxiii. pp. 181-196. 1914.)

GLASTONBURY.

Borough Records, with M.S. Index, at Glastonbury Museum. (*Local Records Comm. Rep.*, 1902. App. III. p. 58.)

Parker (James). Documentary Evidence relating to the Early Hist. of Glastonbury. (*Som. Archæol. & Nat. Hist. Soc. Proc.*, vol. xxvi. pt. i. pp. 40–43. 1880.)

Hill (O'Dell Travers). The Glastonbury Library. (*The Gentleman's Mag.*, vol. 221, pp. 322–332. 1867.)

Catal. of Books at Glastonbury Abbey, 1278. (*John of Glastonbury*, ed. by Thomas Hearne, 1726, pp. 423–444.)

Index to the 'Secretum' (a list of Charters, etc., relating to Glastonbury and other places) **of Walter de Monington, Abbot of Glastonbury, 1341–1374, M.S. Wood, empt. I. Bodl. Lib.** (*Som. & Dor. Notes & Queries*, vol. xii. pp. 273, 321, 356; vol. xiii. pp. 41, 89, 136. 1911–12.)

SOMERSETSHIRE (continued).

LANGPORT.

Ross (D. Melville). The Papers of the former Corporation of Langport, 1596–1886, with a list of Documents at the Town Hall. (*Som. Archæol. & Nat. Hist. Soc. Proc.*, vol. liii. pt. ii. pp. 148–173. 1907.)

MARTOCK.

Bernard (Rev. Canon). A List of Papers relating to the Church of Martock and the Priory of Bruton, in the Archives of St. Lo, Normandy. (*Som. Archæol. & Nat. Hist. Soc. Proc.*, vol. xix. pt. ii. pp. 95-98. 1873.)

NETHER STOWEY,

Wise (Thomas J.). A Biblio. of the Writings in Prose and Verse of Samuel Taylor Coleridge. Bibliographical Soc. London, 1913.

Coleridge (Ernest Hartley). The Lake Poets in Somersetshire. (*Roy. Soc. of Lit. Trans.*, Ser. 2, vol. xx. pp. 105–131. 1899.)

Nichols (William Luke). The Quantocks and their Associations. Second edition. London, 1891. (Relates to the connection of Wordsworth and Coleridge with the District.)

STOKE COURCY.

Goodford (Charles Old), Provost of Eton. Note on some Mediæval Deeds of Stoke Courcy. (*Som. Archæol. & Nat. Hist. Soc. Proc.*, vol. xviii. p. 15. 1872.)

TAUNTON.

Hugo (Rev. Thomas). Collections for the History of Taunton, Brit. Mus. Add. MS. 30289.

Murray (David). 'Museums.' Glasgow, 1904. Biblio. Note on Taunton Museum, vol. iii. p. 208.

Baker (Arthur E.). A Brief Account of the Public Library Movement in the Borough of Taunton. (The Public Lib., Taunton Souvenir.) 1912.

Archdeaconry of Taunton Records. See Biblio. and Descriptive Note in T. Scott Holmes, *ante* p. 233).

WALCOT.

Shickle (C. W.). Notes on an Old Map of the Parish of Walcot. (*Bath Nat. Hist. & Antiq. Field Club. Proc.*, vol. ix. pp. 183–188. 1900.)

WELLINGTON.

Humphreys (Arthur L.). Materials for the Hist. of the Town of Wellington. London, 1889. Biblio., pp. 258–270. A fuller Biblio. will be contained in the new edition of the Hist. of Wellington, now in course of publication.

WELLS.

Wells Records (Corporation, Bishop's Registry, Dean & Chapter, Vicars Choral, &c.), see *ante* Hist. MSS. Comm. Reports, p. 231.

Valuable summary descriptions of the Wells Records are given in the Introductory pages of the Hist. MSS. Comm. Reports, especially those issued in 1907 and 1914. The Indexes to these latter vols. are important.

Wells Cathedral Records, A.D. 958, etc., with MS. Index, at Wells. (*Local Records Comm. Rep.*, 1902. App. III. p. 110.)

Archdeaconry Records of Wells. See Biblio. and Descriptive Note in T. Scott Holmes, *ante* p. 233.

SOMERSETSHIRE (continued).

Indexes to the Record Books of the Dean and Chapter of Wells Cathedral, with notes and preface. Edited by F. H. Dickinson. Bristol, 1876. Issued with the General Index to vol. i.–xx. of the 'Proceedings' of the Som. Archæol. Soc.

The Registers, Charters, Deeds, and Historical Records of the Cathedral Church of St. Andrew's, Wells. See Biblio. and Descriptive Notes in T. Scott Holmes, *ante* p. 233.

Wells Cathedral Statutes, by F. H. Dickinson. (*Som. Archæol. & Nat. Hist. Soc. Proc.*, vol. xvii. pp. 32–34. 1871.)

Church (Charles Marcus). The Documentary Evidence relating to the Early Architecture of the Cathedral, with a List. (*Som. Archæol. & Nat. Hist. Soc. Proc.*, vol. xxxiv. pt. ii. pp. 1–20, and App. pp. 95–97. 1888.)

—— **Notes on the Buildings, Books, and Benefactors of the Library of the Dean and Chapter of the Cathedral Church of Wells.** (*Archaeologia*, vol. lvii. pp. 201–228. 1901.)

Williams (T. W.). Wells Cathedral Library. (*The Library Assoc. Record*, vol. viii. pp. 372–377. 1906.)

Botfield (Beriah). Notes on the Cathedral Libraries of England. 1849. **Wells,** pp. 417–429.

WESTON-SUPER-MARE.

Baker (Ernest E.). A Contribution towards the Biblio. of Weston-super-Mare. Reprinted from the 'Weston Mercury.' 1887.

STAFFORDSHIRE.

SIMMS (RUPERT). BIBLIOTHECA STAFFORDIENSIS; OR A BIBLIOGRAPHICAL ACCOUNT OF BOOKS AND OTHER PRINTED MATTER RELATING TO, PRINTED OR PUBLISHED IN, OR WRITTEN BY A NATIVE, RESIDENT, OR PERSON DERIVING A TITLE FROM, ANY PORTION OF THE COUNTY OF STAFFORD: giving a full collation and biographical Notices of Authors and Printers, together with as full a list as possible of Prints, Engravings, Etchings, &c., of any Part thereof; and Portraits of Persons so connected. Lichfield, 1894.

The 'Bibliotheca Staffordiensis' is arranged in one alphabet under 'Authors' and 'Places.' The entries include items taken from Magazines, Academical Publications, and other Sources. The heading 'Staffordshire' at pp. 427–433 is classified. The following are some of the more important sub-divisions:

List of MSS., p. 429.
List of Maps, Plans, etc., pp. 429–430.
List of Newspapers, with descriptive notes, pp. 430–433.

Rupert Simms issued Nos. 1-3 of 'Nota Staffordiensis,' devoted to Keele Church Registers, combined with Catalogues of Books, Prints, etc., relating to Staffordshire on Sale at his Bookshop at Newcastle-under-Lyme in 1896 and 1897. For Biographical Notes on Rupert Simms, see Preface to the 'Bibliotheca,' and also the particulars given under his name in that work.

Index-Catalogue of the William Salt Library at Stafford. Reprinted from 'The Staffordshire Advertiser.' 1878. Indexes or Lists, Printed and Manuscript, mainly to the Printed Books in the William Salt Library, pp. 45–48. Staffordshire items, pp. 91–94.

The William Salt Library was formed by Thorpe, the famous Bookseller of Piccadilly, assisted by Captain Ferneyhough. After the death of Mr. Salt the Library was Catalogued for Sale by Sotheby's, in 1868, and only narrowly escaped being dispersed, by being transferred to the Trustees of the William Salt Archæol. Soc.

Brough (W. S.). The William Salt Library at Stafford. (*Memorials of Old Staffordshire*, ed. by Rev. W. Beresford, 1909, pp. 259–265.)

STAFFORDSHIRE (continued).

Lawley (George T.). Staffordshire Bibliography. A MS. Catal. of Books relating to, or connected with, the County of Stafford. (Offered for Sale by Messrs. W. N. Pitcher, of Manchester, 1912.)

List of the Contents of the William Salt Archæological Society's 'Collections for a Hist. of Staffordshire,' vols. i.-xviii. 1880-1897, and New Series, vols. i.-xiv. 1898-1911. (In 'Collections' for 1911.)

The Coming of Age of the North Staffordshire Archæological and Naturalists' Field Club. Biblio. of Publications. Newcastle, 1886.

Shaw (Stebbing). Proposals for Publishing by Subscription the 'History and Antiquities of Staffordshire,' 1793.

Two folio circulars advertising the proposed publication, containing interesting details of the MS. Collections and other sources from which this important work was compiled. The copies in the Brit. Mus. Library are bound up in a vol. of 'Unpublished Plates' to Shaw's History. A copy of the 'Hist.' published in 1798–1801, in the Brit. Mus. has MS. additions, corrections, etc., by Samuel Pipe-Wolferstan, of Statfold, co. Stafford.

Centenary of the 'Staffordshire Advertiser,' 5 January, 1895. A Sketch of the Hist. of the Paper, 1795–1895. Stafford, 1895.

Staffordshire Clog Almanack. A Biblio. Note by J. M. Gresley. (*Leics. Archæol. & Archit. Soc. Trans.*, vol. i. pp. 410–413. 1866.)

Catal. of Books at Stafford Castle, 1556. See Hist. MSS. Comm. Rep. on Lord Bagot's Collection at Blithefield, 4th Rep. p. 328.

A List of Private Acts relating to the Counties of Staffordshire and Shropshire. Stevens & Sons, London, 1913.

Special Topographical Collections for Staffordshire are in the Walsall Public Lib. and in the William Salt Library at Stafford.

Hist. MSS. Comm. Reports. Staffordshire Collections.

Bagot, Lord, at Blithefield	4th Rep. p. xiv. and App. pp. 325-344.
Dartmouth, Earl of, at Patshall ...	2nd Rep. p. x. and App. pp. 9–12; 11th Rep. pp. 19–23, and App. V.; 13th Rep. p. 32, App. IV. pp. 495–506; 14th Rep. pp. 25–27 and App. X.; 15th Rep. pp. 30–35 and App. I.
Hatherton, Lord, at Teddesley ...	5th Rep. p. vii. and App. pp. 294, 299.
Sneyd, Rev. Walter, at Keele Hall ...	3rd Rep. p. xvii. and App. pp. 287–290.
Sutherland, Duke of, at Dunrobin ...	2nd Rep. p. xvi. and App. pp. 177–180; 5th Rep. p. vi. and App. pp. 135–214.
Whitgreave, Mr. Francis, at Burton Manor	1st Rep. p. xi. and App. p. 61.
Wrottesley, Lord, at Wrottesley ...	2nd Rep. p. x. and App. pp. 46–49.
Lichfield, Dean and Chapter of ...	14th Rep. pp. 45–46 and App. VIII. pp. 205–236.
Oscott College	1st Rep. p. xi. and App. p. 89; 2nd Rep. p. xiii. and App. p. 125.

The 'Lists and Indexes' of Records at the Public Record Office [with Special Reference to Staffordshire]. (*William Salt Archæol. Soc. Collections for a Hist. of Staffs.* 1912, pp. 210–259.)

Local Ecclesiastical Records of the Diocese of Birmingham (Staffordshire, etc.) Report presented to the Bishop of Birmingham, June, 1911, with List of Registers, etc. 1911.

Salt (William). A List and Description of the MS. Copies of Erdeswick's Survey of Staffordshire which have been traced in public Libraries or private Collections, 1842–43. Only 20 copies issued separately. Reprinted in the 1844 edition of Thomas Harwood's 'Erdeswicke,' pp. lxxix–ci.

Ashmole's Collections for a Hist. of Staffordshire, at Oxford. Ashm. Lib. MSS. 859, 864.

STAFFORDSHIRE (continued).

Lysons (Rev. S.). Collections for Staffordshire in the Brit. Museum. Add. MS. 9459.

Upcott's Topog. Collections for Staffordshire in the Brit. Museum. Add. MS. 15926.

Dove (Patrick Edward). Domesday Studies. 1891. Domesday Biblio. Staffordshire, vol. ii. p. 688.

Davenport (Frances G.). List of Printed Materials for Manorial Hist. 1894. Biblio, Note on Staffordshire Manorial Hist., p. 57.

Lyell (Arthur H.). Biblio. List of Romano-British Remains. 1912. Staffordshire, p. 118.

Whitaker (William). List of Books on the Geology of Staffordshire. (*Brit. Assoc. Report*, 1886, pp. 780–797.)

Ward (John). Summary of Literature relating to the Geology, Mineralogy, and Palæontology of North Staffordshire. (*North Staffs. Field Club. Trans.*, vol. xxxiii. p. 72. 1898–99.) **Additions.** (*Ibid.* vol. xxxvi. pp. 94–97, 1902; vol. xxxix. pp. 129–132. 1905.)

A List of Papers contributed to various Publications by John Ward (mainly on Staffordshire). (*Ibid.* vol. xli. pp. 45–47. 1907.)

Trimen (Henry). Botanical Biblio. of the British Counties. Staffordshire. (*Journ. of Botany*, vol. xii. p. 156. 1874.)

Christy (Miller). Biblio. Note on Staffordshire Birds. (*The Zoologist*, Ser. 3, vol. xiv. p. 259, 1890; and reprinted in pamph. 1891, p. 23.) **Mammals.** (*The Zoologist*, Ser. 3, vol. xvii. p. 184. 1893.) **Reptiles.** (*Ibid.* p. 247. 1893). **Fishes.** (*Ibid.* p. 258. 1893.)

Anderson (John P.). Book of Brit. Topo., 1881. Staffordshire, pp. 257–261.
Gatfield (George). Guide to Heraldry. 1892. Staffordshire, pp. 178–180.
Sims (Richard). Manual. 1861. Staffordshire, pp. 173, 219–220, 239.
Upcott (William). English Topo., 1818. Staffordshire, vol. iii. pp. 1172–1190, 1496–1497.
Smith (Alfred Russell). Catal. of Topo. Tracts, etc. 1878. Staffordshire, pp. 349–353, 475.
Gough (Richard). Brit. Topo., 1780. Staffordshire, vol. ii. pp. 229–239.
Bandinel (Bulkeley). Catal. of Books bequeathed to Bodleian Lib. by Richard Gough, 1814. Staffordshire, pp. 294–296.

BILSTON.

Lawley (George T.). A History of Bilston, a Record of its Archæology, Ecclesiology, Bibliography, etc. Bilston, 1893. Bilston Books and Authors, pp. 195–216.

BURTON-ON-TRENT.

Black (W. H.). Ancient Charters relating to the Abbey and Town of Burton-on-Trent. (*Brit. Archæol. Assoc. Journ.*, vol. vii. pp. 421–428. 1852.)

Knowles (T.). On Some Ancient Burton MSS. (*Burton-on-Trent Nat. Hist. & Archæol. Soc. Trans.*, vol. ii. pp. 90–108. 1892.)

——— **Some Documents from the Burton Parish Chest.** (*Ibid.* vol. iii. pp. 261–264. 1897.)

A Résumé of the Hist. of the Burton-on-Trent Nat. Hist. & Archæol. Soc., by Frank E. Lott. (*Trans.*, vol. iii. pp. 191–204. 1897.)

HANDSWORTH.

Murray (David). 'Museums.' Glasgow, 1904. Biblio. Note on Handsworth Museum, vol. ii. p. 279.

STAFFORDSHIRE (continued).

LICHFIELD.

Borough Records, 1387, etc., at the Guildhall, Lichfield. (*Local Records Comm. Rep.*, 1902, App. III. p. 74.)

Dean and Chapter of Lichfield Records. See *ante* Hist. MSS. Comm. Reports, p. 238.

Diocesan Records, 1298, etc., at Lichfield. (*Local Records Comm. Rep.*, 1902, App. III. p. 104.)

A Catal. of the Printed Books and MSS. in the Library of the Cathedral Church of Lichfield. (Contains Lichfield and Staffordshire items.) London, 1888.

Catal. of the Muniments and MS. Books pertaining to the Dean and Chapter of Lichfield,—Analysis of the Magnum Registrum Album,—Catal. of the Muniments of the Lichfield Vicars. Compiled by J. Charles Cox, 1881–86. (*William Salt Archæol. Soc. Collections for a Hist. of Staffs.*, vol. vi. pt. ii. 1885.)

The Statutes of the Cathedral Church of Lichfield analysed and in part translated (by F. S. Bolton). Stafford, 1871.

Botfield (Beriah). Notes on the Cathedral Libraries of England. 1849. **Lichfield,** pp. 259–267.

Murray (David). 'Museums.' Glasgow, 1904. Biblio. Note on Lichfield Museum, vol. ii. pp. 266, 330.

Bicentenary of the Birth of Dr. Samuel Johnson, Lichfield, 1909. Official Guide. 1909. Catal. of Johnsonian Exhibits (including some lent by Mr. A. M. Broadley, of Bradpole, Dorset) at the Exhibition, pp. 30–55.

Courtney (W. P.). A Bibliography of Samuel Johnson. Oxford, 1915.

SHENSTONE.

A List of the Shenstone Charters contained in the 'Chartulary' or 'Great Coucher Book' of the Duchy of Lancaster in the Public Record Office, by George Grazebrook, with notes by H. S. Grazebrook. (*William Salt Archæol. Soc. Collections for a Hist. of Staffs.*, vol. xvii. pp. 237–298. 1896.)

TIXALL.

Clifford (Sir Thomas). A Topog. and Hist. Description of the Parish of Tixall. Paris, 1817. Privately Printed. For a Biblio. Note on a Special Copy of this work, see John Martin's 'Biblio. Catal. of Privately Printed Books,' 1854, p. 235.

WALSALL.

Borough Records, with Printed Index, at Town Hall, Walsall. (*Local Records Comm. Rep.*, 1902, App. III. p. 40.)

A Calendar of the Deeds and Documents belonging to the Corporation of Walsall, from the reign of King John to the end of James II., by Richard Sims. 1882.

WEST BROMWICH.

Hackwood (Frederick W.). A Hist. of West Bromwich. Reprinted from the 'Midland Sun,' Apr. 1894–Aug. 1895. Birmingham, 1895. Biblio., pp. 117–118.

WILLENHALL.

Hackwood (Frederick W.). The Annals of Willenhall. Wolverhampton, 1908. Biblio., pp. 175–178.

WOLVERHAMPTON.

Lawley (George T.). The Biblio. of Wolverhampton. A Record of Local Books, Authors, and Booksellers. Bilston, 1890.

STIRLINGSHIRE.

Bibliotheca Stirlinensis. Supplementary to items in 'Stirling Notes and Queries.' 2 vols. 1883-86. (*The Stirling Antiquary*, vol. i. pp. 2-6. 1893.)

Local Bibliography. By various compilers. (*Ibid.* vol. i. pp. 123-125; vol. ii. pp. 225-229; vol. iii. pp. 221-224; vol. iv. pp. 220-229, 273-280. 1893-1908.)

Hist. MSS. Comm. Reports. Stirlingshire Collections.

Edmondstone, Sir Archibald, at Colzium	3rd Rep. p. xxiii. and App. pp. 407-408.
Livingstone, Mr. T. Livingstone Fenton, at Westquarter	7th Rep. p. xvi. and App. pp. 732-735.
Montrose, Duke of, at Buchanan Castle	2nd Rep. p. xvi. and App. pp. 165-177; 3rd Rep. p. xxi. and App. pp. 368-402.

Records in Public and Private Custody. (*Local Records Comm. Rep.*, 1902, App. III. p. 132.) The following works have been published on the Burgh Records:—'Charters and other Documents relating to the Royal Burgh of Stirling, 1124-1705,' compiled by Robert Renwick, Glasgow, 1884; and 'Extracts from the Records of the Royal Burgh of Stirling, 1519-1752, with Appendix, 1295-1752,' edited by Robert Renwick. 2 vols. Glasgow, 1887-89.

Gross (Charles). Biblio. of Brit. Municipal Hist. (*Harvard Hist. Studies*, vol. v. 1897.) Stirlingshire, p. 135. Stirling, p. 398.

Livingstone (Matthew). Guide to the Public Records of Scotland. Stirlingshire, pp. 128, 180.

Turnbull (William B.). Scottish Parochial Registers. 1849. List of Stirlingshire Registers, pp. 148-152.

Lyell (Arthur H.). Biblio. List of Romano-British Remains. 1912. Stirlingshire, p. 141.

Anderson (Joseph) and Black (Geo. F.). Reports on Local Museums in Scotland. Museum of the Smith Institute at Stirling. (*Soc. of Antiq. Scot. Proc.*, vol. xxii. p. 354. 1888.) **Bridge of Allan Museum.** (*Ibid.* vol. xxii. p. 355. 1888.)

Murray (David). 'Museums.' Glasgow. 1902. Biblio. Note on Bridge of Allan Museum, vol. iii. p. 97.

Local Contributions of Antiquities, etc., to the Glasgow International Exhib. 1901. (*The Stirling Antiquary*, vol. iii. pp. 265-287. 1904.)

Morris (John Edward). Biblio. Notes on 'The Historians of Bannockburn.' (*Bannockburn*, 1914, pp. 50-56.)

Kerr (Eric Stair-). Stirling Castle in Poetry. (*Stirling Castle: its Place in Scottish History*, 1913, pp. 197-213.)

Macintyre (A. C.). Robert Leprevick, the first Stirling Printer. 30 copies only printed for Private Circulation. n.d.

Edmond (John Philip). Elegies and other Tracts issued on the Death of Henry, Prince of Wales (b. at Stirling Castle, 1594), **1612,** with a List. (*Edinb. Biblio. Soc. Pubns.*, vol. vi. pp. 141-158. 1906.)

Harvey (William). The Harp of Stirlingshire. Paisley, 1897.

Pt. I. Poets connected with the Shire by Birth or Residence.
Pt. II. Ballads, Poems, and Songs connected with the Shire.
Pt. III. Rhymes, etc., of Stirlingshire.

—— **Biblio. Notes on Falkirk Chapbooks.** (*The Stirling Antiquary*, vol. iv. pp. 220-229, 273-280. 1908.)

Trimen (Henry). Botanical Biblio. of the British Counties. Stirlingshire. (*Journ. of Botany*, vol. xii. p. 235. 1874.)

STIRLINGSHIRE (*continued*).

A Special Collection of Books owned by the Stirling Nat. Hist. and Archæol. Soc. is at the Stirling Public Library.

Christy (Miller). Biblio. Note on Stirlingshire Birds. (*The Zoologist*, Ser. 3, vol. xiv. p. 265, 1890; and reprinted in pamph., 1891, p. 38.) **Mammals.** (*The Zoologist*, Ser. 3, vol. xvii. p. 214. 1893.)

Anderson (John P.). Book of Brit. Topo., 1881. Stirlingshire, pp. 411-412.

Gough (Richard). Brit. Topo., 1780. Stirlingshire, vol. ii. pp. 719-722.

Bandinel (Bulkeley). Catal. of Books bequeathed to Bodleian Lib. by Richard Gough, 1814. Stirlingshire, p. 364.

SUFFOLK.

COPINGER (WALTER ARTHUR). COUNTY OF SUFFOLK; ITS HISTORY AS DISCLOSED BY EXISTING RECORDS AND OTHER DOCUMENTS, BEING MATERIALS FOR THE HIST. OF SUFFOLK. 6 vols. London, 1904–07. The sixth vol. is entitled:—

Index Nominum et Locorum, being an Index of Persons and Places mentioned in Copinger's 'County of Suffolk, etc.,' completed by H. B. Copinger. Manchester, 1907.

The work, which is parochially arranged, is a guide to the most important records of the County. Biblio. Notes and Lists of Authorities are in Introduction to vol. i.

——— **On a Scheme for Rendering the Charters and MSS. in the various Repositories available for County Purposes** (including a description of compiling the aforesaid monumental work on the County of Suffolk). A Leaflet published by the Congress of Archæol. Societies in Union with the Soc. of Antiquaries, 3 July, 1907.

——— **The Manors of Suffolk.** 7 vols. 1905–11. Vol. vii. contains 'Index of Holders of Manors,' pp. 285–405, and 'Indexes Rerum, Locorum, and Nominum' to the work.

Index of Articles, Contributions, Papers, published in the Proceedings of the Suffolk Institute of Archæology, vols. i.–ix., 1848–98, with list of Illustrations. Issued with vol. x. of the 'Proceedings' of the Institute.

Catal. of Books, MSS., etc., in the Library of the Suffolk Institute of Archæology. (*Proceedings of the Institute*, vol. x. pp. 97–124. 1900.)

Catal. of Books in the Reference Department of the Ipswich Free Library, compiled by Henry Ogle. Ipswich, 1906. Biblio. Notes on Suffolk Newspapers, pp. 3–4. Lists of Books, etc., relating to Suffolk, pp. 91-108.

Hunt (William Powell). A Catal. of the Collection of Rare Books, MSS. and Illustrated Works relating to the Co. of Suffolk, formed by W. P. Hunt. To be sold by auction by Garrod and Turner, Ipswich, 17 Dec. 1873.

Rix (Samuel Wilton). A Catal. of the Library of Samuel Wilton Rix, including Archæological and Topographical Works, MSS., County Histories, and Local Collections, mostly relating to East Anglia. To be sold by Messrs. Spelman, at Beccles, Oct., 1894.

Catal. of a Collection of Printed Books and MSS., illustrative of the History of the County of Suffolk, formed by William Stevenson Fitch, of Ipswich, including original Collections for each Hundred in the County, and a Series of Pictorial Illustrations, comprising nearly 4500 original drawings and engravings (in 32 vols.). Sold by Puttick & Simpson. London, 2 July, 1855. The Catal. is arranged according to 'Hundreds.'

SUFFOLK (continued).

Catal. of the Collection of Printed Books and MSS. of W. S. Fitch, for the most part illustrative of the Hist. of the County of Suffolk. Sold by Ross at Ipswich, 14 Sept., 1859. 'The Suffolk Collection,' at pp. 6–14.

Catal. of the Remaining Library of W. S. Fitch, comprising Works relating to Suffolk, with his MS. Topographical Collections illustrative of the County, with Deeds, Charters, etc. Sold by Sotheby & Wilkinson, 29 Nov., 1859.

Ashby (Rev. George). Collections for the Hist. of the County of Suffolk, made by the Rev. G. Ashby, with a list of headings. See 'Catal. of MSS., Charters, Books, etc., the property of Thomas Thorpe,' p. 9. Sold by Auction by Evans, Pall Mall, 2 Mar., 1826.

Glyde (John). Suffolk in the Nineteenth Century. London, 1856. Chap. ix. Literary and Scientific Institutions, with notes on Suffolk Libraries, pp. 287–307.

Descriptive Catal. of 'The Jackson Collection' at the Sheffield Public Library, compiled by T. Walter Hall and A. H. Thomas. 1914. **Suffolk items,** pp. 206–246.

Prospectuses of Works published by Authors living in the County of Suffolk, 1819–51. A Collection in the British Mus. Library, 10351. g. 21.

Collections of Miscellaneous Papers, cuttings from Magazines, Newspapers, etc., relating to the County of Suffolk, in the Library of the British Museum. (Formerly in the possession of D. E. Davy, of Ufford.)

Suffolk Scarce Tracts, 1595-1684, in Library of Charles Golding. A Biblio. List. 1873. Privately printed.

Booth (W. H.). Suffolk Books, MSS., Illustrations, etc., including extra-illustrated copies of the County Histories. See List in 'Catal. of the Handford Lodge, Ipswich, Collection, formed by W. H. Booth,' pp. 57–60. Sold by Robert Bond & Sons, Ipswich, 23 Apr., 1906.

Gross (Charles). Biblio. of Brit. Municipal Hist. (*Harvard Hist. Studies*, vol. v. 1897.) Suffolk, p. 104. Ipswich, pp. 262-264. Bury St. Edmunds, pp. 182–184.

Davenport (Frances G.). List of Printed Materials for Manorial Hist. 1894. Biblio. Note on Suffolk Manorial Hist., pp. 57–58.

Dove (Patrick Edward). Domesday Studies. 1891. Domesday Biblio. Suffolk, vol. ii. p. 689.

Lyell (Arthur H.). Biblio. List of Romano-British Remains. 1912. Suffolk, pp. 118–120.

Catal. of Antiquities found principally in East Anglia, in the Norwich Castle Museum. Edited by Walter Rye. Compiled by Frank Leney. Norwich, 1909. Biblio., pp. ix.–x.

Macklin (Herbert Walter). Monumental Brasses. London : George Allen & Co., 1913. Biblio. Note on Suffolk Brasses, with a List, pp. 142, 179–182.

A List of Monumental Brasses remaining in the Co. of Suffolk, 1903. By Edmund Farrer. With Biblio. References. Norwich, 1903.

An Index to Suffolk Monumental Inscriptions in the Davy Collection, Brit. Mus. Add. MS. 29761.

Suffolk Monumental Inscriptions. By Rev. T. W. Oswald-Hicks. (*The Register of English Monumental Inscriptions*, vol. ii. 1914.)

I. Table of Printed Transcripts and where Printed, pp. 126–128.
II. Table of Unprinted Transcripts and where Deposited, pp. 129–131.

Suffolk Churchyard Inscriptions. A contribution towards a Biblio. of Inscriptions, Printed and in MSS. By Harleigh Oswald-Hicks. [In preparation,]

SUFFOLK (continued).

Collection of Brass Rubbings in the possession of the Suffolk Inst. of Archæology, with a List of Brasses arranged under Counties. (*Suff. Inst. of Archæol. Proc.*, vol. x. pp. 237-249. 1900.)

Suffolk Archæological Association. A small Collection of Papers, Circulars, etc. Ipswich, 1846. In the Brit. Mus. Library, 10351. g. 19.

Frost's Drawings of Ipswich and Sketches in Suffolk, with a Memoir, and short descriptive notes on the principal Plates, edited by Frank Brown. 1895.

Ford (James). Notices of Prints relating to Suffolk, extended by W. H. Booth. n.d.

Collections of Water-Colour Drawings, Engravings, etc., illustrative of the Topographical, Biographical, and Domestic Hist. of the County of Suffolk, with lists, formed by W. S. Fitch, J. Pulham, and others. See *ante*, p. 242. Hunt, pp. 27–30.

A Collection of the Proposals for Publishing various Engravings, Books, etc., relating to Suffolk, 1770–1845. In the Brit. Mus. Library, 1891. e. 2. (2).

A Complete Catal. of Engraved Suffolk Portraits, with Notes, Biographical, Historical, etc. Announced as 'in preparation,' 1914.

Farrer (Edmund). Portraits in West Suffolk Houses. London, 1908. A Collective List, with detailed descriptions.

Hunt (William Powell). MS. Catal. of Suffolk Portraits. See *ante*, p. 242. Hunt's Catal. p. 14.

County Folk-Lore. Vol. I. Suffolk. Collected and edited by Lady E. C. Gordon, with introduction by Edward Clodd. With a list of Authorities. Folk-Lore Soc. Pubns. vol. xxxvii. 1895.

Allnutt (W. H.). English Provincial Presses. Earliest Printing at Ipswich. 1547–48. (*Bibliographica*, vol. ii. pp. 33–35, 301. 1896.)

Beck (F. G. M.). A New Ipswich Book of 1548. (*The Library*, New Ser., vol. x. pp. 86–89. 1909.)

A Brief Description of the Art of Anastatic Printing and of the Uses to which it may be applied, as practised by S. H. Cowell, Ipswich. 1870.

The Suffolk Garland, or a Collection of Poems, Songs, Tales, Ballads, Sonnets, etc. relative to that County, and illustrative of its Scenery, Places, etc. [Edited by the Rev. James Ford.] Ipswich, 1818.

Suffolk Garland, 2 vols. (MS.) Collections of Ballads, Songs, etc., formed by the Rev. James Ford (Editor of the 'Suffolk Garland,' in 1818), with the additions made by Augustine Page, also the Papers in print and MS. Additions by W. S. Fitch, for the furtherance of a second edition of the 'Garland.' See *ante* p. 242. 'Sale Catal. of Fitch's Library, 29 Nov. 1859,' p. 23. The Collections are now Brit. Mus. Add. MSS. 23965–23966.

Glyde (John). The New Suffolk Garland, a Miscellany of Anecdotes, Romantic Ballads, Descriptive Poems and Songs, Historical and Biographical Notices, etc. relating to the County of Suffolk. Ipswich, 1866.

Biblio. Notes on Suffolk Ballads. (*East Anglian*, New Ser. vol. iv. pp. 95, 335, 383; vol vi. pp. 56-59, 160, 176, 193, 1891–96.)

Eyre (H. R.). Materials for a Hist. of Suffolk Theatres. (In Ipswich Free Library.) For some Ipswich Theatrical items from the Eyre Collection, see *ante* p. 243, 'Catal. of the Collection of W. H. Booth,' p. 60.

A Collection of Ordinances, Acts of Parliament, and Bills relating to Suffolk. 5 vols. 1654–1817. In the Brit. Museum Library, 5805. d. 1–5.

SUFFOLK (continued).

Special Topographical Collections for Suffolk and East Anglia are in the Public Libraries at Ipswich and Yarmouth, and in the Library of the Suffolk Institute of Archæology.

Hist. MSS. Comm. Reports. Suffolk Collections.

Almack, Mr. Richard, at Melford ...	1st Rep. p. x. and App. p. 55.
Bunbury, Sir Charles, at Bury ...	3rd Rep. p. xvi. and App. pp. 240–242.
Guilford, Earl of, at Glemham Hall ...	17th Rep. p. 122; and Various Collections, vol. iv. pp. 175–190.
Hill, Rev. T. S., at Thorington ...	10th Rep. p. 23, and App. IV. pp. 451–457.
Sewell, Rev. W. H., at Yaxley ...	10th Rep. p. 26, and App. IV. pp. 463–466.
Tollemache, Mr. John, at Helmingham Hall	1st Rep. p. x. and App. pp. 60–61.
Aldeburgh Corporation	17th Rep. pp. 124–125, and Various Collections, vol. iv. pp. 279–312.
Beccles Corporation	Various Collections, vol. vii. pp. 70–79.
Bury St. Edmunds Corporation ...	14th Rep. p. 41, and App. VIII. pp. 121–158.
Dunwich Corporation	Various Collections, vol. vii. pp. 81–113.
Eye Corporation	10th Rep. p. 26, and App. IV. pp. 513–536.
Ipswich Corporation	9th Rep. pp. xi.–xiii. and App. I. pp. 222–262.
Mendlesham Parish	5th Rep. p. xviii. and App. pp. 593–596.
Orford Corporation	17th Rep. p. 123; and Various Collections, vol. iv. pp. 255–278.
Southwold Corporation	Various Collections, vol. vii. pp. 114–118.

County Records, 1639, etc., with MS. Index, at the County Hall, Ipswich, and at the Shire Hall, Bury St. Edmunds. (*Local Records Comm. Rep.*, 1902, App. III. p. 24.)

Davy's Collections for the Hist. of the County of Suffolk, in the Brit. Museum. Add. MSS. 19077–19241. A Series of nearly 160 vols. made by David E. Davy, of Ufford.

Davy's Suffolk Collections. A verbatim Copy of a 'List of the MS. Material enumerated by D. E. Davy for a Hist. of Suffolk,' Brit. Mus. Add. MS. 19172. By W. A. Copinger. (*East Anglian*, Ser. 3, vol. viii. p. 373; vol. ix. pp. 8, 21, 56, 70, 88, 156. 1899–1901.)

Jermyn's Collections for a General Hist. of the County of Suffolk, in the Brit. Museum. Add. MSS. 8168–8218, 17097, 17099.

Suckling's Collections for Suffolk, in the Brit. Museum. Add. MSS. 18476–18478, 18480–18482.

The Topography of Suffolk. References to MSS. in the Brit. Museum, by R. P. Sanderson. (*East Anglian*, Ser. 2, vol. iv. pp. 183–185, 262–266; vol. v. p. 361. 1892–94.)

On MS. Collections relating to Suffolk in the Brit. Museum, by Edward Levien. (*Brit. Archæol. Assoc. Journ.*, vol. xxi. pp. 5–21. 1865.)

MS. Collections relating to the County of Suffolk, by S. W. Rix. (*Ibid.* vol. xxi. pp. 144–158. 1865.)

Suffolk MSS. in the Brit. Museum. A List from the 'Catal. of Additions to MSS. in the Brit. Mus., 1906–10,' by R. F. Bullen. (*East Anglian Miscellany*, 1913, pp. 87, 92.)

SUFFOLK (continued).

A Descriptive Catal. of Ancient (Suffolk) Deeds in the Public Record Office, with an Index, by W. E. Layton. (*Suff. Inst. of Archæol. Proc.*, vol. x. pp. 251–344, 399–413. 1900.) Also issued separately.

Fitch (William Stevenson). Collections of MSS. relating to the Hist. of Suffolk. 28 vols. (In Ipswich Free Library.) Indices to Fitch's Materials for the Bleckbourne and Blything Hundreds, by Edward Cookson, are also in the same Library.

Cookson (Edward). MS. Collections relating to Suffolk. See *ante* p. 242. 'Catal. of the Reference Department of the Ipswich Free Lib.' p. 107.

Bibliotheca Martiniana. Catal. of Library of the late Antiquary, Thomas Martin, of Palgrave, issued by Martin Booth and John Berry. (Contains numerous Suffolk MSS.) (*Norf. Antiq. Misc.*, vol. iii. pp. 394–401. 1887.)

Memoirs of the Life of Thomas Martin, of Palgrave, in Suffolk, with an Account of the disposal and disposition of his large and valuable Collections of MSS., Printed Books, Papers, Pictures, etc., by John Fenn. 1784. (*Norfolk Archæology*, vol. xv. pp. 233–236. 1904.)

Tom Martin's MSS. List of MSS. formerly belonging to Tom Martin, the Palgrave Antiquary. (*East Anglian Miscellany*, 1914, pp. 49–50.

Ford (Rev. Joseph). Collections of Portraits and Materials for the Parochial Hist. of Suffolk. 10 vols. See 'Catal. of MS. Library of Dawson Turner,' pp. 298, 299. Sold by Puttick and Simpson, June 1859.

The Blois MSS. (In possession of the Suff. Inst. of Archæology, formerly in the Library of Robert Hovenden.) 4 vols. By Rev. Edmund Farrer. (*Suff. Inst. of Archæol. Proc.*, vol. xiv. pp. 147–226. 1911.) The following are described :

Vol. I. Pedigrees of Suffolk Families.
Vol. II. Additional Pedigrees, & Index to Pedigrees.
Vol. III. Church Notes, & Index to Church Notes.
Vol. IV. A Suffolk Armory.

Coleman's Suffolk Deeds. A list of those relating to Suffolk in the James Coleman Collection, by H. W. B. Wayman. (*East Anglian*, Ser. 3, vol. xiii pp. 328–329. 1910.)

A Catal. of the Library of John Ives (Suffolk Herald, b. 1751, d. 1776), sold by Baker & Leigh, London, Mar. 3–10, 1777. (Includes important MSS., etc., relating to Suffolk.)

Catal. of Ancient MSS., chiefly Antiquarian and Historical, including the valuable Collections of Sir Henry Spelman, collected by the Rev Dr. Cox Macro, of Little Haugh (Norton), in the County of Suffolk. To be sold by Christie, Pall Mall, Feb. 1820. (Contains a few interesting Suffolk items.) These MSS. were privately purchased by Hudson Gurney, of Keswick Hall, Norwich, and Dawson Turner, of Yarmouth.

Catal. of Suffolk Manorial Registers, Royal Grants, Deeds, etc., collected for the purpose of illustrating a Hist. of the County, by William Stevenson Fitch. Ipswich, 1843. Privately printed.

Suffolk County Records, with a List of the Principal Records in the Custody of the Clerk of the Peace for Suffolk. (*Suff. Inst. of Archæol Proc.*, vol. xv. pp. 144–151. 1914.)

Archdeaconry of Suffolk Records, 1525, etc., at the Registry, Ipswich (*Local Records Comm. Rep.*, 1902, App. III. p. 124.)

Records of Protestant Dissenters in Suffolk, with a List of Suffolk Non-Parochial Registers (before 1750) and Records. By V. B. Redstone. (*East Anglian Miscellany*, 1913, pp. 94, 96.)

SUFFOLK (*continued*).

Trimen (Henry). Botanical Biblio. of the British Counties. Suffolk. (*Journ. of Botany*, vol. xii. p. 110. 1874.)

Christy (Miller). Biblio. Note on Suffolk Birds. (*The Zoologist*, Ser. 3, vol. xiv. p. 259. 1890; and reprinted in pamph., 1891, p. 24.) **Mammals.** (*The Zoologist*, Ser. 3, vol. xvii. p. 184. 1893.)

Anderson (John P.). Book of Brit. Topo., 1881. Suffolk, pp. 261-268.
Gatfield (George). Guide to Heraldry. 1892. Suffolk, pp. 180-182.
Sims (Richard). Manual. 1861. Suffolk, pp. 173, 220-222, 239.
Upcott (William). English Topo., 1818. Suffolk, vol. iii. pp. 1191-1206.
Smith (Alfred Russell). Catal. of Topo. Tracts, etc., 1878. Suffolk, pp. 355-362, 475.
Gough (Richard). Brit. Topo., 1780. Suffolk, vol. ii. pp. 241-260.
Bandinel (Bulkeley). Catal. of Books bequeathed to Bodleian Lib. by Richard Gough. 1814. Suffolk, pp. 297-301.

ALDEBURGH.

Corporation Records. See *ante* Hist. MSS. Comm. Reports, p. 245.

BECCLES.

Corporation Records. See *ante* Hist. MSS. Comm. Reports, p. 245.

Beccles Collections. A Collection of Papers in MS., comprising the materials towards a Hist. of Beccles. See *ante* p. 242. Rix (S.W.). Catal. of Library, 1894, pp. 25-30.

BURY ST. EDMUNDS.

Corporation Records. See *ante* Hist. MSS. Comm. Reports, p. 245.

Borough Records, at Town Hall, Bury St. Edmunds. (*Local Records Comm. Rep.*, 1902. App. III. p. 48.)

Clarke (Sir Ernest). Bury Chroniclers of the Thirteenth Century. Reprinted from the 'Bury Free Press.' 1905.

Bartholomew (A. T.) and Gordon (Cosmo). On the Library at King Edward VI. School, Bury St. Edmunds. (*The Library*, Ser. 3, vol. i. pp. 1-27, 329-331. 1910.)

DUNWICH.

Corporation Records. See *ante* Hist. MSS. Comm. Reports, p. 245.

EYE.

Corporation Records. See *ante* Hist. MSS. Comm. Reports, p. 245.

Borough Records, 1575, etc., at Town Clerk's office, Eye. (*Local Records Comm. Rep.*, 1902. App. III. p. 56.)

FRESTON.

Index to Freston Parish Registers, 1538-1884. (*Freston Parish Mag.*, ed. by Rev. C. R. Durrant, July, 1887-Oct. 1891.)

IPSWICH.

Corporation Records. See *ante* Hist. MSS. Comm. Reports, p. 245.

List of Books specially relating to Ipswich, also a Collection of Water-color and Pencil Drawings, engravings, etc., illustrative of the town of Ipswich. See *ante* p. 242. Hunt (W. P.). Catal. of Books, etc., relating to Suffolk, pp. 24-29.

List of Books relating to Ipswich, see *ante* p. 242. 'Catal. of Books in the Reference Department of the Ipswich Free Library,' 1906, pp. 100-105.

SUFFOLK (*continued*).

Collections of Books and MSS. relating to Ipswich. See *ante* p. 242. 'Catal. of a Collection of the Books, etc., of W. S. Fitch of Ipswich,' pp. 23–29.

Books and MSS. relating to Ipswich, containing many from the Hengrave Hall, the Charles Golding, and the Eyre Collections, and including an extra-illustrated copy of Clarke's 'Hist. of Ipswich,' extended to five vols., with water-colour drawings, sketches, and a loose Index. See *ante* p. 243. 'Catal. of the Collection of W. H. Booth,' pp. 57–60.

Glyde (John). Materials for a Hist. of Ipswich (18 vols.)—**Materials for a Hist. of Municipal Ipswich** (2 vols.) **and Materials for a Parliamentary Hist. of Ipswich.** (In Ipswich Free Lib.) See *ante* p. 242. 'Catal. of Books in the Ipswich Free Lib.,' pp. 101, 103.

White (C. H. Evelyn). The Ipswich 'Domesday' Books, and especially concerning Percyvale's 'Gt. Domesday Book.' (*Suff. Inst. of Archæol. Proc.*, vol. vi. pp. 195–219. 1888.)

Redstone (Vincent B.). Ipswich Port Books. (*Ibid.* vol. xiv. pp. 238–242. 1911.)

Murray (David). 'Museums.' Glasgow. 1904. Biblio. Note on Ipswich Museum, vol. ii. p. 297.

Ogle (Henry). An Old Town Library (Ipswich). (*The Library Assistant*, vol. iv. pp. 141–145. 1904.)

LONG MELFORD.

Deedes (Cecil). Dr. Bisbie's MS. Collections for Long Melford. (*Suff. Inst. of Archæol. Proc.*, vol. vii. pp. 78–90. 1891.)

MENDLESHAM.

Parish Records. See *ante* Hist. MSS. Comm. Reports, p. 245.

ORFORD.

Corporation Records. See *ante* Hist. MSS. Comm. Reports, p. 245.

SOUTHWOLD.

Corporation Records. See *ante* Hist. MSS. Comm. Reports, p. 245.

Borough Records, 1658, etc., with Printed Index, at the Town Hall, Southwold. (*Local Records Comm. Rep.*, 1902. App. III. p. 70.)

Wake (Robert). Southwold and its Vicinity. 1839. For a Note on an extra-illustrated copy of this work, with sketches by the Ipswich Artist, Henry Davy, and original letters, documents, etc., collected and arranged by W. P. Hunt, see *ante* p. 242. Hunt, p. 18.

SUDBURY.

Borough Records, 1340, etc., at Town Hall, Sudbury. (*Local Records Comm. Rep.*, 1902. App. III. p. 70.)

Calendar of the Muniments of the Borough of Sudbury. By Ethel Stokes and Lilian Redstone. (*Suff. Inst. of Archæol. Proc.*, vol. xiii. pp. 259–310. 1909.)

Early Sudbury Records. By Ethel Stokes. (*Ibid.* vol. xiv. pp. 105–109. 1912.)

Records of the Sudbury Archdeaconry. By Vincent B. Redstone.
I. Calendar of Register Returns. 1580–1640.
II. Terriers and Surveys, with a Calendar. (*Ibid.* vol. xi. pp. 252–300. 1903.)

THETFORD. [See Norfolk, p. 181.]

WOODBRIDGE.

Ford (James). MS. Collections of Materials towards a Hist. of Woodbridge, 2 vols. (In Ipswich Free Library.)

SURREY.

[The Entries under 'London' should also be consulted for places regarded as being in the County of Surrey.]

Minet (William) and Courtney (Charles J.). A Catal. of the Collection of Works relating to the County of Surrey in the Minet Public Library (Camberwell), 1901. **Supplement,** 1910. List of Maps and Plans, pp. 131–133, and Supp. pp. 62–64. Index to the MS. Calendar of Deeds, 1512–1842, in the Minet Lib., pp. 134–142, and Supp. pp. 65–71. **Additions to Works relating to the County of Surrey, 1910–1912.**

Stephenson (Mill). Catal. of Surrey Books and MSS. in the Lib. of the Surrey Archæol. Soc. (*Surrey Archæol. Soc. Collections*, vol. x. pp. 173–204. 1891.) Also issued separately.

General Index to vols. i. to xx. (1858-1907) of the Surrey Archæological Collections. (Surrey Archæol. Soc.) Guildford, 1914. App. I. Classified List of Illustrations. App. II. Key to References to the Visitation Pedigrees.

A Schedule of Antiquities in the County of Surrey, by P. M. Johnston, and others. (Surrey Archæol. Soc.) Guildford, 1913. A summary of the specialised information contained in the principal County Histories, the Collections of the Surrey Archæol. Soc., and other works. The earliest dates of Parish Registers are given. Collections of MSS., Pictures, etc., in public and private custody are recorded.

Manning (Owen) and Bray (William). Catal. of Books relating to the County, or particular Parts of it, and List of Prints, Maps, Views, Portraits, Acts of Parliament, etc., relative to the County, in vol. iii. pp. 683–702, and App. pp. i.–viii., lxxxiv.–cvii. of **'The History and Antiquities of the County of Surrey.'** 3 vols. London, 1804–14.

An extra-illustrated copy of Manning and Bray's 'History,' in 30 vols., formed by Richard Percival, Highbury Park, London, in 1847, is in the Lib. of the Brit. Museum. It is illustrated by upwards of six thousand drawings, prints, maps, plans, portraits, &c. The vols. have special title-pages, descriptive of the Collection, with names of Artists, etc.

An Index to the Victoria History of the County of Surrey. London, 1914.

Malden (Henry Elliott). A History of Surrey. London, 1900. Biblio. of Some Books on Surrey, pp. 310–318.

Coutts (H. T.). List of Books on Surrey in the Croydon Public Library. (*The Reader's Index to the Croydon Public Libraries*, vol. vi. pp. 133–140. 1904.)

Bax (A. Ridley). List of Papers and Illustrations relating to the County of Surrey, contained in the 'Archæologia,' 1770–1897, the Archæological Journal, 1845–1893, and the Journal of the Brit. Archæol. Assoc., 1845-1898. (*Surrey Archæol. Soc. Collections*, vol. xv. pp. 128–136. 1900.)

Catal. of the extensive Collection of Original Coloured Drawings, Portraits, Topographical Prints and Books illustrative of the County of Surrey made by Arthur Tyton. Sold by Evans, Pall Mall, 16 Nov. 1838.

For a note on Tyton's Collection, see Upcott's 'English Topography,' 1818, vol. iii. p. 1234.

Collections of Surrey Prints in the Library of the Surrey Archæol. Soc. at Guildford.

Photographic Survey and Record of Surrey. The Photographic Prints, etc., are in the Reference Department of the Croydon Public Libraries.

Dove (Patrick Edward). Domesday Studies. 1891. Domesday Biblio. of Surrey, vol. ii. p. 690.

Lyell (Arthur H.). Biblio. List of Romano-British Remains. 1912. Surrey, pp. 120–122.

Macklin (Herbert Walter). Monumental Brasses. London: Geo. Allen & Co., 1913. Biblio. Note on Surrey Brasses, with a List, pp. 142, 182–184.

SURREY (continued).

A List of Monumental Brasses in Surrey, compiled by Mill Stephenson. (*Monumental Brass Soc. Trans.*, vol. vi. pp. 257–295, 329–353, 377–398. 1913–14.) Also in Surrey Archæol. Collections, vol. xxv. pp. 33–100; vol. xxvi. pp. 1–80; vol. xxvii. pp. 21–87. 1912–14.)

Gross (Charles). Biblio. of Brit. Municipal Hist. (*Harvard Hist. Studies*, vol. v. 1897.) Surrey, p. 105. Guildford, pp. 251–252. Kingston-on-Thames, p. 268.

Davenport (Frances G.). List of Printed Materials for Manorial Hist. 1894. Biblio. Note on Surrey Manorial Hist., p. 58.

A List of Private Acts, etc., relating to the County of Surrey. Stevens and Sons, London, *circa* 1912.

List of Acts of Parliament relating to Surrey. See *ante* p. 249. 'Catal. of Books in the Minet Public Lib.,' pp. 76–126.

Bolton (W.). The County of Surrey in Works of Fiction. (*The Surrey Mag.*, vol. i. pp. 319–321. 1900.)

The Printing Industry in Surrey. See 'A History of Surrey,' edited by H. E. Malden, vol. ii. 1902, pp. 421–424. (Victoria County Histories.)

Pierce (William). The Marprelate Press at East Molesey. See 'An Historical Introduction to the Marprelate Tracts,' 1908, p. 233.

Allnutt (W. H.). English Provincial Presses. The Marprelate Press at East Molesey. (*Bibliographica*, vol. ii. pp. 174–175. 1896.)

Plomer (Henry R.). G. F. Hudson's Private Press at Tadworth Heath. (*Some Private Presses of the Nineteenth Century*, in '*The Library*,' New Ser., vol. i. p. 427. 1900.)

Baker (Alfred A. Bethune-). Surrey Bookplates. (*The Home Counties Mag.*, vol. vii. pp. 116–123. 1905.)

Special Topographical Collections for Surrey are at the Minet Public Library, Camberwell, and in the Lib. of the Surrey Archæol. Soc. at Guildford.

Hist. MSS. Comm. Reports. Surrey Collections.

Hodgkin, Mr. J. Eliot, of Richmond ...	15th Rep. p. 41 and App. II.
Midleton, Viscount	1st Rep. p. ix. and App. p. 44.
Molyneux, Mr. W. More, at Loseley Park	7th Rep. p. xiv. and App. pp. 596–680; 17th Rep. p. 12.
Onslow, Earl of, at Clandon Park ...	14th Rep. pp. 29–31 and App. IX. pp. 458–524.
Kingston-on-Thames Corporation ...	3rd Rep. p. xx. and App. pp. 331–333.

County Records, 1690, etc., with MS. Indexes at the County Hall, Kingston-on-Thames. (*Local Records Comm. Rep.*, 1902, App. III. p. 24.)

Collections for Surrey by Richard Symmes [1670–1680] in the Brit. Museum. Add. MS. 6167.

Topographical Notes for a Hist. of the County of Surrey by Dr. Gibson, in the Brit. Museum, arranged according to Hundreds. Add. MS. 23231.

Index to a Calendar of Deeds concerning the County of Surrey contained in the Minet Public Library, Camberwell. 1914. This Index supersedes the one issued in the Catal. of Books in the Minet Library, see *ante* p. 249.

Archdeaconry of Surrey Records, 1566, etc. (*Local Records Comm. Rep.*, 1902, App. III. p. 118.)

Index to the Monumental Inscriptions in Thorpe's 'Registrum Roffense,' 1769. Privately printed by F. A. Crisp. 1885.

The Diocese of Rochester comprises a part of Surrey.

SURREY (*continued*).

The Antiquary's List of Surrey Deeds and other Documents. Offered for Sale by F. Marcham, Tottenham. The parts were issued, with a continuous pagination, in order to form a volume for reference.

Trimen (Henry). Botanical Biblio. of the British Counties. Surrey. (*Journ. of Botany*, vol. xii. p. 73. 1874.)

Boulger (G. S.). Botanical Biblio. of the South-Eastern Counties. Surrey. (*South-Eastern Union of Scientific Societies, Trans.*, vol. iv. pp. 49–51. 1899.)

Bucknill (John A.). The Birds of Surrey. 1900. Biblio., pp. xv.–xix. xlii.–lvi.

Christy (Miller). Biblio. Note on Surrey Birds. (*The Zoologist*, Ser. 3, vol. xiv. p. 259, 1890; and reprinted in pamph., 1891, p. 24.)

Anderson (John P.). Book of Brit. Topo., 1881. Surrey, pp. 268-275.

Gatfield (George). Guide to Heraldry. 1892. Surrey, pp. 83-181.

Sims (Richard). Manual. 1861. Surrey, pp. 174, 222-223, 240.

Upcott (William). English Topo., 1818. Surrey, vol. iii. pp. 1207-1238, 1498.

Smith (Alfred Russell). Catal. of Topo. Tracts, etc. 1878. Surrey, pp. 363-377, 476.

Gough (Richard). Brit. Topo., 1780. Surrey, vol. ii. pp. 261-284.

Bandinel (Bulkeley). Catal. of Books bequeathed to Bodleian Lib. by Richard Gough, 1814. Surrey, pp. 302-306.

CHERTSEY.

Wheeler (Lucy). Chertsey Abbey. An Existence of the Past. London, 1905. List of Authorities, pp. 197–198. List of Charters relating to Chertsey Abbey, pp. 199–200.

CROYDON.

Johnson's MS. History of Croydon, consisting of miscellaneous cuttings, and other interesting local matter, to 1877. 10 vols. (In Croydon Public Library.)

GUILDFORD.

Stevens (D. M.). The Records and Plate of the Borough of Guildford. (*Surrey Archæol. Soc. Collections*, vol. ix. pp. 317–335. 1888.)

HAM.

Roundell (Julia A. E.). Ham House, its Hist. and Art Treasures. 1904. 2 vols. Books and MSS. of Duke of Lauderdale, vol. ii. pp. 127–130. The Library at Ham House, by W. Y. Fletcher, vol. ii. pp. 135–140.

KINGSTON-ON-THAMES.

Corporation Records. See *ante* Hist. MSS. Comm. Reports, p. 250.

Collectanea for a Hist. of the Parish of Kingston upon Thames, particularly with regard to Richmond (originally a part of that Parish), **also Collections for Twickenham.** By Richard Filkin, of Richmond. In the Brit. Museum. Add. MSS. 36486–36487.

Roots (George). The Charters of the Town of Kingston-upon-Thames. London, 1797.

LOSELEY.

Kempe (Alfred John). MSS. and other rare Documents in the Muniment Room of James More Molyneux, at Loseley House. London, 1835.

SURREY (continued).

MERTON.

Heales (Alfred). The Records of Merton Priory, 1898. List of Documents, in App. pp. i.–viii.

OCKLEY.

Bax (Alfred Ridley). The Church Registers and Parish Account Books of Ockley. (*Surrey Archæol. Soc. Collections*, vol. x. pp. 20–78. 1891.)

REIGATE.

Borough Records, at the Market Hall, Redhill. (*Local Records Comm. Rep.*, 1902, App. III. p. 66.)

An Old Library at Reigate (Reigate Public Lib.), by C. E. A. Bedwell. (*The Home Counties Mag.*, vol. vi. pp. 198–201. 1904.)

RICHMOND.

Chancellor (E. Beresford). The Hist. and Antiquities of Richmond, Kew, Petersham, Ham, etc. 1894. App. A. pp. iii.–vi. List of some of the Principal Authorities quoted.

Hodgkin (John Eliot). Collections of Views, etc., of Richmond and Neighbourhood, its Theatres, Park, etc. See 'Rariora, being Notes on some of the Printed Books, MSS., Historical Documents, etc., collected (1858–1900) by J. E. Hodgkin,' vol. i. pp. 27, 55, 67.

Illustrated Catal. of May Day Exhibition, Richmond, 1889. List of Books on Richmond, pp. 49–62.

Filkin's Collectanea relating to Richmond, see *ante* Kingston-on-Thames.

TWICKENHAM.

Filkin's Collectanea relating to Twickenham, see *ante* Kingston-on-Thames.

SUSSEX.

Butler (G. Slade). Topographica Sussexiana: An attempt towards forming a list of the various Publications relating to the County of Sussex. (*Sussex Archaeol. Collections*, vol. xv. pp. 215–230; vol. xvi. pp. 273–290; vol. xvii. pp. 169–184; vol. xviii. pp. 87–110. 1863–66.) List of Maps of the County, vol. xv. p. 230. Also issued separately.

Sawyer (F. E.). Recent Sussex Bibliography (1864 to 1881). (*Sussex Archaeol. Coll.*, vol. xxxii. pp. 201–212. 1882.) **1882, with Addenda, 1864 to 1881.** (*Ibid.* vol. xxxiii. pp. 207–212. 1883.)

General Index to vols. i. to xxv., 1848–73, of the Sussex Archaeological Collections, by Henry Campkin. The Sussex Archaeol. Soc. Lewes, 1874.

Brief Subject-Indexes to the Collections of the Sussex Archaeol. Soc., vols. xxvi. to xl., 1875–96 (in vol. xli. of 'Collections') **and to vols. xli. to l., 1897–1906** (in vol. li. of 'Collections').

An Index to the first Twenty vols. of the 'Suss. Arch. Coll.' was issued as an Appendix to vol. ii. of Mark Antony Lower's 'Compendious Hist. of Sussex.' 1870.

Index of Illustrations in the Sussex Archaeol. Collections, vols. i. to xxx., 1848–80. By J. Horace Round. (*Sussex Archaeol. Coll.*, vol. xxx. pp. 198–229. 1880.)

SUSSEX (continued).

Catal. of the Library of the Sussex Archaeol. Soc., compiled by Joseph Cooper. (*Ibid.* vol. xxvii. pp. 212–226. 1877.) **List of Books added, 1877–79.** (*Ibid.* vol. xxx. pp. 230–234. 1880.)

Catal. of Books belonging to the Sussex Archaeol. Soc., in the Library at Lewes Castle. (*Ibid.* vol. xxxvi. pp. 193–238. 1888.)

This Catal. includes the books, etc., in the previous lists. Lists of Additions are given in subsequent vols. of the 'Collections' from time to time.

Notices of Books relating to Sussex, recently published. Issued in 'Sussex Archaeol. Collections' from vol. 49. 1906.

Catal. of the Brighton and Sussex Books in the Reference Library of the Brighton Public Lib. (In '*Supplementary Catal. of the Victoria Lending Lib., Brighton,*' pp. 61–83.) 1892.

Catal. of Publications relating to the Topography of Sussex, both generally and arranged according to the names of Places, up to 1860. (Brit. Mus. Add. MS. 37039.)

A List of some Papers in the 'Archaeologia,' relating to Sussex. By N. Comber. (*Sussex Archaeol. Coll.*, vol. xxxiv. pp. 262–263. 1886.)

Fleet (Charles). 'The Sussex Diarists' and the 'Sussex Poets,' in his 'Glimpses of Our Ancestors in Sussex.' First Series, 1878, pp. 1–62 and pp. 226–270.

Gross (Charles). Biblio. of Brit. Municipal Hist. (*Harvard Hist. Studies*, vol. v. 1897.) Sussex, p. 105, Brigton, p. 176, Lewes, p. 276, Rye, p. 381.

Ballard (Adolphus). The Early Municipal Charters of the Sussex Boroughs. (*Sussex Archaeol. Coll.*, vol. lv. pp. 35–40. 1912.)

Davenport (Frances G.). List of Printed Materials for Manorial Hist. 1894. Biblio. Note on Sussex Manorial Hist., p. 58.

Lyell (Arthur H.). Biblio. List of Romano-British Remains. 1912. Sussex, pp. 122–125.

Haverfield (F.). Roman Remains in Sussex. A Biblio. List. (*The Archæol. Review*, vol. i. pp. 434–440. 1888.)

Catal. of Antiquities exhibited at the Annual Meeting of the Archæol. Institute at Chichester, 1853. (*Trans. of the Archæol. Inst., Chichester*, 1853, pp. 55–120.)

The Antiquities preserved in the Museum of Lewes Castle, catalogued and described, by Mark Antony Lower and Robert Chapman. (*Sussex Archaeol. Coll.*, vol. xviii. pp. 60-73. 1866.)

Mantell (Gideon A.). A Descriptive Catal. of the Objects of Geology, Natural History, and Antiquity (chiefly discovered in Sussex) in the Museum of the Sussex Scientific and Literary Institution at Brighton. 6th edn. 1836.

Dove (Patrick Edward). Domesday Studies. 1891. Domesday Biblio. of Sussex, vol. ii. p. 691.

Index of Names of Places in Domesday Survey of Sussex. By F. E. Sawyer. n.d.

Macklin (Herbert Walter). Monumental Brasses. London: Geo. Allen & Co., 1913. Biblio. Note on Sussex Brasses, with a List, pp. 142, 184–185.

Catal. of Authors born or resident within the County of Sussex, and of their published Works down to the year 1851. (MS. in Lib. of Sussex Archaeol. Soc.)

SUSSEX (continued).

The late William Durrant Cooper, F.S.A., and the late Mark Antony Lower, with lists of their Works, and of their Contributions to the Collections of the Sussex Archaeol. Soc., and other Societies. (*Sussex Archaeol. Coll.*, vol. xxvii. pp. 117–151. 1877.

A Collection of Original Articles from the 'Suss. Archaeol. Collections,' 'Cuttings from the 'Gent.'s Magazine,' etc., from 1831 to 1875, by W. D. Cooper, in 6 vols., is in the Lib. of the Suss. Arch. Soc.

The late William Smith Ellis. Biographical Notice by F. W. T. Attree, with a list of papers contributed to the 'Sussex Archaeol. Collections,' and Notes on MSS. bequeathed to the Society. (*Sussex Archaeol. Coll.*, vol. xxxviii. pp. 189–192. 1892).

The Rev. Frederick Henry Arnold. Biographical Notice, with a list of his Contributions to the 'Sussex Archaeol. Collections.' By John H. Mee. (*Sussex Archaeol. Coll.*, vol. l. pp. 189–192. 1907.)

Lower (Mark Antony). Notes and Observations on a volume of Newspaper Cuttings relating to Sussex, from the year 1678 to 1771, with a brief Biblio. Note on Sussex Newspapers. (*Ibid.* vol. xxiv. pp. 139–144. 1872.)

Cooper (W. Durrant). The Sussex Poets. A Lecture. 1842.

Taylor (James). The Sussex Garland, a Collection of Ballads, etc., illustrative of the County of Sussex, with notices, historical, biographical and descriptive. London, 1851.

Cook (C. F.). The Book of Sussex Verse. Foreword by Arthur F. Bell. Hove, 1914.

Sussex Songs and Music. A Lecture to the Brit. Archæol. Assoc. by F. E. Sawyer. Brighton, 1885.

Fleet (Charles). Sheep Shearing Songs, in his 'Glimpses of our Sussex Ancestors.' First Series, 1878, pp. 100–101.

Blencowe (Robert Willis). South-Down Shepherds and their Songs at the Sheepshearings. (*Sussex Archaeol. Coll.*, vol. ii. pp. 247–256. 1849.)

Piper (A. Cecil). Notes on the Introduction of Printing into Sussex up to the year 1850, with a Chronology of Sussex Printers to that date. (*The Library*, Ser. 3, vol. v. pp. 257–265. 1914.)

—— **Private Printing Presses in Sussex.** (*Ibid.* Ser. 3, vol. v. pp. 70–79. 1914.)

Contains Accounts of the following Private Presses :—The Rev. James Hurdis, of Bishopstone, near Newhaven, 1791–1881 ; Howard Dudley, at Easebourne, near Midhurst ; Davies Gilbert, at Eastbourne ; Lord Hampden, at Glynde, about 1770 ; A Private Press, at Haywards Heath ; Lewis Way, at Stanstead ; Albany Wallace, at Worthing. For a further note on Davies Gilbert's Press, at Eastbourne, see Boase and Courtney 'Bibliotheca Cornubiensis,' vol. iii. p. 1195.

The Lewes Newsmen's New Year's Verses, Addresses, etc., for the years 1786 to 1823. (A Collection in the Brit. Museum Library.)

A Pioneer in Local Journalism. William Fleet, with Biblio. Notes on the 'Brighton Herald.' ('*A Peep into the Past': Brighton in the Olden Time*, by J. G. Bishop, 1892, pp. 355–363.)

A List of Private Acts relating to the County of Sussex. Stevens and Sons, London, *circa* 1912.

Dodson (J. G.). On some Old Acts of Parliament concerning Roads in, or connected with the County of Sussex. (*Sussex Archaeol. Coll.*, vol. xv. pp. 138–147. 1863.)

SUSSEX (continued).

Hawkesbury (Lord). Catalogues of Portraits at Compton Place and at Buxted Park, in Sussex. (*Sussex Archaeol. Coll.*, vol. xlvii. pp. 82–108. 1904.)

Simmons (Henry). A Catal. of Drawings in the British Museum relating to the County of Sussex, arranged alphabetically, and, as far as possible, according to Parishes. (*Ibid.* vol. xxviii. pp. 148–179. 1878.)

Grimm (S. H.). Catal. of Drawings relating to Sussex in the Bodleian Library. (*Ibid.* vol. iii. pp. 232–238. 1850.)

Gerard (Ethel). Notes on Some Early Printed Maps of Sussex and their Makers, with Special Reference to those in the Worthing Reference Library. (*The Library*, Ser. 3, vol. vi. pp. 252–275. 1915.)

Ellis (William Smith). Biblio. Notes on Budgen's and other Maps of Sussex. (*Ibid.* vol. xxv. pp. 85–100. 1873.)

The Sussex Archaeol. Soc. have appointed a Committee to deal with Sussex Maps prior to 1815, with a view to a publication on the subject.

Roberts (Richard G.). The Place-Names of Sussex. Cambridge, 1914. Biblio. pp. xxvi.–xxxii.

Special Topographical Collections for Sussex are in the Public Libraries at Brighton, Eastbourne, and Worthing, in the Brassey Institute at Hastings, and in the Lib. of the Sussex Archaeol. Soc. at Lewes Castle.

Hist. MSS. Comm. Reports. Sussex Collections.

Abergavenny, Marquess of, at Eridge Castle	10th Rep. pp. 23–25; and App. VI. pp. 1–72.
Ashburnham, Earl of, at Stowe ...	8th Rep. App. III. pp. 1–127.
Chichester, Earl of, at Stanmer Park...	3rd Rep. p. xv.; and App. pp. 221–223.
Colchester, Lord	3rd Rep. p. xi.; 4th Rep. p. xiv. and App. pp. 344–347.
De-la-Warr, Earl, at Buckhurst ...	3rd Rep. p. xv. and App. pp. 217–220; 4th Rep. p. xiii. and App. pp. 276–317.
Egmont, Earl of, at St. James's Place	7th Rep. p. xiii. and App. pp. 232–249; 17th Rep. pp. 143–153; and Vol. I. 1905.
Field, Rev. Edmund, of Lancing College...	5th Rep. p. xii. and App. pp. 387–404.
Frewen, Col., at Brickwall, Northiam	Various Collections, vol. vii. pp. 351–359.
Gage, Lord, at Lewes	3rd Rep. p. xvi. and App. pp. 223–224.
Leconfield, Lord, at Petworth House...	5th Rep. p. xi.; 6th Rep. p. xii. and App. pp. 287–319.
Othen, Miss, of Midhurst	3rd Rep. p. xviii. and App. p. 277.
Vidler, Mr. J. W. C., of Rye	10th Rep. p. 14.
Chichester, Bishop of	16th Rep. pp. 96–97. Various Collections, vol. i. pp. 177–186.
——— Dean and Chapter of	16th Rep. pp. 97–99. Various Collections, vol. i. pp. 187–204.
Hastings Corporation	13th Rep. p. 50, and App. IV. pp. 354–364.
Rye Corporation	5th Rep. App. pp. 488–516; 13th Rep. pp. 51–55, and App. IV. pp. 1–246.

County Records, with MS. Index, at County Hall, Lewes. (*Local Records Comm. Rep.*, 1902, App. III. p. 24.)

Burrell (Sir William). Collections relating to the Hist. and Antiquities of Sussex, in the Brit. Museum. 41 vols. Add. MSS. 5670–5711.

For a Biblio. Note on the Burrell MSS., see 'Sussex Archaeol. Coll.,' vol. xxiii. pp. 318–320. 1871.

SUSSEX (continued).

Hayley's Collections for a Hist. of Sussex, in the Brit. Museum. Add. MSS. 6343–6361.

Index to Hayley's 'Notitia Sussexiæ.' 2 vols. Brit. Mus. Add. MSS. 6343–6344.

Warburton's Collections for a Hist. of Sussex, in the Brit. Museum. Lansd. MSS. 886, 918.

A Calendar of the Deeds and other Documents in the possession of the Sussex Archaeol. Soc. By E. H. W. Dunkin. (*Sussex Archaeol. Coll.*, vol. xxxvii. pp. 39–110, 190; vol. xxxviii. pp. 137–140; vol. xxxix. pp. 179–196. 1890–94.) The Calendar is divided into the following sections :—

I. Sussex Documents and Deeds.
II. Schedules of Sussex Deeds and Abstracts of Title.
III. Deeds and Documents chiefly relating to London and Norwich.

MS. Collections relating to Sussex, and where Deposited, including descriptions of (I.) The Burrell MSS., 15 vols. in the Brit. Mus.; (II.) The Hayley and Petyt Collections, in the Lib. of the Inner Temple. (*Sussex Archaeol. Coll.*, vol. xxiii. pp. 318–320. 1871.)

MSS. relating to Sussex in the Bodleian Lib., Oxford. By J. H. Mee. (*Ibid.* vol. xlii. pp. 239–241. 1899.)

Sussex MSS. in Lambeth Palace Library. Brief Notes by S. W. Kershaw. (*Ibid.* vol. xl. p. 267; vol. xliii. p. 276. 1896–1900.)

Catal. of the Lambeth MSS. referring to Sussex. By A. C. Ducarel. (Among the Burrell MSS. in the Brit. Museum) Add. MS. 5707.

A Calendar of the Entries relating to Sussex in the Harleian MSS. By L. F. Salzmann. (*Sussex Record Soc. Pubns.*, vol. iv. pp. 69–82. 1904.)

Daniel-Tyssen (J. R.). The Parliamentary Surveys of the County of Sussex, 1649 to 1653. (*Sussex Archaeol. Coll.*, vol. xxiii. pp. 217–313. 1871.) See the Index to the vol. at pp. 335–342 for a Digest of the Surveys.

Descriptive Catal. of the Original Charters, Royal Grants, etc., constituting the Muniments of Battle Abbey, on Sale by Thomas Thorpe, Bedford St., London. 1835. (Contains valuable records of Manor Lands in Sussex and other Counties.)

Suggestions for the Collecting and Printing of Records relating to the Hist. of the County, by Charles Francis Trower. (*Sussex Archaeol. Coll.*, vol. xxvii. pp. 1, 2; vol. xxviii. pp. 1–10. 1877–78.)

The Publication of our County Records. By C. F. Trower. (*Ibid.* vol. xxix. pp. 232–234. 1879.)

Archæological Record and Registration (with special reference to Sussex), by William Law. (*Brighton and Hove Archæologist*, no. 1, 1914, pp. 61–71.)

Some Early Sussex Documents. By J. Horace Round. (*Sussex Archaeol. Coll.*, vol. xlii. pp. 75–86. 1899.)

Charters and Deeds relating to Sussex. A List issued by F. Marcham, New Southgate, London.

Inventories of Sussex Parochial Documents, etc. (*Sussex Archaeol. Coll.*, vol. xlix. pp. 159–161, 1906; vol. lii. pp. 179–187, 1909; vol. liii. pp. 267–271, 1910; vol. liv. pp. 259–264, 1911; vol. lv. pp. 299–304, 1912.)

The following places are dealt with :—Hailsham, Bexhill, East Dean, Friston, Jevington, Ringmer, Waldron, Hove, New Shoreham, Selsey, West Firle Beddingham, Framfield, and Southwick.

'Bishop's Transcripts' for the Archdeaconry of Lewes. A List by W. C. Renshaw. (*Sussex Archaeol. Coll.*, vol. lv. p. 314. 1912.)

SUSSEX (*continued*).

Walcott (**Mackenzie E. C.**) **The Mediæval Registers of the Bishops of Chichester.** (*Roy. Soc. of Literature, Trans.*, Ser. II. vol. ix. pp. 215–244. 1870.)

—— **Kalendar of the Episcopal Registers of Chichester.** (*Ibid.* Ser. II. vol. ix. pp. 245–255. 1870.)

Charters of the Cinque Ports. By Samuel Jeake. London, 1728.

Mantell (**Sir Thomas**). **Cinque Ports Brotherhoods and Guestlings.** New Edn. Dover, 1828. Schedule of Charters, etc. at New Romney, 1812, pp. 35–36.

Indexes of the 'Great White Book,' and of the 'Black Book' of the Cinque Ports (1433–1902), edited by H. B. Walker. London, 1905.

Lucas (**Perceval**). **Some Notes on the Early Sussex Quaker Registers.** (*Sussex Archaeol. Coll.*, vol. lv. pp. 74–96. 1912.)

Trimen (**Henry**). **Botanical Biblio. of the British Counties. Sussex.** (*Journ. of Botany*, vol. xii. p. 71. 1874.)

Boulger (**G. S.**) **Botanical Biblio. of the South-Eastern Counties. Sussex.** (*South-Eastern Union of Scientific Societies.* Trans., vol. iv. pp. 51–52. 1899.)

Reid (**Clement**). **Geology of the Country round Chichester.** 1903. Biblio., p. 48.

Christy (**Miller**). **Biblio. Notes on Sussex Birds.** (*The Zoologist*, Ser. 3, vol. xiv. p. 260, 1890; and reprinted in pamph., 1891, p. 24.) **Mammals.** (*The Zoologist*, Ser 3, vol. xvii. pp. 184–185. 1893.) **Reptiles.** (*Ibid.* p. 247. 1893.) **Fishes.** (*Ibid.* p. 258. 1893.)

Anderson (John P.). Book of Brit. Topo., 1881. Sussex, pp. 275-285.

Gatfield (George). Guide to Heraldry, 1892. Sussex, pp. 185-186.

Sims (Richard). Manual, 1861. Sussex, pp. 174, 223, 240.

Upcott (William). English Topo., 1818. Sussex, vol. iii. pp. 1239-1246, 1499.

Smith (Alfred Russell). Catal. of Topo. Tracts, etc., 1878. Sussex, pp. 379-385, 478.

Gough (Richard). Brit. Topo., 1780. Sussex, vol. ii. pp. 285-298.

Bandinel (Bulkeley). Catal. of Books bequeathed to Bodleian Lib. by Richard Gough. 1814. Sussex, pp. 307-308.

ARUNDEL.

Borough Records, 1586, etc., with MS. Index at Town Hall, Arundel. (*Local Records Comm. Rep.*, 1902, App. III. p. 46.)

Tierney (**Rev. M. A.**). **Hist. and Antiquities of the Castle and Town of Arundel.** 1834–51. An extensively extra-illustrated copy, with rare engravings, was sold at W. B. D. D. Turnbull's Sale, by Sotheby's, 27 Nov. 1863, see pp. 93–94 of the Sale Catalogue.

ASHBURNHAM.

Catal. of the Manuscripts at Ashburnham Place, 1853. London. Printed by C. F. Hodgson. n.d.

The Ashburnham Registers. By Rose Fuller Whistler. (*Sussex Archaeol. Coll.*, vol. xxxiii. pp. 49–68. 1883.)

BATTLE.

Battle Abbey Evidences (from Charters, etc.) By Sir G. F. Duckett. (*Sussex Archaeol. Coll.*, vol. xxxi. pp. 157–168. 1881.)

BERWICK.

Berwick Parochial Records. By George Miles Cooper. (*Sussex Archaeol. Coll.*, vol. vi. pp. 223–243. 1853.)

SUSSEX (*continued*).

BRIGHTON.

Borough Records, with MS. List, at Town Hall, Brighton. (*Local Records Comm. Rep.*, 1902, App. III. p. 42.)

Catal. of the 'Pocock' Collection of Prints and Drawings illustrative of Old Brighton. 1892. In the Brighton Public Lib. A similar collection is the 'Furner' Collection, also in the Brighton Public Lib.

Harrison (Frederic). Historical and Literary Associations of Brighton and Hove. 1906.

The Brighton Public Library, Museums, and Fine Art Galleries. By Henry D. Roberts, (*Lib. Assoc. Record*, vol. x. pp. 439–454. 1908.)

Murray (David). 'Museums.' Glasgow, 1904. Biblio. Note on Brighton Museums, vol. ii. p. 140.

CHICHESTER.

Borough Records, Hen. VI., etc., at Town Clerk's Office, Chichester. (*Local Records Comm. Rep.*, 1902, App. III. p. 50.)

Ecclesiastical Records of Chichester. See *ante* Hist. MSS. Comm. Reports.

Walcott (Mackenzie E. C.). The Early Statutes of the Cathedral Church of the Holy Trinity, Chichester. London, 1877.

Stephens (W. R. W.). Memorials of the South Saxon See and Cathedral Church of Chichester. London, 1876. Biblio. Notes, with a List of the Bishops' Registers, in Preface.

Cooper (J. H.). MSS. relating to the See of Chichester in Corpus Christi Coll. Lib., Cambridge. (*Sussex Archaeol. Coll.*, vol. xliv. pp. 208–209. 1901.)

Hennessy (Rev. George). Chichester Diocese Clergy Lists, or Clergy Succession from the earliest time to 1900. London, 1900. Brief Biblio. Notes in Preface.

Botfield (Beriah). Notes on the Cathedral Libraries of England. 1849. **Chichester,** pp. 74–88.

DURRINGTON.

Snewin (H. E.). Parochial Documents: Durrington. (*Sussex Archaeol. Coll.*, vol. lvi. pp. 194–195. 1914.)

EASTBOURNE.

Chambers (George F.). East Bourne: Memories of the Victorian Period, 1845–1901. Eastbourne, 1910. Chap. X. Literature, Science and Art, contains Biblio. Notes on Local Newspapers, Printers, Old East Bourne Guides, Local Authors, Old Maps, etc.

—— **Biblio. Note on Old Eastbourne Maps.** (*Sussex Archaeol. Coll.*, vol. liii. pp. 276–277. 1910.)

EDBURTON.

Index to the Registers of Edburton, 1558–1673. Privately printed for F. A. Crisp. 1887.

GLYNDE.

Names from the Register Books of the Parish of Glynde, from 1558 to 1812, with an Alphabetical List. By W. de St. Croix. (*Sussex Archaeol. Coll.*, vol. xxiv. pp. 99–114. 1872.)

SUSSEX (*continued*).

HASTINGS.

Corporation Records. See *ante* Hist. MSS. Comm. Reports.

Borough Records, 1590, etc., with MS. Indexes, at the Town Hall, Hastings, and at the Hastings Museum. (*Local Records Comm. Rep.*, 1902, App. III. p. 44.)

Dawson (Charles). History of Hastings Castle. 2 vols. London, 1909. Biblio. Notes in Preface.

Howard (M. M.). Hastings, Past and Present. 1855. List of Books relating to the District, Appendix, pp. i.-xiv., lxiii.-lxiv.

LEWES.

Woolgar (T.). MS. Collections for the Hist. of Lewes and its Neighbourhood, 3 vols. (In the Lib. of the Sussex Archaeol. Soc.)

Daniel-Tyssen (J. R.). Documents relating to Lewes Priory, with translations and notes. (*Sussex Archaeol. Coll.*, vol. xxv. pp. 136-151. 1873.)

Duckett (Sir G. F.). Additional Materials towards the Hist. of the Priory of St. Pancras at Lewes. (*Ibid.* vol. xxxv. pp. 101-126. 1887.)

LINDFIELD.

Lower (Mark Antony). On some old Parochial Documents relating to Lindfield. (*Ibid.* vol. xix. pp. 36-52. 1867.)

RINGMER.

Legge (W. Heneage). The Parish Documents of Ringmer of the Jacobean and Georgian Periods. (*The Reliquary*, New Ser. vol. v. pp. 217-226. 1899.)

ROBERTSBRIDGE.

Calendar of Charters and Documents relating to the Abbey of Robertsbridge, preserved at Penshurst, among the Muniments of Lord de Lisle and Dudley. [By H. Penfold.] Privately Printed, 1873.

Remarks on some Charters and other Documents relating to the Abbey of Robertsbridge, in the possession of the Rev. J. H. Blunt. By Charles Spencer Perceval. (*Archaeologia*, vol. xlv. pp. 427-461. 1880.)

RYE.

Corporation Records. See *ante* Hist. MSS. Comm. Reports.

Borough Records, 14th. cent., etc., at Town Hall, Rye. (*Local Records Comm. Rep.*, 1902, App. III. p. 68.)

Catal. of the Antiquities and Historical MSS. of the Ancient Towns of Rye and Winchelsea. By John Neve Masters. [1895?]

List of Rye Municipal Records Printed. (*Notes & Queries*, Ser. 11, vol. vi. p. 91. 1912.)

SALEHURST.

Hodson (Leonard J.). Biblio. Note on the Parish Records in 'A Short Hist. of the Parish of Salehurst.' 1914. Chap. xi. pp. 82-96.

SELSEY.

Heron-Allen (Edward). Selsey Bill, Historic and Prehistoric. 1911. Biblio., pp. xiii.-xvi.

SUSSEX (continued).

Brown (Rev. J. Cavis-). Maps of Selsey in the County of Sussex, in the years 1672 and 1901. Chichester, 1906.

——— **Maps of Selsey, in the years 1778 and 1901.** Chichester, 1908.

WARNHAM.

Warnham: Its Church, Monuments, Registers, and Vicars, by J. L. André and R. G. Rice. (*Sussex Archaeol. Coll.*, vol. xxxiii. pp. 152–206. 1883.)

WINCHELSEA.

Rice (R. Garraway). Some Notes on the Parish Registers of Winchelsea. (*St. Paul's Ecclesiological Soc. Trans.*, vol. iv. pp. 308–312. 1900.)

WIVELSFIELD.

Attree (F. W. T.). Wivelsfield Parochial Records (The Registers and other Documents), with an alphabetical List of Names from the Registers. (*Sussex Archaeol. Coll.*, vol. xxxvi. pp. 19–42. 1888.)

SUTHERLANDSHIRE.

MOWAT (JOHN). BIBLIOGRAPHY OF CAITHNESS AND SUTHERLAND. Viking Club. London, 1910.

——— **A List of Books and Pamphlets relating to the North of Scotland, with special reference to Caithness and Sutherland.** (*Old-Lore Miscellany—Viking Club*, vol. ii. pp. 238–242; vol. iii. pp. 49, 170, 224; vol. iv. pp. 45, 99, 151, 201; vol. v. pp. 38, 82, 134. 1909–12.)

MS. List of Books and Pamphlets relating to Sutherland and the Burgh of Dornoch, in the possession of Hugh F. Campbell, Advocate, Aberdeen. See p. 47 of Mowat's 'Biblio. of Caithness and Sutherland.' 1910.

Hist. MSS. Comm. Reports. Sutherland Collection.

Sutherland, Duke of, at Dunrobin, 2nd Rep. p. xvi. and App. pp. 177–180;
Golspie ... ... 5th Rep. p. vi. and App. pp. 135–214.

County Council, etc., Records, at Golspie and elsewhere. (*Local Records Comm. Rep.*, 1902, App. III. p. 86.)

Caithness and Sutherland Records. Extracts from Documents, etc., with translations. Viking Club, London, 1909, etc. In progress.

Dornoch Burgh Records, 1729, etc., with MS. Index, at Dornoch. (*Local Records Comm. Rep.*, 1902, App. III. p. 90.)

Livingstone (Matthew). Guide to the Public Records of Scotland. 1905. Sutherland, p. 177.

Turnbull (William B.). Scottish Parochial Registers. 1849. List of Sutherland Registers, pp. 153–155.

Sutherland and the Reay Country, edited by Rev. Adam Gunn and John Mackay. Glasgow, 1897. Songs and Melodies connected with the County, by Henry Whyte and Malcolm MacFarlane, pp. 283–320.

Mackay (Angus). Sutherland and Caithness in Ancient Geography and Maps. (*Soc. of Antiq. Scot. Proc.*, vol. xlii. pp. 79–94. 1908.)

SUTHERLANDSHIRE (continued).

Some References to Witchcraft and Charming from Caithness and Sutherland Church Records, by 'Historicus.' (*Old-Lore Miscellany—Viking Club*, vol. ii. pp. 110–115, 171, 172, 193; vol. iii. pp. 47, 48. 1909–10.)

Cadell (Henry Mowbray). The Geology and Scenery of Sutherland. Edinburgh, 1896. Summary of recent Literature and Maps, in Introduction, pp. 15–17.

Trimen (Henry). Botanical Biblio. of the British Counties. Sutherland. (*Journ. of Botany*, vol. xii. p. 237. 1874.)

Christy (Miller). Biblio. Note on Sutherlandshire Birds. (*The Zoologist*, Ser 3, vol. xiv. p. 265, 1890, and reprinted in pamph., 1891, p. 39.) **Mammals.** (*The Zoologist*, Ser. 3, vol. xvii. p. 214. 1893.) **Reptiles.** (*Ibid.* p. 250. 1893.) **Fishes.** (*Ibid.* p. 262. 1893.)

Anderson (John P.). Book of Brit. Topo., 1881. Sutherlandshire, p. 412.

Gough (Richard). Brit. Topo., 1780. Sutherlandshire, vol. ii. p. 723.

Bandinel (Bulkeley). Catal. of Books bequeathed to Bodleian Lib. by Richard Gough, 1814. Sutherlandshire, p. 365.

TIPPERARY.

Coleman (James). Bibliography of the Counties of Waterford, Tipperary, and Wexford. (*Waterford & South-East of Irel. Archæol. Soc. Journ.*, vol. x. pp. 323–328; vol. xi. pp. 127–128. 1907–08.)

O'Hanlon (John). List of Materials for the Hist. and Topography of the County of Tipperary in the Ordnance Survey Records. (*Kilkenny & South-East of Irel. Archæol. Soc. Journ.*, vol. viii. p. 124. 1864.)

Dix (Ernest Reginald McClintock). Early Printing in the South-East of Ireland. Clonmel, 1771-1825. (*Waterford and South-East of Irel. Archæol. Soc. Journ.*, vol. ix. pp. 217–227. 1906.) **Carrick-on-Suir, 1792-1816.** (*Ibid.* vol. x. pp. 140–146; vol. xiii. pp. 69–70. 1907–10.) **Cashel, 1770-1798.** (*Ibid.* vol. x. pp. 317–319. 1907.) **Roscrea, 1780-1824.** (*Ibid.* vol. xi. p. 236; vol. xii. p. 110. 1908–09.) **Thurles.** (*Ibid.* vol. xi. p. 237. 1908.)

—— **Printing in Clonmel, 1801-25, with a List.** (*Irish Book Lover*, vol. iv. pp. 42–46. 1912.)

—— **Biblio. Note on the old Carrick-on-Suir Press of John Stacy.** (*Ibid.* vol. iii. pp. 33, 60. 1911.)

Casaide (Seamus Ua). Biblio. Note on Clonmel Printing. (*Waterford & South-East of Irel. Archæol. Soc. Journ.*, vol. xvii. p. 184. 1914.)

—— **List of Works projected or published by Patrick Lynch,** with Notes on the Earliest Printing at Carrick-on-Suir. (*Ibid.* vol. xv. pp. 107–120. 1912. See also Casaide's Biog. Sketch of Lynch at pp. 47–61 of the same volume.

—— **Biblio. Note on a Scarce Tipperary Journal,** printed and published by R. D'Alton, Tipperary, 1862. (*Ibid.* vol. xiii. pp. 107–111. 1910.)

Biblio. Note on Printing in Cashel. (*The Irish Literary Inquirer*, No. 2 p. 19. 1865.)

Hist. MSS. Comm. Report. Tipperary Collection.

Donoughmore, Earl of ... ... 12th Rep. pp. 35–38, and App. IX. pp. 227–333.

TIPPERARY (*continued*).

Macalister (R. A. Stewart). Studies in Irish Epigraphy. Part III. Biblio. of Tipperary Epigraphy, 1907.

Anderson (John P.). Book of Brit. Topo., 1881. Tipperary, p. 441.
Gough (Richard). Brit. Topo., 1780. Tipperary, vol. ii. p. 816.
Bandinel (Bulkeley). Catal. of Books bequeathed to Bodleian Lib. by Richard Gough, 1814. Tipperary, p. 383.

CASHEL.

Seymour (Rev. St. John D.). The Chapter-Books of Cashel Cathedral. (*Soc. of Antiq. Irel. Journ.*, vol. xl. pp. 329-339. 1910.)

FETHARD.

Laffan (Thomas). Fethard: Its Charters and Corporate Records. (*Soc. of Antiq. Irel. Journ.*, vol. xxxvi. pp. 143–153. 1906.)

TYRONE.

Crone (John S.). Ulster Bibliography. Tyrone. (*Ulster Journ. of Archæol.*, vol. xv. pp. 95–102. 1909.) See also a brief list of Books on Tyrone in 'Notes & Queries,' Ser. 10, vol. v. p. 172. 1906.

O'Hanlon (John). Index of Materials for the Hist. & Topography of the County of Tyrone in the Irish Ordnance Survey Records, and in the Royal Irish Academy. (*Kilkenny & South-East of Irel. Archæol. Soc. Journ.*, vol. viii. p. 20. 1864.)

Dix (Ernest Reginald McClintock). List of Books and Pamphlets printed in Strabane, co. Tyrone, in the Eighteenth Century. Dublin, 1901. Second and Revised edition. Dundrum, 1908. (Irish Bibliography, No. I.)

——— **Ulster Bibliography. A List of Books and Pamphlets printed in Strabane in the 18th cent.,** with additions by Rev. W. T. Latimer, and A. A. Campbell. (*Ulster Journ. of Archæol.*, vol. vi. pp. 1–3, 183, 246 ; vol. vii. pp. 54–56, 108, 136, 174, 176 ; vol. viii. p. 171. 1900–02.)

——— **Printing in Strabane, 1801-1825, with a List.** (*Irish Book Lover*, vol. iv. pp. 114–116, 134–135. 1912–13.)

Campbell (A. Albert). Early Strabane Newspapers and Magazines. (*Ulster Journ. of Archæol.*, vol. vii. pp. 176-177. 1901.)

——— **Notes on the Literary History of Strabane.** Omagh, 1902. Biblio. Notes on the Strabane Press (with a List, 1771–1875), Printers, Newspapers, etc.

——— **Biblio. Note on 'The Strabane Magazine.'** (*Irish Book Lover*, vol. iii. pp. 144–145. 1912.)

——— **Biblio. Note on Omagh Printing.** (*Ibid.* vol. vii. pp. 7, 46. 1915.)

Dix (Ernest Reginald McClintock). Ulster Bibliography. A List of Books printed in Dungannon, 1797-1800. (*Ulster Journ. of Archæol.*, vol. vii. p. 173 ; vol. ix. pp. 42–43. 1901–03.)

——— **Printing in Dungannon, 1801-1827, with a List.** (*Irish Book Lover*, vol. iv. pp. 188–189. 1913.)

'The Dungannon Weekly Magazine.' A Biblio. Note. (*Ibid.* vol. v. pp. 115–116. 1914.)

Anderson (John P.). Book of Brit. Topo., 1881. Tyrone, p. 442.
Gough (Richard). Brit. Topo., 1780. Tyrone, vol. ii. p. 816.
Bandinel (Bulkeley). Catal. of Books bequeathed to Bodleian Lib. by Richard Gough, 1814. Tyrone, p. 383.

ULSTER.

[The Province of Ulster consists of the Counties of Antrim, Armagh, Cavan, Donegal, Down, Fermanagh, Londonderry, Monaghan, and Tyrone, which should also be consulted.]

Dix (Ernest Reginald McClintock). Ulster Bibliography.

A List of Books and Pamphlets printed in Strabane in the 18th cent., with additions by Rev. W. T. Latimer and A. A. Campbell. (*Ulster Journ. of Archæology*, vol. vi. pp. 1–3, 183, 246; vol. vii. pp. 54–56, 108, 136, 174, 176; vol. viii. p. 83, 171. 1900–02.)

A List of Books and Pamphlets printed in Armagh, with additions by Rev. W. T. Latimer and A. A. Campbell. (*Ibid.* vol. vi. p. 246; vol. vii. pp. 53–55, 57, 108; vol. viii. p. 24. 1900–02.)

A List of Books and Pamphlets printed in Monaghan. (*Ibid.* vol. vii. pp. 103–107, 137; vol. viii. p. 171; vol. xi. p. 48. 1901–05.)

A List of Books, etc., printed in Derry. (*Ibid.* vol. vii. pp. 132–136, 174; vol. viii. p. 24; vol. ix. p. 71. 1901–03.)

A List of Books, etc., printed in Downpatrick, Dungannon, and Hillsborough. (*Ibid.* vol. vii. pp. 172–174; vol. ix. pp. 42–43. 1901–03.)

A List of Books, etc. printed in Newry, by Rev. W. T. Latimer and E. R. McC. Dix. (*Ibid.* vol. vii. pp. 175–176; vol. ix pp. 69–71. 1901–03.)

A List of Books, etc., printed in Cavan. (*Ibid.* vol. viii. pp. 23–24. 1902.)

Biblio. Note on Coleraine Printing. (*Ibid.* vol. xiii. pp. 22–23. 1907.)

Crone (John S.). Ulster Bibliography. Derry. (*Ulster Journ. of Archæology*, vol. x. pp. 151–156; vol. xi. pp. 27–32. 1904–05.) **Antrim.** (*Ibid.* vol. xi. pp. 108–112, 163–167. 1905.) **Down.** (*Ibid.* vol. xii. pp. 35–39, 57–62; vol. xiii. pp. 105–108. 1906–07.) **Armagh.** (*Ibid.* vol. xiii. pp. 120–126. 1908.) **Tyrone.** (*Ibid.* vol. xv. pp. 95–102. 1909.)

Casaide (Seamus Ua). Some Irish Publications in Ulster. (*Ulster Journ. of Archæol.*, vol. xvi. pp. 97–100. 1910.)

MacCarthy (B.). Index to the 'Annals of Ulster; otherwise Annals of Senat, a Chronicle of Irish Affairs, A.D. 431–1541.' 4 vols. Dublin, 1887–1901. The Index is in vol. iv., also the Introduction, with Biblio. Notes.

O'Donoghue (D. J.). Ulster Poets and Poetry. (*Ulster Journ. of Archæol.*, vol. i. pp. 20–22. 1894.)

Shaw (William). Ulster Printers and Poets. (*The Irish Book Lover*, vol. vi. pp. 20–21. 1914.)

WARWICKSHIRE.

Catal. of the Reference Library of the Birmingham Free Libraries, by J. D. Mullins, 1883–90. Birmingham, 1890. **Warwickshire items,** pp. 1225–1238. The sub-divisions are:—

Earls of Warwick, p. 1225.
Town of Warwick, p. 1225.
Warwickshire, pp. 1225-1227.
Warwickshire MSS., etc., pp. 1227-1234.
Warwickshire Maps and Views, pp. 1234-1235.
Warwickshire Pamphlets, pp. 1235-1238.
Warwickshire Poll Books, p. 1238.

Birmingham items, pp. 179–272. **Coventry items,** pp. 418–419. **Stratford-on-Avon items,** pp. 1138–1140.

Timmins (Sam.). A Hist. of Warwickshire. (Popular County Histories.) London, 1889. Biblio., pp. 288–295. List of Maps, p. 296.

—— **Special Collections of Books in and near Birmingham.** (*The Library Chronicle*, vol. iv. pp. 157–163. 1887.)

WARWICKSHIRE (continued).

The Staunton Warwickshire Collection (of **Books, MSS., Prints,** etc.). See George Dawson's 'Shakespeare and other Lectures.' London, 1888, pp. 170–175.

Bates (William). Catal. of Books, Pamphlets, etc., printed at, or relating to Birmingham, Coventry, Lichfield, and the County of Warwick, on sale by J. H. W. Cadby, Birmingham, 1870.

Bloom (J. Harvey). Proposed Biblio. of Warwickshire. 'I am preparing a Biblio. of the Co. of Warwick and should be glad of notes of any scarce pamphlets, etc.'—J. Harvey Bloom, Whitchurch Rectory, Stratford-on-Avon. See *Notes & Queries*, Ser. xi. vol. vii. p. 247. 1913.

List of Warwickshire Books. (*Catal. of the Reference Department, Leamington Spa Free Public Lib.* 1886, pp. 65–67.)

Merridew (John). Catal. of Old Books for 1827 and 1828, including Collection of Warwickshire and Shakespearian Literature. 1828.

Descriptive Catal. of 'The Jackson Collection' at the Sheffield Public Library, compiled by T. Walter Hall and A. H. Thomas. 1914. **Warwickshire items,** p. 205.

Catal. of a Collection of Books, Historical Documents, etc., to be sold by Puttick & Simpson, London, Dec. 17th, etc., 1885. Warwickshire items, pp. 85–88.

Gross (Charles). Biblio. of Brit. Municipal Hist. (*Harvard Hist. Studies,* vol. v. 1897.) Warwickshire, p. 106. Birmingham, pp. 169–171. Coventry, pp. 202–204. Stratford-on-Avon, pp. 400–401. Warwick, pp. 410–411.

Davenport (Frances G.). List of Printed Materials for Manorial Hist. 1894. Biblio. Note on Warwickshire Manorial Hist., p. 59.

Dove (Patrick Edward). Domesday Studies. 1891. Domesday Biblio. Warwickshire, vol. ii. p. 692.

Lyell (Arthur H.). Biblio. List of Romano-British Remains. 1912. Warwickshire, p. 125.

Macklin (Herbert Walter). Monumental Brasses. London: Geo. Allen & Co., 1913. Biblio. List of Warwickshire Brasses, with a List, pp. 142, 185–186.

Bevan (J. O.). A Plea for the Production of an Archæological Map and Index for the County of Warwickshire. (*Birm. and Midl. Inst. Birm. Archæol. Soc. Trans.*, vol. xxiv. pp. 6–17. 1898.)

Civil Wars in Warwickshire; with Biblio. of Local Civil War Tracts. 1876.

Merridew (John). A Catal. of Engraved Portraits of Nobility, Gentry, Clergymen, and others, born, resident in, or connected with the County of Warwick, alphabetically arranged, with the names of painters, engravers, biographical notices, etc. Coventry, 1848.

Malins' Collection of Warwickshire Maps, in the Birmingham Reference Lib. See detailed List in 'Catal. of the Reference Lib.' 1890, pp. 1234–1235.

Jourdain (M.). Notes on Tapestry Maps representing Warwickshire in 'The Tapestry Manufacture at Barcheston.' (*Memorials of Old Warwickshire,* edited by Alice Dryden. 1908, pp. 30–38.)

Biblio. Notes on Early Printed Birmingham Books. (*The Midland Antiquary,* vol. ii. p. 107; vol. iii. pp. 127–128; vol. iv. pp. 43, 90. 1884–86.)

Dent (Robert K.) and Straus (Ralph). John Baskerville: A Memoir. Cambridge, 1907. **Baskerville Biblio.,** pp. 66–93.

Pt. I. Books with Baskerville's Name as printer, or thought to be printed by him.

Pt. II. Handlist with Books as appear to be printed, either before or after 1775, with Baskerville's types.

WARWICKSHIRE (continued).

Reed (Talbot Baines). John Baskerville, Printer. (*Birm. and Midl. Inst. Birm. Archæol. Soc. Trans.*, vol. xviii. pp. 30–43. 1892.)

Handlist [of Books printed by Baskerville]. The Baskerville Club. Publication. No. 1. Cambridge, 1904.

Benton (Josiah Henry). John Baskerville, Type-Founder and Printer, 1706-1775. Printed for Private Circulation at the Merrymount Press, Boston (Mass.), 1914.

Timmins (Samuel). Brief Catal. of Unique Collection of Books printed in Birmingham by John Baskerville, 1757-1773. Birmingham, 1886.

Prosser (Richard B.). John Baskerville, Printer. (*The Bibliographer*, vol. i. pp. 17-18. 1882.) Extracted from Prosser's 'Birmingham Inventors and Inventions,' 1881.

Notes on Baskerville. (*The Midland Antiquary*, vol. i. pp. 7–9, 56. 1882.)

Catal. of Books, Letters, Specimens, etc., of John Baskerville, exhibited on visit of the Biblio. Soc. to the St. Bride Foundation Inst. Technical Lib. London. 1906.

John Baskerville. (*The Bookworm*, vol. i. pp. 100–102. 1888.)

Wesselhaeft (F.). A Letter on Printers in Birmingham established before 1840. 1905.

Bradshaw (Henry). Collection of Birmingham Ballads, etc.

'I happen to have in my own possession 1350 slips and small sheets of Street Songs, all printed at Birmingham by more than 20 different Printers, and hawked about the streets there during the first half of the 19th century. They are neatly mounted in a vol., and arranged according to the Presses at which they were severally printed, etc.

See Henry Bradshaw 'Collected Papers,' 1889, p. 405.

Halliwell-Phillipps (J. O.). Some Account of the Popular Tracts formerly in the Library of Captain Cox, of Coventry. (1575.) 1849.

See also the Ballad Society's 'Captain Cox, his Ballads and Books; or Robert Laneham's Letter,' re-edited by Frederick J. Furnivall, with forewords describing all the accessible books, tales, and ballads, in Captain Cox's List. London, 1871.

Jourdain (M.) The Literary Associations of Warwickshire. (*Memorials of Old Warwickshire*, edited by Alice Dryden, 1908, pp. 112–126.)

Special Topographical Collections for Warwickshire are in the Birmingham Public Library and the Leamington Spa Public Library. Special Shakespeare Collections are at the Birmingham Public Lib. and in the Stratford-on-Avon Museum, and elsewhere.

Hist. MSS. Comm. Reports. Warwickshire Collections.

Davenport, Mr. W. Bromley, at Baginton Hall	2nd Rep. p. xi. and App. pp. 78–81; 10th Rep. p. 20, and App. VI. pp. 98–103.
Denbigh, Earl of, at Newnham Paddox	4th Rep. p. xvi. and App. pp. 254–276; 6th Rep. p. xi. and App. pp. 277–287; 7th Rep. p. xiii. and App. pp. 196–232; 8th Rep. p. xi. and App. pp. 552–572.
Hertford, Marquess of	4th Rep. p. xiii. and App. pp. 251–254.
Merttens, Mr. F., of Bilton Rise ...	Various Collections, vol. vii. pp. 376–388, 1914.
Leigh, Lord	1st Rep. p. xi; 2nd Rep. p. xiii. and App. p. 49.
Shirley, Mr. E. P., at Ettington Hall	5th Rep. p. x. and App. pp. 362–369.
Throckmorton, Sir Nicholas W., at Coughton Court	3rd Rep. p. xxi. and App. pp. 256–258; 10th Rep. p. xxv. and App. IV. pp. 168–176.

WARWICKSHIRE (*continued*).

Coventry Corporation ... ... 1st Rep. App. pp. 100–102; 15th Rep. p. 43, and App. X. pp. 101–160.

Oscott, St. Mary's College ... ... 1st Rep. p. xi. and App. p. 89; 2nd Rep. p. xiii. and App. p. 125.

Stratford-on-Avon Corporation ... 9th Rep. p. xiv. and App. I. pp. 289–293.

County Records, 1612, etc., with MS. Index, at County Hall, Warwick. (*Local Records Comm. Rep.*, 1902, App. III. p. 24.)

Warwick Borough Records, with MS. Index, at Court House, Warwick. (*Ibid.* 1902, App. III. p. 72.)

Report on the Custody of Parochial Documents. Issued by the Warwickshire County Council. 1899.

Dugdale's MS. Collections relating to Warwickshire in the Ashmolean Lib. Oxford. MSS. 6491–6513.

Collections for the continuation of the Hist. and Antiquities of Warwickshire, by Sir William Dugdale and Dr. Thomas, with drawings, etc. [By Rev. Thomas Ward, of Leamington.] Brit. Mus. Add. MSS. 29264, 29265.

Index of Places in Dugdale's Warwickshire, by William Thomas. Privately printed by Sir Thomas Phillipps, Middle Hill, 1844.

Illustrations for Dugdale's Warwickshire. A Collection of Drawings, Prints, etc., formed by the Earl of Aylesford, *circa* 1821, to illustrate a copy of Dugdale (now in the Birmingham Reference Lib.). See a list in the 'Catal. of the Reference Lib.' 1890, p. 1235, and also 'Sale Catal. of the Library of Leonard Lawrie Hartley,' p. 35. Sold by Puttick & Simpson, May 3, 1886.

The Aston Papers. Collections relating to Warwickshire. 12 vols. Brit. Mus. Add. MSS. 36901–36912.

Collections for the Hist. of Warwickshire by Robert Bell Wheler. Brit. Mus. Add. MS. 28564.

Bloom (J. Harvey). Two Warwickshire Muniment Rooms. (*Birm. and Midl. Inst. Birm. Archæol. Soc. Trans.*, vol. xxx. pp. 22–35, 1904.) Descriptions of Documents belonging to Lord Willoughby de Broke at Compton Verney, and the Earl of Warwick at Warwick Castle.

——— **Ancient Warwickshire Deeds,** with Biblio. Notes on Early Charters at Drayton, Alcester, Combe Abbey, Haselor, Kineton, etc. Reprinted from the 'Warwick Advertiser,' 1902.

Brough (W.). Books, MSS., Old Deeds, etc. relating to Warwickshire Families. Birmingham, 1870.

Warwickshire Topographical MSS. See 'Catal. of MSS., etc.', on Sale by Thomas Thorpe, London, 1833, pp. 179–182.

Index to Warwickshire Visitations, in Harl. MSS. By Sir Thomas Phillipps. Privately Printed. Middle Hill, 1838.

Index Locorum to the Subsidy Roll of Warwickshire for 1327, compiled by W. Fowler Carter, and **Index Nominum,** compiled by E. A. Fry. (*Midland Record Soc. Trans.*, vol. vi. Supp. 1902.) A Transcript of the Subsidy Roll was published in earlier vols. of the 'Transactions.'

Local Ecclesiastical Records of the Diocese of Birmingham. (Warwickshire, etc.) Report presented to the Bishop of Birmingham, June, 1911, with List of Registers, etc. 1911.

Bickley (William B.). Parish Registers of Warwickshire, with a List arranged according to 'Hundreds.' (*Birm. and Midl. Inst. Archæol. Section, Trans.*, vol. xix. pp. 71–104, 1893.)

WARWICKSHIRE (continued).

Bagnall (James E.). Biblio. Notes on Botanical Investigations in Warwickshire, and List of Authorities. (*The Flora of Warwickshire*, 1891, pp. xxxi. 490–507.)

Trimen (Henry). Botanical Biblio. of the British Counties. Warwickshire. (*Journ. of Botany*, vol. xii. p. 155, 1874.)

Whitaker (William). List of Books on the Geology of Warwickshire. (*Report of British Assoc. Meeting*, 1886, pp. 806–813.)

Lapworth (Charles). Biblio. to the Birmingham Country, its Geology and Physiography. (*Handbook for Birmingham and the Neighbourhood*, edited by G. A. Auden, for Brit. Assoc. Birmingham, 1913, pp. 610–611.)

Christy (Miller). Biblio. Note on Warwickshire Birds. (*Catal. of Local Lists of British Birds*, London, 1891, p. 25.) **Mammals.** (*The Zoologist*, Ser. 3, vol. xvii. p. 185, 1893.

Anderson (John P.). Book of Brit. Topo., 1881. Warwickshire, pp. 285–293.
Gatfield (George). Guide to Heraldry. 1892. Warwickshire, pp. 186–187.
Sims (Richard). Manual. 1861. Warwickshire, pp. 175, 223–224, 240.
Upcott (William). English Topo., 1818. Warwickshire, vol. iii. pp. 1247–1282.
Smith (Alfred Russell). Catal. of Topo. Tracts, etc. 1878. Warwickshire, pp. 387–396, 479.
Gough (Richard). Brit. Topo., 1780. Warwickshire, vol. ii. pp. 299–310.
Bandinel (Bulkeley). Catal. of Books bequeathed to Bodleian Lib. by Richard Gough, 1814. Warwickshire, pp. 309–311.

BIRMINGHAM.

Catal. of the Reference Library of the Birmingham Free Libraries, by J. D. Mullins, 1883–90. Birmingham, 1890. **Books about, Printed in, or Illustrative of, the Hist. of Birmingham,** 1885, pp. 179–272.

The principal sub-divisions are:

Acts of Parliament, pp. 179–189.
Birmingham Almanacks, p. 189.
Corporation and other official Documents, pp. 190–192.
Directories, pp. 192–193.
Birmingham Exhibitions, pp. 193–194.
Birmingham Hist. Topog., Guides, etc., pp. 195–203.
Birmingham Institutions and Associations, pp. 203–223.
Birmingham Maps, Views, etc., pp. 224–227.
Birmingham Newspapers, etc., pp. 227–234.
Birmingham Poetry and Poems on Birmingham, pp. 235–236.
Pamphlets, etc., relating to Birmingham, pp. 237–249.
Birmingham Printed Books, etc., pp. 249–271.
Birmingham Manuscripts, p. 271.
Birmingham Booksellers, p. 271.
Birmingham Sale Catalogues of Books, p. 272.
Birmingham Theatres, etc., p. 272.
Collection of Maps, Portraits, Views, etc., illustrative of Birmingham, p. 272.

Timmins (Samuel). Old Birmingham Books. (*Birmingham and Midland Inst. Trans.*, vol. xi. pp. 59–68. 1883.)

Index to the Transactions of the Birmingham Archæological Society, vols. i. to xxxi. 1870–1905. [Birmingham and Midland Institute.] 1907.

Pearson (Howard S.). Some Old Birmingham Books. (*Birm. & Mid. Inst. Trans.*, vol. xxiii. pp. 67–71. 1897.)

—— **Birmingham Periodical Literature Half-a-Century Ago.** (*Mid-England*, vol. i. pp. 79–82, 115–120. 1879–80.)

WARWICKSHIRE (continued).

Hill (Joseph). The Book Makers of Old Birmingham—Authors, Printers, and Book Sellers. Birmingham, 1907. (Biblio. Notes on Early Printers, Newspapers, Maps, etc.)

Scarse (Charles Edward). Rough List of Birmingham Books and Pamphlets. Birmingham, 1881.

A List of Contributions to the 'Local Notes & Queries' in the 'Birmingham Journal,' and the 'Birmingham Daily Post,' 1861, etc. (*The Midland Antiquary*, vols. i.–iv. *passim*, 1882–87.)

Downing (W.). Birmingham and Literature. (*The Library Chron.*, vol. v. pp. 49–52. 1888.)

Langford (John Alfred). Biblio. Note on Birmingham Libraries, Newspapers, Maps, etc., in 'A Century of Birmingham Life,' 2 vols. 1868, *passim.*

Dent (Robert K.). Birmingham: Its Libraries and its Booksellers. (*Book-Auction Records*, vol. iv. pt. I. pp. i.–iv. 1906.)

Shaw (A. Capel). The Birmingham Free Libraries. (*The Library Assoc. Record*, vol. iv. pp. 492–518. 1902.)

Langford (John Alfred). The Birmingham Free Libraries, the Shakespeare Memorial Library, and the Art Gallery. Birmingham, 1871. Reprinted from the 'Birmingham Morning News.'

Trommsdorff (Paul). The Birmingham Free Libraries. Birmingham, 1900.

Powell (Walter). Libraries in Birmingham. (*Handbook for Birmingham and the Neighbourhood*, edited by G. A. Auden, for Brit. Assoc., Birmingham, 1913, pp. 248–273.)

Timmins (Samuel). Centenary of the Birmingham Library, 1779–1879. Birmingham, 1879.

Maps, Plans, and Views of Birmingham, with a List, 1731–1860, by 'Este.' (*The Midland Antiquary*, vol. ii. pp. 104–106, 150–151. 1884.)

Maps or Plans of Birmingham. By Samuel Timmins. (*Birm. & Midl. Inst. Birm. Archæol. Soc. Trans.*, vol. xi. pp. 53–58. 1883.)

Some Old Views of Birmingham. By Howard S. Pearson. (*Ibid.* vol. xxxvi. pp. 1-8. 1910.)

Catal. (with descriptive notes) of a Collection of Drawings of Old Birmingham and Warwickshire, in the Birmingham Museum and Art Gallery. 1894.

Murray (David). 'Museums.' Glasgow, 1902. Biblio. Note on Birmingham Museums, vol. ii. p. 119.

Borough Records, 1838, etc., at Council House, Birmingham. (*Local Records Comm. Rep.*, 1902, App. III. p. 30.)

Hill (Joseph). Unpublished Records relating to Birmingham. (*Birm. and Midl. Inst. Birm. Archæol. Soc. Trans.*, vol. xviii. pp. 1–13. 1892.)

Hamper's Collections for Hist. of the Parish of Aston-juxta-Birmingham. List of Contents. (*The Midland Antiquary*, vol. ii. p. 111. 1884.)

COVENTRY.

Catal. of the Reference Library of the Birmingham Free Libraries. By J. D. Mullins, 1883–90. Birmingham, 1890. **Coventry items,** pp. 418–419.

The sub-divisions are:

Coventry MSS., p. 418.
Coventry Maps, Views, etc., p. 419.
Pamphlets on Coventry, p. 419.

WARWICKSHIRE (continued).

Harris (Mary Dormer). List of Books relating to, or printed at Coventry. (*Life in an Old English Town; a Hist. of Coventry from the earliest times*, 1898, pp. 377–380.)

Corporation Records. See *ante* Hist. MSS. Comm. Reports.

Borough Records, Hen. II., etc., with Printed Catalogue, at Coventry. (*Local Records Comm. Rep.*, 1902, App. III. p. 32.)

A Calendar of the Books, Charters, etc., in the New Muniment Room at St. Mary's Hall, made for the Corporation of Coventry. By J. C. Jeaffreson. Coventry, 1896.

Fetherston (John). Selected List of Charters and other Evidences belonging to the Corporation of Coventry. 1871. Privately Printed.

Whitley (T. W.). The Charters and MSS. of Coventry. (*Warw. Nat. & Arch. Field Club. Proc.*, 1897, pp. 35–71.)

Harris (Mary Dormer). The MS. Records of Coventry. (*Birm. & Midl. Inst. Trans.*, vol. xxv. pp. 46–50. 1899.)

——— **The MS. Treasures of Coventry.** (*Memorials of Old Warwickshire*, edited by Alice Dryden, 1908, pp. 157–168.)

EDGE HILL.

Walford (Edwin Alfred). A List of Books and Pamphlets relating to Edge Hill and the Battle. (*Edge Hill: The Battle and Battlefield*, 1904, pp. 97–102.)

KNOWLE.

The Records of Knowle. Collected by T. W. Downing. 1914. Index of Names in the Parish Registers, 1682–1912, pp. 141–204. The muniments of the Dean and Chapter of Westminster relating to Knowle, pp. 360–371.

LEAMINGTON.

List of Leamington Books in the Leamington Spa Public Lib. See 'Catal. of the Reference Department,' 1886, pp. 43–44.

OSCOTT.

Murray (David). 'Museums.' Glasgow, 1902. Biblio. Note on the Museum at St. Mary's College, Oscott, vol. iii. p. 67.

St. Mary's College, Oscott, Records. See *ante* Hist. MSS. Comm. Reports.

ROWINGTON.

Ryland (John William). Records of Rowington. 1896. List of the Deeds, pp. 1–83. Appendix of Notes from Brit. Mus. Public Record Office, etc., pp. 117–216.

RUGBY.

Murray (David). 'Museums.' Glasgow, 1902. Biblio. Note on Rugby School Museum, vol. iii. p. 145.

STRATFORD-ON-AVON.

Catal. of the Reference Library of the Birmingham Free Libraries, by J. D. Mullins, 1883–90. Birmingham, 1890. **Books and Pamphlets on Stratford-on-Avon,** pp. 1138–1140.

Corporation Records. See *ante* Hist. MSS. Comm. Reports.

WARWICKSHIRE (continued).

Halliwell-Phillipps (J. O.). A Descriptive Calendar of the Ancient MSS. and Records in the possession of the Corporation of Stratford-upon-Avon, including notices of Shakespeare and his Family. London, 1863. 75 copies only printed.

——— **A Nominal Index to J. O. Halliwell's Descriptive Calendar of the Ancient Records of Stratford-on-Avon.** London, 1865. 25 copies only printed, of which 15 were destroyed.

——— **A Brief Hand-list of the Records belonging to the Borough of Stratford-on-Avon, showing their general character,** with notes of a few of the Shakespearian Documents in the same Collection. London, 1862. 50 copies only printed.

——— **A Brief Hist. of the Ancient Records of Stratford-on-Avon,** chiefly in reply to a leading article in the 'Stratford-on-Avon Herald.' Brighton, 1884.

Hardy (W. J.). Calendar of Documents of the Mediæval Gild of Stratford. Stratford-on-Avon, 1885.

MS. Collections of Thomas Fisher for a Hist. of the Guild of Stratford. See 'Sale Catal. of the Topographical Library, MSS., etc., of Thomas Fisher,' sold by Southgate & Son, London, 15 Mar., 1837, pp. 11–12.

Brassington (W. Salt). A Note upon the Charters and Muniments of Stratford-on-Avon. (*Memorials of Old Warwickshire*, 1908, pp. 258–266.)

Bloom (J. Harvey). Topographical Notes, Stratford-on-Avon. Reprinted from the 'Stratford-on-Avon Herald,' 1903–05.

Early Stratford Charters, pp. 15–17, 36–43.
Some unpublished Stratford Charters, pp. 19–21.
Documents illustrating the Hist. of the Manor of Clopton, sold at the Severne Sale, pp. 40–42.
Documents illustrating the Hist. of Ruyne Clifford, pp. 45–48.
Ancient Charters of Drayton, pp. 50–54.

Jaggard (William). Shakespeare Bibliography: A Dictionary of every known issue of the Writings of our National Poet, and of recorded opinions thereon in the English Language. Stratford-on.Avon, 1911.

Halliwell-Phillipps (J. O.). A Brief Hand-list of Books, MSS., etc., illustrative of the Life and Writings of Shakespeare, collected between the years 1842 and 1859. London, 1859. 30 copies only printed.

——— **A Brief Hand-list of the Early Quarto Editions of the Plays of Shakespeare,** with notices of the old Impressions of the Poems. London, 1860. 25 copies only printed.

——— **A Brief Hand-list of the Collections respecting the Life and Works of Shakespeare, and the Hist. and Antiquities of Stratford-upon-Avon, formed by the late Robert Bell Wheler, the Historian of Stratford,** and presented by his Sister, Miss Wheler, to that Town, to be preserved for ever in the Shakespeare Lib. and Museum. London, 1863. 100 copies only printed.

——— **A List of Works illustrative of the Life and Writings of Shakespeare, the Hist. of Stratford-on-Avon, etc.** London, 1867.

——— **A Catal. of the Books, MSS., Works of Art, Antiquities, and Relics, illustrative of the Life and Works of Shakespeare, and of the Hist. of Stratford-on-Avon, which are preserved in the Shakespeare Lib. and Mus. in Henley Street.** 1868.

——— **A Catal. of a small portion of the Engravings and Drawings illustrative of the Life of Shakespeare preserved in the Collection formed by J. O. Halliwell.** London, 1868.

WARWICKSHIRE (continued).

Halliwell-Phillipps (J. O.). A Brief List of a selected portion of the Shakespeare Rarities that are preserved in the Rustic Wigwam at Hollingbury Copse, Brighton. 1886.

Halliwelliana. A Biblio. of the Publications of James Orchard Halliwell-Phillipps. By Justin Winsor. (*Biblio. Contributions, Lib. of Harvard University*, no. 10. 1881.)

Jaggard (William). Biblio. of Folklore, Superstition and Witchcraft in Shakespeare. (In 'Shakespeare and the Supernatural,' by Margaret Lucy. 1906, pp. 34–38.)

Murray (David). 'Museums.' Glasgow, 1902. Biblio. Note on Stratford Museum, vol. iii. p. 198.

SUTTON COLDFIELD.

The Corporation Records of Sutton Coldfield. (*Midland Record Soc. Trans.*, vol. iii. pp. 3–9. 1899.)

WATERFORD.

Coleman (James). Bibliography of the Counties of Waterford, Tipperary, and Wexford. (*Waterford & South-East of Irel. Archæol. Soc. Journ.*, vol. x. pp. 323–328; vol. xi. pp. 126–127. 1907–08.)

O'Hanlon (John). List of Materials for the Hist. and Topography of the County of Waterford, in the Ordnance Survey Records. (*Kilkenny & South-East of Irel. Archæol. Soc. Journ.*, vol. viii. p. 129. 1864.)

Buckley (James). Biblio. Note on Earliest Waterford Printing. (*Waterford & South-East of Irel. Archæol. Soc. Journ.*, vol. ii. p. 209. 1896.)

Coleman (James). Productions of the Printing Press in Waterford, 1555-1897. (*Ibid.* vol. 4, no. 17, etc. 1898–1901.)

Dix (Ernest Reginald McClintock). Irish Provincial Printing prior to 1701. Biblio. Note on Waterford Printing. (*The Library*, New Ser. vol. ii. pp. 342–344. 1901.)

—— **The Bonmahon Press (founded by Rev. D. A. Doudney), 1852-58, with a List.** (*The Irish Book Lover*, vol. i. pp. 97–100. 1910.) See also 'Another Bonmahon Press,' by 'Biblio.' in vol. vi. p. 168. 1915.

—— **A Waterford Bookseller's Advt. of Books, etc., sold by him in 1750.** (*Waterford & South-East of Irel. Archæol. Soc. Journ.*, vol. xiii. pp. 5–7. 1910.)

Singleton's Secret Press—Where? (with references to Waterford Printing). (*The Irish Book Lover*, vol. i. pp. 116–118. 1910.) See also Henry R. Plomer's articles on 'The Protestant Press in the Reign of Queen Mary,' in 'The Library,' Ser. 3, vol. i. pp. 54–72, 1910, and 'Ireland and Secret Printing,' in 'The Irish Book Lover,' vol. i. p. 27. 1910.

Power (Rev. Patrick). A Bundle of Old Waterford Newspapers. (*Waterford & South-East of Irel. Archæol. Soc. Journ.*, vol. xii. pp. 128–131; vol. xiii. pp. 1–4. 1910–11.)

Madden (Richard Robert). Biblio. Notes on Early Waterford Printing, and on Waterford Newspapers before 1800. (*Hist. of Irish Periodical Literature*, 1867, vol. i. pp. 129, 134, 154; vol. ii. pp. 189–202.)

Egan (P. M.). Waterford in Literature, including Biblio. and Biog. Notes on Local Writers, Local Ballads, Histories of Waterford, etc. (*Hist., Guide, etc., of the County & City of Waterford.* 1891, pp. 243–286.)

WATERFORD (continued).

Waterford Clerical Authors. By Rev. Thomas Gimlette. (*The Irish Literary Inquirer*, ed. by John Power, no. iii. pp. 27–29. 1865.)

Casaide (Seamus Ua). Bibliographical and Genealogical Notes on Donnchadh Ruadh Mac Con-Mara. (Denis M'Namara, an Irish Poet, born about 1715, died 1810, and connected with the County of Waterford.) (*Waterford & South-East of Irel. Archæol. Soc. Journ.*, vol. xiii. pp. 132–139; vol. xiv. 45–48. 1910–11.)

——— **Some Editions of O'Sullivan's Miscellany.** (Timothy O'Sullivan, a Poet, and connected with the County of Waterford.) (*Ibid.*, vol. xiv. pp. 113–122. 1911.)

Waterford Ballads and Chapbooks. (A small Collection in the Brit. Mus. Library, 11622. e. 14.)

Gross (Charles). Biblio. of Brit. Municipal Hist. (*Harvard Hist. Studies*, vol. v. 1897.) Waterford, pp. 119, 411.

Hist. MSS. Comm. Report. Waterford Collection.

Waterford, Corporation of ... ... 1st Rep. App. pp. 131–132; 10th Rep. p. 45, and App. V. pp. 265–339.

Sargent (W. A.). Old Records of the Corporation of Waterford. (*Waterford & South-East of Irel. Archæol. Soc. Journ.*, vol. i., pp. 240–246; vol. ii. pp. 33–36. 1895–96).

Power (Rev. Patrick). Irish MSS. in Library of St. John's Coll., Waterford. (*The Gaelic Journal*, vol. xiv. *passim* 1904.)

Macalister (R. A. Stewart). Studies in Irish Epigraphy. Pt. iii. Biblio. of Waterford Epigraphy. 1907.

Windle (Bertram C. A.). Archæological Map of Waterford. Biblio. Note. (*Waterford & South-East of Irel. Archæol. Soc. Journ.*, vol. xiv. pp. 44–45. 1911.)

An Old Map of Dungarvan, dated 1760. By Rev. Patrick Power. (*Ibid.* vol. xiv. pp. 103–107. 1911.)

Du Noyer's Waterford Sketches (in the Lib. of the Roy. Irish Acad.). A List by Rev. Patrick Power. (*Ibid.* vol. xvii. p. 182. 1914.)

Christy (Miller). Biblio. Note on Waterford Birds. (*The Zoologist.* Ser. 3, vol. xiv. p. 267, 1890; and reprinted in pamph., 1891, p. 42.)

Anderson (John P.). Book of Brit. Topo., 1881. Waterford, p. 442.

Gough (Richard). Brit. Topo., 1780. Waterford, vol. ii. p. 817.

Bandinel (Bulkeley). Catal. of Books bequeathed to Bodleian Lib. by Richard Gough, 1814. Waterford, p. 383.

WESTMEATH.

Coleman (James). Biblio. of the Counties of Louth, Meath, Westmeath, and Longford. (*Co. Louth Archæol. Journ.*, vol. ii. pp. 24–26. 1908.)

O'Hanlon (John). Index of Materials for the Hist. and Topography of Westmeath in the Irish Ordnance Survey Records and in the Royal Irish Academy. (*Kilkenny & South-East of Irel. Archæol. Journ.*, vol. vi. p. 193. 1860.)

Dix (Ernest Reginald McClintock). Printing in some Irish Provincial Towns in the Eighteenth Century. Mullingar Printing, 1780-1800, with a List. (*Dublin Penny Journ.*, vol. iii. p. 296. 1904.)

——— **Printing in Mullingar, 1773-1900, with a List.** (*The Irish Book Lover*, vol. ii. pp. 120–122; vol. vi. pp. 127–128, 140–141, 160–161. 1911–15.)

WESTMEATH (*continued*).

Tuite (James). John Charles Lyons and the Ledeston Press, 1820-53. (*The Irish Book Lover*, vol. i. pp. 69–71. 1910.) See also Cotton's 'Typographical Gazetteer,' Ser. II. p. 114.

J. C. Lyons and the Ledeston Press. By J. S. Crone. (*Ibid.* vol. iv. pp. 98–99. 1912.)

Anderson (John P.). Book of Brit. Topo., 1881. Westmeath, p. 442.
Gough (Richard). Brit. Topo., 1780. Westmeath vol. ii. p. 819.

WESTMORLAND.

[Numerous entries under Cumberland should also be consulted, as containing material relating to Westmorland.]

HINDS (JAMES PITCAIRN). BIBLIOTHECA JACKSONIANA, being a Catal. of the Collections of William Jackson, F.S.A. Published for the Carlisle Public Library, Tullie House, by Titus Wilson. Kendal, 1909. **Westmorland items,** pp. 185–188.

Sanderson (T.). Biblio. Hist. of Westmorland and Cumberland. 2 vols. (A Collection of Printed and MS. extracts in the 'Jackson Collection.')

Ferguson (Richard Saul). Hist. of Westmorland. 1894. A Classified List of Books, etc., relating to Westmorland, pp. 293–299.

——— **Notes on the Heraldic Visitations of Cumberland and Westmorland.** (*Cumb. & Westm. Antiq. & Archæol. Soc. Trans.*, vol. ii. pp. 20–27. 1876.)

Index to the Trans. of the Cumberland and Westmorland Antiq. and Archæol. Soc., vols. i.–vii., compiled by W. B. Arnison. Kendal, 1885.

Catalogue-Index to the Trans. of the Cumberland and Westmorland Antiq. and Archæol. Soc., vols. i.–xvi., 1866-1900, compiled by Archibald Sparke. Kendal, 1901.

Index to the Trans. of the Cumberland and Westmorland Association, vols. i.–xi. 1875-86. (*Transactions*, vol. xi. pp. 153–167. 1886.)

Topographical Catal. of the Library at Horncop, Heversham. Sect. I. Antiquities, Archæology, Topography (Local Books). Compiled by John F. Curwen. Privately Printed. 1907.

Gross (Charles). Biblio. of Brit. Municipal Hist. (*Harvard Hist. Studies*, vol. v. 1897.) Westmorland, pp. 106–107. Kendal, pp. 265–266.

Dove (Patrick Edward). Domesday Studies. 1891. Domesday Biblio. Westmorland, vol. ii. p. 692.

Lyell (Arthur H.). Biblio. List. of Romano-British Remains. 1912. Westmorland, p. 126.

Ferguson (R. S.) and Cowper (H. S.). An Archaeol. Survey of Cumberland, Westmorland, and of Lancashire North-of-the-Sands. (*Archaeologia*, vol. liii. pp. 485–538, 1893, and reprinted separately.) Biblio. and Topog. Index, pp. 488–520.

Curwen (John F.). An Index to the Heraldry of Cumberland and Westmorland. (*Cumb. & Westm. Antiq. & Archæol. Soc. Trans.*, New Ser. vol. vi. pp. 204–236. 1906.)

Sparke (Archibald). A Biblio. of the Dialect Literature of Cumberland and Westmorland, and Lancashire North-of-the-Sands. (*Cumb. & Westm. Antiq. & Archæol. Soc, Tract Series*, no, ix. 1907.)

WESTMORLAND (*continued*).

Jackson (William). A List of Books illustrating English Dialects.—Westmorland. (*Papers and Pedigrees relating to Cumberland, etc.*, vol. ii. pp. 277–281. 1892.) Reprinted from English Dialect Soc. Pubns., Ser. A, no. 8, p. 104.

Sedgefield (W. J.). The Place-Names of Cumberland and Westmorland. (*Univ. of Manchester Pubns., English Series*, no. vii. 1915.) Biblio. pp. xxxvii.–xliii.

Nightingale (B.). The Ejected of 1662 in Cumberland and Westmorland. (*Univ. of Manchester Pubns., Historical Series*, no. xii. 1911.) Principal authorities consulted, vol. i. pp. xvii.–xxiv. Bibliography, vol. ii. pp. 1409–1423.

Local Chronology; being Notes of the Principal Events published in the Kendal Newspapers since their establishment, compiled by the Editors. Reprinted from the 'Kendal Mercury' and 'Westmorland Gazette.' London, 1865. Biblio. Note on Early Kendal Newspapers, p. xxv. A London newspaper printed at Kendal, p. 120.

Joseph Richardson, Founder of the 'Kendal Times.' Biog. and Biblio. Note by Q. V. (*The Westmorland Note-Book*, vol. i. pp. 58–59. 1888–89.)

Biblio. Note on Kendal Periodicals. (*Ibid.* vol. i. pp. 285–286. 1889.)

Bewick's Cuts in Kendal Printed Books. (*Ibid.* vol. i. p. 265. 1889.)

Pollitt (Charles). De Quincey's Editorship of the 'Westmorland Gazette.' With selections from his work in that Journal from July, 1818, to Nov. 1819. Kendal, 1890.

Ferguson (Richard Saul). Notes on Kendal Chap-Books and Kendal Printers. (*Cumb. & Westm. Antiq. & Archæol. Soc. Trans.*, vol. xiv. pp. 78–80. 1897.)

Catal. of a Collection of Books, Pamphlets and Prints relating to the Counties of Cumberland and Westmorland. Charles Thurnam & Sons, Carlisle [1913].

A List of Private Acts, etc. Westmorland. Stevens & Sons, London. 1913.

List of Local Biographies of Westmorland Worthies in the 'Westmorland Gazette,' for 1884–1886. (*The Westmorland Note-Book*, vol. i. pp. 310–312. 1888–89.)

A Special Topographical Collection for Westmorland is in the Public Library at Lancaster. A Local Collection is in the Kendal Public Library.

Hist. MSS. Comm. Reports. Westmorland Collections.

Bagot, Capt. Josceline F., at Levens Hall	10th Rep. p. 16 and App. IV. pp. 318–347.
Browne, Mr. George, at Troutbeck ...	10th Rep. p. 17 and App. IV. pp. 347–358.
le Fleming, Mr. S. H., at Rydal Hall	12th Rep. pp. 38–39 and App. VII.
Lonsdale, Earl of, at Lowther Castle	13th Rep. pp. 32–35 and App. VII.
Strickland, Mr. Walter C., of Sizergh Castle	5th Rep. p. ix. and App. pp. 329–332.
Kendal Corporation	10th Rep. p. 16 and App. IV. pp. 299–318.

County Records, 1661, etc., with MS. Index, at Kendal Town Hall. (*Local Records Comm. Rep.*, 1902, App. III. p. 24.)

Collections for Westmorland and Cumberland in the Cathedral Library of Carlisle. See 'Notes & Queries,' Ser. 8, vol. ix. p. 498. 1896.

WESTMORLAND (continued).

Hill's MS. Collections for Westmorland and Cumberland. List of Contents of the 9 vols. See 'A Notice of the late John Hill, of Bankfoot, and his Westmorland MSS.' (*Cumb. & Westm. Antiq. & Archæol. Soc. Trans.*, vol. ix. pp. 14–28. 1888.)

Duckett (Sir George). Westmorland, its Tenures, General History, and Post-mortem Inquests, exemplified in the Collection of Rawlinson, among the MSS. of the Bodleian Lib. (A brief Summary of the Contents of the Rawlinson MSS. relating to Westmorland.) (*Ibid.* vol. iv. pp. 13–14. 1879.)

Whitehead (Henry). Westmorland Parish Registers, with a List. (*Cumb. & Westm. Antiq. & Archæol. Soc. Trans.*, vol. xiii. pp. 125–141. 1895.)

Ferguson (Richard Saul). An attempt to trace the missing Episcopal Registers of the See of Carlisle. (*Ibid.* vol. vii. pp. 295–299. 1884.)

Wilson (James). Calendar of Charitable Trusts in the Diocese of Carlisle, 1736–1865, with a Table arranged under Parishes, giving objects of Deeds, and References where Copies are to be found. (*Ibid.* New Ser. vol. ii. pp. 348–379. 1902.)

Whitaker (William). A List of Works relating to the Geology of Cumberland and Westmorland. (*Cumb. & Westm. Assoc. Trans.*, no. vii. pp. 13–39. 1882.)

Trimen (Henry). Botanical Biblio. of the British Counties. Westmorland. (*Journ. of Botany*, vol. xii. p. 182. 1874.)

Christy (Miller). Biblio. Note on Westmorland Birds. (*The Zoologist*, Ser. 3, vol. xiv. p. 260, 1890, and reprinted in pamph., 1891, p. 25.) **Mammals.** (*The Zoologist*, Ser. 3, vol. xvii. p. 185. 1893.) **Reptiles.** (*Ibid.* p. 247. 1893.) **Fishes.** (*Ibid.* p. 258. 1893.)

Anderson (John P.). Book of Brit. Topo., 1881. Westmorland, pp. 294–297.
Gatfield (George). Guide to Heraldry. 1892. Westmorland, pp. 187–188.
Sims (Richard). Manual for the Genealogist. 1861. Westmorland, pp. 175, 224.
Upcott (William). English Topo., 1818. Westmorland, vol. iii. pp. 1283–1285.
Smith (Alfred Russell). Catal. of Topo. Tracts, etc. 1878. Westmorland, pp. 397–398.
Gough (Richard). Brit. Topo., 1780. Westmorland, vol. ii. pp. 311–314.
Bandinel (Bulkeley). Catal. of Books bequeathed to Bodleian Lib. by Richard Gough. 1814. Westmorland, pp. 312–313.

APPLEBY.

Borough Records, 1179, etc., at the Town Hall, Appleby. (*Local Records Comm. Rep.*, 1902, App. III. p. 46.)

Rivington (C. R.). The Appleby Chained Books. (*Cumb. & Westm. Antiq. & Archæol. Soc. Trans.*, vol. xi. pp. 271–278. 1891.)

Hewitson (W.). The Appleby Charters. (*Ibid.* vol. xi. pp. 279–285. 1891.)

INGS.

Reade (Rev. George E. P.). The Ings Registers. (*Ibid.* New Ser. vol. xiii. pp. 79–84. 1913.)

KENDAL.

Corporation Records. See *ante* Hist. MSS. Comm. Reports.

Borough Records, 1575, etc., at Kendal Town Hall. (*Local Records Comm. Rep.*, 1902, App. III. p. 60.)

Moser (G. E.). Kendal Parish Church Registers. (*Cumb. & Westm. Antiq. & Archæol. Soc. Trans.*, vol. iii. pp. 49–63. 1878.)

WESTMORLAND (continued).

Nicholson (Francis). Kendal (Unitarian) Chapel and its Registers. (*Ibid.* New Ser. vol. v. pp. 172–181. 1905.)

Severs (Joseph). A Sketch of the 'Kendal Nat. Hist. Society.' (*The Westmorland Nat. Hist. Record*, vol. i. pp. 28–34. 1888–89.)

A Local Collection is in the Kendal Public Library.

KIRKBY LONSDALE,

Conder (Edward). The Kirkby Lonsdale Parish Registers, 1538-1812, with Biblio. Notes. (*Cumb. & Westm. Antiq. & Archæol. Soc. Trans.*, New Ser. vol. v. pp. 213-242. 1905.)

ORTON.

Nicholson (J. Holme). The Parish Registers of Orton, with Biblio. Notes. (*Ibid.* vol. xi. pp. 250–265. 1891.)

WEXFORD.

Coleman (James). Biblio. of the Counties of Waterford, Tipperary, and Wexford. (*Waterford & South-East of Irel. Archæol. Soc. Journ.*, vol. x. pp. 323–328. 1907.)

O'Hanlon (John). Index of Materials for the Hist. & Topography of Wexford in the Irish Ordnance Survey Records and in the Royal Irish Academy. (*Kilkenny & South-East of Irel. Archæol. Soc. Journ.*, vol. iv. p. 392. 1857.)

Dix (Ernest Reginald McClintock). Early Printing in the South-East of Ireland. Wexford Printing, with a List, 1769-1825. (*Waterford & South-East of Irel. Archæol. Soc. Journ.*, vol. xii. pp. 15-19. 1909.)

Hore MSS. Biblio. Note on the Collections of Herbert Hore, of Pole-Hore, co. Wexford, relating to Irish History and to County Wexford. (*Soc. Antiq. Irel. Journ.*, vol. xxiii. p. 213. 1893.)

Griffiths (George). Chronicles of the County Wexford. 1890. Biblio. Notes in Introduction.

Wheeler (H. F. B.) and Broadley (A. M.). The War in Wexford, 1798. An Account of the Rebellion in the South of Ireland in 1798. London, 1910. Biblio. pp. 327–332.

List of Wexford Municipal Records Printed. (*Notes & Queries*, Ser. 11, vol. vi. p. 91. 1912.)

Flood (W. H. Grattan). The Diocesan MSS. of Ferns during the rule of Bishop Sweetman, 1745-1786. (*Archivium Hibernicum*, vol. ii. pp. 100–105, Catholic Record Soc. of Irel. 1913.)

A Chorographic Account of the Southern Part of the County of Wexford, written 1684, by Robert Leigh, of Rosegarland, in that County. Edited by Herbert F. Hore. (*Kilkenny & South-East of Irel. Archæol. Soc. Journ.*, vol. v. pp. 17–21, 451–467. 1858–59.)

Christy (Miller). Biblio. Note on Wexford Mammals. (*The Zoologist*, Ser. 3, vol. xvii. p. 216. 1893.) **Reptiles.** (*Ibid.* p. 251. 1893.) **Fishes.** (*Ibid.* p. 263. 1893.)

Anderson (John P.). Book of Brit. Topo., 1881. Wexford, pp. 442-443.
Gough (Richard). Brit. Topo., 1780. Wexford, vol. ii. p. 820.

WICKLOW.

Coleman (James). Biblio. of the Counties of Waterford, Tipperary, and Wexford; Kilkenny, Carlow, and Wicklow. (*Waterford & South-East of Irel. Archæol. Soc. Jour.*, vol. xi. pp. 126–133. 1908.)

O'Hanlon (John). Index of Materials for the Hist. & Topography of Wicklow in the Irish Ordnance Survey Records and in the Royal Irish Academy. (*Kilkenny & South-East of Irel. Archæol. Soc. Journ.*, vol. iv. p. 424. 1857.)

Hist. MSS. Comm. Report. Wicklow Collection.
Malony, Rev. Michael, of Kilbride ... 3rd Rep. p. x. and App. p. 432.

Maffett (R. S.). The Roundwood Press, with a list, 1817–20. (*The Irish Book Lover*, vol. i. pp. 37–39; vol. iii. pp. 199–202. 1909–12.) See also supplemental Note by E. R. McC. Dix at vol. i. p. 61.

Macalister (R. A. Stewart). Studies in Irish Epigraphy. 1897–1907. Biblio. Note on Wicklow Epigraphy. Pt. I. 1897.

Christy (Miller). Biblio. Note on Wicklow Birds. (*Catal. of Local Lists of British Birds*, 1891, p. 42.) **Mammals.** (*The Zoologist*, Ser. 3, vol. xvii. p. 216. 1893.)

Anderson (John P.). Book of Brit. Topo., 1881. Wicklow, p. 443.
Gough (Richard). Brit. Topo., 1780. Wicklow, vol. ii. p. 821.
Bandinel (Bulkeley). Catal. of Books bequeathed to Bodleian Lib. by Richard Gough 1814. Wicklow, p. 383.

WIGTOWNSHIRE.

Hist. MSS. Comm. Rep. Wigtownshire Collection.
McDouall, Col. James, at Logan ... 4th Rep. p. xxiii. and App. pp. 535–536.

Livingstone (Matthew). Guide to the Public Records of Scotland. 1905. Wigtownshire, pp. 129, 180.

Turnbull (William B.). Scottish Parochial Registers. 1849. List of Wigtownshire Registers, pp. 155–157.

Black (George Fraser). Descriptive Catal. of Antiquities found in Ayrshire and Wigtownshire. (*Ayrshire and Galloway Archæol. Assoc. Collections*, vol. vii. pp. 1–47. 1894.)

Biblio. of Literature relating to Historical Monuments, etc., in Wigtownshire. See 'Fourth Report and Inventory of Monuments and Constructions in Galloway,' vol. i. Co. of Wigtown, 1912, pp. xiv.–xvi. Hist. Monuments [Scot.] Commission.

Trimen (Henry). Botanical Biblio. of the British Counties. Wigtownshire. (*Journ. of Botany*, vol. xii. p. 234. 1874.)

Christy (Miller). Biblio. Note on Wigtownshire Birds. (*The Zoologist*, Ser. 3, vol. xiv. p. 266. 1890; and reprinted in pamphl., 1891, p. 39.)

Anderson (John P.). Book of Brit. Topo., 1881. Wigtownshire, pp. 412-413.
Gough (Richard). Brit. Topo., 1780. Wigtownshire, vol. ii. p. 723.

WILTSHIRE.

Catal. of the Hoare Library at Stourhead, co. Wilts, compiled by J. Bowyer Nichols. London, 1840. **Wiltshire items,** pp. 412–444 (includes Lists of Wiltshire Drawings, and details of the MS. Collections of Sir Richard Colt Hoare, Sir Thomas Phillipps, Rev. J. Collinson, John Aubrey, and others).

A Chronological List of the Works of Sir R. C. Hoare, pp. xix.–xxv.

An Account of the Museum of British Antiquities at Stourhead, by Sir R. C. Hoare, pp. 723–731.

Catal. of the Paintings and Drawings at Stourhead, with a description of the Mansion, by Sir R. C. Hoare, pp. 733–754.

WILTSHIRE (*continued*).

Some Notices of the Library at Stourhead, with descriptions of the MS. Collections of Sir Richard Hoare. By J. Bowyer Nichols. (*Wilts. Archæol. & Nat. Hist. Mag.*, vol. ii. pp. 119–125. 1855.)

See also notes on the Library in John Britton's 'Essay on Topographical Literature,' 1843, pp. viii.-ix.

Hunter (Joseph). The Topographical Gatherings at Stourhead, 1825–1833. (*The Archaeol. Inst. Salisbury Meeting*, 1849, *Memoirs*, pp. 16–27.)

Murray (David). Biblio. Note on Stourhead Museum, etc. ('*Museums*,' Glasgow, 1902, vol. ii. p. 288.)

Hoare (Sir Richard Colt). Hints on the Topography of Wilts., to which is appended **Queries submitted with a view to promote a General History of the County.** Salisbury, 1818. Privately Printed. Ten Copies only.

The original MS. of Hoare's 'Wiltshire' is in the possession of Mrs. Mackay, The Grange, Trowbridge.

—— **Repertorium Wiltunense; printed with a View to facilitate Inquiry into the Topography and Biography of Wiltshire.** Bath, 1821. Privately Printed.

General Indexes to the Wiltshire Archæol. & Nat. Hist. Mag., vols. i. to viii. 1853–64; vols. ix. to xvi. 1865–76; vols. xvii. to xxiv. 1877–89; vols. xxv. to xxxii. 1890–1902. Issued by the 'Wilts. Archæol. & Nat. Hist. Soc.' as part of the 'Mag.'

Catal. of the Library of the Wilts. Archæol. & Nat. Hist. Society's Museum at Devizes. 1894. Appendices issued in 1895, 1897, 1899.

Wiltshire Books, Pamphlets, Portraits, Illustrations, etc. Lists, Reviews, etc., of Recent Publications relating to Wilts., or by Wilts. Authors. (*Wilts. Archæol. & Nat. Hist. Mag.*, vol. xxvii. to date. 1894, etc.

Catal. of the Collection of Drawings, Prints and Maps, in the Library of the Wilts. Archæol. & Nat. Hist. Soc. at Devizes, compiled by W. Heward Bell and Rev. E. H. Goddard. Devizes, 1898.

List of Original Documents, MSS. and Drawings relating to Wilts., presented to the Wilts. Archæol. & Nat. Hist. Soc., by Richard Mullings, of Stratton, near Cirencester. (*Wilts. Archæol. & Nat. Hist. Mag.*, vol. ii. pp. 392–396. 1855.)

Britton (John). An Essay on Topographical Literature, its Province, Attributes, and varied Utility, with Accounts of the Sources, Objects, and Uses of National and Local Records, etc. London, 1843.

The above was issued as the first publication of the 'Wiltshire Topographical Society,' as an annexe to 'The Hist. of the Parish of Grittleton,' by the Rev. J. E. Jackson. The work has also the following title at the beginning, 'Essay on Topography, embracing a Review of the essential characteristics and utility of that Science :–Opinions of eminent Authors on the Subject : References to, and Accounts of the Sources and Authorities whence the most authentic information is to be obtained, with an Account of the Origin of the Record Commission and of its Publication, etc.' It contains valuable Biblio. Notes on MSS., Printed Books, Topographical Collections, Drawings, etc., relating to Wilts. Fifty copies were printed separately for presentation.

—— **Catal. of Books on Wiltshire.** 1851.

—— **A List of Books, Maps, and Prints that have been published illustrative of the Topography of Wiltshire.** (*The Beauties of Wiltshire*, vol. iii. 1825, pp. 422–436.)

—— **Alphabetical List of Local Acts of Parliament.** (*Ibid.* pp. 402–410.)

—— **Memoir of John Aubrey, F.R.S., embracing his Autobiographical Sketches, and an Account of his Works, etc.** London, 1845. The Second publication of the 'Wilts. Topographical Society.' Brief descriptions and analysis of the MS. and Printed Works of John Aubrey at pp. 83–124.

WILTSHIRE (continued).

Britton (John). The Natural Hist. of Wiltshire, by John Aubrey. Edited and elucidated by notes by John Britton. London, 1847. The Third publication of the 'Wilts. Topographical Soc.' Historical and Descriptive particulars of Aubrey's MSS. in Preface, p. v.

——— **An Address to 'The Wiltshire Archaeol. & Nat. Hist. Inst.'** (formerly The Wilts. Topog. Soc.). 1849.

——— **Address at the inaugural meeting of the Wilts. Archæol. & Nat. Hist. Soc. 1853, with Queries relating to Archæology and Nat. Hist. of Wilts.** (*Wilts. Archæol. & Nat. Hist. Mag.*, vol. i. pp. 45–55. 1854.)

——— **The Auto-Biography of John Britton.** 3 pts. London, 1849–1850.

Pt. I. Personal and Literary Memoir of the Author (including Plans for a Hist. of Wilts. and suggestions for treatment of a County Hist., with Biblio. Notes on John Aubrey, H. P. Wyndham, Sir R. C. Hoare, William Cunnington, and others, pp. 449–459.)

Pt. II. A Descriptive Account of the Literary Works of John Britton, from 1800 to 1849, by T. E. Jones. (Section I. is devoted to Wilts. Topography, and includes 'The Wiltshire Topographical Soc., its Hist. and Publications, 1843–47, with full descriptions.)

Pt. III. (Appendix.) Biog., Archæol., and Critical Essays (including a Chronological List of the Literary Works of John Britton, 1799–1806, pp. 185–192).

——— **Memoirs of the Life, Writings, and Character of Henry Hatcher, author of 'The History of Salisbury.'** (With Biblio. Notes, and an account of his controversy with R. Benson about the 'Hist. of Salisbury,' written for Sir R. C. Hoare's 'Modern Wiltshire.') Printed by John Britton to accompany his 'Auto-Biography.' London, 1847.

——— **Bowood and its Literary Associations,** with Anecdotes of Bowles, Crabbe, and Moore. 1854. 25 copies only printed.

——— **Historical Account of Corsham House, with Catal. of the Celebrated Pictures.** 1806.

Memoir of John Britton, with a Classified List of his Literary Works, in Rev. J. E. Jackson's 'Kington St. Michael.' (*Wilts. Archæol. & Nat. Hist. Mag.*, vol. iv. pp. 109–128. 1857.) See also Memoir of John Britton in Preface to his 'Beauties of Wiltshire,' vol. iii. 1825.

Jackson (Rev. John Edward). Address at the inaugural meeting of the Wilts. Archæol. & Nat. Hist. Soc., 1853, on the reasons for the formation of the Society, and on Wilts. Topography, with Biblio. Notes on Aubrey, Phillipps, Britton, Hoare, and others. (*Wilts. Archæol. & Nat. Hist. Mag.*, vol. i. pp. 25–41. 1854.)

——— **The Topographical Collections of John Aubrey, 1659-70,** collected and enlarged by Rev. J. E. Jackson. Wilts. Archæol. & Nat. Hist. Soc. Devizes, 1862. Biblio. Notes in Introduction, Appendix of Deeds, pp. 419–444.

——— **Lost Volume of Aubrey's MSS. 'Hypomnemata Antiquaria B; or, An Essay towards the Description of Wiltshire.'** (*Wilts. Archæol. & Nat. Hist. Mag.*, vol. vii. pp. 76–80. 1860.)

——— **Memoir of John Aubrey,** in 'Kington St. Michael.' (*Ibid.* vol. iv. pp. 92–108. 1857.)

——— **Index to the 'Wiltshire Institutions' as printed by Sir Thomas Phillipps.** (*Ibid.* vol. xxviii. pp. 210–235. 1895.)

Jackson's Collections for Wilts. Bibliography in the Library of the Soc. of Antiquaries, London. 12 vols. For a description of some important Wilts. items at the Sale of Canon Jackson's Library by Hodgson, May 7–9, 1895, in London, see 'Wilts. Archæol. & Nat. Hist. Mag.,' vol. xxviii. pp. 197–198. 1895.

WILTSHIRE (*continued*).

Holgate (Clifford W.). A Proposed Bibliography of Wiltshire. (*Wilts. Archæol. & Nat. Hist. Mag.*, vol. xxvi. pp. 221–241. 1892. Note on 'The Printing Press in the County of Wilts.,' pp. 233–236.

——— **Wilts. Bibliography.** A Note. (*Ibid.* vol. xxviii. pp. 257–258. 1895.) The following Biblio. Lists are mentioned :—

Catal. of Printed Books and Pamphlets relating to Wiltshire, in the Lib. of James Waylen. 1876.

Henry Cunnington's Brief Alphabetical List of Books relating to Wiltshire.

List of Books relating to Wiltshire, compiled by W. C. Kemm, of Amesbury, with an Alphabetical Index by Canon J. E. Jackson.

Bibliotheca Wiltonensis. 'The Wiltshire Archæol. & Nat. Hist. Soc. are desirous of collecting materials for a complete List of Books, Tracts, or MS. Documents, relating to, or published in Wiltshire, or written by natives of the County.' See 'Wilts. Archæol. & Nat. Hist. Mag.,' vol. xi. p. 346. 1869.

Wilkinson (Rev. John). On Parochial Histories (with special reference to Wilts.). (*Wilts. Archæol. & Nat. Hist. Mag.*, vol. iii. pp. 57–67. 1856.)

——— **Parochial Histories of Wilts. and Dorset, with 'Heads of Information suggested for Parochial Histories.'** (*Ibid.* vol. iv. pp. 253–266. 1858.)

A Collection of Wilts. Books, Prints, etc., was bequeathed to the Salisbury and South Wilts. and Blackmore Museum by Mr. Job Edwards of Amesbury.

Extracts from 'The Gentleman's Magazine,' relating to Wiltshire. (*Wilts. Notes & Queries*, vol. i. pp. 211, 265, 298, 363, 397, 442, 490, 543; vol. ii. pp. 18, 53, 116, 222. 1894–97.)

Gross (Charles). Biblio. of Brit. Municipal Hist. (*Harvard Hist. Studies*, vol. v. 1897.) Wiltshire, p. 107. Salisbury, pp. 384–386.

List of Salisbury Municipal Records Printed. (*Notes & Queries*, Ser. 11, vol. vi. p. 92. 1912.)

Davenport (Frances G.). List of Printed Materials for Manorial Hist. 1894. Biblio. Note on Wilts. Manorial Hist., pp. 59–61.

Dove (Patrick Edward). Domesday Studies. 1891. Domesday Biblio. Wilts., vol. ii. p. 693.

Wyndham (Henry Penruddocke). Wiltshire, extracted from Domesday Book, with Translation, with an Index, and with a Preface in which is included a Plan for a General Hist. of the County. Salisbury, 1788.

Roman Remains in Wiltshire. A Biblio. List. (*The Archæol. Review*, vol. i. pp. 39–40. 1888.)

Lyell (Arthur H.). Biblio. List of Romano-British Remains. 1912. Wilts., pp. 126–130.

Harrison (W. Jerome). A Biblio. of the Great Stone Monuments of Wiltshire:—Stonehenge and Avebury, with other References. (*Wilts. Archæol. & Nat. Hist. Mag.*, vol. xxxii. pp. 1–169. 1901.) Also issued separately.

Goddard (E. H.). A List of Prehistoric, Roman, and Pagan Saxon Antiquities in the County of Wilts., arranged under Parishes, with references to publications where described. (*Ibid.* vol. xxxviii. pp. 153–378. 1913.)

Smith (Rev. Alfred Charles). Guide to the British and Roman Antiquities of the North Wiltshire Downs in a Hundred Square Miles round Abury, being a Key to the large Map of the above. Marlborough Coll. Nat. Hist. Soc. 1884. List of Wilts. Maps, pp. vii.–ix. List of Illustrations with Authorities, pp. xiii.–xv.

Barclay (Edgar). Stonehenge and its Earth-Works. London, 1895. List of Authors on Stonehenge, in chronological order, pp. 131–149.

WILTSHIRE (continued).

Barclay (Edgar). The Ruined Temple: Stonehenge, its Hist. and a Short Account of Questions associated with it. London, 1911. List of Writers on Stonehenge, pp. 56–66.

Long (William). Historical and other Notices of Stonehenge, from Henry of Huntingdon to the date of the publication of Sir R. C. Hoare's 'Ancient Wiltshire,' vol. i. 1812. (*Wilts. Archæol. & Nat. Hist. Mag.*, vol. xvi. pp. 6–53. 1876.)

Upcott (William). List of Books on Stonehenge and Avebury. (*A Biblio. Account of Works on English Topography*, 1818, vol. iii. pp. 1315–1329.)

Murray (David). Biblio. Note on Salisbury Museums. ('*Museums*,' Glasgow, 1904, vol. iii. p. 156.)

Catal. of Antiquities in the Museum of the Wiltshire Archæological and Nat. Hist. Soc. at Devizes. 2 pts. Devizes, 1896, 1911. Pt. I. comprises the Stourhead Collection of Antiquities.

Macklin (Herbert Walter). Monumental Brasses. London: Geo. Allen & Co., 1913. Biblio. Note on Wilts. Brasses, with a List, pp. 142, 186–187.

Biblio. Notes of the Writings of James Waylen (the historian of Devizes, Marlborough, etc.). See Obituary Notice by E. H. Goddard, in 'Wilts. Archæol. & Nat. Hist. Mag.', vol. xxvii. pp. 301–308. 1894.

A Biblio. List of the Writings of William Cunnington, F.G.S. (on the Geology, Archæology, etc., of Wilts., etc.). See Obituary Notice in 'Wilts. Archæol. & Nat. Hist. Mag.', vol. xxxiv. pp. 325–327. 1906. Biblio. Notes on William Cunnington and his MSS. and Drawings made for 'Ancient Wiltshire,' by Sir R. C. Hoare, are in John Britton's 'Auto-Biography,' Pt. I. pp. 468–473.

Dartnell (G. E.) and Goddard (E. H.). A Biblio. of Works relating to Wilts., or illustrating its Dialect. (*A Glossary of Words used in the County of Wiltshire*, App. I. pp. 217–223.) English Dialect Society. London, 1893.

Chubb (Thomas). A Descriptive Catal. of the Printed Maps of Wiltshire from 1576 to 1885. (*Wilts. Archæol. & Nat. Hist. Mag.*, vol. xxxvii. pp. 211–326. 1911.)

Buckler (John). A Collection of Six Hundred and Ninety Water-Colour Drawings of Country Seats, Views, Churches, Monuments, and Antiquities of Wiltshire, executed for Sir Richard Colt Hoare. 1808–10. 10 vols. A List of the principal views was given in Catal. No. 336, March 1914, pp. 62–65, of Francis Edwards, Bookseller, London. See also a reference to this Collection in the 'Catal. of the Hoare Lib. at Stourhead,' p. 412.

Haskins (Charles). The Salisbury Corporation Pictures and Plate, with introduction by Lionel Cust. Salisbury, 1910.

A Catal. of some Portraits and other Prints having to do with the County of Wilts. From the Collection of Ambrose Tucker. Privately Printed. Salisbury, 1908.

Jourdain (M.). Literary Associations. (*Memorials of Old Wiltshire*, ed. by Alice Dryden, 1906, pp. 156–166.)

Macdonald (Hugh). Some Literary Associations of Salisbury. (*Book-Auction Records*, vol. x. pt. i. pp. i.–viii. 1913.)

Some Wiltshire Book-Plates. (*Wilts. Notes & Queries*, vol. ii. pp. 495–500. 1898.)

A Special Topographical Collection for Wiltshire is in the Museum of the Wilts. Archæol. & Nat. Hist. Soc. at Devizes.

WILTSHIRE (continued).

Hist. MSS. Comm. Reports. Wiltshire Collections.

Ailesbury, Marquess of, at Savernake	15th Rep. pp. 18–21, and App. VII. pp. 152–306.
Arundell of Wardour, Lord, at Wardour Castle	2nd Rep. p. xii. and App. pp. 33–36.
Bath, Marquess of, at Longleat ...	3rd Rep. p. xiii. and App. pp. 180–202; 4th Rep. p. xi. and App. pp. 227–251; 16th Rep. pp. 56–59, and vol. i. (1904); 17th Rep. pp. 35–45, and vol. ii. (1907).
Leyborne - Popham, Mr. F. W., at Littlecote	16th Rep. pp. 79–86, and a vol. (1899).
Matcham, Miss M. Eyre, of Newhouse, Salisbury	Various Collections, vol. vi. pp. 1–80, 1909.
Morrison, Mr. Alfred, of Fonthill House	9th Rep. p. xvii. and App. II. pp. 406–493.
Pembroke, Earl of, at Wilton House ...	9th Rep. p. xvi. and App. II. pp. 379–384.
Radnor, Earl of, at Longford Castle, Salisbury	15th Rep. p. 35, and App. X. pp. 161–172.
Somerset, Duke of, at Maiden Bradley	15th Rep. pp. 16–18, and App. VII. pp. 146–151.
Story-Maskelyne, Mr. Neville, of Basset Down House, Swindon	10th Rep. p. 8, and App. IV. pp. 146–152.
Wykeham-Martin, Mr. Cornwallis, of the Hill, Purton	Various Collections, vol. vi. pp. 297–434. 1909.
Salisbury, Dean and Chapter of ...	1st Rep. App. pp. 90, 91; 16th Rep. p. 102; Various Collections, vol. i. pp. 338–388. 1901.
,, Bishop of	17th Rep. pp. 109–112; Various Collections, vol. iv. pp. 1–12. 1907.
,, Corporation of	17th Rep. pp. 122–124; Various Collections, vol. iv. pp. 191–254. 1907.
Wiltshire Quarter-Sessions Records ...	16th Rep. pp. 95–96; Various Collections, vol. i. pp. 67–176. 1901.

County Records, at County Record Office, Devizes. (*Local Records Comm. Rep.*, 1902, App. V. p. 234.)

Wiltshire Records in Public and Private Custody. (*Ibid.* 1902, App. III. p. 134.)

The MSS. of the Wilts. Archæol. & Nat. Hist. Soc. (Mainly copies of Documents, with descriptions, notes, etc., of the Collection of Richard Mullings, presented to the Soc. by Mr. John Mullings. They are grouped according to Parishes.) (*Wilts. Archæol. & Nat. Hist. Mag.*, vol. xxx. pp. 38, 126, 307; vol. xxxi. pp. 49, 135; vol. xxxv. p. 460; vol. xxxvi. pp. 90, 213, 439; vol. xxxvii. p. 1. 1898–1911.)

List of Documents presented to the Wilts. Archæol. & Nat. Hist. Soc. by Miss Hughes, of Bath. (*Ibid.* vol. xxxvi. pp. 439–447; vol. xxxvii. pp. 1–41. 1909–11.)

Lysons (Rev. S.). Collections for Wilts. in the Brit. Museum. Add. MS. 9459.

Upcott's Topog. Collections for Wilts. in the Brit. Museum. Add. MS. 15927.

Aubrey's Collections for Wiltshire. Privately Printed for Sir Thomas Phillipps. 2 parts. 1821.

WILTSHIRE (continued).

An Enquiry into the Conduct of Edmond Malone concerning the MS. Papers of John Aubrey, in the Ashmolean Museum, Oxford. [By J. Caulfield.] London, 1797.

MS. Collections for Wiltshire in the Library of Sir Thomas Phillipps. A List by the Rev. J. E. Jackson, extracted from the privately printed Catal. Pt. I. of the 'Bibliotheca Phillippsiana.' (*Wilts. Archæol. & Nat. Hist. Mag.*, vol. i. pp. 97–104. 1854.) See also Wilts. entries in Sotheby's Sale Catal. of Lib. of Sir T. Phillipps, 2 May, 1903, pp. 158–160.

Wiltshire Topography [1659-1843]. With some Notes on the late Sir Thomas Phillipps and his Historical Collections for the County. By Edward Tite. (*Wilts. Notes & Queries*, vol. vi. pp. 145–161. 1908.)

MS. Collections for Wiltshire, by Thomas Gore. In Lib. of the Wilts. Archæol. & Nat. Hist. Soc. Devizes.

Wiltshire Charters, etc., in the Bodleian Library. (*Calendar of Charters, etc., in the Bodl. Lib.*, ed. by W. H. Turner and H. O. Coxe, pp. 584–588, 686. 1878.)

Historical Documents in Wiltshire. A Memorandum by F. N. Rogers, Chairman of the Wilts. County Council Committee on Charities and Records, appeared in the 'Devizes Gazette,' 17 May, 1900. The Report gives a classified List of the various classes of Documents at the County Record Office, Devizes.

The Tropenell Cartulary, being the Contents of an old Wiltshire Muniment Chest. Edited by J. Silvester Davies. 2 vols. Wilts. Archæol. & Nat. Hist. Soc. 1908. See also article by J. Silvester Davies in 'Wilts. Archæol. & Nat. Hist. Mag.,' vol. xxxii. pp. 194–205, 1902, and 'Tropenell Memoranda,' in the same Magazine, vol. xxxvii. pp. 542–592, 1912, and vol. xxxviii. pp. 48–51, 1913.

Schedule of Ancient Deeds discovered at Kingston House, Bradford, Wilts., with Indexes. By Rev. J. E. Jackson. (*Wilts. Archæol. & Nat. Hist. Mag*. vol. i. pp. 279–295. 1854.)

Salisbury Cathedral Records, 12th cent., etc., with MS. Index, at Salisbury. (*Local Records Comm. Rep.*, 1902, App. III. p. 114.)

Dean and Chapter of Salisbury Records. See *ante* Hist. MSS. Comm. Reports.

Charters and Documents illustrating the Hist. of the Cathedral, City, and Diocese of Salisbury in the 12th and 13th centuries, selected from the Capitular & Diocesan Registers by Rev. William Rich Jones, and edited by W. Dunn Macray. London, 1891. [Rolls Series.]

Index to Register of Sarum Charters, from the Inner Temple Library, 1822. Privately printed by Sir Thomas Phillipps. 1830?

Britton (John). List of Books, Essays, and Prints that have been published relating to Salisbury Cathedral, also a List of Engraved Portraits of its Bishops. (*Hist. and Antiquities of the Cathedral Church of Salisbury*, 1814, pp. 109-113.)

List of Old Deeds and Muniments [*circa* **1445-1720**] **relating to St. Nicholas' Hospital, in the Registry at Salisbury.** (*The Fifteenth Century Cartulary of St. Nicholas' Hospital, Salisbury, with other Records*, ed. by Chr. Wordsworth, pp. 295-311.) Wilts. Record Soc. 1902.

A Catal. of the Library of the Cathedral Church of Salisbury. (Catal. of MSS. by E. Maunde Thompson, Catal. of Books, by S. M. Lakin.) London, 1880.

Botfield (Beriah). Notes on the Cathedral Libraries of England. 1849. **Salisbury,** pp. 405–416.

WILTSHIRE (continued).

Plenderleath (Rev. W. C.). On Some Curiosities and Statistics of Parish Registers (with allusions to Wilts. Parish Registers). (*Wilts. Archæol. & Nat. Hist. Mag.*, vol. xvi. pp. 301-336. 1876.)

Lists of Non-Parochial Registers and Records relating to Wilts., in the Custody of the Registrar-General. By A. Coleman. (*Wilts. Archæol. & Nat. Hist. Mag.*, vol. xxviii. pp. 149–155. 1895.)

Calendar of Enclosure Awards deposited at the County Record Room at Devizes, compiled by the Clerk of the Peace. Marlborough, 1900.

Wiltshire Parochial Terriers, 1542-1836. A Complete List of Parishes for which Terriers exist in the Diocesan Registry at Salisbury, by C. W. Holgate. (*Salisbury Diocesan Gazette*, Aug. 1899.)

Phillipps (Sir Thomas). Collections for Wiltshire, 1818. Printed for J. Agg, Evesham.

——— **Collections for Wiltshire, 1819.** Salisbury.

——— **Index to Feet of Fines for Wilts., from 1 Edw. III. [1326-7] to Richard III. [1483-5], from Lansdowne MS. 306.** Privately Printed. Middle Hill. 1840?

——— **Index to Feet of Fines for Wilts., 1 Geo. I. [1714] to 11 Geo. II. [1737].** Privately Printed. Middle Hill. 1853.

——— **Index to Wilts. Visitation, 1623, with some additions.** Privately Printed. London, 1831.

——— **Wilts. Close Rolls, ex MSS. Phillipps. A List.** Privately Printed. Middle Hill? 1840?

Lukis (Rev. William Collings). Collections for the Parochial Histories of Wilts. 1861.

Cartularies of Wiltshire Abbeys and Monasteries. Lists by Edward Kite, E. Margaret Thompson, and Christopher Wordsworth. (*Wilts. Notes & Queries*, vol. iv. pp. 229–230, 330-331; vol. v. pp. 233–236. 1903–06.)

Whitaker (William). List of Books, Papers, Maps, etc., on the Geology, Mineralogy, and Palaeontology of Wiltshire. (*Wilts. Archæol. & Nat. Hist. Mag.*, vol. xiv. pp. 107–120. 1873.)

Trimen (Henry). Botanical Biblio. of the British Counties. Wiltshire. (*Journ. of Botany*, vol. xii. p. 70. 1874.)

Preston (Rev. T. A.). The Flowering Plants of Wilts. Wilts. Archæol. & Nat. Hist. Soc. 1888. List of Works, etc., quoted and referred to, pp. lix.-lxiii.

Christy (Miller). Biblio. Note on Wiltshire Birds. (*The Zoologist*, Ser. 3, vol. xiv. p. 260, 1890; and reprinted in pamph., 1891, p. 25.) **Mammals.** (*The Zoologist*, Ser. 3, vol. xvii. p. 185. 1893.) **Reptiles.** (*Ibid.* p. 248. 1893.) **Fishes.** (*Ibid.* p. 259. 1893.)

Anderson (John P.). Book of Brit. Topo., 1881. Wilts., pp. 297-303.
Gatfield (George). Guide to Heraldry. 1892. Wilts., pp. 188-190.
Sims (Richard). Manual. 1861. Wilts., pp. 175, 224, 240-241.
Upcott (William). English Topo., 1818. Wilts., vol. iii. pp. 1286-1329.
Smith (Alfred Russell). Catal. of Topo. Tracts, etc. 1878. Wilts., pp. 399-406, 480.
Gough (Richard). Brit. Topo., 1780. Wilts., vol. ii. pp. 315-384.
Bandinel (Bulkeley). Catal. of Books bequeathed to Bodleian Lib. by Richard Gough, 1814. Wilts., pp. 314-317.

CHIPPENHAM.

Borough Records, 1320, etc., at Chippenham. (*Local Records Comm. Rep.*, 1902, App. III. p. 50.)

WILTSHIRE (continued).

Goldney (Frederick Hastings). Records of Chippenham relating to the Borough, 1554 to 1889, with references from the Charters, Deeds, and Documents in the Borough Chest. London, 1889. List of Title Deeds, etc., relating to the Early Hist. of the Borough, pp. 292–298.

DEVIZES.

Borough Records, from reign of King Stephen, with MS. Index at Town Hall, Devizes. (*Local Records Comm. Rep.*, 1902, App. III. p. 54.)

Murray (David). Biblio. Note on Devizes Museum. ('*Museums*,' Glasgow, 1904, vol. II. p. 206.)

Reynolds (Stephen). Biblio. of Works relating to Devizes and Neighbourhood. (*Devizes and Roundabout*, 1907, App. II.)

LACOCK.

Clark-Maxwell (W. G.). The Earliest Charters of the Abbey of Lacock. (*Wilts. Archæol. & Nat. Hist. Mag.*, vol. xxxv. pp. 191–209. 1907.)

LANGLEY BURRELL.

A List of Briefs from the Register Books of Langley Burrell. (*Wilts. Archæol. & Nat. Hist. Mag.*, vol. xxxvi. pp. 448–463. 1909.)

LONGLEAT.

Jackson (Rev. J. E.). The Literary Treasures of Longleat. (*Ibid.* vol. xv. pp. 337–348. 1875.)

Boyle (Mary Louisa). Biographical Catal. of the Portraits at Longleat. London, 1881. See also *ante* Hist. MSS. Comm. Rep. p. 282.

MALMESBURY.

Jackson (Rev. J. E.). List of Malmesbury Cartularies, Registers, etc., and where existing. (*Wilts. Archæol. & Nat. Hist. Mag.*, vol. viii. pp. 49–50. 1863.)

MARLBOROUGH.

Wordsworth (Canon Christopher). Old Marlborough Landmarks. A Series of Papers in 'The Marlborough Times,' 1904. A complete List is in 'Wilts. Archæol. & Nat. Hist. Mag.' vol. xxxiii. p. 423. 1904. Among the items are the following :—

- No. 7. Full description of Paintings of Old Marlborough by George Maton.
- No. 8. A List of Water Colour Views and Drawings of Marlborough in the Wilts. Archæol. & Nat. Hist. Society's Collection, in the Adderley Library, and in possession of Mr. R. W. Merriman, with a List of Portraits in the Adderley Library.
- No. 14. A List of Ancient Bequests registered by the Corporation, and of Chantry Certificates.
- No. 15. A List of Engraved and Lithographed Views of Marlborough, chiefly from the Collections of H. Richardson, J. F. L. Hardy, and the Wilts. Archæol. Soc.
- No. 17. Notes on Dr. Maurice's Collection of Broadsides, etc., connected with the Elections of 1818, 1819, 1820, with a List.
- No. 24. Notes on the Registers, and of Memoranda to be found in the Register Books, etc.

Brentnall (H. C.) and Carter (C. C.). The Marlborough Country. Oxford, 1912. Biblio., pp. 166–167.

WILTSHIRE (*continued*).

STANLEY.

Birch (**Walter de Gray**). **Collections towards the Hist. of the Cistercian Abbey of Stanley,** with texts of a Calendar of the Muniments, and of some unpublished Charters of the Abbey preserved in the British Museum. (*Wilts. Archaeol. & Nat. Hist. Mag.*, vol. xv. pp. 239-307. 1875.)

STONEHENGE. [See entries, pp. 280-281.]

SWINDON.

Borough of Swindon. Catal. of Rare and Valuable Works, Maps, Prints, etc., presented to Swindon, by Alderman James Powell, May, 1907. Swindon, 1907.

WARMINSTER.

MS. Collections and Notes on Hist. of Hundred of Warminster. Collected for Sir R. C. Hoare by H. Wansey. (In Lib. of Wilts. Archæol. & Nat. Hist. Soc.)

WILTON.

Slow (**Edward**). **Chronology of Wilton,** with Biblio. Notes and Lists of Borough Charters, Books relating to Wilton, Wilton Authors, etc. Wilton, 1903.

Murray (**David**). **Biblio. Note on the Collection at Wilton.** ('*Museums*,' Glasgow, 1904. Vol. iii. p. 100.)

Wilkinson (**Nevile Rodwell**). **Wilton House Pictures,** containing a full and complete Catal. and Description of the Three Hundred and Twenty Paintings which are now in the possession of the Earl of Pembroke and Montgomery at his House at Wilton. With an Introduction by Sidney, Earl of Pembroke and Montgomery, A Hist. of Wilton House, and other Matters. 2 vols. London, 1907. Vol. i. App. II. Biblio. of the Wilton House Collection.

Kite (**Edward**). **Wilton House and its Literary Associations.** (*Wilts. Notes & Queries*, vol. v. pp. 433, 494, 529. 1907.)

WORCESTERSHIRE.

BIBLIOGRAPHY OF WORCESTERSHIRE. Published by the Worcestershire Historical Society. 3 parts. Oxford, 1898-1907. A further Part is announced for publication.

Part I. Acts of Parliament relating to the County, 1224-5 - 1897. By John Richard Burton and Frank Shakespeare Pearson, 1898.

Part II. A Classified Catal. of Books, and other Printed Matter relating to the County of Worcester, with descriptive and explanatory notes. By John Richard Burton. 1903.

CONTENTS :

Account of John Oswen, the Earliest Printer in Worcs., with List of Books printed by him at Ipswich and Worcester [1548-1553], pp. 1-13.

Works relating to the County generally :—

I. General Literature, exclusively relating to the County, pp. 14-107.
II. General Literature, containing References to the County, pp. 108-152.
III. A Collection of Works relating to the Geology of Worcs., 1684-1899, pp. 153-216 (by G. R. Mills).

Part III. Works relating to the Botany of Worcestershire, pp. 217-252. Compiled by John Humphreys. 1907.

WORCESTERSHIRE (*continued*).

Nash (Treadway Russell). 'Collections for the Hist. of Worcs.' 2 vols. & Supp. London, 1781–99. For a Description of the work, with Lists of Portraits, Views, Engravings of Monuments, Pedigrees, etc., see *ante* 'Biblio. of Worcs.' Pt. II. pp. 58–66.

An Index to Dr. Nash's 'Collections for a History of Worcestershire.' Compiled by John Amphlett, of Clent, with an Introduction. Worcs. Hist. Soc. Oxford, 1894–95. The Index was also issued in fol., uniform with Nash's 'Collections.'

An Account of Treadway Russell Nash, with Biblio. Notes, in Introduction, pp. v.–xliv.
Index to Names of Persons, pp. 1–224.
Index to Names of Places, pp. 225–335.
Index of Engravings, Arms, Pedigrees, etc., pp. 337–352.
Index to Domesday, pp. 353–358.

Proposals for a County Hist. of Worcestershire. By J. W. Willis Bund. (*Assoc. Archit. Soc. Reports & Papers*, vol. xxi. pp. 119–129. 1891.)

Catal. of the Reference Department of the Worcester Public Library and Hastings Museum, compiled by Samuel Smith, 1887. Worcs. items, pp. 233–243. Additions are included in the 'slip' Catal. in the Reference Library.

Catal. of Books, Pamphlets, MSS., Pedigrees, Engravings, Drawings, Portraits, Maps, Plans, Acts of Parliament, etc., illustrative of the City and County of Worcester. Eaton, Bookseller, Worcester, 1877. A similar Catal. issued in 1879.

Indexes to the 'Reports and Papers of the Associated Architectural Societies, etc.' (includes the 'Worcester Diocesan Archit. & Archæol. Soc.' from vol. iii. 1854). Vols. i.–viii. (1850–66); vols. ix.–xiv. (1867–78); vols. xv.–xix. (1879–88); and vols. xx.–xxv. (1889–1900). Lincoln; 1867–1905.

For a List of some of the Worcs. Papers in the 'Reports,' see *ante* 'Biblio. of Worcs.' Pt. II. pp. 104–107.

Worcestershire Historical Society. For Lists of Publications of the Soc., including Reprints of Early Registers, Records, Visitations, etc., see 'Annual Report' of the Society.

List of Worcs. Items in 'The Archaeol. Journ. of the Royal Archæol. Institute,' vols. i.–xxv. 1844–1868. See *ante* 'Biblio. of Worcs.' Pt. II. pp. 85–87.

List of Items relating to Worcs. in 'The Analyst.' 10 vols. London and Worcester, 1834–40. See *ante* 'Biblio. of Worcs.' Pt. II. pp. 70–72.

List of the Chief References to Worcs. in 'The Midland Antiquary,' vol. i.–iv. 1881–87. London & Birmingham. See *ante* 'Biblio. of Worcs., Pt. II. pp. 143–144.

Gross (Charles). Biblio. of Brit. Municipal Hist. (*Harvard Hist. Studies*, vol. v. 1897.) Worcestershire, pp. 107–108. Worcester, pp. 421–423. Evesham, p. 231.

Davenport (Frances G.). List of Printed Materials for Manorial Hist. 1894. Biblio. Note on Worcs. Manorial Hist., pp. 61–62.

Lyell (Arthur H.). Biblio. List of Romano-British Remains. 1912. Worcs., pp. 130–131.

Allies (Jabez). On the Ancient British, Roman, and Saxon Antiquities, and Folk-Lore of Worcestershire. Second edition. London, 1852.

Descriptive Catal. of the Museum formed at Worcester during the Meeting of the Archæological Institute of Great Britain, July 1862. Edited by Albert Way. Worcester, 1862.

WORCESTERSHIRE (continued).

Murray (David). 'Museums.' Glasgow, 1904. Biblio. Note on Worcester Museum, vol. iii. p. 279.

Dove (Patrick Edward). Domesday Studies. 1891. Domesday Biblio. of Worcs., vol. ii. p. 694.

Bund (J. W. Willis). Domesday Book as far as it relates to Worcs. (*Assoc. Archit. Soc. Reports & Papers*, vol. xxi. pp. 253–270 ; vol. xxii. pp. 88–108. 1892–93.)

Round (J. Horace). Index to the Worcestershire Domesday Survey, also 'Some Early Worcs. Surveys.' (*The Victoria Hist. of Worcs.*, vol. i. pp. 324–340. 1901.)

Macklin (Herbert Walter). Monumental Brasses. London : Geo. Allen & Co., 1913. Biblio. Note on Worcs. Brasses, with a List, p. 187.

Cotton (William A.). Extracts from the 'Calendars of State Papers' having reference to the Hist. of the City and County of Worcester [1547–1667]. Reprinted from the 'Bromsgrove Messenger.'

Leach (Arthur F.). Documents illustrating Early Education in Worcester, A.D. 685 to 1700. Worcs. Hist. Soc. 1913. (A Collection embracing all Records.)

Worcestershire Exhibition, 1882. Catalogue. Compiled by R. W. Binns and C. M. Downes. Worcester, 1882. List of Portraits, pp. 3–30. List of Local Views, Charters, etc., pp. 31–69.

—— **Reports on the various Sections.** Historical Section, by Walter de Gray Birch ; Exhibits of Autographs, by Rev. F. Hopkinson ; Exhibits of Prehistoric, etc., Relics, by A. H. Winnington-Ingram. Worcester, 1883.

See also a note on the Historical Section, in 'The Midland Antiquary,' vol. i. pp. 84–89. 1882.

A Collection of Maps, Views, Portraits, and other Illustrations of Worcestershire. 3 vols. Presented to Birmingham Free Library by R. W. Boodle.

Woof (Richard). Biographical Notes of the Portraits preserved in the Guildhall, Worcester. Worcester, n.d.

Chambers (John). Biographical Illustrations of Worcs., to which is added a List of Living Authors of the County. 1820.

Burton (John Richard). Early Worcestershire Printers and Books. (*Assoc. Archit. Soc. Reports & Papers*, vol. xxiv. pp. 197–213. 1897.) See also *ante* p. 286, 'Biblio. of Worcs.,' Pt. II., for an 'Account of John Oswen, the Earliest Printer in Worcs.'

Allnutt (W. H.). English Provincial Presses. Earliest Printing at Worcester, 1548-1553. (*Bibliographica*, vol. ii. pp. 36–41. 1896.)

Berkeley (Mrs. R.). A Sketch of Early Provincial Journalism. [Biblio. Notes on Worcs. Newspapers, etc.] (*Assoc. Archit. Soc. Reports and Papers*, vol. xxiv. pp. 550–573. 1898.)

The Oldest English Newspaper. 'Berrow's Worcester Journal.' [An Account of its Origin, etc.] Reprinted from 'Berrow's Worcester Journal,' Jan. 4, 1890. Second edition, with Supplementary Notes. Worcester, 1890.

Plomer (Henry R.). The Private Press of Sir Thomas Phillipps at Middle Hill, Worcs. (*Some Private Presses of the Nineteenth Century*, in 'The Library,' New Ser. vol. i. pp. 414–417. 1900.)

Lowndes (William Thomas). List of Privately Printed Publications of the Middle Hill Press of Sir Thomas Phillipps. (*The Bibliographers' Manual*, 1864, vol. iv. pp. 1856–1858, and Appendix, pp. 225–237.)

WORCESTERSHIRE (continued).

The Middle Hill Press. A Short Catal. of some of Sir T. Phillipps' Privately Printed Works. [By T. Fitz-Roy Fenwick.] London, 1886.

A List of Books and Articles printed for Sir Thomas Phillipps, and chiefly at his private Printing Press at Middle Hill, Worcs., between 1817 and 1858. (*Notes and Queries*, Ser. 2, vol. vi. pp. 389-391. 1858.)

Martin (John), The Middle Hill Press, with a List. (*A Biblio. Catal. of Books Privately Printed.* 1834, pp. 441-458.)

Bibliotheca Phillippsiana. Catal. of Printed Books, Middle Hill (The Seat of Sir Thomas Phillipps) **with Supplements,** 1827-48.

Special Topographical Collections for Worcs. are at the Worcester Cathedral Lib. and in the Worcester Public Lib. Special Local Collections are in the Public Libraries at Evesham, Kidderminster, and Malvern.

Hist. MSS. Comm. Reports. Worcestershire Collections.

Coventry, Earl of, at Croome Court ...	1st Rep. p. x. and App. p. 34.
Berington, Mr. Charles M., at Little Malvern Court	2nd Rep. p. xii. and App. p. 72.
Hopkinson, Rev. Francis, at Malvern Wells	3rd Rep. p. xvi. and App. pp. 261-267.
Lechmere, Sir Edmund A. H., of Rhydd Court, Upton-on-Severn	5th Rep. p. viii. and App. pp. 299-304.
Lloyd, Mr. S. Zachary, of Areley Hall, nr. Stourport	10th Rep. p. 20, and App. IV. pp. 444-450.
Lyttelton, Lord, at Hagley Hall ...	2nd Rep. p. xi. and App. pp. 36-39.
Winnington, Sir Thomas, at Stanford Court	1st Rep. p. x. and App. pp. 53-55.
Worcester, St. Andrew's	8th Rep. App. p. 638.
——— Dean and Chapter of	14th Rep. pp. 44, 45, and App. VIII. pp. 165-203.
——— Bishop's Registry	14th Rep. p. 45, and App. VIII. pp. 204-205.
County Records	16th Rep. pp. 100-101. Various Collections, vol. i. pp. 282-326. 1901.

County Records, 1596, etc., at the Shire Hall, Worcester. (*Local Records Comm. Rep.*, 1902, App. III. p. 134.)

Records in Public and Private Custody. (*Ibid.* 1902, App. III. p. 134.)

Borough of Worcester Records, Rich. I., etc., with printed Catal., at the Town Hall, Worcester. (*Ibid.* 1902, App. III. p. 40.)

Catal. of MS. Records and Printed Books in the Library of the Corporation of Worcester, with an Appendix of Local Records not in the Custody of the Corporation. By Richard Woof. Worcester, 1874.

Worcestershire County Records. Division I. Documents relating to Quarter Sessions. Calendar of the Quarter Sessions Papers. Vol. I. 1591-1643. Compiled for the Records and Charities Committee, by J. W. Willis Bund. Worcester, 1900. Also issued by the 'Worcs. Hist. Soc.'

Original Charters relating to the City of Worcester, in possession of the Dean and Chapter, and by them preserved in the Cathedral Lib. Edited for the 'Worcs. Hist. Soc.' by J. Harvey Bloom. 1909. Biblio. Notes on the Deeds in 'Introduction.'

WORCESTERSHIRE (continued).

Habington's MS. Collections for Worcestershire are in Viscount Cobham's Library at Hagley Hall; Library of the British Museum, Harl. MS. 2205; Library of the Soc. of Antiquaries, MSS. Nos. 143–148.

See descriptions of these Collections in the Life of Thomas Habington, prefixed to 'A Survey of Worcestershire by Thomas Habington,' edited for the 'Worcs. Hist. Soc.' by John Amphlett, of Clent, 1895. See also Introduction to Nash's 'Worcestershire,' and the Preface to Valentine Green's 'Hist. of Worcester,' for accounts of the history of Habington's MSS. after his death. For a List of the Habington material in the Lib. of the Soc. of Antiq. see Sir Henry Ellis's 'Catal. of the MSS. Soc. Ant.' pp. 48-49.

For a note on the vol. in the Bodleian Lib. belonging to Jesus Coll. Oxford, entitled 'Habington Manuscripts,' see pp. 22-23 of Amphlett's Life of Thomas Habington aforementioned.

Prattinton's MS. Collections for Worcs. in the Lib. of the Soc. of Antiquaries. 61 vols. consisting of Pedigrees, Lists of Clergy, etc., and General Index of Names.

Descriptive Catal. of the Charters and Muniments of the Lyttelton Family, in the possession of Viscount Cobham, at Hagley Hall, Worcs., with Introduction, Notes, and Index, by Isaac H. Jeayes. London, 1893. See also *ante* Hist. MSS. Comm. Rep.

The Kyre Park Charters, by the permission and with the assistance of Mrs. Baldwyn-Childe. Edited for the Worcs. Hist. Soc. by John Amphlett, of Clent. Oxford, 1905.

Noake (John). Descriptive Notes on Worcs. MS. Collections. (*Worcestershire Nuggets*, by John Noake, 1889, pp. 233–265.)

——— **Worcestershire MSS.** Descriptions of the Dineley MSS., the Jeffries MSS., the Townsend MSS., and others. (*Notes & Queries for Worcs.*, by John Noake, 1856, pp. 135–166.)

Phillipps (Sir Thomas). Topographical, Genealogical, and Miscellaneous Collections for Worcs. See 'Bibliotheca Phillippica,' Sotheby's Sale Catal., 2 May 1903, pp. 161–163.

Indexes to the Visitations of Worcestershire, 1569 and 1684. Compiled by Sir Thomas Phillipps to serve for Nash's 'Collections for the Hist. of Worcs.' Middle Hill, 1838.

Index to the Pedes Finium for Worcestershire [1649-1714]. Impensis Dni Thomæ Phillipps. Ex Zincographia Appelana, 1853.

An Index to Worcestershire Fines, 1649-1714. Edited by John Amphlett for the Worcs. Hist. Soc. Oxford, 1896.

Index Pedum Finium pro Com. Wigorn ab 1 Edw. III. ad Hen. VI. Impensis Dni T. P. Bart. Privately Printed. Cheltenham, 1865.

Botfield (Beriah). Notes on the Cathedral Libraries of England. 1849. **Worcester,** pp. 491–501.

Local Ecclesiastical Records of the Diocese of Birmingham. (Worcestershire, etc.) Report presented to the Bishop of Birmingham, June, 1911, with List of Registers, etc. 1911.

A Digest of the Parish Registers within the Diocese of Worcester, previous to 1812, together with a Table of the Bishops' Transcripts now in existence in Edgar Tower, Worcester, previous to 1700. [Index to the Bishops' Transcripts, compiled by John Amphlett.] Birmingham, 1899.

List of Worcester Diocesan Registers, 1268-1559, Hen. III. to Elizabeth. App. V. pp. ccxlvi.–ccxlvii. of 'Register of Bishop Godfrey Giffard,' 1268–1301. Edited for 'Worcs. Hist. Soc.' by J. W. Willis Bund. 2 vols. 1902.

The Register of the Diocese of Worcester during the Vacancy of the See, usually called 'Registrum Sede Vacante,' 1301–1435. (A Calendar of the Contents of the Register.) Edited for 'Worcs. Hist. Soc.' by J. W. Willis Bund. Oxford, 1893-97.

WORCESTERSHIRE (continued).

Noake (**John**). **Parish Records of the City of Worcester, with Biblio. Notes on the Registers.** (*Notes & Queries, for Worcs.*, by John Noake, 1856, pp. 1-73.)

Urwick (**William**). **List of Non-Parochial Registers and Records for Worcs., at Somerset House.** (*Nonconformity in Worcester*, by Wm. Urwick, 1897, pp. 186–191.)

Catal. of MSS. preserved in the Chapter Library of Worcester Cathedral, with a List of MSS. formerly belonging to the Library, now in other Libraries, compiled by Rev. John Kestall Floyer, and edited and revised by Sidney Graves Hamilton. Worcs. Hist. Soc. 1906.

Floyer (**John Kestall**). **The Mediæval Library of the Benedictine Priory of St. Mary, in Worcester Cathedral Church.** (*Archaeologia*, vol. lviii. pp. 561–570. 1902.)

——— **The Early Monastic Writers of Worcester,** with a List of Writers connected with Worcester Monasteries. (*Assoc. Archit. Soc. Reports & Papers*, vol. xxv. pp. 146-164. 1899.)

Accounts of the Priory of Worcester, A.D. 1521–2. Edited by Rev. Canon James Maurice Wilson, and a **Catal. of the Rolls of the Obedientiaries,** prepared by Rev. J. Harvey Bloom. Worcs. Hist. Soc. Oxford, 1907.

Wilson (**Canon James Maurice**). **The Library of Printed Books in Worcester Cathedral.** (*The Library*, Ser. 3, vol. ii. pp. 1–33. 1911.) Also issued separately.

——— **Introductory Notes on some of the Ancient MSS. now shown in Worcester Cathedral.** (*Assoc. Archit. Soc. Reports & Papers*, vol. xxxi. pp. 577–584. 1912.)

——— **On Two Fragments of Geometrical Treatises found in Worcester Cathedral Library.** (*Ibid.* vol. xxx. pp. 167–172. 1909.)

Birch (**Walter de Gray**). **The Anglo-Saxon Charters of Worcester Cathedral,** with a Calendar. (*Brit. Archaeol. Assoc. Journ.*, vol. xxxviii. pp. 24–53. 1882.)

Hooper (**John H.**). **On Some Documents Restored to the Dean and Chapter of Worcester.** (*Assoc. Archit. Soc. Reports & Papers*, vol. xiii. pp. 276–280. 1876.) See also 'Brit. Archaeol. Assoc. Journ.', vol. xxxii. pp. 210–214. 1876.

Bloom (**J. Harvey**). **Catal. of certain Rolls in the Archives of the Dean and Chapter of Worcester.** (*Worcs. Hist. Soc. Collectanea*, 1912, pp. 91–136.)

——— **Charters from St. Swithun's, Worcester.** [A Calendar.] (*Ibid.* pp. 1-67.)

Duckworth (**Thomas**). **Biblio. of Natural History, with Special Reference to Works of Local Interest.** (*Worcs. Naturalists' Club Trans.*, vol. iv. pp. 12–20. 1908.)

Whitaker (**William**). **List of Works on the Geology, Mineralogy, and Palæontology of Worcs.** (*Brit. Assoc. 55th Report*, 1885, pp. 797–806.)

List of Works relating to the Geology of Worcs., 1684-1899. See *ante* p. 286 'Biblio. of Worcs.', Part II. Sect. III. pp. 153-216.

Trimen (**Henry**). **Botanical Biblio. of the British Counties. Worcs.** (*Journ. of Botany*, vol. xii. p. 155. 1874.)

Amphlett (**John**) and **Rea** (**Carleton**). **The Botany of Worcestershire.** Birmingham, 1909. Biblio. Notes, with List of Books referred to, pp. xx.–xxxiii. See also *ante* p. 286 'Biblio. of Worcs.', Part III. Works relating to the Botany of Worcs., by John Humphreys.

WORCESTERSHIRE (continued).

Christy (Miller). Biblio. Note on Worcs. Birds. (*The Zoologist*, Ser. 3, vol. xiv. p. 261, 1890; and reprinted in pamph., 1891, p. 26.) **Mammals.** (*The Zoologist*, Ser. 3, vol. xvii. p. 186. 1893.) **Reptiles.** (*Ibid.* p. 248. 1893.) **Fishes.** (*Ibid.* p. 259. 1893.)

Anderson (John P.). Book of Brit. Topo., 1881. Worcs., pp. 303-308.
Gatfield (George). Guide to Heraldry. 1892. Worcs., pp. 190-191.
Sims (Richard). Manual. 1861. Worcs., pp. 176, 224-225, 241.
Upcott (William). English Topo., 1818. Worcs., vol. iii. pp. 1330-1350.
Smith (Alfred Russell). Catal. of Topo. Tracts, etc. 1878. Worcs., pp. 407-413, 480.
Gough (Richard). Brit. Topo., 1780. Worcs., vol. ii. pp. 385-394.
Bandinel (Bulkeley). Catal. of Books bequeathed to Bodleian Lib. by Richard Gough, 1814. Worcs., pp. 318-319.

BEWDLEY.

Borough Records, Edw. IV. etc., at Town Clerk's Office, Bewdley. (*Local Records Comm. Rep.*, 1902, App. III. p. 48.)

BOSCOBEL.

[For items relating to Boscobel, and the Battle of Worcester, see under Shropshire, p. 221.]

CLENT.

Amphlett (John). The Parochial Records of Clent. (*The Midland Antiquary*, vol. iii. pp. 49-54. 1884.)

DROITWICH.

Borough Records, 1275, etc., with MS. Catalogues, at Town Hall, Droitwich. (*Local Records Comm. Rep.*, 1902, App. III. p. 56.)

DUDLEY.

Blocksidge (E.). Dudley Parish Registers from the Earliest Period, described, tabulated, and illustrated. Dudley, 1894.

Rollason (Arthur A.). The Old Non-Parochial Registers of Dudley, with Index Nominum. Dudley, 1899.

EVESHAM.

Borough Records, at Town Hall, Evesham. (*Local Records Comm. Rep.*, 1902, App. III. p. 56.)

HAGLEY.

Hoare (Sir R. Colt). A Catal. of the Pictures and Portraits at Hagley Hall. (A MS.) See 'Catal. of the Hoare Lib. at Stourhead,' 1840, p. 446.

HALES OWEN.

Roth (H. Ling). Biblio. and Chronology of Hales Owen. (*Index Soc. Occasional Index*, No. II. 1887.)

KIDDERMINSTER.

Borough Records, 1102, etc., at Town Hall, Kidderminster. (*Local Records Comm. Rep.*, 1902, App. III. p. 60.)

MALVERN (GREAT).

Nott (James). Some of the Antiquities of 'Moche Malverne' (Great Malvern). Malvern, 1885. Biblio. Notes on the 'Scudamore Papers,' the Parish Registers, etc., with Lists.

YORKSHIRE.

BOYNE (WILLIAM). THE YORKSHIRE LIBRARY: A BIBLIOGRAPHICAL ACCOUNT OF BOOKS ON TOPOGRAPHY, TRACTS OF THE SEVENTEENTH CENTURY, BIOGRAPHY, SPAWS, GEOLOGY, BOTANY, MAPS, VIEWS, PORTRAITS, AND MISCELLANEOUS LITERATURE, RELATING TO THE COUNTY OF YORK, with Collections and Notes on the Books and Authors. London, 1869.

Catal. of a Collection of Historical and Topographical Works and Civil War Tracts, relating to the County of York, Tracts concerning Sir Thomas Fairfax, also Sermons and other Works connected with the County, in the Library of Edward Hailstone, at Horton Hall. Bradford, 1858.

Privately Printed. The Hailstone Collection was bequeathed to the Minster Library at York in 1891. In the 'Catal. of the Printed Books in the Lib. of the Dean and Chapter of York,' by James Raine, 1896, it is stated that 'a large series of Books, etc., will be catalogued with the Hailstone Collection.' See a note on this Collection by James Raine in the 'Obituary Notice of Edward Hailstone' by G. W. Tomlinson in 'Yorks. Archæol. & Topog. Journ.,' vol. xi. pp. 204-207. 1891.

Catal. of the Second Portion of the Library of Edward Hailstone, of Walton Hall, Wakefield, sold by Sotheby's, 23 Apr. 1891. **Yorks. items,** pp. 185-193, 200, 202. Many of the Yorkshire pamphlets, etc., from this Sale are now in the Lib. of the Brit. Museum.

List of Books in the Local Collection of the City of York Public Library, relating to the City and County of York. 1912.

Part I. Classified List.
Part II. York Printed Books.
Part III. Photographs, Engravings, etc.
Part IV. Author List.

Catal. of the Books and Pamphlets relating to Yorkshire, in the Central Reference Library, Bradford. 1892.

Yorkshire Bibliographer, edited by Joseph Horsfall Turner. Vol. I. Bingley, 1888. Contains much Biblio. information, including an unfinished Biblio. of Yorks. Authors and Places (A—Ayton), at pp. 1-26, 34-56, 73-89, 111-122, 140-145, arranged alphabetically, also Notices of New Books (mostly Yorks. Publications). A Biblio. entitled 'Ten Thousand Yorkshire Books,' by J. Horsfall Turner, was compiled and announced, but not published.

Macmichael (J. Holden). The Biblio. of Yorkshire (A—Boroughbridge). (*Yorks. Notes & Queries*, ed. by Chas. F. Forshaw. Supp. vol. 4, 5. 1907-08.)

Ross (Frederick). 'Biographia et Bibliographia Eboracenses.' This work was announced as 'ready for publication,' and was stated to consist of thousands of names of persons and book-titles, the result of thirty years' research. See 'Yorks. County Mag.' vol. i. pp. 20-21, 1891. A complete Biblio. of Yorks. books was under consideration by the 'Yorks. Archæol. Soc.' about 1892.

Hotten (John Camden). Biblio. Account of nearly 1500 curious and rare Books, Tracts, MSS. and Engravings relating to the History and Topography of Yorkshire, collected by Mr. Hotten, with numerous descriptive Notes, etc. 1863.

Index of the Papers contained in Vols. I. to XVII. of the 'Journal,' and of the 'Excursions,' 1867 to 1903, of the Yorkshire Archæological Society. Compiled by William F. Lawton. Leeds, n. d.

YORKSHIRE (*continued*).

Catalogues of the Library of the Yorks. Archæol. Soc., 1897, 1901, and 1909. Leeds, 1898–1909.

Catal. of MSS. in the Library of the Yorks. Archæol. Soc., 1912, compiled by W. T. Lancaster. Leeds, 1912. The bulk of the MSS. was bequeathed to the Soc. by Sir Thomas Brooke (a large proportion of them came from the Lib. of Sir Thomas Phillipps, at Middle Hill, Worcs.). The following Collections of MSS. are described in the Catal.: Thoresby, Fairfax, Woodhead, Beckwith, Dade, Radcliffe, Hunter, Paver, and others.

The Yorks. Archæol. Soc. An Account of its Origin in 1863 and of its Progress from that date to 1913. By S. J. Chadwick. (*Yorks. Archæol. Journ.* vol. xxiii. pp. 1–91. 1914.) Contains a Classified List of Selected Articles in the 'Journal,' and Lists of the Publications, and Excursion Programmes of the 'Society,' pp. 39–44.

The Huddersfield Archæol. and Topographical Assoc. (afterwards the **Yorks. Archæol. Soc.**), **founded in 1864.** An Account of the Assoc., 1864–70, by Sir Thomas Brooke. (*Yorks. Archæol. Journ.*, vol. xvi. pp. 227–237. 1901.)

Bradford Historical and Antiq. Soc. A Record of the Work of the Soc., with List of Papers read before the Soc., 1878-1911, and a List of Excursions, also a Rough Index of the chief Papers printed in 'The Bradford Antiquary,' 1881–1910. (*The Bradford Antiquary*, New Ser. vol. iii. pp. 458–466. 1911.)

A 'Résumé of the Society's Operations since 1883, with List of Papers read since Dec. 1880,' by William Cudworth, appeared in vol. ii. pp. 98–101. 1892.

Catal. of the Books, MSS., etc., belonging to the Bradford Hist. and Antiq. Soc. Bradford, 1886.

Indexes to the Reports and Papers of the Associated Architectural Societies, etc. (includes the Yorkshire Architectural Society. Vols. i.–viii. (1850-66); vols. ix.–xiv. (1867–78); vols. xv.–xix. (1879–88); and vols. xx.–xxv. (1889-1900). Lincoln, 1867–1905.

General Index of the First Six Volumes of the 'Miscellanea,' being vols. ii. iv. ix. xi. xv. and xxii. of the Publications of the Thoresby Soc., compiled by James Singleton. (*Publications*, vol. xxii. pp. 409–421. 1915.)

Catal. of Books in the Lib. of the Mechanics' Inst., Wakefield. 1895. **Yorks. Books,** pp. 110-114. **Supp. Catal.** 1911. **Yorks. Books,** pp. 45–48.

A Consolidated Index to Paver's Marriage Licenses (1567 to 1630). [Printed in the '*Yorks. Archæol. & Topog. Journ.*' vols. vii. ix.–xiv. xvi. xvii. xx.] Yorks. Archæol. Soc. Extra Series, vol. ii. 1912.

Index to Articles on Yorkshire County Families, in 'Leeds Mercury' Supplement, 1885-90. (*Bradford Pub. Lib. Catal. of Books, etc., relating to Yorks.* 1892, p. 38.)

Stansfeld (John). Sale Catal. of the valuable Lib. of John Stansfeld, of Leeds, comprising a Collection of Yorks. Topography, a Collection of Yorks. Illustrations, in 10 vols. and a valuable Series of MSS. relating to Yorks. known as the 'Walker Collection,' in 60 vols. Sold by Sotheby's, London, 13-15 June, 1898. **Yorks. items,** pp. 47–54, 58-63, 65–69.

Brooke (Thomas). A Catal. of the MSS. and Printed Books, collected by Thomas Brooke, and preserved at Armitage Bridge House, near Huddersfield. 2 vols. London, 1891. Privately Printed. **Yorks. items,** pp. 709–717 and *passim.*

YORKSHIRE (*continued*).

Burton (**John**). **A Scheme and Proposals, in order to form a Society for Compiling a complete Civil and Natural Hist. of the Antient and Present State of Yorkshire,** with a Chorographical and Topographical Description thereof, to this is added, as a Specimen, part of the History, etc. of the Parish of Hemingbrough.

The above is appended to Burton's 'Monasticon Eboracense, and the Ecclesiastical Hist. of Yorks,' 1758, pp. 426-448. The preface to the latter work contains Biblio. Notes on various Yorks. Collections, and a Catal. of the Records at York consulted by the Author.

Johnston (**Nathaniel**). **Enquiries for information towards the illustrating and compleating the Antiquities and Natural Hist. of Yorks.** A single-sheet. London? 1685?

Copies are in the Brit. Mus. Lib. at 816 m. 16 (44) and Lansd. MS. 889. For the Yorks. Collections of Nathaniel Johnston in the possession of Mr. Bacon Frank, at Campsall Hall, see 17th Rep. Hist. MSS. Comm. p. 188. See also a note at p. 126 of Freemantle's 'Biblio. of Sheffield,' 1911.

Smythe (**John**). **Catal. of the MSS., Printed Books, of the Hist. and Antiquities, Medals, Coins, Portraits, Topographical Engravings and Drawings, Charts, Maps and Surveys, relating to the Co. of York, in the Collection of John Smythe, at Heath, Pontefract.** 1809.

Ross (**Frederick**). **Yorkshire in the 'Archaeologia.'** A List of Yorks. Contributions to the Journal. (*Old Yorkshire*, ed. by Wm. Smith, vol. i. pp. 56-66; vol. iii. pp. 37-48. 1881-82.)

—— **Yorkshire Authors and the Royal Society.** A List of Yorks. Contributions to the 'Philosophical Transactions.' (*Ibid.* vol. i. pp. 46-56; vol. iii. pp. 48-49. 1881-82.)

Yorkshire in the 'Monasticon.' A brief Abstract of the Contents of Dugdale's 'Monasticon' relating to Yorks., by R. V. Taylor. (*Ibid.* vol. iv. pp. 259-260. 1883.)

Index to the Visitation of the County of York, 1665-66, by William Dugdale, compiled by Sir George John Armytage. London, 1872.

Auden (**George A.**). **Historical and Scientific Survey of York and District.** Prepared for the 75th Meeting of the Brit. Assoc. 1906. York, 1906. Among the Biblio. items are:—

The Minster Library, by Rev. Canon Watson, pp. 243-245.
Notes on the more important Historical MSS. in Public Custody in the City of York, pp. 246-247.
Biblio. of the Churches of York, p. 127.
Biblio. of the Merchant Adventurers of York, p. 227.

Widdrington (**Sir Thomas**). **Analecta Eboracensia, or Some Remaynes of the Ancient City of York.** Edited by Caesar Caine. 1897. Some Account of the 'Analecta Eboracensia,' pp. vii-xix. Life of the Author, with Biblio. Notes, pp. xx.-xxxiii.

Drake (**Francis**). **Eboracum, or the Hist. and Antiquities of the City of York.** London, 1736. Biblio. Notes in Preface on Camden, Dodsworth, James Torr, and others. A 'Memoir of Francis Drake,' by Robert Davies, is in 'Yorks. Archæol. & Topog. Journ.', vol. iii. pp. 33-54. 1875.

Joseph Horsfall Turner. Biographical Notice, with a Biblio. (*The Bradford Antiquary*, New Ser. Pt. xviii. pp. 194-198. 1915.)
Turner's Collection of Yorks. Books, Pamphlets, etc., left to the Belle Vue Public Library at Halifax, 'Horsfall Turner Section.'

Gross (**Charles**). **Biblio. of Brit. Municipal Hist.** (*Harvard Hist. Studies*, vol v. 1897.) Yorks., pp. 108-110. York, pp. 427-430. Bradford, pp. 173-174. Halifax, p. 253. Hull, pp. 259-261. Leeds, p. 272. Sheffield, pp. 388-389.

YORKSHIRE (continued).

Davenport (Frances G.). List of Printed Materials for Manorial Hist. 1894. Biblio. Note on Yorks. Manorial Hist. pp. 62–64.

Lyell (Arthur H.). Biblio. List of Romano-British Remains. 1912. **Yorks.**, pp. 131–136.

Price (John E.). Roman Remains in Yorks. A Biblio. List. (*The Archæol. Review*, vol. ii, pp. 337–342. 1889.)

Catal. of Antiquities exhibited at the Annual Meeting of the Archæol. Institute at York, 1846. (*Memoirs, etc., of the Archæol. Inst., York*, 1846, pp. 1–25.)

Hand-Book to the Antiquities in the Grounds and Museum of the Yorks. Philos. Soc., by Charles Wellbeloved. Seventh Edn. York, 1881.

Catal. of the Bateman Collection of Antiquities in the Sheffield Public Museum. By Elijah Howarth. London, 1899.

Murray (David). Biblio. Note on Museums at York. ('*Museums*,' Glasgow, 1904, vol. iii. pp. 283–284.)

Dove (Patrick Edward). Domesday Studies. 1891. Domesday Biblio. of Yorks., vol. ii. p. 695.)

Keyser (Charles E.). List of References to Books with notices of Norman Doorways in Yorkshire. [Arranged under Churches, etc.] Appendix to 'The Norman Doorways of Yorkshire.' (*Memorials of Old Yorkshire*, ed. by T. M. Fallow, 1909, pp. 211–219.)

Old York Views and Worthies Exhibition, 1905. A Handbook, with a Preface by J. Solloway. 1905.

Sheppard (Thomas). Descriptions of Lord Burleigh's MS. Chart of East Yorks. and of Early Maps of East Yorks. (*The Lost Towns of the Yorks. Coast.* London, 1912, pp. 207–238.)

——— **East Yorks. History in Plan and Chart.** (*East Riding Antiq. Soc. Trans.*, vol. xix. 1912.)

Speed's Map of Yorkshire, 1627. A Biblio. Note. (*The Yorks. County Mag.* vol. i. pp. 1–8. 1891.)

Turner (J. Horsfall). Yorkshire Place Names, as recorded in the Yorks. Domesday Book, 1086, comprising all the References to Places in the Three Ridings. Bingley. [1900.]

Moorman (F. W.). The Place-Names of the West Riding of Yorks. The Thoresby Soc., vol. xviii. Leeds, 1910. Biblio. pp. xlix–liv.

Goodall (Armitage). Place-Names of South-West Yorks. (Cambridge Archaeol. and Ethnological Series.) Cambridge, 1913, and Revised edn. 1914. Biblio. pp. 46–51.

Federer (Charles A.). A Biblio. of Yorks. Dialect Literature. (*Yorks. Dialect Soc. Trans.*, vol. i. pp. 86–114. 1900.)

Yorks. Dialect Soc. Some Work for the Society. A suggested scheme as a basis on which to carry out the objects of the Society, by J. Horsfall Turner, with Biblio. references. (*Yorks. Dialect Soc. Trans.*, vol. i. pp. 34–40. 1898.)

County Folk-Lore, vol. ii. Examples of Printed Folk-Lore concerning the North Riding of Yorkshire, York, and the Ainsty. Edited by Mrs. Gutch. Folk-Lore Soc. London, 1901. List of Authorities, pp. xxiii–xxxix.

County Folk-Lore, vol. vi. Printed Extracts—East Riding of Yorkshire. Edited by Mrs. Gutch. Folk-Lore Soc. London, 1912. List of Sources, pp. xix–xxvii.

Page (W. G. B.). Biblio. of Folk-Speech of Yorkshire. (*The Folk-Speech of East Yorks.*, by John Nicholson, 1889, pp. 97–100.)

YORKSHIRE (*continued*).

Davies (Robert). A Memoir of the York Press, with Notices of Authors, Printers, and Stationers, in the Sixteenth, Seventeenth, and Eighteenth Centuries. Westminster, 1868.

Duff (E. Gordon). The Printers, Stationers, and Bookbinders of York up to 1600, with a List of Books printed at York, or for Sale in York, before 1600. (*Biblio. Soc. Trans.*, vol. v. pp. 87–108. 1899.)

——— **Notes on a Book Printed at York in 1579.** (*Edinburgh Biblio. Soc. Pubns.*, vol. iii. pp. 133–136. 1899.)

Allnutt (W. H.). English Provincial Presses. Earliest Printing at York. (*Bibliographica*, vol. ii. pp. 26–27, 282–286. 1896.)

The Printing Press in Yorkshire; List of Places, with dates of introduction of Printing, and Biblio. Notes, by Chas. A. Federer, Simeon Rayner, and others. (*The Yorks. Mag.*, vol. ii. pp. 288, 336, 384, 432. 1873.) There are also Notes in vol. iii.

Scruton (William). Early Yorkshire Journalism. ('*Leeds Mercury*' *Supplement*, 19 May, 1883.)

——— **Yorkshire Journalism in 1802.** (*The Yorkshireman*, 19 May and 2 June, 1877.)

Gent (Thomas). The Life of Thomas Gent, Printer, of York, written by himself. London, 1832.

Dobson (Austin). Thos. Gent, Printer. (*Eighteenth Century Vignettes*, Ser. III. 1896, pp. 104–133.)

Ross (Frederick). Thomas Gent, Printer, York, with a List of his Writings. (*Old Yorkshire*, ed. by Wm. Smith, vol. v. pp. 90–96. 1886.)

Clephan (James). The Early Press of York. Biblio. Notes. (*Monthly Chron. North-Country Lore and Legend*, vol. i. pp. 459–462. 1887.)

Blackett (F.). Yorkshire Typographers and the Early Press of York. [1880?) A Contribution to a Newspaper.

Yorkshire Printer-Authors. Joseph Richardson, Anthony Hewitson, and Abraham Holroyd. (*Yorkshire Bibliographer*, ed. by J. Horsfall Turner, vol. i. pp. 159–160, 181–190, 227–229. 1888.)

Holroyd (Abraham). Old Books and Old Authors of Yorks.
I. Cædmon, the Saxon Poet of Whitby, pp. 235–240.
II. Thos. Gent, Printer, of York, with a list of Books printed and published by him, pp. 411–415, 444–448. (*The Yorks. Mag.* vol. i. 1872.)

Dibdin (Thomas Frognall). Books, Booksellers, Bookbinders, etc., at York. (*Northern Tour*, 1838, vol. i. pp. 166–230.)

Wood (Butler). The Bradford Newspaper Press. (*The Bradford Antiquary*, New Ser., vol. iii. pp. 49–67. 1907.)

Scruton (William). The First Bradford Newspaper (the 'Bradford Courier'). (*The Yorkshireman*, 1 Sept. 1887.)

——— **Extinct Bradford Magazines, etc.** (*Yorkshire Bibliographer*, ed. by J. Horsfall Turner, vol. i. pp. 105–110. 1888.)

Early Bradford Printers. [A Biblio. Note on the 'Nicholsons,' by W. S.] (*The Bradford Antiquary*, New Ser., vol. iv. p. 116. 1914.)

Page (W. G. B.). Notes on Hull Authors, Booksellers, Printers, and Stationers, etc. (*Book-Auction Records*, vol. vi. pt. i. pp. i.–vii. 1908.)

List [typewritten] of Printers in Hull having been established since before 40 years ago. 1905. (In the Blades Library at the St. Bride's Foundation, London.)

YORKSHIRE (continued).

Hand (Thomas W.). The Leeds Booksellers, Printers, and Libraries. (*Book-Auction Records*, vol. viii. pt. 2, pp. xxxiii.-xxxix. 1911.)

Old Leeds Printers and Booksellers. A Catal. of Books and Pamphlets, printed in Leeds before 1800. [Announced for publication about 1879.]

Petty (W.). Leeds Printers of Fifty Years Ago. (*Federation of Master Printers' Souvenir*, 1906.)

The Private Printing Press of Sir George Reresby Sitwell at Scarborough. Several important works were printed at this press in 1889–1901.

List of Publications of John Cole of Scarborough. See 'Sale Catal. of J. Walter K. Eyton's Library of Privately Printed Books,' Sotheby's, 1848, pp. 49–50, and also John Martin's 'Biblio. Catal. of Books Privately Printed,' 1834, pp. 271–272.

Bibliotheca Coleiana, a Catal. of the Collection of Books, the Private Property of John Cole, of Scarborough, comprising illustrated copies of all works of which he is the Author, etc. Scarborough, 1829.

James Montgomery, the Poet, and his connection with Sheffield Newspapers, Printing, etc. See 'Memoirs of the Life and Writings of James Montgomery,' by John Holland and James Everett. 7 vols. London, 1854–56.

A History of the 'Sheffield Independent,' from 1819 to 1892. (Seventy-three years of Progress.) Sheffield, 1892.

Porter (W. S.). Old Sheffield Newspapers. A Lecture. (*The Hunter Archæol. Soc. Trans.*, vol. i. pp. 110–111. 1914.)

Hester (Giles). Nevill Simmons, Bookseller and Publisher. With Notices of Literature connected with Old Sheffield. London, 1893. See also 'Who was Nevill Simmons?' by Henry Jackson, in 'Notes and Queries,' 31 Jan. 1863.

A Yorkshire Magazine of the last Century. (The Yorkshire Mag. 1786.) (*The Yorkshire Mag.*, vol. i. pp. 268–270, 354–358. 1872.)

Paterson (Alexander). Yorkshire Journalism, Past and Present. Barnsley, 1901.

Taylor (Richard Vickerman). Yorkshire Novels and Novelists. Contributed to 'The Yorkshire Weekly Post.'

Halliwell-Phillipps (J. O.). The Yorkshire Anthology, a Collection of Ancient and Modern Ballads, Poems and Songs relating to the County of York. London, 1851.

Holroyd (Abraham). A Garland of Poetry; by Yorkshire Authors, or relating to Yorks., with Biog. Notes. Saltaire, 1873.

——— **A List of Yorkshire Ballads and Songs.** (*Old Yorkshire*, ed. by Wm. Smith, vol. v. pp. 99–105. 1884.)

Holroyd's Collection of Yorkshire Ballads, with some remarks on Ballad Lore, by W. J. Kaye, and a Life of Abraham Holroyd, by William Scruton. With Biog. & Biblio. Notes. Edited by Chas. F. Forshaw. London, 1892.

Turner (J. Horsfall). Yorkshire Anthology: Ballads and Songs, Ancient and Modern, covering a Period of a Thousand Years of Yorks. History in Verse, with Notes, Bibliographical, Biographical, Topographical, Dialectic, etc., and quaint & original illustrations. Bingley, 1901. Four vols. were compiled, but only one was issued.

Ingledew (C. J. Davison). The Ballads and Songs of Yorkshire, transcribed from private MSS., rare Broadsides, and scarce publications. London, 1860.

Newsam (William C.). The Poets of Yorkshire, comprising Sketches of their Lives, etc. London, 1845.

YORKSHIRE (continued).

Axon (**William E. A.**). **The Ballads and Songs of Yorkshire.** (*Manchester Literary Club. Proc.*, 1873–74, pp. 57–60.)

Grainge (**William**). **The Poets and Poetry of Yorks.**, with Biog. Notes, etc. 2 vols. Wakefield, 1868.

Andrews (**William**). **Modern Yorkshire Poets**, with Biog. & Critical Notes. Hull, 1885.

Federer (**Charles A.**). **Yorkshire Chap-Books.** First Series. London, 1889. Biblio. Notes in Introduction. Sketch of Life of Thomas Gent, pp. 10–23.

Ballads, Chapbooks, Broadsides, etc., relating to Yorkshire, 1803-67. A Collection of the Publications of J. Kendrew, of York, and others, is in the Brit. Mus. Library, 1870, c. 2.

Fowler (**Joseph Thomas**). **Biblio. Notes on 'Ballets' in Ripon Minster Library.** (*Yorks. Archæol. & Topog. Journ.*, vol. xi. pp. 200–201. 1891.)

Forshaw (**Charles F.**). **John Hartley: Poet and Author** (**Author of 'Yorkshire Ditties,' etc.**). An Appreciation. Bradford, 1909.

Rowe (**J. Hambley**). **Yorkshire Almanacks.** A Lecture before the Bradford Hist. & Antiq. Soc., 10 Feb. 1915.

Camidge (**William**). **Loyal York. Coronations and Proclamations in York, from the Days of the Romans.** 1902.

——— **Richard Naylor, the last of the Corporation Bellmen.** [1893.]

Schedule of Broadside Royal Proclamations of King Charles I., in the possession of Godfrey Wentworth, Esq., of Woolley Park, near Wakefield. 1887.

War Ballads and Broadsides of Previous Wars, 1779-1795. By H. Ling Roth and J. T. Jolley. (*Bankfield Museum Notes*, Ser. 2, no. 5. 1915.) A Selection from the Collections of F. A. Leyland, in Bankfield Museum, Halifax, mostly printed in Halifax.

Stuart (**J. A. Erskine**). **The Literary Shrines of Yorkshire—The Literary Pilgrim in the Dales.** London, 1892.

The Venerable Francis Wrangham, F.R.S., Archdeacon of the East Riding of the County of York. A Memoir, with a list of his publications, and a brief note on his Printing. [1830.] For lists of his works, mostly privately printed, see 'Sale Catal. of Lib. of Archdeacon Wrangham,' First Portion, 12 July, 1843, pp. 149–151. Second Portion, 29 Nov., 1843; pp. 151–156, and 'Dict. Nat. Biog.' art. Wrangham.

Cooper (**T. P.**). **Literary Associations of the City of York.** (*Book-Auction Records*, vol. x. pt. 3. 1913.)

Morrell (**William Wilberforce**). **A Public Library for York.** A Letter to the Lord Mayor of York. York, 1891.

Gilson (**J. P.**) **The Library of Henry Savile, of Banke.** With the Catalogue. (*Biblio. Soc. Trans.*, vol. ix. pp. 127–210. 1908.)

A List of Private Acts, etc., relating to the County of Yorkshire. Stevens and Sons. London, n.d. *circa* 1912.

Special Topographical Collections for Yorkshire are in the Public Libraries at Bradford, Brighouse, Dewsbury, Huddersfield, Leeds, Sheffield (the Jackson Collection), Wakefield, and York, also in the Dean and Chapter Library at York (the Hailstone Collection) and in the Library of the Yorks. Archæol. Soc. at Leeds. Special Local Collections are in the Public Libraries at Bradford, Dewsbury, Halifax, Leeds, Wakefield, and York.

YORKSHIRE (*continued*).

Hist. MSS. Comm. Reports. Yorkshire Collections.

Carlisle, Earl of, at Castle Howard ...	15th Rep. pp. 27–30, and App. VI.
Cathcart, Earl, at Thornton-le-Street	2nd Rep. p. x. and App. pp. 24–30.
Cooke, Mr. P. B. Davies, at Owston Hall, near Doncaster	6th Rep. p. xv. and App. pp. 418, 426.
Devonshire, Duke of, at Bolton Abbey	3rd Rep. p. xiv. and App. pp. 36–45.
Darwin, Mr. Francis, of Creskeld ...	11th Rep. p. 23, and App. VII. pp. 90–93.
Effingham, Earl of	3rd Rep. p. xv. and App. p. 223.
Fawkes, Mr. Ayscough, at Farnley Hall	7th Rep. p. xiv. and App. pp. 509–511.
Frank, Mr. F. Bacon, at Campsall Hall	5th Rep. p. x. ; 6th Rep. p. xiv. and App. pp. 448–465 ; 17th Rep. p. 188.
Graham, Sir Reginald	5th Rep. p. xi. ; 6th Rep. p. xii. and App. pp. 322–344.
Hailstone, Mr. Edward, at Walton Hall, near Wakefield	8th Rep. p. xiii. and App. pp. 636, 637.
Harford, Mrs., at Holme Hall... ...	16th Rep. p. 108 ; Various Collections, vol. ii. pp. 348–366.
Harvey, Mr. John, at Finningley Park	1st Rep. p. x. and App. pp. 62–63 ; 2nd Rep. App. pp. 89–91.
Herries, Lord, at Everingham Park ...	1st Rep. p. xi. and App. p. 45.
Ingilby, Sir Henry, at Ripley Castle ...	5th Rep. p. x. ; 6th Rep. p. xiii. and App. pp. 352–395.
Lawson, Sir John, at Brough Hall ...	3rd Rep. p. xvi. and App. pp. 255, 256 ; 4th Rep. p. xv. and App. p. 367 ; 5th Rep. p. viii. and App. pp. 305–307.
Leeds, Duke of, at Hornby Castle ...	11th Rep. pp. 11–13, and App. VII. pp. 1–58.
Meadley, Mr. Cornelius...	1st Rep. App. p. 110.
Ridgway, Mr. Matthew, of Dewsbury	4th Rep. App. p. 404.
Ripon, Marquess of, at Studley Royal	5th Rep. p. vii. and App. p. 294 ; 6th Rep. p. xi. and App. pp. 243–250.
Wentworth, Mrs., at Woolley Park ...	16th Rep. pp. 109–110; Various Collections, vol. ii. pp. 367–432.
Wilson, Sir Matthew, at Eshton Hall	3rd Rep. p. xviii. and App. pp. 293–300.
Wharncliffe, Earl of, at Belmont, Perthshire	3rd Rep. p. xvi. and App. pp. 224–226 ; 4th Rep. p. xxiii. and App. p. 518 ; 5th Rep. p. xx. and App. pp. 621, 622.
Wombwell, Sir George, at Newburgh Priory	16th Rep. pp. 103–104 ; Various Collections, vol. ii. pp. 1–226. (1903.)
Zetland, Earl of	1st Rep. p. xi. and App. p. 44.
York Corporation of	1st Rep. App. pp. 108–110.
——— Dean and Chapter of	1st Rep. App. p. 97.
——— Company of Merchant Adventurers	1st Rep. App. p. 110.
Yorkshire, Philosophical Society ...	1st Rep. App. p. 110.
——— West Riding Sessions Rolls ...	9th Rep. p. xvi. and App. I. pp. 324–329.
——— North Riding Sessions Rolls ...	9th Rep. p. xvi. and App. I. pp. 324–329.
Ampleforth, St. Lawrence's College ...	2nd Rep. p. xiii. and App. p. 109.
Beverley Corporation	16th Rep. pp. 91–93, and vol. (1900).
Pontefract Corporation	8th Rep. p. xvi. and App. pp. 269–276.

County Records, 1637, etc., with MS. Indexes, at the Court House, Northallerton, and at the County Hall, Wakefield. (*Local Records Comm. Rep.*, 1902, App. III. p. 26.)

Borough of York Records, 12th cent., etc., with MS. Index, at the Guildhall, York. (*Ibid.* App. III. p. 42.)

YORKSHIRE (*continued*).

Jeaffreson (**J. Cordy**). **MSS. of West Riding of Yorks. A List of Rolls, Registers, etc., at Wakefield, 1880.** (*Yorks. Archæol. & Topog. Journ.* vol. viii. pp. 163–174. 1884.)

—— **MSS. of the North Riding of Yorks. A List of Documents at Northallerton, 1881.** (*Ibid.* vol. viii. pp. 175–178. 1884.)

Registry of Deeds relating to the West Riding of Yorks., at Wakefield, II. and III. Anne. See S. R. Scargill-Bird, '*Guide to Documents in the Public Record Office*,' 1908, p. 23.

Registry of Deeds for the East Riding of Yorks., at Beverley, VI. Anne. (*Ibid.* p. 23.)

Registry of Deeds for the North Riding of Yorks., at Northallerton, VIII. Geo. II. (*Ibid.* p. 24.)

Report of a Committee of Solicitors in the West Riding respecting the Indexes kept at the Register Office, Wakefield. 1831.

Meek (**Ernest E.**). **Registration of Deeds and Wills. Are the Registries worth preserving?** A Paper read before the 'York Law Students' Soc.', Jan. 1884.)

A Bill for the Publick Registering of all Deeds, Wills, etc., within the North Riding. [17—].

Report of an Inspection of the Records of the Commission of Sewers for Hatfield Chase, Oct. 1913. (*Local Records Comm. Rep.*, 1914, vol. ii. pt. 2, p. 166.) See also 'The Stovin MS.' (Drainage of the Level of Hatfield Chase), by Charles Jackson, in 'Yorks. Archæol. & Topog. Journ.', vol. vii. pp. 194–238. 1882.)

Catal. of the Charters, House Books, Accounts, Freemen's Rolls, Gild Ordinances, and other Old Records and Documents belonging to the Corporation of York, together with a Report on their Renovation. Compiled by William Giles, Deputy Town Clerk, 1912.

Farrer (**William**). **Early Yorkshire Charters, being a Collection of Documents anterior to the Thirteenth Century,** made from the Public Records, Monastic Chartularies, Roger Dodsworth's MSS., and other available sources. Edinburgh, 1914–15. The work is to be in 4 vols. Vols. i. and ii. only as yet published. A List of the Charters is at the beginning of each vol., and Biblio. Note in Preface to vol. i.

Descriptive Catal. of the Charters, Rolls, Deeds, Pedigrees, Pamphlets, Newspapers, Monumental Inscriptions, Maps, and Miscellaneous Papers, forming 'The Jackson Collection,' at the Sheffield Public Reference Library. Compiled by T. Walter Hall and A. Hermann Thomas. Sheffield, 1914. Yorks. items, pp. 1–104.

Catal. of the Charters, Deeds and MSS. in the Public Reference Lib. at Sheffield, prepared by T. Walter Hall. Sheffield, 1912. App. Schedule of Deeds in the 'Leader Collection.'

Dodsworth's MS. Collections in the Bodleian Library relating to Yorks. Bodl. Lib. MSS. 4143–5105.

Collections relating to the County of York, consisting of extracts from the Dodsworth MSS., etc. By Henry Paget. Brit. Museum, Add. MS. 26737.

List of the Dodsworth MSS. in the Bodleian Library. By Samuel Margerison. (*Old Yorkshire*, ed. by Wm. Smith, vol. iii. pp. 181–185. 1882.

YORKSHIRE (continued).

Index of Persons and Places in the First Seven Volumes of the Dodsworth MSS., compiled by W. H. Turner. Privately printed for the Bodleian Lib. Oxford, 1879. This Index continued in MS. for a further portion of the Collection by W. F. Thurland.

For an account of this Collection, see Macray, 'Annals of the Bodleian,' 1890, pp. 137–139. For a Catal. of the MSS., see Bernard's 'Catalogi Librorum Manuscriptorum Angl. et Hib., 1697, pp. 187–233.

Synopsis of the Contents of the Dodsworth MSS., with an Account of Dodsworth's Life and Labours, by Joseph Hunter. (*Report of the Record Commission of* 1837.) Reprinted with two other Indexes in 1838 as a separate work.

Paver's MS. Collections in the British Museum relating to Yorks. Add. MSS. 29644–29703. 60 vols.

Brooke's MS. Collections relating to Yorks. in the College of Arms, London. MSS. I.C.B.

Warburton's MS. Collections relating to Yorks. in the British Museum. Lansd. MSS. 899–901, 908–919.

Warburton's Account of his MSS. relating to Yorkshire. Brit. Museum Lansd. MS. 1219, fol. 111.

List of MSS. relating to Yorks. in the Lansdowne Collection at the British Museum. By Samuel Margerison. (*Old Yorkshire*, ed. by Wm. Smith, vol. iii. pp. 174–181. 1882.)

Hunter's MS. Collections relating to Yorks. in the British Museum (Add. MSS. 24436–24630, 25459–25483) **and in Leeds Public Library.**

Hunter's Collections for a Hist. of South Yorkshire; in the Brit. Museum, Add. MS. 24439.

A Brief Memoir of the late Joseph Hunter, F.S.A., with a Descriptive Catal. of his principal separate Publications, and Contributions to the 'Archaeologia.' [By Sylvester Hunter.] Privately Printed. London, 1861.

Joseph Hunter, F.S.A., the Historian of Hallamshire, with a List of his Principal Works and MS. Collections. (*The Hunter Archæol. Soc., Trans.* vol. i. pp. 12–17. 1914.)

List of MSS. relating to Yorks. in the Cottonian Collection at the British Museum. By Samuel Margerison. (*Old Yorkshire*, ed. by Wm. Smith, vol. iv. pp. 244–250. 1883.)

List of MSS. relating to Yorks. among the Harleian MSS. in the British Museum. By Samuel Margerison. (*Ibid.* vol. ii. pp. 174–183. 1881.)

List of Yorkshire MSS. in various places. By Richard Vickerman Taylor. (*Ibid.* vol. ii. pp. 183–184. 1881.)

Collections relating to Yorks., by Charles Devon. Brit. Mus. Add. MSS 24831–24833.

Torr's Yorkshire Collections at York, made between 1670 and 1687 from the Archbishops' Registers. (In Custody of the Dean and Chapter at the Minster Lib., York.)

A Catal. of James Torr's MSS. relating to the Hist. and Antiquities of Yorks. Brit. Museum, Lansd. MS. 889.

Burton Constable MSS. A Collection of MSS. illustrating the various Branches of the Hist. of Yorks. from 1066 to 1760, collected by John Burton, M.D., Author of 'Monasticon Eboracense.' 42 vols.

For a list of this Collection, see pp. 10–12 of the 'Sale Catal. of the Burton Constable MSS.,' collected by William Constable. Sold by Sotheby's, 24–26 June 1889, and see also List of the Contents of vols. in Gough's 'Brit. Topography,' vol. ii. 1780, pp. 408–416. For other Yorks. MSS. see pp. 59–62. For 'Memoir of John Burton' (b. 1710, d. 1771), by Robert Davies, see 'Yorks. Archæol. & Topog. Journ.,' vol. ii. pp. 403–440. 1873.

YORKSHIRE (*continued*).

Walker Collection of Genealogical, Antiquarian and Historical MSS. relating to Yorks., compiled, or collected, by Edward Johnston Walker, of Halifax. 60 vols. For a list, see 'Sale Catal. of the Lib. of John Stansfeld, of Leeds,' 1898, *ante* p. 294.

Hunter (Joseph). A Memoir of the Collection of Charters, and other Documentary Matters, illustrative of the Topography and History of England, but especially of the County of York, made by John Wilson, of Bromhead, between 1735 and 1783, also a Schedule of the Deeds which relate to the Estate of Bromhead and to the Wilsons. With a Prefatory Letter to Wilson's Yorks. Deeds, 1843. See 'A Memoir of the Wilsons of Bromhead,' by the Rev. Joseph Hunter, 1824, in 'Yorks. Archæol. & Topog. Journ.,' vol. v. pp. 64–68, 111–125. 1879. See also Wilson's Yorkshire Deeds, in the Brit. Museum, Add. MS. 24467.

M'Call (Hardy Bertram). Calendar of the Historical MSS. of R. H. Prior-Wandesforde, Esq., preserved at Castlecomer House, co. Kilkenny, in 'Story of the Wandesforde Family, of Kirklington and Castlecomer.' London. 1904. App. Pt. I. pp. 171–330. (Mostly Yorks. Deeds.)

A Mediæval Index (in Custody of the Dean and Chapter) **of the Charters and Muniments of the Dean and Chapter of York.** For Hist. MSS. Comm. Report on the Dean and Chapter Records, see *ante* p. 300.

Raine (James). The Historians of the Church of York and its Archbishops. 3 vols. (*Chronicles and Memorials of Great Britain.*) London, 1879–94. Biblio. Notes in Prefaces to vols. i. & ii.

The Records of the Northern Convocation, edited by the Dean of Durham. (*Surtees Soc. Pubns.*, vol. cxiii. 1907.) Report on the Convocation Records of the Province of York, by the Rev. W. D. Macray, App. pp. ciii.–cv.

Botfield (Beriah). Notes on the Cathedral Libraries of England. 1849. **York,** pp. 502–527.

Taylor (Richard Vickerman). List of Old Yorkshire Church Registers, in chronological order. (*Old Yorkshire*, ed. by Wm. Smith, vol. iii. pp. 188–190. 1882.)

Norcliffe (Charles Best). Lists of East Riding, North Riding, & West Riding Registers. (*Ibid.* vol. v. pp. 247–250. 1884.)

James (Montague R.). The Catal. of the Library of the Augustinian Friars at York, now first edited from the MS. at Trinity Coll. Dublin. (*John Willis Clark Memorial Volume*, Cambridge, 1909, pp. 2–96.)

Brode (T. Ainsworth). The Old Parish Account Books of St. John the Evangelist, York. (*Assoc. Archit. Soc. Reports & Papers*, pp. 304–322. 1907.)

Stevenson (W. H.). Yorkshire Surveys and other Eleventh-Century Documents in the York Gospels. (*The English Hist. Rev.*, vol. xxvii. pp. 1–25. 1912.)

Dale (Bryan). Non-Parochial Registers in Yorks. (*The Bradford Antiquary*, New Ser. vol. i. pp. 447–469. 1900.) Also in 'Congregational Hist. Soc. Trans.,' vol. i. pp. 5–25. 1901.

Macklin (Herbert Walter). Monumental Brasses. London: Geo. Allen & Co., 1913. Biblio. Note on Yorks. Brasses, with a List, pp. 142, 188–190.)

Churchyard Inscriptions in Yorkshire. List of Transcriptions and where to be found. (A Leaflet.) Yorks. Archæol. Soc. 1913.

Yorks. Monumental Inscriptions. A List of 84 Transcripts Printed and in MS. (*The Register of English Monumental Inscriptions*, vol. ii. pp. 89–93. 1914.) Compiled by T. W. Oswald-Hicks from the preceding List.

YORKSHIRE (continued).

Hist. of the Yorks. Geol. & Polytechnic Soc., 1837-87, with Biog. Notices of some of its Members, by James W. Davis. (*Yorks. Geol. & Poly. Soc. Proc.* vol. x. 1889.)

Classified Index of the Proceedings of the Yorks. Geol. & Poly. Soc., vols. i.-xiv. 1839-1902, by W. Lower Carter. (*Ibid.* vol. xv. pp. 96-153. 1903.)

Classified Index of the Transactions of the Leeds Geol. Assoc., vols. i.-xiv. 1883-1908. (*Trans. of the Soc.*, vol. xiv. pp. 59-67. 1908.)

Sheppard (Thomas). List of Papers referring to the Geology, etc., of the East of Yorks. and North Lincolnshire, which have been published during 1895-1898. (*Hull Geol. Soc. Trans.*, vol. iii. pp. 25-27; vol. iv. pp. 37-39; vol. v. pp. 27-28. 1895-1900.)

—— **Biblio. of Papers and Records published with respect to the Geology and Palæontology of the North of England, 1902-1908.** (*Yorks. Naturalists' Union. Trans.*, 1908.) Lists for 1884 to 1901 appeared in 'The Naturalist,' for 1885 to 1903.

—— **List of Papers, Maps, etc., relating to the Erosion of the Holderness Coast, and to changes in the Humber Estuary.** (*Hull Geol. Soc. Trans.*, vol. vi. pp. 43-57. 1906.)

Strangways (C. Fox-). Biblio. of Yorks. Geology, 1534-1914. (C. Fox-Strangways Memorial volume.) Edited by Thomas Sheppard, with considerable additions. (*Yorks. Geol. and Poly. Soc. Proc.*, vol. xviii. 1915.)

Davis (James William). Summary of Geological Literature relating to Yorks. (*Ibid.* vols. vi.-ix., xi., xii. 1874-90.)

List of Memoirs, Papers, etc., by James William Davis [principally on Yorks. Geology]. See Obituary Notice in 'Yorks. Geol. & Poly. Soc. Proc.' vol. xii. pp. 319-334. 1894.

List of Memoirs and Papers by Dr. W. Crawford Williamson (a Yorks. Naturalist), b. 1816, d. 1896. See Obituary Notice in 'Yorks. Geol. & Poly. Soc. Proc.,' vol. xiii. pp. 95-111. 1895.

Harker (Alfred). List of the Principal Publications dealing with the Petrology of the English Lake District. (*Yorks. Geol. & Poly. Soc. Proc.*, vol. xiv. pp. 494-496. 1902.)

Cuttriss (S. W.). The Yorkshire Caves. Biblio. 1781-1903. (*Ibid.* vol. xv. pp. 293-304. 1904.)

Whitaker (William). Biblio. of Yorks. Geology. (*Illustrations of the Geology of Yorks.*, by John Phillips and R. Etheridge, 1875.)

Davis (James W.) and Lees (F. A.). Biblio. on Geology and Physical Geography of West Yorks. (*Physical Geography & Botanical Topography of West Yorks.* 1880.) See also the same compilers' Biblio. (1674-1876) in 'West Yorkshire, an account of its Geology, etc.,' 1878, pp. xiii.-xl.

Marr (John Edward) and Tiddemann (R. H.). Biblio. of the Geology of the West of Yorkshire.) (*Geology*, 1891.)

Reid (Clement). Biblio. of the Geology of Holderness. (*Memoirs of the Geol. Survey of England & Wales*, 1885, pp. 163-170.)

Biblio. of Geology of Sheffield and District. (*Brit. Assoc. Handbook and Guide to Sheffield*, 1910, pp. 399-404.)

Trimen (Henry). Botanical Biblio. of the British Counties. Yorks. (*Journ. of Botany*, vol. xii. p. 180. 1874.)

YORKSHIRE (continued).

Baker (John Gilbert). List of Authorities for details of the Topography of Plants in 'North Yorkshire; Studies in its Botany, Geology, etc.' 1863. App. B. pp. 341–344.

Robinson (James Fraser). Biblio. of the Flora of the East Riding, in 'The Flora of the East Riding of Yorkshire.' London, 1902. Biblio. Notes in Introduction, and a List at pp. 55–56.

Lees (Frederick A.) Biblio. of West Yorkshire Botany, 1548–1885, in 'The Flora of West Yorkshire,' 1888, pp. 85–100, 815–818. (Yorks. Naturalists' Union.)

Nelson (T. H.). The Birds of Yorks. 2 vols. London, 1907. Biblio., vol. ii., pp. 776–777.

Christy (Miller). Biblio. Note on Yorks. Birds. (*The Zoologist*, Ser. 3, vol. xiv. p. 261, 1890; and reprinted in pamph., 1891, p. 26). **Mammals.** (*The Zoologist*, Ser. 3, vol. xvii. p. 186, 1893.) **Reptiles.** (*Ibid.* p. 248, 1893.) **Fishes.** (*Ibid.* p. 259. 1893.)

Anderson (John P.). Book of Brit. Topo., 1881. Yorks., pp. 308–333.
Gatfield (George). Guide to Heraldry. 1892. Yorks., pp. 191–199.
Sims (Richard). Manual. 1861. Yorks., pp. 176, 225–226, 241.
Upcott (William). English Topo., 1818. Yorks., vol. iii. pp. 1351–1426, 1500.
Smith (Alfred Russell). Catal. of Topo. Tracts, etc. 1878. Yorks., pp. 416–436, 481–482.
Gough (Richard). Brit. Topo., 1780. Yorks., vol. ii. pp. 395–478.
Bandinel (Bulkeley). Catal. of Books bequeathed to Bodleian Lib. by Richard Gough, 1814. Yorks., pp. 320–329.

ACKWORTH.

Nodal (John Howard). The Biblio., Biography, and Topography of Ackworth School. Manchester, 1889.

AGBRIGG.

Raine (James). On the Materials for the Topography of the Wapentake of Agbrigg. (*Yorks. Archæol. & Topog. Journ.*, vol. i. pp. 13–23. 1870.)

Hopkinson (John). MS. Collections for the Hist. of Agbrigg, at Eshton Hall, and at the Brit. Museum (from Heath Hall).

ALDBOROUGH.

Lyell (Arthur H.). Biblio. of Roman Remains at Aldborough. (*Biblio. List of Romano-British Remains*, 1912, p. 132.)

BARNSLEY.

Biblio. of Barnsley Literature. In preparation. To be issued by the Barnsley Public Lib. Committee.

BEVERLEY.

Corporation Records. See *ante* Hist. MSS. Comm. Reports, p. 300.

Catal. of a Selection from the Muniments of the Corporation of Beverley. (*The Yorks. County Mag.* vol. i. pp. 316–317. 1891.) See also 'Beverley Town Documents,' ed. by Arthur F. Leach. Selden Soc. Pubn., vol. xiv. London. 1900.

Brown (William). Documents from the Record Office relating to Beverley. (*East Riding Antiq. Soc.*, vol. v. pp. 35–49.)

YORKSHIRE (*continued*).

Printed and MS. Collections relating to Beverley, including a memoranda of Books and MSS. Brit. Mus. Lansd. MS. 896.

Collection of MS. and Printed Matter relating to Beverley. 20 vols. See 'Catal. of Lib. of Edward Hailstone,' Second Portion. Sold by Sotheby's 23 April, 1891, p. 22.

BRADFORD.

Dickons (James Norton). A Catal. of Books, Pamphlets, etc., published at Bradford. Privately Printed. Bradford, 1895.

The Appendix contains Lists of Acts of Parliament, Corporation Reports and Papers, Hymn Books published at Bradford, Magazines and Newspapers, Reports of various Institutions, List of Hailstone MSS., etc. Biblio. Notes on Bradford Printers and Printing, Booksellers, Newspapers, etc., in Prefatory Note.

Empsall (T. T.) and Federer (C. A.). Biblio. of Bradford and Neighbourhood, being a List of Books, Pamphlets, etc., by Authors, natives of or connected with the District. (*The Bradford Antiquary*, vol. i. pp. 39–44, 98–101, 154–159, 204–209, 279–284; vol. ii. pp. 9–14, 102–105, 148–155, 229–234, 256–259. 1881–95.)

List of MSS. relating to Bradford and District formed by Samuel Hailstone, purchased at the Edward Hailstone Sale, and presented to the Bradford Free Lib. See Dickons. Catal. of Books, etc., pp. 222–223.

Catal. of the Books, MSS., etc., belonging to the Bradford Historical and Antiquarian Soc. Bradford, 1886. One of the aims of the Soc. is the acquirement and conservation of Local Documents, Books, Plans, Genealogical Charts, etc.

Bradford Books, etc., in the Bradford Public Lib. See 'Catal. of the Books and Pamphlets relating to Yorks., in the Central Reference Lib.,' 1892, pp. 5–17. A Collection of Books, Prints, and MSS. was bequeathed by J. Norton Dickons to the Library. It is rich in Civil War Tracts, and Books, etc., relating to Yorks. Topography.

An Account of the Bolling Hall Museum, Bradford. (*The Museums Journ.*, vol. xv. pp. 157–161. 1915.) Broadsides, Portraits, Maps, Bookplates, Documents, etc., relating to Bradford are among the Objects exhibited.

Speight (Harry). The Bradford Manor Court Rolls. (*The Bradford Antiquary*, New Ser. vol. iii. pp. 185–199. 1909.)

Federer (Charles A.). Yorkshire Bibliography.—William Scoresby, Jun., 1789–1857. 1887. A complete account of Scoresby's writings, whether published at Bradford or elsewhere, with a List.

—— **William Cudworth. Obituary Notice and Biblio.** (*The Bradford Antiquary*, New Ser. vol. iii. pp. 94–95. 1907.)

Bailey (Samuel Oldfield). Plans of Bradford, with additions by the Editor. (*The Bradford Antiquary*, New Ser. vol. ii. pp. 225–231. 1903.) See also 'An Old Bradford Plan,' by W. Scruton, in vol. iii. p. 368. 1911.

BRETTON.

Hunter (Joseph). Catal. of the Library of the Priory of Bretton. 1831.

DARLINGTON.

Borough Records, at the Town Hall, Darlington. (*Local Records Comm. Rep.*, 1902, App. III. p. 52.)

YORKSHIRE (continued).

DONCASTER.

Borough Records, 1194, etc., at the Mansion House, Doncaster. (*Local Records Comm. Rep.*. 1902, App. III. p. 54.)

A Calendar to the Records of the Borough of Doncaster. 4 vols. 1899–1903.

ECCLESFIELD.

Collections for a Hist. of the Parish of Ecclesfield, by Joseph Hunter, Brit. Mus. Add. MS. 24438.

Freemantle (William Thomas). The Rev. Alfred Gatty, D.D. (Vicar of Ecclesfield). A Biblio. (*The Hunter Archæol. Soc. Trans.*, vol. i. pp. 81–83, 1914.)

ESHTON.

Catal. of the Library Collected by Miss Frances Mary Richardson Currer, at Eshton Hall, Craven, Yorks., by C. J. Stewart. Privately Printed. The principal portion of the Library was sold by Sotheby's, 30 July, 1862.

HALIFAX.

Turner (J. Horsfall). Halifax Books and Authors. A Series of Articles on the Books written by Natives and Residents, Ancient and Modern, of the Parish of Halifax, with Notices of their Authors and of the Local Printers, etc. Reprinted from the 'Brighouse News.' Privately Printed. Bradford, 1906.

Crossland (Charles). Halifax Bibliography and Authors. (*Halifax Antiq, Soc. Papers*, 1909, pp. 317–346; 1910, pp. 273–295; 1911, pp. 253–268; 1912, pp. 25–72; 1913, pp. 45–75; 1914, pp. 23–60.)

Catal. of Books, etc., of the Halifax Antiquarian Soc. (*Ibid.* 1904–05, pp. 149–150.)

Savage (Henry Edwin), Dean of Lichfield. Some Local Gleanings from the Bookstalls. [With Biblio. Notes.] (*Ibid.* 1912, pp. 201-214.)

Hanson (T. W.). 'Edwards of Halifax.' A Family of Booksellers, Collectors, and Bookbinders. (*Ibid.* 1912, pp. 141–200.)

Rouse (E. P.). Old Halifax Circulating Library, 1768–1866. (*Ibid.* 1911, pp. 45–59.)

Hanson (T. W.). John Brearcliffe, the Antiquary. (*Ibid.* 1907, pp. 213–243; 1908, pp. 321–348.)

Walker Collection of Genealogical, Antiquarian and Historical MSS. relating to Halifax. See *ante* p. 303.

Walker (Walter James). Chapters on the Early Registers of Halifax Parish Church, from the local archæological Collection of Edward Johnston Walker, with Biblio. Notes on the Histories of Halifax. 1885.

Murray (David). Biblio. Note on Halifax Museums. ('*Museums*,' Glasgow, 1904, vol. ii. p. 275.)

Exhibitions of Books, Pictures, Prints, and Curios of Local Antiquarian Interest, by the Halifax Antiq. Soc. in 1904 & 1905. (*Halifax Antiq. Soc. Papers*, 1904–05, pp. 1–2, 151–156.)

Cox (J. L.) Halifax Directories. (*Ibid.* 1914, pp. 271–282.)

HOLDERNESS.

Holmes (L.). Alphabetical List of Parish Registers in the Seigniory of Holderness. (*Old Yorkshire*, ed. by Wm. Smith, vol. iv. p. 255. 1883.)

YORKSHIRE (continued).

HUDDERSFIELD.

Borough Records, at Town Hall, Huddersfield. (*Local Records Comm. Rep.*, 1902, App. III. p. 44.)

HULL.

Boulter (W. Consitt). Hull Bibliography. A few pages only issued as a specimen. For a reference to this work, see 'Yorkshire Bibliographer,' ed. by J. Horsfall Turner, vol. i. p. 13. 1888.

Page (William G. B.). Biblio. of Hull. A Catal. of Books, Pamphlets, Music, and articles by Local Authors, for the years 1880–1881, 1887, 1888, and 1889. Reprinted from the 'Weekly Express.' Hull, 1883–91.

The Biblio. was only issued for the above years, the one for 1887 appeared in 'The Hull and East Riding Portfolio.' The compiler intends to continue the Biblio. to date. For 'Notes on Hull Authors, etc.,' see *ante* p. 297.

Catal. of Hull Books and Pamphlets in the Wilberforce Historical Museum at Hull. [Nearly ready for publication.]

Frost (Charles). Address to the Literary & Philos. Society at Hull (comprising a Literary Hist. of the Town). Hull, 1831.

Corlass (Reginald W.). Sketches of Hull Authors. Hull, 1879.

Kingston-on-Hull. Borough Records, Edw. I., etc., with MS. Index, at the Town Hall, Hull. (*Local Records Comm. Rep.*, 1902, App. III. p. 34.) 'Charters and Letters Patent granted to Kingston-upon-Hull,' translated by John Roberts Boyle, was printed for the Corporation in 1905.

Woolley (William). A Collection of Statutes relating to the Town of Kingston-upon-Hull, the County of the same town, and the parish of Sculcoates, with a Chronological Table of Acts of Parliament, from the earliest period to the end of the reign of Geo. IV. London, 1830.

Collections relating to the Hist. and Antiquities of the Town of Kingston-upon-Hull. Brit. Museum. Lansd. MSS., 890, 891.

Cook (John). Ancient Hull Deeds. (*Old Yorkshire*, ed. by Wm. Smith, vol. v. pp. 242–247. 1884.)

Index and Notes of Searches relating to Kingston-on-Hull. Brit. Museum, Add. MS. 21343.

Murray (David). Biblio. Note on Hull Museum. ('*Museums*,' Glasgow, 1904, vol. ii. p. 293.)

Sheppard (Thomas). The Evolution of Kingston-upon-Hull, as shewn by its Plans. (A List of Plans, Views, etc., with descriptive notes.) Published for the Hull Corporation. 1911.

Some Old Plans of Kingston-upon-Hull. (*The Hull Quarterly*, ed. by W. G. B. Page, vol. ii. pp. 169–170. 1885.)

ILKLEY.

Collyer (Rev. Robert) and Turner (J. Horsfall). Biblio. of Ilkley, and Ben Rhydding, in 'Ilkley: Ancient and Modern.' Otley, 1885, pp. 277–282.

Murray (David). Biblio. Note on Ilkley Museum. ('*Museums*,' Glasgow, 1904, vol. ii. p. 296.)

KIRKBY MALHAM.

Index Transcript of the Register of Kirkby Malham. (Presented to the Bradford Public Library, by Rev. Edward Cookson, of Ipswich.)

YORKSHIRE (continued).

KIRKLEES.

A Catal. of the Muniments at Kirklees [1200-1800] in the possession of Sir George J. Armytage. Privately Printed. London, 1900.

KIRKSTALL.

Stansfeld (John). List of Charters and other Documents relating to Kirkstall Abbey now in the Brit. Museum. (*Thoresby Soc. Pubns.*, vol. ii. pp. 19-21. 1891.)

KNARESBOROUGH.

Parkinson (Thomas). Lays and Leaves of the Forest. A Collection of Poems, and Historical, Genealogical, and Biographical Essays and Sketches relating chiefly to men and things connected with the Royal Forest of Knaresborough. 1882.

Watson (Eric R.). Biblio. of the Trial of Eugene Aram, in 'Eugene Aram, his Life and Trial,' 1913. App. VI. pp. 207–219. Biblio. Notes in Chap. I. For descriptions of Eugene Aram relics exhibited at the 'Greenland Fishery Museum,' King's Lynn, see 'Guide to the Museum,' 1912, pp. 37–40.

LEEDS.

Extracts from the 'Leeds Mercury,' 1721-1729. (*Thoresby Soc. Pubns.*, vol. xxii. pp. 183–233. 1913.)

Wilson (Edmund). Two Old Plans of Leeds. (*Ibid.* vol. ix. pp. 196–204. 1899.) See also 'A "Waterloo" Map of Leeds,' by E. Wilson, in vol. xi. pp. 281–288. 1904.

Ford (John Rawlinson). Plan of Leeds, 1806. (*Ibid.* vol. xi. pp. 130-136, 1904.) See also 'Map of Leeds, 1781,' by Frank Gott, in vol. xv. pp. 46-47. 1909; and 'Thorp's Map of Leeds, 1819-21,' in vol. xv. p. 152. 1909.

The Early Years of the Leeds Library (the first Subscription Library in Leeds). Printed for the Editor. Leeds, 1879.

MS. Collections relating to Leeds. Brit. Museum, Add. MS. 33770.

Atkinson (D. H.). Ralph Thoresby, the Topographer, his Town and Times. 2 vols. Leeds, 1885.

Musæum Thoresbyanum; or, a Catal. of the Antiquities, and of the Natural and Artificial Rarities preserved in the Repository of Ralph Thoresby, at Leeds, 1712 (including a Cat. of the MSS., Printed Books, etc.). Appended to Thoresby's 'Ducatus Leodiensis.' Second Edn. 1816. Edited by T. D. Whitaker.

Murray (David). Biblio. Notes on Ralph Thoresby's Museum, Leeds. ('*Museums*,' Glasgow, 1904, vol. iii. p. 211. **Biblio. Note on Leeds Museum.** (*Ibid.* vol. ii. p. 320.)

PONTEFRACT.

Corporation Records. See *ante* Hist. MSS. Comm. Reports.

List of Pontefract Municipal Records Printed. (*Notes and Queries*, Ser. 11, vol. v. p. 478. 1912.)

PUDSEY.

Rayner (Simeon). Biblio. of Books, Pamphlets, etc., relating to Pudsey, including those issued from the Pudsey Press, in 'The Hist. and Antiquities of Pudsey,' pp. 177–184. Edited, with a Memoir of Rayner, by William Smith. London, 1887.

YORKSHIRE (continued).

RICHMOND.

Borough Records, 16th cent., etc., with MS. List, at Richmond. (*Local Records Comm. Rep.*, 1902, App. III. p. 68.)

RIPON.

Borough Records, at Town Hall, Ripon. (*Local Records Comm. Rep.*, 1902, App. III. p. 68.)

Ripon Cathedral Records, 14th cent., etc., with MS. Catal., at Ripon. (*Ibid.* 1902, App. III. p. 114.)

Fowler (Joseph Thomas). Ripon Minster Library and its Founder. (Dean Antony Higgin), with a List of MSS., Printed Books, Ballads, Broadsides, etc. (*Yorks. Archæol. & Topog. Journ.*, vol. ii. pp. 371–402. 1873.)

Botfield (Beriah). Notes on the Cathedral Libraries of England. 1849. **Ripon**, pp. 384–389.

Ripon Millenary, a Record of the Festival, also a Hist. of the City arranged under its Wakemen and Mayors from the year 1400. Ripon, 1892. Exhibition of Antiquities, etc., pp. 44–45.

ROCHDALE.

Records in Public and Private Custody. (*Local Records Comm. Rep.*, 1902, App. III. p. 138.)

SCARBOROUGH.

Baker (J. B.). Biblio. of Scarborough, in 'Hist. of Scarborough,' 1882, pp. 518–520.

A Catal. of Charters, Corporate Transactions, Letters, Records, and other Documents, in the possession of the Corporation of Scarborough. 1893.

Murray (David). Biblio. Note on Scarborough Museum. ('*Museums*,' Glasgow, 1904, vol. iii. p. 162.)

SHEFFIELD.

Freemantle (William Thomas). A Biblio. of Sheffield and Vicinity, Section I. to the end of 1700. Sheffield, 1911. Section II. is intended to cover 1701–1800 inclusive. See also 'Lib. Assoc. Record,' vol. xi. pp. 435–455, 1909, for a Paper on 'Our Local Bibliography,' by W. T. Freemantle.

Curtis (E.) A Short Biblio. of the Hist. of Sheffield. (*Historical Assoc. Leaflet*, No. 25, June, 1911.)

Catal. of the Sheffield Central Library, 1890. **List of Books and Pamphlets relating to the Hist. of Sheffield,** in Parts III. and IV.

Derry (John). The Story of Sheffield. London, 1915. The Writers of Sheffield History, pp. 173–183. Notes on Sheffield Museums, Libraries, etc., pp. 271–284.

MS. Collections in Sheffield Public Reference Lib. See *ante* p. 301.

The 'Jackson Collection' of Books, Charters, etc., relating to Sheffield, in the Public Ref. Library, Sheffield. See *ante* p. 301. 'Descriptive Catal. of the Charters,' etc., by T. W. Hall and A. H. Thomas.

A Catal. of the Ancient Charters belonging to the Twelve Capital Burgesses and Commonalty of the Town and Parish of Sheffield, 1297-1554. By T. Walter Hall. Sheffield, 1913.

YORKSHIRE (continued)

Collections for a Hist. of Sheffield, by Joseph Hunter. Brit. Museum, Add. MSS. 24437, 24440.

Murray (David). Biblio. Note on Sheffield Museums. ('*Museums*,' Glasgow, 1904, vol. iii. pp. 173–174.)

SWINE.

Duckett (Sir George). Charters of the Priory of Swine in Holderness [among the Rawlinson MSS. in the Bodleian], with a list of some in the Dodsworth Collection. (*Yorks. Archæol. & Topog. Journ.*, vol. vi. pp. 113–124. 1881.)

TODMORDEN.

Holden (Joshua). Township Records in the Todmorden District. (*Halifax Antiq. Soc. Papers*, 1908, pp. 1–22.)

WAKEFIELD.

Federer (Charles A.). Catal. of the Lib. of Wakefield Books in the possession of Charles Skidmore, of the Inner Temple [now at the City Library, Wakefield]. Privately Printed, 1897.

Borough Records, at Town Hall, Wakefield. (*Local Records Comm. Report*, 1902, App. III. p. 72.)

WHITBY.

Smales (Gideon). Whitby Authors and their Publications, with the titles of all the Books printed in Whitby, A.D. 670–1867. Whitby, 1867.

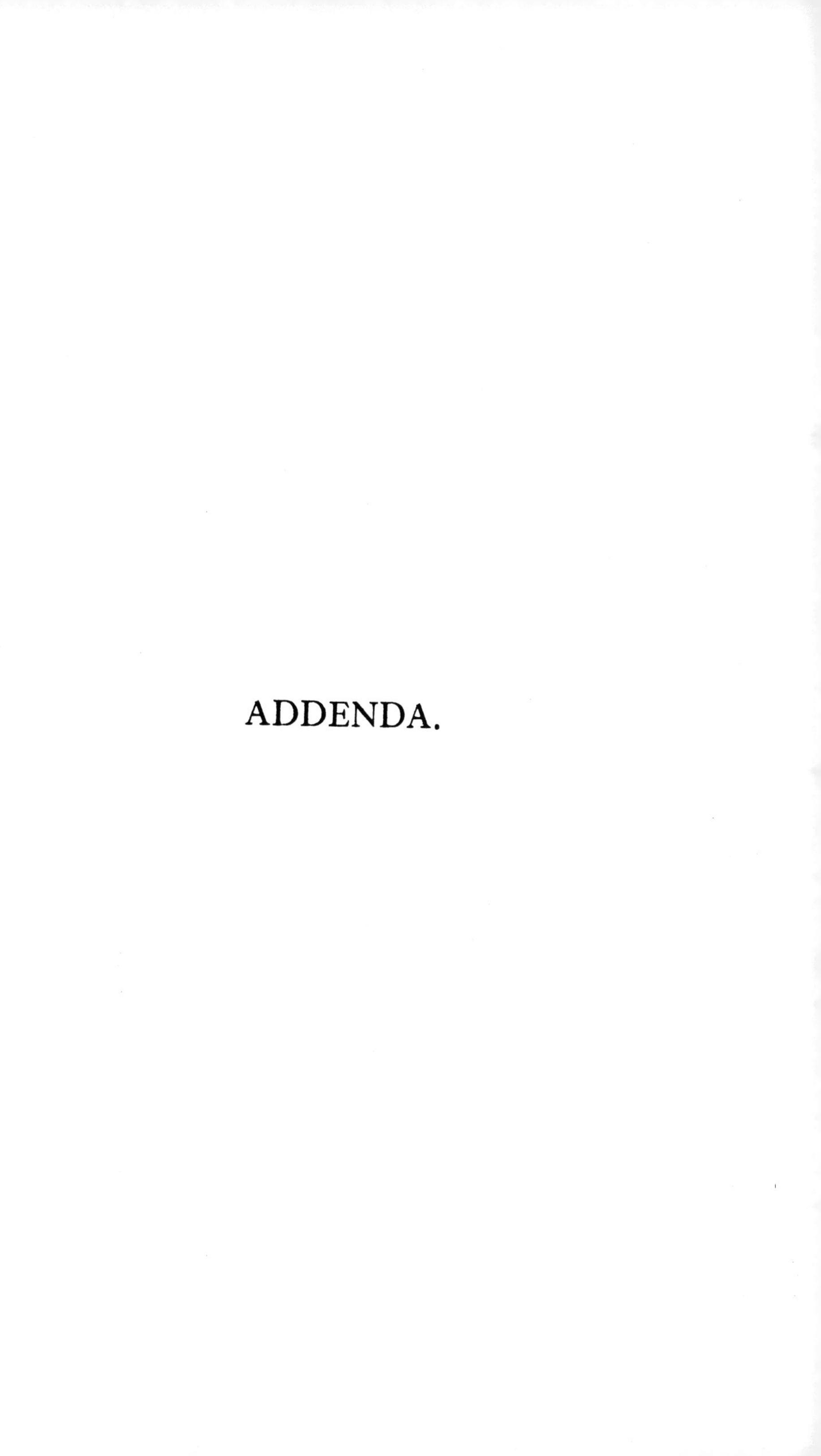

ADDENDA.

ADDENDA.

ABERDEENSHIRE.

Johnstone (James Fowler Kellas). A Concise Biblio. of the Hist., Topography, and Institutions of the Shires of Aberdeen, Banff, and Kincardine. (*Aberdeen Univ. Studies*, No. LXVI.) 1914. First published in 'Aberdeen Univ. Lib. Bull.,' vols. i. & ii. 1913–14.

Thomson (James B.). Biblio. of Aberdeen. Kincardine, and Banff, 1912. ('*Aberdeen Journal' Notes & Queries*, vol. vi. pp. 68–71, 74–77. 1913.) A continuation of entry on p. 2.

Aberdeen Public Library. Catal. of Local Collection to be found in the Reference Department. Edited by G. M. Fraser. Aberdeen, 1914.

Anderson (Peter John). Aberdeen Friars, Red, Black, White, Grey. A Preliminary Calendar of illustrative Documents, with a List of 'Accounts in Print of Scottish Friars,' 1622–1909. (Univ. of Aberdeen Studies, No. XL.) Aberdeen, 1909.

Inventory of Charters relating to the Blackfriars in Aberdeen. (*Scottish Notes & Queries*, vol. vii. pp. 120–121, 134–136. 1894.)

Walker (George). Aberdeen Bibliographer's Manual. (Articles contributed to 'Aberdeen Herald,' 20 Nov. 1858 to 26 Mar. 1859.) Aberdeen, 1859.

—— **Aberdeen Awa', Sketches of its Men, Manners, and Customs, as delineated in Brown's Book-Stall, 1892–94.** Aberdeen, 1897. Biblio. Notes on Aberdeen Printers, Booksellers, Publishers, Book-Sales, etc. *passim.*

—— **The Bards of Bon-Accord, 1375–1860.** Aberdeen, 1887. A Biblio. of Local Poetry to 1860 is appended to the work. A few copies were separately printed.

Leask (W. Keith). The Story of the University Magazine, 1836–1914, with Biblio. notes on Aberdeen and other University Magazines. (*Aberdeen Univ. Rev.*, vol. ii. pp. 1–20. 1914.)

Johnstone (J. F. Kellas). The Lost Aberdeen Theses, with lists. (*Aberdeen Univ. Lib. Bulletin*, vol. ii. pp. 739–751. 1915.)

The 'Aberdeen Journal,' 1748–1897. Our 150th Year. A unique Journalistic Record. (From the 'Aberdeen Journal,' 5 Jan. 1897.) Aberdeen, 1897.

Anderson (Peter John). Aberdeen References in the Privy Seal Register, 1498–1707. (*Scottish Notes & Queries*, Ser. 2, vol. v. pp. 101–103, 114–117. 1904.)

Bulloch (John Malcolm). Biblio. and Iconography of all the Battalions, etc., of the Gordon Highlanders, 1794–1914, in 'Territorial Soldiering in the North-East of Scotland during 1759–1814,' pp. 397–441. New Spalding Club. Aberdeen, 1914.

—— **An Ideal for the University Library.** (*Aberdeen Univ. Lib. Bulletin*, vol. i. pp. 249–256. 1912.)

Ballads Old and New, of Local and General Interest. Aberdeen, 1886.

The Ballad Book. (With a Biographia Leslyana, or Life of Charles Lesley, the Aberdeen Ballad-monger.) Edinburgh, 1827.

Fraser (G. M.). Aberdeen Maps and Views. A List. (*Scottish Notes & Queries*, Ser. 2, vol. vii. pp. 25, 41, 69. 1905.)

ABERDEENSHIRE (continued).

Anderson (Peter John). MS. Maps of Aberdeen in the Brit. Museum. A List. (*Scottish Notes & Queries*, Ser. 2, vol. vi. pp. 186–187. 1905.)

Aberdeen Almanacks. An extract from J. F. K. Johnstone's 'Concise Biblio. of Aberdeen, etc.' (*Aberdeen Book Lover*, vol. i. pp. 21–22. 1913.)

PETERHEAD.

Taylor (William L.). Biblio. of Peterhead Literature, 1593–1900, also Presidential Address on '**Peterhead Literature during the 19th cent.**' (*Buchan Field Club. Trans.*, vol. vi. 1901.)

The Book of Buchan, a Scientific Treatise, in Six Sections, on the Natural History of Buchan, Prehistoric Man in Aberdeenshire, and the Hist. of the North-East in Ancient, Medieval and Modern Times, by Twenty-nine Contributors, edited and arranged by J. F. Tocher. Peterhead. The Buchan Club, 1910. Bibliographies are appended to each Section, at pp. 58, 96, 130, 246, 348, 443. Among the Chapter headings are the following :—

Men of Literature in the North-East during tbe Stuart Period, by James Middleton, pp. 209-227.

The Traditional Minstrelsy of Buchan (with lists of Ballads), by Gavin Greig, pp. 228-245.

Men of Literature in the North-East in Modern Times, by James Middleton, pp. 377-387.

Catal. of the Private Library of Peter Buchan, consisting of rare and curious Books and unpublished MSS., chiefly old Scottish Poetry, History, Antiquities, etc. To be sold 13 Apr. 1837 at William Smith's Sale-Rooms, Aberdeen. Aberdeen, 1837. (Contains some scarce Aberdeen items.)

Fairley (John A.). Biblio. of the Works of Peter Buchan. (*Buchan Field Club. Trans.*, vol. vii. 1903.)

Buchan (Peter). Gleanings of Scotch, English, and Irish Scarce Old Ballads, many of them connected with Aberdeenshire. Peterhead, 1825.

ANGLESEY.

List of Anglesey Illustrations in the 'Archæologia Cambrensis,' 1884–1900. See Alphabetical Index to 'Archæol. Camb.,' 1884–1900, by Francis Green, p. 97.

ANTRIM.

Crone (John S.). Ulster Bibliography. Antrim. (*Ulster Journ. of Archæol.*, vol. xi. pp. 108–112, 163–167. 1905.)

Dix (Ernest Reginald McClintock). The Earliest Belfast Printing. (*The Irish Book Lover*, vol. vi. pp. 157–158. 1915.)

——— **Early Belfast Printing.** Biblio. Note. (*Ulster Journ. of Archæol.*, vol. xii. pp. 44–45. 1906.)

——— **The Private Press at Duncairn, Belfast, 1850-1892.** (*The Irish Book Lover*, vol. i. pp. 7–8, 25–26. 1909–10.)

The Duncairn Printing Press, Belfast. (Extract from Cotton's 'Typographical Gazetteer,' Ser. II. pp. 62–63), with a List. (*Ulster Journ. of Archæol.*, vol. xi. pp. 76–78. 1905.)

ANTRIM (continued).

Young (R. M.). A Forgotten Belfast Evening Paper. (*Ibid.* vol. iii. p. 201. 1897.)

Bigger (Francis Joseph). 'The Northern Star.' (*Ibid.* vol. i. pp. 33-35. 1894.) A brief item on 'Belfast Book Printing,' by F. J. Bigger, is at vol. ii. p. 210. 1896.

—— **Thomas Beggs, an Antrim Poet; and the Four Towns Book Club,** with a Biblio. (*Ibid.* vol. viii. pp. 119-127. 1902.)

—— **A Sketch of the Magees, the famous Printers and Journalists in Belfast and Dublin.** (*Belfast Art Gallery, Quarterly Notes*, No. xxxi. 1915.)

Madden (Richard Robert). Biblio. Notes on Belfast Newspapers, in 'Hist. of Irish Periodical Literature,' 1867, vol. ii. pp. 207-235.

The Belfast Booksellers. A Biblio. note. (*The Irish Book Lover*, vol. vi. pp. 5-7. 1914.)

McCance (Stouppe). Biblio. Note on Greenisland Printing. (*Ibid.* vol. vii. p. 7. 1915.)

Ewart (Lavens M.). Belfast Maps. A Record of Plans of the Town, chronologically arranged. (*Ulster Journ. of Archæol.*, vol. i. pp. 62-69, 99-105. 1894-95.)

Young (Robert M.). Early Notices and Engraved Views of the Giants' Causeway. (*Ibid.* vol. iii. pp. 40-49. 1896.)

CARRICKFERGUS.

Swanston (William). Maps of Carrickfergus. (*Ulster Journ. of Archæol.*, vol. ii. pp. 2-3. 1895.)

—— **Unpublished View of Carrickfergus.** (*Ibid.* vol. v. pp. 1-4. 1898.)

Notes on a Plan of Carrickfergus, temp. Elizabeth. (*Ibid.* Old Ser. vol. iii. pp. 276-291. 1855.)

Davis (Thomas). Samuel McSkimmin, Historian of Carrickfergus. (From 'The Nation,' 4 Mar. 1843.) (*The Irish Book Lover*, vol. vi. pp. 85-87. 1915.)

ARMAGH.

Crone (John S.). Ulster Bibliography. Armagh. (*Ulster Journ. of Archæol.*, vol. xiii. pp. 120-126. 1908.)

Dix (Ernest Reginald McClintock). Ulster Bibliography. A List of Books and Pamphlets printed in Armagh, with additions by Rev. W. T. Latimer and A. A. Campbell. (*Ibid.* vol. vi. p. 246; vol. vii. pp. 53-55, 57, 108; vol. viii. p. 24. 1900-02.)

—— **Printing in Armagh, 1801-24, with a List.** (*The Irish Book Lover*, vol. iv. pp. 83-84. 1912.)

—— **The First Printing Presses in Armagh and Newry.** (*Ulster Journ. of Archæol.*, vol. xvi. p. 46. 1910.)

—— **Printing in Portadown, with a List.** (*The Irish Book Lover*, vol. vii. pp. 123-124. 1916.)

Garstin (John Ribton). List of Documents transferred from Armagh Diocesan Registry to the Public Record Office, Dublin. (*County Louth Archæol. Soc. Journ.*, vol. iii. pp. 347-356. 1915.)

AYRSHIRE.

Finlayson (James). Biblio. of the Writings of Robert Watt, Author of 'Bibliotheca Britannica,' 1824, b. at Stewarton, in 'An Account of the Life and Works of Dr. Robert Watt,' 1897, pp. 42–46. The MS. of the 'Bibl. Brit.', in 69 vols., is in the Paisley Free Lib.

ALLOWAY.

Memorial Catal. of the Burns Exhibition, 1896. Glasgow, 1898. Chronological List of Dated Editions of the Works of Burns, pp. 437–450. Index of Writers on Robert Burns, pp. 451–454.

BANFFSHIRE.

Johnstone (James Fowler Kellas). A Concise Biblio. of the Hist., Topography, and Institutions of the Shires of Aberdeen, Banff, and Kincardine. See *ante* p. 315.

Ramsay (Sir James H.). Bamff Charters, A.D. 1232–1703. Biblio. Summary and Notes. Oxford, 1915.

See also article by Sir Archibald Geikie, 'A Scottish Charter-Chest: The Bamff Charter,' in 'The Scottish Historical Rev.', vol. xiii. pp. 105–110. 1916.

A List of the Publications of Dr. William Cramond, 1880–1907. (*Scottish Notes & Queries*, Ser. 2, vol. viii. pp. 154–156. 1907.)

BEDFORDSHIRE.

References to County Collections. Bedfordshire. (*Geneal. Queries & Memoranda*, ed. by G. F. Tudor Sherwood, vol. i. pp. 88, 95–96; vol. ii. pp. 6–8. 1897–99.)

BERKSHIRE.

References to County Collections. Berkshire. (*Geneal. Queries & Memoranda*, ed. by G. F. Tudor Sherwood, vol. ii. pp. 14–16, 23–24, 30–32. 1897–99.)

Mores (Edward Rowe). Parochial Queries for the County of Berks., 1759. See 'Sale Catal. of his Library,' p. 134. Sold by Paterson, London. 1779.

Baker (Alfred a Bethune-). Berks Bookplates. (*The Home Counties Mag.*, vol. vii. pp. 44–51. 1905.)

Brain (John Alfred). Berkshire Ballads, and other Papers. Reading, 1904.

READING.

Whitaker (S. P.). Newspaper and other Sources for the Hist. of Reading, 1643–45. (*The Reading Univ. Coll. Rev.*, vol. vi. pp. 215–227. 1914.)

Ditchfield (P. H.). The Literature and Writers of Reading and the District. (*The Library*, vol. ii. pp. 401–420. 1890.

Barfield (S.). Lord Fingall's Cartulary of Reading Abbey (15th cent.). (*The English Hist. Rev.*, vol. iii. pp. 113–125. 1888.) The Cartulary includes a Catal. of Books in the Library of the Abbey, which is printed in this article. See also pp. xlv.–l. of G. Laurence Gomme's Introduction to Macfarlane's 'Legend of Reading Abbey,' 1898.

BERKSHIRE (*continued*).

WINDSOR.

Report on Dean and Chapter of Windsor Records, by Reginald Lane Poole. (*Hist. MSS. Comm. Reports of MSS. in various Collections*, vol. vii. pp. 10–43. 1914.)

Botfield (Beriah). Notes on the Cathedral Libraries of England. 1849. **Lib. of Dean & Chapter of Windsor,** pp. 484–490.

BERWICKSHIRE.

Black (George F.). Descriptive Catal. of Loan Collections of Prehistoric and other Antiquities from the Shires of Berwick, etc. See also p. 217.

Biblio. of Historical Monuments in the Co. of Berwick, in 'Inventory of Monuments, etc.' (*Hist. Monuments* (*Scot.*) *Comm. 6th Rep.*, pp. x.–xii. 1915.) Revised issue.

BRECKNOCKSHIRE.

Jones (M. H.). The Trevecca MSS. and Library. (*Welsh Biblio. Soc. Journ.*, vol. i. pp. 1–16. 1910.)

List of Brecknockshire Illustrations in the 'Archæologia Cambrensis,' 1884–1900. See Alphabetical Index to 'Archæol. Camb.,' 1884–1900, by Francis Green, p. 97.

Morgan (G. E. F.). Theophilus Jones, F.S.A. (the Historian of Brecknockshire). See Memoir in the 1898 reprint of 'Hist. of the Co. of Brecknock,' by Theophilus Jones, 1805–09.

BUCKINGHAMSHIRE.

References to County Collections. Bucks. (*Geneal. Queries & Memoranda*, ed. by G. F. Tudor Sherwood, vol. ii. pp. 36–40. 1897–99.)

Bucks. Churchyard Inscriptions. (Appendix A. to Report of Committee, vol. i. pp. 77–78.) List of Parishes, with particulars of Transcribers, if Printed, and where to be found. (*The Reg. of English Monumental Inscriptions*, vol. ii. pp. 26–31. 1913.)

Cocks (Alfred Heneage). Biblio. of Bells of Bucks., in 'Church Bells of Bucks.' London, 1897, pp. xiii.–xix.

Baker (Alfred a Bethune-). Bucks. Bookplates. (*The Home Counties Mag.*, vol. vi. pp. 85–91. 1904.)

BURNHAM.

Williams (William H.). Burnham (Bucks.) Church Deeds. Privately Printed, 1913. List of Deeds in Prefatory Notice.

ETON.

Leigh (R. A. Austen). The Savile Types. (*Etoniana*, No. 2, pp. 17–22; No. 4, pp. 49–51. 1904–05.)

Eton in Prose and Verse. An Anthology. Selected by Arthur Campbell Ainger. London. [1910.]

BUTESHIRE.

The Book of Arran. Vol. I. Archæology. Edited by J. A. Balfour. Vol. II. History and Folklore. Edited by W. M. Mackenzie. (The Arran Soc. of Glasgow), 1910–14. Gaelic Songs of Arran, with Notes, vol. ii. pp. 314–350. List of Works on the Island of Arran, pp. 378–379.

CAITHNESS.

[See also Sutherlandshire, pp. 260–261.]

Mowat (John). List of Books, Pamphlets, etc. relating to Caithness. See Div. II. Literature, in 'The County of Caithness,' edited by John Horne. Wick. 1907, pp. 205–248.

—— **List of Books by Caithnessian Authors, prepared for the Glasgow Caithness Literary Association.** A series of Articles contributed to the 'Northern Ensign.' 1908.

—— **Caithness Geographers.** Address before the Glasgow Caithness Literary Assoc. (Reprinted from 'John O'Groat Journ.' Sept., 1912.)

CAMBRIDGESHIRE.

Shadwell (L. L.). Enactments in Parliament specially concerning the Universities of Oxford and Cambridge, etc. 1912. This work supersedes that by J. Griffiths, published in 1869. See p. 205.

Graces, Documents, and other Papers in the University Registry, which concern the University Library. A Chronological List. Cambridge, 1870.

James (Montague R.). Collections of MSS. at Cambridge. (The Sandars Lectures for 1903.) Cambridge, 1903.

—— **The Sources of Archbishop Parker's Collection of MSS., at Corpus Christi Coll., with a Reprint of the Catal. of Thomas Markaunt's Library.** (*Camb. Antiq. Soc. Octavo Pubns.*, No. xxxii. 1899.)

Sinker (Robert). Biographical Notes on the Librarians of Trinity Coll. on Sir Edward Stanhope's Foundation. (*Ibid.* No. xxix. 1897.)

Sayle (Charles). Annals of Cambridge Univ. Lib. [1278–1900]. (*The Library*, Ser. 3, vol. vi. pp. 38–76, 145–182, 197–227, 308–345. 1915.)

Gray (Arthur). The Priory of Saint Radegund, Cambridge. (*Camb. Antiq. Soc. Octavo Pubns.*, No. xxxi., 1898.) Catal. of Charters, pp. 74–144.

Report on the Pepys MSS. preserved at Magdalene College, Cambridge, By E. K. Purnell. (Hist. MSS. Comm. 1911.)

ELY.

Botfield (Beriah). Notes on the Cathedral Libraries of England. 1849. **Ely,** pp. 124–131.

CARDIGANSHIRE.

Evans (George Eyre). One Hundred Years of Printing at Aberystwyth. (*The Aberystwyth Almanack*, 1909.)

—— **Aberystwyth, A.D. 1909. Centenary of the Introduction of Printing in 1809.** Aberystwyth, 1909.

CARDIGANSHIRE (continued).

Samuel (David). Aberystwyth Printers and Printing Houses. Aberystwyth, 1909.

Cardigan Printer's Files, 1825-65. (M. & W. R. Thomas of Cardigan.) A Collection in the Nat. Lib. of Wales, including Broadsides, Election Literature, etc. See 'Report of Council,' 1913, pp. 49-50.

Vaughan (H. M.). The Hafod Press, and Colonel Thomas Johnes, Author and Publisher. (*Soc. of Cymmrodorion. Trans.*, 1911-12, pp. 1-22.)

List of Cardiganshire Illustrations in the 'Archæologia Cambrensis,' 1884-1900. See Alphabetical Index to 'Archæol. Camb.,' 1884-1900, by Francis Green, p. 98.

CARLOW.

Coleman (James). Biblio. of the Counties of Waterford, Tipperary, and Wexford, Kilkenny, Carlow, and Wicklow. (*Waterford and South-East of Irel. Archæol. Soc. Journ.*, vol. xi. pp. 131-132. 1908.)

Dix (Ernest Reginald McClintock). Early Printing in the South-East of Ireland. Pt. I. **Carlow, 1778-1825.** (*Ibid.* vol. ix. pp. 112-119. 1906.)

Maffett (R. S.). Biblio. Note on Carlow Printing. (*The Irish Book Lover*, vol. vii. p. 6. 1915.)

CARMARTHENSHIRE.

Davies (John). List of Books printed by John Ross at Carmarthen, 1763-1807. Welsh Biblio. Soc. (Announced for publication.)

List of Carmarthenshire Illustrations in the 'Archæologia Cambrensis,' 1884-1900. See Alphabetical Index to 'Archæol. Camb.,' 1884-1900, by Francis Green, p. 98.

List of Old Carmarthenshire Engravings in the Brit. Museum, by A. W. Matthews. (*Carm. Antiq. Soc. Trans.*, vol. x. pp. 74-75. 1915.)

Lists of Carmarthenshire Plea Rolls, Rentals, Surveys, etc., by A. W. Matthews. (*Ibid.* vol. x. pp. 57-58, 86-87. 1915.)

CARNARVONSHIRE.

List of Carnarvonshire Illustrations in the 'Archæologia Cambrensis, 1884-1900. See Alphabetical Index to 'Archæol. Camb.,' 1884-1900, by Francis Green, p. 99.

Public Record Office for Wales—The Case for Carnarvon. Carnarvon Borough Council. [1912.]

CAVAN.

Dix (Ernest Reginald McClintock). Ulster Bibliography. A List of Books, etc., printed in Cavan. (*Ulster Journ. of Archæol.*, vol. viii. pp. 23-24. 1902.)

—— **Printing in the Town of Cavan, 1790-1860.** (*The Irish Book Lover*, vol. i. pp. 83-84. 1910.)

—— **Printing in Cavan, 1801-1827, with a List.** (*Ibid.* vol. iv. pp. 165-167. 1913.)

CHANNEL ISLANDS.

Vallaux (**Camille**). **L'Archipel de la Manche.** Paris, 1913. Biblio. des Livres et Cartes, pp. 249–253.

Channel Islands Records. (*Local Records Comm. Rep.*, 1914, vol. ii. pt. 2, pp. 75-77 ; vol. ii. pt. 3, pp. 74–79.)

CHESHIRE.

Local Biblio. of Cheshire, by W. H. Allnutt, J. P. Earwaker, and others. See 'Local Gleanings relating to Lancs. & Ches.' Edited by J. P. Earwaker. Vols. i. & ii. *passim.* 1875–78.

Gower (**Foote**). **An Address to the Public relative to the proposed Hist. of Cheshire,** dated Chelmsford, Feb. 1, 1772.

Report on the Records on the County Palatine of Chester and the Co. of Flint. (*Deputy Keeper's Report.* I., 1840. Appendix, pp. 78–122.)

Index to Inquisitions, Edward III.–Charles I., Counties of Chester and Flint. (*Ibid.* xxv. 1864. Appendix, pp. 32-60.)

Cheshire Books and MSS. collected **by Thomas Hughes, of Chester, with additions by T. Cann Hughes.** A List of some of the items in the Collection. See 'Special Collections of Books in Lancs. & Cheshire,' by C. W. Sutton, 1900, p. 45.

Plomer (**Henry R.**). **A Chester Bookseller, 1667–1700 ; Some of his Customers and the Books he sold them.** (*The Library*, New Ser., vol. iv. pp. 373–383. 1903.)

Leigh (**Egerton**). **Ballads and Legends of Cheshire.** London, 1867.

Botfield (**Beriah**). **Notes on the Cathedral Libraries of England.** 1849. **Chester,** pp. 55–73.

Robson (**John**). **On the Early Charters of St. Werburgh's in Chester.** (*Hist. Soc. of Lancs. & Cheshire. Trans.*, vol. xi. pp. 187–198. 1859.)

CHURCH LAWTON.

Renaud (**Frank**). **Church Lawton Manor Records.** An analysis of the contents of a bundle of Records. (*Lancs. & Cheshire Antiq. Soc. Trans.*, vol. v. pp. 19–63. 1887.)

MACCLESFIELD.

Biblio. Notes on Macclesfield Books. By W. H. Allnutt, J. P. Earwaker, and others. (*Local Gleanings for Lancs. & Cheshire*, vol. i. pp. 111, 120, 121, 127 ; vol. ii. p. 172. 1875–78.)

STOCKPORT.

Biblio. Notes on Stockport Books, by W. H. Allnutt, J. P. Earwaker, etc. (*Ibid.* vol. i. pp. 124, 137 ; vol. ii. pp. 172, 837. 1876–78.)

Borough Records, 1464, etc., at Public Museum, Stockport. (*Local Records Comm. Rep.*, 1902, App. III. p. 40.)

CLARE.

Early Printing in Limerick and Ennis. (*The Irish Book Lover*, vol. iii. pp. 157–158. 1912.)

O'Gormon and Steele's MS. Collections chiefly relating to the County of Clare. See 'Sale Catal. of the Lib. of Thomas Crofton Croker,' p. 33. Sold by Puttick & Simpson, 19 Dec. 1854.

CONNAUGHT.

[The Counties of Galway, Leitrim, Mayo, Roscommon, and Sligo, which comprise the Province of Connaught, should also be consulted.]

Kelly (R. J.). Some Connaught Literary Men. (*The Irish Book Lover*, vol. vi. pp. 1-3. 1914.)

CORK.

Dix (Ernest Reginald McClintock). A Cork Bibliographical Puzzle. [A Note on the printing of Worth's Sermons.] (*The Irish Book Lover*, vol. i. pp. 128–129. 1910.)

—— **Facsimile of an Early Cork Title-page.** (*Ibid.* vol. iii. pp. 129–131. 1912.)

—— **Printing in Youghal, 1770–1826, with a List.** (*Ibid.* vol. iv. pp. 24–25. 1912.)

Maffett (R. S.). Cork Printing. A Biblio. Note. (*Ibid.* vol. vii. p. 45. 1915.)

Day (Robert). The Business Cards of Printers, Publishers, and Booksellers. (*Cork Hist. & Archæol. Soc. Journ.*, Ser. 2, vol. viii. pp. 95–103. 1902.)

O'Dowd (D. J.). 'The Cork Magazine,' 1847–48. A Biblio. Note. (*Ibid.* vol. vi. pp. 125–127. 1915.)

Madden (Richard Robert). Biblio. Notes on Cork Newspapers, in 'Hist. of Irish Periodical Literature,' 1867, vol. ii. pp. 164–189.

Three Memorable Cork Archæologists (John Windele, Richard Rolt Brash, and Richard Caulfield), with a List of Writings. (*Cork Hist. & Archæol. Soc. Journ.*, Ser. 2, vol. vi. pp. 32–47. 1900.)

Lunham (T. A.). Memoir of the late Richard Caulfield, with a Biblio. List. (*Royal Hist. & Archæol. Assoc. of Irel. Journ.*, vol. xviii. pp. 171-175. 1887.)

—— **Memoir of the late Canon Hayman,** with a Biblio. List. (*Ibid.* vol. xviii. pp. 165-170. 1887.)

Lee (Philip G.). Robert Day, F.S.A., with a List of Contributions to the 'Cork Archæol. Journ.', and the 'Journ. of the Roy. Soc. of Antiq. Irel.' (*Cork Hist. & Archæol. Soc. Journ.*, Ser. 2, vol. xx. pp. 109–113. 1914. An Account of the Sale of the Library of Robert Day, of Myrtle Hill, Cork, is in 'The Irish Book Lover,' vol. vii. pp. 63–64. 1915.

A List of Papers and Illustrations on the Antiquities of Youghal, which have appeared in the 'Journ. of the Roy. Soc. of Antiq. Irel.' (*Royal Soc. Antiq. Irel. Journ.*, vol. xxxiii. p. 344. 1903.)

CORNWALL.

List of Cornwall Illustrations in the 'Archæologia Cambrensis,' 1884–1900. See Alphabetical Index to 'Archæol. Camb.,' 1884-1900, by Francis Green, p. 100.

Index to Vols. I.–VI. of Cornwall Parish Registers. [Marriages], compiled by A. Terry Satterford. (*Phillimore's Parish Registers, Index Series*, vol. i. 1915.)

Jenner (Henry). Thomas Hodgkin, Historian. (*Royal Cornwall Polytechnic Soc. Ann. Report*, New Ser., vol. ii. pp. 82–100. 1914.)

Worth (Richard Nicholls). The West Country Garland, selected from the Writings of the Poets of Devon and Cornwall, from the 15th to 19th century, with folk songs, etc. Plymouth, 1875.

CORNWALL (continued).

Biblio. of the Works of Robert Stephen Hawker, in 'The Poetical Works of R. S. Hawker.' Edited, with a prefatory notice, by Alfred Wallis. London, 1899, pp. xxiii.–xxxi.

A Collection of Broadsides, Single-sheets, etc., printed at Hayle, mostly by J. O. Harris, *circa* 1844 to 1866. (In Brit. Mus. Library, 1876, f. 28.)

A Collection of MSS. and Printed Books relating to Cornwall, including the MSS. collected by Sir Thomas Phillipps, and sold at his Sales [owned by Samuel H. Brooks, Levenshulme, Manchester]. See 'Special Collections of Books in Lancs. and Cheshire,' by C. W. Sutton. 1900, p. 37.

Oliver (Rev. George). An Index to the 'Monasticon Dioecesis Exoniensis.' See under 'Devonshire,' p. 45.

PENZANCE.

Lach-Szyrma (W. S.). Libraries of Penzance. (*The Library Chron.*, vol. iii. pp. 169–173. 1886.)

TRURO.

Moor (A. P.). The Libraries of Truro. (*The Library Chron.*, vol. iii. pp. 105–107. 1886.)

SCILLY ISLES.

List of Books relating to the Scilly Isles, by Ronald Dixon. (*Notes & Queries*, Ser. 11, vol. iv. pp. 286–287. 1911.)

CUMBERLAND.

Botfield (Beriah). Notes on the Cathedral Libraries of England. 1849. **Carlisle,** pp. 49–54.

Anderson (Robert). Cumberland Ballads, with Notes. Carlisle. 1805. A List of the various editions of Anderson's writings is given in the 'Biblio. List of Works on Dialects,' of the English Dialect Soc., 1877, p. 36.

Dialogues, Poems, Songs, and Ballads, by various Writers, in the Westmorland and Cumberland Dialects, now first collected. London, 1839.

Sedgefield (W. J.). The Place-Names of Cumberland and Westmorland. Biblio. See under Westmorland, p. 274.

Wilson (James). Calendar of Charitable Trusts in the Diocese of Carlisle, 1736-1865. See under Westmorland, p. 275.

CROSTHWAITE.

Wilson (James). Charters of Crosthwaite. (*Northern Notes & Queries*, vol. i. pp. 79–83, 106–114, 145–152. 1906–07.)

DENBIGHSHIRE.

List of Denbighshire Illustrations in the 'Archæologia Cambrensis,' 1884-1900. See Alphabetical Index to 'Archæol. Camb.', 1884-1900, by Francis Green, p. 101.

Axon (W. E. A.). On the Seventeenth Century Ballad, entitled 'A Warning for all Murderers.' (*Y Cymmrodor*, vol. xxii. pp. 171–179. 1910.)

DERBYSHIRE.

Descriptive Catal. of 'The Jackson Collection,' at the Sheffield Public Lib. 1914. **Derbyshire items,** pp. 105–199. See *ante* under 'Yorkshire,' p. 301.

Catal. of the Charters, etc., in the Public Ref. Lib. at Sheffield. 1912. The Library is rich in Deeds, etc., in respect to the Peak District and Derbyshire. See *ante* under 'Yorkshire,' p. 301.

Joseph Hunter's Topographical Collections for Derbyshire, in the Brit. Museum. See 'The Hunter Archæol. Soc. Trans.,' vol. i. p. 16. 1914.

Jeayes (Isaac Herbert). Descriptive Catal. of Charters and Muniments of R. W. Chandos-Pole at Radbourne Hall (*circa* 1170–1558). London, 1896.

—— **Descriptive Catal. of the Charters and Muniments of the Gresley Family,** *circa* **1148–1676,** in the possession of Sir Robert Gresley, at Drakelowe. London, 1895. See also notes on the Muniments, etc., in 'The Gresleys of Drakelowe,' by Falconer Madan, in the 'William Salt Archæol. Soc. Collections,' vol. xix. 1898.

Jewitt (Llewellynn). The Ballads and Songs of Derbyshire. London, 1867.

Stronach (G.). The Chatsworth Library, its Treasures and Librarians. A Paper read before the 'Edinb. Biblio. Soc.,' 12 Nov. 1914.

DEVONSHIRE.

Devonshire Bibliography. The 'Devonshire Assoc.' has appointed a Committee for the compilation of a Biblio. of Devon. See 'Report and Trans. of the Assoc.,' vol. xlvii. p. 19. 1915.

Milles (Jeremiah), Dean of Exeter. Collections for a Hist. of Devonshire. 20 vols. See 'Sale Catal. of his Library,' pp. 58–60. Sold by Sotheby's, 10 Apr., 1843.

A set of 'Queries' to elicit information for the Hist. was sent out by Milles soon after 1739, see 'Bib. Top. Brit.,' vol. i. p. 1.

Tapley-Soper (H.). Some Recent Devonshire Literature. (*The Devonian Year Book*, 1915, pp. 137–138; 1916, pp. 107–108.) See also *ante* p. 41.

—— **William Henry Kearley Wright.** A Biog. Notice. With a list of Wright's Contributions to West Country Literature, by R. E. Wellington. (*Devon & Cornwall Notes & Queries*, vol. viii. pp. 193–198. 1915.)

Worth (Richard Nicholls). The West Country Garland, selected from the Writings of the Poets of Devon and Cornwall, from the Fifteenth to the Nineteenth Century. 1875.

Report of an Inspection of the Admiralty, War Office, and Customs Records, at Plymouth, April 1911. (*Local Records Comm. Rep.*, 1914, vol. ii. pt. 2, pp. 187–188.)

BARNSTAPLE.

Account of Public Records of the Town of Barnstaple. (*The Saturday Review*, vol. xlvi. pp. 335–337. 14 Sept. 1878.)

DARTMOOR.

Biblio. of Dartmoor Prison, in 'The Diary of Benjamin F. Palmer.' The Acorn Club, Hartford, Conn. 1914, pp. xv.–xvi.

EXETER.

Randolph (F. C. Hingeston), and others. The Episcopal Registers of the Diocese of Exeter. (Mainly Indices to the Contents of the Registers.) 10 vols. London, 1886–1915. The following Registers are fully Indexed :—

Edmund Stafford, 1395–1419; Bronescombe, 1257–1280; Quivil, 1280–1291; Bytton, 1292–1307; Walter de Stapeldon, 1307–1326.

DEVONSHIRE (*continued*).

List of Charters in the Cartulary of St. Nicholas Priory at Exeter. (*Collectanea Topog. & Geneal.*, vol. i. pp. 60–65, 184–189, 250–254, 374–388. 1834.)

Botfield (Beriah). Notes on the Cathedral Libraries of England. 1849. **Exeter,** pp. 132–158.

TORQUAY.

Roberts (William James). Literary Landmarks of Torquay. London, 1905.

DORSETSHIRE.

Hutchins (John). 'Queries' circulated for his 'Hist. of Dorset,' 1739. See 'Bibl. Topog. Brit..' 1790, vol. i. p. 1, and also preface to the first edn. of 'History,' 1774.

Mayo (Charles Herbert). The Municipal Records of the Borough of Dorchester. Exeter, 1908.

Gray (H. St. George). Index to 'Excavations in Cranborne Chase' and 'King John's House, Tollard Royal.' Also a Memoir of General Pitt Rivers, and a Biblio. List of his Works, 1858–1900. See vol. v. of 'Excavations in Cranborne Chase, near Rushmore,' by A. H. L. Fox-Pitt-Rivers. 5 vols. Privately Printed, 1887–1903.

Fry (Edward A.). The Augmentation Books (1650-1660) in Lambeth Palace Lib., with a Table of Contents. (*Dorset Nat. Hist. & Antiq. Field Club. Proc.*, vol. xxxvi. pp. 48-105. 1915.

DOWN.

Crossle (Ph.). Printers of Newry. (*Newry Reporter*, 1911.)

Maffett (R. S.). Printing in Newry. A Biblio. Note. (*The Irish Book Lover*, vol. vi. pp. 17–18. 1914.) See also a note by J. B. in vol. vii. p. 7. 1915.)

Marshall (J. J.) and Reid (B.). Donaghadee Printing. A Biblio. Note. (*Ibid.*, vol. vii. p. 46. 1915.)

DUBLIN.

M'Cready (C. T.). Dublin Bibliography, Historical and Topographical. A List of Books relating to the City and Suburbs of Dublin. Dublin, 1892. A reprint of Appendix to 'Dublin Street Names, Dated and Explained.'

Dix (Ernest Reginald McClintock). Dublin Printers between 1619 and 1660. (*Dublin Penny Journ.*, vol. ii. p. 104.)

——— **Notes of General Literature printed, etc., in Dublin in the 17th century.** (*Ibid.* vol. ii. pp. 140, 167 ; vol. iii. p. 136.)

——— **Dublin Publishing in 1663.** (*Irish Eccles. Gaz.*, 22 Dec. 1899.)

——— **Note on the 1664 edition of Book of Common Prayer.** (*Ibid.*)

——— **Another XVIIth Century Dublin Printed Prayer Book.** (*Ibid.* 11 Nov. 1898.)

——— **Printing Restrictions in Dublin in the First Quarter of the 17th century.** (*Ireland Illustrated*, New Ser. vol. iv. no. 11, p. 598.)

DUBLIN (*continued*).

Dix (Ernest Reginald McClintock). Dublin Newspapers prior to 1701. (*Irish Daily Independent*, 18 & 20 Jan. 1905.)

—— **An Early 18th Century Broadside on Printing.** (*Royal Irish Acad.* Proc., vol. xxvii. Sect. C, pp. 401–403. 1909.

—— **The Earliest Dublin editions of Shakespeare's Plays.** (*The Athenæum*, 3 Feb. 1903.)

Madden (Richard Robert). Biblio. Notes on Dublin Newspapers, in 'Hist. of Irish Periodical Literature,' 1867, vols. i. & ii. *passim.*

Collections of Dublin Books, MSS., Maps, Broadsides, etc. See 'Sale Catal. of the Literary Collections of William Monck Mason.' Sold by Sotheby's, 29 Mar. 1858.

Catalogues of Dublin Booksellers. A Collection of John O'Daly's Catalogues in the National Lib. Dublin, and also in the Brit. Mus. Lib. London. See a note by E. R. McC. Dix in 'The Irish Book Lover,' vol. vi. p. 42. 1914.

The complete Dublin Catal. of Books, from the beginning of this century to the present time, with prices affixed and alphabetically classed. Luke White, Dublin, 1786.

List of Dublin Corporation Records exhibited at meeting of Roy. Soc. of Antiquaries of Ireland, 11th Mar. 1891. By John Beveridge, Town Clerk. (*Roy. Soc. Antiq. Irel. Proc.*, vol. xxi. pp. 421–425. 1891.)

Stokes (George Thomas). Dudley Loftus: A Dublin Antiquary of the 17th century. (*Ibid.* vol. xxi. pp. 17–30. 1890.)

White (Newport J. D.). An Account of Marsh's Library, Dublin. (*The Library Assoc. Record*, vol. i. pt. i. pp. 133–145. 1899.)

McDonnell (Randal). The Story of Marsh's Library. (*The Irish Book Lover*, vol. vi. pp. 91–93. 1915.)

Le Fanu (T. P.). Dean Swift's Library. (*Roy. Soc. Antiq. Irel. Journ.*, vol. xxvi. pp. 113–121. 1896.).

Keatinge (Charles T.). The Guild of Cutlers, Painters-Stainers, and Stationers (with notes on Printing, etc.). (*Ibid.* vol. xxx. pp. 136–147. 1900.)

Berry (Henry F.). The Records of the Dublin Gild of Merchants. (*Ibid.* vol. xxx. pp. 44–68. 1900.)

—— **The Records of the Feltmakers' Company of Dublin, 1687–1841, their Loss and Recovery.** (*Ibid.* vol. xli. pp. 26–45. 1911.)

—— **Additions to List of 'Existing Records, etc., of the old Dublin City Gilds.'** (*Ibid.* vol. xli. pp. 45, 393. 1911.) See *ante* p. 52.

DUMBARTONSHIRE.

Macleod (Donald). Poets and Poetry of The Lennox. Dumbarton, n.d. [1889 ?]

DUMFRIESSHIRE.

Couper (W. J.). The Date of the 'Drumfries Mercury.' A Paper read before the Glasgow Biblio. Soc. Dumfries, 1915.

Miller (Frank). The Poets of Dumfriesshire (with Biblio. Notes on Ballads, etc.). Glasgow, 1910.

DURHAM.

[Entries under Northumberland should also be consulted.]

Rud (Thomas). Codicum Manuscriptorum Ecclesiæ Cathedralis Dunelmensis Catalogus classicus, descriptus a Thoma Rud, cum Appendice. Edited by James Raine. Durham, 1825.

Appendix, pp. 317–456. Manuscripts purchased by the Dean & Chapter of Durham at different periods since the completion of the preceding Catalogue. (Contains detailed lists of the MS. Collections of Dr. Christopher Hunter, the Rev. Thomas Randall, and George Allan, of Darlington.)

'Rud compiled with much labour and learning, and with beautiful penmanship, a Catal. of the MSS. at Durham Cathedral, which he completed at Northallerton on 15 Sept. 1727. It was printed for the Dean & Chapter under the editorship of the Rev. James Raine, and with an Appendix by him in 1825. To Rud, Raine owed much of the material embodied in the latter's "Catalogi veteres Librorum Ecclesiæ Cathedralis Dunelm."'—*D. N. B.*

Durham Records. Calendar of the Cursitors' Records, Chancery Enrolments. (*Ann. Rep. Dep. Keeper of Public Records*, xxxi. pp. 42–168; xxxii. App. I. pp. 264–330; xxxiii. pp. 43–210; xxxiv. pp. 163–264; xxxv. pp. 76–156. 1870–74.) Continued to 1617 in Reports, xxxvi., xxxvii., xl.

—— **Inventory and Lists of Documents transferred from the County Palatine of Durham, pursuant to Warrant dated 17 Nov. 1868.** (*Ibid.* xxx. pp. 44–98. 1869.)

—— **Report by Sir T. Duffus Hardy on the Durham Records.** (*Ibid.* xvi. pp. 44–93; xxix. pp. 104–112. 1855–68.)

Botfield (Beriah). Notes on the Cathedral Libraries of England. 1849. **Durham,** pp. 89–123.

Sharp (Sir Cuthbert). The Bishoprick Garland, or a Collection of Legends, Songs, Ballads, etc., belonging to the County of Durham. London, 1834.

Hill (B. Rowland). A Sketch of the Life of Sir Cuthbert Sharp, with a Biblio. of his Writings. (*Antiquities of Sunderland*, vol. x. pp. 115–131. 1909.)

Works relating to the County of Durham. See pp. 87–89 of the 'Sale Catal. of the Thomas Bell Library,' 1860, *ante* p. 189.

Darlington Private Press. List of Tracts issued from the Private Press of George Allan, of Darlington, and of 'Allan' MSS. relating to the County. See 'Sale Catal. of the Lib. of Leonard Lawrie Hartley (Third Portion).' Sold by Puttick & Simpson, London, 25 Apr. 1887, pp. 261–263.

Wetherald's Printing Press at Sunderland. A brief note. (*Sunderland Public Lib. Circular*, vol. i. p. 244. 1901.)

EDINBURGHSHIRE.

Murray (David). David Laing, Antiquary and Bibliographer. Reprinted from 'The Scottish Hist. Rev.', vol. xi. pp. 345–369. 1914.) Glasgow, 1915.

See also a Memoir of David Laing in John Small's edition of Laing's 'Select Remains of the Poetry of Scotland.' 1885.

Report on the Laing MSS. preserved in the Univ. of Edinburgh, by Rev. Henry Paton. Vol. i. 1914. (Hist. MSS. Comm.)

Cuthbertson (David). The Edinburgh University Library. An Account of its origin, with a description of its rarer Books and MSS. Edinburgh, 1910.

EDINBURGHSHIRE (continued).

Black (William). Biographical Notices of some Eminent Edinburgh Librarians. (*Lib. Assoc. Trans.*, Third Meeting, Edinb. 1880, pp. 30–48.)

Small (John). Historical Account of the Lib. of the Univ. of Edinburgh. (*Ibid.* pp. 95–103.)

Fairley (John A.). Biblio. of Robert Fergusson [b. at Edinb. 1750, d. 1774.] (*Glasgow Biblio. Soc. Records*, vol. iii. pp. 115–155. 1915.)

Oliphant (Margaret Oliphant). Annals of a Publishing House. William Blackwood and his Sons, their Magazine and Friends. 3 vols. Edinburgh, 1897–98. The third vol. is by Mrs. Gerald Porter, and deals with John Blackwood.

Chalmers (George). The Life of Thomas Ruddiman, Librarian of the Advocates' Library, Edinburgh. London, 1794.

Kerr (Robert). Memoirs of the Life, Writings, and Correspondence of William Smellie, late Printer in Edinburgh. 2 vols. Edinburgh, 1811.

Johnstone (J. F. Kellas) and Cowan (William). Biblio. Notes on 'Peter Williamson's Press,' with a List. (*Scottish Notes & Queries*, vol. ix. pp. 29, 47. 1895.)

Lawlor (Hugh Jackson). Notes on the Library of the Sinclairs of Rosslyn. (*Soc. of Antiq. Soc. Proc.*, vol. xxxii. pp. 90–120. 1898.)

Whibley (Charles). The Library of an Old Scholar. (Drummond of Hawthornden). (*Blackwood's Edinburgh Mag.*, vol. clxvi. pp. 753–767. 1899.)

Couper (W. J.). Andrew Symson, Preacher, Printer and Poet. (*The Scottish Historical Review*, vol. xiii. pp. 47–67. 1915.)

Sampson (R. A.). Biblio. of Books exhibited at the Napier Tercentenary Celebration, July 1914, with an Index. (*Memorial Volume*, ed. by C. G. Knott, pp. 177–242.) Roy. Soc. of Edinb. 1915.

Inventory of Original Documents in the Archives of George Heriot's Hospital. Edinb., 1857.

Stevenson (Thomas George). Edinburgh in the Olden Time displayed in a series of Sixty-three original Views between 1717 and 1828, with Lists and Descriptive Notices. Edinburgh, 1880.

RESTALRIG.

Index to the Register of Burials in the Churchyard of Restalrig, 1728-1854, by Francis James Grant. (*Scottish Record Soc. Pubns.*, Part xli. 1908.)

ELGIN OR MORAY.

Ree (Rev. Stephen). Biblio. of the Counties of Moray and Nairn. Aberdeen, 1916.

ESSEX.

Cole (William). John Norden's Map of Essex. (*The Essex Naturalist*, vol. i. pp. 41–45. 1887.)

Avery (John). Christopher Saxton, Draughtsman of the oldest known Map of Essex. (*Ibid.* vol. xi. pp. 240–242. 1900.)

Green (Joseph J.). Chapman and André's Map of Essex, 1777. (*The Essex Review*, vol. xix. pp. 78–88. 1910.)

Baker (Alfred A. Bethune-). Essex Bookplates. (*The Home Counties Mag.*, vol. v. pp. 175–179. 1903.)

ESSEX (continued).

The Old Parish Register Books (prior to 1813) of the Archdeaconry of Colchester. A revised and verified List for the 199 old Parishes of the Archdeaconry. (*St. Albans Diocesan Mag.*, vol. vii. no. 8-vol. ix. no. 10. 1902-4.)

A similar list appeared in 'The Essex Review,' vol. vii.-x. 1898-1901. See also Report presented to the St. Albans Dioc. Conference, with specimen page of list, in 'Report of Joint Committee of Convocation of Canterbury on Local Eccles. Records,' 1905. App. iv. pp. 18-19.

Christy (Miller). Biblio. Note on Essex Printing and Newspaper Publishing, in 'The Victoria County Hist. of Essex,' vol. ii. 1907, pp. 470-473.

COLCHESTER.

Jeayes (Isaac Herbert). Court Rolls of Colchester. (*Essex Archæol. Soc. Trans.*, vol. xiv. pp. 81-89. 1915.)

HARWICH.

Dale (Samuel) and Taylor (Silas). A Catalogue of Authors made use of . . . with the Place and Time of the Publication of each. *See* 'The Hist. and Antiquities of Harwich and Dovercourt.' 1730. 2nd Edn. 1732, pp. xiii.-xxiv.

SAFFRON WALDEN.

Saffron Walden Local Authors and Authoresses. Collected by R. Heffer. Additions by Joseph J. Green. (*The Essex Review*, vol. xxiv. pp. 126-130, 192-196. 1915.)

FERMANAGH.

Dix (Ernest Reginald McClintock). Printing in Enniskillen, 1830-1900, with a List. (*The Irish Book Lover*, vol. vii. pp. 3-5. 1915.)

FIFESHIRE.

ST. ANDREWS.

Inventories of Buikis in the Colleges of Sanctandrois, 1588-1612. (*Miscellany of the Maitland Club*, vol. i. pp. 303-329. 1834.

Votiva Tabella: A Memorial Volume of St. Andrews University in connection with its Quincentenary Festival, 1411-1911. St. Andrews, 1911. The Library, by James Maitland Anderson, pp. 93-112. The Poets of the University, by Alexander Lawson, and others, pp. 243-292.

FLINTSHIRE.

Deputy-Keeper of Public Records. Reports on Flintshire Records and Index to Inquisitions, see *ante* p. 322.

An Inventory of the Ancient Monuments in Wales and Monmouthshire. II. County of Flint. London, 1912. (Royal Commission on Ancient & Hist. Monuments, etc., in Wales, etc.) Biblio. references are given to many items in the 'Inventory.'

The Henry Taylor Flintshire Historical Collection in the Nat. Lib. of Wales at Aberystwyth. A Schedule of the Contents. (*Rep. of Council, Nat. Lib. of Wales*, 1913, pp. 29-32.) A short account of the Collection is in the above 'Report,' 1911, pp. 26-27.

FORFARSHIRE.

Millar (Alexander H.). 'The Dundee Advertiser,' 1801-1901. A Centenary Memoir. Dundee, 1901.

GALWAY.

Falkiner (C. Litton). Some Suggestions towards a County Hist. of Galway. (*Galway Archæol. & Hist. Soc. Journ.*, vol. ii. pp. 91–102. 1902.)

Dix (Ernest Reginald McClintock). Printing in Loughrea, 1825-1862, with a List. (*The Irish Book Lover*, vol. vi. pp. 175–176. 1915.)

—— **Printing in Tuam, 1825-1900,** with a List. (*Ibid.* vol. vii. pp. 40–41. 1915.)

—— **Printing in Ballinasloe, 1828-1900,** with a List. (*Ibid.* vol. vii. pp. 147–148. 1916.)

Maffett (R. S.). Biblio. Note on Ballinasloe Printing. (*Ibid.* vol. vii. p. 6. 1915.)

GLAMORGANSHIRE.

Aberdare Printers' Files. (Josiah Thomas Jones.) A summary of the Collection in the Nat. Lib. of Wales, which includes Ballads, Almanacs, Broadsides, Newspaper Prospectuses, etc. See 'Report of Council,' 1913, pp. 50–53.

Descriptive Catal. of the Penrice and Margam Abbey MSS., by W. de Gray Birch. Third and Fourth Series, 1895, 1905. See also *ante* p. 74.

GLOUCESTERSHIRE.

Hyett (Francis Adams) and Austin (Roland). Supplement to the Bibliographer's Manual of Gloucestershire Literature, being a Classified Catal. of Biographical and Genealogical Literature, relating to Men and Women connected by birth, office, or many years' residence with the County of Gloucester or the City of Bristol, with descriptive and explanatory notes. 2 vols. Gloucester, 1915–16.

Mr. Francis Adams Hyett, of Painswick House, presented in Sept. 1914 to the Reference Department of the Gloucester Public Library his important Gloucestershire Collection, consisting of 1414 tracts and pamphlets, and 1877 broadsides, leaflets, and election squibs, bound in 99 vols., with special title-pages, arranged in series and subjects. Mr. Hyett also presented earlier in the year, a Collection of 264 pamphlets, etc., by Gloucestershire Writers. The pamphlets, etc., in the Local Collection now number 6984. The Library of the 'Cotteswold Club' and the Lib. of the 'Bristol & Glos. Archæol. Soc.' are housed at the Public Library. See 16th Ann. Report for 1914-15, pp. 5-7, 11.

Catal. of the temporary Museum at Gloucester formed for the Meeting of the Bristol & Glos. Archæol. Soc., 1883, consisting of Portraits, Views, Charters, Antiquities, etc., connected with the Hist. of Gloucester. See 'Trans.' of the Soc. vol. xiii. pp. 72–84. 1888.

Austin (Roland). 'The Gloucester Journal.' Numbering of Volumes. (*Notes and Queries*, Ser. 11, vol. xi. p. 317. 1915.)

—— **Robert Raikes, the Elder, and the 'Gloucester Journal.'** (*The Library*, Ser. 3, vol. vi. pp. 1–24. 1915.)

—— **Samuel Rudder [of Cirencester, Printer and County Historian].** (*The Library*, Ser. 3, vol. vi. pp. 235–251. 1915.)

GLOUCESTERSHIRE (continued).

Austin (Roland). 'The Cirencester Flying Post,' a Biblio. Note. (*Notes & Queries*, Ser. 11. vol. x. pp. 325–326. 1914.)

Norris (Herbert E.). Cirencester Booksellers and Printers, with a List. (*Ibid.* Ser. 11, vol. xi. pp. 141–142. 1915.)

Account of Early Bristol Printing. Extracts from the 'Bristol Times and Mirror,' 6 & 8 Feb. 1911, probably by Charles Wells.

George (William). The Oldest Bristol Newspapers. Reprinted from the 'Bristol Times and Mirror,' 4 Aug. 1884.

Butler (Miss R. F.). Biblio. Note on Gloucestershire Printing and Paper, in 'The Victoria County Hist. of Glos.,' vol. ii. 1907, pp. 208–209.

Hyett (F. A.). 'Annalia Dubrensia.' [A rare Gloucestershire Book.] (*Bristol & Glos. Archæol. Soc. Trans.*, vol. xiii. pp. 103–117. 1889.)

Biblio. Note on Haslewood's Collection of Samuel Harward's Tewkesbury Chap-Books, 1760-75, with a List. (*Glos. Notes & Queries*, vol. iii. pp. 226–228. 1885.)

Botfield (Beriah). Notes on the Cathedral Libraries of England. 1849. **Gloucester,** pp. 159–171.

Report on the MSS. of the Diocese of Gloucester, by W. Dunn Macray. (*Hist. MSS. Comm. Reports of MSS. in various Collections*, vol. vii. pp. 44–69. 1914.)

List of Charters in the Winchcombe Cartularies, in the possession of Lord Sherborne. (*Collectanea Topog. et Genealogica*, 1835, vol. ii. pp. 16–39.)

BRISTOL.

'The Bristol Collection,' in the Bristol Public Library. For a List, see Faber's 'Catal. of the Library collected by George Weare Braikenridge,' 1894, pp. 203–258.

Catal. of the Bristol Books in the Canynge Room, Redcliff Street, Bristol. (A MS. vol. in Bristol Public Library.)

Collections for Bristol. Selections from Barrett's 'Hist. of Bristol,' Newspaper Extracts, MS. Notes, etc., towards forming a complete Hist. of Bristol, 1326–1874. 36 vols. (In the Braikenridge Collection at the Bristol Public Library.)

Nicholls (J. F.). The Early Bristol Charters and their chief object. (*Roy. Hist. Soc. Trans.*, vol. i. pp. 88-95. 1875.)

Botfield (Beriah). Notes on the Cathedral Libraries of England, 1849. **Bristol,** pp. 1–4.

Atchley (E. G. Cuthbert F.). On the Mediæval Parish Records of the Church of St. Nicholas, Bristol. (*St. Paul's Eccles. Soc. Trans.*, vol. vi. pp. 35–67. 1906.)

White (James Walter). The Flora of Bristol, 1912. Biblio. of Books consulted, pp. 104–108.

HADDINGTONSHIRE.

Bibliographies of John Knox. See Henry Cowan's 'John Knox.' New York, 1905, pp. xxiii.-xxxiii., and David Laing's edition of 'The Works of John Knox,' 1846, vol. i. pp. xxix.-xliv.

HAMPSHIRE AND THE ISLE OF WIGHT.

Duthy (John). Sketches of Hampshire. Winchester, 1839. Index of Authorities, pp. 488–491.

MS. Collections of Sir Frederick Madden relating to Hampshire. See 'Sale Catal. (Third Portion) of the Library of Leonard Lawrie Hartley,' sold by Puttick & Simpson. London, 18 Apr. 1887.

Hampshire Printing. See slight Biblio. Note by Ethel M. Hewitt, in the 'Victoria County Hist. of Hampshire,' vol. v. p. 461. 1912.

Cave (C. J. P.). A List of Hampshire Brasses. (*Monumental Brass Soc. Trans.*, vol. v. pp. 247, 295, 343; vol. vi. pp. 1, 121. 1908–11.)

ANDOVER.

Clutterbuck (Rev. R. H.). The Museum at Andover. (*Wilts. Archæol. & Nat. Hist. Mag.*, vol. xxi. pp. 315–316. 1884.)

SELBORNE.

Mullens (W. H.). Gilbert White of Selborne. London, 1907. Biblio. of the earlier and rarer editions, pp. 24–32.

SOUTHAMPTON.

Jeaffreson (J. Cordy). List of Charters, Letters Patent, and other Muniments of the Corporation of Southampton. Privately Printed, 1886.

WINCHESTER.

Botfield (Beriah). Notes on the Cathedral Libraries of England. 1849. **Winchester,** pp. 465–483.

Madge (Francis Thomas). Winchester Cathedral Lib. Early Printed Books, 1479-1640. [1902.]

Cassan (Stephen Hyde). Charters & Records in the Tower of London, relating to the Church of Winton, several religious Houses, Chapels, Colleges, and Hospitals, in and about that City. (In Cassan's 'Lives of the Bishops of Winchester,' vol. i. pp. 18–28. 1827.)

A Catal. of Books, Prints, etc., mainly in connection with Winchester College and the City of Winchester. Published and Sold by P. & G. Wells. Winchester, 1911.

ISLE OF WIGHT.

Edward Vernon Utterson. (1777-1856.) Note on the Private Press at Beldornie, from which issued reprints and facsimiles of rare old Tracts. (*Contributions towards a Dictionary of English Book-Collectors.* London. B. Quaritch. Part VII. 1895.)

Andrews (S.). Notes on the Parish Registers of Newport, Isle of Wight. (*Brit. Archæol. Assoc. Journ.*, New Ser. vol. xxii. pp. 81–84. 1916.)

HEREFORDSHIRE.

Notes on the Pilley Local Collection in the Hereford Free Library. (*The Pedigree Register*, ed. by G. F. Tudor Sherwood, vol. iii. pp. 314–317. 1915.)

Botfield (Beriah). Notes on the Cathedral Libraries of England. 1849. **Hereford,** pp. 172–188.

HERTFORDSHIRE.

Fordham (Sir Herbert G.). Index-List of Hertfordshire Maps, 1579-1900. (*Studies in Carto-Bibliography*, 1914, pp. 17–22.)

——— **County Maps and the Books in which they are found, with special reference to the Maps of Herts.** A Paper read before the St. Albans & Herts. Archit. & Archæol. Soc., 2 Dec. 1902. See 'Trans. of the Society,' New Ser., vol. ii. p. 112. 1905.

Pollard (Alfred W.). John Herford, Printer, at St. Albans, 1534-38, at London, 1544-48, Katherine Herford, 1549-50. (*Biblio. Soc. Handlists of English Printers*, vol. iii. 1905.)

Blades (William). The Printer at St. Albans, 1480-1486. (*The Book-Worm*, ed. by J. P. Berjeau, vol. i. pp. 169–172. 1866.)

Plomer (Henry R.). Hertfordshire Printing. See '*Victoria County Hist. of Hertfordshire*,' vol. iv. pp. 258–264. 1914.)

Baker (Alfred A. Bethune-). Herts. Bookplates. (*The Home Counties Mag.*, vol. v. pp. 300–306. 1903.)

Hist. MSS. Comm. Reports. Hertfordshire Collections.

Salisbury, Marquess of, at Hatfield ...	Vol. xiii. (1915) now issued.
Essex, Earl of, at Cassiobury Park, Watford	MSS. in Various Collections, vol. vii. pp. 297–350. 1914.

Brown (A. W. Payne). The Hatfield MSS. in 'Our Old Mansions and their Historic Records.' (*The Archivist*, vol. iv. p. 59; vol. v. pp. 14, 31, 43, 55; vol. vi. pp. 12, 26. 1891–93.)

Hall (H. R. Wilton). Transcripts of Parish Registers existing among the Records of the Old Archdeaconry of St. Albans, now in St. Albans Cathedral, with a List. (*Herts. Archæol. Soc. Trans.*, vol. v. p. 287. 1915.)

The Parish Register Books (prior to 1813) of the Archdeaconry of St. Albans. A revised and verified List for the 132 old Parishes of the Archdeaconry. (*Middx. & Herts. Notes & Queries*, vols. iii.-iv. Jan. 1897—Oct. 1898.)

Classified Subject-Index to the 'Transactions' of the Herts. Nat. Hist. Soc. for the 40 years, 1875-1914. (*Herts. Nat. Hist. Soc. Trans.*, vol. xv. pp. 257–271. 1915.)

ST. ALBANS.

Page (William). List of MSS. relating to the Hist. of St. Alban's Abbey, in his 'St. Alban's Cathedral.' London, 1898, pp. 90–98.

HUNTINGDONSHIRE.

Norris (Herbert E.). Huntingdonshire Almanacs, with a List. (*Notes & Queries*, Ser. 12, vol. i. pp. 5–8. 1916.)

——— **Huntingdon Civil War Tracts, with a List.** (*Ibid.* Ser. 12, vol. i. pp. 86–87, 105-107. 1916.)

——— **The Witches of Warboys,** a Biblio. Note. (*Ibid.* Ser. 12, vol. i. pp. 283, 304. 1916.)

INVERNESS-SHIRE.

Anderson (P. J.). A Concise Biblio. of the Hist., Topography and Institutions of the Burgh, Parish, and Shire of Inverness. (*Aberdeen University Lib. Bulletin*, vol. ii. pp. 415–447, 575–594, 805–837; vol. iii. pp. 88–132, 222–269. 1914-16.) The Biblio. when completed will be recast and issued in separate form as one of the 'Aberdeen Univ. Studies.'

ISLE OF MAN.

Booksellers and Newspapers in the Isle of Man. (*The Bookseller*, 15 Aug. 1882, pp. 689–690.)

Ralfe (P. G.). Biblio. of Isle of Man Birds, in his 'Birds of the Isle of Man.' Edinb. 1905, pp. 287–289.

KENT.

Plomer (Henry R.). James Abree, Printer and Bookseller of Canterbury. London, 1913.

Hammant (Walter). Crayford and its great Printer, Augustus Applegarth. (*Woolwich District Antiq. Soc. Rep.*, vol. xv. pp. 50–51. 1909.)

Freeman (Roland). Kentish Poets, a Series of Writers in English Poetry, Natives, or Residents in Kent, with specimens of their Compositions, and some Account of their Lives and Writings. 2 vols. Canterbury, 1821.

Odo of Cheriton Romances. See 'Catal. of Romances in the Dep. of MSS. in the Brit. Mus.', ed. by J. A. Herbert, 1910, vol. iii. pp. 50–78.

Baker (Alfred A. Bethune-). Kent Bookplates. (*The Home Counties Mag.*, vol. vii. pp. 202-211. 1905.)

Churchill (Irene J.). A Handbook to Kent Records. (*Kent Archæological Soc.*) 1915.

A List of Somner's Posthumous MSS., now in the Library of Christ's Coll. Canterbury, in Somner's 'Treatise of Gavelkind.' 1726.

CANTERBURY.

Botfield (Beriah). Notes on the Cathedral Libraries of England. 1849. **Canterbury,** pp. 5–48.

FAVERSHAM.

Catal. of Anglo-Saxon and other Antiquities discovered at Faversham. 1873.

GREENWICH.

Montmorency (J. E. G. de). Early and Mediæval Records of Greenwich. (*Greenwich Antiq. Soc. Trans.*, vol. i. pp. 13–33. 1907.)

——— **Greenwich MSS. and Maps in the British Museum.** A List. (*Ibid.* vol. i. pp. 61–66. 1910.)

——— **Greenwich Records in the Record Office.** (*Ibid.* vol. i. pp. 67–74. 1910.

ROCHESTER.

Botfield (Beriah). Notes on the Cathedral Libraries of England. 1849. **Rochester,** pp. 390–404.

Rye (W. Brenchley). A Memorial of the Priory of St. Andrew at Rochester, with a Catal. of the Monastic MSS. A.D. 1202. (Reprinted from the 'Archæologia Cantiana,' vol. iii.) Privately Printed, 1861.

KILDARE.

Maffett (R. S.). Biblio. Note on Naas Printing. (*The Irish Book Lover*, vol. vii. p. 6. 1915.)

KILKENNY.

Hist. MSS. Comm. Reports. Kilkenny Collection.

Tighe, K. B., of Woodstock, co. Kilkenny ... ... Various Collections, vol. vi. pp. 435–437. 1909.

Coleman (James). Biblio. of the Counties of Waterford, Tipperary, and Wexford; Kilkenny, Carlow, and Wicklow. (*Waterford & South-East of Irel. Archæol, Soc. Journ.*, vol. xi. pp. 128–130. 1908.)

Madden (Richard Robert). Biblio. Note on Kilkenny Newspapers, in 'Hist. of Irish Periodical Literature,' 1867, vol. ii. pp. 236–240.)

KINCARDINESHIRE.

Johnstone (James Fowler Kellas). A Concise Biblio. of the Shires of Aberdeen, Banff, and Kincardine. See *ante* p. 315.

Bulloch (J. M.). Biblio. of Stonehaven Periodical Literature. (*Scottish Notes & Queries*, vol. ii. pp. 60–61. 1888.)

KING'S COUNTY.

Dix (Ernest Reginald McClintock). Local Printing. Birr, 1775–1892. (*Leinster Reporter*, 7 Sept. 1901 and 22 Aug. 1903.)

Macalister (R. A. Stewart). Materials for a Hist. of the Monastery of Clonmacnois. Appendix to 'Memorial Slabs of Clonmacnois,' Dublin, 1909.

LANARKSHIRE.

Records of the Glasgow Biblio. Society. Vol. iii. Glasgow, 1914–15.

CONTENTS:

Biblio. of 'Blind Harry's Wallace,' by Rev. J. F. Miller, pp. 1–25.

Robert Sanders the Elder (Printer in Glasgow), by Rev. W. J. Couper, pp. 26–88.

Robert Urie—Printer in Glasgow, with a Hand-List of Books printed by or for Robert Urie, by Hugh A. McLean, pp. 89–108.

Biblio. of Douglas Moore, Poet and Bookseller, by William Sinclair, pp. 109–114.

Baird (Agnes). Review of the Historical & Topographical Works of James Cleland on Glasgow, containing a detection of errors and misrepresentations in his Works. Glasgow, 1830.

Catal. of the Library of Thomas A. Mathieson, compiled by F. T. Barrett. Glasgow, 1891. **Glasgow items,** pp, 38–56.

Notes as to Ancient Documents in Glasgow. 1856.

LANARKSHIRE (continued).

Ewing (J. C.). A Great Scottish Book-printing Society—The Maitland Club. A Paper read before the Glasgow Biblio. Soc.

Norrie (Joseph). Stirling's: An Episode in Glasgow Library History. A Paper read before the Glasgow Biblio. Soc.

Motherwell Collection of Chap-Books. For Biblio. Notes on the Contents, see William Walker's 'Peter Buchan,' 1915, pp. 280–281.

LANCASHIRE.

Biblio. Notes on Lancashire Books, Newspapers, Ballads, Songs, etc. (*Local Notes & Queries from the 'Manchester Guardian,'* 1874–76, *passim.*)

Axon (William E. A.). Folk Song and Folk Speech of Lancs. On the Ballads and Songs of the County Palatine. Manchester. [1870.]

Fishwick (Henry). Tim Bobbin. (John Collier.) With Biblio. Notes. (*Rochdale Lit. & Scient. Soc. Trans.*, vol. ii. pp. 78–95. 1890.)

M. (W.). Liverpool's Printing Bi-Centenary. (*The Liverpool Post*, 5 July, 1912.)

Hadley (W. W.). Rochdale Newspapers. (*Rochdale Lit. & Scient. Soc. Trans.*, vol. ix. pp. 8–24. 1908.)

LEICESTERSHIRE.

Peck (Francis). 'Queries' for the Natural Hist. & Antiquities of Leicester and Rutland Shires. Single sheet. 1729. See 'Bibl. Topog. Brit.' 1790, vol. i. p. 1.

Hist. MSS. Comm. Report. Leicestershire Collection.

Merttens, F., of Rothley Temple, Leics., and Bilton Rise, co. Warwick ...	Various Collections, vol. vii. pp. 376–388. 1914.

Lyte (Sir H. Maxwell). The MSS. of the Duke of Rutland, preserved at Belvoir Castle. (*Leics. & Rutland Notes & Queries*, vol. i. pp. 26–29. 1889.) See also *ante* Hist. MSS. Comm. Rep. p. 136.

List of Documents relating to the Archdeaconry of Leicester preserved in the Leicester Archdeaconry Registry. Appendix to Report of the Joint Committee of the Convocation of Canterbury on Local Eccles. Records, 1906, in 'The Chron. of Convocation,' 1906, no. III.

LINCOLNSHIRE.

Lincoln Diocese Documents, 1450–1544. Edited with Notes and Indexes, by Andrew Clark. [Early English Text Soc.] London, 1914. List of Documents, in Forewords.

Thompson (Pishey). Topographical and Historical Notices of various Towns, Villages, etc., in the Co. of Lincs. (*Collections for a Topog. and Hist. Account of Boston*, 1820. App. pp. 27–66).

Waterfield (A. J.). The Literary Associations of Stamford. (*The Rutland Mag.*, vol. iii. pp. 110–120. 1907.)

The Numbering of the Volumes of the 'Stamford Mercury.' (*Notes and Queries*, Ser. 11, vol. vii. pp. 365, 430, 471. 1913.)

BRIGG.

Sheppard (Thomas). Biblio. to article on 'The Pre-historic Boat from Brigg.' (*E. Riding Antiq. Soc. Trans.*, vol. xvii. pp. 52–54. 1910.)

LINLITHGOWSHIRE.

Bisset (Alexander M.). The Poets and Poetry of Linlithgowshire, an Anthology of the County. Paisley, 1896.

LONDON.

Flenley (Ralph). A List of the Chronicles of London, in his 'Six Town Chronicles of England,' Oxford, 1911, pp. 96–98.

Report on MSS. of the Bishop of London, by Reginald Lane Poole. (*Hist. MSS. Comm. Reports on MSS. in various Collections*, vol. vii. pp. 1-9. 1914.)

Deeds and Documents relating to London in the possession of the Sussex Archaeol. Soc. See *ante* under Sussex, p. 256.

Catal. of the Maps, Plans, and Views of London collected by Frederick Crace, lent for exhibition in the South Kensington Museum, by John Gregory Crace. London, 1879.

ARCHÆOLOGY.

Some Museums of Old London. A Series.
I. The Leverian Museum. By W. H. Mullens. (*The Museums Journ.*, vol. xv. pp. 123–129. 1915.)

CITY PARISHES.

Davis (E. Jeffries). A List of Parochial Records of the City Parishes, in 'The Victoria Hist. of London,' vol. i. 1909, pp. 404–405.

WESTMINSTER ABBEY.

Burtt (Joseph). Some Account of the Muniments of the Abbey of Westminster. (*Archæol. Journ. of the Roy. Archæol. Inst.* vol. xxix. pp. 135–150. 1872.)

Legg (J. Wickham). On an Inventory of the Vestry in Westminster Abbey in 1388. (*Archaeologia*, vol. lii. pp. 195–286. 1890.)

BANK OF ENGLAND.

Andréadès (A. M.). Biblio. of the Bank of England, in his 'Hist. of the Bank of England, 1640–1903.' London, 1909, pp. 429–445.

PRINTERS.

Welch (Charles). Biblio. Note on London Printing, in 'The Victoria Hist. of Middlesex,' vol. ii. 1911, pp. 197–200.

Peddie (R. A.). The St. Bride Typographical Lib.: its Methods and Classification. (*The Library Assoc. Record*, vol. xviii. pp. 235–258. 1916.)

A Note by William Morris on his aims in founding the Kelmscott Press, with a description of the Press, and a List of the Books printed thereat. 1898. The last book printed at the Press.

LAMBETH.

Botfield (Beriah). Notes on the Cathedral Libraries of England. 1849. **Lambeth Palace Library,** pp. 189–258.

James (Montague R.). MSS. in the Library at Lambeth Palace. (*Camb. Antiq. Soc. Octavo Pubns.*, no. xxxiii. 1900.)

SOUTHWARK.

Report on Deeds and Documents relating to the Parish Property of St. Saviour, Southwark. 1841.

MIDDLESEX.

TWICKENHAM.

Merritt (E. Percival). An Account of Descriptive Catalogues of Strawberry Hill, and of Strawberry Hill Sale Catalogues, together with a Bibliography. Privately Printed. Boston, Mass. 1915.

Journal of the Printing-office at Strawberry Hill, by Horace Walpole. (A MS. in the Waller Collection at Woodcote, Warwick.) See a note in 'Bodleian Quarterly Record,' vol. i. pp. 206–207. 1915.

MONMOUTHSHIRE.

Coxe (William). An Historical Tour in Monmouthshire. London, 1801. A List of the principal Works consulted, pt. II. p. 432.

A Digest of the Parish Registers within the Diocese of Llandaff previous to 1836. (Comprises Monmouthshire.) See *ante* under 'Glamorganshire,' p. 73.

Haines (William). Notes on Charles Heath, Printer, etc., of Monmouth. Reprinted from 'Monmouthshire Beacon,' 1908.

A Collection of Prints and Drawings relating to the Co. of Monmouth, collected by John Proctor Eeles of Penarth, is in the National Library of Wales at Aberystwyth. See 'Report of Council of the Library,' 1911, p. 10.

MUNSTER.

Art Catal. of the First Munster Exhibition, with notes by Robert Day. (*Cork Hist. & Archæol. Soc. Journ.*, Ser. 2, vol. iv. pp. 308–317. 1898.)

NAIRNSHIRE.

Ree (Rev. Stephen). Biblio. of the Counties of Moray and Nairn. Aberdeen, 1916.

NORFOLK.

Blomefield (Francis). 'Queries' circulated for his 'Hist. of Norfolk.' 1736. See 'Bibl. Topog. Brit.' 1790, vol. i. p. 1.)

Rye (Walter). Norfolk Families. Pt. II. Index Nominum, being an Index to Christian Names and Surnames in the Work, by Charles Nowell. Norwich, 1915.

—— **An Appendix to Rye's Index to Norfolk Topography.** [Rye's Norfolk Hand Lists, Ser. II. no. 1.] Norwich, 1916.

—— **References to all Printed Accounts of Roman Camps and Remains in Norfolk.** [*Ibid.* Ser. I. no. 2.]

—— **Castles and Manor Houses from the Conquest to the present time,** being references to all Printed Accounts. [*Ibid.* Ser. I. no. 3.]

Stephen (George A.). Norfolk Celebrities. I. Horatio, Viscount Nelson. Biblio. (*Norw. Public Lib. Readers' Guide*, vol. iv. no. 4. July, 1915. **II. Norfolk Artists. An Annotated Catal. of the Books, Pamphlets, and Articles relating to deceased Norfolk Artists, in the Norwich Public Lib.** (*Ibid.* vol. iv. nos. 5 & 6. Sept. & Nov. 1915.)

Hist. MSS. Comm. Reports. Norfolk Collections.

Norfolk, Duke of	Various Collections, vol. vii. pp. 153–246. 1914.
Thetford Corporation	—— vol. vii. pp. 119–152. 1914.

NORFOLK (*continued*).

Deeds and Documents relating to Norwich in the possession of the Sussex Archaeol. Soc. See *ante* under Sussex, p. 256.

HOLKHAM.

Roscoe (W.) Some Account of the Manuscript Library at Holkham, belonging to T. W. Coke, Esq. (*Roy. Soc. of Lit. Trans.*, vol. ii. pp. 352–379. 1834.)

KING'S LYNN.

Parkin (Charles). The Topography of Freebridge Hundred and Half, containing the Hist. & Antiquities of the Borough of King's Lynn. Lynn, 1762.

An Extra-illustrated copy enlarged by numerous water-colour drawings, engravings, etc., is in the Lib. of the Brit. Museum at 1853, d. 15.

Guide to the Contents of the Greenland Fishery Museum, King's Lynn. 1912. (Lynn Views, Maps, Drawings, Antiquities, the Eugene Aram Relics, Lynn MSS., Scarce Lynn Books, Norfolk and Lynn Printing.)

Nelson (Robert C.). A Collection of Engravings, Drawings, Autographs, Newspaper Cuttings, etc., relating to King's Lynn, formed prior to 1870. [In the Lib. of the Brit. Museum.]

Rye (Walter). Index to Red Book of Lynn. [Typewritten.] 1915.

THETFORD.

Corporation Records, see *ante* Hist. MSS. Comm. Reports.

NORTHAMPTONSHIRE.

List of Books and Documents in the Peterborough Diocesan Registry, with introduction by A. P. Moore. Appendix to Third Report of the Joint Committee of the Convocation of Canterbury on Local Eccles. Records, 1910, in 'The Chron. of Convocation,' 1910, no. II.

MOULTON.

Madge (Sidney J.). Materials for a Hist. of Moulton, being a short chronological summary of the Collections formed by S. J. Madge. Northampton. [1903.] 25 copies only privately printed.

NORTHUMBERLAND.

Catal. of the MSS., Books, Roman and other Antiquities, belonging to the Soc. of Antiquaries of Newcastle-upon-Tyne. Privately printed. Newcastle, 1839.

Anderton (Basil). Thomas Bewick, the Tyneside Engraver. (*The Library*, Ser. 3, vol. vi. pp. 365–384; vol. vii. pp. 1–17. 1915–16.) Also issued separately.

Budge (E. A. T. Wallis). An Account of the Roman Antiquities preserved in the Museum at Chesters, Northumberland. Second edn. London, 1907.

Chap. I. Antiquarian labours of John Clayton, F.S.A.
,, II. The Clayton Collection in the Museum at Chesters.
,, III. A List of the Papers contributed to 'Archaeologia Aeliana' by John Clayton, F.S.A., with Appendix 'A List of the Papers on the Antiquities in the Museum at Chesters which have been contributed to 'Archaeologia Aeliana' by various writers.
,, X. Ancient and Modern Authorities on the Roman Wall. Catal. of the Roman Antiquities in the Museum at Chesters. List of Water-Colour Drawings at Chesters.

NOTTINGHAMSHIRE.

Nottinghamshire County Records. Notes and Extracts from the Notts. County Records of the 17th. cent. Compiled by H. Hampton Copnall, with Biblio. Notes and Lists. [County Records Comm. of the Notts. County Council.] Nottingham, 1915.

Hist. MSS. Comm. Reports. Nottinghamshire Collections.

Lloyd, Sir Hervey Juckes, at Clifton Hall, Nottingham	Various Collections, vol. vii. pp. 247–296, 389–433. 1914.
Staunton, Mr. H. C., of Staunton, Notts.	——— pp. 360–375.

Notts. MSS., collected by William Constable. See Sale Catal. of the Burton Constable MSS., Sold by Sotheby's, 24–26 June, 1889, pp. 50–52.

ORKNEY AND SHETLAND.

A Short Biblio. of Orkney and Shetland, by Alfred W. Johnston. (*The Reliquary & Illustrated Archæol.*, vol. ii. p. 101. 1896.) See also *ante* p. 16, Mowat, Biblio. of Caithness, 1909.

Records of the Earldom of Orkney, 1299-1614. Edited with introduction and notes by J. Storer Clouston. (*Scottish Hist. Soc. Pubns.*, Ser. 2, vol. vii. 1914.)

Jo. Ben's Description of Orkney, 1529. Biblio. Notes in Preface to Macfarlane's 'Geog. Collections, etc.,' vol. iii. pp. vii.–xiii. See *ante* p. 201.

OXFORDSHIRE.

Indexes [in vol. iii.] to 'Survey of the Antiquities of the City of Oxford composed in 1661-1666, by Anthony Wood,' edited by Andrew Clark. [Oxf. Hist. Soc.] Oxford, 1899.

Rawlinson (Richard). 'Queries' circulated for a description of Oxfordshire. See 'Bibl. Topog. Brit.', vol. i. p. 1.

Early Oxford College MSS. A rough List of Oxford College MSS. written before 1200. (*The Bodleian Quarterly Record*, vol. i. pp. 157–162. 1915.)

Bodleian Catalogues of the Seventeenth Century. Résumé of Paper read before the Biblio. Soc. by Strickland Gibson. (*Ibid.* vol. i. pp. 228–232. 1915.)

The Lives of those eminent Antiquaries John Leland, Thomas Hearne, and Anthony à Wood; with an Authentick Account of their respective Writings and Publications. 2 vols. Oxford, 1772.

Christ Church, Oxford. An Anthology in Prose and Verse, selected by Arthur Hassall. London, 1911.

Jeffery (Reginald W.). The Oxford Press, in 'The Victoria Hist. of Oxfordshire,' vol. ii. 1907, pp. 229–235.

Index to the 'Transactions' and 'Reports' of the Oxfordshire Archæol. Soc., 1853-1915. (In 'Report' for 1915.)

PEMBROKESHIRE.

Owen (Henry). Calendar of the Public Records relating to Pembrokeshire. Vol. i. Haverford, 1204–1547. (*Cymmrodorion Soc. Record Series*, 1911.)

Haverfordwest Books. Additions to List by T. L. Jones. (*Welsh Biblio. Soc. Journ.*, vol. i. p. 259. 1915.)

ROSCOMMON.

Dix (Ernest Reginald McClintock). Printing in Athlone in 19th century. (*The Irish Book Lover*, vol. vi. pp. 106–108. 1915.)

——— **Printing in Boyle, with a List.** (*Ibid.* vol. vii. pp. 24–26. 1915.)

RUTLANDSHIRE.

Peck (Francis). 'Queries' for Rutlandshire. See *ante* p. 337.

Hist. MSS. Comm. Rep. Report on the MSS. of Allan George Finch, of Burley-on-the-Hill, vol. i. 1913. See also *ante* p. 218.

SHROPSHIRE.

Shropshire MSS. (Church Notes, Extracts from Parish Registers, Records, Pedigrees, etc.), from Halston Library. See 'Sale Catal. of the Library (First Portion) of Leonard Lawrie Hartley,' sold by Puttick & Simpson, 12 June, 1885, pp. 164–165.

Shropshire MS. Collections by Hardwicke, of Bridgnorth. See Sale Catal. of the Library (Third Portion) of Leonard Lawrie Hartley, sold by Puttick & Simpson, 18 April, 1887, p. 286.

Extracts from the Cartulary of St. Peter's Abbey at Shrewsbury, comprising an Index of the Charters. (*Collectanea Topog. et Geneal.*, 1834, vol. i. pp. 23–28, 190–196.)

Thomas Jones, the Almanacer (of Shrewsbury, Printer, etc.). (*Welsh Biblio. Soc. Journ.*, vol. i. pp. 239–245. 1915.)

SOMERSETSHIRE.

Cassan (Stephen Hyde). List of Portraits of Bishops of Bath and Wells, in 'Lives of the Bishops of Bath and Wells.' London, 1829–30, pt. I. pp. 69–70.

Hewitt (Ethel M.) Biblio. Note on Somerset Printing, in 'The Victoria Hist. of Somerset,' vol. ii. 1911, pp. 357–358.

WELLS.

Reynolds (Herbert Edward). Wells Cathedral: Its Foundation, Constitution, History, and Statutes. n.d. Biblio. Notes in Introduction, with List of Books in possession of the Dean and Chapter.

STAFFORDSHIRE.

Index-Catal. of the Reference Department of the Wolverhampton Free Library. 1895. Sect. I. Local Section. (Staffs. & Wolverhampton Books), pp. 1–29.

Whitfield (A. S.). William Henry Duignan, Bibliography, 1865-1912. (*Notes & Queries*, Ser. 11, vol. xi. pp. 373–374. 1915.)

SUFFOLK.

MS. Collections for Suffolk, by Ford and others. See Sale Catal. of the Library (Second Portion) of Leonard Lawrie Hartley, sold by Puttick & Simpson, 3 May, 1886.

Unwin (George). Biblio. Note on Suffolk Printing, in 'The Victoria Hist. of Suffolk,' vol. ii. 1907, pp. 288–289.

SURREY.

Giuseppi (Montague S.). Biblio. Note on Surrey Printing, in 'The Victoria Hist. of Surrey,' vol. ii. 1907, pp. 421–424.

LOSELEY.

Calendar of the Loseley MSS.

[A. J. Kempe's work (see *ante* p. 251) has recently been supplemented by a valuable and well-arranged Calendar (so far only in the typewritten stage). The Loseley MSS. are well known to be of the highest historical value and contain a large number of documents connected with the County and elsewhere.]

SUSSEX.

A Bookseller and Stationer's Shop-Bill. (Lewis Meryon, a Bookseller at Rye). Printed for Brash & Reid, Glasgow. 1810?

Phillipps (Sir Thomas). Battle Abbey MSS. Descriptive Account of the Collection of original Charters, and Muniments of the Abbey of Battle, together with Papers of the Browne and Webster families. 1835.

HASTINGS.

Cousins (Henry). Hastings of Bygone Days—and the Present. Hastings, 1911. (Contains Notes on Old Maps and Views of Hastings, with a List; a List of the Principal Guide Books, 1794–1812, and Biblio. Notes on Hastings and St. Leonards Newspapers.)

TIPPERARY.

Dix (Ernest Reginald McClintock). John Davis White and Cashel Printing, with a List of Books printed in Cashel in the 19th century. (*The Irish Book Lover*, vol. vi. pp. 193–197. 1915.)

TYRONE.

Dix (Ernest Reginald McClintock). Printing in Strabane, 1825-1900, with a List. (*The Irish Book Lover*, vol. vii. pp. 68–69. 1915.)

ULSTER.

McCance (Stouppe). Some Old Ulster Song Books, with a List. (*The Irish Book Lover*, vol. vii. pp. 108–110. 1916.)

WARWICKSHIRE.

COVENTRY.

Harris (Mary Dormer). The MSS. of Coventry. (*Bristol & Glos. Archæol. Soc. Trans.*, vol. xxxvii. pp. 187–193. 1914.) A Catal. of 350 Deeds relating to Coventry, by the same authoress, appeared in the 'Coventry Herald,' in 1912–14.

A Local Collection to be called 'The Coventry and Warwickshire Library' is being formed at the Coventry Public Library, but is not yet catalogued.

WATERFORD.

Dix (Ernest Reginald McClintock). Printing in the City of Waterford in the Seventeenth Century. (*Royal Irish Acad. Proc.*, vol. xxxii. sec. C. pp. 333–344. 1916.) See also pamphlet reprinted from the 'Waterford News.'

Printing in Waterford in 17th. and 18th. Centuries. (*The Irish Book Lover*, vol. vii. pp. 170–172. 1916.)

WILTSHIRE.

Old Wiltshire Newspapers. [Notes from the Centenary No. of 'The Wiltshire Gazette,' by Edward Kite.] (*Wilts. Notes & Queries*, vol. viii. pp. 414–417. 1916.)

The Centenary of 'The Wiltshire Gazette.' Centenary No. 1916. See review in 'The Wilts Archæol. & Nat. Hist. Mag.' vol. xxxix. p. 298. 1916.

Richardson (Mrs. Herbert). The Old 'Salisbury Journal' and Early Newspaper Enterprise in Salisbury. (In 'Salisbury, South Wilts and Blackmore Museum, 1864–1914; The Festival Book of Salisbury.' 1915. See also 'The Wilts Archæol. & Nat. Hist. Mag.' vol. xxxix. p. 285. 1916.

Baker (Thomas Henry). Monumental Inscriptions and Heraldry in Salisbury Cathedral [Baker MSS. Collection]. Index by H. B. W. (*Notes & Queries*, Ser. 12, vol. i. pp. 425–426. 1916.)

WORCESTERSHIRE.

Williams (J. B.). Biblio. Note on 'Berrow's Worcester Journal.' (*Notes & Queries*, Ser. 11, vol x. pp. 21–22, 46. 1914.)

Report of Parish Register Committee of the Worcester Dioc. Conference, with specimen pages of Digest. See Report of Joint Committee of the Convocation of Canterbury on Local Eccles. Records, 1905. App. III. pp. 11–17. Also issued in 'The Chron. of Convocation,' 1905. No. 1.

WORCESTERSHIRE (continued).

The Middle Hill Press. A List of the Privately Printed Publications of Sir Thomas Phillipps. See 'Sale Catal. of the Library (Second Portion) of Leonard Lawrie Hartley,' sold by Puttick & Simpson, 5 May, 1886, pp. 120-130.

The List contains 272 items, and is stated to be the most complete set ever offered for sale. It embraces the entire collections of Sir C. G. Young and Sir F. Madden, as well as that collected by L. L. Hartley.

——— **List of Privately Printed Works of Sir Thomas Phillipps.** See Lord Crawford's 'Bibliotheca Lindesiana. Catal. of the Printed Books at Haigh Hall, Lancs.' 1910, vol. iii. cols. 7041-7058.

YORKSHIRE.

Ellis (A. S.). Yorkshire circa A.D. 420, according to Ptolemy's Geography. (*Thoresby Soc. Pubns.*, vol. xxii. pp. 339-346. 1914.)

Sheppard (Thomas). Yorkshire's Contribution to Science, with a Biblio. of Nat. Hist. Publications. Hull, 1916.

ENGLAND.

[GENERAL WORKS.]

[The List of Books and References in this Section attempts only to give a few of the leading well-known Guides. Its chief purpose is to direct attention to many of the less-known bibliographies, indexes, etc.]

Anderson (John Parker). The Book of British Topography. A Classified Catal. of the Topog. Works in the Lib. of the Brit. Mus. relating to Great Britain & Irel. 1881. A New edition in preparation.

Gough (Richard). British Topography, or, an Hist. Account of what has been done for illustrating the Topog. Antiquities of Gt. Brit. & Irel. 2 vols. London, 1780.

For an account of Gough's own copy, in 5 vols., at the Bodleian Lib., Oxford, which he had prepared for a Third edn., see Macray's 'Annals,' 1890, p. 289.

Bandinel (Bulkeley). A Catal. of the Books relating to Brit. Topog., etc., bequeathed to the Bodl. Lib. in 1799, by Richard Gough. Oxford, 1814.

Upcott (William). A Biblio. Account of the principal Works relating to English Topography. 3 vols. London, 1818.

Spalding (John Tricks). A Biblio. Account of the Works relating to English Topography in the Lib. of John Tricks Spalding, Nottingham. 5 vols. Exeter, 1912–13. Privately printed.

Hotten (John Camden). A Hand-book to the Topog. and Family Hist. of Engl. & Wales. London, n.d.

Smith (Alfred Russell). A Catal. of Ten Thousand Tracts and Fifty Thousand Prints and Drawings, illustrating the Topography & Antiquities of England, Wales, Scotland, and Ireland. Collected by William Upcott and John Russell Smith. London, 1878.

Daniell (Walter V.) and Nield (Frederick J.). Manual of Brit. Topography. A Catal. of County and Local Histories, etc. London, 1909.

Sonnenschein (William Swan). The Best Books. 3rd edn. London, 1912. Pt. II. (includes Topography).

Hoare (Sir R. C.). A Catal. of Books relating to the Hist. & Topog. of Engl., Wales, Scot., & Irel., at Stourhead, Wilts. 1815. 25 copies only printed.

——— **Catal. of the Hoare Lib. at Stourhead, co. Wilts.,** compiled by J. Bowyer Nichols. London, 1840.

Catal. of the Library in the Public Record Office, and Supplement. [Compiled by T. Craib.] Third Edition. London, 1902, 1909.

List of Topographical Works relating to Great Britain and Ireland, printed for official use, by the Library of the Public Record Office. 1907.

List of Works relating to British Genealogy and Local History. (*Bulletin of the New York Public Lib.*, vol. xiv. 1910.) Also issued separately.

Bibliotheca Phillippica. Sale Catalogues of the Library of Sir Thomas Phillipps, of Middle Hill, Worcs., and Thirlestaine House, Cheltenham, containing Historical, Topographical, Genealogical, and other Books and MSS. Sold by Sotheby's. London.

The followihg are the dates of the various Sales:—I. Aug. 3, 1886; II. Jan. 22, 1889; III. July 15, 1891; IV. Dec. 7, 1891; V. July 4, 1892; VI. June 19, 1893; VII. Mar. 21, 1895; VIII. June 10, 1896; IX. May 17, 1897; X. June 6, 1898; XI. June 5, 1899; XII. Apr. 27, 1903; XIII. June 15, 1908; XIV. June 6, 1910; XV. Apr. 24, 1911; XVI. May 19, 1913. See a list of the first eleven sales in 'The Times,' Apr. 6, 1903. For other items relating to Sir Thomas Phillipps, see under 'Worcestershire,' pp. 289, 315.

Sale Catal. of the Library of Leonard Lawrie Hartley, of Middleton Tyas, Yorks., and St. Leonards-on-Sea, containing an extensive collection of Topographical Books, MSS., Prints, Publications of Societies, etc. Compiled by J. Corbet Anderson. Sold by Puttick & Simpson, June 1–12, 1885; May 3–14, 1886; Apr. 18–27, 1887. The Topographical and Antiquarian Collections are arranged under Counties.

Guide to the Victoria History of the Counties of England. By H. Arthur Doubleday and William Page. London [1912].

(Contains Lists of Records in Public Depositories, arranged under Counties, pp. 49–120.)

Index to 'The Life and Times of Anthony Wood, Antiquary, of Oxford, 1632-1695, described by himself.' Edited by Andrew Clark for the Oxford Hist. Soc. 5 vols. Oxford, 1891–1900. The Index is Index II. Topographical, in Vol. V. pp. 85–142, and 'England' is arranged under Counties.

Rawlinson (Richard). The English Topographer, or an Historical Account of all the Pieces that have been written relating to the Antiquities or Topographical Description of any Part of England. London, 1720.

(Contains quaint Biblio. and other information arranged under Counties.)

Tymms (Samuel). The Family Topographer. 7 vols. London, 1832–43.

A useful and little-known work. Arranged under Counties.

Nichols (John). Queries proposed with a view of obtaining the most perfect Account of the Antiquities of Great Britain and Ireland, with a list of Topographical Queries circulated by compilers of various County Histories. See 'Bibliotheca Topographica Britannica,' vol. i. 1780, pp. i.–xiv.

A Catal. of Pamphlets, Tracts, Proclamations, Speeches, etc., from 1506 to 1700 in the Library of the Honourable Soc. of Lincoln's Inn. London, 1908.

Catal. of the Pamphlets, Books, Newspapers, and MSS. relating to the Civil War, the Commonwealth, and Restoration, collected by George Thomason, 1640-1661 [in the Brit. Mus. Library]. 2 vols. London, 1908.

Catal. of the Library of the London Institution, systematically classed. 4 vols. London, 1835–1852. Vol. ii. is devoted to valuable Collections of Topog. Tracts and Pamphlets.

Catal. of the Contents of Eighty Vols. of Antiquarian and Topographical Tracts at Stourhead, in 'Catal. of the Hoare Lib. at Stourhead,' compiled by J. Bowyer Nichols, 1840, pp. 106–119.

Bibliotheca Lindesiana. Catal. of the Printed Books at Haigh Hall, Wigan. Compiled for James Ludovic Lindsay, Earl of Crawford. 4 vols. 1910.

Arber (Edward). The Term Catalogues, 1668-1711. 3 vols. London, 1903–06. Privately printed.

Catal. of a Collection of Tracts illustrative of British History from the Accession of Chas. I. to the Present time. Printed for John Stevenson. Edinburgh, 1837.

Wheatley (Henry B.). Preliminary List of English Indexes, in his 'What is an Index?' London, 1879. (Index Soc. Pubn. I.)

A General Index to the 'Gentleman's Mag.', 1731-1786 [compiled by Samuel Ayscough]. 2 vols. London, 1789; **General Index, 1787-1818,** with a prefatory introduction descriptive of the Hist. of the Mag., by John Nichols, and a List and Index to Plates, 1731-1818. 3 vols. London, 1821. **An Index to the Biographical and Obituary Notices, 1731-1780,** by R. H. Farrar. British Record Soc. (Index Soc. Pubns. vol. xv.). 1891.

Ayscough (Samuel). 1745-1804. For Notes on Indexes compiled by Ayscough, and others, see vol. i. under 'Ayscough,' in Allibone (S. A.), 'Critical Dictionary of English Literature, etc.,' 1859-91.

A General Index to the 'Annual Register,' 1758-1780. 3rd edn. London, 1799.

General Index to Dodsley's Annual Register, vol. i.-lxi. 1758 1819. London, 1826.

'Notes and Queries.' General Indexes to Series I.-X. London, 1856-1910. Separate Indexes for each Series.

The Camden Society, 1838-1897. A Descriptive Catal. of the First Series of the Works of the Soc., stating the nature of their principal Contents, the periods of Time to which they relate, their MS. Sources, Authors, and Editors, with a Classified arrangement, and an Index. By John Gough Nichols. Second edn. London, 1872. A 'Catal. of the First Series, with a General Index' (A-Bau), unfinished, was issued in 1881.

Contents of the Harleian Miscellany (12 vols. London, 1808-11), with an Index. Compiled at the Public Library, Sydney, N.S.W., 1885.

Hazlitt (W. Carew). A General Index to Hazlitt's Handbook and his Biblio. Collections, 1867-1889, by G. J. Gray. London, 1893.

British Record Society. The Index Library, 1890, etc. London.

Sandys (Sir John Edwin). Scholars, Antiquaries, and Bibliographers, with a Biblio., in 'The Cambridge Hist. of English Literature,' vol. xii. chap. xv. pp. 323-371, and pp. 479-523. 1915.

Fuller (Thomas). The Hist. of the Worthies of England, with Notes by J. Nichols. New edition. 2 vols. London, 1811. (The work has a County arrangement.)

The Gentleman's Magazine Library; being a Classified Collection of the Chief Contents of the 'Gentleman's Mag.', from 1731 to 1868. Edited by G. Laurence Gomme. 30 vols. London, 1883-1905.

Gross (Charles). The Sources and Literature of English Hist. from the earliest times to about 1485. Second edn. London, 1915. Chronological Tables of the Principal Chronicles, Biographies, etc., pp. 712-718.

Hall (Hubert). The Biblio. of English Official Historical Documents, with lists of Depositories, etc., in his 'Studies in English Official Historical Documents,' 1908, pp. 101-118.

Gardiner (Samuel R.) and Mullinger (J. Bass). Introduction to the Study of English Hist. Third and Enlarged edition. London, 1894. List of Authorities, pp. 207-442.

Gairdner (James). Early Chroniclers of Europe. England. London, 1879.

Nicholas (Sir Nicholas Harris). Notitia Historica, containing Tables, Calendars and Miscellaneous Information, for the Use of Historians, Antiquarians, etc. London, 1824.

Turner (Dawson). Guide to the Historian, the Biographer, the Antiquary, etc. Yarmouth, 1848.

A Select Biblio. for the Study, Sources, and Literature of English Mediæval Economic History. Compiled by a Seminar of the London School of Economics. Edited by Hubert Hall. London, 1914.

Moore (Margaret Findlay). Two Select Biographies of Mediæval Historical Study. I. A Classified List of Works relating to the Study of English Palæography and Diplomatic. II. A Classified List of Works relating to English Manorial and Agrarian History from the Earliest Times to 1660. London, 1912.

Sutherland (Alexander Hendras). Collections in Illustration of Clarendon's 'Hist. of the Rebellion' and 'Life,' and Burnet's 'Own Times.' 61 vols. in elephant folio, containing 19224 Portraits, Views, etc. [In the Bodleian Library at Oxford.] A Printed Catal. in 3 vols. was issued in 1837 and a Supplement in 1838. See a note on the Collection in Macray's 'Annals,' pp. 332–333.

Index to Articles, Notes, Documents, and selected reviews of Books contained in vols. i.-xx. 1886-1905, of the 'English Historical Review.' London, 1906.

Catal. of Parliamentary Papers, 1801-1900, with a few of earlier date. Supplement, 1901-10. P. S. King & Son. London.

Index to the Local and Personal and Private Acts, 1798-1839. London, 1840.

Index to Local Acts, consisting of Classified Lists of the Acts from 1801 to 1899. London, 1900.

The Local and Private Acts, with an Index. Published at end of each Session.

Index (MS.) to the Contents of Sir George Nayler's Private Acts of Parliament, 1733-1835, 37 vols. in the Guildhall Library, contained in each vol. See note in 'Genealogical Queries and Memoranda,' edited by G. F. Tudor Sherwood, vol. i. p. 21. 1899. A list of the Pedigrees in the Collection is at pp. 21, 31, 53, 62, 85.

Firth (C. H.) and Rait (R. S.). Indices to their 'Acts and Ordinances of the Interregnum, 1642-1660,' with chronological Tables, in vol. iii. 1911.

Wheatley (Henry B.). Lists of Indexes to the Statutes (in his 'What is an Index?' 1879, pp. 96–98). **Indexes to the Journals of the Houses of Lords and Commons.** (*Ibid.* pp. 98–99.) **Indexes of Parliamentary Papers.** (*Ibid.* pp. 99–101.)

List of Places on the Inclosure Awards from 1757-1837. See App. I. 26th Report of Deputy Keeper of Public Records, 1865. **List of Awards, from 1756-1853.** See App. I. 27th Report of Deputy Keeper of Public Records, 1866.

Andrews (Charles M.) and Davenport (Frances G.). Guide to the Manuscript Materials for the Hist. of the United States to 1783, in the Brit. Museum, in Minor London Archives, and in the Libraries of Oxford & Cambridge. Washington, 1908. (Carnegie Instn. Pubn., 90.)

This work, with the next two items, contains valuable accounts of various important Collections, with lists of Catalogues, etc., which are accessible to the student either for English or American History.

Andrews (Charles M.). Guide to the Materials for American Hist., to 1783, in the Public Record Office of Gt. Britain. 2 vols. Washington, 1912, 1914. (Carnegie Instn. Pubn., 90. A.)

Paullin (Charles O.) and Paxson (Frederic L.). Guide to the Materials in London Archives for the Hist. of the United States since 1783. Washington, 1914. (Carnegie Instn. Pubn., 90. B.)

Biblio. of American Historical Societies, by A. P. Clark Griffin, in 'Annual Report of the Amer. Hist. Assoc. for 1905–07,' vol. ii. Washington, 1907.

Adam (Margaret I.), Ewing (John) and Munro (James). Guide to the Principal Parliamentary Papers relating to the Dominions, 1812–1911. Edinburgh, 1913.

Ellis (Sir Henry). A General Introduction to Domesday Book. 2 vols. London, 1833.

Index of Tenants in the time of William the Conqueror who held their lands immediately from the King, ordinarily styled Tenants in Capite. Vol. i. pp. 361-515.

Index of Persons, Monasteries, etc., entered in Domesday Book as holding lands in the time of K. Edwd. the Confessor, and through later years anterior to the formation of the Survey. Vol. ii. pp. 1-273.

Index of the Under-Tenants of lands at the formation of the Domesday Survey. Vol. ii. pp. 276-416.

Dove (Patrick Edward). Domesday Studies. London, 1891.

Domesday Commemoration, 1886. Notes on the MSS. and Printed Books exhibited at the Public Record Office and the Brit. Museum, pp. 623–662.

Domesday Bibliography. Edited by H. B. Wheatley, pp. 663-669.

Inman (A. H.). Domesday and Feudal Statistics. London, 1900. Population Statistics at various Periods, in 'Epitome,' pp. xxxvi.-xxxvii.

The Population of England in former times has also been dealt with by William Cunningham, Macaulay, Thorold Rogers, McCulloch in his 'Statistical Dictionary,' William Denton in his 'England in the Fifteenth Century,' and others, as well as in the succeeding items.

Abstract of the Population of the different Counties of England at the close of the reign of William the Conqueror, as far as the same is actually recorded in the Domesday Survey. See 'A General Introduction to Domesday Book,' by Sir Henry Ellis, 1833, vol. ii. pp. 417–514.

Return of the Population in 1676 of the Parishes of the Province of Canterbury, over sixteen years of age. (A MS. in the William Salt Lib. at Stafford.) See a note in 'How to Write the Hist. of a Parish,' by J. Charles Cox, 1909, p. 207.

List of Towns and Counties with approximate population in 1337, according to the Poll Tax of 51. Edwd. III. See 'Subsidy Roll of 51 Edwd. III.' by John Topham, in 'Archaeologia,' vol. vii. pp. 340–347. 1785. See also 'Remarks on the Population of English Cities, *temp.* Edw. III.', by Thomas Amyot, in 'Archaeologia,' vol. xx. pp. 524–531. 1824.

Report of the Commissioners appointed to inquire into the State, Custody, and Authenticity of Registers or Records of Births, etc., in England and Wales, other than the Parochial Registers. 1838.

Index of Archæological Papers, 1665–1890. Edited by George Laurence Gomme. London, 1907. **Indexes of Archæological Papers published in 1891,** etc., issued separately for each year, edited by G. Laurence Gomme, Bernard Gomme, Allan Gomme and William Martin.

Godwin (Henry). The English Archæologist's Handbook. Oxford, 1867. Alphabetical List of Castles having Royal Licenses to fortify, granted 1256–1478, pp. 233–251. Chronological Table of English Armour and Arms from the 11th to the 17th cent., pp. 252–268.

Armitage (Ella S.). A Key to English Antiquities. Sheffield, 1897.

Clinch (George). Handbook of British Antiquities. London, 1905.

Lyell (Arthur H.). A Biblio. List descriptive of Romano-British Architectural Remains in Great Britain. Cambridge, 1912.

Haverfield (F.). Roman Britain in 1913 and 1914. Biblio. of Publications. (*The British Academy, Supp. Papers*, II. and III., 1914, 1915.)

Summary of Discoveries relating to Roman Britain, with Biblio. notes. By F. Haverfield. (*The Year's Work in Classical Studies*, 1906–07); by H. B. Walters. (*Ibid.* 1908–09); by F. A. Bruton. (*Ibid.* 1910, etc.)

Evans (Sir John). The Ancient Bronze Implements, etc., of Gt. Brit. & Irel. London, 1881. 'England' arranged under Counties in Geog. & Topog. Index.

—— **The Ancient Stone Implements, etc., of Gt. Britain.** Second edition. London, 1897. 'England' arranged under Counties in Geog. & Topog. Index.

Scheme for Recording Ancient Defensive Earthworks and Fortified Enclosures. 1903. Appendix II. 1905.

Report of the Committee on Ancient Earthworks and Fortified Enclosures. Congress of Archæol. Societies, 1905, etc. With Biblio. lists of recent literature on the subject.

Kemble (J. M.). List of Anglo-Saxon Towns, Cities, and Boroughs mentioned in the 'Anglo-Saxon Chronicle,' in his 'Saxons in England,' 1876, vol. ii. pp. 551–558.

Searle (William George). Onomasticon Anglo-Saxonicum. A List of Anglo-Saxon Proper Names, etc. Cambridge, 1897. Biblio. of Works consulted, pp. xxxii.–lvii.

Birch (Walter de Gray). An Index to all the Names of Persons and Places in the 'Cartularium Saxonicum,' 3 vols. 1883-99. London, 1899.

Cunningham (William). List of Towns declared to be decayed in the time of Henry VIII. See his 'Growth of English Industry and Commerce during the Early & Middle Ages,' 5th edn., 1910, p. 507.

Sims (Richard). List of Towns of which MSS. exist in the Brit. Museum, in his 'Handbook to the Library of the Brit. Museum,' 1854, pp. 177–209.

Harvey (Alfred). List of Castles in England and Wales, existing or known to have existed, in his 'Castles and Walled Towns of England.' London, 1911. See also Godwin's 'English Archæologist's Handbook,' 1867, pp. 183–232.

Clay (Rotha Mary). Tabulated List (arranged under Counties) of Mediæval Hospitals in England, with Biblio., in her 'Mediæval Hospitals of England,' 1909, pp. 277–342.

Index to the 'Archæological Journal' of the Royal Archæological Institute of Great Britain, vols. i.–xxv. 1844–68. London, 1878.

General Index to the 'Journal of the British Archæological Association,' vols. i.–xxx. 1845–74; vols. xxxi.–xliii. 1875–86; and to 'Collectanea Archæologica,' vols. i.–ii., etc. London, 1875, 1887.

An Index to the 'Archaeologia,' vols. i.–l. 1704 1887, published by the Soc. of Antiquaries of London. 1889.

A General Index to the 'Proceedings' of the Soc. of Antiq., London, First Series, vols. i.–iv. 1843–58 (in vol. iv.). **Second Series, vols. i.–xx. 1859–1905, with Classified List of Illustrations.** London, 1908.

Index to Engravings in the 'Proceedings' of the Soc. of Antiq., London. By Edward Peacock. London, 1885. (Index Soc. Occasional Indexes, No. 1.)

Catal. of Printed Books in the Library of the Soc. of Antiq. London, 1887. **Supplement, 1887-1899.** London, 1899.

Year-Book of Scientific and Learned Societies of Gt. Brit. & Irel. London, 1884, etc. Issued yearly, and contains lists of the Contents of the Publications of various Societies.

A List of County Associations in London, by Rev. J. Leonard E. Hooppell, in Bernau's 'International Genealogical Directory.' Second edn. Second Supp., 1910, pp. xlvi.–xlviii.

Murray (David). List of Museums in the United Kingdom, with Biblio., in his 'Museums, their History, etc.' 3 vols. Glasgow, 1904.

Keyser (Charles E.). A List of Buildings in Gt. Brit. & Irel. having Mural and other Painted Decorations, of dates prior to the latter part of the Sixteenth Century (with a County Classification). Third edn. London, 1883.

Nelson (Philip). County Lists of Ancient Glass, in his 'Ancient Painted Glass in England, 1170–1500.' (The Antiquary's Books.) London, 1913, pp. 51–260.

Dryden (Sir Henry). A Catal. of the Collection of Drawings, Plans, Notes on Churches, Houses, and various Archæol. matters made by the late Sir Henry E. L. Dryden, of Canons Ashby, Northants. Northampton, 1912. See *ante*, p. 184.

Boyne (William). Trade Tokens issued in the Seventeenth Century in England, Wales, and Ireland. New Edition, by G. C. Williamson. 2 vols. London, 1889–91. The Work is arranged according to Counties.

Catal. of Seals in the Dep. of MSS. in the Brit. Museum. By Walter de Gray Birch. 6 vols. London, 1887–1900. The first 4 vols. deal with English, Scottish & Irish Seals, arranged under Places.

Macklin (H. W.). Monumental Brasses, with a selected Biblio., & County Lists of Brasses remaining in the Churches of the United Kingdom. London, 1913. For Biblio. purposes this book supersedes the same author's 'The Brasses of England,' 1907.

Haines (Herbert). A Manual of Monumental Brasses. 2 vols. Oxford, 1861. A List of Monumental Brasses in the Brit. Isles arranged under Counties, in vol. ii. pp. 1–242.

List of Books on Sepulchral Monuments, Inscriptions, Obituaries, and Epitaphs. See Gatfield's 'Guide to English Heraldry,' 1892, pp. 231–239.

The Register of English Monumental Inscriptions. Published by the English Monumental Inscriptions Soc. from 1911, contains County Lists of Transcripts.

Monumental Brass Society. Transactions. 6 vols. 1887–1914. Lists of Brasses for Hampshire, Surrey, Derbyshire, Cambs., Essex, Hunts., Beds., and other Counties have appeared in the 'Transactions.' An Index of Places arranged according to Counties occurs in each volume.

A List of Illustrations in Druitt's 'Costume on Brasses,' and Macklin's 'Brasses of England,' arranged topographically (under Counties). See 'Trans. Mon. Brass Soc.,' vol. v. pp. 235–241. 1909.

Weever (John). Ancient Funerall Monuments within the United Monarchie of Great Britain. London, 1631.

Bibliographies of the Lives of Antiquaries and Topographers. See 'The Cambridge Hist. of English Literature,' edited by A. W. Ward and A. R. Waller, vols. i.–xii. 1907–15, *passim*.

Rye (Walter). A Short Antiquarian, etc., Directory, in his 'Records and Record Searching,' pp. 180–192. Second edn. London, 1897. Similar lists are in 'A Select Biblio. of English Mediæval Economic Hist.,' edited by Hubert Hall, 1914, pp. 272–283, and in 'The Sources and Literature of Engl. Hist.,' by Charles Gross, 1915, pp. 20–30.

Quaritch (Bernard). Summary of an Address on 'The Great Learned Societies and Chief Printing Clubs of Gt. Brit. & Irel.' [Sette of Odd Volumes. Miscellany. No. xv.] London, 1886.

De Mély (Fernand) and Bishop (Edmund). Bibliographie Générale des Inventaires Imprimés. Paris, 1892. A valuable and little-known book. England is dealt with in vol. i. pp. 136–335, and vol. ii. pp. 335–370.

Brand's Popular Antiquities of Gt. Britain, largely extended and now first alphabetically arranged by W. Carew Hazlitt. 2 vols. London, 1905.

Northall (G. F.). English Folk-Rhymes. A Collection of Traditional Verses relating to Places and Persons, etc. (arranged under Counties). London, 1892.

County Folk-Lore. Examples of Printed Folk-Lore. 7 vols. The Folk-Lore Soc. 1895–1914.

Vol. 1. Gloucestershire, Suffolk, Leicestershire & Rutland.
Vol. 2. N. R. of Yorkshire, etc.
Vol. 3. Orkney & Shetland Islands.
Vol. 4. Northumberland.
Vol. 5. Lincolnshire.
Vol. 6. E. R. of Yorkshire.
Vol. 7. Fife, etc.

Gomme (Alice Bertha). The Traditional Games of England, Scotland, and Ireland, with annotations. 2 vols. 1894–98. (In 'A Dictionary of British Folk-Lore,' edited by G. Laurence Gomme.) Lists of Authorities arranged under Counties in both vols.

A Biblio. List of the Works that have been published, or are known to exist in MS. of the various Dialects of England. Compiled by Members of the English Dialect Soc. and Edited by Walter W. Skeat and J. H. Nodal. London, 1877.

Wright (Joseph). Biblio. of the Principal Books, MSS. etc. quoted, with an Index (arranged under Counties), in his 'English Dialect Dictionary,' vol. vi. 1905.

Notestein (Wallace). Biblio. of Witchcraft Trials, etc. in England, in Appendices to his 'Hist. of Witchcraft from 1558 to 1718.' Amer. Hist. Assoc. Washington, 1911.

Phillimore (W. P. W.). The Parish Historian: A short initial Guide for Writing, Printing, and Illustrating the Hist. of a Parish. London, 1905.

Cox (J. Charles). How to Write the Hist. of a Parish. An outline Guide to Topog. Records, MSS. and Books. Fifth edn. London, 1909.

Smith (Joshua Toulmin). The Parish, its Obligations and Powers, its Officers and their Duties. Second edn. London, 1857. Parish Records, pp. 486–541.

Eden (Sir Frederick Morton). Parochial Reports (arranged under Counties) and Catal. of English Publications concerning the poor, in his 'State of the Poor.' 1797, vols. ii. & iii.

Biblio. of Parish Records. In preparation by the Librarian of the London School of Economics, see 'Library Assoc. Record,' Aug. 1915.

Gross (Charles). Biblio. of Guilds in England, in his 'The Gild Merchant,' Oxford, 1890, vol. i. pp. 301–332. The second vol. is mainly a list of Towns in Gt. Britain, with documentary proofs of the existence and history of Guilds in each place.

——— **A Biblio. of Brit. Municipal Hist.** (*Harvard Hist. Studies*, vol. v.) New York, 1897.

——— **List of Town Records of Gt. Britain.** (*The Amer. Hist. Rev.*, vol. ii. pp. 191–200. 1896.)

Gomme (G. Laurence). The Literature of Local Institutions. London, 1886.

Rhodes (A.). Lists of Municipal Records Printed. (*Notes and Queries*, Series 11, vol. ii. pp. 450, 529; vol. iii. p. 493; vol. iv. pp. 131, 390, 451; vol. v. pp. 73, 297, 352, 398, 478; vol. vi. p. 91. 1910–12.)

Webb (Sidney and Beatrice). English Local Government from the Revolution to the Municipal Corporations Act. 3 vols. London, 1906–08. (Biblio. footnotes.)

Flower (Cyril Thomas). Public Works in Mediaeval Law. [Records relating to the maintenance of Roads, Bridges, etc., arranged under Counties.] Vol. i. (Beds.—Lincs.) Selden Soc. London, 1915.

Ballen (Dorothy). Biblio. of Road-Making and Roads in the United Kingdom. London, 1914.

Davenport (Frances G.). A Classified List of Printed Original Materials for English Manorial and Agrarian History during the Middle Ages. (Radcliffe Coll. Monographs, No. 6.) Boston, U.S.A., 1894.

Reports of the Royal Commission on Market Rights and Tolls. Parliamentary Papers. 1888, liii.–lv.; 1889, xxxviii.; 1890–91, xxxvii.–xli. 14 vols. in 17.

Index to the Reports of the Commissioners for enquiry concerning Charities in England and Wales. London, 1840.

An Account of Public Charities in England and Wales, abridged from the Reports of the Commissioners on Charitable Foundations. London, 1826. (Arranged under Towns.)

Hone (Nathaniel J.). Biblio. of Manorial Literature, in his 'The Manor and Manorial Records.' 2nd edn. London, 1912. App. II. pp. 312–336.

——— **List of Court Rolls in various Depositories.** (Public Record Office, Brit. Museum, Lambeth Palace, and Bodleian Library.) (*Ibid.* App. I. pp. 243–301.)

The Public Rec. Off. 'Lists & Indexes,' No. VI., does not include the Court Rolls kept there which are indexed in the foregoing list.

Lists of Manor Court Rolls in Private Hands. Edited by Alfred L. Hardy, with introductions by Charles Greenwood and N. J. Hone. Pts. I.–III. 1907–10. (The Manorial Society's Monographs.) A General Index is to be published. The Manorial Soc. is preparing a card-index to all the references to Manors and Manorial Documents in the Reports of the Hist. MSS. Comm.

Phillipps (Sir Thomas). Indexes of Leases of Manors and Lands in England granted since the Reformation, annis 4 & 5 Edw. VI. 1832.

Hearnshaw (F. J. C.). List of Printed and Unprinted Court Rolls, in his 'Leet Jurisdiction in England,' 1908, pp. 156–160. (Southampton Record Soc. Pubns.)

Matthews (George F.). Contemporary Index to Printed Parish (**and Non-Parochial Registers**), **1908 edition,** with a Supplementary List of MS. Transcripts to be found in the Public Libraries of England and Wales. London, 1908.

Marshall (George W.). Parish Registers: A List of those Printed, or of which MS. Copies exist in Public Collections, etc. London, 1900. Appendix, 1904. (Parish Register Soc. vols. xxx. and l.)

Burke (Arthur Meredyth). Key to the Ancient Parish Registers of England and Wales. London, 1908. Supplement, 1909.

Cox (J. Charles). The Parish Registers of England. London, 1910.

App. I. A List of some Bishops' Transcripts of Parish Registers whose dates are older than the Parish Registers, pp. 261–263.
App. II. List of Parish Registers beginning in 1538, pp. 264–269.
App. III. List of Parish Registers beginning in 1539, pp. 270–271.
App. IV. List of Printed Parish Registers, pp. 272–282.

List of Episcopal and other Registers. See Stubbs, 'Registrum Sacrum Anglicanum,' 1897, pp. vii. xiii.-xvi.

Crisp (Frederick A.). List of Parish Registers and other Genealogical Works, issued at the Private Press of F.A.C. London, 1899.

Phillimore (W. P. W.). Parish Registers, with suggestions for their Transcription. London, 1907.

Index Series of Phillimore's Parish Registers. London, 1915, etc. These Indexes are being issued County by County. Cornwall, vol. i. has appeared.

Blagg (Thomas M.). Catal. of Phillimore's Parish Register Series. London, 1913. A useful list with a County arrangement.

Williams (John Foster). List of Early Churchwardens' Accounts, in his 'The Early Churchwardens' Accounts of Hampshire,' pp. lxiii.-lxviii. Winchester, 1913.

Cox (J. Charles). Chron. List of Wardens' Accounts of the Sixteenth & Seventeenth Centuries, in his 'Churchwardens' Accounts,' pp. 44-52, 353. (The Antiquary's Books.) London, [1913].

—— **Index to Wardens' Accounts,** arranged under Counties. (*Ibid.* pp. 355-359.)

Hutchins (B. L.). Lists of reprinted Parish and other Accounts, etc., of the 15th to 17th centuries. (*Notes & Queries*, Ser. 9, vol. iv. pp. 301, 414, 452; vol. v. p. 63. 1899-1900.)

Philipps (Elsbeth). A List of Printed Churchwardens' Accounts. (*The English Hist. Rev.*, vol. xv. pp. 335-341. 1900.)

Report on the Transcription and Publication of Parish Registers, etc., 1892, with lists of Parish Registers printed or in MS., etc. Reprint, 1896. **Second Report, with Calendar of Registers printed and transcribed since the first Report of 1892.** Congress of Archæological Societies, 1896.

List of MSS. formerly in the possession of Cathedrals, Monasteries, Colleges and Churches in Engl., Scot. & Irel., & now in the Bodleian Lib. See W. D. Macray, 'Annals of the Bodl. Lib. Oxford,' 1890, pp. 439-450.

Ecclesiastical Records. First Report of the Joint Committee of the Convocation of Canterbury on the Collection and Custody of Local Ecclesiastical Records, 1905. (Issued in '*The Chronicle of Convocation*,' 1905, no. I.) **Second Report, 1906.** (*Ibid.* 1906, no. III.) **Third Report, 1910.** (*Ibid.* 1910, no. II.) Also issued separately.

Shaw (William A.). A Hist. of the English Church during the Civil Wars and under the Commonwealth, 1640-1660. 2 vols. London, 1900. The information is largely under a County arrangement.

Chronological List of Effigies of Anglican Bishops from 1547 to 1907 (with Biblio. references). See Appendix B, pp. 110-120, of Report of the Sub-Committee of the Upper House of the Convocation of Canterbury on 'The Ornaments of the Church and its Ministers,' 1908. The latter Report also contains Biblio. references and authorities.

Bond (Francis). Tables of Dedications of English Churches in Selected Counties, in his 'Dedications and Patron Saints of English Churches,' pp. 203-218. Oxford, 1914. The book has a Biblio.

List of Books on Parish Registers, in Gatfield's 'Guide to Books on Heraldry,' 1892, pp. 227-229.

The Registers of Protestant Dissenters. Biblio. note by A. L. Humphreys. (*Notes & Queries*, Ser. 11, vol. x. pp. 30-31. 1914.)

Calendar and Description of the Monastic and other Chartularies in the Public Record Office. See Deputy-Keeper's Report, 1847, viii. App. II. pp. 135–166.

Nichols (J. B.). List of Monastic Cartularies at present existing, or which are known to have existed since the Dissolution of Religious Houses. (*Collect. Topog. et Geneal.*, vol. i. pp. 73, 197, 399; vol. ii. pp. 102, 400. 1834–35.)

Lists of Monastic Chartularies. See Gross, 'Sources & Literature of English Hist.' 1915, p. 493; Sims, 'Manual for the Genealogist,' 1856, pp. 14–28, and 'Handbook to Lib. of Brit. Mus.,' 1854, pp. 210–220; 'Guide to the Victoria Hist. of the Counties of England,' 1912, pp. 49–120.

Phillipps (Sir Thomas). Index to Cartularies now, or formerly, existing since the Dissolution of Monasteries. Middle Hill Press, 1839.

Birch (Walter de Gray). Fasti Monastici Aevi Saxonici, or an alphabetical list of the Heads of Religious Houses in England previous to the Norman Conquest, etc. London, 1872.

Clapham (Alfred W.). List of the principal Remains of the Augustinian Order in England, with Biblio. References to the best published Plans, in his 'Lesnes Abbey, in the Parish of Erith, Kent.' App. C, pp. 82–84. (Woolwich Antiq. Soc.) London, 1915.

Luard (Henry R.). Index and Glossary to his 'Annales Monastici,' 1864–69, in vol. v. London, 1869. (*Chronicles & Memorials of Gt. Brit. & Irel.*)

General Index to Dugdale's 'Monasticum Anglicanum,' in vol. vi. pt. III. pp. 1665–1851, of New Edn. 1846, edited by John Caley, Sir Henry Ellis, & Rev. Bulkeley Bandinel.

A Hand-Book of English Ecclesiology (with notes on English Churches, classified under Counties, in Appendix. [Ecclesiological, late Cambridge Camden Soc.] London, 1847.

Gasquet (Francis Aidan). List of English Religious Houses, in his 'English Monastic Life,' 1904, pp. 251-317. 2nd Edn. London, 1904.

Keyser (Charles E.). A List of Norman Tympana and Lintels, still or till recently existing in the Churches of Great Britain. London, 1904. (With a County classification and an alphabetical Catal., with Biblio. references.)

Madge (Sidney J.). Comprehensive Biblio. on Bells, 'Bibliotheca Campanalogica,' in his 'Moulton Church and its Bells,' 1895, pp. 78-98.

Cox (J. Charles) and Harvey (Alfred). List of Early Lecterns, in their 'English Church Furniture,' 1907, pp. 80–81. **List of Churches with Screens and Rood-lofts.** (*Ibid.* pp. 101–143.) **List of Pre-Reformation Pulpits, Hour-Glasses and Stands.** (*Ibid.* pp. 148–159.) **List of the principal Church Fonts.** (*Ibid.* pp. 185–231.) **List of Stalls and Misericords in English Churches.** (*Ibid.* pp. 259–261.) **List of Seats and Benches in English Churches.** (*Ibid.* pp. 261–282.) The Lists are arranged under Counties. Biblio. references are interspersed in the descriptions of each.

Stride (Edward Ernest). A Biblio. of some Works relating to the Huguenot Refugees, whence they came, and where they settled. (*Huguenot Soc. of London*, Proc., vol. i. pp. 130–149. 1886.)

Ten Years' Work of the Catholic Record Soc., with List of Contents of vols. issued 1904-1914, and a short Classified List. By Rev. John H. Pollen. July, 1914.

Crippen (T. G.). Early Nonconformist Bibliography. (*Congregational Hist. Soc. Trans.*, vol. i. pp. 44, 99, 171, 252, 410; vol. ii. pp. 61, 219, 432. 1901–06.)

Biblio. of Congregational Church History. (*Ibid.* vol. ii. pp. 119–135, 337–338. 1905–06.)

Turner (G. Lyon). Original Records of Early Nonconformity under Persecution and Indulgence. 3 vols. London, 1911–14. Vol. II. contains County Classification and Indexes.

The Nonconformist's Memorial, by Edmund Calamy. Second edition, by Samuel Palmer. 3 vols. London, 1802–03. The work has a County arrangement.

List of Nonconformist Academies, 1680-1770, appended to 'The Literature of Dissent,' by W. A. Shaw, in 'The Cambridge Hist. of Eng. Lit., vol. x. 1913, pp. 384–387.

Evans (George Eyre). Vestiges of Protestant Dissent, being Lists of Ministers, Sacramental Plate, Registers, Antiquities, etc. [with Biblio. Notes.] Liverpool. 1897.

'The Seconde Parte of a Register,' being a Calendar of MSS. under that title intended for Publication by the Puritans about 1593, and now in Dr. Williams' Lib. London. Edited by Albert Peel, with a preface by C. H. Firth. 2 vols. Cambridge, 1915.

Newman (Josiah). The Quaker Records, in 'Some Special Studies in Genealogy,' pp. 37–65. (The Genealogist's Pocket Library, vol. i. 1908.)

Devonshire House Index to Births, Marriages and Deaths, of which any record is preserved by the Soc. of Friends from *circa* 1650 to the present time, with List of Registers at Devonshire House with date when earliest records commence. See *ante* 'The Quaker Records,' by Josiah Newman, 1908, pp. 39–44.

Quaker Records. Being an Index to 'The Annual Monitor,' 1813-1892. Edited by Joseph J. Green. London, 1894.

Besse (Joseph). A Collection of the Sufferings of the People called Quakers, etc. 1650–1689. 2 vols. London, 1753. Contains Lists of Deaths, etc.

Smith (Joseph). A Descriptive Catal. of Friends' Books, or Books written by members of the Soc. of Friends. 2 vols. London, 1867. Supplement. London, 1893.

List of Local Histories on Methodism (arranged under Places), compiled chiefly by George Stampe from his Collection, with a Supplemental List of Local Methodist Histories in George Stampe's Collection. (*Wesley Hist. Soc. Proc.*, vol. i. pp. 3–14; vol. vi. pp. 70–74. 1898, 1907.)

Gatfield (George). Guide to Printed Books and MSS. relating to English and Foreign Heraldry and Genealogy. London, 1892.

Marshall (George W.). The Genealogist's Guide. Guildford, 1903. Privately Printed. The 1893 edn. includes a 'List of Parish Registers, etc.'

Rye (Walter). Index to 'Records and Record Searching.' Second edition. London, 1897, pp. 193–253.

In this Index are incorporated many references to subjects treated of in the works on the Public Records by Cooper, Sims, Thomas, Ewald, Phillimore, and Scargill-Bird, which are not dealt with in the book itself.

Sims (Richard). Manual for the Genealogist. London, 1856. List of Family Chartularies, etc., pp. 28–29.

The Classed Lists of Genealogical and Topographical MSS. in the Dep. of MSS. in the Brit. Museum greatly amplify the items in this work.

Classed Catal. of Printed Books on Heraldry in the National Art Library, South Kensington. London, 1901. **Great Britain & Ireland,** pp. 17–58.

Catal. of Works on the Peerage and Baronetage of England, Scotland, and Ireland, in the Library of Sir Charles George Young. London, 1827.

Index to Burke's 'Dictionary of the Landed Gentry of Great Britain and Ireland' [3 vols. 1843-49], comprising upwards of 100,000 names mentioned in the work. London, 1849.

The Index was issued as part of vol. 3, and also separately.

Index of Family Names in Burke's 'Landed Gentry,' 1863, in Bridger's 'Index to Pedigrees,' 1867, pp. 178–258.

Index to Pedigrees in Burke's 'Commoners,' originally prepared by George Ormerod (the Cheshire Historian) in 1840. Oxford, 1907. The Index serves for the editions of the work in 4 vols. issued in 1833, and the small-paper edn. of 1837.

Phillimore (W. P. W.). How to Write the Hist. of a Family. A Guide for the Genealogist. London, 1887. **Supplement,** 1896. Contains useful Lists for England, Scotland, and Ireland.

—— **Pedigree Work.** A Handbook for the Genealogist, with a New Date Book, 1066 to 1914. Second edn. London, 1914.

—— **The Family Charter Chest.** Hints for the Preservation, Arrangement, and Calendaring of Family Muniments. London, 1905.

—— **The Family Historian.** A Short initial guide for Writing, Printing, & Illustrating the Hist. of a Family. Part I. London, 1905.

This was intended to replace the Author's 'How to Write the Hist. of a Family,' which had gone out of print. No other part was issued.

Lea (James Henry). Genealogical Research in England, Scotland, and Ireland. A Handbook. Boston, Mass., 1906.

Waters (Henry F.). Genealogical Gleanings in England. 2 vols. Boston, U.S.A., 1901, and New Ser. Pt. I. (A—Anyon). Salem, 1907. A full Index is contained in Vol. II.

Bernau (Charles Allan). The International Genealogical Directory. Second edn. Walton-on-Thames, 1909, and Supplements I.-III. London, 1909–11. Pt. 1. is an Index of Names of Persons, with special lines of Research indicated in which they are interested. The First Supplement is 'An Index of Places,' by G. F. Tudor Sherwood, arranged under Counties.

—— **Sixteenth Century Marriages. (1538-1600.)** Vol. I. London, 1911. Vol. II. not yet published. List of Parish Registers Indexed, pp. vii.-xvi. List of Parish Registers arranged under Counties, pp. 333–335.

—— **The Genealogist's Pocket Library.** 8 vols. Walton-on-Thames. 1908–10.

Vol. I. 1908. Chap. I. American Emigrants: How to Trace their English Ancestry, by Gerald Fothergill.
Chap. II. The Quaker Records, by Josiah Newman.
Vol. VIII. 1910. The Records of Naval Men, by Gerald Fothergill.

Hitching (F. K. and S.). References to English Surnames in 1601 and 1602. Indexes with references to Surnames in Printed Registers of English Parishes. 2 Pts. Walton-on-Thames, 1910. London, 1911.

Index of Baptisms, Marriages, and Burials, in English Parish Registers prior to 1837.

The foregoing Index was formerly in the possession of Messrs. Stokes & Cox, Record Agents, of Chancery Lane, London, and contained about a million entries. It has now passed out of their hands.

Foster (Joseph). Index to the Marriages of the Nobility and Gentry, 1650-1880 (Aa—Alexander), in 'Collectanea Genealogica,' Part IV. 1881.

Indexes to Wills proved in the Prerogative Court of Canterbury, 1383-1629. [*The Index Library.*] 6 vols. Brit. Record Soc. London. 1893–1912.

Indexes to 'Miscellanea Genealogica et Heraldica.' London, 1866, etc. Issued separately for each vol.

An Index of Subjects contained in 'The Genealogist.' New Series. Vols. i.-xx. Exeter, 1905. Issued separately, and also as part of vol. xx.

The Consolidated Index of the Soc. of Genealogists of London. The Index [in MS.] consists of about a million entries of Records of various kinds to which Sub-Committees, representing Parish Registers, Monumental Inscriptions, etc., and Members of the Soc. contribute from time to time. See 'Annual Reports of the Soc.'

Index to 'Genealogical Queries and Memoranda,' edited by G. F. Tudor Sherwood. Vol i. 1896–99. London, 1900.

Indexes to the County Visitations in the Library at Middle Hill, 1840, and to a few others in the Harl. MSS. Brit. Mus., the Bodl. Lib., and Queen's College, Oxford. By Sir Thomas Phillipps. Typis Medio-Montanis. 1841. Privately Printed.

Sims (Richard). An Index to the Pedigrees and Arms contained in the Heralds' Visitations, etc. in the Brit. Museum. [Arranged under Counties.] London, 1849.

Return of Owners of Land, England and Wales (exclusive of the Metropolis). 1873. (Arranged under Counties.) 2 vols. London, 1875.

List of Unclaimed Dormant Funds in Chancery, etc., with an Index. Issued as a Supplement to 'The London Gazette' every three years.

Records of Soldiers [at the War Office]. A Register of Soldiers' Services kept by Officers in charge of Records, which brings together in one book a great mass of detail with regard to every soldier who serves in the Army, showing his age, date of enlistment, place of birth, military services, marriage, and other details, forming a complete compendium of his life while in the Army. See 'Second Rep. of Royal Comm. on Public Records,' 1914, II. pt. iii. p. 13.

Venn (John and J. A.). List of College Admission Registers of the Univ. of Cambridge in introduction to 'The Book of Matriculations and Degrees,' a Catal. from 1544–1659. Cambridge, 1913.

Roll of Attorneys-at-Law and Solicitors from circa 1200, in 17 vols., compiled by W. U. Richards. (In the Record Department of the Law Society).

Munk (William). The Roll of the Royal College of Physicians of London, 1518–1825. 3 vols. Second Edition. London, 1878.

Members of Parliament. Index to Return of the Names, etc. of every Member in each Parliament, from 1213 to 1885. Printed by order of the House of Commons. 1879 and 1891.

Perrin (G. H.). Biblio. of Printed Navy Lists. See 'The Mariner's Mirror,' vol. i. pp. 257–264, 321–329. 1911.

Fothergill (Gerald). The Records of Naval Men. (*The Genealogist's Pocket Library*, ed. by C. A. Bernau, vol. viii. 1910.) Contains full information as to Indexed material, etc. relating to men of all grades in the Navy.

Jackson (Sir George). Naval Commissioners from 1660–1760. A List, with Historical Notices by Sir G. F. Duckett. Privately Printed. Lewes, 1889.

Return giving in Chronological order, a list of all Enquiries made into Naval and Military Affairs since 1800, the Reports of which have been published as Parliamentary Papers. Ordered to be printed by the House of Commons, 12 Oct. 1908.

Reports from the Select Committee appointed to inquire into the State of the Public Records of the Kingdom, 4 July, 1800, with Table of Records, etc. systematically classed, pp. 519–667.

Report from the Commissioners appointed to execute the measures recommended by a Select Committee of the H. of Commons respecting the Public Records, with an Account of their Proceedings, 1800–1812. 5 June, 1812.

Reports (1st, 2nd, with Appendices, etc.) from the Commissioners on the Public Records, 1800–1819. 2 vols. 1819.

General Report of the Commissioners on the Public Records, with an Appendix and Index. 24 Feb. 1837.

Reprint of Statutes, Rules and Schedules governing the disposal of Public Records, by destruction or otherwise, 1877–1913. For Official Use. H.M. Stationery Office, London, 1914.

Catal. of English, Scottish, and Irish Record Publications, Reports of the Hist. MSS. Comm. and the Annual Report of the Deputy Keepers of the Public Records, England and Ireland. H.M. Stationery Office, London. [Issued occasionally.]

Index of Titles of Works contained in the 'Chronicles and Memorials of Great Britain and Ireland.' (Rolls Series.) London, 1858, etc. See Gross' 'Sources and Literature of Eng. Hist.' 1915. App. C, pp. 704–711.

Catal. of Works (other than Parliamentary Papers and Acts of Parliament) published by H.M. Stationery Office. London, Harrison & Sons, 1915. List of Record Works, with Index, pp. 65-104.

Reports of the Deputy Keeper of the Public Records. Index to the Printed Reports of Sir Francis Palgrave, 1840-61. London, 1865. **Index to the Printed Reports of Sir Thomas Duffus Hardy, 1862-78.** London, 1880.

Catal. of the Library of the House of Lords (exclusive of the Legal Section), by Edmund Gosse. London, 1908.

App. I. Lists of Calendars of State Papers, Record Commission Pubns., Hist. MSS. Comm. Reports, etc.
App. II. List of the Peel Collection of Tracts.
App. III. Catal. of Treaties.

Catal. of Parliamentary Reports and a breviate of their Contents, arranged under Subjects, 1696–1834. London, 1836.

Catal. of Papers, etc., printed by Order of the House of Commons, 1731–1800. London, 1807.

General Alphabetical Index to the Accounts and Papers, etc., printed by Order of the House of Commons, 1801 to 1852, 1852 to 1899, 1900–1909. London, 1863–1914. 3 vols.

Soule (Charles C.). Year-Book Bibliography, with Tables. (*Harvard Law Review*, vol. xiv. pp. 557–587. 1901.)

Local Records Committee. Report on Existing Arrangements for the Collection and Custody of Local Records. H.M. Stationery Office. London, 1902.

Royal Commission on Public Records. First Report of the Commission appointed to Inquire into and Report on the State of the Public Records and Local Records of a Public Nature of England and Wales. Vol. I. 3 pts. H.M. Stationery Office. 1912.

A 'Biblio. of the Hist. of the Public Records' is contained in App. XII. of vol. i. pt. 2, 1912.

——— **Second Report & Appendices.** Vol. II. H.M. Stationery Office. 1914.

Below are given a number of headings from the Second Report which are dealt with by the Commissioners in a manner most helpful to the student of local history. The pagination is in each case to the Appendix matter in Pt. II., but much more will be found in the Report itself over and above what is specified below. The Third Part contains a useful Index to the whole.

The Contents of the Commissioners' First Report dealing with Local Records, issued in 1912, will be found in this work embodied under Counties and Towns in the classified arrangement.

The Second Report appeared while this book was in course of compilation.

App. I. no. 3.—Replies to Questions addressed by the Commission to the several Courts, Registries, Government Departments, and Public Authorities which do not transmit Records to the Public Record Office. [These questions relate to the condition, etc., attached to research, etc., and as to existing Indexes to the various Records.]

The Principal Probate Registry, Somerset House. Pp. 36–37.
Ely Diocesan Registry. Pp. 39–40.
Vicar-General's Office, Doctors' Commons. P. 41.
General Register Office, Somerset House. Pp. 43–45.
Royal Establishments and Public Offices. Pp. 47–68.

App. I. no. 4.—List of Records in the Government House, Guernsey, and in the Government Office, St. Helier, Jersey. P. 75.

App. I. no. 5.—Classified List of Official Archives under the control of the Courts of Justice, Registries, Public Departments, Public Authorities, Trusts or Institutions, and the Dependencies of the English Crown. Pp. 87-90.

App. II. no. 3.—Some Notes on the Ancient Ecclesiastical Records now deposited in the Principal Probate Registry. Pp. 92-93.

App. II. no. 4.—Report of Inventories, Prerogative Court of Canterbury. By J. C. Challenor Smith. P. 93.

App. II. no. 5.—Report (dated 1865) on the Records of the 'Four Courts' of the Diocese of London transferred to the Principal Probate Registry under the Probate and Divorce Court Acts of 1857. Pp. 93-96.

[Contains a reference to the existence of 'A List of the Muniments in the Registry of the Lord Bishop of London in the Cathedral Church of St. Paul,' about 1761. See p. 93.]

App. II. no. 15.—A List of the different kinds of Records belonging to the Vicar-General's Office and Court of Peculiars. P. 102.

App. II. no. 20.—Note on the Records of the Lord Steward's Department of His Majesty's Household. P. 104.

App. II. no. 33.—List of the Principal Military Record Offices, with a note on the duties of the officers in charge of Records. Pp. 123-124.

App. II. no. 37.—A List of Books and Documents, etc., of a date prior to the 19th Century at the Inland Revenue Department. Pp. 127-128.

App. II. no. 39.—A Short Summary of Records in the custody of and under the control of His Majesty's Office of Works, other than those in the Public Record Office. P. 128.

App. II. no. 41.—Official Memorandum on the Custody of Public Records within Urban Areas. P. 129.

App. II. no. 42.—List of the Chief Classes of Documents kept in the Record Room of the Board of Agriculture and Fisheries at 3 St. James's Square. P. 129.

App. III. no. 8.—Report of an Inspection of the Records of the Palatinate Courts at Preston and Lancaster. P. 141.

App. III. no. 11.—Memorandum on the Custody of the Records of the Coroners' Courts. P. 143.

App. III. no. 12.—Returns relating to the Custody of Coroners' Records [arranged under Counties]. Pp. 145-163.

App. III. no. 17.—Report of an Inspection by the Commission of the Records of the Guildhall, London. P. 164.

App. III. no. 22.—Report of an Inspection by the Commission of the Records of the Lord Great Chamberlain's Office. P. 167.

App. III. no. 23.—Reports of Inspections of the Records of the Ecclesiastical Courts at Lambeth Palace and St. Paul's Cathedral, Dec. 1912 and Jan. 1913. Pp. 167-168.

App. III. nos. 27, 28.—Report of an Inspection of the Records of the General Register Office, Somerset House, Jan. 1913. Pp. 170-171.

App. III. no. 29.—Report of an Inspection of the Records of the Lord Steward's Department (Buckingham Palace), Jan. 1911. P. 171.

App. III. no. 32.—Reports on the Records of the Royal Almonry, the King's Body-Guard of the Yeomen of the Guard, the Honourable Corps of Gentlemen-at-Arms, the Coroner of the Verge, the Master of the Buckhounds, the Groom of the Stole, and the Mistress of the Robes, July, 1913. Pp. 172-173.

App. III. no. 44.—Reports of Inspections of the Records of the War Office (1910-13). Pp. 178-179.

App. III. no. 48.—Reports of Inspections of the War Office Records at Dover (1911-13). P. 181.

App. III. no. 49.—Reports of Inspections of the Records of the Admiralty. Pp. 182-184.

App. III. no. 50.—Report upon and List of Records at Deptford Dockyard. Pp. 184-185.

App. III. no. 52.—Report of an Inspection of the Records of the Admiralty and War Office, at Portsmouth (Jan. 1911). Pp. 185-187.

App. III. no. 53.—Report of an Inspection of the Admiralty, War Office, and Customs Records at Plymouth [April 1911]. Pp. 187-188.

App. III. no. 54.—Report of Inspections of the Admiralty and War Office Records at Sheerness and Chatham (1911). Pp. 188-189.

App. III. no. 64.—Reports of Inspections of the Records of the Office of His Majesty's Woods, Forests, and Land Revenues (1910-11). P. 191.

App. III. no. 77.—Select Summary Lists of the Records of the Courts of Justice, Registries, Government Departments, and Public Institutions. Pp. 197-198.

App. III. no. 77.—Summary List of the Records prior to 1858 in the Strong-Room of the Principal Probate Registry, Somerset House, and some in Room A. By F. W. X. Fincham. Pp. 199-204.

Ibid.—Summary of the Records preserved in the General Register and Record Office of Shipping and Seamen (1912). P. 207.

Ibid.—Summary of the Records of the Privy Council Office. P. 209.

Ibid.—Summary Lists of War Office Records. Pp. 211-224.

Ibid.—Summary Lists of Admiralty Records. Pp. 225-237.

Ibid.—Summary List of the Customs and Excise Records, including the Records of the local Excise Offices of the United Kingdom. Pp. 237-248.

Ibid.—Summary Lists of the Records in the Custody of the Commissioners of His Majesty's Woods, Forests, and Land Revenues. Pp. 248-251.

App. IV. no. 10.—List of Documents transferred to the Public Record Office from 1911 to the present time. Pp. 265-267.

App. VI. no. 1.—Regulations concerning the admission of Literary Inquiries to the Principal Probate Registry at Somerset House. By F. W. X. Fincham. Pp. 287-288.

App. VI. no. 2.—List of Calendars, Indexes, etc., prior to 1858 in the Literary Search Department at Somerset House. By F. W. X. Fincham. Pp. 288-290.

App. VI. no. 4.—[Critical] Notes on the Literary Search Department at Somerset House. By Gerald Fothergill. Pp. 290-291.

App. VI. no. 15.—Memorandum as to Searches by Solicitors at the Registrar-General's Office in connection with Proceedings in the Courts of Justice. Pp. 296-7.

App. VI. no. 16.—List of Registers and Records of which the Originals or Certified Copies are deposited in the Custody of the Reg.-Gen., Somerset House [states whether indexed or not]. Pp. 297-300.

App. VI. no. 20.—List of Official Agents in England, Scotland, and Ireland, appointed for the Sale of Ordnance Survey Maps. Pp. 302-3.

App. VI. no. 21.—Regulations concerning the Inspection of Books and Documents belonging to the various Departments of the Government, deposited in the Public Record Office, and open to public inspection. Pp. 303-304.

App. VII. no. 1.—Memorandum on the Publication of the Admiralty Records. By C. H. Firth. P. 304.

App. VIII. no. 1.—Tabular List of Archive Establishments, with Notes, etc., on the Officers having Custody of Records therein. Pp. 307-336.

Hist. MSS. Commission. A Guide to the Reports on Collections of MSS. of Private Families, Corporations and Institutions in Gt. Brit. & Irel. Part I. Topographical. Report for Scotland and Ireland. London, 1914.

——— **List of Reports issued, Names of Owners of MSS. whose Collections have been reported on, and places of Deposit, with a List of Collections reported on arranged under Counties.** See Appendix to the 'Annual Reports.'

Scargill-Bird (S. R.). A Guide to the various classes of Documents preserved in the P.R.O. Third edn. London, 1908.

Catal. of the Library of the P.R.O. Third edition. London, 1902. **Supplement, 1902-1908.** London, 1909. [Compiled by T. Craib.]

Public Record Office. Lists and Indexes [of Records preserved in the Public Record Office]. 1892, etc.

For a List of Nos. i.-xl. see Gross, 'Sources & Literature of English Hist.,' 1915, pp. 81-82. 44 vols. have appeared, many containing a County classification. A complete list is given in the 'Catal. of Works published by H.M. Stationery Office,' issued yearly, and which can be obtained gratis from the Printers. See *ante* p. 360.

Wedgwood (Josiah C.). The 'Lists and Indexes' of Records at the P.R.O. (*William Salt Archæol. Soc, Collections for a Hist. of Staffs.*, 1912, pp. 209-259.) A Review of the first 34 vols.

Maxwell-Lyte (Sir H. C.). Catal. of MSS. and other Objects in the Museum of the P.R.O., with Notes. London, 1915.

Martin (Charles Trice). The Record Interpreter. Second edn. London, 1910.

Wright (Andrew). Court-Hand Restored, etc., with an Appendix containing the Names of Places in Gt. Brit. & Irel. Tenth edn., edited by Charles Trice Martin. London, 1912.

Classified Catal. of the MSS. in the British Museum. 108 vols. (In the Students' Room of the Dep. of MSS. at the Museum.) For a list of the divisions of the Catal. see *ante* p. 349. Andrews & Davenport, 'Guide to the MS. Materials, etc.,' 1908, pp. 6–7.

Index to the Charters and Rolls in the Department of MSS. at the Brit. Museum. Vol. I. (Index Locorum). By Henry John Ellis and Francis B. Bickley; Vol. II. (Religious Houses and other Corporations, and Index Locorum, 1882–1900). By Henry John Ellis. London, 1900, 1912.

Annual Return to Parliament of the Brit. Museum. (Contains statements as to progress in the arrangement and description of the Collections, Lists of Acquisitions, to the various Departments, etc.) H.M. Stationery Office, London.

List of Catalogues, Guide Books, and other Publications published by the Trustees of the Brit. Museum. [Gratis.]

Guide to the use of the Reading Room, British Museum, with lists of Catalogues of Books, Bibliographies, Maps, Newspapers, etc., and Synopsis of the Rules of the General Catal. of Printed Books. London, 1912.

Turner (W. H.). Calendar of Charters & Rolls preserved in the Bodleian Lib. Oxford, 1878. For notes on this Work and the Author, see Macray's 'Annals of the Bodleian,' 1890, p. 392.

Index to the Catal. of the Rawlinson MSS. in the Bodleian Lib., by W. Dunn Macray, in 'Catal. Cod. MSS. Bibl. Bodl.,' Part V. fasc. I., II. Oxon., 1862–78, pp. 565–592.

Lists of Printed Catalogues of MSS. in European Languages in the Brit. Museum, the Bodl. Lib. at Oxford, the Cambridge Univ. Lib., etc. See 'Books in Manuscript,' by Falconer Madan, 1893, App. B, pp. 166–174.

Black (William Henry). Catal. of the Arundel MSS. in the Lib. of the Coll. of Arms. Privately Printed for Sir Charles Young. London, 1829. Two MS. Catalogues are in the Brit. Museum; Lansd. MS. 689, and Hargrave MS. 497. See also note in John Martin's 'Biblio. Catal. of Books Privately Printed,' 1854, p. 384.

Fincham (F. W. X.). A rough List of all the Ancient Records in the Strong Room, Somerset House Probate Registry. [For Official Use at Somerset House.] See Second Rep. Royal Comm. on Public Records, 1914, vol. ii. pt. 3, p. 51.

Todd (H. J.). Catal. of the Archiepiscopal MSS. at Lambeth Palace. London, 1912.

Marshall (George W.). A Handbook to the Ancient Courts of Probate and Depositories of Wills. London, 1895.

A List of the District Probate Registries of the High Court of Justice appears in the 'Law List' annually.

Bartholomew (John George). The Cartography of England and Wales. A List of the Principal Maps and Atlases from the Earliest Times to the Present Day, in his 'Survey Atlas of England & Wales.' Edinburgh, 1903, pp. 25 27.

—— **The Survey Gazetteer of the British Isles, Topographical, Statistical and Commercial.** Edinburgh, 1914.

Fordham (Sir Herbert G.). Studies in Carto-Bibliography, British and French, and in the Biblio. of Itineraries and Road-Books. Oxford, 1914.

British & Irish Itineraries & Road-Books, pp. 23–60.

Descriptive Catalogues of Maps. Their arrangement and the details they should contain, pp. 92–118.

An Itinerary of the 16th. cent. 'La Guide des Chemins d'Angleterre,' by Jean Bernard. Paris, 1579, pp. 120–127.

A Biblio. of Works of Reference relating to British & French Topography and Cartography, pp. 169–174.

Fordham (Sir Herbert G.). Descriptive Catalogues of Maps. (*Biblio. Soc. Trans.*, vol. xi. pp. 135-164. 1912.)

——— **Notes on the Cartography of the Counties of England and Wales.** Hertford, 1908.

——— **Notes on British & Irish Itineraries and Road-Books.** Hertford, 1912.

——— **Road-Books and Itineraries Bibliographically considered.** [Reprinted from 'Trans. of the Biblio. Soc.,' vol. xiii.] 1916.

Catal. of the Printed Maps, Charts and Plans in the Brit. Museum. 2 vols. London, 1885. An interleaved copy with additions up to date, in 46 vols. is in the Reading Room, and forms the present Catal. of Maps.

Catal. of the MS. Maps, Charts & Plans, and of the Topographical Drawings in the Brit. Museum, by John Holmes. 3 vols. London, 1844–61.

Catal. of Maps, Prints, Drawings, etc., in the King's Lib. of the Brit. Museum. London, 1829.

Chubb (Thomas). A Descriptive List of Atlases of Great Britain and Ireland. [Ready for Publication.]

General Index to 'The Itinerary of John Leland, in or about 1535-1543,' in vol. v. pp. 245-352, ed. by Lucy Toulmin Smith. 5 vols. London, 1907–10. For a Biblio. of Leland, see Edward Burton's 'Life of John Leland' (the First English Antiquary). London, 1896.

Wesley's Journals. A complete and classified Index (to suit all editions) of the Journals of the Rev. John Wesley, by Rev. Henry Skewes. London, 1872.

Dictionary of the Parishes, Townships, Hamlets, etc., in England and Wales. London, 1879.

Alphabetical List of Parishes and Places in England and Wales. H.M. Stationery Office. London, 1897.

Itineraries and Tours. See 'General Catal. of Printed Books in the Lib. of the British Museum,' under England, pp. 1331-1347.

Smith (Edward). Biblio. of Tours by Foreigners in England, in his 'Foreign Visitors in England,' 1889, pp. viii.-xvi. (The Book-Lover's Library, ed. by H. B. Wheatley.)

Summary of the Publications of the Ordnance Survey of the United Kingdom, with Indexes to the Scale Maps, etc. London. [Issued annually.]

Ordnance Survey of Great Britain: England and Wales. Indexes to the 1/2500 and 6-inch Scale Maps, and Small Specimens of different Maps published. [n.d.]

Garlick (F. O.). MS. Catal. of the Richard Gough Collections of Maps, Prints and Drawings, in the Bodleian Lib. at Oxford.

Ellis (W. P.). Index to the Gough Prints and Drawings in the Bodl. Lib. at Oxford. [In preparation.]

Catal. of Topographical Drawings and Prints, by John Buckler and others, illustrative of the Counties of England. See 'Catal. of the Hoare Lib. at Stourhead,' by J. B. Nichols, 1840, pp. 122–128.

Topographical Index to measured Drawings of Architecture which have appeared in the principal British Architectural Publications. H.M. Stationery Office. London, 1908.

Lindsay (James Ludovic), Earl of Crawford. Handlist of Proclamations issued by Royal and other Constitutional Authorities, 1714 1910, with an Index of Names and Places. (*Bibliotheca Lindesiana*, vol. viii.) Wigan, 1913. Privately Printed.

Lindsay (James Ludovic), Earl of Crawford. Catal. of a Collection of English Ballads of the 17th. and 18th. centuries printed for the most part in black letter. (*Bibliotheca Lindesiana.*) Aberdeen, 1890. Privately Printed.

Contents.
- Ballads, in alphabetical order.
- List of Printers, Publishers, and Booksellers.
- General Index.
- Titles of Ballads in Thackeray's List.
- Titles of Ballads in the Huth and Euing Collections.

—— **Catal. of English Broadsides, 1505-1897,** with Preface by Lord Crawford and Introduction by J. P. Edmond. (Bibliotheca Lindesiana.) Aberdeen, 1898. Privately Printed.

[The student of local history has long seen the importance of studying single sheet literature and Ballad journalism so as to unearth any old Local Ballads, Garlands, Broadsides, etc., as well as more important and authoritative sheets such as Proclamations. These are of both topographical as well as historical and typographical value, and from the time of Pepys and indeed earlier they have been collected with enthusiasm by the few. They reflect the opinions of the day upon special subjects or events. The Ballad and the Broadside were forerunners of the pamphlet.

Under the headings of numerous counties, there are given in this work references to the literature of local Ballads, etc., but I think it necessary here under the General heading of 'England' to refer to the various sources which exist for the study of street journalism and single local sheets in general. The pioneers of the study of this branch of our subject were the promoters of the Percy Society in 1840, and J. O. Halliwell-Phillipps who worked independently for many years. In 1866, Robert Lemon issued his valuable 'Catal. of Printed Broadsides in the possession of the Soc. of Antiquaries,' and in 1868, the Ballad Society began the publication of the Roxburghe, the Bagford, and other Collections of Street Ballads; Frederick J. Furnivall, William Chappell, and E. F. Rimbault being chiefly concerned in this admirable work, followed by J. W. Ebsworth, who gave up the greater part of his life to it. There is no necessity to pursue the history of the subject further, except to allude to the munificent and princely contributions made by the late Lord Crawford, references to whose chief publications are here given.]

Steele (Robert Reynolds). Biblio. of Royal Proclamations of the Tudor and Stuart Sovereigns, etc., 1485-1714, vol. i. England and Wales, vol. ii. Scotland and Ireland. (*Bibliotheca Lindesiana*, vols. v.-vi. 1910.) A most important section deals with Collections, and where preserved.

Halliwell-Phillipps (J. O.). A Catal. of Proclamations, Broadsides, Ballads, and Poems, presented to the Chatham Library, Manchester, by J. O. Halliwell. 1851. Privately Printed.

—— **A Catal. of Chapbooks, Garlands, and Popular Histories in the possession of J. O. Halliwell.** 1849.

The Ballad Society. Publications. 38 parts. London, 1868–1899. Certain sections of this magnificently edited series have Indices, but the General Index which Joseph Woodfall Ebsworth had prepared in part has never been completed. The work as it stands is a monument of learning and curious local lore. The two final parts of the Roxburghe Ballads contain the most important notes for the researcher.

Gray (George John). A General Index to Hazlitt's 'Handbook' and 'Biblio. Collections,' 1867–1889. London, 1893.

Newton (T. W.). Catal. of Old Ballads in the possession of Frederic Ouvry. London, 1877. Privately Printed.

Catal. of Books in the Library of the Brit. Museum printed in England, etc., up to 1640. 3 vols. London, 1884. See Index in vol. iii. under Ballads. For Collections of Ballads, see the General Cat. of Printed Books under 'Ballads.'

The Brit. Museum at one time considered the question of issuing a complete Catal. of its Ballads (see article by J. Winter Jones in 'North British Review,' Nov. 1846). The Collections of Ballads in the Museum include the Roxburghe and Bagford Collections and several others. At present each Ballad is entered in the General Catal. under its title.

Pepys's Collection of English Broadside Ballads at Magdalene College, Cambridge. This is probably the largest Collection in existence outside the Brit. Museum. See *ante* under London, p. 161.

Smith (John Russell). A Catal. of an unique Collection of ancient English Broadside Ballads printed entirely in the Black Letter. London, 1856.

This is known as the Euing Collection and is now in the Glasgow University Library.

Collmann (Herbert L.). Ballads and Broadsides, chiefly of the Elizabethan period, now in the Library at Britwell Court, Bucks. Roxburghe Club. 1912.

Welsh (Charles). Catal. of English and American Chap-books and Broadside Ballads in Harvard College Lib., Cambridge, Mass. (*Harvard Univ. Lib. Biblio. Collections*, No. lvi. 1905.)

Symonds (H.), Brown (Arthur), and Coxe (H. O.). Catal. of the Douce Collection in the Bodleian Lib. at Oxford. 1840. See Macray's 'Annals,' 1890, p. 328. For details of Ballads, Chapbooks, etc., in the Anthony Wood Collection in the Bodleian, see Introduction to 'The Life and Times of Anthony Wood,' by Andrew Clark, vol. i.

Ellis (Frederick Startridge) and Hazlitt (W. Carew). Catal. of the Huth Library. 5 vols. London, 1880. List of the Collection of Ballads, vol. i. pp. 85–105.

Lilly (Joseph). Catal. of a Collection of Ballads and Broadsides printed between 1559 and 1597. London, 1867.

Daniel (George). An Elizabethan Garland, being a descriptive Catal. of Seventy Black Letter Ballads printed between 1559 and 1597, in the possession of George Daniel of Canonbury. London, 1856.

This was Daniel's private issue of the Catal. published by Lilly, 1867. Only 25 copies printed.

Collier (John Payne). A Collection of Old Ballads anterior to the reign of Charles I. Percy Society. London, 1840.

The Bagford Ballads. Edited by J. W. Ebsworth. 2 vols. The Ballad Soc., 1876–78, and Supplement, 1880. See also 'John Bagford & his Collections,' by W. Y. Fletcher (Biblio. Soc., vol. iv.), and 'On the Track of John Bagford,' (Biblio. Soc., vol. iv.).

Evans (Thomas). Old Ballads, historical and narrative, with some of modern date, etc. New Edition, revised and enlarged by Robert Harding Evans. 4 vols. London, 1810.

Catal. of the Books, Tracts, Ballads, Prints, etc., of William Hone. Sold by Henry Southgate & Co., London, 25 Feb. 1843.

The Ballads, Tracts, etc., collected by Hone for forming 'The Every Day Book.'

Grant (Francis). Catal. of the extraordinary Collection of Broadsides, Proclamations, Black Letter Ballads, etc., of the late Col. Francis Grant. Sold by Sotheby's, 9 May, 1900.

Popular Ballads of the Olden Time, selected and edited by Frank Sidgwick. Series I.–III. London, 1903-06.

List of Books for Ballad Study (*a.* The Literary Hist. of Ballads ; *b.* Collections of Ballads), pp. lii.–liv.

Dixon (J. H.). Ancient Poems, Ballads and Songs of the Peasantry of England. [Percy Soc.] London, 1846.

Hodgkin (John Eliot). Catal. of Historical Broadsides, with an Index, in his 'Rariora,' 1903, vol. iii. pp. 1–161.

Catalogues of Newspapers in the Library of the Brit. Museum. These Catalogues are in four divisions, as follows:—London and Suburbs, England and Wales, Scotland, and Ireland, arranged under Places, with an Index to the Titles in each division.

List of Newspapers, 1641-1663, in the Thomason Collection at the Brit. Museum, in 'Catal. of the Thomason Collection,' 1908, vol. ii. pp. 371–446. See *ante* p. 347.

Catal. of a Collection of Early Newspapers, etc., in the Bodleian Lib. at Oxford, formed by John Thomas Hope, compiled by J. H. Burn. Oxford, 1865. See a note on the Collection in Macray's 'Annals of the Bodleian,' 1890, pp. 375–376.

A Chronological List of Early Newspapers, 1640, etc., in 'Life of Thomas Ruddiman, Librarian of Advocates' Lib., Edinburgh,' by George Chalmers. London, 1794. App. VI. pp. 404–442.

Williams (Joseph Batterson). Catal. of Periodicals, Newspapers, etc., from 1641 to 1666, in his 'Hist. of English Journalism to the Foundation of the Gazette.' London, 1908.

——— **The Beginnings of English Journalism,** with a Biblio., in 'The Cambridge Hist. of English Literature,' vol. vii. 1911, pp. 343-365, 494–503.

Ellis & Elvey's Catal. of Early Newspapers, etc. No. 156. London, 1914–15.

List of Existing Newspapers & Periodicals of the 17th. and 18th. centuries, arranged chronologically, in 'Willing's Press Guide,' 1916, pp. 419–420.

A Dictionary of Printers and Booksellers in England, Scotland, and Ireland, and of Foreign Printers of English Books, 1557-1640. By H. G. Aldis, Robert Bowes, E. R. McC. Dix. General Editor, R. B. McKerrow. Biblio. Soc. London, 1910.

Allnutt (W. H.). English Provincial Presses, with Biblio. Notes. (*Bibliographica*, vol. ii. pp. 23, 150, 276. 1896.)

Mr. Allnutt's Collections and Notes relating to Printing are in the Greenwood Library of Bibliography at the Manchester Public Library.

——— **Notes on the Introduction of Printing-Presses into the smaller Towns of England and Wales,** after 1750, to the end of the 18th cent. (*The Library*, New Ser. vol. ii. pp. 242–259. 1901.)

——— **Notes on Printers and Printing in the Provincial Towns of England and Wales.** Oxford, 1878. London, 1879.

Martin (John). A Biblio. Catal. of Books Privately Printed. 2 vols. London, 1834, and Second Edition, 1854.

An interleaved copy in the Brit. Mus. Lib. has MS. notes by the Author.

List of Catalogues of English Book-Sales, 1676-1900, now in the British Museum. London, 1915.

List of Catalogues of Books and MSS. sold by Auction, Booksellers and Library Catalogues. See 'Bibliotheca Lindesiana.' Catal. of the Printed Books at Haigh Hall, co. Lancs., 1910, cols. 1450–1502.

A General List of Provincial Booksellers (arranged under Towns). (*Notes & Queries*, Ser. 10, vol. v. pp. 141, 183, 242, 415; Ser. 11, vol. i. pp. 304, 363; vol. ii. pp. 52, 112. 1906–10.)

SCOTLAND.

List of Works in the New York Public Lib. relating to Scotland, compiled by George F. Black. (*New York Public Lib. Bulletin*, vol. xviii. 1914.)

The List includes articles in Magazines and in publications of learned Societies. It has since its periodical issue been greatly enlarged, and is now reissued in 1 vol. with an Index.

General Catal. of Printed Books in the Library of the Brit. Museum. 'Scotland.' A separate vol. containing works that are not entered in the General Cat. under the authors' names or elsewhere, and comprising official and anonymous publications, etc. A Key to the arrangement and an Index to Subheadings is at the beginning of the vol.

Terry (Charles Sanford). A Catal. of the Publications of Scottish Historical and Kindred Clubs and Societies, and of the volumes relative to Scottish Hist. issued by H.M. Stationery Office, 1780–1908, with a subject index. Glasgow, 1909. Also issued as 'Aberdeen University Studies.' No. xxxix. 1909.

—— **An Index to the Papers relating to Scotland, described or calendared in the Hist. MSS. Comm. Reports.** Glasgow, 1908.

Index volume to 'The Hist. of Scotland,' by John Hill Burton. (Second edition. 8 vols. Edinb. 1873.) Edinb. 1873.

Index to [the First edition and to the Second edition of the] 'Hist. of Scotland,' by Patrick Fraser Tytler. Edinb. 1850. Both indexes were issued in 1850.

Index to 'Caledonia, or an Historical & Topographical Account of North Britain,' by George Chalmers. [7 vols. Paisley, 1887-1902.] Paisley, 1902.

A List of Books relating to Scotland and the Scots, preserved in the Reference Department of the Wigan Public Lib., by H. T. Folkard. Wigan, 1910.

Brown (Peter Hume). Hist. of Scotland to the present time. 3 vols. Cambridge, 1911. **Biblio.** vol. i. pp. 322–328; vol. ii. pp. 359–366; vol. iii. pp. 387–394.

Catal. of the Printed Books in the Signet Lib., Edinburgh. 2 pts. **Supplement and List of MSS.** Edinb. 1871–82. **Second Supp. 1882-87, with a Subject Index to the whole Catal.** 1891. **List of Books added, 1888-1911.** Edinb. 1889–1912.

Catal. of the Printed Books in the Lib. of the Faculty of Advocates. 7 vols. Edinb. 1863–79.

Catal. of Books in the Lib. of the Faculty of Procurators in Glasgow, with Index of Subjects, by John Muir. Glasgow, 1903. For books on Scotland generally, see Index of Subjects, pp. 1008–1018.

Sibbald (Sir Robert). An Account of the Writers, antient and modern, Printed, and MSS. not Printed, which treat of the Description of North-Britain, called Scotland, as it was of old, and is now at present, with a Catal. of the Mapps, Prospects, etc. Edinb. 1710.

(In 'A Collection of several Treatises in Folio concerning Scotland, etc.,' by Sibbald, 1739.) For Notes on Sibbald's Collections in the Advocates' Library, see 'Macfarlane's Geographical Collections,' ed. by Sir Arthur Mitchell, vol. ii. pp. vi.–li. Scottish Hist. Soc. 1907.

Sibbald (Sir Robert.) An Advertisement and General Queries for the Description of Scotland, 1682. (*The Bannatyne Miscellany*, vol. iii. pp. 369–380.) The Bannatyne Club. Edinb. 1855.

General Index and Index of Illustrations to the Proceedings of the Soc. of Antiquaries of Scotland, vols. i.–xxiv. 1851–90. Edinb. 1892.

Smellie (William). An Historical Account of the Soc. of Antiquaries of Scotland. (*Archæologia Scotica*, vol. i. pp. iii.–xxxiii. 1792.)

Scottish Exhibition of National History, Art, and Industry, Glasgow, 1911. Palace of History. Catal. of Exhibits (Portraits, Sir Walter Scott Literature, Ramsay Literature, Burns MSS., Burghal Deeds, Maps, etc.). Glasgow, 1911.

Catal. of Antiquities, Works of Art, and Historical Relics, exhibited at the Meeting of the Archæol. Inst. of Gt. Brit. at Edinburgh, 1856. Compiled by Albert Way. Edinb. 1859.

Notices relative to the Bannatyne Club, including Critiques on some of its Publications. Edited by James Maidment. Edinb. 1836. 50 copies only printed for private circulation.

Bannatyniana. Catal. of the Privately Printed Publications of the Bannatyne Club from 1823 to 1848, with an Introductory Note and Illustrative Notes by Thomas George Stevenson. Edinb. 1848.

Catal. of the Books printed for the Bannatyne Club since its institution in 1823. Edinb. 1867.

Catal. of Books printed for the Abbotsford Club since its institution in 1833. Edinb. 1866.

A Great Scottish Book-printing Society: The Maitland Club. A Paper by J. W. Ewing read before the Glasgow Bib. Soc., Feb. 1915.

Stuart (John). Notices of the Spalding Club, with the Annual Reports, Lists of Members and Works printed for the Club, 1839–71. Edinb. 1871.

Lyman (Alice). Reading List on Scotland. (*New York State Lib. Bull.*, No. 112. 1907.)

Bibliotheca Historica, Scotica, Curiosa et Rarissima. Descriptive Catal. of Interesting, Curious and Rare Books, pertaining chiefly to the Hist., Antiquities, Topography, and Poetry of Scotland, including the largest Collection in Scotland of the Privately Printed Books issued by various Literary Societies. On Sale by Thomas George Stevenson. Edinburgh, n.d.

A valuable store of Biblio. information.

Laing (William). Supplement to a Catal. of Books connected with the Hist. & Literature of Scotland, on sale by William Laing. Edinburgh, 1819. See 'Glasgow Courier,' 31 May, 1832.

'At its date probably the best record in existence of early Scottish Literature.'—David Murray.

Catal. of the Lib. of David Constable, containing an extraordinary assemblage of rare and curious Books and MSS. 22 days' Sale at Edinburgh, 1828.

Catal. of the Lib. of William Barclay David Donald Turnbull, consisting of Books on English and Scottish Topography, etc. Sold by C. B. Tait and T. Nisbet, Edinburgh, 12 Nov. 1851.

Catal. of the Lib. of David Laing, comprising an extraordinary Collection of Works by Scottish Writers and relating to Scotland, Sold by Sotheby's, 1 Dec. 1879, 5 Ap. 1880, 20 July 1880, 21 Feb. 1881.

The Laing Collection of MSS. chiefly relating to Scotland is in the Edinburgh Univ. Lib.

List of Communications to the Soc. of Antiq. of Scot. by David Laing. (*Soc. Ant. Scot. Proc.*, vol. xiii. pp. 6–16. 1879.)

De Mély (Fernand) and Bishop (Edmund). A List of Scotch Inventories, in their 'Biblio. Gén. des Inventaires Imprimés,' Paris, 1892, pp. 74–86.

Catal. of the Library at Abbotsford, compiled by John George Cochrane, with a Preface by John Gibson Lockhart. [The Maitland Club.] Edinb. 1838. A group of works on Scottish Hist., pp. 1–23. Collections of Ballads and Songs, pp. 32, 57, 156, 288.

Inventories of Ecclesiastical Records of North-Eastern Scotland, compiled by the Church Records Committee of the Council of the New Spalding Club. (*The Miscellany of the New Spalding Club*, vol. i. pp. 163–356. 1890.)

Turnbull (W. B. D. D.). Fragmenta Scoto-Monastica. Memoir of what has been already done, and what Materials exist towards the formation of a Scotish Monasticon. Edinburgh, 1842.

List of Scottish Monastic Chartularies. See Sims' 'Manual for the Genealogist,' 1856, p. 28. See also *ante* p. 356.

Leith (William Forbes). Pre-Reformation Scholars in Scotland in the XVIth. Century. Their Writings, etc., with a Biblio., and a list of Graduates from 1500 to 1560. Glasgow, 1915. **Biblio.**, pp. 23–98. **Index to Biblio.**, pp. 154–155.

——— **Biblio. des Livres publiés à Paris et à Lyon par les Savants Écossais réfugiés en France au XVIe siècle.** Paris, 1912.

Bellesheim (Alphons). Hist. of the Catholic Church of Scotland. 4 vols. Edinb. 1887–90. List of Authorities, vol. i. pp. xxi.–xxxiv.

Law (Thomas Graves). The Biblio. of the Lives of Two Scottish Capucins, John Forbes and George Leslie, both named in religion 'Archangel.' (*Edinb. Biblio. Soc. Pubns.*, vol. i. no. 3. 1891.)

Handbook and Index to the Principal Acts of Assembly of the Free Church of Scotland, 1843–68. Edinb. 1869.

Cowan (William). The Biblio. of the Book of Common Order of the Church of Scotland. (*Edinb. Biblio. Soc. Pubns.*, vol. i. no. 2. 1891.)

——— **A Biblio. of the Book of Common Order and Psalm Book of the Church of Scotland, 1556–1644.** (*Ibid.* vol. x. pp. 53–100. 1913.)

Johnston (John C.). Biblio. of the Scottish Covenant, in his 'Treasury of the Scottish Covenant,' 1887.

Mackinlay (James M.). Ancient Church Dedications in Scotland. 2 vols. Edinb. 1910–14. Biblio. vol. i. pp. ix.–xxiii. ; vol. ii. pp. ix.–xxxvi.

Evans (George Eyre). Vestiges of Protestant Dissent, being Lists of Ministers, Sacramental Plate, Registers, Antiquities, etc. [With Biblio. Notes.] Liverpool, 1897. **Scotland,** pp. 267–271.

Murray (David). Scottish Collectors and Scottish Museums, in his 'Museums.' Glasgow, 1904, vol. i. pp. 151–169.

Royal Commission on the Ancient and Historical Monuments and Constructions of Scotland. Reports and Inventories. Edinb. 1909, etc.

Allen (John Romilly) and Anderson (Joseph). The Early Christian Monuments of Scotland. A Classified, Illustrated, Descriptive List of the Monuments, with an analysis of their symbolism, etc. (*The Rhind Lectures for 1892.* 3 pts. [Soc. Antiq. Scot.] Edinb. 1903. List of Books of Reference in pt. ii. pp. 415–419.

Black (George F.). Catal. of the National Museum of Antiquities of Scotland. [Soc. Antiq. Scot.] Edinb. 1892.

Edmond (John Philip). Biblio. of the Sculptured Stones of Scotland. (*The Antiq. Mag. & Bibliographer*, vol. iii. pp. 185–189. 1883.)

Allen (John Romilly). List of Books and Papers relating to cup-marked Stones in Scotland, etc. (*Soc. Antiq. Scot. Proc.*, vol. xvi. pp. 139–143. 1882.

List of Works on Scottish Numismatics. (*New York Public Lib. Bull.*, vol. xviii. pp. 1379–1382. 1914, and in enlarged re-issue, '*A List of Works relating to Scotland*,' 1916, pp. 727–730.)

Laing (Henry). Descriptive Catal. of Impressions from Ancient Scottish Seals, embracing a period from 1094 to the Commonwealth, taken from original Charters, etc. preserved in public and private archives. Edinb. 1850.

—— **Supplemental Descriptive Catal. from 1150 to the 18th. cent.** Edinb. 1866.

Thomson (Thomas). A Collection of Inventories and other Records of the Royal Wardrobe and Jewel-House, and of the Artillery and Munitions, in some of the Royal Castles, 1488-1606. Privately printed. Edinb. 1815.

Mackinlay (James M.). Biblio. of Place-Names of Scotland, in his 'Influence of the Pre-Reformation Church on Scottish Place-Names.' Edinb. 1904, pp. vii.–xvii.

List of Books on the Place-Names of Scotland. (*New York Public Lib. Bull.*, vol. xviii. pp. 944–947. 1914, and in enlarged re-issue, '*A List of Works relating to Scotland*,' 1916, pp. 425-428.)

Hogan (Edmund). Onomasticon Goedelicum Locorum et Tribuum Hiberniae et Scotiae. An Index, with identifications, to the Gaelic Names of Places and Tribes. Dublin, 1910.

List of MS. and Printed Sources, pp. xi.–xiv.

List of Books on Scottish Folk-Lore. (*New York Public Lib. Bull.*, vol. xviii. pp. 1382–1402. 1914, and in enlarged re-issue, '*A List of Works relating to Scotland*,' 1916, pp. 731–750.)

Mackinlay (James M.). 'Folk Lore of Scottish Lochs and Springs.' Glasgow, 1893, Biblio. pp. ix.–xii.

Ferguson (John). Biblio. Notes on the Witchcraft Literature of Scotland, with a List. (*Edinb. Biblio. Soc. Pubns.*, vol. iii. pp. 37–124. 1897.)

A Short Biblio. of the Border Gypsies. (*Gypsy & Folk-Lore Gazette*, vol. i. p. 133. 1912.)

List of Scottish Criminal and other Trials. (*New York Public Lib. Bull.*, vol. xviii. pp. 1295–1311. 1914, and in enlarged re-issue, '*A List of Works relating to Scotland*,' 1916, pp. 643–659.)

Nodal (J. H.). Biblio. of the Scottish Dialects, in 'A Biblio. List of Works illustrative of the various Dialects of England, compiled by Members of the English Dialect Soc.' 1877, pp. 133–154.

Maidment (James). Scotish Ballads and Songs, Historical and Traditionary. 2 vols. (With Biblio. notes.) Edinb. 1868.

Macmath (William). The Biblio. of Scottish Ballads in MS. (*Edinb. Biblio. Soc. Pubns.*, vol. i. no. 3. 1891–92.)

—— **The Ballad MSS. of Charles Kirkpatrick Sharpe and James Skene of Rubislaw.** (*Ibid.* vol. i. no. 18. 1893–94.)

Geddie (William). A Biblio. of Middle Scots Poets. (*The Scottish Text Soc. Pubns.* vol. lxi.) Edinb. 1912.

Glen (John). Biblio. of MSS. and Printed Works relating to Early Scottish Melodies, in his 'Early Scottish Melodies,' Edinb. 1900, pp. xi.–xvi.

Watt (Lauchlan Maclean). Scottish Life and Poetry. London, 1912. List of Notable MSS. referred to, pp. 499–500. Biblio. pp. 501–502.

List of Scottish Chapbooks. (*New York Public Lib. Bulletin*, vol. xviii. pp. 1576–1593. 1914, and in enlarged re-issue, '*A List of Works relating to Scotland*,' 1916, pp. 773–895.)

Harvey (William). Scottish Chapbook Literature. Paisley, 1903. List of Chapbooks, pp. 145–147.

Watkins (James Hutton). Early Scottish Ballads. (*Glasgow Archæol. Soc. Trans.*, vol. i. pp. 438–485. 1868.)

The Sempill Ballates, a Series of Historical, Political and Satirical Scotish Poems, ascribed to Robert Sempill, 1567–1583, with descriptive and Biblio. Notes and Preface by Thomas George Stevenson. Edinb. 1872.

Fraser (John). The Humorous Chap-books of Scotland. 2 pts. New York, 1873.

Decennial Indexes to the Services of Heirs [recorded in Chancery] in Scotland, 1700–1859. 4 vols. H.M. Stationery Office. Edinb. 1863–89.

For 1546–1699, see 'Inquisitionum ad Capellam Regis Retornatarum Abbreviatio.' [Record Commission.] 3 vols. London, 1811–16. Indices with County arrangement in vol. iii.

Annual Indexes to the Services of Heirs in Scotland, 1860, etc. H.M. Stationery Office. Edinb. 1871, etc. [In progress.]

Paul (Sir James Balfour). A Biblio. of Scottish Family Histories. [In course of compilation.]

——— **Index Volume to 'The Scots Peerage,' edited by Sir James Balfour Paul** (8 vols. Edinb. 1904–11), compiled by Mrs. Alexander Stuart. Edinb. 1914.

Catal. of MSS. relating to Genealogy and Heraldry in the Lib. of the Faculty of Advocates, Edinburgh. Preface by W. B. D. Turnbull. London, 1852. Ten copies only printed. Compiled exclusively for W. B. D. Turnbull and Sir Charles George Young, Garter King-at-Arms.

List of Books on the Heraldry, Blazonry and Seals of Scotland. (*New York Public Lib. Bull.*, vol. xviii. pp. 1153–1157. 1914, and in enlarged re-issue, '*A List of Works relating to Scotland*,' 1916, pp. 554–558.)

List of Books on Scottish Genealogy. (*Ibid.* vol. xviii. pp. 1157–1233. 1914, and in enlarged re-issue, '*A List of Works relating to Scotland*,' 1916, pp. 558–634.)

List of Books on Scottish Surnames. (*Ibid.* vol. xviii. pp. 1157–1158. 1914, and in enlarged re-issue, '*A List of Works relating to Scotland*,' 1916, pp. 558–559.)

Grant (Francis James). Index to Genealogies, Birth briefs, and Funeral Escutcheons recorded in the Lyon Office, Edinburgh. (*Scottish Record Soc. Pubns.*, Pt. xl.) Edinb. 1908.

Stevenson (John Horne). Heraldry in Scotland. 2 vols. Glasgow, 1914. The Records of Early Practice, in vol. i. pp. 102–124.

Murdoch (Robert). Biblio. of Works on the Stewart and Stuart Families. (*Scottish Notes & Queries*, Ser. 2, vol. viii. pp. 113–114, 171. 1907.)

An Index of Places mentioned in Bernau's 'Genealogical Directory' [includes the Scotch Counties], by Geo. F. T. Sherwood. See the First Supplement to the Second edition of the 'International Genealogical Directory,' 1909.

List of Works on Clan History. By Peter John Anderson. (*Scottish Notes & Queries*, vol. v. pp. 125, 126; Ser. 2, vol. i. pp. 190, 191. 1892–1900.)

Biblio. of Clan Literature, by Robert Murdoch (afterwards R. Murdoch-Lawrance), with Notes. (*Scottish Notes and Queries*, Ser. 2, vol. viii. pp. 183–185. 1907; *Aberdeen Journal Notes and Queries*, vol. i. p. 137; vol. ii. pp. 116, 203; vol. iv. pp. 133, 139; vol. v. pp. 192, 197, 245; vol. vi. pp. 196, 203, 209; vol. vii. pp. 130, 137, 269, 278. 1908–14.)

List of Books on Clan History, Tartans, Arms, Regimental Histories, etc. (*New York Public Lib. Bull.*, vol. xviii. pp. 947–953. 1914, and in enlarged re-issue, '*A List of Works relating to Scotland*,' 1916, pp. 428–434.)

Douglas (Loudon M.). The Kilt. A Manual of Scottish National Dress, with a Biblio. of Scottish Dress. Edinb. 1914.

Scott (John). A Biblio. of Printed Documents and Books relating to the Scottish Company, commonly called the Darien Company. Revised by George P. Johnston. (*Edinb. Biblio. Soc. Pubns.*, vol. vi. pp. 19–70. 1904.) **Additions and Corrections,** by G. P. Johnston. (*Ibid.* vol. vi. pp. 159–179. 1906.)

Dunbar (Sir Archibald Hamilton). Scottish Kings. A Revised Chronology of Scottish Hist., 1005-1625. Edinb. 1899. List of Authors, Books, Chronicles, etc., referred to, pp. 381–392. Second edn. 1906, pp. 389–401.

Terry (Charles Sanford). A Biblio. of Jacobite History, 1689-1788, in his 'The Rising of 1745, with a Biblio.' London, 1903.

Wyckoff (Charles Trumen). Feudal Relations between the Kings of Engl. and Scot. under the early Plantagenets. [Univ. of Chicago.] Chicago, 1897. **Biblio.,** pp. 155–159.

A List of Persons concerned in the Rebellion, 1746, with a Preface by the Earl of Rosebery, and annotations by Walter Macleod. (*Scottish Hist. Soc. Pubns.*, vol. vii. 1890.) The List is arranged according to Districts.

Scott (John). A Biblio. of Works relating to Mary, Queen of Scots, 1544-1700. (*Edinb. Biblio. Soc. Pubns.*, vol. ii. 1896.)

An extensive and interesting Collection of Books and MSS. from the 16th. to 19th. centuries, in 'Catal. of the Lib. of John Scott,' sold by Auction, 27 March, 1905, pp. 141–182.

Includes the greater portion of the items in the preceding Biblio. of Mary, Queen of Scots, and some that are not entered there.

Law (Thomas Graves). Mary Stewart. Biblio. of the Period. (In 'Cambridge Modern Hist.,' vol. iii. pp, 810-815. 1904.)

Cameron (James). First Provisional Handlist of Proclamations. Mary, Queen of Scots. 14 Dec. 1542-24 July 1567. (Bibliotheca Lindesiana.) Aberdeen, 1891.

Steele (Robert Reynolds). Biblio. of Royal Proclamations of the Tudor and Stuart Sovereigns, etc., 1485-1714, vol. ii. Scotland. (*Bibliotheca Lindesiana.*) Oxford, 1910.

Robertson (William). An Index drawn up about 1629 to Charters granted by Scottish Kings, between 1309 and 1413, with a description of the ancient Records of Scotland in 1292, with Indexes. Edinb. 1798.

General Index to 'The Acts of the Parliaments of Scotland, 1124-1707.' 11 vols. 1814-75. H.M. Gen. Register House, Edinburgh. 1875.

Return of the Names of every Member returned to Parliament [Parliaments and Estates of Scotland, 1357-1707.] 4 vols. 1878–91.

Shearer (John E.). Old Maps and Map Makers of Scotland. A complete Hist. of the Cartography of Scotland. Stirling, 1905.

Harker (Alfred). On Some Old Maps [of Scotland]. (*The Scottish Mountaineering Club Journ.*, vol. xiii. pp. 273–281, 310-320; vol. xiv. pp. 18–25. 1915–16.)

Douglas (William). Note on Old Scottish Maps. (*Ibid.* vol. ii. pp. 283–284. 1893.)

Catal. of the County Maps and Town Plans of the Ordnance Survey of Scotland, to Jan. 1908. H.M. Stationery Office, London.

Cameron (James). A Biblio. of Slezer's 'Theatrum Scotiæ,' with an Analytical Table of the Plates, by W. Johnston. (*Edinb. Biblio. Soc. Pubns.*, vol. iii. pp. 141–147. 1899.) See also a note on 'Papers relating to the Theatrum Scotiæ,' and other Works in the Register House, in Livingstone's 'Guide to the Public Records of Scotland,' 1905, p. 203.

Papers relating to the 'Theatrum Scotiæ,' and 'History and Present State of Scotland,' by Capt. John Slezer, 1693-1707, with lists of Plates and Contents in various editions. (*The Bannatyne Miscellany*, vol. ii. pp. 307–344.) The Bannatyne Club. Edinb. 1836.

Papers relative to Captain John Slezer, in 'Analecta Scotia.' Edinb. 1834, vol. vii. pp. 47–51.

Jamieson (John). Life of Slezer, in Jamieson's edition of the 'Theatrum Scotiæ.' London, 1874, pp. vii.–xv.

Papers relating to the Geographical description, Maps and Charts of Scotland, by John Adair, Geographer for the Kingdom of Scotland, 1686–1723. (*The Bannatyne Miscellany*, vol. ii. pp. 347–388.) The Bannatyne Club. Edinb. 1836.

Geographical Collections relating to Scotland made by Walter Macfarlane, edited by Sir Arthur Mitchell and James Toshach Clark. 3 vols. [Scottish Hist. Soc. Pubns., vols. li.–liii.] Edinb. 1906–08. The Prefaces contain Biblio. notes on the Collections of Macfarlane and Sibbald, with lists, etc.

Macbain (Alexander). Ptolemy's Geography of Scotland. (*Gaelic Soc. of Inverness. Trans.*, vol. xviii. pp. 267–288. 1894.)

Cash (C. G.). The First Topographical Survey of Scotland, with Biblio. notes on Maps, etc. (*The Scottish Geog. Mag.*, vol. xvii. pp. 399–414. 1901.)

——— **MS. Maps by Pont, the Gordons, and Adair in the Advocates' Lib., Edinb.,** with Biblio. of Maps. (*Ibid.* vol. xxiii. pp. 574–592. 1907.)

Bartholomew (J. G.). A Biblio. of the Cartography of Scotland, from the earliest times to present date, in 'The Royal Scottish Geographical Society's Atlas of Scotland,' 1895, pp. 16–18.

Mitchell (Sir Arthur). A List of Travels, Tours, Journeys, Voyages, etc., relating to Scotland. (*Soc. Antiq. Scot. Proc.*, vol. xxxv. pp. 431–638. 1901.)

——— **Supplementary List, with Index.** (*Ibid.* vol. xxxix. pp. 500-527. 1905.)

——— **Second and final Supplementary List, with an Index.** (*Ibid.* vol. xliv. pp. 390–405. 1910.) See also 'Early Travellers in Scotland, 1295–1689,' Edinb. 1891, and its Supplement, 'Tours in Scotland, 1677 and 1681,' Edinb. 1892, both edited by P. Hume Brown.

Leyden (John). Journal of a Tour in the Highlands and Western Islands of Scotland in 1800, with a Biblio. of Dr. John Leyden, by James Sinton. Edinb. 1903.

Index to the 'Scottish Mountaineering Club Journal,' vols. i.-x. 1890-1909, compiled by William Garden & James A. Parker. Edinb. 1911.

Catal. of the Western Scottish Fossils, compiled by James Armstrong, John Young, and David Robertson. [Brit. Assoc. Glasgow meeting.] Glasgow, 1876. Biblio. pp. 25–28, 93–98, 153–156.

Aldis (Harry G.). A List of Books printed in Scotland before 1700, including those printed furth of the Realm for Scottish Booksellers, with brief notes on the Printers and Stationers. (*Edinb. Biblio. Soc. Pubns.*, vol. vii. 1904.)

Aldis (**Harry G.**). **Scottish Bibliography.** (*The Scottish Review*, vol. xxix. pp. 101–115. 1897.)

Dickson (**Robert**) and **Edmond** (**John Philip**). **Annals of Scottish Printing**, from the Introduction of the Art in 1507 to the beginning of the 17th. century. Cambridge, 1890.

Dickson (**Robert**). **Introduction of Printing into Scotland.** Aberdeen. 1885.

——— **Who was Scotland's first Printer.** London, 1881.

Duff (**E. Gordon**). **The Two First Books printed in the Scottish Language.** (*Edinb. Biblio. Soc. Pubns.*, vol. i. no. 3. 1893.)

Clark (**J. T.**). **Notes on Early Printing in Scotland, 1507-1600.** (*Library Assoc. Trans. Third Meeting*, 1880, pp. 22–29.)

Wilson (**Robert**). **Notes on the Introduction of Printing into Scotland.** (*Hawick Archæol. Soc. Trans.*, 1913, pp. 25–27.)

Johnstone (**J. F. Kellas**). **The Introduction of Printing into Scotland re-studied.** A Paper read before the Edinb. Biblio. Soc., Mar. 1915.

Lee (**John**). **Memorial of the Bible Societies in Scotland**, with the Additional Memorial on Printing and Importing the Bibles and Lists of the various editions of the Bible printed in Scotland. 2 vols. Edinb. 1824–26.

These vols. contain much information relating to Early Scottish Printers. They were issued in connection with the dispute between the King's Printers for Scotland and the Bible Societies, as to the right of the latter to introduce and sell Bibles printed in England.

Information anent His Majesties Printers in Scotland. By Robert and James Bryson against Robert Young, Printer to Charles I. (*Spottiswoode Miscellany*, 1844, vol. i. pp. 295–302.)

Answers for James Anderson, His Majestys Printer, and Agnes Campbell, his Mother, to the Petition of Robert Saunders, Printer in Glasgow. [Illustrates the history of the Press in the Reign of Charles II.] (*Ibid.* vol. i. pp. 303–310.)

Couper (**William James**). **Scottish Rebel Printers.** Privately Printed. Edinburgh, 1912.

Blaikie (**Walter Biggar**). **The Printers to Prince Charles Edward in 1745.** (*The Scottish Typographical Circular*, Apr. 1901.)

Mackay (**Æneas J. G.**). **A Short Note on the Local Presses of Scotland, etc.** (*Edinb. Biblio. Soc. Pubns.*, vol. iii. pp. 33–35. 1899.)

Macleod (**Robert D.**). **The Early Scottish Typefounders.** (*Scottish Library Assoc.* 12 May, 1909.)

Cameron (**Alexander**). **Oldest Printed Gaelic Books**, in his 'Reliquiæ Celticæ,' 1894, vol. ii. pp. 524–532.

Documents relative to the Printers of some Early Scottish Newspapers, etc., 1686-1705. (*Miscellany of the Maitland Club*, vol. ii. 1840, pp. 227–280.)

Wallace (**W.**). **Early Scottish Journalists and Journalism.** Stirling, 1899.

Cockburn (**James D.**). **Beginnings of the Scottish Newspaper Press.** (*The Scottish Review*, vol. xviii. pp. 366-377 ; vol. xxi. pp. 399-419. 1891-93.)

The Earliest Scottish Newspaper. An Account of the 'Mercurius Caledonius.' (*Good Words*, vol. xlii. pp. 58–63. 1901.)

Catal. of Scotch Newspapers in the British Museum, arranged under Places, with an Index of Titles.

A List of Scotch Newspapers is in Chalmers' 'Life of Thomas Ruddiman,' 1794, pp. 441-442.

Alexander Russell of the 'Scotsman.' A Collection of Obituary Notices. Privately Printed. Edinb. 1876.

Niven (G. W.). The Biblio. of 'The Scots Magazine.' (*The Library*, vol. x. p. 310. 1898.)

Robertson (Joseph). Sketch of the Hist. of Scottish Almanacs. Reprinted from Oliver & Boyd's 'New Edinb. Alm.,' 1838, pp. 454–457. (*Scottish Notes & Queries*, vol. x. pp. 145–147. 1897.)

List of Scottish Booksellers and of Scottish Book Auctions. See Nichols, 'Literary Anecdotes of the Eighteenth Century,' vol. iii. 1812, pp. 689-693, and also 'Notes and Queries,' Ser. 11, vol. i. p. 423, vol. ii. pp. 170, 418. 1910.

Cameron (James). A Biblio. of Scottish Theatrical Literature. (*Edinb. Biblio. Soc. Pubns.*, vol. i. no. 4. 1892.) **Supplement.** (*Ibid.* vol. i. no. 24. 1896.)

Hist. MSS. Commission. A Guide to the Reports on Collections of MSS. of Private Families, Corporations, and Institutions in Gt. Brit. & Irel. Part I. Topographical. Report for Scotland and Ireland. London, 1914.

Calendar of Documents relating to Scotland in the Public Record Office, London, 1108–1509. Edited by Joseph Bain. 4 vols. H.M. Register House. Edinb. 1881–88.

Calendar of Letters and Papers relating to the Affairs of the Borders of England and Scotland, preserved in the Public Record Office, London, 1560-1603. Edited by Joseph Bain. 2 vols. Edinb. 1894–96.

Calendar of the State Papers relating to Scotland and Mary, Queen of Scots, 1547-1603, preserved in the Public Record Office, the British Museum, and elsewhere in England. Edited by Joseph Bain and William K. Boyd. 9 vols. [1547–1588]. Edinb. 1898–1915.

Calendar of the State Papers relating to Scotland in the Public Record Office, London. By Markham J. Thorpe. 2 vols. London, 1858.

Report from the Select Committee appointed to inquire into the State of the Public Records of the Kingdom. 1800. **Scotland,** pp. 393–495, 657–667.

Annual Reports of the Deputy Clerk Register of Scotland [on General Records, Local Registries, etc.]. Edinb. 1807–1868.

Livingstone (Matthew). Guide to the Public Records of Scotland deposited in H.M. General Register House, Edinburgh. Edinb. 1905.

Bryce (William Moir). Handbook of Records in H.M. General Register House. 1885. Privately Printed.

Johnson (J. Bolam). The Scottish Records, in 'The Genealogist's Pocket Library,' ed. by C. A. Bernau, vol. iii. pp. 39–97. 1908.

Descriptive Catal. of the State Papers and other Historical Documents preserved in the Archives at Hamilton Palace, 1309–1759. (*Miscellany of the Maitland Club*, vol. iv. pp. 59–208. 1847.) See also 'Hist. MSS. Comm. Rep.', xi. App. VI. 1887.

Campbell (Duncan). The Exchequer Rolls of Scotland. (*Gaelic Soc. of Inverness. Trans.*, vol. xxii. pp. 210–233. 1900.)

Notices of Original Unprinted Documents preserved in the Office of the Queen's Remembrancer and Chapter-House, Westminster, illustrative of the Hist. of Scotland. Edited by Joseph Stevenson. [Maitland Club.] 1842.

Parliamentary Records of Scotland in the General Register House, Edinburgh, 1244–1569. Vol. i. only published. 1804.

Palgrave (Sir Francis). Documents and Records illustrating the Hist. of Scotland, preserved in the Treasury of the Exchequer. (Record Commission.) 1837.

Teulet (Alexandre). Inventaire Chronologique des Documents relatifs à l'Histoire d'Écosse, conservés aux Archives du Royaume à Paris. [Abbotsford Club.] Edinb. 1839.

——— **Papiers de État, etc. de l'Écosse au XVIe Siècle, tirés des Bibliothèques de France, publiés pour le Bannatyne Club d'Edimbourg.** 3 vols. Paris, 1852–60. Table Alphabétique des Noms de Personnes, de Lieux et de Matières contenus dans les Trois Volumes. Paris [1859].

Robertson (William). An Index, drawn up about the year 1629, of many Records of Charters, granted by the different Sovereigns of Scotland between the years 1309 and 1413, most of which Records have been long missing. Edinb. 1798.

Livingstone (Matthew). A Calendar of Charters and other Writs relating to Lands or Benefices in Scotland, in possession of the Soc. of Antiquaries of Scotland. (*Soc. Antiq. Scot. Proc.*, vol. xli. pp. 303–392. 1907.)

Laing (David). A Note on the subject of Protocol Books as connected with Public Records. (*Ibid.* vol. ii. pp. 350–353. 1859.)

Innes (Cosmo). Notes of some MSS. in English Libraries examined while preparing the materials for the 'National MSS. of Scotland.' (*Ibid.* vol. vii. pp. 362–371. 1870.)

Reid (Alexander George). Note as to the Recovery of Three Volumes of the MS. Collections of Scottish Antiquities of Robert Riddell, of Friars Carse and Glenriddell. (*Ibid.* vol. xxx. pp. 222–224. 1896.)

Grant (Francis James). Charter Chest of the Earldom of Dundonald, 1219-1672. (*Scottish Record Soc. Pubns.*, Part L. 1910.)

Scottish Burgh Records Society. The Soc. has Calendared and Indexed large quantities of Scottish Records, and issued printed Indexes from 1868 onwards. See 'Complete List of Publications, 1868–1911,' in last vol. published.

Index to Extracts from the Records of the Convention of the Royal Burghs of Scotland, 1295-1738. Edinb. 1890.

Records of the Scottish Universities. By Peter John Anderson. I. St. Andrews, II. Glasgow, III. Aberdeen, IV. Edinburgh. (*Scottish Notes & Queries*, vol. v. pp. 162–163. 1892.)

The New Club. Founded in Paisley in 1877 to print a series of Works illustrative of the Antiquities, History, Literature, Poetry, Bibliography, and Topography of Scotland in former times. For a List of Publications see 'A List of Works relating to Scotland' (New York Public Lib.), 1916, p. 12.

Keith (Theodora). Commercial Relations of England and Scotland, 1603–1707. [Girton College Studies. No. I.] Camb. 1910. **Biblio.** pp. 207–210.

——— **Biblio. of Scottish Economic History.** (*Historical Assoc. of Scot. Pamphlet*, No. V.) 1914.

Turnbull (W. B. D. D.). Memoranda of the State of the Parochial Registers of Scotland. [Arranged under Counties.] Edinb. 1849.

Dundas (W. Pitt). Detailed List of the Old Parochial Registers of Scotland. Edinb. 1872.

Seton (George). Sketch of the History and imperfect Condition of the Parochial Records of Births, Deaths, and Marriages in Scotland. Edinb. 1854.

Cleland (James). Letter to the Duke of Hamilton respecting the Parochial Registers of Scotland. Glasgow, 1834.

List of Parish Registers in Scotland. (*Northern Notes and Queries*, vol. i. pp. 89–90, 130–131; vol. iii. pp. 57–58, 143–145; *The Scottish Antiquary*, vol. viii. pp. 175–179. 1888–94.)

Maxwell (Sir Herbert E.). The Early Chronicles relating to Scotland. Glasgow, 1912.

Anderson (Alan O.). Scottish Annals from English Chroniclers, A.D. 500 to 1286. London, 1908. Table of References, pp. ix.–xiii.

Skene (William Forbes). Notice of the existing MSS. of Fordun's 'Scotichronicon.' (*Soc. Antiq. Scot. Proc.*, vol. viii. pp. 239–256. 1871.)

——— **Additional Notice of the MS. of Fordun's Chronicle.** (*Ibid.* vol. ix. pp. 13–24. 1873.)

——— **Notice of an early MS. of Fordun's Chronicle, the property of Alexander Pringle, of Whytbank.** (*Ibid.* vol. x. pp. 27–30. 1875.) See also David Murray's 'The Black Book of Paisley, and other MSS. of the "Scotichronicon."' 1885.

Amours (Francis Joseph). Editions and MSS. of 'Wyntoun's Cronykil.' (*Philos. Soc. of Glasgow, Proc.*, vol. xxxiii. pp. 219–231. 1902.) Also appeared in 'The Original Chronicle of Andrew of Wyntoun,' ed. by F. J. Amours, vol. i. pp. xliii.–lxvii. Scottish Text Soc., vol. lxiii. 1914.

Craigie (William A.). The St. Andrews MS. of Wyntoun's Chronicle. (*Anglia.* Halle-a-S. vol. xx. pp. 363–380. 1898.)

——— **Wyntoun's 'Original Chronicle.'** (*The Scottish Review*, vol. xxx. pp. 33–54. 1897.)

Law (Thomas Graves). Biblio. of John Major and his Disciples (David Cranstoun, George Lokert, William Manderston and Robert Caubraith), in 'A Hist. of Greater Britain, as well England as Scotland,' compiled by John Major, 1521, with Notes by Archibald Constable and Life by Æneas J. G. Mackay [Scottish Hist. Soc. vol. x.]. Edinb. 1892.

Giles (Peter). The Earliest Scottish Literature. (In 'The Cambridge Hist. of English Literature,' vol. ii. pp. 100–132. 1908.)

Catalogue of Scottish Writers. Edited by James Maidment. Edinb. 1833.

Ferguson (John). Biblio. of the 'Nobilis Scotus' of William Davisson [b. about 1593, d. about 1669] in his 'Bibliotheca Chemica,' 1906, vol. i. pp. 200–201.

Finlayson (James). Biblio. of Peter Lowe, Founder of the Faculty of Physicians and Surgeons of Glasgow, in his 'Account of the Life and Works of Maister Peter Lowe.' Glasgow, 1889.

——— **Biblio. of Sylvester Rattray (Physician in Glasgow, fl. 1650–1666)** published in 'Janus,' Amsterdam, 1900.

Biblio. of Barbour's 'Bruce,' in Walter W. Skeat's edn. of 'The Bruce,' published by 'The Scottish Text Soc.' 2 vols. 1894. See also 'Scottish Notes & Queries,' vol. ix. p. 34. 1895.

Hewison (James King). Biblio. of Ninian Winzet (1518-1592) in his edition of 'Certain Tractates, etc. by Ninian Winzett.' Vol. i. Introduction, p. lxxv. [Scottish Text Soc.] 2 vols. Edinb. 1888–90.

Hutcheson (Thomas S.). Bibliotheca Wallasiana. List of the various Works relating to Sir William Wallace from 1488 to 1858. Glasgow, 1858.

Laing (David). A few Remarks on the Portraits of Sir William Wallace. (*Soc. Antiq. Scot. Proc.*, vol. ii. pp. 308–313. 1859.)

——— **Biblio. of Robert Baillie,** in his 'Letters and Journals of Robert Baillie, Principal of the Univ. of Glasgow, 1637–1662. [Bannatyne Club.] Edinb. 1841.

Murray (David). Biblio. of George Buchanan, in 'George Buchanan. Glasgow Quatercentenary Studies, 1906,' edited with a Preface by George Neilson. Glasgow, 1907. See also 'George Buchanan: A Memorial, 1506–1906,' by various Writers, compiled and edited by D. A. Millar. St. Andrews, 1907.

—— **The Scot Abroad and the Biblio. of his Writings.** (*Records of the Glasgow Biblio. Soc.*, vol. i. pp. 59–65. 1914.) See also Chap. I. pp. 1–130, of 'The Scot abroad,' by John Hill Burton, 1864, on 'The Scholar and the Author.'

Innes (Cosmo). Memoir of Thomas Thomson, Advocate. The Bannatyne Club. Edinb. 1854. List of Thomson's Works, pp. 248–251.

Index to the First, Second, and Third Series of the Trans. of the Highland and Agricultural Soc. of Scotland from 1799 to 1865. Edinb. 1869; **Index to the Fourth Series, 1866-88.** Edinb. 1888; **Index to the Fifth Series, 1889-1909** (in 3 pts.). Edinb. 1896–1910.

IRELAND.

List of Works in the New York Public Lib. relating to Ireland, the Irish Language and Literature, etc. (*New York Public Lib. Bull.* vol. ix. pp. 90-104, 124-144, 159-184, 201-229, 249-280. 1905.) Also issued separately. The list includes articles in Magazines and publications of learned Societies.

Shirley (Evelyn Philip). Catal. of the Library at Lough Fea, in illustration of the Hist. and Antiquities of Ireland. London, 1872. Privately printed.

Best (Richard Irvine). Biblio. of Irish Philology and of Printed Irish Literature. [National Library of Ireland.] Dublin, 1913.

Of Topographical as well as Philological value.

King (Jeremiah). King's Irish Biblio. A Subject Guide to Irish Books. (Pt. I. of 'Irish Researches.') London, 1903.

Casaide (Seamus ua). Bibliographies of Irish Subjects. A Classified List of Bibliographies, arranged under Subject, Author, and Reference. (*The Irish Book Lover*, vol. iii. pp. 22-23. 1911.)

Biblio. of Histories of Irish Counties and Towns. (Arranged under places.) By William MacArthur. (*Notes and Queries*, Ser. 11, vol. xi. pp. 103, 183, 315; vol. xii. pp. 24, 210, 276, 375; Ser. 12, vol. i. p. 422; vol. ii. pp. 22, 141. 1915-16.)

Lowdermilk (W. H.). Bibliotheca Hibernica. A Collection of scarce and valuable works on Ireland and the Irish People. Washington, U.S.A. 1890?

Dix (E. R. McClintock). Irish Bibliography. The Use and Need of its Study. (*Dublin Penny Journ.* New Ser. vol. i. pp. 200, 217. 1902.)

——— **Irish Librarians and Irish Bibliography.** (*An Leabharlann—The Library.*) Dublin, vol. i. no. 1. Jan. 1905.)

——— **Irish Pirated Editions.** (*Ibid.* vol. ii. no. 1, p. 67. 1906.)

Ireland and the Irish. A Catal. of Works relating to Ireland in the Reference Department of the Wigan Public Lib. Wigan, 1896.

Quarterly Supplement of Irish Bibliography, afterwards Quarterly Biblio. of Irish Literature, etc. In 'The Irish Book Lover,' edited by J. S. Crone, vol. i. no. iv. etc. 1909, etc.

Power (John). Bibliotheca Hibernica. A Manual of Irish Literature, being a list of all Writings by Irishmen, and Persons enjoying preferment or office in Ireland, and also of Works relating to Ireland, printed in other parts, from the Invention of Printing to the present time, with Biog. notices, Biblio. remarks, Critical Notices, Collations of the rarer articles, to which is prefixed a dissertation on early Printing in Ireland. Dublin, 1865.

Irish Literary Inquirer, or Notes on Authors, Books, and Printing in Ireland, Biographical and Bibliographical, Notices of Rare Books, Memoranda of Printing in Ireland, Biographical Notes of Irish Writers, etc. Conducted by John Power. No. 1-4. July 1865—April 1866. London.

For a note on John Power and his Biblio. works, see 'The Irish Book Lover.' vol. i. pp. 2-4. 1909.

O'Reilly (Edward). A Chronological Account of nearly Four Hundred Irish Writers, commencing with the earliest account of Irish History and carried down to 1750, with a descriptive Catal. of such of their Works as are still extant, etc. (*Iberno-Celtic Soc. Trans.* vol. i. pt. i. Dublin, 1820.)

'Historicus.' The Best Hundred Irish Books, with annotated Index. Reprinted from the 'Freeman's Journal.' [1886.]

Blacker (Beaver Henry). Contributions towards a Bibliotheca Hibernica. (Irish Eccles. Gazette. No. 1, etc. 1875, etc.)

Ware (Sir James). The Hist. of the Writers of Ireland, with an Account of all the Works they published, written in Latin, translated, revised, and continued down to the beginning of the present century, by Walter Harris. Dublin, 1764.

Brown (Stephen James). A Guide to Books on Ireland. Vol. i. Prose Literature, Poetry, Music, and Plays. Dublin, 1912. Vols. ii. and iii. are not yet issued. See also 'The Irish Book Lover,' vol. i. pp. 81–82, 102–104. 1910.

Irish Books in the Library of the Brit. Museum. A separate vol. of the 'Catal. of Printed Books' is devoted to 'Ireland,' and contains publications of a miscellaneous character which are not entered elsewhere under the Authors' names. A Key to the arrangement is at the beginning of the vol. with an Index of Sub-headings.

Dix (E. R. McClintock). Suggestions for Irish Book Collectors. (*The Irish Book Lover*, vol. i. pp. 144–146. 1910.)

——— **Irish Bookbinding. Primary Introduction to its Study.** (*Dublin Penny Journ.* New Ser. vol. i. p. 344. 1903.)

Early Book Auctions in Ireland. (*The Irish Literary Inquirer*, ed. by John Power, no. iii. pp. 29–30. 1865.)

Sale-Catal. of the Library of Thomas Crofton Croker, relating to Irish History, etc. [Collections of MSS., Historical Tracts, Ballad Literature, Broadsides, Prints, etc.] Sold by Puttick & Simpson, London, 18–20 Dec. 1854.

Sale-Catal. of the Library of Denis H. Kelly, containing rare Books and MSS. on the History, Antiquities, etc. of Ireland. Sold by John Fleming Jones, Dublin, 28 Oct. 1875.

Sale-Catal. of the Library of Dr. Thomas Willis, senior, containing a remarkable collection of MSS. Books, Maps, Ballads, etc. relating to Ireland. Sold by John Fleming Jones, Dublin, 22 Nov. 1876.

Sale-Catal. of the Library of James Weale, relating to the Hist., Literature, and Antiquities of Ireland. [Collections of MSS. in the Irish Language, Proclamations, etc.] Sold by Evans, London, 5–11 Feb. 1840. Weale's 'Collectanea Hibernica Historico-Bibliographica' was included in the sale; see entry with descriptive note at p. 53.

Great Irish Book Collectors, with notes on the sales of their Libraries. No. I. Dr. John Murphy, Bishop of Cork; No, II. William Chadwick Neligan; No. III. William Horatio Crawford; No. IV. Sheffield Grace; No. V. Canon Jeremiah Murphy; No. VI. William Monck Mason; No. VII. Dr. Sheehan, Bishop of Waterford. (*The Irish Book Lover*, vol. vii. pp. 1–3, 21–23, 38–39, 59–60, 89–90, 107–108, 125–126, 180–181. 1915–16.)

The Henry Bradshaw Irish Collection, presented to the Camb. Univ. Lib. in 1870 and 1886 by Henry Bradshaw. (*Cambridge University Lib. Bulletin*, Extra Series, 1909.) 'A full Catal. of the whole Collection is in preparation,' June, 1909. See a note in 'The Irish Book Lover,' vol. i. pp. 134–135. 1910.

Mason (W. Shaw). Bibliotheca Hibernicana, 1820, or a Descriptive Catal. of a Select Irish Library, collected for the Rt. Hon. Sir Robert Peel. Dublin, 1823. Privately printed. For a Biblio. Note on the above see 'The Irish Book Lover,' vol. vii. pp. 117–118. 1916.

Halliday (Bernard). Catal. of a Special Collection of Books on Ireland, and a remarkable collection of original MSS. and Deeds from 1500 to 1850, relating to the principal families of Ireland, mostly from the collection of Rev. J. Graves. Leicester, 1904.

The Haliday Pamphlets. A Biblio. Note on the Collection formed by Charles Haliday, presented to the Royal Irish Academy. (*The Irish Book Lover*, vol. vii. pp. 121–122. 1916.)

A Collection of Catalogues of Irish Books, MSS., Maps, etc. on Sale by John O'Daly and by Thomas Connolly, Booksellers in Dublin, 1854-1876. (In the Library of the Brit. Museum.)

A List of Irish Booksellers. (*Notes & Queries*, Ser, 11, vol. i. p. 424. 1910.)

Arbois de Jubainville (Henri d'). Essai d'un Catal. de la Littérature Épique de l'Irlande, précédé d'une étude sur les manuscrits en langue Irlandaise conservés dans les Iles Britanniques et sur le continent. Paris, 1883.

Hull (Eleanor). A Text Book of Irish Literature. 2 vols. Dublin, 1906, 08. **Biblio.** vol. ii. pp. 237–246.

Catal. of the Literary Collections and original Compositions of William Monck Mason, in the department of Irish History and General Philology, with a descriptive note. [Comprises Books, MSS., Newspapers, Maps, Broadsides, etc.] Sold by Sotheby's, 29–31 Mar. 1858. See an account of William Monck Mason and his Library in 'The Irish Book Lover,' vol. vii. pp. 125–126. 1916.

Catal. of the Sixth and Final Portion of the Lib. of Dr. John Murphy, Bishop of Cork. Sold by Sotheby's, 18 Dec., 1848.

The Irish items are in this portion. The Library was described as 'the largest ever formed by a private individual.'

Mackinnon (Donald). A Descriptive Catal. of Gaelic MSS. in the Advocates' Lib., Edinburgh, and elsewhere in Scotland. Edinb., 1912.

Nutt (Alfred). Ossian and Ossianic Literature. (*Popular Studies in Mythology, etc., No. III.*) London, 1899. Biblio Appendix, pp. 51–54.

Biblio. of Irish Tales, Sagas, etc. See *ante* p. 380. Best's 'Biblio. of Irish Philology, etc.', 1913, pp. 78–126.

Brown (Stephen James). A Reader's Guide to Irish Fiction. London, 1910. Also an edition, Dublin, 1910.

—— **Ireland in Fiction. A Guide to Irish Novels, Tales, Romances, and Folk-Lore.** 1916. An expansion of the preceding work.

Maxwell (Constantia). A Brief Biblio. of Irish History. Dublin, 1911.

Morris (William O'Connor). Ireland, 1494–1905, revised by Robert Dunlop. [Camb. Hist. Series.] Cambridge, 1909. **Biblio.** (arranged under periods) pp. 389–402.

D'Alton (Edward A.). Hist. of Ireland, from the earliest times to the present day. 3 vols. Dublin, 1903–10. **Biblio.** vol. ii. pp. 571–576.

Condon (J.). A Short Biblio. of Irish History. (*An Leabharlann—The Library*, Dublin, vol. i. no. 1, Jan. 1905.)

Steele (Robert Reynolds). Biblio. of Royal Proclamations of the Tudor and Stuart Sovereigns, etc., 1485–1714. Vol. II. Ireland. (*Bibliotheca Lindesiana*. Oxford, 1910.

For a Chronological List of Irish Proclamations from 1618-1875, see *infra* p. 385, Reports of the Dep. Keeper of Public Records in Ireland.

Gilbert (Sir John Thomas). The Historic Literature of Ireland. An Essay on the Publications of the Irish Archæol. Soc. Reprinted from the 'Irish Quarterly Review.' Dublin, 1851.

O'Curry (Eugene). Lectures on the MS. Materials of Ancient Irish History, delivered at the Catholic Univ. of Ireland, in 1855 and 1856. Dublin, 1861.

Nicolson (William), Bishop of Derry. The Irish Historical Library, pointing at most of the Authors and Records in Print and Manuscript, which may be serviceable to the compilers of a general Hist. of Ireland. Dublin, 1724.

Dunlop (Robert). Ireland to the Settlement of Ulster. From beginning of 16th cent. to 1611, **Biblio.** (*The Cambridge Modern Hist.* vol. iii. pp. 852–859. 1904); **Ireland from the Plantation of Ulster to the Cromwellian Settlement (1611–1659), Biblio.** (*Ibid.* vol. iv. pp. 913–918. 1906); **Ireland from the Restoration to the Act of Resumption (1660–1700), Biblio.** (*Ibid.* vol. v. pp. 829–837. 1908); **Ireland from 1700–1789, Biblio.** (*Ibid.* vol. vi. pp. 913–924. 1909); **Ireland and the Home Rule Movement, Biblio.** (*Ibid.* vol. xii. pp. 856-862. 1910.)

Joyce (Patrick Weston). A Social History of Ancient Ireland. 2 vols. London, 1903. List of Authorities consulted, vol. ii. pp. 585–609.

Chapters xii.–xv. in vol. i. deal with Irish Literature, Ecclesiastical and Religious Writings, Annals, Histories, and Genealogies, and Historical and Romantic Tales.

Murray (Alice Effie). A Hist. of the Commercial and Financial Relations between England and Ireland. London, 1903. Biblio. pp. 445–467.

Index to the Transactions of the Royal Irish Acad. from 1786 to the present time, compiled and published in London, 1813, by Nicholas Carlisle.

Index to Vols. i.–vii. 1836–61 of the Proceedings of the Royal Irish Acad. [In 'Proceedings,' vol. vii. 1862.] Compiled by William Reeves, Bishop of Down and Connor and Dromore.

List of Papers published in the Transactions, Cunningham Memoirs, and Irish MSS. Series, of the Roy. Irish Acad., 1786-1886. Compiled by Robert Macalister. 1887.

Index to the Serial Publications of the Royal Irish Academy (Transactions, Proceedings, Cunningham Memoirs, Todd Lecture Series, and Irish MSS. Series) from 1786 to 1906. Dublin, 1912.

Douglas (John M.). Sir Charles Gavan Duffy. A Biblio. (*The Irish Book Lover*, vol. vii. pp. 177-180; vol. viii. p. 17. 1916.)

Index to the Journ. of the Royal Soc. of Antiquaries of Ireland, vols. i. to xix. 1849–1889. [Forms vol. xx. of 'Journal.'] Dublin, 1902. **Index to the Journ. vols. xxi.–xl. 1891-1910.** Dublin, 1915.

A Descriptive Catal. of the Antiquities, etc., in the Museum of the Royal Irish Academy. By Sir W. R. W. Wilde. 2 pts. Dublin, 1857–61.

Hints and Queries, intended to promote the Preservation of Antiquities, and the Collection and Arrangement of Information on the subject of Local History and Traditions. Published by the Kilkenny and South-East of Ireland Archæol. Soc. Dublin, 1858.

Catal. of a Collection of Antiquities formed by Thomas Crofton Croker. London, 1854.

Westropp (Thomas Johnson). Address on the Progress of Irish Archæology, with Biblio. references. (*Soc. Antiq. Irel. Journ.*, vol. xlvi. pp. 2–26. 1916.)

Wakeman (W. F.). Statement of his Services to Irish Archæology, with lists of articles contributed to various publications. (*Roy. Hist. & Archæol. Soc. of Irel. Journ.*, vol. xviii. pp. 486–490. 1888.)

Consolidated Index of Surnames and Place-Names in the Journ. of the Assoc. for the Preservation of the Memorials of the Dead, Ireland, vols. i. to vii. 1888–1909, compiled by Miss Vigors and Mrs. Peirce G. Mahony. Dublin, 1914.

Martin (William Gregory Wood). Pagan Ireland, an Archæol. Sketch: a Handbook of Irish Pre-Christian Antiquities. London, 1895. Biblio. of Papers and Works on Irish Pre-Christian Archæology (arranged by Subjects and Authors), pp. 595–655.

Martin (William Gregory Wood). Traces of the Elder Faiths of Ireland. 2 vols. London, 1902. Biblio. of Papers and Works on Irish Pre-Christian Archæology and Folklore (arranged by Subjects and Authors), vol. ii. pp. 329–422.

Macalister (R. A. Stewart). Studies in Irish Epigraphy. 3 pts. London, 1897–1907.

Petrie (George). Christian Inscriptions in the Irish Language. Edited by M. Stokes, with Biblio. and Hist. Notes. 2 vols. [Roy. Hist. & Archæol. Assoc. of Irel.] Dublin, 1872, 78.

Atkinson (George Mouncey). Some account of Ancient Irish Treatises on Ogham writing. (*Hist. and Archæol. Assoc. of Irel. Journ.*, vol. xiii. pp. 202–236. 1874.

Biblio. of Books on Ancient Irish Inscriptions. See *ante* p. 380, Best's 'Biblio. of Irish Philology, etc.', 1913, pp. 54–56.

Catal. of Georgian Houses in Ireland, arranged under Counties, with authorities, etc. [The Georgian Soc.] (*Records of 18th cent. Domestic Architecture, etc., in Ireland*, vol. v. App. pp. 81–107. 1913.)

Joyce (Patrick Weston). The Origin and Hist. of Irish Names of Places. 3 vols. Dublin, 1870–1913. Vol. iii. is a List of Place-Names with their Irish forms and translations, alphabetically arranged.

List of Books on Place Names. See *ante* p. 380, Best's 'Biblio. of Irish Philology, etc.', 1913, pp. 19–21.

Hogan (Edmund). Onomasticon Goedelicum Locorum et Tribuum Hiberniae et Scotiae. Dublin, 1910. See *ante* under Scotland, p. 371.

O'Donoghue (David James). Feis Ceoil, 1899. Catal. of the Musical Loan Exhibition held in the Nat. Library and Nat. Museum, Dublin, May, 1899. Dublin, 1899.

'A nearly complete Biblio. of Collections of Irish Music.'

Skey (William). The Heraldic Calendar; a list of the Nobility and Gentry whose Arms are registered, and Pedigrees recorded in the Herald's Office in Ireland. Dublin, 1846.

An Index to the Marriages in 'Walker's Hibernian Mag.', 1771 to 1812, by Henry Farrar, with an Appendix from the Notes of Sir Arthur Vicars, of the Births, Marriages, and Deaths in the 'Anthologia Hibernica,' 1793 and 1794. 2 vols. 1897.

Biblio. of Irish Family History. (*The Irish Book Lover*, vol. v. pp. 110–112, 151–152. 1914.)

List of Books on Personal Names. See *ante* p. 380, Best's 'Biblio. of Irish Philology, etc.', 1913, pp. 17–19.

Matheson (Sir Robert Edwin). Special Report on Surnames in Ireland, with Notes as to numerical strength, derivation, ethnology, & distribution, based on information from the Indexes of the Gen. Reg. Office. Dublin, 1909. Originally issued as an Appendix to the 29th. Rep. of the Reg.-Gen. for Irel.

—— **Varieties and Synonymes of Surnames and Christian Names in Ireland,** for the guidance of Registration Officers, & the Public in searching the Indexes of Births, Deaths, & Marriages, with Lists. Dublin, 1890.

List of Names of Irish Biographies in the 'D. N. B.', Second Supplement, vols. i.-iii. (*The Irish Book Lover*, vol. iii. pp. 205–207; vol. iv. pp. 80–82, 116–117. 1912–13.)

Register of Historical Portraits [connected with Ireland]. Edited by Rev. James Graves. (*Kilkenny & South-East of Irel. Archæol. Soc. Journ.*, vol. v. pp. 232–238; vol. vii. pp. 138–140. 1858–62.)

Bellesheim (Alphons). Geschichte der Katholischen Kirche in Irland. 3 vols. Mainz, 1890–91. Each vol. has a good Biblio.

List of Irish Monastic Chartularies. See Sims' 'Manual for the Genealogist, etc.', 1856, p. 27.

Evans (George Eyre). Vestiges of Protestant Dissent, being Lists of Ministers, Sacramental Plate, Registers, Antiquities, etc. [With Biblio. Notes.] Liverpool, 1897. **Ireland,** pp. 273–306.

The Historian of the Presbyterian Church in Ireland (The Rev. William Thomas Latimer), with a Biblio. by A. A. Campbell. (*The Irish Book Lover*, vol. vi. pp. 173–175. 1915.)

Irish Quaker Records, dating from about 1650, are preserved at 6 Eustace St. Dublin (Miss Edith Webb, Registering Officer).

Irish Record Commission. Reports [1st to 15th, 1810–25] **from the Commissioners respecting the Public Records of Ireland,** with Supplements and Appendices. 3 vols. London, 1813–29.

A Classified Schedule and General Inventory of the Plea Rolls, Pipe Rolls, Books of Reference, etc. in the Record Tower, Dublin Castle. (8th Rep. 1819, Supp. pp. 79–150.)

A Catal. of the Contents of the Parliamentary Record Office, Record Tower Dublin Castle. (*Ibid.* pp. 153–216.)

Catal. of Books and Papers in the State Paper Room, Record Tower, Dublin Castle. (*Ibid.* pp. 220–246.)

Catal. of the Reports and Schedules of the Court of Claims in the Surveyor General's Office, Record Tower, Dublin Castle. (*Ibid.* pp. 248–300.)

A Press Catal. of the Records and other Public Documents in the Auditor General's Office, Dublin Castle. (*Ibid.* pp. 302–352.)

Inventory of the Statute and other Rolls, etc. in the Rolls Office, Four Courts, Dublin. (*Ibid.* pp. 353–520.)

A Classified Schedule and General Inventory of the Memoranda and other Rolls etc. in the Chief Remembrancer's Office, Four Courts, Dublin. (*Ibid.* pp. 522–626.)

Classified Schedule of the Contents of the Quit Rent Office in the Customs House, Dublin. (*Ibid.* pp. 627–632.)

Report and Inventory of the Contents of the Prerogative Office, Dublin. (*Ibid.* pp. 633–637.)

Index of Persons in the Grants under the Acts of Settlement and Explanation, with Index of the Baronies, Towns, and Liberties in the respective Counties. (County arrangement.) (15th Rep. 1825, App. I. pp. 329–340.)

Index Nominum to the Original Certificates of the Court of Claims in the Rolls Office of the Court of Chancery in Ireland. (*Ibid.* App. II. pp. 341–347.)

Index Nominum and Locorum to Inrolments of the Certificates for Adventurers Soldiers, etc. in the Office of the Chief Remembrancer of the Exchequer, Dublin. Compiled by Thomas Tyrrell. (*Ibid.* App. IV. pp. 403–521.)

Index Nominum and Locorum to the Inrolments of the Decrees of Innocents in the Office of the Chief Remembrancer of the Exchequer. (*Ibid.* App. V. pp. 526–575.)

Index Nominum and Locorum to the Inrolments of the Connaught Certificates in the Office of the Chief Remembrancer of the Exchequer. (*Ibid.* App. VI. pp. 580–609.)

Index Nominum and Locorum to the Adjudications in favour of the (1649) Officers, preserved in the Office of the Chief Remembrancer of the Exchequer. (*Ibid.* App. VII. pp. 616–647.)

Repertory to MS. vols. in the Record Tower, Dublin Castle, with Indexes of Names of Persons and Places. (*Ibid.* pp. 648–694.)

Reports of the Deputy Keeper of Public Records in Ireland. Dublin, 1869, etc.

Index to Reports I.–V. (in 5th Rep.), VI.–X. (in 10th Rep.), XI.–XV. (in 15th Rep.), XVI.–XX. (in 20th Rep.), XXI.–XXV. (in 25th Rep.), XXVI.–XXX. (in 30th Rep.), XXXI.–XL. (in 40th Rep.).

Reports of Sir J. Bernard Burke. (1st and later Reports, 1869, etc.)

Index to Deeds in Collection of Records of Edward Litton. (2nd Rep. 1870, App. III.

Schedule of the Records of the Law Exchequer, Equity Exchequer Records, etc. (2nd Rep. 1870, App. III.)

Calendar of 'Fiants' of Hen. VIII. with Index. (7th Rep. 1875, App. X.)
" " Edw. VI. with Index. (8th Rep. 1876, App. IX.)
" " Philip and Mary, with Index. (9th Rep. 1877, App. IV.)
" " Elizabeth (11th Rep. 1879, App. III.; 12th Rep. 1880, App. V.; 13th Rep. 1881, App. IV.; 15th Rep., 1883, App. I.; 16th Rep. 1884, App. II.; 17th Rep. 1885, App. IV.; 18th Rep. 1886, App. VI.). Index A–C (21st Rep. 1889, App. III.), D–Z (22nd Rep. 1890, App. VI.).

Index to the 'Liber Munerum Publicorum Hiberniæ' [compiled by Rowley Lascelles, 1812–30], 2 vols. 1852 (9th Rep. 1877, App. III.). See also a Biblio. note, pp. 6–7 of the same Report.

An Index of the Decrees abstracted of the Court of Claimes for the Tryall of Innocents, 1662–1663. (19th Rep. 1887, App. pp. 84–87.)

Index to Calendar of Christ Church Deeds, 1174 to 1684, contained in Appendices to the 20th, 23rd, and 24th Reports. (27th Rep. 1895, App.)

Report on Insolvency Records. (22nd Rep. 1890, App. IV.)

Catal. of Proclamations from 1618 to 1875. (22nd Rep. 1890, App. V.; 23rd Rep. 1891, App. II.; 24th Rep. 1892, App. V.)

Report on Bankruptcy Records, 1772–1857. (23rd Rep. 1891, App. I.)
" " 1857–1872. (26th Rep. 1894, App. II.)

Schedule of Records of the Manor of St. Sepulchre, Dublin. (24th Rep. 1892 App. VI.)

Table of Contents of the Red Book—Exchequer. (*Ibid.* App. VII.)

Report on the Early Plea Rolls to 51 Edw. III. with a Catal. of Justiciary and other Rolls. (26th Rep. 1894, App. III.; 28th Rep. 1896, App. II.)

Index to the Act or Grant Books, and to Original Wills of the Dioc. of Dublin, 1275–1800. (26th Rep. 1894, App. IV.) Index, etc. 1800–58. (30th Rep. 1898, App.) Corrections to Addenda in 26th Rep. (31st Rep. 1899, App. I. pp. 39–88.)

Table of the Parochial Records of Ireland, distinguishing the several Parishes, etc. the Records of which are at the P.R.O., Dublin, from those which are in the Local Custodies, corrected to May, 1896. (28th Rep. 1896, App. II.)

Reports on MSS. purchased at Sale of Sir Thomas Phillipps' Library. (30th Rep. 1898, App. I.)

Reports on Records of the Clerks of the Crown and Peace. (32nd Rep. 1900, App.

Reports on the Books of the Treasury and Accounting Departments of Irel. (33rd Rep. 1901, App. II.)

List of Original Barony Maps of the Down Survey formerly in the Headfort Collection. (34th Rep. 1902, App. I.)

Report on Registers of Irregular Marriages, 1799–1844. (*Ibid.* App. II.)

List of Classes of Records found in sacks from former Record Office in Custom House. (35th Rep. 1903, App. I.)

Catal. of Accounts on the Pipe Rolls of the Irish Exchequer, Hen. III. to ix. Edw. III. (35th Rep. 1903, to 39th, 1907; 42nd, 1911, to 44th, 1912.)

Report on Records transferred from former Landed Estates Record Office. (40th Rep. 1908, App. I.)

List of Parishes for which Registers of Baptisms are preserved in the Record Office. (41st Rep. 1909, App. I.) List of Parishes for which Returns to Visitations supply deficiencies in Parish Registers. (*Ibid.* App. II.)

List of Deeds deposited by Edward J. French. (43rd Rep. 1912, App. 1.)

Calendar of Documents relating to Ireland in the Public Record Office, London, 1171-1307. Edited by H. S. Sweetman and G. F. Handcock. [Rolls Series.] 5 vols. London, 1875–86.

Reports from the Select Committee appointed to inquire into the State of the Public Records of the Kingdom, 1800. (Reports to House of Commons, 1800, vol. xv.)

Collections of Records in Dublin and elsewhere. (*Local Records Comm. Rep.* 1902, App. III. pp. 102, 256, 286.)

Hist. MSS. Comm. A Guide to the Reports on Collections of MSS. of Private Families, Corporations and Institutions in Gt. Brit. & Irel. Pt. I. Topographical. London, 1914.

An Account of the Proceedings taken for the Recovery, Arrangement, and Preservation of the Public Records of Ireland. (*The Monthly Museum*, Dublin, vol. i. pp. 397–399; vol. ii. pp. 140–142. 1814.)

List of Books containing Facsimiles of Irish MSS. See *ante* p. 380. Best's 'Biblio. of Irish Philology, etc.', 1913, pp. 63–68.

Gilbert (Sir John T.). Record Revelations. A Letter on the Public Records of Ireland and on the 'Calendars of Patent and Close Rolls of Chancery in Ireland,' recently published. London, 1863.

—— **Record Revelations Resumed.** A Letter on statements in Parliament on the Public Records of Ireland, and on the 'Calendars of Patent and Close Rolls of Chancery in Ireland,' lately published. By an Irish Archivist. London, 1864.

—— **On the History, Position, and Treatment of the Public Records of Ireland.** By an Irish Archivist. Second edition. London, 1864. The two previous entries are included in this work.

—— **English Commissioners and Irish Records.** A Letter in reference to the publication of 'The Calendars of the Patent and Close Rolls of Ireland.' By an Irish Archivist. London, 1865.

—— **Account of Facsimiles of National MSS. of Ireland, to 1719.** London, 1884. The Introductions to the 'Facsimiles of the National MSS. of Ireland,' ed. by Sir J. T. Gilbert. Dublin, 1874-84. (4 vols. in 5 pts.) are republished in this work.

Biblio. of the Works of Sir John Thomas Gilbert, Irish Historian and Archivist, in his 'Life,' by Lady Gilbert, 1905, App. XV. pp. 445–448.

Lhwyd (Edward). A Catal. of Irish MSS. in his 'Archæologia Britannica, vol. i. pp. 435–436. Oxford, 1707.

O'Grady (Standish Hayes). Catal. [Classified] of the Irish MSS. in the British Museum. London [1894]. The Catal. was not completed.

Flower (Robin E. W.). The Irish MSS. in the British Museum. (*Philological Soc. Trans.*, 1911–14, pp. 118–122.)

Calendar of the Carew MSS. preserved in the Archiepiscopal Library at Lambeth, 1515–1600. Edited by J. S. Brewer and William Bullen. 6 vols. London, 1867–69.

Report upon the Carte and Carew Papers in the Bodleian and Lambeth Libraries, 1863, by Sir Thos. Duffus Hardy and J. S. Brewer. London, 1864.

Catal. of Irish MSS. and such as relate to Irish Affairs, in the Lambeth Palace Lib. (*The Monthly Museum*, Dublin, vol. i. pp. 440–441. 1814.)

Abbott (Thomas Kingsmill). Catal. of the MSS. in the Lib. of Trinity College, Dublin. Dublin, 1900. **Index to Irish MSS.**, pp. 582–592.

Todd (James Henthorn). On the Irish MSS. in the Bodleian, Oxford. (*Roy. Irish Acad. Proc.*, vol. v. pp. 162–176. 1853.)

Hardiman (James). Ancient Irish Deeds and Writings from the 12th to the 17th Century. Dublin, 1826.

O'Donovan (John). The Lost and Missing Irish Manuscripts. (*Ulster Journ. of Archæol.*, vol. ix. pp. 16–28. 1861.)

O'Conor (Charles). Bibliotheca MS. Stowensis. A descriptive Catal. of the MSS. in the Stowe Library. 2 vols. Buckingham, 1818–19.

MSS. in the Irish Language, vol. i. pp. 21–207. MSS. relating to Ireland, vol. i. pp. 207–290.

Bibliotheca Phillippica. List of Irish MSS. and other items from the Sale of the Lib. of Sir Thomas Phillipps, June, 1910, and Apr. 1911. (*The Irish Book Lover*, vol. i. pp. 164–165; vol. iii. pp. 10–11. 1910–11.)

John D'Alton's MS. Collections relating to Ireland. Biblio. Notes by William MacArthur and others. (*Ibid.* vol. vii. pp. 75, 101, 116. 1915–16.)

Hore MSS. Biblio. Note on Collections of MSS. relating to Irish Hist. See *ante* under Wexford, p. 276.

Peddie (Robert Alexander). MSS. relating to Ireland in the Libraries of France. (*The Irish Book Lover*, vol. i. pp. 86–87. 1910.)

Bindon (S. H.). Catal. of the MSS. relating to Ireland in the Burgundian Lib. at Brussels. (*Roy. Irish Acad. Proc.*, vol. iii. pp. 477–502. 1847.)

Catal. of Maps and Plans relating to Ireland in H.M. State Paper Office, Whitehall, London. (*Ulster Journ. of Archæol.*, vol. iii. pp. 272–276. 1855.)

Notes on Old Irish Maps. (*Ibid.* vol. iv. pp. 118–127. 1856.)

Hore (Herbert F.). Notes on a Facsimile of an Ancient Map of Leix, Ofaly, Irry, etc., in the Brit. Museum. (*Kilkenny and South-East of Irel. Archæol. Soc. Journ.*, vol. vii. pp. 345–372. 1863.)

Orpen (Goddard H.). Ptolemy's Map of Ireland. (*Soc. Antiq. Irel. Journ.*, vol. xxiv. pp. 115–128. 1894.)

Westropp (Thomas J.). Early Italian Maps of Ireland from 1300 to 1600, with lists. (*Royal Irish. Acad. Proc.*, vol. xxx. Sect. C, pp. 361–428. 1913.)

Dunlop (Robert). Sixteenth-Century Maps of Ireland [in the Brit. Mus., P.R.O., Trinity Coll. Dublin, and elsewhere]. (*Eng. Hist. Rev.*, vol. xx. pp. 309–337. 1905.)

Corry (Somerset R. Lowry), Earl of Belmore. Descriptive Notes on the Irish Historical Atlas, 1609. Belfast, 1903.

Hardiman (James). A Catal. of Maps, Charts, Plans, etc., in the Lib. of Trinity Coll. (*Royal Irish Acad. Trans.*, vol. xiv. pt. 2, pp. 57–77. 1825.)

Petty (Sir William). The Hist. of the Survey of Ireland, commonly called 'The Down Survey.' Edited by T. A. Larcom. [Irish Archæol. Soc.] Dublin, 1851.

For an Account of the Irish Ordnance Survey, see an article on Eugene O'Curry, by Rev. Timothy Lee, in 'Limerick Field Club Journ.', vol. i. no. iii. 1899.

A Catal. of the Maps of the 'Down Survey' (arranged under Counties) and the Barony Maps copied by General Vallancey. (In *3rd Ann. Rep. on the Public Records of Irel.*, 1813, Supp. pp. 502–539.)

For accounts of the Maps of the 'Down Survey,' made by Sir William Petty, and the Barony Maps of Gen. Vallancey, see 'The Monthly Museum,' Dublin, vol. i. p. 489; vol. ii. p. 141. 1814.

O'Hanlon (John). A General Index of the Ordnance Survey Records of Irish Counties. (*Soc. Antiq. Irel. Journ.*, vol. iv.–ix. *passim*, 1856–67.)

Biblio. of Irish Surveys (Counties), by 'Lector.' (*Dublin Penny Journ.*, 31 Jan. 1903.)

Anderson (John Parker). Biblio. to 'Arthur Young's Tour in Ireland during the years 1776–1779,' edited with Introduction and Notes by Arthur W. Hutton, 1891, vol. ii. pp. 349–374.

Catal. of the County Maps and Town Plans and other Publications of Ireland of the Ordnance Survey of the United Kingdom to Jan. 1908. London, 1908.

Maps of Ireland. See Lists in 'Sale Catal. of the Lib. of William Monck Mason,' 29. Mar. 1858, pp. 71, etc., and in 'Catal. of the Lib. of Dr. Thomas Willis,' sold by John Fleming Jones, Dublin, 22 Nov. 1876, pp. 99–105. See *ante* pp. 381, 382.

Dix (E. R. McClintock). A List of Irish Towns and Dates of Earliest Printing in Each. London, 1903. Second edition. Dublin, 1909. (Irish Biblio. Pamphlets, no. vi.)

—— **Dates of Earliest Printing in Irish Towns.** (*The Irish Book Lover*, vol. vii. pp. 110–111. 1916.)

—— **Irish Provincial Printing prior to 1701.** (*The Library*, New Ser. vol. ii. pp. 341–348. 1901.)

—— **Provincial Printing in Ireland.** A Series of Lists. (*The Irish Book Lover*, vol. iv. etc., 1912, etc.)

—— **List of Irish Books, 1571-1820.** (In 'An Claidheamh Soluis' [a newspaper]. Dublin, Jan.–Apr. 1904.)

—— **An Early Eighteenth-century Broadside on Printing.** (*Roy. Irish Acad. Proc.*, vol. xxvii. Sect. C, pp. 401–403. 1909.)

—— **and Casaide (Séamus ua). List of Books, Pamphlets, etc., printed wholly, or partly, in Irish, from the Earliest period to 1820.** Dublin, 1905. New and enlarged edition. Dublin, 1913.

E. R. McC. Dix and the History of Irish Printing. (*The Irish Book Lover*, vol. vi. pp. 124–125. 1915.) See also 'The Library World,' vol. xvii. pp. 196–197. 1915.

Gilbert (Sir John T.). Irish Bibliography. Edited with Introduction, Notes and Appendices, by E. R. McC. Dix, with lists of 16th. and 17th. cent. books and printers. (*Roy. Irish Acad. Proc.*, vol. xxv. sect. C, pp. 117–142. 1904.) Reprinted in Lady Gilbert's 'Life of Sir J. T. Gilbert,' 1905, pp. 437–442.

Casaide (Séamus ua). Biblio. of Local [Irish] Printing. A Table giving Towns, Periods, & references to Publications where Lists have appeared. (*The Irish Book Lover*, vol. ii. pp. 4–6. 1910.)

Peddie (Robert A.). Biblio. of Irish Printing; A List of Books, Pamphlets, and Articles on Printing, in the Typographical Lib. of the St. Bride Foundation, London. (*Ibid.* vol. ii. pp, 51–53. 1911.)

Plomer (Henry R.). Ireland and Secret Printing. (*Ibid.* vol. i. pp. 27–28. 1909.) See also notes by Dix and others, at pp. 7, 116, 150, 169.

Lennox (P. J.) Early Printing in Ireland. Washington, U.S.A. Reprinted from 'The Catholic University Bulletin,' vol. xv. nos. 3 & 4. 1909.

Reed (Talbot Baines). Rough List of Books printed in the Irish Character and Language. (*The Celtic Mag.*, vol. x. pp. 584–586. 1885.)

Bradshaw (Henry). Printing in the Irish Character. Letters to T. B. Reed. (*Biblio. Register*, No. I. pp. 6–13; No. II. pp. 23–29. 1905.)

—— **Printing in Ireland.** (*Brit. & Col. Printer*, vol. xiii. p. 259. 1884.)

—— **On Printing in Ireland.** A Speech before the 'Lib. Assoc.' at Trinity Coll., Dublin, 1884, reproduced from the 'Freeman's Journal,' 3 Oct. 1884, with a note by E. R. McC. Dix, and a Biog. note by John S. Crone.

Madden (Richard Robert). The Hist. of Irish Periodical Literature from the end of the 17th to the middle of the 19th century. 2 vols. London, 1867.

Dix (E. R. McClintock). Rare Ephemeral Magazines of the 18th cent. (*The Irish Book Lover*, vol. i. pp. 71–73. 1910.)

—— **The First Irish Papers.** A Biblio. Note. (*Ibid.* vol. iv. pp. 97–98. 1912.) See also a note on pp. 61–62 of the same vol.

—— **Biblio. of Irish Newspapers, 1660-1700.** (*Irish Independent*, 18–20 Jan., 1905.)

Power (John). List of Irish Periodical Publications (chiefly Literary), from 1729 to the present time. London, 1866. Reprinted from 'Notes and Queries,' Ser. 3, vol. ix. pp. 173, 231, 316, 342, 1866, and 'The Irish Literary Inquirer,' No. IV. pp. 45–52, 1866, with additions and corrections.

Irish Newspapers in the British Museum. A Printed Catal. arranged under Towns, with an Index of Titles, is in the Reading Room.

Evans (Edward). Historical and Bibliographical Account of Almanacks, Directories, etc., published in Ireland from the 16th cent. Dublin, 1897.

Lynch (Patrick). An Historical Account of Irish Almanacks. (*The Irish Magazine*, Dublin, 1810, pp. 330, 378, 476, 524; 1811, p. 36.)

Casaide (Seamus ua). Irish Almanacks. (*The Irish Book Lover*, vol. iii. pp. 128-129. 1912.)

O'Donoghue (David James). The Poets of Ireland. A Biographical and Bibliographical Directory of Irish Writers of English Verse. Dublin, 1912.

Dix (E. R. McClintock). Irish Song Books in the Royal Irish Academy, (*The Irish Book Lover*, vol. ii. pp. 81–83. 1911.)

——— **Irish Chap Books, Song Books, and Ballads.** (*Ibid.* vol. ii, pp. 33–35. 1910.)

Historical Ballad Poetry of Ireland. Arranged by M. J. Brown, with an Introduction by Stephen J. Brown. London, 1912.

Davis (Thomas). 'A Ballad Hist. of Ireland,' and **'Ballad Poetry of Ireland,'** in 'Prose Writings of Thomas Davis,' with an introduction by T. W. Rolleston, London [n.d.], pp. 192-207.

Colum (Padraic). Broad-Sheet Ballads, being a Collection of Irish Popular Songs, with an Introduction by P. C. Dublin, 1913.

Irish Chap Books. By John J. Marshall. (*The Irish Book Lover*, vol. i. pp. 157–159. 1910.)

The Harvard Chap Books. A Biblio. Note on the Irish items in the 'Catal. of the Chap Books and Broadsides,' in the Lib. of Harvard Univ. (*Ibid.* vol. ii. pp. 35–36. 1910.)

Denny (H. L. L.). Anglo-Irish Genealogy. [With Biblio. Notes.] A Paper read before the Soc. of Genealogists of London, May, 1916.

Frazer (William). List of Works on Irish Music. (*Notes and Queries*, Ser. 7, vol. iv. p. 510. 1887.)

Praeger (R. Lloyd). A Biblio. of Irish Glacial and Post-Glacial Geology, with a Key Index arranged under Counties. (*Belfast Naturalists' Field Club. Proc.*, App. vol. ii. no. 6, 1895-96, 'Systematic Lists,' vol. ii. pp. 237–316.)

——— **Biblio. of Irish Topographical Botany.** (*Roy. Irish Academy. Proc.*, Ser. iii. vol. vii. pp. xcix–cxlvii. 1901.)

Christy (Miller). Biblio. Note on Irish Birds. (*The Zoologist*, Ser. III. vol. xiv. p. 266, 1890, and reprinted in pamph., 1891, p. 40.) **Mammals.** (*The Zoologist*, Ser. III. vol. xvii. p. 215. 1893.) **Reptiles.** (*Ibid.* p. 251. 1893. **Fishes.** (*Ibid.* p. 262. 1893.)

WALES.

Blackwell (Henry). Bibliography of Welsh Bibliographies. [Announced for publication.] **Biblio. of Welsh Books published in America.** [In active preparation.] See 'The Publishers' Weekly,' New York, 5 Apr. 1913, p. 1233.

Rowlands (William). Cambrian Bibliography: containing an Account of the Books printed in the Welsh Language, or relating to Wales, from 1546 to the end of the Eighteenth Century, with Biog. Notices. Edited and enlarged by Daniel Silvan Evans. Llanidloes, 1869.

Williams (Moses). Catal. of all the Books, mostly printed, in the Welsh Language. London, 1717. The book is in Welsh. An interleaved copy in the Brit. Museum has notes and additions. See also the List of Welsh Books in 'Y Gwyliedydd' (Bala), Dec. 1831.

Cardiff Free Libraries. Catal. of Printed Literature in the Welsh Department. By John Ballinger and James Ifano Jones. Cardiff, 1898.

Recent additions to the Welsh Department. 'A Record of Current Literature in Wales or relating to Wales,' 1909, etc., in 'The Cardiff Libraries' Review, vol. i. No. 4, etc. Jan. 1910, etc.

University College of Wales, Aberystwyth. A Catal. of Welsh Books, Books relating to Wales, Books written by Welshmen, Books relating to Celtic Literature, etc. Aberystwyth, 1897.

Swansea Public Libraries. Catal. of Welsh Books, with English and other Literature relating to Wales and Celtic Countries. Pt. I. Authors. Pt. II. Subjects. Compiled by D. Rhys Phillips. Swansea, 1911.

Blackwell (Henry). Biblio. of Local and County Histories relating to Wales and Monmouth. (*Old Welsh Chips*, vol. i. 1888, pp. 138–145, 171–181, 198–216, 224–230.)

For a note on a proposed Biblio. of Wales by Charles Ashton, see 'Bye-Gones, vol. xiii. p. 215. 1895.

The National Library of Wales. Bibliotheca Celtica. A Register of Publications relating to Wales and the Celtic Peoples and Languages for 1909, etc. Aberystwyth, 1910, etc. Issued annually.

Catal. of the Cambrian Books at Glen-Aber, Chester, 1500-1799, not mentioned in the 'Cambrian Bibliography.' Compiled by Enoch Gibbon R. Salisbury. Carnarvon, 1874.

Catal. of Welsh Books, Books on Wales, and Books by Welshmen, 1800-1862, at Glan Aber, Chester. Carnarvon, 1880?

Hotten (John Camden). Bibliographical Account of nearly one thousand Books, Tracts, etc., relating to the Hist. and Topography of North and South Wales. London, 1863.

Biblio. of Wales. A Record of Books in Welsh, or relating to Wales, 1899-1911. Nos. 1 to 14, Apr. 1900—June, 1903, issued in 'The Public Library Journal,' Cardiff. Nos. 15 to 29, Sept. 1903—Sept. 1912, issued separately.

Archæologia Cambrensis.' An Alphabetical Index to the First Four Series, 1846-1884. By D. Rowland Thomas. London, 1892.

—— **An Alphabetical Index to the Fifth Series, 1884–1900.** Compiled by Francis Green. London, 1902.

Index to 'Bye-Gones, relating to Wales and the Border Counties.' Vols. I. to VII. 1871–1885. Compiled by G. H. Brierley. Oswestry and Wrexham, 1887.

Index to the Publications of the Hon. Soc. of Cymmrodorion from 1877 to 1912. Supplement to 'Trans.' of the Soc. 1911–12, pp. 1–59.

List of Books in the Library of the Hon. Soc. of Cymmrodorion, catalogued by Dr. Alfred Daniell. Supplement to 'Trans.' of the Soc. 1901–02.

Mee (Arthur). Wales and the Border in 'Notes and Queries.' (*Bye-Gones*, New Ser. vol. xi. pp. 2, 25, 49, 63, 77, 138, 215, 242, 254, 269; vol. xii. pp. 9, 33, 76, 80, 85, 96, 99, 130, 138, 243, 247, 272, 294; vol. xiii. pp. 10, 50, 52, 69, 74, 79, 84, 125, 129, 141, 155. 1909–14.)

Poole (Edwin). Sale oı the Library of Edward Breese, F.S.A. of Portmadoc. Sold by Sotheby's, 31 May, 1888. Descriptive notes on the Welsh Books. (*Old Welsh Chips*, vol. i. 1888, pp. 231, 253, 292, 329.)

Index to Welsh Periodicals. Compiled by Rev. David Davies and T. C. Evans ('Cadrawd'.) See 'The Journ. of the Welsh Biblio. Soc.' vol. i. pp. 195, 255. 1914–15.)

Lewis (Edward Arthur). A Biblio. Note on some of the Printed and MS. Sources of the Medieval Hist. of the Welsh Boroughs. (*Welsh Biblio. Soc. Journ.*, vol. i. pp. 65–75. 1911.)

Skeel (Caroline A. J.). The Council in the Marches of Wales. A Study in Local Government during the Sixteenth and Seventeenth Centuries. [Girton College Studies, II.] London, 1904. List of Authorities, pp. vii.–xvi. See also Miss Skeel's article in 'English Historical Rev.' Jan. 1915.

Davies (John Humphreys). Bibliography and its Aims. A Paper read at the Second Meeting of the Cymmrodorion Section of the National Eisteddfod, with a view of promoting the objects of the proposed 'Welsh Bibliographical Society.' See Report of the Meeting held at Swansea, 1907.

—— **Early Welsh Bibliography.** (*Soc. of Cymmrodorion. Trans.*, Sess. 1897–98, pp. 1–22.)

The Ideal of a Welsh National Library. I. By Sir John Williams; II. By Sir Isambard Owen; III. By Sir Marchant Williams. (*Ibid.* 1903–04, pp. 84–99.)

Ballinger (John). The National Library of Wales in Relation to other Libraries and Institutions. (*Welsh Biblio. Soc. Journ.*, vol. i. pp. 33–42. 1911.)

The National Library of Wales. Charter of Incorporation and Report on the Progress of the Library, to March, 1909. Oswestry, 1909.

Report on the Library of Sir John Williams, pp. 33–38.
Report on the Hengwrt and Peniarth MSS. pp. 25–26, 43–51.

—— **Reports on tbe Progress of the Library, from April, 1909, etc.** Aberystwyth, 1911, etc.

Sir John Williams's Collection of Prints, Drawings, etc. relating to Wales. (Report, 1911, p. 9.)
Notes on Welsh Books and MSS. presented by Sir John Williams. (Reports, 1909, 1911, 1913.)
Report on the Ty Coch (near Carnarvon) Collection of Edward Humphrey Owen [mainly Books, MSS. etc. relating to North Wales]. (Report, 1911, App. pp. 14–25.)
Biblio. Notes on MSS., Books, etc. presented to the Library, Lists of Welsh Newspapers, Periodicals, etc. [arranged under Counties]. (Reports, 1909, 1911, 1913.)

—— **Catal. of a Selection of MSS. and Books from Sir John Williams' Library, exhibited July and August, 1909.** Aberystwyth, 1909.

Stephens (Thomas). The Literature of the Kymry. Second edition. Edited by Daniel Silvan Evans, with Life of Stephens by B. T. Williams. London, 1876. List of Collections of Cambrian MSS., pp. 335-338.

Prys (Robert John). Hist. of Welsh Literature, 1300-1650. Liverpool [1885]. The book is in Welsh.

Wilkins (Charles). The Hist. of the Literature of Wales from 1300 to 1650. Cardiff, 1884.

Chap. IV. MS. Collections of Wales, List of Hengwrt MSS., Iolo MSS., Civil War Literature, etc.

Ashton (Charles). Hist. of Welsh Literature, 1651-1850. Liverpool [1893]. The book is in Welsh.

Special Bibliographies. No. I. Dr. Lewis Edwards, of Bala [b. 1809, d. 1887]. Compiled by James Ifano Jones. (*The Cardiff Libraries' Rev.*, vol. i. pp. 37–41. 1910.)

——— **No. II. David Jones, of Llangan** [b. 1736, d. 1810]. (*Ibid.* vol. i. pp. 94–96; vol. ii. pp. 9–12. 1910–11.)

Ballinger (John). Vicar Prichard. (Rees Prichard, Vicar of Llandovery, b. 1579, d. 1644. Author of 'Canwyll y Cymry.') **A Study in Welsh Bibliography.** (*Y Cymmrodor*, vol. xiii. pp. 1–75. 1899.)

Biblio. of Quaker Literature in the English Language relating to Wales. (*Welsh Biblio. Soc. Journ.*, vol. i. pp. 203–225. 1914.)

John ap John and Early Records of Friends in Wales. Compiled by William Gregory Norris. (*Friends' Hist. Soc. Journal Supplement*, No. 6, 1907.)

A Biblio. of Welsh Calvinistic Methodism. By John Humphreys Davies and others. (*Calvinistic Meth. Hist. Soc. Journ.*, vol. i. pp. 3–9. 1916.)

Evans (George Eyre). Vestiges of Protestant Dissent, being Lists of Ministers, Sacramental Plate, Registers, Antiquities, etc. [With Biblio. Notes.] Liverpool, 1897. **Wales,** pp. 307–325.

Phillips (D. Rhys). The Romantic Hist. of the Monastic Libraries of Wales from the Fifth to the Sixteenth Centuries. (Reprinted, with additions, from the 'Library Assoc. Record,' July & Aug. 1912. Swansea, 1912.)

Davies (John Humphreys). Welsh Book Collectors. I. Rev. Owen Jones. II. Richard Williams. III. Rev. Robert Williams. (*Welsh Biblio. Soc. Journ.*, vol. i. pp. 17–20, 56–57, 142–145. 1910–13.)

Vaughan (Herbert M.). Old Book Plates of West Wales. (*West Wales Historical Records, Hist. Soc. of West Wales*, vol. iv. pp. 177–192. 1914.)

Catal. of Halliwell's (the Shakesperian Scholar) very curious Collection of Books on North Wales. [London.] 1861.

National Museum of Wales. Catal. of an Exhibition of Welsh Topographical Prints, from Drawings made during the 18th. and 19th. centuries, held June-Oct. 1915. Compiled by Isaac J. Williams. 1915.

——— **Handbook to the Exhibition of Welsh Antiquities, June-Oct. 1913.** Cardiff, 1913.

Catal. of Historical Works and Historical Novels relating to Wales. (Cardiff Library Rev. Special List.) Cardiff, 1909.

National Library of Wales. Catal. of Tracts of the Civil War and Commonwealth Period relating to Wales and the Borders. (Index Locorum at end.) Aberystwyth, 1911.

Evans (Howell T.). Wales and the Wars of the Roses. Cambridge, 1915. List of Original Authorities, pp. 231–234.

Phillips (D. Rhys). A Select Biblio. of Owen Glyndwr. (Glyndwr Quincentenary, 1415–1915. Welsh Biblio. Soc. 1915.

Banks (Richard William). On the Welsh Records in the time of the Black Prince. (*Archæol. Cambrensis*, Ser. IV. vol. iv. pp. 157–188. 1873.)

Phillimore (Egerton). The Publication of Welsh Historical Records. (*Y Cymmrodor*, vol. xi. pp. 133–175. 1892.)

Lloyd (John Edward). The Organization of Welsh Historical and Archæol. Research. (*Soc. of Cymmrodorion, Trans.*, 1910–11, pp. 116–124.)

Bosanquet (Robert Carr). The Organization of Welsh Historical and Archæol. Research. (*Ibid.* 1910–11, pp. 125–129.)

Firth (Charles Harding). Suggestions for the Study of Welsh History. (*Ibid.* 1914–1915, pp. 1–10.)

Williams (Moses). Proposals for printing by subscription a Collection of Writings in the Welsh Tongue, to the beginning of the Sixteenth Century. July 31, 1719. [With a specimen page.] London.

Williams (Edward). Prospectus of Collections for a new History of Wales, consisting of Historical Documents from Ancient Welsh MSS. 1819. See 'Recollections, etc., of Edward Williams,' by Elijah Waring, 1850, pp. 177–185.

Lhwyd (Edward). Parochial Queries in order to a Geographical Dictionary, and Natural History, etc. of Wales. [n.d.]

The 'Queries' were printed at length in 'Arch. Camb.' 1857, pp. 260-264. See also 'Parochialia,' being a Summary of Answers to 'Parochial Queries in order to a Geographical Dictionary, etc., of Wales.' Pts. I.-III. Edited by Rupert H. Morris, and issued by the 'Cambrian Archæol. Assoc.' as Supplements to 'Archaeologia Cambrensis.' 1909-11. See also 'Some Incidents in the Life of Edward Lhwyd,' by Richard Ellis, in 'Soc. of Cymmrodorion. Trans.', 1906-7, pp. 1-51.

Evans (E. Vincent). List of Books written by Sir John Rhŷs, with Bibliographical details. (*Soc. of Cymmrodorion. Trans.*, 1914-15, pp. 243–246.)

Evans (George Eyre). Aberystwyth, 1909, Centenary of the Introduction of Printing in 1809. Exhibition of Books, Portraits, Relics, etc. in the Public Library, June–Sept. 1909. Aberystwyth, 1909.

Ashton (Charles). The Old Welsh Printers. See articles (in Welsh) in 'Y Geninen,' vol. ix. pp. 240–244; vol. x. pp. 19–24. 1891–92.

Quaritch (Bernard). Names of Printers and Publishers of Welsh Books. (*Y Cymmrodor*, vol. v. pp. 159–160. 1882.) See also vol. vii. pp. 230-232. 1886.

Lloyd (Howel William). Welsh Books printed Abroad in the 16th. and 17th. Centuries and their Authors. (*Ibid.* vol. iv. pp. 25–69. 1881.) Also issued separately.

Parry (Morris). List of the Welsh Books printed at Chester from 1713 onwards. [Announced for publication by Welsh Biblio. Soc.]

Catal. of Welsh Newspapers in the British Museum. [Arranged under Towns with an Index of Titles.] Newspapers before 1700 are not included in the Catal., but are entered under the heading 'Periodical Publications.'

Jones (T. M.). Literature of my Country, or a Hist. of Newspapers and Welsh Periodicals in Wales, America, Australia, etc. Holywell, 1893. [The book is in Welsh.]

Davies (John Humphreys). A Biblio. of Welsh Ballads printed in the 18th. century. Issued by the Hon. Soc. of Cymmrodorion and the Welsh Biblio. Soc. London, 1911.

A Collection of Ballads, etc. made by J. D. Lewis, of Llandyssul, is in the Nat. Lib. of Wales at Aberystwyth. They are printed in 30 different Towns in Wales by 45 different Printers. See Report of Council of Nat. Lib. of Wales, 1913, p. 57. See also 'Catal. of Printed Literature in the Welsh Department of the Cardiff Free Libraries,' by John Ballinger and James Ifano Jones, 1898, under Ballads and Fugitive Pieces, pp. 26-35.

Poole (Edwin). List of Novels relating to Wales. (*Old Welsh Chips*, vol. i. 1888, pp. 69, 159–165, 247–248.)

Hist. MSS. Comm. Reports on MSS. in the Welsh Language, by J. Gwenogvryn Evans.

Vol. I. pt. I. 1898. Mostyn Hall, co. Flint. (Lord Mostyn.)
,, pt. II. 1899. Peniarth, Towyn, etc. (W. R. M. Wynne.)
Vol. II. pt. I. 1902. Jesus College, Oxford. Free Library, Cardiff. Havod. Wrexham. Llanwrin. Merthyr. Aberdâr.
,, pt. II. 1903. Plas Llan Stephan. Free Library, Cardiff.
,, pt. III. 1805. Panton. Cwrtmawr.
,, pt. IV. 1910. The British Museum.

Reports from the Select Committee appointed to inquire into the State of the Public Records of the Kingdom. (*Reports to House of Commons*, 1800, vol. xv.)

Valuable for Accounts of the Welsh County Records.

General Report of the Commissioners on the Public Records, with an Appendix and Index. (*Reports to House of Commons*, vol. xxxiv. pt. 2. 1837.)

Supplements the Account of Welsh County Records in the 1800 Report.

Black (William Henry). Report on a Survey and Examination of the Records of the Courts of Session and Exchequer of the County Palatine of Chester and the Courts of Great Sessions of the Principality of Wales. See 1st Rep. of Dep. Keeper of the Public Records, 1840, App. pp. 78-122.

Memorandum on the Records of the Crown Lordships or Manors in Wales and Monmouthshire. (*Local Records Comm. Rep.*, 1914, vol. ii. pt. 2, pp. 259–260.

Roberts (Charles). Lists of the Welsh Records, Books, etc. See 20th Rep. Dep. Keeper of the Public Records, 1859, App. pp. 160–183, and 21st Rep. 1860, p. 26.

Turner (Peter). Calendars and Lists of Welsh Records, in 'Reports of the Dep. Keeper of the Public Records,' from the 20th Rep., 1859, onwards.

Catalogues of Welsh MSS. [References to Catalogues in various Publications.] (*Bye-Gones*, Ser. II. vol. i. pp. 282–283. 1889.)

Roberts (Richard Arthur). The Public Records relating to Wales. (*Soc. of Cymmrodorion. Y Cymmrodor*, vol. x. pp. 157–206. 1890.)

Birch (Walter de Gray). Notes on the importance of preserving the Records and Literary Antiquities of Wales, as illustrated by some recent publications. (*Brit. Archæol. Assoc. Journ.*, New Ser. vol i. pp. 25–48. 1895.)

Pollock (Sir Frederick). The Use of Local Records, with an Appendix, 'Welsh Local Records: Details and Classified Topographical List,' by Hubert Hall. (*Soc. of Cymmrodorion. Trans.*, 1914–15, pp. 11–42.)

The Appendices are grouped under the following headings:

(*a*) Details of Welsh Local Records.

I. Definition of the Title.
II. Differentiation of Welsh Local Records.
III. Classification of Welsh Local Records.
IV. General Comparison between Welsh and English Records.
V. Printed Works relating to Welsh Local Records.
VI. Conclusions as to the present Condition and future Disposal of Welsh Local Records.

(*b*) A Classified Topographical List of the Local Records of Wales and Monmouthshire.

I. Public Records in Local Custody.
II. Local Records in Public Custody.
III. Local Records of a Semi-Public Nature.

Lewis (John Herbert). On the Importance of a National Collection of Public Documents for Wales, with a rough List of the classes of documents suggested for preservation in the National Lib. of Wales. (*Welsh Biblio. Soc. Journ.*, vol. i. pp. 97–113. 1912.) Also issued separately. The List is reprinted in 'Report' of the Council of the Nat. Lib. of Wales, 1913, pp. 19–25.

Catal. of Welsh MSS. in North Wales. By Miss Angharad Llwyd. (*Cymmrodorion Soc. Trans.*, vol. ii. pp. 36–58. 1828.)

Catal. of Welsh MSS. in North Wales. By Aneurin Owen. (*Ibid.* vol. ii. pp. 400–418. 1843.)

Yeatman (John Pym). Welsh Records. (*Archæol. Camb.*, Ser. 5, vol. xvii. pp. 277–293; Ser. 6, vol. i. pp. 126–132. 1900–01.)

MSS. relating to Wales. (*Ibid.* New Ser. vol. i. pp. 65–66. 1850.)

Account of Welsh Collections in Hist. MSS. Comm. Reports. (*Ibid.* Ser. 4, vol. ix. pp. 66, 141, 225, 302; vol. x. p. 304. 1878–79.)

Old Records on Wales and the Marches, temp. Edwd. I.-III. A Short List, by 'Cambrensis.' (*Bye-Gones*, Ser. 2, vol. i. pp. 477–478. 1890.)

Banks (Richard William). On the Early Charters to Towns in South Wales. (*Archæol. Camb.*, Ser. 4, vol. ix. pp. 81–101. 1878.)

Taylor (Henry). The First Welsh Municipal Charters. (*Ibid.* Ser. 5, vol. ix. pp. 102–119. 1892.)

Owen (Edward). Catal. of MSS. relating to Wales in the British Museum. *Cymmrodorion Soc. Record Ser.*, No. IV. 1900.)

Pts. I.-III. issued. Pt. IV. expected to complete the work.

Welsh Records and Welsh MSS. in the Brit. Museum. (*Archæol. Camb.*, Ser. 3, vol. i. pp. 247–249. 1855.)

MSS. of the Rev. Edward Llwyd, including an Account of the Collection of Sir W. W. Wynn, a List of MSS. lost, etc. (*Cymmrodorion Soc. Trans.*, vol. i. pp. 173–176. 1822.)

A Catal. of the Myvyrian MSS. belonging to the Cymmrodorion (the Owen Jones Collection). Compiled by W. Owen Pughe. (*Ibid.* vol. i. pp. 177–202. 1822.)

Coleman Deeds. Documents relating to Wales (about 950) collected by James Coleman, in the Nat. Lib. of Wales, at Aberystwyth. See Report of Council of Nat. Lib. of Wales, 1911, p. 36.

Welsh Records in Paris. Edited, with an Introduction, etc. by Thomas Matthews. Carmarthen, 1910.

See also 'Welsh Records in Foreign Libraries,' by Thomas Matthews in Cardiff Naturalists' Soc. Rep. and Trans.,' vol. xliii. pp. 20-31. 1910.

Hall (Hubert). The Foreign Aspect of the Welsh Records. (*Y Cymmrodor*, vol. xxii. pp. 1–21. 1910.)

——— **The Diplomatics of Welsh Records,** with List of Repositories of Welsh Records, a Classification of Welsh Records, etc. (*Soc. of Cymmrodorion. Trans.*, 1900–1901, pp. 40–52.)

Collections of Browne Willis relating to the Four Welsh Cathedrals, in the Bodleian Lib. See Macray, 'Annals of the Bodl. Lib. Oxford.' 1890, p. 259.

List of Welsh Monastic Chartularies. See Richard Sims' 'Manual for the Genealogist, etc. 1856, p. 27.

Williams (Edward). A Short Review of the Present State of Welsh MSS. Merthyr, 1836.

Thomas (D. Lleufer). Biblio. List of Works relating to Welsh Agriculture and Land Tenure, Appendix to 'Minutes, etc. of the Royal Comm. on Land in Wales, etc.' 5 vols. London, 1894–96.

Whitaker (William.) List of Works on the Geology, Mineralogy, and Palæontology of Wales [to end of 1873]. British Association. 1880. For Additions up to 1896, see Report of the Royal Comm. on Land in Wales and Monmouthshire.

Cantrill (Thomas Crosbee). Geological Biblio. of South Wales and Monmouthshire, in 'Memoirs of the Geol. Survey,—The Country around Cardiff.' 1902, and Appendices compiled by O. T. Jones in 'Memoirs,—The Country around Swansea.' 1907.

Christy (Miller). Biblio. Notes on Welsh Mammals, Reptiles, and Fishes. (*The Zoologist*, Ser. 3, vol. xvii. pp. 185, 247, 258. 1893.)

Forrest (Herbert Edward). 'The Vertebrate Fauna of North Wales.' London, 1907. Biblio. pp. xliii.–li.

INDEX.

List of the Principal Subject-Headings.

INDEX.

ERRATA AND CORRIGENDA.

Page 2. Bulloch. 'Chron. List of Aberdeen Newspapers, etc.' *For* 1889 *read* 1887.

,, 7. Johnson. 'Biblio. of the Shires of Aberdeen, etc.' *For* Johnson *read* Johnstone.

,, 15. Cust (Sir Lionel). 'Eton College Portraits.' *For* Sir Lionel *read* Lionel Henry, *and add* 1910 as date of book.

,, 19. Roberts (T. C.) The University Press. *For* T. C. Roberts *read* S. C. Roberts.

,, 26. 'Index to Trans. of Hist. Soc. of Lancs. & Cheshire.' *For* 1849–1909 *read* 1849–1900.

,, 30. Macalister (A. A. Stewart). 'Studies in Irish Epigraphy.' *For* A. A. Stewart *read* R. A. Stewart.

,, 33. 'Archdeaconry Court Records at Bodmin,' *is by* Rev. W. Iago.

,, 54. 'Catal. of Books, etc. on Genealogy, etc. Central Public Libraries, Newcastle-on-Tyne.' *For* Basil Anderson *read* Basil Anderton.

,, 96. Allnutt. 'English Provincial Presses.' *For* Earliest Printing of Canterbury *read* Earliest Printing at Canterbury.

,, 152. Orridge (B. R.) 'The Corporation of London and their Records.' *For* B. R. Orridge *read* B. B. Orridge.

,, 178. 'Kempe's Heraldical & Historical Collections, etc.' *For* Kempe *read* Kemp.

,, 187. Elliott (H. L.) 'The Parish Registers of Northampton, etc.' *For* Elliott *read* Elliot.

,, 253. Gross (Charles). 'Biblio. of Brit. Municipal Hist.' *For* Brigton *read* Brighton.

,, 323. O'Dowd (D. J.) 'The Cork Magazine, etc.' *For* O'Dowd *read* O'Donoghue, *and for Ibid.* read *The Irish Book Lover.*

,, 336. 'Records of the Glasgow Biblio. Soc.' Biblio. of Douglas Moore. *For* Douglas *read* Dugald.

,, 365. Halliwell-Phillipps. 'A Catal. of Proclamations, etc. presented to the Chatham Lib. Manchester.' *For* Chatham Library *read* Chetham Library.

,, 391. 'Archæologia Cambrensis.' An Alphabetical Index, etc. By D. Rowland Thomas. *For* D. Rowland Thomas *read* David Richard Thomas.

,, 395. 'Hist. MSS. Comm. Reports on MSS. in the Welsh Language,' vol. ii. p. iii. 1805. Panton, Cwrtmawr. *For* 1805 *read* 1905.

,, 403. Balfour, John Alexander, 320. Omitted from Index.